The Legal Environment of the New Millennium

seventh edition

Samuel D. Hodge, Jr.

Temple University

McGraw-Hill Primis Custom Publishing

New York St. Louis San Francisco Auckland Bogotá
Caracas Lisbon London Madrid Mexico Milan Montreal
New Delhi Paris San Juan Singapore Sydney Tokyo Toronto

McGraw-Hill Higher Education

A Division of The McGraw-Hill Companies

The Legal Environment of the New Millennium

Previous editions of this book were published using the title *Law in Society* by The McGraw-Hill Companies, Inc.

1 2 3 4 5 6 7 8 9 0 QPD QPD 0 9 8 7 6 5 4 3 2 1

ISBN 0-07-250723-3

Editor: Constance Ditzel
Cover Design: Maggie Lytle
Printer/Binder: Quebcor World

ACKNOWLEDGMENTS

The author gratefully acknowledges the research
and editorial assistance of Theresa Parkhill,
Jasmine Park, Sheila Lawson, John Bongiovanni, IV,
Bindu Jacob, David Lieberman, Franklin Love
and Daniel Tobin.

Special thanks is also extended to
Jakarta M. Eckhart of NiteOwl Creations for her
desktop publishing assistance.

DEDICATION

This book is dedicated to Rhonda Hodge,
without whose patience and understanding this project
would not have been possible.

TABLE OF CONTENTS

CHAPTER 1

THE LEGAL ENVIRONMENT OF THE NEW MILLENNIUM, AN OVERVIEW

SECTION 1.1
INTRODUCTION

Law is a dynamic force that is not capable of a single or simple definition. It affects all aspects of life and establishes the parameters of acceptable conduct within our society. These rules can be created by legislative enactment or be imposed by court decision. While one may not always agree with the law, deviations from these mandates can result in both criminal and civil liability.

In the face of expanding governmental regulation and a litigation-oriented society, individuals must be cognizant of the legal implications of their actions. Seemingly minor violations of the law can have devastating financial and emotional consequences. Multi-million dollar verdicts are commonplace and the courts are continually recognizing new theories of liability.

Law books tend to be theoretical in nature and present the economic, sociological and political implications of the law. This book, however, focuses on the practical side of the legal system and allows the reader to become a participant in a variety of legal disputes. Through the use of biographical sketches, students are introduced to a cast of characters who live in the same neighborhood. As the semester unfolds, the families become involved in a variety of squabbles that threaten to destroy the peace and harmony of a once quiet street. Minor disturbances become major confrontations. Tempers flare and the neighbors are soon embroiled in various civil and criminal proceedings.

The law firm of *Hodge, Dodge and Lodge* is retained by one of the neighbors because the family is related to the senior partner. Needing help to deal with the added caseload, *Hodge, Dodge and Lodge* has hired you as its new legal assistant. Your sole responsibility will be to assist the senior partner in dealing with the problems of his relatives.

The law firm is unable to offer financial remuneration for your services, because of your inexperience. The management committee, however, is grateful for your efforts and will direct its attorneys to provide you an overview of the legal system. Arrangements have already been made with your college to grant academic credit if your work product is satisfactory.

Great care has also been used in selecting the legal cases for this text. The court discussion on a particular point of law will focus on recent

1

decisions or cases involving famous people. For example, a student will learn about punitive damages by reading about a case involving Whitney Houston. Domain name disputes will focus on litigation involving Madonna and Sting. The enforcement of an arbitration agreement deals with Latrell Sprewell and his assault of the head coach of the player's former basketball team. It is believed that this approach will stimulate interest in the materials since the players to the litigation will be known to the general public and students should enjoy learning about the legal exploits of these famous people.

SECTION 1.2
THE STUDY OF LAW

The legal system seems to thrive on a host of rules, regulations and judicial decisions that defy logic and common sense. Ambiguity appears commonplace. Loopholes and technicalities abound. What should be said in one paragraph ends up being many pages in length, laced with phrases from another century and typed in fine print. In this way, lawyers perpetuate the system, justify their existence and charge large fees. Perhaps Shakespeare was right when he said, "The first thing we should do is to kill all the lawyers." I think not!

The law is not perfect, but it does attempt to establish a system of order and justice. What would automobile traffic be like if we didn't have a motor vehicle code? How could we be secure in our homes if we didn't have the threat of imprisonment for those who commit crimes? How would we protect those harmed by the wrongful misconduct of others if the courts did not order compensation to be paid to the aggrieved party?

The law naturally operates in an adversarial setting. There are two sides to every story and one party must lose. Who is to obtain custody of the children in a divorce proceeding? If the court awards custody to the mother, does this mean that the father loves the children any less than his former spouse? Judges make difficult decisions which are not always popular among all members of society. It is the best system that exists, however, and is clearly superior to the alternative-uncontrolled chaos or a dictatorship where the people have no rights or say in the operation of the government.

Trying to understand the law is complicated by the use of multi-syllable words and Latin phrases. Instead of saying a person has filed an appeal to the United States Supreme Court, we label such an appeal a writ of certiorari. Precedent becomes **stare decisis** and legal documents are filled with "wherefores and hereinafters."

Judges and attorneys are aware of the public's perception of the legal system. Great care is now taken to eliminate "legalese" and to use simple English. But yet, would we have confidence in a physician who dictates a medical report to another doctor by noting, "the patient hurt his funny bone" instead of saying, "the patient sustained an injury to his ulnar nerve on the posterior aspect of the left forearm?"

Change is occurring, but reform takes time. More and more contracts are being written in easy to understand language. In fact, the drafters of contracts are penalized by construing ambiguities in the document against the author.

The study of law can be an intimidating and frustrating process. Students are forced to confront the stereotypes and misconceptions they have learned over the years about the legal system. At times, the law does seem to protect the criminal by the use of technicalities. These "loopholes," however, stem from the basic rights of the people as established by the United States Constitution. It is only through the vigorous enforcement of our constitutional rights that all people are protected. Isn't justice better served by a guilty person being set free than by an innocent person going to jail?

This course will attempt to simplify the law by explaining how the legal system works. Legal terms will be presented and translated into common English. Controversial issues will be discussed. It is only through this learning process that one can gain a better appreciation for the law.

SECTION 1.3
THE COURTROOM

The courtroom is like a stage filled with drama and suspense. It is through this forum that stories unfold with lives hanging in the balance. Did the suspect really kill his wife to collect the proceeds of a million dollar life insurance policy that he purchased the week before, or was his car forced off the road by an unknown assailant who robbed him at gun point and killed his wife because she started to scream? The outcome is always in doubt until the verdict is announced.

There is no better place to start this educational experience than to introduce the players in the courtroom.

The master of ceremonies is the judge who sits facing the parties on an elevated platform. All are bound by her rulings as the jurist oversees everything that occurs within the courtroom. The starting and concluding time of court and legal determinations are all within the province of the judge.

The directors in the drama are the attorneys. They orchestrate the presentation of evidence and determine the sequence of witnesses to maximize the impact of the testimony.

The parties to the suit are the plaintiff and the defendant. The plaintiff initiates the case, and the defendant is the one being sued. The easiest way to remember the difference between the two is to look at the word "defendant." The term contains the word "defend" in its spelling.

The positioning of the parties in the courtroom is predetermined by custom. The party with the burden of proof sits closest to the jury box. In a civil case, the plaintiff has the burden of proof and in a criminal case the government must prove that the accused is guilty of the crime. The other side of the courtroom is reserved for the defense.

The jury sits to the side of the court and is segregated from all others in the courtroom. This is done to guard against tampering and undue influence. Jurors are instructed not to discuss the case with anyone and to refrain from any type of contact with those involved in the dispute. Jurors are brought into and leave the courtroom separately.

Cases are tried by the presentation of evidence. Witnesses are called to testify as to the facts and occasionally to act as character witnesses. The witness stand is located next to the judge, and is in close proximity to the jury.

COURTROOM

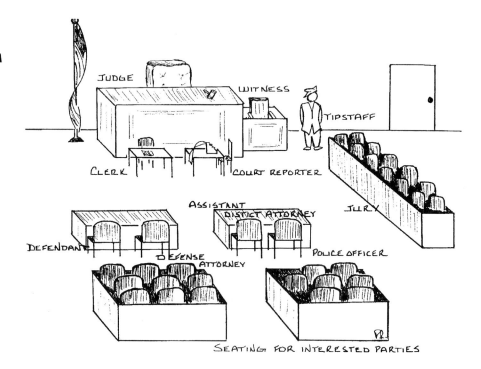

All dramas need an audience and trials are no different. Courtrooms are generally open to the public for observation and spectators are seated in the back of the room.

As a theater needs a production crew, a courtroom needs a staff. A stenographer is present to record and transcribe everything that is said for appellate review. A court clerk keeps track of the exhibits, administers the oath to all who testify, and oversees the jury. Each judge has a tipstaff or personal that acts as a bodyguard, helps run the courtroom, and assists the jurist in the daily operation of the office.

**SECTION 1.4
THE EVOLUTION OF
THE JURY TRIAL**

The right to be judged by one's peers is so basic to a fair hearing that a trial by jury is constitutionally guaranteed. In turn, the power of a jury is immense. Did O.J. Simpson murder his former wife? Did the Menedez brothers really murder their parents? How many people were behind the Oklahoma City Bombing? The jury decides these types of factual questions and their answers determine innocence or guilt.

The evolution of the jury system is presented in the following article prepared by the **Association of Trial Lawyers of America**:

The U.S. Jury system has its source in English history. Before there were juries, there were three general methods of "trial" in England. The first, **the wager of law**, simply required the accused person to take an oath, swearing to a fact. In those days, a person's oath carried great weight. In fact, the word "jury" derives from the term "jurare" which means to swear, to take an oath. Those with good reputations who were accused of a crime had only to swear that they were innocent to be acquitted.

If others swore against the accused, however—in effect challenging the truth of the accused's oath—a **compurgation** was necessary. The accused had to bring in 11 supporters called **compurgators**, making 12 people in all who would be willing to take an oath on behalf of the accused. The **compurgators** did not swear that what the accused said was true. They served more as character witnesses, swearing that the accused was considered a credible person. If the accused was found guilty, the compurgators might also be punished because they were then implicated in the defendant's guilt.

An accused who was a repeat offender, or who was unable to find enough compurgators willing to swear to his good character, would be subjected to a **trial by ordeal**, some sort of physical test, the results of which were supposed to indicate guilt or innocence. Unfortunately, the trials were usually designed so that, in proving innocence, the physical ordeal often resulted in bodily harm or even death to the accused.

For instance, in a **trial by hot water**, a ring might be suspended by a string in a cauldron of boiling water, either wrist-deep or elbow-deep, depending upon the severity of the crime. The accused was first "cleansed" by prayer and fasting and then was instructed to reach into the boiling water to grab the ring. If the accused's hand and arm were burned, that was considered a sign of guilt. If not burned, the obvious miracle was treated as a sign of innocence.

In a **trial by cold water**, used in the American colonies at the time of the Salem witch trials, the accused was bound and placed in a body of water that had been purified by prayer. An accused who sank was considered innocent because the water would "accept" one who was pure; floating indicated that the accused's body was polluted by sin and the water was rejecting it. Apparently the object of this ordeal was not always to drown the innocent or the guilty—the accused might be removed from the water after sinking or floating for a while.

There were various types of **trial by fire**. Some entailed having the accused show innocence by either walking across hot coals or holding a white-hot iron rod. In these trials, the accused was guilty if burned or innocent if not burned. Sometimes the test was not whether the person was burned, but how the burn healed after a certain period of time. For instance, if the burn healed well after a few days, it was a sign of innocence because the body was "clean." But if the wound showed signs of infection, it was considered a sign that the body was defiled by evil.

Not all trials by ordeal were so dramatic. For example, one trial consisted only of taking a large piece of bread from an altar and eating it. An accused who could eat the bread without difficulty was considered innocent; choking or gagging was thought to show an evil presence in the body rejecting the bread. Another less dramatic trial required the accused to wear a blindfold and choose between two pieces of wood, one of which had a cross drawn on it. If an accused selected the one with the cross it was considered that divine intervention had proved innocence.

One common aspect of all of the trials by ordeal was that the outcomes were often a matter of chance or placed the accused in a "no-win" situation. To prove innocence, an accused had to risk death or serious bodily injury. Yet, since survival was often considered a sign of guilt, an accused lucky enough to survive the ordeal was often immediately judged guilty and put to death.

Most of these trials had a religious context and were conducted by clergymen or other church officials. Most were preceded by purifying prayer for either the accused or the object used in the trial—water, bread, etc. If the trial required purification of the body before the ordeal, the accused was often sequestered and forced to fast and pray for up to three days prior to the trial.

These kinds of trials had no juries, and often citizens did not want to be chosen for "jury duty" as compurgators because they faced the possibility of punishment for "incorrect" verdicts. As trial by jury began to develop, the situation for the jurors did not improve much. When the courts were under royal control, the jurors were often punished if they decided against the king. Often, "incorrect" jurors had their property seized, were imprisoned, or were separated from their families as punishment for not "properly" fulfilling their duties as jurors. And since the jurors were still considered witnesses, they were also subject to punishment for perjury.

Trial by jury did not fully come into being until the trial by ordeal was abolished. The move to jury trial took longer for criminal matters than for civil cases, since trials by ordeal were used mainly to resolve common crimes or offenses against the king, the state, or the church. Corrupt rulers were known to "plant" witnesses or jurors to manipulate the outcomes of trials. In order to guard against this, the church began to support the principle that jurors should have no interest in the case at issue. With the church's influence, the courts began to insist on impartiality in jurors. The separation of the roles of witness and juror, and the desire for protection against royal manipulation, combined to spark the evolution of the system of trial with an impartial and unbiased jury.

New developments brought additional changes to the nature of the jury. For instance, when attorneys began to bring in witnesses to corroborate facts in a case, it was no longer necessary for the jurors to know the accused. And witnesses began to testify before the judge as well as the jury, not before the jury alone. Since both the judge and the jury were to hear the facts, it became more desirable for all persons to be at the same place, hear the same facts, and base their decisions solely upon the information presented in open court, instead of having some persons on the jury who knew more about the case than others. Gradually, juries came to decide only questions of fact, while judges ruled on questions of law.

By the time the colonists were settled in America, the right to **trial by jury** was considered essential. British rulers attempted to deny the colonists this right but were met by strong resistance. The importance and value the colonists placed on this right was clearly evidenced in the Declaration of Independence, and in the Sixth and Seventh Amendments to the U.S. Constitution. Today the jury is a mainstay of the America's legal system.[1]

SECTION 1.5
THE CAST OF CHARACTERS

HODGE, DODGE AND LODGE
ATTORNEYS AT LAW
MEMORANDUM

To: All Law Clerks
From: Gregory Olan Dodge
Re: Biographical Sketches

My name is Gregory Olan Dodge and I am the managing partner of the law firm, *Hodge, Dodge and Lodge*. On behalf of the firm, I would like to welcome you. In the past, we only hired law clerks from Ivy League Schools. I am skeptical about an education that offers an undergraduate legal studies course and have decided to give you a variety of research assignments to ascertain your legal skills.

Hodge, Dodge and Lodge is a multi-faceted law firm handling all types of cases. Our biggest problem client happens to be my partner's brother, Joe Hodge and his family. They are a constant source of embarrassment and take up a lot of our time. Since we do not charge Joe for our legal representation, I will delegate much of this work to you for handling and advice.

I am providing you with biographical sketches of the various people whose cases you will be working on during the next few months. Learn their identities and background. As for Joe Hodge, he is constantly fighting with his neighbors. You will painfully learn of these problems as you start researching the answers to his family's cases.

Estelle Worthington Hodge

Estelle Worthington met Joe Hodge when he delivered groceries to her parent's home as part of his clerk's job with the supermarket. They immediately hit it off and started dating. Their relationship soon blossomed and they saw no one else during their last two years of high school. Joe was offered a scholarship to attend an out-of-state college, but Estelle convinced him to attend Temple University. During Joe's junior year at Temple, the couple got married.

As fate would have it, Estelle became pregnant on her honeymoon. Nine months later, Estelle gave birth to a son, Anthony. Joe soon had to drop out of Temple University and obtain a job to support his new family. Joe took a position with a construction company. After a few years, they bought a nice home in Northeast Philadelphia. Six years later, she became bored with her routine and decided to become pregnant. This led to the birth of her daughter, Kathy. During the next few years, she had two more children. These boys are Brad, who is now 12, and Gregory, who is 6 years old.

To keep busy, Estelle immerses herself in one cause after another. She soon developed a reputation as a tenacious consumer advocate and lobbied for a variety of reforms on issues such as woman rights, tax reform and the educational needs of children with learning disabilities.

There was one period, however, when Estelle's life almost fell apart. Joe developed a drinking problem which nearly destroyed their marriage but that's all in the past.

Joseph Hodge   Joe does not remember the early years when his parents struggled to make ends meet and could barely speak English. Things eventually worked out and his parents purchased their own grocery store. A second son was born five years after Joe. Mr. and Mrs. Hodge always encouraged their children to do well in school. Their parents believed that education was the gateway to success. Joe heeded his parents' advice and excelled in academics. Fate was kind to Joe when he met Estelle Worthington while delivering groceries to her parent's house. They fell in love and eventually married.

Joe never finished college and obtained work as a bulldozer operator. As the pressures of married life mounted, Joe started to drink and was rarely seen without a beer in his hand.

Joe's drinking caused numerous conflicts at work. The climax occurred when Joe drove his bulldozer over his supervisor's new BMW. Joe was fired immediately. He was unemployed with four kids to feed, a mortgage to pay and a very unhappy wife. The bills mounted and his marriage deteriorated. Joe's creditors eventually brought suit and his house was sold at Sheriff's Sale.

With his last bit of money, Joe jumped on a bus and headed to the casinos in Atlantic City. Much to his disbelief, Joe hit the jackpot and won a million dollars while down the shore. With this new found wealth, Joe purchased the construction company that had previously fired him. He renamed the entity, Joho Construction Company and assumed the title of President and CEO. Joe quickly doubled his funds and made two unusual purchases. Believe it or not, Joe bought a baby gorilla named "Harry" from a bankrupt circus and he acquired a yacht which he named *"ONLY IN AMERICA,"* to reflect his life story.

Anthony Hodge   Joe and Estelle's son, Tony, is 22 years old. Throughout high school, Tony excelled in athletics and was the goalie on the soccer team.

During his junior year in high school, Tony took up football. His soccer background enabled him to become an outstanding place kicker and his high school team went on to win the Pennsylvania State Championship.

Temple University offered Tony a full-paid scholarship to play football. During Tony's last year at college, he set a number of school records for points and field goal accuracy. The various scouting combines rated him as one of the top kickers in collegiate football. While Tony attended a Philadelphia Eagles mini-camp, he realized that he was tired of living in the Philadelphia area and wanted a change. He subsequently worked out for the Stallions, the latest expansion team in the N.F.L. This new franchise was impressed with Tony's ability to put the ball in the end zone and he was signed by the expansion team to three, one-year contracts.

Kathleen Hodge

Kathy is 16 years old and her sole interests in life seem to focus on her cell phone, TV, clothes, and the beach. She spends hours gossiping on the telephone and watching television. On the face of things, she appears to be an average teenager. Kathy, however, has a grave problem.

Ever since she started experimenting with drugs, her grades have gone from A's to F's. She has now completely detached herself from the day to day life of her family. Whenever her parents try to communicate with her, Kathy reacts with great hostility. Since her parents increasingly avoid any sort of confrontation with her, Kathy's decline accelerates.

Peter Christopher

Peter Christopher was born one of a pair of identical twins in Tampa, Florida. Since no one was able to tell them apart, their father gave each boy an identical tattoo of a shark on opposite shoulders. After lying about their age, the Christopher brothers enlisted in the military service at age 16. They spent their time in the service specializing in military intelligence and photographic analysis.

After leaving the military, the Christopher brothers started a small but lucrative business in Texas performing investigative services with a specialization in surveillance and industrial espionage. Following a business dispute with his brother over the handling of a sensitive file, Peter relocated to the Philadelphia area and took up residence next to Joe Hodge.

Donald Feelgood, M.D.

Donald Feelgood always wanted to be a physician but he did not excel in the sciences. Nonetheless, Donald studied day and night and was accepted at a medical school in Grenada. Even though he wasn't that academically talented, Donald had hands of gold. He was a master craftsman and knew that his manual dexterity would enable him to become an excellent surgeon. Eventually, he graduated from medical school and became a resident at Cook County Memorial Hospital in

Chicago. After several years, he became an adequate doctor, relocated to the Philadelphia area and is now a successful surgeon. Dr. Feelgood lives in the home on the other side of Joe.

Officer John O'Brien

John O'Brien is the oldest of five children. Both his father and grandfather were members of the police force, and it has always been his ambition to follow in their footsteps.

While all of the other children in the neighborhood were playing sports, John would religiously read his father's police manuals. With the help of his father, John became quite a marksman. At the age of 22, John graduated from college with a degree in police science and chose to become a police officer with a suburban Philadelphia police department. Presently, he is assigned to the Patrol Division and is also a field-training officer for new recruits. Due to his proficiency as a marksman, Officer O'Brien is also a member of the department's S.W.A.T. Team.

Because of Officer O'Brien's size and demeanor, he is affectionately known as *"Big, Bad John."*

SECTION 1.6
CASE ANALYSIS

COMMON LAW AND STATUTORY LAW

The laws of the United States originate either by legislative enactment or judicial pronouncement. The study of law requires an analysis of both processes. This will be accomplished by examining court cases on each subject.

When analyzing a statute, one must disregard the ordinary meaning of a word. It is more important to ascertain how the term is defined by statute. In trying to understand a court decision, remember that the judge is attempting to balance the economic, political and sociological forces of the day to reach a just result.

Two decisions are presented for analysis. The first case deals with whether the owner of a tree is entitled to recover pain and suffering because of the damage done to a tree by an errant car. The Michigan Appellate Court denied the claim and limited the recovery to the cost of having a tree surgeon repair the damage to the tree. The decision is an example of court made law and is presented in a poem. The second case deals with the interpretation of a statute and presents the question of whether a pony is a small bird. The reader will learn that the court is only interested in whether a horse is a small bird in the eyes of the law and not whether it is one in fact.

COMMON LAW CONSTRUCTION
WILLIAM FISHER V. KAREN LOWE
122 MICH. APP. 418 (1983)

We thought that we would never see
A suit to compensate a tree.
A suit whose claim in tort is prest
Upon a mangled tree's behest;

A tree whose battered trunk was prest
Against a Chevy's crumpled crest.
A tree that faces each new day
With bark and limb in disarray;

A tree that may forever bear
A lasting need for tender care.
Flora lovers though we three,
We must uphold the court's decree.

Apply this holding to the following case. Our client owns a Mazda. As she was driving home, another vehicle ran a red light and struck her car. It will cost $1,000.00 to repair the rear fender. The person who hit the Mazda offered our client $1,000.00 for the property damage. The client demands an additional sum of money since the car has now been in an accident. She says that the car will always carry the scars of the collision. Based upon the tree case, can the client collect an additional sum of money beyond the $1,000.00?

STATUTORY CONSTRUCTION
REGINA V. FRED OJIBWAY[2]
8 CRIMINAL LAW QUARTERLY 137 (1965-66)

BLUE, J.: —THIS IS AN APPEAL BY THE CROWN by way of a stated case from a decision of the magistrate acquitting the accused of a charge under the *Small Birds Act*, R.S.O., 1960, c.724, s.2. The facts are not in dispute. Fred Ojibway, an Indian, was riding his pony through Queen's Park on January 2, 1965. Being impoverished, and having been forced to pledge his saddle, he substituted a downy pillow in lieu of the said saddle. On this particular day the accused's misfortune was further heightened by the circumstance of his pony breaking its right foreleg. In accord with Indian custom, the accused then shot the pony to relieve it of its awkwardness.

The accused was then charged with having breached the *Small Birds Act*, Section 2 of which states:

> Anyone maiming, injuring or killing small birds is guilty of an offense and subject to a fine not in excess of two hundred dollars.

The learned magistrate acquitted the accused holding, in fact, that he had killed his horse and not a small bird. With respect, I cannot agree.

In light of the definition section my course is quite clear. Section 1 defines "bird" as "a two legged animal covered with feathers." There can be no doubt that this case is covered by this section.

Counsel for the accused made several ingenious arguments to which in fairness, I must address myself. He submitted that the evidence of the expert clearly concluded that the animal in question was a pony and not a bird, but this is not the issue. We are not interested in whether the animal in question is a bird or not in fact, but whether it is one in law. Statutory interpretation has forced many a horse to eat birdseed for the rest of its life.

Counsel also contended that the neighing noise emitted by the animal could not possibly be produced by a bird. With due respect, the sounds emitted by an animal are irrelevant to its nature, for a bird is no less a bird because it is silent.

Counsel for the accused also argued that since there was evidence to show the accused had ridden the animal, this pointed to the fact that

it could not be a bird but was actually a pony. Obviously, this avoids the issue. The issue is not whether the animal was ridden or not, but whether it was shot or not, for to ride a pony or a bird is of no offense at all. I believe counsel now sees his mistake. Counsel contends that the iron shoes found on the animal decisively disqualify it from being a bird. I must inform counsel, however, that how an animal dresses is of no concern to this court. Counsel relied on the decision **In Re Chicadee**, where he contends that in similar circumstances the accused was acquitted. However, this is a horse of a different color. A close reading of that case indicates that the animal in question there was not a small bird, but, in fact a midget of a much larger species. Therefore, that case is inapplicable to our facts.

Counsel finally submits that the word "small" in the title *Small Birds Act* refers not to "Birds" but to "Act", making it *The Small Act* relating to Birds. With respect, counsel did not do his homework very well, for *The Large Birds Act* R.S.O. 1960, c. 725, is just as small. If pressed, I need only refer to *The Small Loans Act* R.S.O. 1960, c.727 which is twice as large as *The Large Birds Act*.

It remains then to state my reason for judgment which, simply, is as follows: Different things may take on the same meaning for different purposes. For the purpose of the Small Birds Act, all two legged, feather-covered animals are birds. This, of course, does not imply that only two-legged animals qualify, for the legislative intent is to make two legs merely the minimum requirement. The statute therefore contemplated multi-legged animals with feathers as well. Counsel submits that having regard to the purpose of the statute only small animals "naturally covered" with feathers could have been contemplated. However, had this been the intention of the legislature, I am certain that the phrase "naturally covered" would have been expressly inserted just as 'Long' was inserted in the Longshoreman's Act.

Therefore, a horse with feathers on its back must be deemed for the purposes of this Act to be a bird, and a fortiori, a pony with feathers on its back is a small bird.

Counsel posed the following rhetorical question: If the pillow had been removed prior to the shooting, would the animal still be a bird? To this let me answer rhetorically: Is a bird any less of a bird without its feathers?

Appeal allowed.

Reported by: H. Pomerantz and S. Breslin

SECTION 1.7
ELEMENTS OF A
JUDICIAL OPINION

It is important to be familiar with the elements of a judicial opinion so one may better understand the law that the court has established. For the purpose of this discussion, we will analyze the case entitled *Spitzer v. Tucker*.

The **caption** of a case identifies the parties to the lawsuit. The full name of the case being reviewed is *Spitzer v. Tucker*. In other words, Mary Jo Spitzer has sued her ex-husband, Francis J. Tucker. Because Spitzer sued Tucker, she is the plaintiff and Tucker is the defendant. When a case is appealed to a higher court, the names of the parties change to appellant and appellee. The person who appeals the lower court's decision is the **"appellant."** The party against whom the appeal is filed is the **"appellee."**

The **citation** tells a person how to locate the case. The citation identifies the book that contains the decision, the volume number of that book and the first page of the case. In this instance, the citation is 591 A.2d 723 (Pa. Super. 1991). "A.2d" refers to the *"Atlantic Reporter, Second Series."* The *Atlantic Reporter* is a series of books that contain appellate court decisions in a specific region of the United States. "591" is the volume number of the book that contains the case and "723" is the page number on which the case first appears. "Pa. Super." is the abbreviation for the court in which the case was decided. **Spitzer** was decided in the Pennsylvania Superior Court—the intermediate appellate court in Pennsylvania. If a Federal court decided the case, the initials F. or F. Supp. would appear. "1991" is the year that the case was decided.

The next item that appears after the caption is the name of the judge who authored the opinion. On appeal, one judge writes the opinion or body of the case, for the "majority" of the court. Because an appellate court consists of a panel of three or more judges, a decision reached by more than half of the judges constitutes the **"majority opinion."** A decision rendered by the majority is the law. **Spitzer** contains a second opinion that is called a **"dissenting opinion."** A judge writes a dissent when he or she disagrees with the result reached by the majority. The dissent has no value as precedent. A judge may also write a **"concurring opinion"** when the jurist agrees with the outcome of the case but wants to note a difference in logic for reaching the decision.

SECTION 1.8
BRIEFING OF A CASE

Breaking a case down into its component parts simplifies one's understanding of the opinion. An opinion has four main parts:

1. The Action;
2. The Facts;
3. The Issue; and
4. The Opinion of the Court.

The Action — What kind of case is it? What remedy is being sought?

The Facts — What happened? The reader should be concerned with the three *W's*. Specifically, *Who* did *What* to *Whom?* The facts of a case are discussed in a narrative form.

The Issue — What question is presented to the court for it to decide?

The Opinion of the Court — First, the reader must ascertain what the court decided. In other words, how does the court answer the question posed in the Issue section? Second, and more importantly, what justification does the court provide for coming up with its answer? For example, what sociological, economic or political policies does the court use to justify its decision? Any dissenting or concurring opinions should also be noted in this section, but the discussion will be less detailed than that of the majority opinion.

An appellate court can affirm, reverse or remand the decision of a lower court. When a decision is **affirmed**, the appellate court determines that the lower court reached the correct decision. The appellate court **reverses** a decision when it finds that the lower court's decision was incorrect. A case may also be **remanded** to the trial court. This occurs when the appellate court finds that the trial judge committed an error in deciding the case or additional evidence must be obtained.

The reader should now examine *Spitzer v. Tucker* and break the case down into its component parts. A sample brief follows the opinion.

MARY JO SPITZER V. FRANCIS TUCKER
591 A.2D 723 (PA. SUPER. 1991)

CAVANAUGH, Judge

OPINION: THE PRESENT APPEAL is from a support order following a petition initiated by appellee, Mary Jo Spitzer, against her ex-husband, Francis J. Tucker, to obtain from Tucker additional support to fund his son Will's educational expenses at Syracuse University. The court entered an order which found that each parent had sufficient resources to allow for payment of the educational expenses and that each, after consideration of personal living expenses, had sufficient discretionary income available for this purpose. After ordering the payment of a modest contribution by the student, the court directed that each parent contribute one-half of the tuition, board and related expenses.

Appellant Tucker attacks this order and argues that undue discretion was vested in the student's choice of school and that the court erred in refusing to assign a sufficient earning capacity to the student's mother.

The obligation of a parent with adequate financial resources to furnish support for a child's college education is well settled in Pennsylvania. See e.g., *Miller v. Miller*, 353 Pa. Super. 194, 509 A.2d 402 (1986); *Sutliff v. Sutliff*, 339 Pa. Super. 523, 489 A.2d 764 (1985). A court will impose this obligation on a parent only if the burden of college support will not cause undue hardship. Furthermore, if it can be shown that "a parent can meet the support needs of a college-age child with ease, a court is free to impose a complete obligation." *Miller v. Miller*, supra, 509 A.2d at 404.

We find that the arguments of appellant are without merit and we affirm the order of the trial court. We believe that the goal of the court in higher education support cases should be to "replicate, as nearly as possible the decision the intact family would have made." In such a situation one would expect, for example, that a father who was only subject to minimal support obligations for almost eighteen years would have made economic preparations to assist in his only son's post-secondary education; that a well-educated parent would not resort to a claim of entry level employment competence, or shield personal trust resources to resist what should ordinarily be considered a paramount family aspiration; and finally, that the prospective student would recognize the enormous variety of excellent educational institutions available and yield in his personal preferences to choices dictated by familial resources and wisdom. Thus, there is substantial evidence that both parents can make equal contributions to the educational enterprise without undue hardship and there is no necessity for a circumscribed evaluation of Mrs. Spitzer's earning capacity. Moreover, the record supports the trial court's conclusion with respect to this issue, and we find the court's reasoning and disposition to be a valid exercise of discretion.

Order affirmed.

DISSENTING OPINION BY CIRILLO, J.

Because I feel that Francis J. Tucker should not be required to contribute to his son's education at Syracuse University, I respectfully dissent.

Mr. Tucker and Mary Jo Spitzer were divorced in 1973. Mr. Tucker, pursuant to a support order, was providing $40.00 per week for the support of his son Will Tucker. On January 31, 1989, Ms. Spitzer filed a petition seeking financial contributions from Mr. Tucker for Will's college expenses. The trial court found that Mr. Tucker, an attorney, earns approximately

$60,000.00 annually, while Ms. Spitzer, who is the beneficiary of a trust fund and who is a certified teacher, was assigned an earning capacity of $40,000.00 per year. Ms. Spitzer's current husband is an attorney with gross annual earnings of over $200,000.00. The Honorable Thomas J. Gavin ordered that Will would be responsible for the first $2,000.00 of his college expenses and that the remaining expense would be borne equally by both parties. This appeal followed.

On appeal, father argues that he should not be required to contribute to the cost of Will's Syracuse education because Will's college selection was arbitrary and because Will could receive a comparable education at the Pennsylvania State University ("PSU") for less than half the cost of Syracuse. I agree.

It is imperative that we examine the reasons underlying Will's decision to attend Syracuse and whether there is any evidence of record which would indicate that Syracuse would offer Will a superior education.

Ms. Spitzer stated that Will liked Syracuse because his best friend from Conestoga was going to attend Syracuse and because Will was interested in watching Syracuse sporting events. Apparently, the academic curriculum at Syracuse was not a factor in Will's decision. Essentially, since there was no indication that Syracuse offered Will a superior education, there was no academic reason for Will to attend Syracuse over PSU.

Moreover, if Will's biological family had remained intact, I do not feel that Will would have been afforded a Syracuse education.

There was testimony at the hearing that Will's father lived a frugal life. Clearly, cost, as Ms. Spitzer admitted, has always been a factor for Mr. Tucker. Moreover, there was no indication that Will harbored any animosity for his father; indeed, Will worked for his father during the summers of 1988 and 1989. These two factors, Mr. Tucker's frugality and the apparently friendly relationship between father and son, lead me to conclude that Mr. Tucker would not have agreed to fund Will's Syracuse education if the family had remained intact.

On the contrary, from the testimony it appears that Mr. Tucker would have insisted that, for financial reasons, Will attend PSU. In sum, because Will offered no academically legitimate reason for attending Syracuse instead of PSU and because Mr. Tucker's history of frugality convinced me that he would have been opposed to funding a Syracuse education if the family had remained intact, I find that the trial court abused its discretion when it ordered Mr. Tucker to contribute to Will's educational pursuits at Syracuse when Will could have enjoyed a comparable education at PSU for less than half the cost.

Questions for Discussion:

1. Should a student have complete discretion in deciding which college to attend when the parents are divorced and they will be required to pay the tuition?

2. Should a court have the right to enforce family obligations between divorced parents and their children?

3. Should the significantly higher income of a woman's second husband alter the apportionment of tuition contributions between the woman and her first husband?

SAMPLE BRIEF
SPITZER V. TUCKER
591 A.2D 723
(PA. SUPER. 1991)

Action: The plaintiff, Mary Jo Spitzer, seeks to obtain additional support from her ex-husband.

Facts: Mr. Tucker was divorced from the plaintiff, Mary Jo Spitzer, and had not lived with his son, Will, for many years. Spitzer had remarried and had a combined income with her new husband of four times that of Tucker. Mr. Tucker refused to fund Will's educational expenses at Syracuse University. Ms. Spitzer and her son believed that Mr. Tucker was financially responsible for sending Will to the college of his choice.

Issue: Is a divorced father financially responsible for sending his child to the child's choice of college even though it is more expensive than a state related institution?

Opinion of the Court: Yes. Mr. Tucker is responsible for funding his son's education at Syracuse. The court based its decision on the fact that "the obligation of a parent with adequate financial resources to furnish support for a child's college education is well settled in Pennsylvania." The court wanted to protect a child's right to receive any educational opportunities available to him or her.

The dissenting opinion by Justice Cirillo stressed that Mr. Tucker should not be forced to contribute to his son's education at Syracuse, because Will could receive a comparable educational experience at Penn State for less than half the price of Syracuse University.

SECTION 1.9
STATUS AND PROCESS

Status and Process is synonymous with an essay on how to make the law simple in five hundred words or less. The concept is quite simple. The law favors certain institutions rather than individual members of society. If one is able to ascertain who enjoys favored status with the law it is often possible to predict the outcome of a case without even knowing the law.

Status and process requires an examination of the parties to the litigation. The outcome of the case will depend on whom we want to protect and what goals society wants to achieve.

For example, consider the institution of marriage. Does the law favor or frown upon marriage? The laws obviously support the concept of marriage and the outcome of a case will frequently be decided to uphold that institution. From a sociological point of view, marriage serves three functions:

1. It is a way of regulating the struggle between men and women. This is amply reinforced during the marriage vows of the wedding. One takes a spouse for better or for worse, through sickness and in health and until death do they part.

2. The law recognizes marriage as the accepted way of producing children, albeit not the only way. A child born out of wedlock is frowned upon and labeled "illegitimate."

3. Marriage is favored since it offers a logical way of transferring assets from generation to generation. Assets are passed down to children and spouses rather than being given to the first person that arrives at the home of the decedent.

To prove that the law favors the institution of marriage, one merely has to think of how easy it is to become married and how difficult it is to obtain a divorce. Everyone is aware that a marital union can be created through a religious or civil ceremony. The law, however, goes out of its way to establish marital relationships and has created the fiction of a common law marriage. Most would say that the parties have to live together for seven years and hold themselves out as a man and wife to establish such a marriage. This response would be incorrect. No magical time period is necessary.

This is demonstrated in the case of **In re Estate of Garges, 378 A.2d 307 (Pa. 1977)** where the court stated:

> A marriage contract does not require any specific form of words. In particular, words of taking or explicit utterances, such as "*I take you to be my wife*" or "*I hereby marry you*" are unnecessary. All that is essential is proof of an agreement to enter into a legal relationship of marriage at the present time. For example,…a marriage contract was found where a man gave a woman a ring and said, "*Now you have the ring and you are my wife*," whereupon she replied, "*That is fine, I love it.*"

Those individuals who have not stopped reading this section to call their attorneys should know that a common law marriage is just as valid as a religious or civil ceremony and requires a formal divorce decree to dissolve.

What other institutions enjoy favor with the law? These groups would include children, incompetents, the government and religious organizations. The saying that, "You can't sue City Hall," is a lot truer than one would believe. The government, its agencies and high ranking officials enjoy immunity from suit in most cases.

When using the concept of status and process, one must analyze the institution as it existed at the time of the court decision. As the times change, so do the institutions that the law protects. Returning to marriage, women were traditionally viewed as the weaker of the sexes. Therefore, women were automatically awarded one-third to one-half of the husband's net income in a support proceeding. With Equal Rights and the shifting of public opinion, the role of women in today's society has vastly changed. They are considered equal to men and have made significant inroads in the market place. It is now common to see a female doctor, lawyer, construction worker, police officer or soldier. This equality of the sexes has resulted in change in the support laws. The courts now examine the earning capacity of each person instead of making an automatic award to the wife. This has resulted in court decisions requiring wives to pay support to husbands and giving husbands custody of the children.

Court cases are complicated and difficult to understand. Courts sometimes appear to reach a conclusion that is not supported by the facts, or the logic of the opinion seems flawed. When this occurs, perhaps the court is engaging in the protection of a certain institution and wants to achieve an end result even though logic would suggest a different outcome.

SECTION 1.10
CHRISTOPHER V. HODGE

PROBLEM ONE—A

HODGE, DODGE AND LODGE
ATTORNEYS AT LAW
MEMORANDUM

To: All Law Clerks

From: K. Bradford Lodge

Re: Kathy Hodge and the Purchase of Her Car

During the period of time that you work at the firm, you will get to know Kathy Hodge quite well. Kathy is 16 years old and she related the following story to me.

She recently purchased a ten year old Honda with a Blaupunkt tape deck and sun roof for $1,000.00. Immediately after passing her driving test, Kathy decided she must have a car. Unfortunately, she and her father, Joe Hodge, disagreed as to whether she was ready for and deserving of what her father considered an "unnecessary extravagance." Kathy felt that after finally passing the driving test, she deserved some reward.

After grueling, yet unsuccessful, negotiations with her father, Kathy decided to purchase the vehicle on her own. She had saved $1,000.00 from her work last summer as a waitress. With this sum of money, Kathy was sure that she could purchase the car of her dreams. An extensive examination of the car ads, however, shattered these illusions. As luck would have it, though, she happened to stumble across a Honda in the parking lot of a McDonald's restaurant. The car was just like the one owned by her neighbor, Peter Christopher. But this car had a "For Sale" sign in its window, so Kathy jotted down the telephone number.

Kathy called the number and was shocked to learn that the vehicle was, in fact, the car owned by Christopher. He was selling the Honda for $1,000.00 to pay for a plane ticket to California.

When Kathy's father learned of the purchase, he exploded. "How dare you buy a car after I told you, no." Kathy had never seen her father more outraged. Even her sweetest smile couldn't calm him down. Not only did he suspend her driving privileges, but he even attempted to return the car to Christopher. The neighbor refused to take the car back claiming that a "deal is a deal." Two days later, Kathy figured that her father had calmed down enough for her to start driving the vehicle. Unfortunately, being a novice driver, Kathy was unable to negotiate a turn a block from home and demolished the Honda. As she sat on the curb crying, the hubcap of the vehicle rolled by her. Since this was the only thing left of the car, she picked it up and walked home.

Kathy spent the rest of the day calling friends for advice. One girl-friend told Kathy that she could obtain the return of her money from Christopher since she was only sixteen. The girlfriend had received the return of her money from a record club that she had joined when she was fifteen. Relying on this advice, Kathy approached her neighbor and demanded her money back. She even offered Christopher the return of the hubcap. After all, that was all that was left of the car. Christopher laughed and said that she had entered into a valid contract and had destroyed the car.

I told Kathy that I didn't have time to talk to her, but that I would have the law clerks research the law. Please read the **Lemke** decision and apply the case to Kathy's problem. You must decide the following:

1. Can Kathy rescind the contract and receive the return of her money from Christopher?

2. Does it matter that the only thing she can return to Christopher is the hubcap, or must she pay to have the car repaired before she can disaffirm the contract?

3. Did status and process play any part in the **Lemke** decision? Explain your answer.

JAMES HALBMAN V. MICHAEL LEMKE
298 N.W.2D 562 (WIS. 1980)

ON THIS REVIEW WE MUST DECIDE whether a minor who disaffirms a contract for the purchase of a vehicle must make payment to the seller for damage sustained by the vehicle prior to the time the contract was disaffirmed.

This matter was before the trial court upon stipulated facts. On or about July 13, 1973, James Halbman, Jr. (Halbman), a minor, entered into an agreement with Lemke whereby Lemke agreed to sell Halbman a 1968 Oldsmobile for the sum of $1,250. Lemke was the manager of L & M Standard Station in Greenfield, Wisconsin, and Halbman was an employee at L & M. At the time the agreement was made, Halbman paid Lemke $1,000 in cash and took possession of the car. Arrangements were made for Halbman to pay $25 per week until the balance was paid, at which time title would be transferred to him. About five weeks after the purchase agreement, and after Halbman had paid a total of $1,100 of the purchase price, a connecting rod on the vehicle's engine broke. Lemke, while denying any obligation, offered to assist Halbman in installing a used engine in the vehicle if Halbman, at his expense, could secure one. Halbman declined the offer and in September took the vehicle to a garage where it was repaired at a cost of $637.40. Halbman did not pay the repair bill.

In October of 1973, Lemke endorsed the vehicle's title over to Halbman, although the full purchase price had not been paid by Halbman, in an effort to avoid any liability for the operation, maintenance, or use of the vehicle. On October 15, 1973, Halbman returned the title to Lemke by letter which disaffirmed the purchase contract and demanded the return of all money theretofore paid by Halbman. Lemke did not return the money paid by Halbman.

The repair bill remained unpaid, and the vehicle remained in the garage where the repairs had been made. In the spring of 1974, the garage removed the vehicle's engine and transmission and then towed the vehicle to the residence of James Halbman, Sr., the father of the minor since the bill was not paid. Lemke was asked several times to remove the vehicle from the senior Halbman's home, but he declined to do so, claiming he was under no legal obligation to remove it. During the period when the vehicle was at the garage and then subsequently at the home of the plaintiff's father, it was vandalized and unsalvageable.

Halbman initiated this action seeking the return of the $1,100 he had paid toward the purchase of the vehicle.

The sole issue before us is whether a minor, having disaffirmed a contract for the purchase of an item which is not a necessity and having tendered the property back to the seller, must make payment to the seller for damage to the property prior to the disaffirmance. Lemke argues that he should be entitled to recover for the damage to the vehicle up to the time of disaffirmance, which he claims equals the amount of the repair bill. Neither party challenges the absolute right of a minor to disaffirm a contract for the purchase of items, which are not necessities.

That right, known as the doctrine of incapacity or the "infancy doctrine," is one of the oldest and most venerable of our common law traditions. *Grauman, Marx & Cline co. v. Krienitz*, **142 Wis. 556, 560, 126 N.W. 50 (1910).** Although the origins of the doctrine are obscure, it is generally recognized that its purpose is the protection of minors from foolishly squandering their wealth through improvident contracts with crafty adults who would take advantage of them in the marketplace. *Kiefer v. Fred Howe Motors, Inc.,* **39 Wis.2d 20, 24, 158 N.W.2d 288 (1968).** Thus it is settled law in this state that a contract of a minor for items which are not necessities is void or voidable at the minor's option. **Id. at 23, 158 N.W.2d 288;** *Schoenung v. Gallet,* **206 Wis. 52, 55, 238 N.W. 852 (1931).**

Once there has been a disaffirmance, however, as in this case between a minor buyer and an adult seller, unresolved problems arise regarding the rights and responsibilities of the parties. As a general rule a minor who disaffirms a contract is entitled to recover all consideration he has paid incident to the transaction. In return the minor is expected to return as much of the consideration as, at the time of disaffirmance, remains in the minor's possession. The minor's right to disaffirm is not contingent upon the return of the property, however, as disaffirmance is permitted even where such return cannot be made. *Olson v. Veum,* **197 Wis. 342, 345, 222 N.W. 233 (1928).** The return of property remaining in the hands of the minor is not the issue presented here. In this case we have a situation where the property cannot be returned to the vendor in its entirety because it has been damaged and therefore diminished in value, and the seller seeks to recover the depreciation.

A minor is under an enforceable duty to return to the seller, upon disaffirmance, as much of the consideration as remains in his possession.

When the contract is disaffirmed, title to that part of the purchased property which is retained by the minor revests in the seller; it no longer belongs to the minor. The rationale for the rule is plain: a minor who disaffirms a purchase and recovers his purchase price should not also be permitted to profit by retaining the property purchased. The infancy doctrine is designed to protect the minor, sometimes at the expense of an innocent seller, but it is not to be used to bilk merchants out of property and proceeds of the sale. Consequently, when the minor no longer possesses the property which was the subject matter of the contract, the rule requiring the return of property does not apply. The minor will not be required to give up what he does not have.

Here Lemke seeks the value of the vehicle prior to disaffirmance. Such a recovery would require Halbman to return more than what was remaining in his possession. This would bind the minor to a part of the obligation which by law he is privileged to avoid.

Modifications of the rules governing the capacity of infants to contract are best left to the legislature. Until such changes are forthcoming, however, we hold that, absent misrepresentation…, a minor who disaffirms a contract for the purchase of an item which is not a necessity may recover his purchase price without liability for use, depreciation, damage, or other diminution in value.

PROBLEM ONE—A
ANSWER SHEET

Name   **Please Print Clearly**

1. Can Kathy rescind the contract and receive the return of her money from Christopher?

_____

_____

_____

_____

_____

_____

_____

_____

_____

_____

_____

_____

_____

_____

_____

_____

_____

_____

_____

_____

_____

2. Does it matter that the only thing Kathy can return to Christopher is the hubcap, or must she pay to have the car repaired before she can disaffirm the contract?

_____

_____

_____

_____

_____

_____

_____

_____

3. Do you think that the concept of status and process played any part in the Lemke decision? Explain your answer.

_____

_____

_____

_____

_____

_____

_____

_____

_____

_____

SECTION **1.11**
PRECEDENT:
THE BACKBONE OF
AMERICAN JURISPRUDENCE

Precedent is the process whereby judges apply the decisions and rules of prior cases to the present case over which they are presiding. The correct legal term for this concept is **stare decisis**. This doctrine forms the backbone of the American legal system and offers litigants certainty and uniformity in the application of the law.

Judges will generally follow precedent but are not bound to do so in every situation. The court has the discretion to change the law as the social, political or economic conditions change. Changes in the law are also observed as members of the court, especially the United States Supreme Court, are replaced by members with different judicial or political philosophies.

The following materials chronicle the changing law in Pennsylvania with respect to a separated or divorced parent's obligation to pay for the college education of a child. In *Blue v. Blue*, the reader will learn that the court has overruled the **Spitzer** decision and 30 years of case law in declining to recognize a divorced or separated parent's obligation to pay for a child's college education since no legal duty exists to support a child past the age of 18.

REGINALD BLUE v. RONALD BLUE
616 A.2D 628 (PA. 1992)

ZAPPALA, JUSTICE

IN THIS APPEAL, WE ARE ASKED TO DETERMINE to what extent a parent must pay for a child's college education and whether that child must contribute to his or her own college education through the use of loans and grants.

Reginald V. Blue's father and mother separated in October of 1987, with the mother leaving the marital residence. Prior to separation, Reginald had attended three semesters of college at Pennsylvania State University. However, the emotional trauma of his parents' separation caused him to take a leave of absence during his second year at Penn State.

The father is an assistant professor at Lehigh County Community College with an annual salary of approximately $43,000.00. Reginald's mother is also employed by the college, as a secretary, with an annual gross income of approximately $12,000.00. Prior to separation, while Reginald was attending Penn State, all college expenses were paid for by Reginald's parents from their joint incomes.

During the spring of 1988, Reginald attended Lehigh County Community College. Because Reginald's parents were employees of the college, no tuition had to be paid. It is also during this time that Reginald resided with his father in the marital residence. The monthly mortgage on the marital residence was $280.00. In addition, it appears that the father alone paid for all of Reginald's needs including $40.00 a week spending money, a car payment and automobile insurance.

During the summer and fall of 1988, Reginald worked as a ride operator at Dorney Park and as a temporary for Kelly Services. Through both jobs, Reginald earned approximately $6,265.44.

In August of 1988, Reginald's father decided that he needed to "get on with his life" and purchased a $114,000.00 five-bedroom home. The monthly mortgage payment for this new home was $1,187.00 a month or a monthly mortgage payment increase of $900.00. The father then left his son and the marital residence and moved into his new home with his girlfriend and her two minor children where the father pays all the monthly living expenses. Approximately 30 days after father left the marital residence, mother, her boyfriend and his emancipated son moved into the marital residence. During his semester breaks, Reginald now lives with his mother who provides free room and board.

Because he did not have the funds to pay the required college expenses, Reginald postponed returning to Penn State until January 1989. At that time, the cost of tuition, room and board was approximately $6,440.00 with an additional $400.00 needed for books and other expenses.

[T]he trial court entered an order requiring the father to pay $4,600.00 a year towards Reginald's college education. In addition, the trial court required Reginald to apply for and accept any educational loans or grants he received. The father would then be entitled to a reduction in support to the extent of any grants and/or loans received.

On appeal, the Superior Court affirmed the assessment of support but reversed the trial court with regard to the requirement that Reginald seek financial assistance and that the father's support obligation be reduced by the amount of any assistance received. The Superior Court reasoned that since parents bear the financial responsibility for college expenses, a child should not have to obtain loans and/or grants but should that

child choose to do so, a parent's obligation to provide support should not be reduced.

The trial court determined that the father caused his own undue hardship as the result of his real estate purchase. Therefore, the trial court determined that the father had a duty to provide financial assistance to Reginald. However, the trial court also concluded that the father did not have limitless financial resources and therefore Reginald had the primary obligation for his own college education. This added requirement is what caused Superior Court to reverse the trial court.

Neither statute nor specific case law had enunciated the legal axiom relied upon by the lower courts. To the contrary, all that had been articulated was that set forth in *Emerick v. Emerick*, **445 Pa. 428 (1971).**

In *Emerick* the mother and father had entered into an agreement which required the father to provide a four-year college education for each of his children. When the father refused to pay the educational expenses of two college age children, the mother sought enforcement of the agreement. We were persuaded by the fact that the father had entered into an agreement to pay educational expenses. We did not unequivocally adopt a legal principle that a parent has a legal obligation to provide college expenses but rather permitted recovery of college expenses if a parent had the financial ability to do so, because the parties' agreement had required that result. Therefore, our research having found no legal authority to require a parent to provide for college educational support, we must reverse the Superior Court and decline to adopt the reasoning of either lower court.

The Superior Court's reasoning seems to have evolved from its opinion in *Commonwealth v. Gilmore*, **97 Pa. Super. 303 (1929).** In refusing to grant the father's petition to terminate support, Superior Court noted that case law tended to include some education within the purview of a parent's obligation to provide support and maintenance.

The duty to provide educational support beyond the minimum state-required attendance, however, was tempered by the parent's ability to pay and the child's commitment to completing his high school studies.

In recent history, the Superior Court has adopted and applied the *Gilmore* analysis to college educational support of a child. In essence, the Superior Court has transferred this "principle of necessity" of basic fundamental education to a requirement that each child be entitled to an "enhanced" education. We do not agree with this transformation.

Under the common law, a parent had a duty to support a minor child. Consequently, the common law duty to support a minor child must by necessity cease at age 18.

Since no legal duty has been imposed by our legislature, nor have we developed such a duty by our case law, we decline to do so. The judgment of the Superior Court is reversed and the complaint for support for aid to higher education is dismissed.

DISSENTING OPINION BY LARSEN, J.

I would affirm the Superior Court's order as to the holding that parents have an obligation to provide support for their children. I would reverse the Superior Court order as to the parents not getting a reduction or credit toward this obligation from the children's grants, scholarships, loans, financial worth, etc. No windfalls should occur here.

QUESTIONS FOR DISCUSSION:

1. Do you agree with the decision in **Spitzer** or in **Blue**?

2. Why did the Supreme Court change the law as it was expressed in **Spitzer**?

3. Why didn't the Pennsylvania Supreme Court in **Blue** discuss the **Spitzer** decision?

4. Do you think that the court's decision in **Blue** is arbitrary, or is it based on sound legal reasoning?

The Pennsylvania legislature promptly accepted the challenge of the court in *Blue v. Blue* by enacting legislation to re-establish the support obligation of divorced or separated parents for their college-bound children. As a pre-condition for obtaining postsecondary educational expenses, the statute requires a child to first make reasonable efforts to obtain scholarships, grants, and work-study. After deducting these proceeds from the cost of education, the court may order one or both of the parents to pay the remaining educational costs based upon a number of factors such as the financial resources of both parents and the ability of the child to raise funds through employment

The relevant portions of the statute are as follows:

SECTION 4327
POSTSECONDARY
EDUCATIONAL
EXPENSES

GENERAL RULE

a. Where applicable under this section, a court may order either or both parents who are separated, divorced, unmarried or otherwise subject to an existing support obligation to provide equitably for educational costs of their child whether an application for this support is made before or after the child has reached 18 years of age. The responsibility to provide for postsecondary educational expenses is a shared responsibility between both parents. The duty of a parent to provide a postsecondary education for a child is not as exacting a requirement as the duty to provide food, clothing and shelter for a child of tender years unable to support himself. This authority shall extend to postsecondary education, including periods of undergraduate or vocational education after the child graduates from high school. An award for postsecondary educational costs may be entered only after the child or student has made reasonable efforts to apply for scholarships, grants and work-study assistance.

OTHER RELEVANT FACTORS

b. Calculating educational costs and deducting grants and scholarships, the court may order either parent or both parents to pay all or part of the remaining educational costs of their child The court shall consider all relevant factors which appear reasonable, equitable and necessary, including the following:

1. The financial resources of both parents.

2. The financial resources of the student.

3. The receipt of educational loans and other financial assistance by the student.

4. The ability, willingness and desire of the student to pursue and complete the course of study.

5. Any willful estrangement between parent and student caused by the student after attaining majority.

6. The ability by the student to contribute to the student's expenses through gainful employment. The student's history of employment is material under this paragraph.

7. Any other relevant factors.

WHEN LIABILITY MAY NOT BE FOUND

c. A court shall not order support for educational costs if any of the following circumstances exist:

1. Undue financial hardship would result to the parent.

2. The educational costs would be a contribution for post-college graduate educational costs.

3. The order would extend support for the student beyond the student's twenty-third birthday. If exceptional circumstances exist, the court may order educational support for the student beyond the student's twenty-third birthday.

Since its passage, the Pennsylvania courts have had to interpret the statute in a number of situations. For example, the court has ruled that parental support obligations for college do not include living expenses for personal items such as clothing and supplies as well as bookstore purchases. Parents also cannot claim that estrangement from their child negates an obligation to pay educational costs when the relationship is one of disagreement and misunderstanding because the child and parent are not getting along. Furthermore, a widowed parent is considered "unmarried," and is obligated to pay educational expenses.

On October 10, 1995, the Pennsylvania Supreme Court once again dealt a blow to the ability of a child to obtain parental assistance for college education. In *Curtis v. Kline*, the high court overturned the legislation requiring divorced or estranged parents to help out with college costs. The court held that the statute violates the Equal Protection Clause of the Fourteenth Amendment because it granted children from broken homes the right to obtain financial assistance for college that children of married parents did not enjoy.

It should be noted, however, that the courts in several other states have found laws similar to the one in Pennsylvania constitutional and not violative of the Equal Protection Clause.

According to the American Bar Association Journal, the following states allow the court to order divorced parents to support their children after the children reach majority:

STATES THAT ALLOW SUPPORT AFTER MAJORITY

Alabama	Iowa	Oregon
Colorado	Massachusetts	South Carolina
Connecticut	Missouri	Tennessee
Hawaii	Michigan	Utah
Indiana	Nevada	Washington
Illinois	New Hampshire	West Virginia
		Wyoming

SECTION 1.12
COMMONWEALTH OF
PENNSYLVANIA
V. JOSEPH HODGE

PROBLEM ONE—B

HODGE, DODGE AND LODGE
ATTORNEYS AT LAW
MEMORANDUM

To: All Law Clerks

FROM: K. Bradford Lodge

RE: Joe Hodge and His Skating Accident

You have probably heard the rumors about Joe Hodge's drinking problems. Unfortunately, not all of the stories are rumors. Joe was fired from his job when he became so drunk that he drove his bulldozer over the supervisor's new BMW. Well, once again, Joe's drinking has gotten him into trouble once again.

Recently, Joe joined "Skateboarders of America." Joe takes his skateboard to the park and spends the day practicing all of the latest stunts. In fact, Joe has become so proficient that he often leaves the car at home and skateboards to work.

Last weekend, there was a meeting of "Skateboarders of America" in the park. Joe was so excited to show off his talents, that he arose early to practice in the driveway. Joe soon worked up a sweat so he drank several cans of beer to quench his thirst. Feeling especially adventurous, Joe decided to skateboard to the park which is five miles from Joe's home.

As Joe was skateboarding down the street, he waived to a neighbor who was sitting in a lounge chair on the front of her lawn. Joe, however, was going so fast that he lost his balance and crashed into officer John O'Brien who was crossing the street. As Officer O'Brien helped Joe to his feet, the police officer smelled the strong odor of alcohol on Joe's breath. A breathalyzer revealed a blood alcohol level of .11, so Joe was arrested for driving under the influence of alcohol. Joe is shocked by the absurdity of the whole situation and has come to our office for advice. He cannot understand how a person can be arrested for driving under the influence when he is using a skateboard and not an automobile. Joe is particularly distressed since he will lose his driver's license if found guilty of the charge.

I told Joe that I was confident that you would do a fine job researching the law for his case. Please read *Commonwealth of Pennsylvania v. Lee Brown* and decide the following:

1.   Does *Section 3731* of the Motor Vehicle Code apply to an individual riding a skateboard while under the influence of alcohol?

2. According to the case, what factors should the Court consider in determining the intention of the legislature in enacting a statute?

3. Is there enough evidence to convict Joe of driving under the influence?

COMMONWEALTH OF PENNSYLVANIA v. LEE BROWN
620 A.2D 1213 (PA. SUPER. 1993)

ON SEPTEMBER 20, 1990, BROWN WAS RIDING her bicycle in the wrong lane of Miller Avenue, Clairton, Pennsylvania, and traveling in the wrong direction. As the bicycle weaved down the street, Brown struck an automobile whose driver had attempted to avoid her by swerving his vehicle. After the accident, a state police officer observed a strong odor of alcohol on Brown's breath. She consented to a blood alcohol test which revealed a blood alcohol content of 0.29%. She also admitted to the police officer that she had been consuming beer.

Based on this incident, the Commonwealth charged Brown with two counts of driving under the influence of alcohol or controlled substances, and with riding on the wrong side of the roadway, a summary offense. The Commonwealth raises the following issue: Whether the trial court erred in holding that bicycles are not "vehicles" for purposes of *75 Pa.C.S.A. Section 3731*, and therefore, that a person cannot be convicted of driving under the influence for operating a bicycle on a public highway while under the influence of alcohol or controlled substances?

Because this case presents a question of the proper interpretation of a legislative enactment, we will review the relevant rules of statutory construction. The cardinal principle in interpreting legislative enactments is "to ascertain and effectuate the intent of the General Assembly."

When the words of a statute are clear and free from all ambiguity, the letter of the law is not to be disregarded under the pretext of pursuing its spirit. A court interpreting a statute must ascertain and effectuate the intention of the legislature and give full effect to each provision of the statute if at all possible. *Fireman's Fund Insurance Company v. Nationwide Mutual Insurance Company*, **317 Pa. Super. 497, 464 A.2d 431 (1983)**. "When the words of a statute are not explicit, the intention of the General Assembly may be ascertained by considering, among other factors:"

1. The occasion and necessity for the statute.

2. The circumstances under which it was enacted.

3. The mischief to be remedied.

4. The object to be attained.

5. The former law, if any, including other statutes upon the same or similar subjects.

6. The consequences of a particular interpretation.

7. The contemporaneous legislative history.

8. Legislative and administrative interpretations of such statute.

The statute which requires interpretation herein is *Section 3731 of the Motor Vehicle Code*, which provides:

a. Offense defined. A person shall not drive, operate or be in actual physical control of the movement of any vehicle while:

1. under the influence of alcohol to a degree which renders the person incapable of safe driving;

2. under the influence of any controlled substance, to a degree which renders the person incapable of safe driving;

3. under the combined influence of alcohol and any controlled substance to a degree which renders the person incapable of safe driving; or

4. the amount of alcohol by weight in the blood of the person is 0.10 percent or greater.

The issue presented by this case is whether *Section 3731* applies to an individual operating a bicycle, as opposed to a motor vehicle.

Keeping in mind the principle that a statute must be construed to give effect to all of its parts, we note the definitions of "vehicle" and "motor vehicle" as set forth in the Vehicle Code. A *"vehicle"* is defined as *"[e]very device in, upon or by which any person or property is or may be transported or drawn upon a highway, except devices used exclusively upon rails or tracks."* 75 Pa.C.S.A.§102. *"Motor vehicle"* is defined as *"a vehicle which is self-propelled except one which is propelled solely by human power or by electric power obtained from overhead trolley wires, but not operated upon rails."* Section 3731 prohibits the driving or operating of a "vehicle"—while under the influence of alcohol. A bicycle clearly falls within the confines of that definition. It is a "device" upon which a person

or property may be "transported or drawn upon a highway," and it is not a device which is "used exclusively upon rails or tracks." See Section 102, supra ("vehicle.") A bicycle is clearly not a motor vehicle as it is a vehicle "which is propelled solely by human power." However, it is the operators of vehicles, not the operators of motor vehicles, who are regulated under Section 3731. Since Section 3731 applies to the operators of vehicles, and since the bicycle which appellee was riding falls within the definition of that term, the lower court erred in holding that appellee could not be prosecuted under Section 3731 for operating her bicycle while purportedly under the influence of alcohol.

For these reasons, we hold that the lower court abused its discretion in dismissing the charges against appellee under Section 3731.

Order reversed; case remanded for further proceedings in accordance with this memorandum.

DEL SOLE, J., concurring.

I join the opinion of my distinguished colleague, Judge Cercone. I only wish to point out that the Vehicle Code evidences the Legislature's understanding that the word "vehicle" does include bicycles. At Pa. C.S.A. Section 1101, all vehicles are required to be titled except those exempted in Section 1102. There, in subparagraph 7, vehicles "moved solely by human or animal power" are excluded from this requirement. This same limitation also applies to the registration requirements of Section 1301 at. seq. These sections demonstrate to me that the members of the General Assembly fully understood that bicycles were included in the definition of "vehicle" when used in Section 3731.

PROBLEM ONE—B
ANSWER SHEET

Name _Niraj Shah_   **Please Print Clearly**

1. Does Section 3731 of the Motor Vehicle Code apply to an individual riding a skateboard while under the influence of alcohol?

No, because a skate board is operated by human power. In sub paragraph 7, "vehicles" moved solely by human or animal power" are excluded from this requirement.

2. According to the case, what factors should the Court consider in determining the intention of the legislature in enacting a statute?

3. Is there enough evidence to convict Joe of driving under the influence? Please explain.

_No_

SECTION **1.13**
LEGAL RESEARCH
AND THE INTERNET

When was the last time you saw a movie or read a magazine without seeing something about the *Internet*? Probably not too long ago! The Internet has become a major source of information, communication, and even entertainment for people all over the world. Materials on a variety of subjects can be accessed at the touch of a key including law-related topics. Court decisions, law review articles and legislation are now instantly accessible. The following is a simplistic overview on how to use the Internet to do legal research.

Directories and search engines are research tools that can be used to search the Internet for information on particular topics. These research tools can be used to search for information on all kinds of topics, including legal information. Search engines, such as Alta Vista, Lycos, Webcrawler and Excite, use robots crawling the Web which try to index every word on every Web page. Search engines are powerful, and some of them index more than 30,000,000 pages. Search Engines are good searching for a specific item. Directories, such as Yahoo and Magellan have lists of Web sites described in a few words and classified by specific examples. Directories are ideal when you are looking for general topics.

In order to use these research tools, you can enter the address of the Search Engine or Directory in the *text entry box*. This will take you to the homepage of that particular research tool. Some of these addresses are:

- **http://www.lycos.com**
- **http://www.yahoo.com**
- **http://webcrawler.com**
- **http://aol.com**
- **http://www.askjeeves.come**
- **http://www.about.com**

Type the address **http://www.yahoo.com** in the text entry box and press enter. You should travel to the *Yahoo* homepage. You should see many different categories. Click on the ***Business and Economy*** category. You should then travel to a page which has many different business selections, such as Business Schools, Employment, Law and Television. Choose the **Employment** category. If you are interested in looking up different types of resumes, you can click on the Resumes category. Now, return to the previous **Employment** page.

Say you've decided to pursue a career in Business and you are uncertain as to what you want to do. In order to effectively use a search engine or directory, you have to narrow the search to an area that you might be interested in. For instance, if you decide you might like to learn more about **the corporate side of business,** you can enter the words **"corporate business"** into the *text entry box* of the **Employment** page. This should provide you with over one hundred category matches to corporate business employment opportunities and information.

> **NOTE:** When you want to print out a page from the Internet, simply go to the upper lefthand corner of your computer screen under the *File* menu and drag your mouse down to print. You should be able to print a page from the Internet just as you would print out other information on your computer.

If you wish to locate law related topics on Yahoo's Internet site, merely click on the word "law" in the *Business and Economy* section and you will be linked to a site that provides a variety of legal resources, including: **(1)** the America Bar Association's Section on Business Law topics, **(2)** federal and state statutes, **(3)** tax forms, **(4)** articles on high tech law, and **(5)** the corporate counselor, which link contains articles on employment law, securities, antitrust and other business related issues.

A good start for legal research on the Internet is to visit a law oriented directory or Search Engine. These resources can help you find subjects from different types of law to specific cases, legal news and even U.S. Government sites. Several specific legal research sites are:

- **http://www.lawcrawler.com**
  Lawcrawler is a legal search engine that is powered by Alta Vista and allows for a comprehensive legal search on the topic of your choice.

- **http://www.findlaw.com**
  Findlaw is a legal subject index.

- **http://www.hg.org**
  Hieros Games has information on legal organizations, including every government in the world. This is a good research tool for those interested in practicing law.

- **http://www.ilrg.com**
  Internet Legal Resource Guide is a categorized index of over 3100 select web sites in 238 nations, islands, and territories.

- **http://www/nolo.com**
  Legal Encyclopedia is a self-help center on the Internet.

- **http://www,cclabs.missouri.edu/~tbrown/lawmarks**
  Law Marks is a legal resource database that contains legal, political and governmental resources.

- **http://www.lawguru.com**
  This is the Web site for a law firm. This site contains answers to frequently asked legal questions and has many interesting links.

- **http://www.lectlaw.com**
  The *Lectric Law Library* contains practical links such as "Legal help for the poor' and 'How to fight your traffic ticket."

- **http://www.legis.state.pa.us**
  This Internet site allows access to information from the Pennsylvania legislature including the text of bills and the history of the legislation.

- **http://www.fedworld.gov**
  This site provides access to the search engine of the Federal government.

- **http://www.lawoffice.com**
  West Publications has created this link to allow the public to gain access to the profiles of law firms and attorneys around the country.

- **http://www.aclu.org**
  This is the official site for the American Civil Liberties Union and offers information on civil liberty controversies, such as lesbian and gay rights and women's rights.

- **http://www.uslaw.com**
  This comprehensive site covers all aspects of the legal field, including articles, current events and chat rooms where you can ask lawyers questions.

- **http://www.megalaw.com**
  This site discusses recent legal developments in the news and provides access to information in different legal fields, as well as information on state and federal court decisions.

- **http://www.itslegal.com**
  This site provides links to different legal topics, including real estate law, personal injury, credit and debt issues, family law, and employment law.

- **http://www.law.indiana.edu/v-lib**
  Indiana University School of Law-Bloomington's virtual law library allows searches about the legal field and will provide links relating to the search.

- **http://www.law.com**
  The law.com connection features law related articles and stories, summaries from local, state, and federal court decisions, law links, and other legal information.

- **http://www.prairielaw.com**
  Through articles, columns and online discussions, this site offers information about the law including consumer concerns, crime, immigration and work related issues.

Now its time to try one of these legal research tools. The 1997 Steven Spielberg movie, *Amistad,* is based upon a United States Supreme Court decision that decided the fate of African slaves who staged a ship board revolt off the cost of Cuba in an attempt to gain their freedom. The slaves ended up in America, but Spain demanded their return in order to face criminal prosecution for the ship uprising. American abolitionists became involved in the frey and the matter ended up in the courts. In a landmark decision, our highest court established the principle that all people are "presumptively free" and entitled to the protections of American law. This holding granted the African slaves the freedom they so desperately desired in order to return to their home land. *The Amistad, 40 U.S. 518 (1841).* If you wish to read the case or learn more about the story, you merely have to access the internet. If you type the word, *Amistad* on a search engine, it will take you to a variety of stories and references on the topic. You may also type **http://www.findlaw.com** in the text entry box and press enter. This will take the user to the home page for Find Law, whose research engine may be used to find court cases and other legal information on most legal topics. Go to the box marked Supreme Court and click on it. The Supreme Court decision in the *Amistad* case should be visible when the page opens. You may also gain access to the case by typing *40 U.S. 518* in the appropriate box.

More and more courts are placing their dockets and other court related information on the Internet. For instance, a person may gain access to the records of the Philadelphia Court of Common Pleas by going to **http://courts.phila.gov**. Depending upon the search, one may check the dockets of a specific court case, conduct a judgment search involving a specific person or conduct a litigation search involving a person's name.

FOR GENERAL INFORMATION ON THE INTERNET

- **http://info.isoc.org/guest/zakon/Internet/History/HIT.html**
  Hobbs' Internet Timeline. For information about the Internet, the people who use it and on-line culture

- **http://www.columbia.edu/~hauben/netbook/**
  Netizens: On the history and *Impact of Usenet and the Internet.* For a collection of essays about the history, nature and impact of the Internet.

- **http://home.netscape.com/eng/mozilla/3.0/handbook**
  To obtain a more detailed transcription of how to use Netscape Navigator, you can access the *Navigator Handbook* on-line.

SECTION 1.14
INTERNET RESEARCH
ON MALPRACTICE

PROBLEM ONE—C

HODGE, DODGE AND LODGE
ATTORNEYS AT LAW
MEMORANDUM

To: All Law Clerks

From: Gregory Olan Dodge

Re: Internet Research on Medical Malpractice

Because it is so expense to maintain a law library, I am interested in learning how to conduct legal Research on the Internet. I have decided that you would be an excellent candidate to become the firm's resident computer expert. I would like you to do some research on the Internet and report back to me on your findings. This will allow me to assess whether the firm should reduce its library and buy more computers

Hodge, Dodge and Lodge has been consulted by a client who suffered a tragic loss as the result of the amputation of her foot due to the negligence of Dr. Feelgood. The client was found to have a cancerous tumor on the right foot that required the amputation. For some unknown reason, Dr. Feelgood became confused in the operating room and mistakenly amputated the left foot. I believe this is a clear case of medical malpractice and we should recover millions.

Please research the question of medical malpractice on the Internet. I want to learn if there are any legal resources out there on this topic. Let me know what you find and give me an explanation on how you uncovered the information. Since I am not computer conversant, I would like you to printout a copy of the resources that you find so that I may review the information on my own. Your research should not be confined to cases involving the amputation of a leg.

SECTION 1.15
REVIEW CASES

1. A 16 year old youth went to a local car dealer in order to purchase an automobile. When the salesman learned of the child's age, he refused to sell the car unless the purchase was made by an adult. A few hours later, the minor returned with an adult that the child had just met. The salesman sold the car to the adult and then assisted the buyer in having the title transferred to the youth. A few days later, the 16 year old returned with his father and attempted to rescind the contract. Will the car dealer be required to take the automobile back and return the money? *Quality Motors, Inc. v. Johnny Hayes, 225 S. W. 2d 326 (Ark. 1949).*

2. The mother of a mentally challenged female was concerned that her 15 year old daughter would become pregnant without understanding the consequences of her act. The mother filed a "Petition To Have A Tubaligation Performed On A Minor" with the court. Even though there was no legal authority for the court to order the sterilization, the judge felt that the procedure would be in the best interest of the child in order "to prevent unfortunate circumstances..." The child was taken to the hospital under the pretext of having her appendix removed and the tubaligation was performed. Several years later, the child married and attempted to become pregnant. At this time, she learned that she had been sterilized. As a result of her inability to have children, she sued the judge claiming that he violated her constitutional rights. Under the concept of status and process, will the judge be immuned from suit for his actions? *Judge Harold Strump v. Linda Sparkman, 435 U.S. 349 (1978).*

3. The parties to a lawsuit attended a settlement conference before the trial judge. During a break, the judge confronted the plaintiff in the hallway, and in a loud angrily voice, yelled at the plaintiff that his settlement demand was "Bull _ _ _ _ "and if he thought that there was money in the case, the plaintiff had "s _ _ _ for brains!" The judge then told counsel for the plaintiff that the client "had to deal with him and now he was their enemy." Sometime later, the judge was interviewed by a reporter about the incident and denied that he had acted improperly as the plaintiff was alleging. This made it appear as though the plaintiff was lying. Subsequently, the plaintiff filed suit against Judge Williams for his improper conduct. Will the judge enjoy immunity for his actions or should he be held responsible for the outbursts? Do you see a difference between the statements that the judge made during the settlement conference as opposed to those he made to the reporter? *Robert Soliz v. Alexander Williams, III, 74 Cal. App. 4th 577 (1999).*

4. Charles Kuralt, the former "On The Road" correspondent with CBS, maintained a long time and intimate relationship with Elizabeth Shannon. This relationship was kept secret because Kuralt was married. Kuralt was the primary source of financial support for Shannon. In 1989, the television personality sent Ms. Shannon a letter indicating that in the event of his death, he wanted her to own the property in Montana which was used as their retreat. In 1994, Kuralt executed a will naming his wife and children as the beneficiaries of his Estate. The will said nothing about the Montana property. In 1997, Kuralt decided to transfer the property to Shannon. The transaction was disguised as a sale but it was Kuralt's intention to give Shannon the money for the transfer. Prior to the completion of the sale, Kuralt become critically ill. While in the hospital, he wrote a letter to Shannon and enclosed a check to complete the transfer with a notation that was his intent for her to inherit the Montana property. Before the transfer could take place, Kuralt died. Subsequently, conflicting claims were made against the Montana property by both Kuralt's family and Ms. Shannon. Who do you believe is entitled to the property? Does status and process play any part in your decision? *In re: The Estate of Charles Kuralt, 2000 Mont. LEXIS 375 (2000).*

Footnotes

1. Reprinted with permission from **"When Justice Is Up To You,"** 1992 by the Association of Trial Lawyers of America and the National Institute for Citizen Education in the Law.

2. Reproduced with the permission of Hart Pomerantz, Steve Breslin and Canada Law Book, Inc., 240 Edward Street, Aurora, Ontario, Canada L4G 3S9 and *The Criminal Law Quarterly*. This article is also reproduced with the permission of the Canadian Copyright Licensing Agency.

CHAPTER 2

CLASSIFICATIONS OF LAW

SECTION 2.1
PUBLIC LAW V. PRIVATE LAW

The major classifications of law are public law and private law. Public law involves the rights of society as a whole, and those interests are usually represented by a governmental agency. The most common forms of public law are criminal law, constitutional law and administrative law. On the other hand, private law involves those matters between individuals. The classifications of private law are contract law, tort law and property law. These topics are of such importance that they constitute the bulk of courses taken by most first year law students. This chapter will provide an overview of each subject.

SECTION 2.2
CRIMINAL LAW

A crime is a violation of those duties, which an individual owes to the community and the breach of which requires the offender to make satisfaction to the public. As a result, a crime is a violation of the rights of society and not the individual victim. This distinction is immediately apparent when the victim of a crime does not want to prosecute the criminal. While the prosecutor will usually follow the victim's wishes, a district attorney can force a victim to testify against the criminal if there is a compelling societal interest, such as in cases of child abuse or rape. Since the government is responsible for taking action against a criminal defendant on behalf of society, the caption of the case contains the name of the governmental unit such as the "United States," "The State" or "The People" versus the defendant.

Crimes are classified into several categories, depending upon the penalty for the offense. These classifications are treason, felonies, misdemeanors and summary offenses. Treason is the only crime defined in the United States Constitution. Article III, section 3 states that, "Treason against the United States shall consist only in levying war against them or in adhering to their enemies, giving them aid and comfort." Although penalties for most crimes vary from state to state, a felony is a crime generally punishable by more than one year in jail. Examples include such offenses as murder, rape and arson. A misdemeanor is usually punishable by less than one year in jail and includes such matters as assault, criminal trespass and harassment. A defendant accused of a summary offense will generally be responsible for the payment of a fine, such as that which occurs with a traffic ticket.

The government has the burden of proving a defendant guilty **beyond a reasonable doubt**. This burden requires that the prosecution prove that the defendant actually committed the crime and that he or she had the necessary state of mind to commit the crime. This requisite state of mind, or criminal intent, is called **mens rea**. The legal system is concerned with what the defendant intended, knew or should have known when he acted.

COMMONWEALTH OF PENNSYLVANIA V. JAMES CHEATHAM
615 A.2D 802 (PA. SUPER. 1992)

JAMES S. CHEATHAM APPEALS HIS CONVICTION on charges of homicide by vehicle and aggravated assault. We affirm.

On August 3, 1990, Cheatham lost control of his car when it jumped the curb, and ran into three children sitting on a fence, killing one child and injuring the other two. Cheatham was found lying across the front seat of the car after the accident. He was described as "dazed" and "swaying" when he stood up. Cheatham has a history of seizure disorder dating to October, 1988. Cheatham's last reported seizure before the accident occurred on April 15, 1990. Cheatham's driver's license was recalled in early 1989. A physician at Allegheny General notified the Commonwealth of Pennsylvania, on January 5, 1989, that Cheatham suffered from seizure disorder and Cheatham's license was recalled. Both the physician and state Department of Transportation notified Cheatham he was not entitled to drive; Cheatham himself complained before the accident to his treating physician about the recall of his license.

Cheatham argues that a seizure-induced blackout is an involuntary act without the mens rea necessary to raise the conduct from negligence as required for a criminal conviction.

The statute under which Cheatham was charged, homicide by vehicle, provides in relevant part:

Any person who unintentionally causes the death of another person while engaged in the violation of any law of this Commonwealth...is guilty of homicide by vehicle, when the violation is the cause of death.

Cheatham was charged with operating a motor vehicle while his operating privileges were suspended. On the face of it, the charges against Cheatham appear to satisfy the elements of the statute. His violation of the law, driving while his license was recalled, caused the death of a child.

Cheatham was barred from driving because he had not gone seizure-free for a year. Cheatham's illegal act, driving when he was not seizure-free, bears the direct and substantial relationship to the fatal result demanded. When Cheatham had his seizure while driving it was not an unnatural or obscure result which would exempt him from criminal culpability. His seizure was foreseeable and, perhaps, likely.

Our next inquiry is directed to the mental element necessary to make a person criminally culpable for the fatal result which his acts cause, the mens rea. The applicable mens rea requirements of culpability are enumerated in **18 Pa.C.S. Section 302(a)** which establishes four degrees of culpability: intentionally, knowingly, recklessly or negligently. "Negligently" is intended to be criminal negligence which is defined as a gross deviation from the standard of care that a reasonable person would observe.

The question becomes: Do the facts of the case at hand present a "gross deviation?"

An epileptic seizure while driving and an ensuing fatal accident is an example law school textbooks use to distinguish cases in which there is no criminal culpability from those in which there is criminal responsibility. The case most often cited is *People v. Decina*, 2 N.Y. 2d 133 (1956). In that case, Decina killed four children when he lost control of his car during an epileptic seizure. The question before the Decina court was whether the evidence was sufficient to indict. Decina argued the state had no evidence of the mens rea required to indict for involuntary manslaughter. The New York court held that Decina knew he was subject to epileptic seizures. That knowledge and the choice to drive amounted to culpable negligence. The court distinguished Decina's behavior from that of a person for whom the seizure was unexpected. An unexpected attack, the Court reasoned, is altogether different, suggesting a lack of criminal culpability. The defining difference between the epileptic who drives with the knowledge that he or she is seizure prone and the unsuspecting epileptic who drives is one of choice. One chooses to take the risk; the other does not know he is taking the risk.

In this case, Cheatham knew the frequency of his seizures even with medication, he knew that his seizures came on without warning, and he knew that the Commonwealth of Pennsylvania required that he be seizure-free for one year before being licensed to drive. Despite that knowledge, Cheatham choose to drive. That choice to drive raises Cheatham's conduct to the level of a gross deviation from the standard of care that a reasonable person would observe.

SECTION 2.3
CONSTITUTIONAL LAW

In order to establish a better-centralized government, a meeting was held during the summer of 1787 to revise the Articles of Confederation under which the original thirteen states operated. The major issues in dispute resolved by compromise that establishd a national republic with the unique feature of both a federal and state government. The issue of state representation on the national level was resolved by the creation of a system whereby the states are equally represented in the Senate and are represented in the House of Representatives in proportion to their population.

On September 17, 1787, thirty-nine delegates signed the Constitution and sent the document to the Congress of Confederation for approval. In turn, the Congress of Conferderation sent the document to the original states for ratification. One year later, the Constitution became the law of the land.

The United States Constitution is the most important legal document in American jurisprudence. It establishes the fundamental rights of the people and protects them from unlawful governmental interference.

The Constitution is written in very broad and vague terms. This was done intentionally so the Constitution could adapt to changing times. This important concept is called "constitutional relativity" and insures that this legal document will maintain its vitality. How does this occur? The courts continually interpret and apply the Constitution to current problems. This power of the judiciary was established by John Marshall, Chief Justice of the United States Supreme Court, in the landmark decision of *Marbury v. Madison*, **1 Cranch 137 (1803).**

The application of constitutional relativity is demonstrated by the evolution of the Fourth Amendment protections. This Amendment provides:

> The right of the people to be secure in their persons, houses, papers, and effects, against unreasonable searches and seizures, shall not be violated, and no warrants shall issue, but upon probable cause.

How could this Amendment, which was adopted more than 200 years ago, have application to a police search of a computer hard drive when this technology was clearly not within the contemplation of the drafters of the Constitution? Quite simply, the 4th Amendment does not identify what is to be searched but merely specifies that warrants must be issued upon probable cause. This allows the court to decide what is and is not subject to police searches over the course of time.

The Constitution consists of seven Articles and twenty-seven Amendments. The framework of the document creates an intentional distribution of power. The framers realized the need for a Federal or National system rather than a confederation of states. They also realized the need to prevent a concentration of power in a single branch of the government. With this in mind, the drafters created a framework of limited government through the concept of separation of powers. The first three Articles of the Constitution apportion the power to run the country among the legislative, executive and judicial branches of the government. Article I empowers the legislature to make the laws which the executive branch enforces pursuant to the authority granted to the President in Article II. Article III designates the judiciary as that branch of the government which interprets the Constitution.

The first ten Amendments to the Constitution were adopted in 1791 and are labeled the Bill of Rights. These personal safeguards include such things as the right to freedom of speech and the prohibition against self-incrimination.

While many people think that the last Amendment to the Constitution granted 18-year-olds the right to vote, the last Amendment was passed in May 1992. The 27th Amendment provides:

> *No law, varying the compensation for the services of the Senators and Representatives, shall take effect, until an election of Representatives shall have intervened.*

In other words, the Constitution now prohibits the legislature from granting itself a raise that is effective before those representatives run for re-election.

Passing an amendment to the Constitution is a very difficult task. This is amply demonstrated by the fact that over 11,000 amendments have been proposed since the Constitution's inception but only 27 have been adopted. Article V of the Constitution requires that an amendment be passed by two-thirds of each House and by three-fourths of the State Legislatures. The framers did not want the Constitution to be amended every time the population was impassioned by a controversial court decision or legal issue.

The call for an amendment to protect the American flag from desecration is a prime example of such constitutional politics. Whether an amendment to prevent the burning of a flag is necessary, let alone appropriate, has become the source of great debate. To put the matter in the proper context, should an amendment be passed to protect the American flag when the country could not agree that women are equal to men when the Equal Rights Amendment was proposed? It is possible that a constitutional amendment to prevent flag burning may be adopted by appealing to the emotional support of the population. This, however, is the type of issue the framers hoped to avoid by making the amendatory process so difficult.

Another proposed amendment that has sparked much discussion is an amendment to limit the terms of those in Congress. The proposed amendment stems from disgruntled voters who think that career politicians have lost touch with the American people and should not be allowed to stay in office for an indefinite period. The United States Supreme Court in *U.S. Term Limits Inc. v. Thronton* decided that a state cannot limit service in Congress without amending the Constitution. The Court stated that any change in term limits must not come by legislation adopted by Congress or an individual state, but through amendment procedures. The passage of such a constitutional amendment would require a two-thirds vote in the House of Representatives and the Senate, as well as ratification by thirty-eight states.

THE CONSTITUTION IN EVERYDAY LANGUAGE

To better understand the rights guaranteed to citizens of the United States, it is important to review briefly the Constitution and its Amendments. However, the archaic language of this more than 200-year old document is often difficult to understand. The following is a summary of the Constitution written in simple, everyday language.

WE THE PEOPLE OF THE UNITED STATES ESTABLISH THIS CONSTITUTION FOR THE UNITED STATES OF AMERICA.

ARTICLE I	The power to make the laws of the United States will be given to Congress, which will consist of a Senate and House of Representatives.
ARTICLE II	All power to enforce and execute the laws of the United States will be given to an elected President and Vice President.
ARTICLE III	The power to interpret the laws of the United States will be given to the Supreme Court and other federal courts.
ARTICLE IV	Each state will enforce and recognize the laws, legal records, and results of lawsuits from every other state. No state shall discriminate against citizens from another state.
ARTICLE V	Congress may propose Amendments to the Constitution based upon a two-thirds vote of both Houses of Congress or two-thirds of the states can call a convention to propose Amendments. Three-fourths of the states must ratify the proposed change before it may become an Amendment to the Constitution.
ARTICLE VI	This Constitution, and the laws and treaties made under it, are the supreme law of the land.
ARTICLE VII	The Constitution became effective on September 17, 1787.

AMENDMENTS TO THE CONSTITUTION OF THE UNITED STATES OF AMERICA

AMENDMENT I	Citizens have the right to freedom of religion, speech, press and to assemble peaceably.
AMENDMENT II	Citizens have the right to bear arms.
AMENDMENT III	Citizens cannot be required to house soldiers in their homes during peace time.
AMENDMENT IV	Citizens are protected against unreasonable searches and seizures of both their person and property.
AMENDMENT V	No person can be tried twice for the same crime or be forced to testify against himself. A person's life, liberty or property cannot be taken away by the government without going through the proper and fair legal procedures.
AMENDMENT VI	A defendant in a criminal trial is entitled to legal representation and must be provided with a speedy and public trial by an impartial jury.
AMENDMENT VII	Citizens are entitled to jury trials in civil cases involving more than twenty dollars.
AMENDMENT VIII	A court cannot impose cruel and unusual punishment or excessive bail on defendants.
AMENDMENT IX	Rights that are not specifically mentioned within the Constitution are held by the citizens.
AMENDMENT X	Rights that are not delegated to the federal government are reserved for the states and the citizens.
AMENDMENT XI	Citizens are not permitted to sue states where they are not residents.
AMENDMENT XII	The Electoral College will select the President and Vice President.
AMENDMENT XIII	Slavery and involuntary servitude is abolished.
AMENDMENT XIV	No state can make or enforce any law which will take away the privileges and immunities of citizens; nor deprive any person of life, liberty or property, without due process of law; nor deny any person within its borders the equal protection of its laws.

AMENDMENT **XV**	Citizens of all races and colors have the right to vote.
AMENDMENT **XVI**	Congress may tax income.
AMENDMENT **XVII**	When a Senator is required to leave office before his or her term in Congress expires, the governor of the Senator's state can appoint another to fill the position until the citizens of the state elect a new Senator.
AMENDMENT **XVIII**	The manufacture, sale or transportation of intoxicating liquors is prohibited. [REPEALED]
AMENDMENT **XIX**	Both male and female citizens have the right to vote.
AMENDMENT **XX**	The President and Vice President begin their terms January 20; Senators and Representatives January 3. If the President-Elect dies before being sworn in, the Vice-President-Elect becomes President.
AMENDMENT **XXI**	The Eighteenth Amendment enforcing the prohibition of intoxicating liquors is repealed.
AMENDMENT **XXII**	The President may not be elected more than twice.
AMENDMENT **XXIII**	The District of Columbia is entitled to representation at the Electoral College.
AMENDMENT **XXIV**	Citizens cannot be charged a fee in order to vote.
AMENDMENT **XXV**	When the President cannot perform his official duties, the Vice President will assume the duties of the President. The President can be impeached upon a two-thirds vote of Congress.
AMENDMENT **XXVI**	Citizens who are eighteen (18) years of age and older have the right to vote.
AMENDMENT **XXVII**	Members of Congress cannot raise their pay while in office. Any law that provides for a pay raise for Congress can not take effect until after the election, which follows the vote, granting the raise.

SECTION 2.4
JOE HODGE'S
CONSTITUTIONAL
LAW PROBLEMS

PROBLEM TWO—A

HODGE, DODGE AND LODGE
ATTORNEYS AT LAW
MEMORANDUM

TO: All Law Clerks

FROM: Gregory Olan Dodge

RE: Joe Hodge's Constitutional Law Problems

We are very glad we hired you at the firm. The Hodge family is at it again and we need you to research the legal mess they got themselves into this time. It all has to do with the last Election Day.

Joe started brewing beer in the basement of his summer home at the New Jersey shore. He calls it "Jersey Joe's Home Brew" and he transported the liquor into Pennsylvania on Election Day to sell it to his neighbors. Joe has a bar in the basement of his Montgomery County house and enough neon signs to light up a street. Unfortunately for Joe, Pennsylvania doesn't allow anyone to bring liquor into the state to sell to customers on Election Day. The state wants to make sure people are sober when they vote.

As Joe was unloading the last keg of beer, Officer O'Brien showed up with the FBI. Even though they had no search warrant, these law enforcement officials stormed past Joe, went into his basement and confiscated the beer, taps and the neon signs. They then began loading the contraband into their cars.

"Hey, Tony," Joe yelled, calling to his son, who was asleep on the living room couch. "Help me; I'm being robbed." Tony ran to his father's aid, carrying a 9-mm pistol. An FBI agent grabbed the gun and confiscated the weapon. "Only cops are allowed to have these types of guns," O'Brien told them.

Joe protested, claiming that he had the right to keep guns in his house. It was the American way, he said, but O'Brien ignored him. I have since learned that there is a law in Pennsylvania that prohibits citizens from having semi-automatic weapons.

Suddenly, two men walked out of the house. Joe told O'Brien they worked for him. "For how much?" O'Brien asked. "For nothing," Joe said. "They work when I tell them to, and they don't go anywhere else. They live here in the basement." Indeed, the men told Officer O'Brien, they owed Joe several thousand dollars in gambling debts, and Joe was forcing them to pay it back by working for him.

Officer O'Brien took Joe to the police station, and tossed him into a holding cell. "Hey, how come you're doing this to me?" Joe asked. "It'll be a cold day in hell before I tell you," O'Brien replied. "You'll stay in there until you tell us where you obtained the ingredients for the beer. Or else, you can pay a million dollars bail, and then we'll let you out."

Meanwhile, New Jersey state officials read about Joe's arrest and used the opportunity to seize Joe's summer home. The state has a law that provides for the confiscation of property used in the commission of a crime. Joe doesn't buy it. The state has been after his land for years to use it for a public parking lot for one of the nearby casinos. Joe swears this is a scheme by the state to take his property without paying for it. In addition, the state wants Pennsylvania to return Joe to New Jersey, since Joe made the mistake of starting his brewery in a "dry town." But Pennsylvania refuses to do it.

The Internal Revenue Service informed Joe he owes the government back taxes for the money he made on selling his beer. And, to make matters worse, the National Guard has decided that the shore home would make a great barracks, so they moved a couple of soldiers from an Air Force base into Joe's living room.

Estelle got into the act, too. She put on her most patriotic shirt—the one she stitched together from an American flag—and went to the police station. Estelle then started to yell insults at Officer O'Brien. A crowd started to form around her. "She's right," said a woman in the crowd, "O'Brien was mean to me, too. Let's go to the mayor's office and complain." Just as Estelle was building momentum, several police officers grabbed her microphone and threatened to arrest Ms. Hodge for inciting a riot and defacing the American flag.

"Since this is Election Day," Estelle said, shaking her finger at the police, "I'm going to write in the name of Bill Clinton for a third term as president. Besides, this is America and I can say anything I want." She then stormed off to the polling place, but the election officials told her that she couldn't vote until she paid a "Voting Tax." And, anyway, they told her, state law says women are not allowed to vote—or anyone under 21. The election official told Estelle the state can do whatever it wants, and the federal government couldn't do a thing to stop it.

Joe and Estelle want to sue the states of Pennsylvania and New Jersey, but we're not sure they can do it. Read the Constitution and answer the following questions so that we can advise our clients on how to proceed.

QUESTIONS FOR DISCUSSION:

1. Which provisions in the Constitution support the actions of Joe and Estelle; which provisions prohibit what they did?

2. Is there anything in the Constitution that shows that O'Brien, the township police, the FBI and the election officials were wrong in their actions?

3. How does someone propose other amendments to the Constitution?

4. What other amendments do you believe should be in the Constitution?

Name   **Please Print Clearly**

1. Which provisions in the Constitution support the actions of Joe and Estelle; which provisions prohibit what they did?

_____

_____

_____

_____

_____

_____

_____

_____

2. Is there anything in the Constitution that shows that O'Brien, the township police, the FBI and the election officials were wrong in their actions?

_____

_____

_____

_____

_____

_____

_____

_____

_____

_____

3. How does someone propose other amendments to the Constitution?

_____

_____

_____

_____

_____

_____

_____

_____

_____

4. What new amendments would you propose to the Constitution?

_____

_____

_____

_____

_____

_____

_____

_____

_____

_____

SECTION 2.5
ADMINISTRATIVE LAW

As the United States has grown in size, power and population, the task of running the country has become extremely difficult, and the needs of the population too great for the legislative branch to handle alone. The growth of the nation, the increases in technical innovations and the demands of the people have placed great burdens on the government. In an effort to ease its burden, Congress created administrative agencies to deal with specialized areas and have staffed the agencies with experts who know how to deal with the particular problems encountered in each area.

An administrative agency is a "governmental body charged with administering and implementing particular legislation." Administrative agencies have greatly increased in number over the past several decades in order to effectuate general policy mandates of the legislative and executive branches of the government at the national, state, and local levels. Administrative agencies are created through congressional action called *Enabling Acts*. The following are examples of federal administrative agencies:

- *Environmental Protection Agency or EPA.* This agency is designed to protect human health and to safeguard the environment including the air, water and land upon which life depends. The *EPA* has been responsible for environmental safeguards including the banning of DDT which is used in pesticides and has been found to be a cancer causing agent. They have also banned the use of lead in gasoline, limited discharges by factories of pollution into the waterways and monitor how motor vehicles perform under the new fuel economy standards. The *EPA's* website is: **http://www.epa.gov.**

- *Securities and Exchange Commission or SEC.* This regulatory body is designed to protect investors and maintain the integrity of the securities market. This agency was created following the economic collapse in the 1930s. The *SEC* oversees the various stock exchanges, mutual fund markets, broker/dealers and public utility holding companies. The *SEC* is aggressive in its enforcement function and brings between 400 to 500 enforcement actions each year against individuals and companies that break the security laws. Examples of infractions include insider trading, and providing false or misleading information about securities or the companies that issue them. The website for the *Securities and Exchanges Commission* can be found at: **http://www.sec.gov.**

- *Occupational Safety and Health Administration or OSHA.* The bureau is designed to reduce the number of occupational, safety and health hazards at work. *OSHA* is empowered to make sure the work environment is free from recognized hazards that are likely to cause death or serious physical harm to workers. This goal is accomplished by work place inspections and by establishing protective standards. Since this agency was created in 1970, the overall workplace death rate has been cut in half. The website for this agency is: **http://www.osha.gov.**

- *Food and Drug Administration or FDA.* This agency protects the health of the public by monitoring products for safety and the *FDA* promotes public health by helping safe and effective products reach the market place in a timely fashion. The *FDA* regulates the sale of food, drugs, medical devices, and radiation-emitting products such as cell phones, lasers and microwaves. The agencies website is: **http://.www.fda.gov.**

- *Federal Trade Commission or FTC.* The *FTC* is the governmental agency which enforces the anti-trust and consumer protection laws. The bureau investigates and prosecutes unfair or deceptive business practices, seeks monetary damages for conduct detrimental to consumers, is responsible for the labeling of cigarettes with health related warning labels, requires the labeling of ingredients for food, drugs, and cosmetics products and regulates automatic teller machines. The agencies website is: **http://www.ftc.gov.**

- *Federal Communications Commission or FCC.* The agency was created in 1934 and is responsible for regulating communications by radio, television, satellite, wire and cable. It also oversees the nation's emergency alert system which notifies the public about a local or national emergency. The *FCC* has the responsibility to regulate the cable and satellite industry, to establish rules and regulations concerning long distance and local telephone services and to grant licenses to radio and television stations. The *FCC's* website is **http://www.fcc.gov.**

The functions of administrative agencies include the imposition of sanctions; licensing and other regulatory decisions; environmental and safety decisions; awards of benefits, loans, grants and other subsidies; inspections, audits, and approvals; and planning and policy-making.

Administrative agencies are unique since they are created with legislative, executive and judicial powers. An agency acts as a legislative body in the sense that it can issue rules and regulations. An agency's regulations are promulgated through a daily publication called **The Federal Register**. Agencies have executive power when enabling legislation grants the administrative body, investigative powers to the agency. This power allows the agency to investigate alleged violations of the Act.

Administrative agencies also possess a judicial power called agency adjudication. Administrative hearings are very similar to court proceedings. Witnesses are heard, and evidence is presented so that an administrative law judge can decide the case. Because agencies possess rule-making, adjudicating and investigative powers, they have been considered by some to be a fourth branch of government.

The theory behind the creation of administrative agencies is that the administrator's expertise allows them to resolve problems within a particular area or industry quickly and effectively. The administrator's expertise should lead to proper decisions in the problem areas, as opposed to improper decisions that might be handed down by Congress or the courts due to good intentions but inadequate knowledge.

Because administrative agencies are empowered to regulate and develop the law for a specific area, the scope of review of an agency's adverse determination is very limited. The courts feel that the agency possesses the expertise in the field being regulated so their decision will not be disturbed unless it is arbitrary, capricious, or an abuse of discretion. Factual findings, however, are conclusive so long as they are supported by "substantial evidence." Under this standard, a finding will not be changed on appeal if it is supported by relevant evidence that a reasonable mind *might accept* as adequate to support a conclusion. This is a very difficult burden for an aggrieved party to overcome.

Howard v. Federal Aviation Authority provides an example of this standard. The decision involved a pilot who landed at an airport in adverse weather conditions. Whenever weather conditions provide a visibility level of less than three miles, a pilot must land the aircraft with the guidance of radar controlled instruments. Instead of landing the aircraft by instruments, Howard used a visual approach even though the visibility level was below the acceptable standard for this type of landing. The pilot appealed the suspension of his pilot's license to federal court.

DENNIS HOWARD V. FEDERAL AVIATION ADMINISTRATION
17 F. 3D 1213 (9TH CIR. 1994)

DENNIS F. HOWARD ("PETITIONER") SEEKS REVIEW of the order of the National Transportation Safety Board (NTSB) temporarily suspending Howard's commercial pilot certificate.

On March 23, 1987, Howard landed a Bell B206 helicopter at Dubois-Jefferson County Airport in Pennsylvania. The airport was operating under Instrument Flight Rules (IFR) because of poor visibility when Petitioner arrived. Instrument Flight Rules prevail when weather conditions make approach via Visual Flight Rules (VFR) unsafe.

Although the IFR beacon was on when Petitioner made his approach, he nevertheless landed under visual observation without obtaining a clearance from air traffic control. Both parties agree that Petitioner did not make radio contact with the flight service specialist on duty.

Periodic weather reports, taken before and after the landing, recorded by the flight service specialist showed the conditions as 2 ½ miles visibility with fog and an estimated ceiling of 700 feet to 800 feet. Petitioner disputed this assessment of the conditions, recalling that during his flight, he encountered "good VFR weather, three miles, a thousand feet, at least."

In connection with this landing, Petitioner was charged with violating three Federal Aviation Regulations: (1) in that he operated an aircraft, under VFR when the ceiling was less than 1000 feet; (2) he landed an aircraft, or entered the traffic pattern of an airport, under VFR, when the ground visibility was not at least three statute miles; and (3) he operated an aircraft in a careless or reckless manner endangering the life or property of others.

An order of the *NTSB* shall not be set aside unless the agency's conclusions are arbitrary, capricious, an abuse of discretion, or otherwise not in accordance with law." The Board's factual findings, however, are conclusive if supported by "substantial evidence" in the record.

Petitioner argues that the Board's ruling is not supported by "substantial evidence" of record. He disputes that the flight ceiling was less than 1000 feet at the time of his landing. A review for "substantial evidence" is one undertaken with some deference. Under this standard, a finding will not be disturbed if supported by "such relevant evidence as a reasonable mind

might accept as adequate to support a conclusion." *Consolidated Edison Co. v. NLRB*, **305 U.S. 197 (1938).** The evidence before the Board easily meets this standard.

We cannot reach Petitioner's argument because he did not raise the claim below. Under the Administrative Code, "No objection to an order of the Board or Secretary of Transportation shall be considered by the court unless such objection shall have been urged before the Board. In the proceeding appealed from, Petitioner did not challenge the evidence presented to establish that flight conditions were below 1000 feet/three miles. Because Petitioner failed either to raise this issue in the *NTSB* proceeding or to justify that forbearance, he has defaulted on this argument, and we are deprived of jurisdiction to address this claim.

Petitioner also argues that substantial evidence does not support the Board's finding "that ground visibility at the airport was reported to be less than three statute miles" at the time of his landing. Petitioner's claim turns not on what the official visibility actually was, but rather on whether that figure was "reported." Petitioner claims the visibility was not "reported" as it was not shown by substantial evidence that it was communicated to anyone. Because the ground visibility was "not reported," he claims that this makes "flight visibility," the relevant factor.

The proper inquiry is whether the information that the ground visibility was below Visual Flight Rules minimums was existent and available to Petitioner when he made his approach. Substantial evidence exists in the record that it was, through the weather information network, via the rotating airport beacon, and through radio contact with the tower.

Petitioner complains that "[T]he agency's interpretations of Federal Aviation Regulations are arbitrary and capricious." This argument appears to be grounded in a misunderstanding of the role of this court in reviewing agency action. We do not have plenary power to oversee the actions of the Board. Congress' grant of jurisdiction conveys only the power to "affirm, modify, or set aside the order complained of." This court could not act in any event to remedy even a blatant "abuse of discretion" by the Board in a case apart from and prior to the instant proceedings.

Board precedent recognizes the reality that changing weather conditions may create situations in which a pilot may properly substitute his more cautious judgment of the prevailing weather conditions. A pilot must be allowed this latitude. The logic behind the rule is that a pilot must be permitted to act with additional caution when the conditions he is actually encountering demand it.

Petitioner has made no showing that his was such a circumstance. Nor could he. He did not substitute his judgment that prevailing conditions were more dangerous, and required more safety precautions, than those officially reported. He was cited precisely because he was operating the craft in an unsafe manner, in apparent ignorance of the official conditions.

For the foregoing reasons, we deny the petition for review of the order of the *NTSB*.

SECTION 2.6
CONTRACT LAW

We enter into hundreds of contracts every day. Because of the informal nature of these agreements, no one thinks in terms of having entered into a contract. The purchase of gas, buying lunch, taking public transportation or buying a newspaper are all examples of agreements entered into by the parties creating valid contracts. Merely walk out of a restaurant without paying for lunch, and the legal significance of your actions will be quickly realized.

The courts face a dilemma, however, when asked to enforce a promise that seems social in nature. For instance, how should a court decide a case where a high school student sues her prom date who never showed up for the prom? Suppose the student bought a prom dress and had her hair done. Should a court allow her to collect damages from her date in the form of payment for her dress and beauty treatment? Is this the type of agreement that will give rise to an enforceable contract, or is it merely a social agreement?

A **contract** is the exchange of promises voluntarily made by the parties which agreement is enforceable in court. While the terms may vary from bargain to bargain, five essential elements must be present. They are:

1. an offer
2. acceptance
3. consideration
4. capacity
5. legality

On the rare occasion that a party does enter into a formal written contract, each term must be carefully analyzed and understood. An Agreement of Sale to purchase a home, an employment contract, an apartment lease or the loan documentation from a bank are complex written documents containing many provisions, each paragraph of which has legal significance.

Nothing is more frustrating than when a client seeks legal advice about a contract that has already been signed without review by the attorney. This is reinforced over and over again when a distraught client calls about the purchase of a home. A buyer will eagerly sign an Agreement of Sale without the advice of counsel. Disputes over the perfect house soon arise when the buyer fails to qualify for the mortgage or learns that the refrigerator is not included in the purchase. There is little an attorney can do at this time to overcome the deficiencies in the legal document.

When a party breaches a contract, an immediate question arises as to damages. The penalty can vary from nothing, to forfeiting the down payment or losing a substantial amount of money. A written contract will frequently dictate the penalty for the breach of the agreement. In fact, the contract can even specify how the dispute is to be resolved. Do the parties resort to the traditional remedies of court, or does the contract provide for an alternative dispute resolution process such as binding arbitration? Only a review of the document will provide an answer to a party's legal rights and obligations.

The following is sample contract.

MOTION PICTURE CONTRACT

THIS AGREEMENT made by and between **Five Star Motion Pictures**, hereinafter referred to as "Employer" and **Jason Versace** (hereinafter **"Actor"**) .

1. **Employer** agrees to employ the **Actor**, and **Actor** agrees to render services exclusively to the **Employer** during the duration of the filming of the motion picture *"Hot Ice,"* in the parts of such characters or roles and in such plays or subjects as the **Employer** may select.

2. The **Actor** agrees that he will, during the term of this contract, devote his services exclusively to the **Employer** and will not engage in any other occupation.

3. The **Actor** grants the right to the **Employer** to use his name and photograph in any way **Employer** deems fit in connection with the advertising of said motion picture film.

4. The **Employer** agrees to pay the **Actor** for his services, the sum of $100,000.00 payable at the end of the filming of the Motion picture.

5. It is agreed that the services of said **Actor** are extraordinary and unique, and there is no adequate remedy at law for breach of contract by the **Actor** and that a case of such a breach, the **Employer** shall be entitled to equitable relief by way of injunction or otherwise.

6. The **Employer** is to supply the **Actor** with all of the costumes required for the assignment under the terms of this contract.

IN WITNESS WHEREOF, we hereto set our hands and seals.

Jason Versace   *Theresa Brown*
JASON VERSACE   FIVE STAR MOTION PICTURES

CHAUSSEE V. DALLAS COWBOYS FOOTBALL CLUB, LTD.
1997 WL 739556 (TEX. APP. 1997)

AFTER THE DALLAS COWBOYS BUILT A ROW A in front of Row 1 at Texas Stadium in 1993, several Row 1 season ticket holders sued the Cowboys for breach of contract. The season ticket holders argued they were entitled to front row seats and that the Cowboys' construction of Row A deprived them of that right.

To finance the construction of Texas Stadium, the city of Irving issued revenue bonds and **Ordinance 1705** authorized the creation of seat options. A seat option gave its holder the contractual right to purchase season tickets to Cowboys games for particular seats.

John Chaussee, Carolyn Cowden, Wright Cowden, and Sam Seabury purchased seat options for upper-deck Row 1 seats at Texas Stadium for Dallas Cowboy games. Until 1993, this meant they sat in the first row of the upper deck. On January 21, 1993, however, Irving passed a resolution allowing the Cowboys to make improvements to Texas Stadium. In June 1993, the Cowboys began building a row in front of Row 1 and labeled it Row A. When the season ticket holders subsequently attended Cowboy games in 1993, they discovered they were now sitting in second row seats and that Row A partially obscured their view of the field.

The Cowboys argue that the season ticket holders' certificates were unambiguous, that the season ticket holders had seat options for Row 1 before 1993, and that they continue to have seat options for Row 1 in 1993 and thereafter. The Cowboys argued that nothing in the seat options correlates "Row 1" with "first row" or "front row." They contend the section, row, and seat numbers were merely coordinates corresponding to a stadium seating chart. Since the season ticket holders do not dispute the location of their seats has not changed, the Cowboys conclude they have not breached their contractual obligations under the seat options.

The season ticket holders first argue that "Row 1" is not ambiguous because it unambiguously means the first row. In the alternative, they argue "Row 1" is ambiguous, because at one time it meant first row and now it means second row.

The seat options define the season ticket holders seat by section, row, and seat number. These numbers have meaning only in the context of a stadium seating chart. For example, the season ticket holders do not argue they are entitled to Row 1 seats on the lower deck or mezzanine, if any, of Texas Stadium. The seat options do not guarantee the season ticket holders options for the "first" or "front" row of their respective sections; they guarantee options for Row 1 of their respective sections. The season ticket holders do not have seat options for Row A. We conclude the seat options are not ambiguous. They definitely and clearly correspond to a specific seat location in Texas Stadium that at one time was a first row, but no longer is.

The season ticket holders have no cause of action for breach of contract because their Row 1 seats are no longer first row seats.. They purchased Row 1 seats. They still have Row 1 seats. If the season ticket holders have a cause of action for breach of contract, it is not because the Cowboys promised them first row seats and breached that promise. The Cowboys promised Row 1 seats and delivered Row 1 seats. We conclude the trial court correctly ruled the seat options were unambiguous and that the season ticket holders should take nothing on their breach of contract claims.

We affirm the trial court's judgment in favor of the Dallas Cowboys.

SECTION 2.7
TORT LAW

A tort is a private or civil wrong against an individual for which the court will award money damages. The word "tort" is derived from the Latin term "torquer," meaning "to twist." Torts are classified into the categories of negligence or intentional torts. Negligence arises when one fails to act as a reasonable person under the circumstances. For example, a motorist is negligent when the driver loses concentration and unintentionally runs into another car. The motorist did not intentionally try to injure the driver of the second car, however, he will be responsible for money damages in causing the accident.

A tort can also be intentional in nature. Examples of intentional torts include assault, battery, intentional infliction of emotional distress, defamation and false imprisonment.

One must always be mindful, however, that the mere fact someone suffers a loss does not mean that he or she is entitled to recover money. The claimant must prove that another person was at fault in causing the harm and that the law recognizes a theory of liability.

For instance, in *Ali v. Gates,* an individual instituted suit against Bill Gates and a number of other people alleging that they violated Ali's constitutional rights under a *Section 1983* action, by engaging in a conspiracy to murder him through a *Windows 95* program. The plaintiff's claim was based upon an alleged violation of federal law that prohibits an individual from violating a person's constitutional rights when acting as the agent of the state. For instance, a police officer carries out the duties of that law enforcement job clothed with the authority that the officer is acting on behalf of the government. If the law enforcement officer knowingly violates a person's constitutional rights in carrying out the duties of the office, the police officer may be responsible for money damages based upon a violation of federal law. A private citizen, however, such as Bill Gates, is not a governmental official so he cannot be sued for violating a person's civil rights.

YOUSEFF ALI V. BILL GATES
1998 WL 317584 (W.D. N.Y. 2000)

YOUSEFF ALI, AN INMATE OF the Southport Correctional Facility, has filed this action and claims that Microsoft World Wide Web, Bill Gates, the State of New York, Governor George E. Pataki, NBC, Fox, ABC, CBS, AT & T and TCI, violated his constitutional rights. For the reasons discussed below, plaintiff's complaint is dismissed.

Plaintiff alleges that the defendants are engaged in a conspiracy to murder him. Plaintiff further alleges that there is a *Windows 95* program hooked to his mind so that the defendants have constant mental and administrative surveillance of him and that a prison security system called *MERLIN* is centered in his brain. Plaintiff claims that this was done in an attempt to murder him. Plaintiff seeks protection from the surveillance, appointment of an attorney to represent him and compensatory and punitive damages.

Plaintiff brings this action pursuant to **42 U.S.C. '1983.** In order to state a claim under § 1983, a plaintiff must allege: (1) that the challenged conduct was attributable at least in part to a person acting under color of state law; and (2) that such conduct deprived the plaintiff of a right, privilege, or immunity secured by the Constitution or laws of the United States.

Plaintiff's claim against the State of New York must be dismissed. The state is protected by the Eleventh Amendment from legal or equitable claims brought by private parties for alleged constitutional violations. Neither a State nor its officials acting in their official capacities are persons under § 1983. Accordingly, plaintiff's complaint against the State of New York is dismissed.

Plaintiff lists Governor George Pataki as the individual presiding over the State of New York. To the extent that plaintiff raises any claim against Governor Pataki in his official capacity, the claim is also barred by the Eleventh Amendment. To the extent that plaintiff may be claiming against Governor Pataki in his individual capacity, the claim is also subject to dismissal because plaintiff has failed to show the personal involvement of Governor Pataki in any alleged constitutional deprivation.

Plaintiff's claims against the remaining defendants are also subject to dismissal. To state a claim for relief under § 1983, a plaintiff must allege both a violation of a right secured by the Constitution or by federal law, and that the alleged deprivation was committed by a person acting under color of state law. All of the defendants appear to be private parties who cannot be said to be "acting under color of state law." The claims against the remaining defendants are therefore dismissed with prejudice.

IT HEREBY IS ORDERED, that the complaint is dismissed with prejudice.

SECTION 2.8
SHOOTING OF
PETER CHRISTOPHER

PROBLEM TWO—B

HODGE, DODGE AND LODGE
ATTORNEYS AT LAW
MEMORANDUM

To: All Law Clerks

FROM: Gregory Olan Dodge

RE: Shooting of Peter Christopher

Tony Hodge needs your advice concerning his recent arrest for attempted murder. Tony shot his neighbor, Peter Christopher, to prevent him from stealing Tony's expensive Corvette. Tony claims he was merely defending his property and questions the fairness of prosecuting him for shooting a thief. The following story emerged after I spoke to Tony at the police station.

Tony came home from football practice around 4 p.m. He was surprised to find the house empty, but then remembered that his little brother, Brad, had invited the family to school for some event. Just as Tony was about to sit down and watch a game film, he heard rattling noises coming from outside. The house was so quiet that he couldn't miss even the slightest sound. Tony peered out his bedroom window and saw Peter Christopher standing by the Corvette in the driveway. Christopher was trespassing, and Tony was aware of the recent encounter the neighbor had with Kathy over the Honda. Tony also knew that Christopher was furious over what happened to the Honda.

When Tony's requests that Christopher get away from the car went unheeded, he ran into his father's study. From there he had access to the deck overlooking the driveway. Tony thought that from this vantage point, he would be able to scare his neighbor away.

Tony was enraged! Tony never allowed anyone near his car. It was a special edition Corvette worth more than $75,000.00.

Tony again warned Christopher to get away from the car. When it became apparent that the neighbor was determined to steal the vehicle, Tony decided to make his request a little more threatening. He ran back into the study and grabbed a gun from his father's collection. He warned Christopher that he would shoot if the neighbor didn't leave immediately. Christopher responded with obscene words and gestures while continuing to break into the car.

Tony really hadn't expected any trouble. He didn't want to shoot Christopher, but he refused to stand there helplessly while Peter drove away with his most prized possession. So Joe's son fired a single shot, which pierced the neighbor's left arm. Tony is an expert marksman and knew he could easily hit his target at such a short distance.

Having apprehended the neighbor, Tony called the police to report the attempted theft. He also called Dr. Feelgood to provide medical attention to the neighbor. Officer O'Brien arrived almost immediately. Tony greeted the policeman with a big smile but was shocked when O'Brien drew his service revolver and handcuffed Tony. He knew there must be some mistake. Tony thought O'Brien was just joking. In fact, he expected O'Brien to pat him on the back. Tony continued to smile. After all, Tony had just caught a thief. But, there was no mistake. O'Brien took the football player to headquarters where Tony was fingerprinted, booked and thrown in jail.

An important decision on the topic is *Katko v. Briney,* **183 N.W.2d 657 (Iowa 1971).** According to the rules set forth in that case, decide whether Tony can escape liability. You must decide the following:

1. Is Tony allowed to use force to protect his property? As Tony said, "I warned him to get away from the car. He made an obscene gesture, so I shot him in self-defense."

2. Was this a reasonable degree of force under the circumstances?

3. Does it matter that Tony warned his neighbor before he shot him?

4. Can Tony be criminally prosecuted and sued civilly for the shooting?

5. Do you agree with the law?

Your decision should include an analysis of these questions along with anything else you believe is relevant in accessing Tony's culpability.

MARVIN KATKO V. EDWARD BRINEY
183 N.W.2D 657 (IOWA 1971)

THE PRIMARY ISSUE PRESENTED here is whether an owner may protect personal property in an unoccupied boarded-up farm house against trespassers and thieves by a spring gun capable of inflicting death or serious injury.

At defendants' request plaintiff's action was tried to a jury consisting of residents of the community where defendants' property was located. The jury returned a verdict for plaintiff and against defendants for $20,000 actual and $10,000 punitive damages.

Most of the facts are not disputed. In 1957 defendant, Bertha L. Briney inherited her parents' farm land. Included was an 80-acre tract in southwest Mahaska County where her grandparents and parents had lived. No one occupied the house thereafter.

There occurred a series of trespassing and housebreaking events with loss of some household items, the breaking of windows and "messing up of the property in general."

Defendants boarded up the windows and doors in an attempt to stop the intrusions. They had posted "no trespass" signs on the land. The nearest one was 35 feet from the house. Defendants set "a shot-gun trap" in the north bedroom where they secured it to an iron bed with the barrel pointed at the bedroom door. It was rigged with wire from the doorknob to the gun's trigger so it would fire when the door was opened. Briney first pointed the gun's trigger so an intruder would be hit in the stomach but at Mrs. Briney's suggestion it was lowered to hit the legs. Tin was nailed over the bedroom window. The spring gun could not be seen from the outside. No warning of its presence was posted.

Plaintiff worked regularly as a gasoline station attendant seven miles from the old house and considered it as being abandoned. He knew it had long been uninhabited. Plaintiff and McDonough had been to the premises and found several old bottles and fruit jars which they took and added to their collection of antiques. About 9:30 p.m. they made a second trip to the Briney property. They entered the old house by removing a board from a porch window which was without glass. While McDonough was looking around the kitchen area plaintiff went to another part of the house. As he started to open the north bedroom door the shotgun when off striking him in the right leg above the ankle bone. Much of his leg, including part of the tibia, was blown away.

Plaintiff testified he knew he had no right to break and enter the house with intent to steal bottles and fruit jars therefrom. He further testified he had entered a plea of guilty to larceny in the nighttime of property of less than $20 value from a private building. He stated he had been fined $50 and costs and paroled during good behavior from a 60-day jail sentence.

The main thrust of defendant's defense in the trial court and on this appeal is that "the law permits use of a spring gun in a dwelling or warehouse for the purpose of preventing the unlawful entry of a burglar or thief."

The overwhelming weight of authority, both textbook and case law, supports the trial court's statement of the applicable principles of law.

Prosser on Torts, Third Edition, pages 116-118, states:

> The law has always placed a higher value upon human safety than upon mere rights in property, it is the accepted rule that there is no privilege to use any force calculated to cause death or serious bodily injury to repel the threat to land or chattels unless there is also such a threat to the defendant's personal safety as to justify a self-defense... Spring guns and other man-killing devices are not justifiable against a mere trespasser, or even a petty thief. They are privileged only against those upon whom the landowner, if he were present in person would be free to inflict injury of the same kind.

Restatement of Torts, section 85, page 180 states: "The value of human life and limb, not only to the individual concerned but also to society, so outweighs the interest of a possessor of land in excluding from it those whom he is not willing to admit thereto that a possessor of land has no privilege to use force intended or likely to cause death or serious harm against another whom the possessor see about to enter his premises or meddle with his chattel, unless the intrusion threatens death or serious bodily harm to the occupiers or users of the premises.

The facts in *Allison v. Fiscus,* **156 Ohio 120, 100 N.E.2d 237, 44 A.L.R.2d 369,** decided in 1951, are very similar to the case at the bar. There plaintiff's right to damages was recognized for injuries received when he feloniously broke a door latch and started to enter defendant's warehouse with intent to steal. As he entered a trap of two sticks of dynamite buried under the doorway by defendant owner was set off and plaintiff seriously injured. The court held the question whether a particular trap was justified as a use of reasonable and necessary force against the trespasser engaged in the commission of a felony should have been submitted to the jury. The Ohio Supreme Court recognized plaintiff's right to punitive or exemplary damages in addition to compensation damages. The jury's findings of fact including a finding defendants acted with malice and with wanton and reckless disregard, as required for an allowance of punitive or exemplary damages, are supported by substantial evidence. We are bound thereby.

Affirmed.

ANSWER SHEET
PROBLEM TWO—B

Name _____   **Please Print Clearly**

1. Is Tony allowed to use force to protect his property?

_____

_____

_____

_____

_____

_____

_____

_____

_____

2. Was this a reasonable degree of force under the circumstances?

_____

_____

_____

_____

_____

_____

_____

_____

_____

3. Does it matter that Tony warned his neighbor before he shot him?

_____

_____

_____

_____

_____

_____

_____

_____

_____

4. Can Tony be criminally prosecuted and sued civilly for the shooting? Do you agree with the law?

_____

_____

_____

_____

_____

_____

_____

_____

_____

_____

_____

Katko v. Briney addressed the issue of how a person can protect personal property against an intruder. What happens, however, when the issue becomes how much force a person can use against an intruder in self-defense? The following case answers that question.

COMMONWEALTH OF PENNSYLVANIA V. EARL JOHNSTON
263 A.2D 376 (PA. 1970)

EAGEN, Judge.

EARL F. JOHNSTON WAS TRIED FOR THE MURDER of Charles Pittman, and found guilty of voluntary manslaughter. We reverse.

On October 8, 1966, a group gathered for social purposes on the business property of defendant Johnston. Among others, the group included Johnston, Pittman, Mrs. Pittman and Mrs. Wolfe. Strong ill feeling existed between Mrs. Pittman and Mrs. Wolfe, and an argument started between them which culminated in a physical tussle. When the pair were separated, Mrs. Wolfe began to berate Pittman and called him obscene names. Pittman became angry, drew a knife and threatened to kill her. He chased her from the building and inflicted two knife wounds on her arm as she fled.

Johnston separated the two, led Pittman to his automobile and asked him to leave. Pittman and his wife got in the car. Mrs. Wolfe then threw a brick through the rear window of the Pittman automobile. Pittman jumped from his automobile and chased Mrs. Wolfe into the building with the knife in his hand, saying, *"I'm going to kill you."*

Johnston tried to stop Pittman from entering his building, and when this effort failed, he went to his automobile, parked nearby, and secured a loaded .45 automatic revolver. He then followed Pittman into the building, grabbed him by the left arm (Pittman had the knife in his right hand) and pulled him back several feet from the area where Mrs. Wolfe was standing.

Pittman then approached Johnston with the knife in an upraised hand, saying he was going to kill Mrs. Wolfe and what was that to Johnston. Johnston retreated 10 to 15 feet, then stood his ground and drew his gun, saying to Pittman: "Charles, don't come any closer I don't want to hurt you." Despite this Pittman kept approaching Johnston with the knife held in a menacing position. When Pittman was about 11 feet distant from him, Johnston fired one shot at his feet. When Pittman was about 6 feet away, Johnston fired two shots into Pittman's body, one of which entered his heart causing instant death.

The killing of another human being without justification or excuse is felonious homicide. However, a killing is excusable if it is committed in self-defense. At trial, Johnston did not deny killing Pittman, but maintained that he did so in defense of his own life.

The following conditions must be satisfied before one can successfully invoke the defense of self-defense:

1. The slayer must have been free from fault in provoking or continuing the difficulty which resulted in the killing.

2. The slayer must have reasonably believed that he was in imminent danger of death, great bodily harm, or some felony, and that there was a necessity to kill in order to save himself therefrom.

3. The slayer must not have violated any duty to retreat or avoid the danger.

Even though a person has entered the business premises of another, at the invitation of the owner, his subsequent conduct may be such as to justify the revocation of the invitation to remain as a guest. As owner of the business premises, defendant Johnston had the right to order the deceased, Pittman, from the premises, and in case of refusal had the right to remove him by force, if necessary. Since the difficulty ensued in the exercise of Johnston's legal right of ejection, Johnston is without fault in provoking the controversy within the meaning of the first element of self-defense.

In view of Pittman's actions immediately prior to and at the time of the killing involved, Johnston had reasonable grounds to believe that he was in imminent danger of his life or great bodily harm from his attacker.

But, it is argued by the Commonwealth that Johnston could have retreated from the building through a nearby door and escaped harm without resorting to shooting Pittman. In a long line of decisions, we have held that the right to take life in self-defense does not arise while there are means of escape open to the person attacked. Life is sacred and if it is merely a question of whether one man should flee or another should die, then certainly the taking of life should be avoided and the person under attack should flee.

There is an exception to this rule, however. Where a man is dangerously assaulted or attacked in his own dwelling house, he need not retreat, but may stand his ground and meet deadly force with deadly force to save his own life or protect himself from great bodily harm.

Since, in this case, defendant Johnston was in his own place of business and was in imminent danger of serious personal harm or death from an unjustified attack, he was not required to retreat and will not be denied the right of self-defense.

Judgment is reversed.

Katko v. Briney clearly demonstrates that a person cannot use force that will inflict death or serious bodily injury in the protection of property. Human life is simply more important than property. In *Commonwealth v. Johnston,* however, the court was confronted with the issue as to whether a person can use deadly force in order to protect human life. While the killing of another without justification is illegal, a killing is excusable if it is committed in self-defense. This will occur when **(1)** the slayer reasonably believes that he is in imminent danger of great bodily harm, **(2)** he has attempted to flee the harm, and **(3)** deadly force is the only way to protect human life.

While the use of a shotgun in the protection of property is clearly excessive force, is the owner of a store liable for an attack by a vicious dog that is allowed to roam the store at night in order to stop trespassers? Based upon the reasoning in *Katko v. Briney,* the storeowner will be liable for the attack. The dog has been kept on the premises for the sole purpose of protecting property by inflicting serious harm to the intruder. Will liability, however, be imposed on a homeowner whose pet dog attacks a burglar that enters a home when no one is present?

The answer is no. The dog is not kept at the family dwelling for the sole purpose of attacking people. Dogs are territorial and they will protect their master's home against an intruder.

Will the owner of a dog be liable if the animal bites a guest or if a large playful dog, that has a habit of jumping on people, knocks someone down? The law is well settled that a dog's owner will be liable for the actions of the pet if the owner knows or has good reason to know of the dog's dangerous or vicious propensities and fails to take reasonable measures to protect the guest from the pet's actions. The saying that "every dog is entitled to one bite" is not true. If a dog has displayed a vicious propensity in the past, the owner will be liable to another for a dog bite even if the animal has not bitten anyone in the past. Likewise, the law imposes a duty of restraint on the owner of a dog when the owner knows of the animal's playful but dangerous propensity of jumping on people and knocking them down.

THOMAS FONTANA v. MORELLI & SONS, INC.
No. 10025 OF 1995 (COURT OF COMMON PLEAS, LAWRENCE COUNTY, PA. 1999)

THE GENESIS OF THIS DOG BITE CASE was on January 27, 1994 when Plaintiff Thomas Fontana entered the office portion of the Defendant's place of business, a beer distributorship. The defendant's dog, a cocker spaniel named Sparky, was asleep on the floor of the business premises at the time. Unwilling to let sleeping canines lie, Mr. Fontana approached Sparky and attempted to pet him. Sparky reciprocated by biting Mr. Fontana on his left hand. Although the injury suffered by Plaintiff Thomas Fontana was not unusually severe, the hand developed an infection for which Mr. Fontana was hospitalized for a number of days. In response, the Plaintiffs filed their cause of action based on the theory of the Defendant's negligence. Following a jury trial, a verdict was returned for the Plaintiff and damages were awarded in the amount of $22,533.78.

Defendant contends that the verdict of the jury is not supported by sufficient evidence. Specifically, Defendant claims that the Plaintiff's evidence was inadequate to establish the vicious propensities of Defendant's dog, which is required in proving the negligence of an owner of a dog.

In order to show that a dog manifests vicious or dangerous propensities, the past conduct of the dog must be such as to furnish a reasonable inference that the animal is likely to commit an act of the kind complained of. The evidence must show that the dog had an intentional and often urgent natural inclination to be vicious or dangerous. As soon as the owner knows, or has good reason to believe that the animal is likely to do mischief, he must take care of him; it makes no difference whether this suspicion arises from one act or from repeated acts. A dog may show ferocious propensities without biting anyone and it is his master's duty to see to it that he is not afforded an opportunity to take a "first bite."

Here, Plaintiff Bonnie Fontana testified that, two days after Sparky had bitten her husband, she and Michael Morelli, owner of the beer distributorship and the owner of Sparky, were casually talking about Sparky biting her husband.

On direct examination, Bonnie Fontana testified as follows:

Q. *What were the contents of your conversation with Mr. Morelli?*

    A. Mr. Morelli told me about the dog. He said the dog even went at my son one time. His son went to get a sandwich, and the dog must have wanted the sandwich, and he said the dog went after his son.

On cross-examination the colloquy was:

Q. *What I want you to do for us, please, is I want you to relate to the jury exactly as you can with as much specificity as you can everything Michael Morelli said about this incident.*

    A. Just that the dog had gone at his son – I don't know if he actually bit him or just went after him to get the sandwich, like whose going to get it first, me or you. You know, how a dog is. And that is it.

Q. *Do you know the circumstances under which it occurred? For instance, was the boy sitting at the table eating the sandwich and the dog attacked him or was he on the floor?*

    A. All he told me is his son went to reach for the sandwich. Now, if he had taken a bite out of the sandwich and set it down and went back to get it, I don't know. I have never been down there, I don't know.

Q. *Do you know if the dog even bit the son?*

    A. All I know is he said he went at the son . . .

Q. *So, you do not know whether the dog bit the boy?*

    A. No, I don't.

If the jury believed Bonnie Fontana's testimony, this evidence was sufficient to show that Sparky, prior to biting the Plaintiff, manifested vicious or dangerous propensities, and that the Defendant knew or had reason to know that Sparky had these tendencies and may bite someone in the future, unless the defendant took appropriate steps to protect potential victims or adequately warn them, including those who entered Defendant's place of business.

Accordingly, the defendant's Motion for a new trial must fail.

SECTION 2.9
PROPERTY LAW

Property law deals with the rights and duties that arise out of the ownership or possession of real property and personal property. **Real property** includes the land and everything attached to the land. For instance, a building, a tree or ground are all considered part of the realty. **Personal property** consists of all other property and would include a book, a car, money or a folding chair. In other words, personal property includes everything not attached to the land.

Personal property is further divided by type into tangible and intangible property. Tangible property is a physical object such as this textbook. Intangible property, on the other hand, is personal property that is not a physical object. The ownership of intangible property is usually evidenced by a legal document. Examples of such property include a patent or invention, a copyright for published material or a trademark to identify a manufacturer or merchant's product.

The purchase of a home has certain inherent problems. Disputes frequently arise as to what was included in the sale. When the buyer inspected the home, a crystal chandelier hung in the foyer. At the time of settlement, a plastic fixture has replaced the chandelier. The seller refuses to give the buyer the chandelier claiming that it is a family heirloom worth several thousand dollars. The buyer maintains that the fixture was part of the realty since it was on display at the time the home was inspected. Who is correct? The answer will depend upon whether the item is real or personal property.

O'Donnell v. Schneeweis
73 D. & C. 2d 400 (Chester County Ct. Common Pleas, Pa. 1975)

Plaintiffs filed a complaint against defendants alleging that plaintiffs and defendants entered into a written Agreement of Sale whereby plaintiffs agreed to purchase certain real property and improvements from defendants and which agreement provided that all fixtures attached to the property were to remain thereon.

Defendants admit to the removal of some items, and aver that the items so removed were the personal property of defendants not intended to pass to the ownership of plaintiffs.

The parties agree that the following articles were removed from the premises by defendants subsequent to execution of the agreement of sale: (1) wall-to-wall carpeting in place in three rooms of the building; (2) a full length mirror affixed to a door in the said building; (3) a wall mirror and glass or spectacle; and (4) café doors. Plaintiffs assert that such articles were either "fixtures" included in the agreement of sale, or "permanent improvements to the realty," title to which passed to plaintiffs along with title to the realty.

A (seller) and purchaser may, of course, specifically agree that (personal property) affixed to the realty is to be treated as fixtures passing with the realty or, conversely, they may agree that such fixtures are to be detached and treated as personalty: *Wick v. Bredin*, **189 Pa. 83, 42 Atl. 17 (1899)**. The paragraph in the Agreement of Sale which plaintiffs rely to sustain their position follows:

"The gas and electric fixtures, heaters, ranges, etc., annexed to the said building are included in the sale, as also any water pipe laid on any street bounding said lot, except for refrigerators located on 2nd and 3rd floors."

It appears evident that the parties intended only gas and electric fixtures, heaters, ranges, water pipes in any street abutting the premises, and chattels of a similar nature, to be the items included within the clause. Hence, the question of whether the disputed items are fixtures, title to which was intended to pass with the realty, must be resolved within the framework of the well-established principles relating to fixtures.

A "fixture" is an article of personal property which, by reason of physical annexation to a building, becomes in legal contemplation a part of the real estate.

(Personal property) used in connection with real estate are of three classes: First, furniture always remains personalty. The second class consists of those things so annexed to the property that they cannot be removed without material injury to the real estate. (These items are fixtures.) The third class includes those things which, although physically connected with the real estate, are so affixed as to be removable without destroying or materially injuring the items themselves; such (fixtures) become part of the realty or remain personalty, depending upon the intention of the parties at the time of annexation.

Wall-to-Wall Carpeting

We believe that carpeting falls within the third class of property so we must determine the intention of defendants at the time of installation.

Wall-to-wall carpeting, although generally cut to fit specific floor areas, may be re-cut and thus re-used. Nonetheless, the carpet (in question) was fitted to the precise dimensions and contours of the floors by the use of woodstripping and nails. We conclude, therefore, that the carpet was specially fitted to the rooms in question and thus adapted to the permanent use and enjoyment of defendants at the time of annexation. Hence, the wall-to-wall carpet became and remains a fixture.

Mirrors

Two mirrors are in issue, one a full-length mirror affixed to a door in the building upon the premises, and the other affixed to a wall.

In *Waltman v. Mayer*, **97 Pa. Superior Ct. 236 (1929),** the question was the same: Whether a mirror was a fixture, passing with the real estate, or personalty; properly removed and retained by the seller. At trial, the purchaser testified that molding was attached to the frame of the mirrors and, in turn, nailed directly to a wall. The seller testified to the contrary that the mirrors she took lifted off.

We find that the wall mirror was personalty, not intended to become a fixture, and properly removed by defendants. We note, however, that the mirror on the door appears to have been attached with the intention to make it a permanent part. The mirror was obviously cut and fitted to the door. Upon its removal, unseemly molding remained and the door presents the appearance of an unfinished structural member. Accordingly, we conclude that defendants intended the door mirror to be a fixture and so find.

Spectacle Cases and Wall Racks

A part of the building was used as the professional office of defendant, an optometrist. In connection with such profession, spectacles were displayed on racks and in cases or cabinets. The photographic exhibits appear to indicate that these items were fitted to and built into the walls of the building upon the premises and, as such, became a part of the real estate at the time of annexation within the second enumerated category, above. At the very least, it appears that upon annexation, defendants intended that the glass or spectacle cases and wall racks become fixtures within the third enumerated category, above.

Café Doors

The café doors appear to be the so-called "swinging" or "saloon" type doors attached to the walls of a passage-or-entryway between two rooms in the building.

The testimony indicates that the doors appeared to be fitted to the passageway and permanently affixed by hinges. Accordingly, we conclude that defendants intended at the time of annexation that such café doors become and remain a part of the realty, as fixtures.

Judgment is entered in favor of plaintiffs and against defendants.

SECTION 2.10
VIOLATIONS OF PUBLIC
AND PRIVATE LAW

Can one incident give rise to a violation of both public and private law? Yes. This is a frequent occurrence in situations involving criminal misconduct. For instance, an intoxicated person who is involved in an accident may be criminally prosecuted for drunken driving and sued civilly by the aggrieved party for personal injury. An election of remedies between public and private law need not be made since both forms of action may be pursued. The government prosecutes the criminal case in the name of the State, and the aggrieved party is merely a witness. A civil lawsuit may be instituted for the same misconduct by the individual harmed to seek monetary compensation. Each suit is independent of the other.

This distinction is demonstrated by the O.J. Simpson criminal and civil trials. The former football player was criminally prosecuted for the murder of his ex-wife and Ronald Goldman. Simpson was found not guilty following a highly publicized criminal trial that was filled with dramatic and theatrical moments such as when John Cochran uttered his famous line, *"If the glove doesn't fit, you must acquit."* Everyone has an opinion on Simpson's guilt or innocence. Nevertheless, the jury did not believe that the government satisfied its burden of proof which is "beyond a reasonable doubt." Following the acquittal, the families of Nicole Simpson and Ronald Goldman filed civil lawsuits against Simpson to recover money for the wrongful death of the two murder victims. Much of the same evidence used during the criminal prosecution was presented in the civil trial. Using the lower burden of proof for a civil trial, the jury found the former football player responsible for the two murders and awarded the families $8.5 million dollars in compensatory damages and $25 million dollars in punitive damages. Simpson appealed that finding.

RONALD GOLDMAN V. O.J. SIMPSON
CASE #B112612 (CAL. CT. APP. 2001)

THESE CIVIL ACTIONS ARISE FROM THE MURDERS of Nicole Simpson and Ronald Goldman. In a prior criminal trial, Simpson was acquitted of these murders. In the present civil trial, the jury concluded that Simpson killed Nicole and Ronald. Simpson does not contend on appeal that the evidence is legally insufficient to support the jury's verdict. He contends that the judgments should be reversed on the grounds that the evidence was erroneously admitted and the award of damages is excessive.

Nicole and Ronald were stabbed to death on June 12, 1994, in front of Nicole's home in Los ·Angeles. Plaintiffs contended that Nicole's ex-husband had the motive to kill Nicole in a rage. On several prior occasions during their marriage, Simpson had physically abused Nicole. On June 7, 1994, Nicole telephoned a battered women's shelter hotline and stated she was frightened because her ex-husband was stalking her. On June 12, 1994, Simpson's and Nicole's young daughter performed in a dance recital. Simpson was in a foul mood that day. At the dance recital, Simpson and Nicole sat apart and did not interact. When the recital ended, Nicole excluded Simpson from a post-recital family dinner.

Ronald was a waiter at the restaurant where the dinner occurred. Afterwards, Nicole telephoned the restaurant about a pair of eyeglasses left at the dinner. Ronald may have been killed because he encountered the murder of Nicole while delivering the eyeglasses to her home. Shortly after the killings, Nicole and Ronald's bodies were found in front of her residence.

Simpson contends the court erred in admitting evidence that Simpson previously abused Nicole. This evidence showed: **(1)** outside a veterinary clinic around the spring of 1983, Simpson approached Nicole's car, tried to pull off Nicole's fur coat, and hit Nicole in the face, saying he "didn't buy this fur coat for you to go f _ _ _ somebody else"; **(2)** in 1984, Simpson lost his temper and struck Nicole's Mercedes with a baseball bat; **(3)** at a public beach in July 1986, Simpson slapped Nicole and she fell to the sand; **(4)** on New Years Day 1989, Simpson and Nicole had a violent argument during which he pulled her hair and struck her on the face or head, for which Simpson pleaded nolo contendere to spousal abuse; and (5) during a rage in October 1993, Simpson broke a door of Nicole's residence.

Simpson contends that prior instances of abuse did not establish a motive for these killings and were not similar to these killings. The courts have concluded that evidence of prior quarrels between the same parties is relevant on the issue whether the accused committed the charged acts. Where a defendant is charged with a violent crime and has or had a previous relationship with a victim, prior assaults upon the same victim, when offered on disputed issues, e.g., identity, intent, motive are admissible based solely upon the consideration of identical perpetrator and victim.

Here the trial court correctly concluded the evidence of Simpson's prior abuse of Nicole was relevant to motive, intent, and identity.

Sharon Rufo and Fredric Goldman, the parents of Ronald, were awarded compensatory damages of $8.5 million dollars. The jury rendered this award under instructions that for death, the heirs are entitled to reasonable compensation for the loss of love, companionship, comfort, affection, society, solace, or moral support suffered as a result of the death. Simpson contends the amount is excessive.

The appellate court will interfere with the jury's determination only when the award is so disproportionate to the injuries suffered that it shocks the conscience and compels the conclusion the award is attributable to passion or prejudice. Here, Fredric Goldman testified about his close and affectionate relationship with Ronald, which continued to the time of the death. As Simpson points out, Sharon Rufo's relationship with Ronald was much less close and regular. The jury award, however, was in the aggregate with no allocation between the father and mother. Although the verdict is very large, this alone does not compel the conclusion the award was attributable to passion or prejudice. "That result which requires reversal, should clearly appear from the record. We are unable to say, as a matter of law, that the judgment in this case is so excessive as to warrant us in interfering with the finding of the jury." *DiRosario v. Havens*, supra, 196 Cal.App.3d 1224.

The jury also awarded punitive damages of $12.5 million to Ronald's estate and $12.5 million to Nicole's estate. Punitive damages are awardable based on the cause of action the decedent would have had if he or she had survived. Simpson contends that, even taking his projected income into account, the amount of punitive damages awarded was excessive as a matter of law. There is no merit to this contention.

Mark Roesler is chairman of CMG Worldwide, which is engaged in marketing and licensing for sports and entertainment personalities. Roesler prepared a financial estimate of the income Simpson could earn for the rest of his life from his name and likeness. Roesler opined that Simpson could earn $2 million to $3 million a year for the rest of his life. In Roesler's opinion, $25 million was a reasonable amount that a person in Roesler's business would pay in present dollars for the exclusive right to use Simpson's name and likeness for the rest of Simpson's life.

Simpson's business manager testified Simpson's net worth at the time of trial was a negative $856,000. He testified that since the murders, Simpson had basically been selling assets to pay expenses. Over the past year, he had vigorously attempted to market Simpson memorabilia and autographs, to secure personal appearance contracts, to secure a book deal based on the criminal trial, and to market a video, all without significant commercial success.

Simpson contends the trial court should not have admitted Roesler's testimony into evidence. Simpson contends that his ability to earn income in the future is irrelevant as a factor to be considered by the jury in assessing punitive damages.

The simple answer is that the evidence at trial contradicts it. Roesler testified the right to exploit Simpson's name and likeness had a present market value, for which a person in Roesler's business would pay. The conflict between this evidence and the defense evidence that the market for Simpson memorabilia and services had dried up, was for the jury to resolve. In denying the motion for new trial, the trial court called plaintiffs' evidence credible.

Simpson contends the verdict totaling $25 million in punitive damages is excessive. An appellate court will not reverse the jury's determination unless the award, as a matter of law, is excessive or appears so grossly disproportionate that it raises a presumption it was the result of passion or prejudice.

In this case, the reprehensibility of the defendant's conduct and the severity of harm to the victims, have the greatest weight legally possible. In effect, the jury found that Simpson committed two deliberate, vicious murders. This is the most reprehensible conduct that society condemns. The harm suffered by the victims was the maximum possible; they were intentionally killed. Considering the outrageousness of Simpson's conduct and the enormity of its consequences, the amount of $25 million is not offensive and does not raise a presumption that the verdict resulted from passion or prejudice. Considering all these factors, the punitive damages award, "in light of the defendant's wealth and the gravity of the particular act," does not exceed "the level necessary to properly punish and deter." *Neal v. Farmers Ins. Exchange*, **21 Cal. 3d at 928.**

The judgments are affirmed.

SECTION 2.11
REVIEW CASES

1. Lawmakers from Virginia approved specialty license plates for a number of organizations. However, the state legislature refused to allow the Sons of Confederate Veterans to obtain license plates that contained a rebel flag logo because it would offend African Americans. Does this action by the lawmakers violate the Sons of the Confederate Veterans' First Amendment freedom of speech rights?

2. Morris released a computer program known as a "worm" on the internet which spread and multiplied, eventually causing computers at various educational institutions to crash or cease functioning. Morris was charged with violating the *Computer Fraud and Abuse Act* which punishes anyone who intentionally accesses, without authorization, a category of computers known as "federal interest computers," or prevents authorized use of information in such computers. Morris argues that the government did not prove that he had the necessary mens rea to have committed the computer crime since it was necessary for the government to show not only that (1) he intended the unauthorized access of a federal interest computer, but also (2) that he intended to prevent others from using it. The government argued that the criminal intent requirement required then to prove only one part of the crime. Which side do you believe is correct? *United States v. Robert Morris*, **928 F.2d 504 (1991).**

3. Following the entry of a civil judgment against O.J. Simpson, Fred Goldman attempted to seize a Grand Piano at Simpson's home in order to help satisfy the multi-million dollar judgment. O.J. Simpson's mother testified that the piano was given to her as a gift in 1984. Although the Grand Piano was still in the football player's house, Simpson claimed that it belonged to his mother and that she was the only one who could play the musical instrument. Who do you think should obtain possession of this item of personal property? *Ronald Goldman v. O.J. Simpson*, **Los Angles Superior Court (Sept. 1997).**

4. Bernard Getz boarded a New York subway and sat down on a bench. Four individuals surrounded Getz and ask him for five dollars. Getz stood up and fired four shots striking the individuals that surrounded him. Getz told the police that two youths stood to his left and two stood to his right. After he was asked for the money,

Getz said the four had smiles on their faces and they wanted to "play with me." While he did not think that any of the people had a gun, Getz had a fear of harm based upon prior experiences of being "maimed". Will Getz have any liability for using deadly force in either a criminal or civil context? *People of New York v. Bernard Getz,* **68 N.Y. 2d 96 (Ct. App. N.Y. 1986).**

5. Clark owned a fifty pound puppy named Rocky that had a habit of jumping on people. In fact, Rocky had a talent for playing football, and striking people with his body just as a tackler would do. Clark asked a friend to watch the dog while he was out of town. He did not, however, inform the friend of the dog's playful habits. When the good Samaritan let the puppy out in the back yard, Rocky ran up behind the woman and struck her forcibly at the back of the knees. The friend fell and fractured her left hip. Is Clark liable for the actions of the playful puppy? *Alice Clark v. Kenneth Clark,* **215 A.2d 293 (Pa. Super. 1965).**

SECTION 2.12
INTERNET REFERENCES

For more information on public and private law, see the following internet sites:

A. Criminal Law

- **www.fbi.gov/homepage.htm**
  The Federal Bureau of Investigation's website provides information on major criminal investigations, their most wanted list, and crime reports.

- **www.thebestdefense.com**
  This criminal law firm's web site provides information about various crimes and the judicial process in a criminal case.

- **www.talkjustice.com**
  At this site, a person can post notes on message boards about the criminal justice system and access "Cybrary," an online library which provides 12,000 links to different web sites relating to criminal law.

- **http://www.law.indiana.edu/law/crimlaw.html**
  Indiana University School of Law at Bloomington provides downloads of short lectures on different aspects of criminal law, such as double jeopardy and being called as a witness in a criminal trial.

B. Constitutional Law

- **http://www.usconstitution.net/index.html**
  This site focuses on the U.S. Constitution and provides a general overview of this historic document, its history, and other related information on the constitution.

- **http://w3.trib.com/fact**
  The First Amendment Cyber-Tribune sponsors this web site which focuses on issues relating to the First Amendment.

- **http://www.supremecourtus.gov**
  The Supreme Court's official site is located at this address. This link provides access to court opinions court, rules, and other general information about the Supreme Court of the United States.

C. *Administrative Law*

- **www.law.fsu.edu/library/admin.com**
  The American Bar Association's Administrative Procedure Database is located at this address. The site provides information about the organization, federal and state resources, and other related links.

D. *Contract Law*

- **http://www.ira-wg.com/library/contract.html**
  This site is devoted to issues involving contract law.

E. *Tort Law*

- **http://www.ljx.com/practice/negligence/index.html**
  News related to the law of torts, including malpractice and negligence as well as court decisions on these topics is available at this web address.

- **http://www.itslegal.com/infonet/injury/injurymain.html**
  This link provides answers to frequently asked questions about tort issues, specifically involving transportation accidents, injury to property, medical malpractice, and defamation.

- **http://www.prairielaw.com**
  This web address provides a general overview of personal injury claims and the law of torts. Information is provided about the statute of limitations, airline liability, products liability and wrongful death.

F. *Property Law*

- **http://propertymart.net**
  Advertisements and other related links dealing with real estate may be accessed through this site.

CHAPTER 3

THE JUDICIAL SYSTEM

SECTION 3.1
THE JURY SYSTEM

"A Court is only as sound as its jury, and a jury is only as sound as the men who make it up."

Harper Lee
"To Kill a Mockingbird," 1960

The Sixth and Seventh Amendments to the United States Constitution guarantee a party the right to a jury where the value in controversy exceeds $20. This is the American system, and allows a party to be judged by his peers. The judge presides over the trial and decides questions of law. The jury is the ultimate arbiter of questions of fact. The jury decides which party should win the controversy based upon the evidence presented at trial.

To better understand the distinction between a question of law and a question of fact, consider the following hypothetical:

> Joe Hodge is driving his car south on Broad Street and enters the intersection on what he maintains is a green light. Bill Smith is proceeding east on Montgomery Avenue and enters the intersection on what he alleges is a green light. The vehicles collide on Broad Street, and Hodge maintains that he is injured. Joe institutes suit against Smith for personal injuries.

The judge will inform the jury that a party who enters an intersection against a red light is negligent and responsible for the injuries caused by that negligence. This is a statement of law. On the other hand, it is up to the jury to decide which party entered the intersection after the light turned red. This is a determination of fact.

Pennsylvania does not require the decision of a jury to be unanimous in all cases. In a criminal case, the defendant is entitled to a trial by twelve people and all members of the jury must agree on the verdict. In a civil case, the verdict need not be unanimous, and the jury will consist of eight jurors unless a party specifically demands a trial by twelve. Seven out of eight jurors must agree upon the verdict in a civil case or ten out twelve jurors if a larger panel has been selected.

Is the jury system the best way of having a matter decided in a court of law? Most experts agree that it is the best system available despite certain recognized short comings and occasional erroneous verdicts. After all, it is better to be tried by the collective judgment of one's peers than by the wisdom of a single individual. This is the backbone of a democracy.

The jury system does have inherent weaknesses. The law is very complicated, and a trial is an intimidating proceeding. Jurors are thrust into the role of deciding complex cases without the proper legal training or experience. They tend to be plaintiff oriented and are more apt to award money than to find for the defense. In fact, Philadelphia County happens to be one of the most plaintiff oriented forums in the country. Attorneys will look for any type of reason to file suit in Philadelphia as opposed to one of the surrounding counties. This results in disparity of verdicts for the same injury depending upon where the trial takes place.

On the other hand, some have found the very weaknesses of the jury system to be its strength. In a speech given by Oliver Wendell Holmes on January 17, 1899, he stated:

> *"I confess that in my experience I have not found juries especially inspired for the discovery of truth…they will introduce into their verdict a…large amount…of popular prejudice, and thus keep the administration of the law in a court with the wishes and feelings of the community."* Shrager and Frost, "The Quotable Lawyer," Facts on File, at 152.

SECTION 3.2
VOIR DIRE

The process for selecting a jury is called the "**voir dire**." It is through this procedure that prospective members of the jury are questioned by the judge or attorneys to ascertain whether they are suitable to serve at the trial. Issues of prejudice, conflicts of interest and philosophies on life will be explored.

In theory, the attorneys are trying to find objective and unbiased citizens who can render a fair decision. In reality, the individual attorneys are trying to find prospective jurors who are most sympathetic to his or her cause.

As was noted by a famed criminal attorney, Percy Foreman:

> The classic adversary system in the United States not only encourages, it demands that each lawyer attempt to empanel the jury most likely to understand his argument or least likely to understand that of his opponent. You don't approach the case with the philosophy of applying abstract justice. You go in to win. "New York Times," February 3, 1969 as cited in the "Quotable Lawyer" at 154.

The O.J. Simpson trial, dubbed by the media as the trial of the century, generated a great deal of controversy regarding the actual fairness and impartiality of juries and whether the process of voir dire is a successful means of obtaining a fair and impartial jury. Indeed, a Gallup Poll showed that public interest in serving on juries dropped more than 50 percent during the duration of the Simpson trial. *American Bar Association Journal*, November 1995, page 72.

A prominent concern is that juries do not reflect the racial make-up of the community. Voter rolls don't always reflect minority participation, and some minority communities feel alienated from the process. Minnesota has taken direct action by posting billboards in predominately minority communities encouraging jury participation. New York has added unemployment and welfare participants to its jury lists. *Id.* at 73. Some counties in Pennsylvania obtain their jury pool from both the voter registration lists and the drivers license records in order to have a better cross section of the population.

There are also concerns that jurors feel unappreciated. While most states have laws that prohibit employers from firing people who are called for jury duty, only six states (Alabama, Colorado, Connecticut, Massachusetts, Nebraska and Tennessee) require employers to keep paying the person while on jury duty. According to surveys, however, jurors are more concerned about inconvenience than a lack of adequate compensation. *Id.* Often times jurors are left sitting around for days waiting to be called. To help solve this problem, many states have switched to a one-day, one-trial jury process where a person is summoned to appear only on one day. If not chosen for service that day, the individual's jury duty is over.

A prospective juror may be challenged on two grounds. Counsel may challenge a juror for cause or exercise a peremptory challenge. A challenge for cause is utilized when an individual is biased or unable to render a fair verdict. For instance, the court will exclude a relative of the victim or a person that has a preconceived opinion on innocence or guilt. The number of challenges for cause is unlimited, and the judge is the final arbiter as to whether the juror can be fair and impartial. Peremptory challenges are discretionary with the attorney and are used to exclude those who are perceived to be least sympathetic to a litigant's position. These individuals are dismissed without reason or justification. The number of peremptory challenges will vary. In a civil suit, an attorney generally receives three peremptory challenges. In a criminal case, the number will differ depending upon the severity of the crime.

The peremptory challenge serves as a very important litigation tool. It is the only way of removing an unwanted juror who can survive a challenge for cause. It is not always possible, however, for an attorney to know which potential jurors should be removed until all members of the panel have been questioned. If an attorney passes over a potential juror but has not used up the allotted peremptory challenges, may counsel go back and remove a juror who was passed over? This is the issue in *Michigan v. Schmitz* involving the shooting death of Scott Amedure, who had appeared on the Jenny Jones talk show and disclosed that he had a secret crush on another male guest.

STATE OF MICHIGAN V. JONATHON SCHMITZ
231 MICH. APP. 521 (1998)

THIS CASE ARISES FROM DEFENDANT'S KILLING of Scott Amedure with a shotgun on March 9, 1995. Three days before the shooting, defendant appeared with Amedure and Donna Riley in Chicago for a taping of an episode of the Jenny Jones talk show, during which defendant was surprised by Amedure's revelation that he had a secret crush on him. After the taping, defendant told many friends and acquaintances that he was quite embarrassed and humiliated by the experience and began a drinking binge.

On the morning of the shooting, defendant found a sexually suggestive note from Amedure on his front door. Defendant then drove to a local bank, withdrew money from his savings account, and purchased a 12-gauge pump-action shotgun and some ammunition. Defendant drove to Amedure's trailer, where he confronted Amedure about the note. When Amedure just smiled at him, defendant walked out of the trailer, stating that he had to shut off his car. Instead, defendant retrieved the shotgun and returned to the trailer. Standing at the front door, defendant fired two shots into Amedure's chest, leaving him with no chance for survival. Defendant left the scene and telephoned 911 to confess to the shooting.

Defendant was charged with first-degree murder but the jury returned a verdict of second-degree murder.

Defendant argues that the trial court erred in refusing to allow him to exercise a peremptory challenge against a potential juror he had previously "passed." On the basis of the current state of the law, we agree and reverse defendant's convictions.

Jury selection took more than three days to complete and was filled with probing questions regarding highly personal matters such as mental illness, homosexuality, past embarrassing moments, and betrayal by others. The jury panel completed individual questionnaires before the start of voir dire, and many potential jurors were dismissed for cause on the basis of their answers to the questionnaires.

Each side was allotted twelve peremptory challenges. On the final day of jury selection, the defense sought to peremptorily challenge a person that had been on the panel when the defense "passed" for peremptory challenges on the second day of jury selection. The prosecutor objected and stated that defendant should be deemed to have accepted the individual and that defendant's request to later peremptorily challenge the potential juror should be denied. The trial court denied defendant's request to exercise a peremptory challenge and noted that the defendant could not "open up the preemptory challenges again."

On appeal, defendant argues that reversal of his convictions is required because the trial court denied him the opportunity to exercise a peremptory challenge in accordance with the court rules. We note that defendant had exercised only five of his twelve peremptory challenges at the completion of jury selection.

A criminal defendant has a constitutional right to be tried by a fair and impartial jury. Peremptory challenges have long been an important tool for ensuring a fair trial, both in fact and in appearance.

Michigan common law has long provided that peremptory challenges may be exercised at any time before the swearing of the jury. The court rule governing the exercise of peremptory challenges provides:

a. First the plaintiff, and then the defendant may exercise one or more peremptory challenges until each party successively waives further peremptory challenges or all the challenges have been exercised, at which point jury selection is complete.

b. A "pass" is not counted as a challenge but is a waiver of further challenge to the panel as constituted at that time.

c. If a party has exhausted all peremptory challenges and another party has remaining challenges, that party may continue to exercise his or her remaining peremptory challenges until they are exhausted.

d. After the jurors have been seated in the jurors' box and a challenge for cause is sustained or a peremptory challenge exercised, another juror must be selected and examined before further challenges are made. This juror is subject to challenge as are other jurors.

The plain language of this rule is clear. If the composition of the panel is changed after a party passes a panel (either by challenges for cause or the exercise of peremptory challenge by another party), the party is free to exercise further peremptory challenges to any member of the new panel. Any other interpretation would ignore the phrase "as constituted at that time." It is not until both parties pass for peremptory challenges, and there has been no change in the makeup of the panel, that the party's pass may be deemed conclusive. Accordingly, we hold that the trial court erred in equating a pass of the panel as an acceptance of each potential juror thereon.

The length of jury duty will vary depending upon the jurisdiction. Jury duty in Federal Court is between two and three weeks unless an individual is selected to serve on a case that extends beyond this time period. While the length of jury duty in state court will vary upon the jurisdiction, a number of courts utilize the "One Day or One Trial" program.

**SECTION 3.3
JURY SELECTION
IN PHILADELPHIA**

The following is an explanation of the jury selection process in Philadelphia.

1. The Jury Board is the department in the Criminal Justice Center that is responsible for assembling prospective jurors. The Board obtains the names of residents of Philadelphia County through the voter registration list.

2. Registered voters are then randomly selected to receive a questionnaire. Upon receipt of the completed questionnaires, they are reviewed by the Jury Board to determine whether a person is eligible to serve as a prospective juror. The names of those that are eligible are placed into a computer.

3. The computer randomly picks several hundred people and forwards a summons to each eligible juror to appear on a certain date for jury duty. Those selected must report to the jury assembly room where they wait to be taken to a courtroom that needs jurors for a trial.

4. If there is no response to the initial summons to appear for jury duty, a second subpoena is sent. If within 30 to 60 days there is still no response, the person is charged with committing a misdemeanor and can be fined up to $500.00.

To Prospective Juror:

You have been selected at random as a Prospective Juror to serve in the Court of Common Pleas of Philadelphia. If you are qualified, you may be subpoenaed to serve for one day or one trial.

In accordance with the Act of Legislature, you are requested to fill out this qualification form and return it in the enclosed envelope within ten (10) days from receipt hereof.

You are cautioned that failure to return form properly and truthfully answered will subject you to a fine or imprisonment or both in accordance with the Act of Legislature. Any false answer will subject you to the Penalty of Perjury. These questions are necessary to determine your qualifications to serve as a juror. Your answers are treated as Confidential. If you are unable to fill out this form, have another person do it for you and indicate the reason for the assistance.

Detach this stub and return card in enclosed envelope

CITY AND COUNTY OF PHILADELPHIA JURY SELECTION COMMISSION CRIMINAL JUSTICE CENTER, 1301 FILBERT STREET	QUESTIONNAIRE FOR PROSPECTIVE JUROR

YOUR PRESENT OCCUPATION **SEAMSTRESS**

NUMBER

YOUR PRESENT EMPLOYER'S NAME AND ADDRESS **McGREGOR CLOTHING**

BAILEY SIMONS
6344 Cresecentville Road
Philadelphia PA 19122

☐ MR.

HAVE YOU EVER BEEN CONVICTED OF ANY CRIME *(If Yes, State Nature of Crime)*
☐ Yes ☒ No

☐ MRS.

CAN YOU READ, WRITE, SPEAK AND UNDERSTAND THE ENGLISH LANGUAGE
☒ Yes ☐ No   Highest grade of school attended: _11_

☒ MISS

ARE YOU PHYSICALLY AND MENTALLY ABLE TO SERVE AS A JUROR | ARE YOU A U.S. CITIZEN
☒ Yes ☐ No *(If No, State Reason on back)* ☒ Yes ☐ No

☐ MS.   **PLEASE COMPLETE BOTH SIDES**

WERE YOU ABLE TO COMPLETE THIS FORM WITHOUT ASSISTANCE? | MARITAL STATUS
☒ Yes ☐ No

☐ Single ☐ Married ☐ Widowed
☐ Divorced ☒ Separated

PLEASE INDICATE ANY CORRECTIONS TO NAME & ADDRESS BELOW:

I hereby certify that the above answers are true and correct

Bailey Simons   9/5
(Sign Your Name)   (Date)

IF YOU DESIRE, YOU MAY RETURN THIS CARD IN PERSON TO ROOM 204 CRIMINAL JUSTICE CENTER
30-31
(Rev. 11/95)

DATE OF BIRTH
Month Day Year
06   08   69

PLACE OF BIRTH *(City & State)*
PHILADELPHIA

HOW MANY YEARS HAVE YOU LIVED AT YOUR PRESENT ADDRESS
10

HOME PHONE NO.
555-7152

BUSINESS PHONE NO.
522-1200

JURY QUESTIONNAIRE
(Please Print)

NAME (Last)	(First)	(Middle Initial)	JUROR NO.
FIGG	SPENCER	B	534

SECTION OF CITY	OTHER SECTIONS OF CITY LIVED IN WITHIN PAST TEN YEARS
WARRINGTON	WARMINSTER

MARITAL STATUS

[x] Married   [ ] Single   [ ] Divorced   [ ] Separated   [ ] Widowed

OCCUPATION	OTHER OCCUPATIONS WITHIN PAST TEN YEARS
GRAPHIC DESIGNER	ADVERTISING

OCCUPATION OF [x] SPOUSE (or deceased spouse)   [ ] OTHER   OTHER OCCUPATIONS WITHIN PAST TEN YEARS   [X] SPOUSE   [ ] OTHER

PHYSICIAN   SOCIAL WORKER

| No. of Male Children ___1___ Ages ___14___ | YOUR LEVEL OF SCHOOLING COMPLETED | RACE [ ] White [ ] Hispanic |
| No. of Female Children ____ Ages ____ | COLLEGE DEGREE | [ ] Black [x] Other ___ |

STOP HERE
Writing below this line is prohibited until the juror video is shown

QUESTIONS TO BE ANSWERED IN THE JURY ASSEMBLY ROOM

1. Do you have any physical or psychological disability or are you presently taking any medication? [ ] Yes [x] No

2. (a) Have you ever been a juror before? [ ] Yes [x] No

   (b) If so, were you ever on a hung jury? [ ] Yes [ ] No

Questions 3 through 15 apply to criminal cases only

3. Do you have any religious, moral or ethical beliefs that would prevent you from sitting in judgment in a criminal case and rendering a fair verdict? [ ] Yes [x] No

4. Have you or anyone close to you ever been a victim of a crime? [x] Yes [ ] No

5. Have you or anyone close to you ever been charged with or arrested for a crime, other than a traffic violation? [ ] Yes [x] No

6. Have you or anyone close to you ever been an eyewitness to a crime, whether or not it ever came to Court? [ ] Yes [x] No

7. Have you, or has anyone close to you, ever worked as a police officer or in other law enforcement jobs? This includes prosecutors, public defenders, private criminal defense lawyers, detectives, and security or prison guards. [x] Yes [ ] No

8. Would you be more likely to believe the testimony of a police officer or any other law enforcement officer just because of his job? [x] Yes [ ] No

9. Would you be less likely to believe the testimony of a police officer or other law enforcement officer just because of his job? [ ] Yes [x] No

10. Would you have any problem following the Court's instruction that the defendant in a criminal case is presumed to be innocent until proven guilty beyond a reasonable doubt? [ ] Yes [x] No

11. Would you have any problem following the Court's instruction that the defendant in a criminal case does not have to take the stand or present evidence, and it cannot be held against the defendant if he or she elects to remain silent? [ ] Yes [x] No

12. Would you have any problem following the Court's instruction in a criminal case that just because someone is arrested, it does not mean that the person is guilty of anything? [ ] Yes [x] No

13. In general, would you have any problem following and applying the judge's instructions on the law? [ ] Yes [x] No

14. Would you have any problem during jury deliberations in a criminal case discussing the case fully but still making up your own mind? [ ] Yes [x] No

15. Is there any other reason you could not be a fair juror in a criminal case? [ ] Yes [x] No

30-58 (1) (Rev. 3/92)

Page 1
JUDGE

SECTION 3.4
COMMONWEALTH
v. CHRISTOPHER

SELECTION OF
THE JURY

PROBLEM THREE—A

HODGE, DODGE AND LODGE
ATTORNEYS AT LAW
MEMORANDUM

To: All Law Clerks

FROM: Gregory Olan Dodge

RE: Commonwealth of Pennsylvania v. Peter Christopher
Selection of The Jury

I must inform you of an unfortunate incident involving Kathy Hodge that occurred last month. A man wearing a ski mask assaulted Joe's daughter at school and stole her handbag. I had my secretary transcribe the news broadcast for your review.

TRANSCRIPTION OF NEWS BROADCAST

In local news, a 16 year old girl was assaulted at her high school gym last night and her handbag was stolen. Kathy Hodge was confronted around 8:00 p.m. while working out in the nautilus room. The victim is unable to identify her attacker since he was wearing a green and white ski mask. She did, however, notice a tattoo of a shark on his bare left shoulder. According to police, the suspect is 5' 10" and weighs 160 pounds. He was last seen wearing a red and white stripped shirt, denim pants and sneakers.

The community has offered a $10,000 reward for information leading to the arrest and conviction of the criminal. According to Dr. Donald Feelgood, the President of the Community Civic Association, "We are deeply saddened and shocked by this event. None of us will rest until the assailant is apprehended."

School officials were not available for comment but Superintendent James Nolan released a statement promising to tighten security in order to reduce the chance that a similar incident could happen again.

Following the publicity surrounding this incident, the case took a bizarre twist when the police arrested Peter Christopher. As you may remember, he is the next door neighbor of the Hodge family and is the individual that sold Kathy the car that she destroyed in an accident. Based upon a tip supplied to the witness hotline, police were notified that Christopher had a tattoo of a shark on his shoulder and held a grudge against the Hodge family. Christopher has been charged with the crime and has been released on $100,000 bail.

The District Attorney was informed of our interest in the matter and the firm has been granted permission to act as the special prosecutor for the criminal trial. We will work on various aspects of the case including the selection of a jury.

I have retained the services of a jury consultant to provide the firm with profiles of perspective jurors. A composite of 21 biographical sketches has been constructed in order to give us a good prediction of the jury panel in the criminal case. You should review the biographical data for each prospective juror to see which individuals should be challenged for cause and which people should be considered for use of a peremptory challenge. When reviewing the sketches, first analyze the problem as though you represent Peter Christopher and make your selections. You should then examine the biographical sketches and assume that you represent the Commonwealth of Pennsylvania on behalf of Kathy Hodge.

For the purposes of this exercise, each side is given three peremptory challenges. The goal is to end up with twelve jurors suitable to both the prosecution and defense. A worksheet is provided for your selections and is attached following the biographical sketches.

Sample questions have been provided and will be used by the defense and prosecution at the time of the jury selection process. They will give you an idea of the types of issues that are of concern to each side.

QUESTIONS FOR DEFENSE COUNSEL TO ASK THE PANEL:

1. Does anybody know any of the parties, counsel, or the judge in this case?

2. Does anybody know anything about this case?

3. Has anyone ever been the victim of a crime?

4. Is anyone a member of the police force or have a close family member on the police force?

5. Has anyone ever been a member of "Women Organized against Rape" or a similar organization?

6. Does anyone believe that the testimony of a police officer should be given more credence than any other witness?

7. The government has the burden of proving the defendant guilty. Would anyone draw an adverse inference if the defendant didn't testify?

QUESTIONS FOR THE DISTRICT ATTORNEY TO ASK THE PANEL:

1. Has anybody ever been accused of committing a crime?

2. Does anyone believe that they cannot be fair and impartial in the hearing of this matter?

3. Does anyone believe that they will have a difficult time in finding the defendant guilty if he could go to jail as a result of the conviction?

4. Will serving on this jury be a hardship or an inconvenience?

BIOGRAPHICAL SKETCHES OF PROSPECTIVE JURORS:

The consultant service that the firm hired has provided us with 21 biographical sketches of the types of jurors that we can anticipate encountering at trial. Please review the sketches and make your decision on jury selection for both the prosecution and defense.

JUROR 1   *Marilyn Trainer*—Female, 40-year-old mother with three daughters, 18, 15 and 12. She claims that she can be fair in the case, even though she has three daughters. She is an unemployed housewife.

JUROR 2   *John McNamara*—Male, 35 years old, married, no children. He is a Police Sergeant.

JUROR 3   *Hans Forrestor*—Male, Single, 30-year-old philosophy professor at Penn who has been mugged on the subway. The police never found his attacker. He claims that he can be fair in the rape case.

JUROR 4   *Star Jackson*—Female, 26-year-old rock singer, single, and involved with Women Organized Against Rape.

JUROR 5   *Chip Wright*—Male, 22-year old single, college student who resides in fraternity house.

JUROR 6   *Jeanette Williams*—Female, 29-year-old civil litigation paralegal, married, no children. Her husband is a doctor (gynecologist).

JUROR 7   *Duke Septa*—Male, 50-year-old, divorced bus driver with four sons. Marriage was the worst years of his life. He believes women should not work and should merely take care of the household.

JUROR 8   *Vincent Serino*—Male, 60-year-old gym teacher ,not married. Teaches at a girl's Catholic school.

JUROR 9   *Lola Thomas*—Female, 21-year-old exotic dancer. Single, but lives with her boyfriend.

JUROR 10   *Alice B. Davis*—Female, 58-year-old housewife with two sons, 28 and 30. She has never worked since her household duties keep her busy enough. Her husband is a traveling salesman for an encyclopedia company.

JUROR 11   *Andrew Hoffman*—Male, 23 years old and single. He knows about the case from the neighborhood. Defendant has a bad reputation. He can't be fair.

JUROR 12   *Jack Joseph Hammer*—Male, 23-year-old, unemployed construction worker who lives at home with family. He has two sisters and a brother.

JUROR 13   *Louis Waterman*—Male, 40-year-old, retired sailor who was in the Navy for 20 years. He is single.

JUROR 14   *Anna Klein*—Female, 43-year-old, widowed fashion designer with no children.

JUROR 15   *Desmond Lovejoy*—Male, 28-year-old florist. He is not married.

JUROR 16   *Aileen Wheeler*—Female, 33-year-old, divorced cab driver. She has one 16 year old son.

JUROR 17   *Elizabeth Addis*—Female, college student at Princeton. She is awaiting trial for streaking.

JUROR 18   *Thomas Bradford*—Male, 50-year-old, disabled veteran on social security. He is married with eight children and ten grandchildren.

JUROR 19   *Rose Kelly*—Female, 45-year-old, married waitress whose husband is a roofer. She was convicted of prostitution when 18 years old.

JUROR 20   *Margaret Jones*—Female, 35-year-old, single, psychiatrist. Practice involves drug therapy. She was in Peace Corp.

JUROR 21   *Jane Sullivan*—Female, 28-year-old lawyer who works for the Office of the Public Defender. She is single.

JURY SELECTION WORKSHEET

Juror Number (For Government)		Juror Number (For Defense)	
1. Yes/No	12. Yes/No	1. Yes/No	12. Yes/No
2. Yes/No	13. Yes/No	2. Yes/No	13. Yes/No
3. Yes/No	14. Yes/No	3. Yes/No	14. Yes/No
4. Yes/No	15. Yes/No	4. Yes/No	15. Yes/No
5. Yes/No	16. Yes/No	5. Yes/No	16. Yes/No
6. Yes/No	17. Yes/No	6. Yes/No	17. Yes/No
7. Yes/No	18. Yes/No	7. Yes/No	18. Yes/No
8. Yes/No	19. Yes/No	8. Yes/No	19. Yes/No
9. Yes/No	20. Yes/No	9. Yes/No	20. Yes/No
10. Yes/No	21. Yes/No	10. Yes/No	21. Yes/No
11. Yes/No		11. Yes/No	

Record of Peremptory Challenges:		Record of Challenges For Cause:	
Government:	Defendant:	Government:	Defendant:
1.	1.	1.	1.
2.	2.	2.	2.
3.	3.	3.	3.

**SECTION 3.5
DISCHARGE OF
AN EMPLOYEE FOR
JURY SERVICE**

Employers are often confronted with the difficult problem of what to do when an employee announces that he or she has been selected for jury duty. The worker's absence can have a disruptive influence on production schedules and cause economic hardship. Can the employer discharge the worker and hire a replacement to minimize the impact of the juror's absence?

Federal law prohibits the discharge, intimidation, or coercion of any permanent employee because of jury service (**28 U.S.C.A. § 1875**). Penalties for a violation of the statute include reinstatement of the worker, recovery of lost wages, other loss of benefits suffered by the employee, and attorney's fees.

An individual claiming that the employer has violated this law may file an application with the Federal District Court in the locale where the employer maintains a place of business. Upon a finding of probable merit in the claim, the court will appoint counsel to represent the employee in any Federal court action necessary to resolve the dispute.

Court cases that have dealt with this legislation have prohibited the recovery of mental pain and suffering for the employer's actions and have based the recovery of attorney's fees on a per hour basis rather than on a percentage of recovery. Recently, a court granted a discharged employee a preliminary injunction reinstating him to his job pending the outcome of the trial for wrongful discharge.

The Pennsylvania Legislature has enacted a similar statute prohibiting the discharge or intimidation of an employee who has been called for jury duty. This law provides in pertinent part:

Section 4563 Protection of Employment of Petit and Grand Jurors

a. An employer shall not deprive an employee of his employment, seniority position or benefits, or threaten or otherwise coerce him because the employee receives a summons, responds thereto, serves as a juror or attends court for prospective jury service. Nothing in this section shall be construed to require the employer to compensate the employee for employment time lost because of such jury service.

SECTION 3.6
JURISDICTION

Jurisdiction refers to the power of a court to determine the merits of a dispute and to grant an aggrieved party relief. In order for a court to properly entertain an action, it must have jurisdiction over the subject matter in dispute and jurisdiction over the parties involved.

Subject matter jurisdiction is quite simple. The particular court where the dispute is heard must have the power to hear the kind of case that is in controversy. The courts are very specialized, and the plaintiff must institute suit before the proper court. For instance, a divorce proceeding may not be instituted in tax court. The court's power to hear these specific types of cases is usually granted by the legislature.

Jurisdiction over the person requires the court to have power to exercise its authority over the defendant. Traditionally, suit was instituted where the defendant could be found. This was either in the state where he resided or where he worked. Now, a court is considered to have jurisdiction over the parties when the defendant has "minimum contacts" with the state where the court is located (the forum state). "Minimum contacts" are generally deemed to exist when the defendant takes actions that are purposefully directed toward the Forum State.

The rule of serving a defendant where the defendant can be found was expanded over time by the passage of longarm statutes that allow a jurisdiction to reach beyond the state boundaries to serve a defendant with the lawsuit. The most common longarm statutes deal with a non-resident who commits a tort within a state, a party who owns property in a state, and one doing business in a state.

In order to satisfy the requirements of Due Process, the Supreme Court has ruled that a state court may exercise personal jurisdiction over a nonresident defendant as long as there are *minimum contacts* between the defendant and the state in which the suit has been filed. The concept of minimum contacts protects defendants against the burdens of litigating in a distant or inconvenient court. Usually, a defendant will have some kind of presence in the forum. In the case of transacting business within a state, however, it is not necessary to have an office in that jurisdiction. Soliciting business through sales representatives or by placing an advertisement in a local newspaper have been held to constitute minimum contacts.

OM V. GEORGE FOREMAN
1992 U.S. Dist. LEXIS 8915 (N.D. ILL. 1992)

OM BROUGHT THIS ACTION ALLEGING that defendants appropriated and used his boxing promotion concepts without his consent. Defendants now move to dismiss plaintiff's action based on lack of personal jurisdiction.

Plaintiff is a citizen of Illinois. None of the defendants is a citizen of Illinois. None of the defendants has employees or offices in Illinois, and they do not maintain phone listings, mailing addresses or bank accounts in Illinois.

Ron Weathers is George Foreman's manager, and both reside in Texas. From Illinois, Om initiated contact with Weathers in Texas about a promotional boxing concept conceived by Om. Om created the concept of the "Ages" promotion, a three-fight series of boxing matches pitting an older fighter (George Foreman) against a younger fighter such as Evander Holyfield, Mike Tyson or Buster Douglas. The concept included titles for each of the fights ("Challenge of the Ages," "Battle of the Ages,"

and "Fight of the Ages") as well as promotional epithets characterizing two of the fighters ("the Foreman Factor" and "the Tyson Triangle"). Plaintiff met with Weathers at Caesar's Palace in Las Vegas, Nevada. Weathers assured Om of his authority to act on Foreman's behalf. A follow up meeting occurred between Weathers and Om at the Las Vegas offices of Top Rank, Inc. At some point Weathers signed a nondisclosure agreement that presumably limited Weathers' use of the concepts Om shared with him. Weathers indicated that he or Om could draft a letter of intent in order to begin planning the first fight, the "Battle of the Ages," between George Foreman and Mike Tyson.

At the request of Weathers, Om prepared the letter of intent for Weathers to put either on Weathers' own or his attorney's letterhead. The letter was not placed on letterhead. Om repeatedly requested a copy of the letter on letterhead in order to satisfy investors in the promotion. Weathers subsequently informed Om that he would not comply with this request. Negotiations between the parties ceased shortly thereafter.

Some months later, Foreman and Holyfield agreed to fight each other, and the "Battle of the Ages" concept was used to promote the fight. Om alleges that his concepts have been used by the defendants without his permission and that he has received no compensation for that use.

Defendants conducted some promotional and advertising activity in Illinois. Defendants Foreman and Weathers attended a press conference in Chicago, Illinois. The press conference was to promote the "Battle of the Ages." The fight between Foreman and Holyfield was allegedly broadcast in Illinois by defendant TVKO.

An Illinois court can obtain jurisdiction over a nonresident defendant if the defendant is "doing business" in Illinois or is subject to jurisdiction under the Illinois long-arm statute.

Personal jurisdiction must be found under the provisions of the Illinois long-arm statute. Under **section 2-209(c)** of that statute, Weathers and Foreman may be sued in Illinois if they made sufficient or "minimum" contacts so as to comport with due process. We must look at whether the defendant "purposely established" minimum contacts with Illinois. Also, Weathers and Foreman must have contacts with Illinois "such that the maintenance of the suit does not offend traditional notions of fair play and substantial justice.

It is "foreseeability," and not physical presence, that is critical; the due process analysis entails a determination of whether Weathers' and Foreman's conduct and connection with the forum State are such that they should reasonably anticipate being haled into court there."

While the question is a close one, we believe that this court has personal jurisdiction over Weathers and Foreman. Weathers and Foreman, among others, attended the pre-fight press conference in Chicago to promote the "Battle of the Ages." Om also alleges other advertising activities, promoting the "Battle of the Ages," in Illinois by defendants.

Going to Illinois to promote the fight, using promotional concepts that are alleged to be the basis of a breach of contract claim, is sufficient to satisfy due process concerns. Defendants maintain that because plaintiff did not allege the press conference as a basis of relief, we cannot, consistent with due process, use those contacts to justify asserting.

Defendants' attendance at the press conference and advertising in Illinois does have a connection to "the contracts and actions which provide the basis for Om's complaint." Sufficient jurisdictional allegations can be fairly read from Om's complaint.

Defendants purposely established minimum contacts with Illinois in a way that does not offend traditional notions of fair play and substantial justice. It was reasonably foreseeable that coming into Illinois to promote a fight using Om's concepts, could result in litigation arising out of those promotional activities. We also find defendants' alleged contacts with Illinois sufficient to satisfy Illinois due process concerns; that is, it is "fair, just and reasonable" to subject defendants to suit here.

Defendants made sufficient minimum contacts with Illinois to satisfy the due process concerns of the United States Constitution and the Illinois constitution. Therefore, defendants' motion to dismiss for lack of personal jurisdiction is denied.

With the advent of websites and their ability to convey information to people around the world, additional jurisdictional issues arise. For instance, is a business that places information about itself on the Internet subject to suit in any place where an individual can access the site even though the business has no presence in that state and has not solicited business in that state? This is the issue in *Michael Hurley v. Cancun Playa Oasis International Hotels.* Basically, the court found that a website by itself is not a sufficient contact to confer jurisdiction in a state just because a person may be able to access the site from that state. The plaintiff must still establish that the defendant has maintained continuous, systematic and substantial business contacts within the state where the lawsuit has been filed.

MICHAEL HURLEY V. CANCUN PLAYA OASIS INTERNATIONAL HOTELS
U. S. DISTRICT COURT, E.D. PENNSYLVANIA (1999)

PLAINTIFF MICHAEL HURLEY ("HURLEY") has filed this action against defendants Cancun Playa Oasis International Hotels ("Cancun Playa") and Reserve Hotel ("ReservHotel"). Hurley alleges that as a result of defendant's negligence, he suffered personal injuries while staying at Cancun Playa's hotel in Mexico. Defendant ReservHotel, a Georgia corporation which Hurley claims is liable as an agent of Cancun Playa, has filed a motion to dismiss for lack of personal jurisdiction.

Pennsylvania law permits courts to "exercise personal jurisdiction over nonresidents within the constitutional limits of the [D]ue [P]rocess [C]lause of the [F]ourteenth [A]mendment."

For a court properly to exercise jurisdiction under the Due Process Clause, the plaintiff must satisfy a two- part test. First, the plaintiff must demonstrate that the defendant had the constitutionally sufficient "minimum contacts" with the forum. Second, the court must determine that the exercise of specific jurisdiction is consistent with traditional notions of fair play and substantial justice.

In his response to defendant's motion to dismiss, Hurley offers no evidence that his contacts with ReservHotel gave rise to his personal injury claim. In fact, Hurley never demonstrates that he actually had contacts with defendant. For example, Hurley notes that ReservHotel maintains a web site and a 1-800 telephone number. Hurley does not contend, however, that he visited the web site, knew of the phone number prior to filing his complaint, or used either medium to make reservations in Cancun. In sum, Hurley's personal injury claim does not arise out of ReservHotel's contacts with Pennsylvania. Hurley's asserted facts, therefore, are insufficient for this court to exercise jurisdiction over ReservHotel.

The exercise of general personal jurisdiction does not require that the subject matter of the cause of action ha[ve] any connection to the forum. Rather, a court has jurisdiction over a nonresident corporation only if the corporation's contacts with the forum are continuous, systematic, and substantial. In fact, only a showing of "significantly more than mere minimum contacts" will suffice.

It is undisputed that ReservHotel is not registered to conduct business in Pennsylvania. It has no assets, bank accounts, or property in Pennsylvania. No officers, agents, or employees of ReservHotel reside or work in Pennsylvania. ReservHotel does not have a Pennsylvania telephone listing. Finally, ReservHotel "has never met, contracted with, or been in contact with any individual traveler or travel agent" in Pennsylvania, including the plaintiff.

Hurley nevertheless asserts that ReservHotel maintained "continuous and systematic business contact" with Pennsylvania through its 1-800 telephone number and Internet web site, both of which are accessible in Pennsylvania. The use of a 1-800 telephone number by a nonresident corporation does not create the "extensive and per[v]asive" contacts with the forum state needed to assert general jurisdiction over a corporation. ReservHotel's web site, however, is a more complicated matter. As noted in *Blackburn v. Walker Oriental Rug Galleries, Inc.*, **999 F. Supp. 636, 639 (E.D. Pa. 1998)**, the type of Internet contacts a foreign corporation can have with a state can vary.

The first type of contact is when the defendant clearly does business over the Internet.... The second type of contact occurs when "a user can exchange information with the host computer. In these cases, the exercise of jurisdiction is determined by examining the level of interactivity and commercial nature of the exchange of information that occurs on the Website." The third type of contact involves the posting of information or advertisements on an Internet Website "which is accessible to users in foreign jurisdictions."

ReservHotel's web site meets the requirements of the second type of Internet contact. ReservHotel's web site accepts and confirms reservations for various hotels. The website publicizes a 1-800 telephone number for voice reservations. The web site also provides e-mail address by which viewers of the site can contact the company. These characteristics give ReservHotel's web site an interactive quality that goes beyond a passive web site that simply advertises.

Personal jurisdiction, however, requires more than a recognition that a nonresident corporation has an "interactive" web site. Rather, the "nature and quality of the commercial" contacts actually conducted over the Internet must be continuous, systematic, and substantial. In other words, there must be some proof that ReservHotel purposefully availed itself of the privilege of conducting activities within the forum State, thus invoking the benefits and protection of [Pennsylvania's] laws.

In this case, the record lacks a single instance of deliberate contact between ReservHotel and Pennsylvania through the Internet. Hurley, for example, has not demonstrated that ReservHotel has formed contracts with any Pennsylvania entity. In fact, Hurley has not shown that any resident of the Commonwealth has even visited ReservHotel's Web page. On the contrary, he "relies solely on the national and international nature of the Internet to demonstrate that [ReservHotel's] web site had the potential to reach and solicit [Pennsylvania] residents." As stated in *E-Data Corp. v. Micropatent Corp.*, **989 F. Supp. 173 (D. Conn. 1997)**, "[i]f such potentialities alone were sufficient to confer personal jurisdiction over a foreign defendant, any foreign corporation with the potential to reach or do business with [the forum state] by telephone, television or mail would be subject to suit in [that forum state].... ReservHotel's web site, as far as the record in this case demonstrates, has not been a place of any commercial activity here. Plaintiff has simply not established that ReservHotel has maintained continuous, systematic, and substantial business contacts with Pennsylvania.

This court, therefore, cannot exercise specific personal jurisdiction. Hurley also has not shown that ReservHotel's contacts with Pennsylvania through its 1-800 telephone number and its web site are continuous, systematic, and substantial. Accordingly, the court will grant ReservHotel's motion to dismiss plaintiff's complaint for lack of personal jurisdiction.

SECTION 3.7
VENUE

Venue is the place where a case should be heard. The plaintiff decides where to institute suit. This decision will rarely be disturbed unless the defendant can demonstrate a compelling reason to remove the matter to another jurisdiction. This will occur if the defendant cannot obtain a fair trial in the location where the lawsuit was filed because of prejudice or bias or because of *forum non conveniens*. This latter term means that the place of the trial is inconvenient for the parties and for the witnesses involved in the trial. A court can refuse to exercise its jurisdiction over the parties on the grounds that it would be more convenient for a court in another jurisdiction to hear the case.

The following criminal case involving the beating of Rodney King by Los Angeles police officers is an example of where a change of venue was ruled necessary by the court due to the continuing and pervasive nature of the publicity against the police.

LAWRENCE POWELL V. SUPERIOR CT. OF CALIFORNIA FOR THE COUNTY OF LOS ANGELES
232 CAL. APP. 3D 785 (1991)

DEFENDANTS SEEK TO ORDER THIS CASE transferred to another county because of pretrial publicity. We are compelled to direct a change of venue and grant the petition.

Unbeknownst to the Los Angeles Police Department (LAPD) officers involved, the incident was videotaped by a nearby resident who sold it to a local TV station. The initial showing caused shock, revulsion, outrage and disbelief among viewers. A fire storm immediately developed in the Los Angeles area, so intense and pervasive was the reaction to the videotape.

Questions developed about the integrity of the LAPD and its chief. The mayor of Los Angeles called for the resignation of the chief of police.

That action polarized the community. The incident and the resultant political turmoil received massive local media coverage, including newspaper, radio and TV which has impacted the residents. We emphasize, however, that were this simply a matter of extraordinary publicity we might have reached a different conclusion. What compels our decision in this case is the high level of political turmoil and controversy which this incident has generated, which continues to this day and appears likely to continue at least until the time when a trial of this matter can be had.

In making an independent evaluation of the likelihood pretrial publicity has prejudiced a defendant's right to a fair trial in the county of original venue, judicial notice of news media coverage of the case is appropriate. Accordingly, we take judicial notice of the continuing and pervasive publicity involving the ongoing political controversy in the City of Los Angeles and all other matters pertinent to our determination of the venue issue.

We have duly considered such political controversy along with the size of the jury pool, the status of the victim and the accused, and the nature of the offense and conclude we must direct a change of venue. So extensive and pervasive has been the trial coverage, and so intense has become the political fallout, potential jurors have been infected the extent there is a reasonable likelihood that a fair and impartial trial cannot be had in Los Angeles County.

The question is whether the potential jurors can view the case with the requisite impartiality. Material factors to be considered in resolving the question include the size of the potential jury pool, the nature and extent of the publicity, the status of the accused and the victim, the nature and gravity of the offense, and the existence of political turmoil arising from the incident.

Size of the potential jury pool is one of the factors considered on a motion for change of venue. "The larger the local population, the more likely it is that preconceptions about the case have not become embedded in the public consciousness." Los Angeles County covers 4,083 square miles. The source list used in the selection of potential jurors in Los Angeles Superior Court includes the list of persons who voted in recent elections and the records of the Department of Motor Vehicles. The potential jury pool in Los Angeles County is 6.526 million according to the Jury Services Division of the Los Angeles County Superior Court.

In support of the motion for change of venue, defendants rely, in part, on polls of residents of Los Angeles County as reported in the Los Angeles Times. On March 10, 1991, within a week of the incident, the Los Angeles Times reported 86 percent of those surveyed had seen the videotape of the offense and 92 percent believed excessive force had been used. In another poll almost two-thirds believed the force used was racially motivated.

Here, questions peculiar to the county of original venue have rendered the seating of a jury panel without preconceived opinions as to some aspects of the case practically impossible.

It cannot be disputed that difficulty in obtaining a fair trial in Los Angeles County is exacerbated by the fact the defendants are police officers. The fact that the videotape depicts local officers in such conduct threatens the community's ability to rely on its police and has caused a high level of indignation, outrage, and anxiety.

Every person charged with a criminal offense is entitled to a trial free of the "unacceptable risk...of impermissible factors coming into play." *Estelle v. Williams* **(1976) 425 U.S. 501.** "The potential of community bias mounts in direct ratio to the pervasiveness of publicity. ... In counties geographically removed from the locale of the crime, lack of a sense of community involvement will permit jurors a degree of objectivity unattainable" in the locale of the crime itself. Most significantly, such jurors are far less likely to be involved in the prevailing political controversies which we have set out in some detail and which appear to be reasonably limited to the greater Los Angeles area.

The record presented before the trial court was sufficient to support defendants' contention they cannot receive a fair trial in Los Angeles

County and their contention becomes increasingly more obvious as each day passes. Under the totality of the circumstances, a change of venue is clearly necessary to assure that defendants have a fair and impartial trial.

We leave the ultimate selection of a site for a fair trial to the trial court with directions to weigh the various factors bearing upon the selection of a forum free from the unacceptable risk that a fair trial cannot be conducted.

The Oklahoma City bombing is another case in which the defendants requested a change of venue. The 1995 bombing destroyed a large part of the Alfred P. Murrah Federal Building and left 169 people dead and 500 injured. The original trial judge was removed from the case because of doubts about his impartiality because the bombing had destroyed his office. The defense also asserted the trial should take place outside of the state to insure an unbiased jury because of the pretrial publicity, and the effect the criminal activity had on people in Oklahoma. The trial was eventually removed and tried in Denver, Colorado.

SECTION 3.8
STANDING

In accordance with the United States Constitution, courts are only permitted to hear actual cases or controversies. That is, courts cannot offer advisory opinions to people who are not actually involved in a dispute. The plaintiff in a lawsuit must have a direct and substantial interest in the outcome of the case that he or she intends to bring. This concept is referred to as **standing**. To meet this requirement, the plaintiff must show that he or she has actually been injured by the action that is the subject of the lawsuit. The injury can be physical, economic, environmental, or aesthetic, but must injure the plaintiff in fact. To have standing to have a case heard, it is also necessary that the relief sought by the plaintiff either correct or compensate for the harm alleged in the lawsuit.

Consider this example: Estelle was in the process of researching the environmentally fragile nature of the Nevada mountains when she discovered that someone planned to build an amusement park in that area. The park would have a detrimental effect on the environment in the mountain region. If Estelle makes no allegation of the way in which the building of the park would cause an actual injury to her personally, she will be denied standing to bring that case.

Elton John authored the composition *Can You Feel the Love Tonight* as the featured song in the film, *The Lion King.* Subsequently, two publishing companies instituted suit over the composition claiming it infringed on their copyright to the previous work, *Listen to Your Heart.* Since only one company may be the proper owner of the song, the court had to ascertain which publisher had standing to maintain the action for copyright infringement.

Halwill Music, Inc., v. Elton John
2000 U.S. Dist. LEXIS 7067 (S.D. N.Y. 2000)

Two different companies seek to assert the same copyright against the same purported infringers; but only one has the right to do so, and the other must be dismissed.

The first suit was brought by plaintiff Gold-Rhyme Music Company ("GoldRhyme") against The Walt Disney Company and other defendants, alleging that the Elton John composition *Can You Feel the Love Tonight,* featured and marketed in connection with the film *The Lion King,* infringed the copyright on a previous work, *Listen To Your Heart,* composed by Glenn Medeiros. GoldRhyme further alleged that it was duly authorized to protect and administer Medeiros' copyright in this work. Subsequently, however, Halwill Music, Inc. ("Halwill") filed suit, making essentially the same claim against essentially the same defendants and further alleging that Medeiros had conveyed to Halwill the sole and exclusive right to sue for copyright infringement with respect to *Listen To Your Heart.*

After the two cases were joined, Halwill moved for summary judgment that it was the only plaintiff with standing to bring the instant copyright infringement action against the defendants. The Court hereby grants Halwill's motion and dismisses the action brought by GoldRhyme for lack of standing.

Under the **Copyright Act of 1976,** "the legal or beneficial owner of an exclusive right under a copyright is entitled…to institute an action for any infringement of that particular right committed while he or she is the owner of it." **17 U.S.C. § 501(b).** Furthermore, "any of the exclusive rights comprised in a copyright… may be transferred…and owned separately [and the] owner of any particular exclusive right is entitled, to the extent of that right, to all of the protection and remedies accorded to the copyright owner by this title." **See §201(d)(2).**

It is undisputed that in 1988, as part of an agreement conveying to Halwill an undisputed half-interest in certain of Medeiros' musical compositions (including *Listen to Your Heart),* Medeiros agreed that Halwill shall have the sole and exclusive right to administer and protect the Musical Compositions on behalf of both parties throughout the world. Pursuant to that 1988 agreement, Halwill registered a claim for copyright in *Listen To Your Heart* in 1993.

In 1996, Medeiros entered into a separate agreement with GoldRhyme that gave GoldRhyme the exclusive right to initiate all actions for infringements of any Medeiros compositions covered by that agreement. This 1996 agreement, however, was limited to compositions "that have not been assigned in writing to any third party as of the date hereof." Therefore, the 1996 agreement does not in any way pertain to *Listen To Your Heart* which was covered by the 1988 agreement. Indeed, quite aside from the terms of the 1996 agreement itself, Medeiros could not in any event have transferred to Gold-Rhyme the exclusive right to sue for infringement of *Listen To Your Heart,* since Medeiros had already transferred such right exclusively to Halwill in 1988.

Although GoldRhyme attempts to attack the validity of the 1988 agreement between Halwill and Medeiros, its arguments in this regard are without merit. For example, GoldRhyme contends that the 1988 agreement is not signed and is therefore invalid. In fact, however, the signed amended agreement between Halwill and Medeiros specifically refers to and incorporates prior agreements,

Accordingly, the Court hereby grants plaintiff Halwill's motion and dismisses with prejudice GoldRhyme's action against defendants for lack of standing.

SECTION 3.9
FULL FAITH AND CREDIT

Article Four of the United States Constitution provides that "full faith and credit shall be given in each state to the public acts, records, and judicial proceedings of every other state." Essentially, this means that a judgment in one state will be enforced in another state as long as the first state had jurisdiction. How does this concept work in reality?

Assume that John Smith, a Pennsylvania resident and Temple student, decides to go to Daytona Beach for spring-break. Upon his arrival in Florida, he rents a car and runs over the clerk as he is pulling away from the rental agency. He is so distraught by the incident that he takes the next plane back to Philadelphia. He is in Florida for a total of 30 minutes. The clerk files suit in Florida for her injuries. John ignores the lawsuit since he has no plans of ever returning to Florida, and a judgment is rendered against him in the amount of $100,000.00. Is Smith correct in assuming that nothing can be done to him as long as he stays out of Florida? Pursuant to the Full Faith and Credit Clause of the Constitution, the Florida judgment can be transferred to Pennsylvania and be enforced in that jurisdiction. Florida had jurisdiction over the Pennsylvania resident since he committed a tort in that state.

Are traffic tickets that are received in another jurisdiction enforceable in the state of domicile of the driver under the doctrine of Full, Faith and Credit? The answer depends upon the jurisdiction. Forty-five states and the District of Columbia have entered into the **Driver's License Compact,** which governs the enforcement of motor vehicle violations committed by a driver in another jurisdiction. Based upon this agreement, a traffic ticket received in a sister state will be enforced in the state where the driver is licensed. The only jurisdictions that do not belong to the Compact are Georgia, Massachusetts, Michigan, Tennessee, and Wisconsin. The purpose of the Compact is to maximize law enforcement efforts nationwide and to create a "one driver record" concept which requires that the complete driving record of an individual be maintained in one location–the state of licensing. The benefits enjoyed by the member states are varied and include the following: (a) law enforcement officers are not burdened with traffic ticket procedures and are able to devote more time to highway patrol, surveillance, and apprehension; (b) court revenues are increased because non-residents can ignore member state's citations without facing driver licenses penalties at home; and (c) there is a decrease in the number of "Failure to Appear" cases.

The **Compact** requires that member states report all traffic convictions which occur within its boundaries to the state where the violator was licensed. This report must describe the violation and the disposition of the charges. In return, the licensing state shall give the same effect to "serious" motor vehicle violations, as though the offense had occurred in the state of licensing in cases of vehicular manslaughter, driving under the influence, using a motor vehicle to commit a felony, or failure to stop and render aid in the event of a motor vehicle accident. Minor traffic violations, such as speeding, disregarding a stop sign, or going through a red light will be reported to the licensing state, but the conviction will not appear on the individual's driving record nor will points be assigned.

A driver will also not be detained in another jurisdiction if that state is a member of the **Compact**. Instead, the individual will merely receive a traffic ticket. If the operator fails to pay the fine, the licensing state will be notified of the non-compliance and the driver's license will be suspended until the ticket is paid. Notice of non-compliance is reported to the home jurisdiction within six months from the date of the issuance of the ticket. If a traffic violation is committed in a state that is not a member of the **Compact,** the driver will be brought before a judge for an emergency hearing and will be required to make arrangements for the payment of the fine before being allowed to leave the jurisdiction.

A conviction for driving under the influence of alcohol in a sister state will result in the automatic suspension of a driver's license in the motorist's state of domicile. In *Hession v. Pennsylvania Department of Transportation,* the court had to decide whether a guilty plea entered under the condition that it may not be used in another proceeding, may be utilized to suspend the driver's license of the individual in another state which is part of the **Compact.**

HARRY HESSION V. PENNSYLVANIA DEPARTMENT OF TRANSPORTATION
2000 WL 33127456 (PA. CMWLTH. 2000)

HARRY HESSION APPEALS FROM AN ORDER of the court affirming the one-year suspension of his driving privileges resulting from his guilty plea in New Jersey for driving under the influence of alcohol (DUI). The issue before this Court is whether the Department of Transportation, Bureau of Driver Licensing (DOT) must honor a New Jersey Municipal Court order which contained Hession's guilty plea with a civil reservation precluding the use of Hession's plea in any later civil proceedings.

Hession was arrested in New Jersey and charged with operating a motor vehicle while under the influence of liquor or drugs. Hession entered a plea of guilty with a "civil reservation" before a municipal court in New Jersey. As a result of the plea, Hession was convicted of the DUI charge. Thereafter, New Jersey acting according to the provisions of the **Driver's License Compact,** notified DOT of the conviction. The Pennsylvania DOT suspended Hession's driving privileges for a one-year period, treating the New Jersey conviction as though Hession had been convicted in Pennsylvania of violating the corresponding Pennsylvania DUI statute.

Hession filed an appeal from the suspension. Hession relied upon the defense that his New Jersey guilty plea could not be used in any subsequent civil proceeding, including a license revocation proceeding. In concluding that the civil reservation did not preclude DOT from using Hession's plea as a basis for the license suspension, the trial court relied on *Bourdeev v. Department of Transportation,* 755 A.2d 59 **(Pa. Cmwlth. 2000).**

Hession argues that the Court should overrule Bourdeev because its holding is contrary to the dictates of the Full Faith and Credit Clause of the United States Constitution. That clause provides in pertinent part that "Full Faith and Credit shall be given in each State to the Public Acts, Records, and Judicial Proceedings of every other State." Hession maintains that the Court's decision in Bourdeev impermissibly al-

lowed DOT to consider Hession's plea despite the New Jersey proceeding which resulted in an order precluding the use of his guilty plea.

In **Bourdeev,** this Court upheld a one-year suspension of operating privileges in similar circumstances. That case involved an appeal by a Pennsylvania motorist from DOT's suspension of his driving privileges as a result of the motorist's guilty plea with a civil reservation to DUI charges in New Jersey. The trial court reversed DOT's suspension concluding that DOT could not rely upon the plea entered in the sister jurisdiction. The trial court further concluded that ignoring the civil reservation would violate the Full Faith and Credit Clause. In reversing that trial court decision, we stated in Bourdeev:

> While the New Jersey Rule of Court, which allows a civil reservation with guilty pleas prohibits the use of the plea itself in any civil proceeding, it does not bar the introduction of evidence of the conviction that resulted from the guilty plea. It is the conviction, not the guilty plea, that triggered New Jersey's report to DOT.

This case presents a similar situation in which DOT is merely acting upon the conviction itself. How the conviction came about, i.e., judgment, admission of guilt or plea with civil reservation, is of no import. Hence, we do not believe that the civil reservation has any impact on DOT's suspension of the individual's driving privileges. Thus, relying upon the decision in **Bourdeev,** this Court concludes that the trial court properly denied Hession's appeal.

SECTION 3.10
COMITY

Comity is the principle that allows the recognition of the rules and laws of a foreign jurisdiction in this country. Each state determines on its own the extent to which it will provide courtesy and respect to a foreign sovereign. Generally, as long as the laws of another country are not contrary to public policy or prejudicial to the interests of the forum jurisdiction, the law will be upheld.

The death penalty is not uniformly supported around the world. This philosophical difference can strain relations between counties—even those sovereignties that enjoy have good relations with each other. This fact is evident in two recent cases in which the United States has sought the return of a person from a foreign country in order to face murder charges in which the death penalty could be imposed.

A new generation of Americans has learned the name of Ira Einhorn. This 1960s activist was charged with the murder of Holly Maddux, whose mummified body was found in a steamer trunk in Einhorn's closet. Shortly before his criminal trial, the defendant disappeared. Nevertheless, the trail went on in his absence and Einhorn was found guilty of first-degree murder and was sentenced to death. After twenty years on the run, Einhorn was located in France but that country refused to return him to the United States because of their opposition to the death penalty. It was only after the Pennsylvania legislature agreed that Einhorn would not face the death penalty, and he would be granted a new trial, that the French court ordered the fugitive's return to Philadelphia.

A similar situation occurred in Canada where two young men, who are living in that country, are accused of killing three people in the state of Washington. Despite the requests by the United States government to return the suspects, Canada has refused because of their opposition to the death penalty. In a case that ended before the Canadian Supreme Court, that judicial body ruled the suspects would not be returned until the United States guaranteed that they would not face the death penalty.

UNITED STATES OF AMERICA v. DAN BURNS
SUPREME COURT OF CANADA (2001)

BURNS AND RAFAY ARE EACH WANTED on three counts of first-degree murder in the State of Washington. If found guilty, they will face either the death penalty or life in prison without parole. The defendants are both Canadian citizens and were 18 years old when the father, mother and sister of Rafay were found bludgeoned to death in their home in Washington. Both Burns and Rafay, who had been friends at high school in British Columbia, admit that they were at the

Rafay home on the night of the murders. They claim to have gone out and when they returned, they say, they found the bodies of the three murdered Rafay family members. Thereafter, the two returned to Canada. They were eventually arrested. United States authorities commenced proceedings to extradite the defendants to the State of Washington for trial. The Minister of Justice for Canada ordered their extradition without seeking assurances from the United States that the death penalty would not be imposed. The Court of Appeal set aside the Minister's decision and directed him to seek assurances as a condition of surrender.

In respect of seeking assurances, the Minister took the position that assurances were not to be sought routinely in every case in which the death penalty was applicable; such assurances should be sought only in circumstances where the particular facts of the case warranted that special exercise of discretion. Although it is generally for the Minister, not the court, to assess the weight of competing considerations in extradition policy, the availability of the death penalty opens up a different dimension. Death penalty cases are uniquely bound up with basic constitutional values and the court is the guardian of the Constitution.

Countervailing factors favor extradition only with assurances. In Canada, the death penalty has been rejected as an acceptable element of criminal justice. Capital punishment engages the underlying values of the prohibition against cruel and unusual punishment. It is final and irreversible. Its imposition has been described as arbitrary and its deterrent value has been doubted. The abolition of the death penalty has emerged as a major Canadian initiative and reflects a concern increasingly shared by most of the world's democracies. Canada's support of international initiatives opposing extradition without assurances, combined with its international advocacy of the abolition of the death penalty itself, leads to the conclusion that in the Canadian view of fundamental justice, capital punishment is unjust and should be stopped. While the evidence does not establish an international law norm against the death penalty, it does show significant movement towards acceptance internationally of the abolition of capital punishment. International experience thus confirms the validity of concerns expressed in the Canadian Parliament about capital punishment. It also shows that a rule requiring that assurances be obtained prior to extradition in death penalty cases not only accords with Canada's principled advocacy on the international level, but also is consistent with the practice of other countries with which Canada generally invites comparison, apart from the retentionist jurisdictions in the United States.

While the government objective of advancing mutual assistance in the fight against crime is entirely legitimate, the Minister has not shown that extraditing the respondents to face the death penalty without assurances is necessary to achieve that objective. There is no suggestion in the evidence that asking for assurances would undermine Canada's international obligations or good relations with neighboring states. While international criminal law enforcement including the need to ensure that Canada does not become a "safe haven" for dangerous fugitives is a legitimate objective, there is no evidence that extradition to face life in prison provides a lesser deterrent to those seeking a "safe haven" than does the death penalty. Whether fugitives are returned to a foreign country to face the death penalty or to face eventual death in prison from natural causes, they are equally prevented from using Canada as a "safe haven."

A review of the factors for and against unconditional extradition leads to the conclusion that assurances are constitutionally required.

SECTION 3.11
THE FEDERAL
COURT SYSTEM

The are two separate court systems in the United States: Federal and State. Each is independent of the other and subject to different rules and regulations.

Article III of the Constitution establishes the United States Supreme Court and gives Congress the power to create all other inferior Federal Courts. The court of original jurisdiction or trial court in the Federal system is the District Court and appeals are entertained by the Circuit Court of Appeals. On rare occasions, the Supreme Court will grant certiorari and review a lower court's decision.

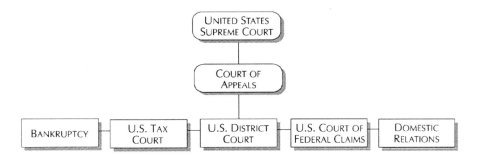

SECTION 3.12
DISTRICT COURTS

The United States District Court, or trial court, is in direct contact with the parties, hears the evidence, and applies the appropriate law to the facts of a case. There are ninety-four district courts in the United States and its territories. A state may have one or more district courts within its boundaries depending on its population. For example, Pennsylvania has three district courts. They are located in the Eastern, Middle, and Western parts of the state.

The type of cases the Federal Court may hear are limited to questions involving Federal Law, the United States Constitution, and disputes between citizens of different states where the amount in controversy exceeds $75,000. Congress has also created a few specialized courts that hear very narrow issues such as tax matters and custom or patent appeals.

SECTION 3.13
CIRCUIT COURT
OF APPEALS

The Court of Appeals is the intermediate appellate court within the Federal Court System. There are thirteen circuit courts throughout the United States. Eleven of the circuit courts hear cases on appeal from the district courts. The twelfth circuit is devoted to hearing cases from the District of Columbia. Congress has also created one specialized court called the United States Court of Appeals for the Federal Circuit. This Federal Circuit hears appeals involving tort claims against the United States government, patent and plant protection cases, and appeals from the United States Court of Federal Claims and the Court of International Trade. Parties may appeal to the Circuit Courts of Appeal as a matter of right.

Because the Supreme Court's decision to hear a case is discretionary, the Courts of Appeal are usually the last place that a party can appeal a Federal case. When a Court of Appeals decides a case, that decision is binding on all of the district courts within the circuit.

SECTION 3.14
THE UNITED STATES
SUPREME COURT

The Supreme Court of the United States is the final arbiter over all legal disputes. As a result, they decide very controversial issues that affect our daily lives. Their decisions establish precedent and bind all other courts. Commentators and constitutional scholars analyze each word of an opinion and predict how a particular holding will impact upon society. Identifiable trends emerge, and many attempt to predict the future direction of the Court.

The Court has undergone a metamorphosis during the past thirty to forty years. Established legal doctrines have changed. For many years the death penalty was unconstitutional but is now considered appropriate punishment. Suspects in criminal proceedings were guaranteed certain rights, but these rights have been eroded as long as the police act in good faith.

What has caused this change in judicial philosophy? Shifting attitudes of the public certainly has an influence in court interpretation. The modification of the law, however, is more a reflection of the personalities of the members of the Supreme Court. There has been a dramatic turnover of Supreme Court justices during the past three decades. These changes in Court personnel have altered the judicial philosophy of the Court.

The Warren Court, named after the Chief Justice during the 1960's, was viewed as a liberal body that went to great lengths to insure that all individuals be treated equally regardless of status. Suspects in criminal proceedings were guaranteed the right to have an attorney present when questioned, and busing of students was the only way that children of all races could receive an equal education. The death penalty was viewed as cruel and unusual punishment, and affirmative action programs were the only way to overcome the discrimination that took place over centuries.

Warren Burger was elevated to Chief Justice in 1969, and the court started to undergo a subtle transformation. As liberal members of the court resigned, middle of the road or conservative jurists took their place. The liberal tendency of the Court became more tempered and reflective of the opinions of the conservative jurists. Decisions were frequently decided by a single vote.

President Reagan dramatically altered this balance of power during his tenure. Members of the Supreme Court are appointed by the President and tend to support the political philosophies of the President.

President Reagan had the luxury of appointing three members to the bench and elevating William Rehnquist to Chief Justice. This changing of the guard brought about a conservative Court that firmly spoke its mind and did not take a middle of the road position on most controversial issues. The death penalty was found to be clearly constitutional, and affirmative action programs became suspect.

President Bush had the opportunity to appoint two new justices to the Supreme Court. William Brennan, Jr. and Thurgood Marshall were the two most liberal members of the court, but were forced to retire because of their advancing ages. David H. Souter replaced Justice Brennan, and Clarence Thomas replaced Justice Marshall, thereby strengthening the voting block of the justices who are Judicial Restraint Oriented.

But it's never easy to predict how a certain justice will vote just by gauging the politics of the president who appointed the judge. For example, Justice Byron White, who retired from the Court in 1993, was appointed by John Kennedy, yet he consistently voted against such liberal issues as the right to an abortion. By contrast, Justice Harry Blackman, who wrote the controversial *Roe v. Wade* decision, was appointed by Richard Nixon.

There are three groups within the Court. Justices Sandra Day O'Connor and Anthony Kennedy, Reagan appointees, have joined with Justice Souter and Stephen Bryer to form a more moderate group backing a middle-of-the-road position. Rehnquist, Thomas and Antonin Scalia form the Judicial Restraint group. John Paul Stevens, a Ford appointee, usually maintains the Activist position.

Judge Ruth Bader Ginsburg was appointed by President Clinton to replace Justice White. As a federal judge in the District of Columbia Circuit for 13 years, Ginsburg worked with Thomas and Scalia, who both were members of that court. Her association with them has helped to bring about more of a consensus on many opinions. Yet despite her familiarity with Scalia and Thomas, Ginsburg has joined O'Connor, Souter, and Kennedy to solidify the middle-of-the-road philosophy. This has halted the Court's movement toward the conservative ideology of Reagan and Bush, and has shifted the Court's opinions to a more moderate position. As a lawyer before joining the Circuit Court, Ginsburg argued before the Supreme Court and won some of the most influential women's rights cases of the 1970's and 80's. It's less clear how she would vote on abortion decisions, since she has publicly criticized *Roe v. Wade*, but, nevertheless, says she believes in a woman's right to choose.

In 1994, President Clinton made a second appointment when Justice Blackman retired. Stephen Breyer was appointed to replace Blackman and has further solidified the position of the moderate members of the Court. During the Clinton presidency, the Supreme Court took steady, incremental steps toward a middle of the road approach. For example, the Court limited the broadness of affirmative action programs by ruling that federal affirmative action programs must show that they are dealing with the effects of past discrimination. Nonetheless, after 10 successive appointments by Republican presidents, beginning with Warren Burger and ending with Clarence Thomas, one would expect such a radical shift to the right. But that hasn't exactly happened. Instead the justices in the middle have been able to limit the outcome of significant, divisive cases. For example, a majority of the justices have upheld the right to abortion and have ruled against public school graduation prayers.

By understanding that decisions are influenced by judicial philosophies, it is much easier to predict the outcome of future cases before the Supreme Court. In overly broad and simplified terms, one merely has to think in terms of conservative philosophies to anticipate the probable outcome of a case. Many surprises, however, have occurred over the years, and no one can predict with certainty what will happen in any given case.

It is not technically accurate to use the label *"Liberal v. Conservative"* when speaking about members of the Court. The proper term to reflect judicial philosophies is *"Activist v. Judicial Restraint Oriented."* An activist is one who views his or her role as bringing about social change. If there is something wrong with the system, the jurist will take an active stance in imposing remedial measures to correct a problem. A justice that is judicial restraint oriented tends to be conservative. These justices believe that their sole role is to make sure that a rule is constitutional. If there is something wrong with the system, it is up to the legislature to bring about the necessary change.

A writer from the Associated Press analyzed the voting records of the Justices for the 1999-2000 judicial term. The jounalist ascertained that a mere seventy-three cases were decided by the Supreme Court and twenty of those decisions were determined by a 5 to 4 vote. Justice Sandra Day O'Connor emerged as the key swing vote that was needed to achieve a majority consensus and she sided with the conservatives more often that not. Justices Ginsberg, Souter and Breyer exhibited a more liberal vent and tended to team up with Justice Stevens. "Justices Make Liberal Calls on Abortion and Prayer," **Bucks County Courier Times,** July 2, 2000.

George W. Bush may have the opportunity to appoint one or two Justices during his Presidential tenure. Depending upon which Justices retire, Bush may be able to shift the philosophy of the Supreme Court to a much more conservative position.

The following chart shows the judicial philosophies of the present members of the Court:

Justices of the Supreme Court		
RESTRAINT ORIENTED	MODERATE	ACTIVIST
William H. Rehnquist, C.J. Antonin Scalia Clarence Thomas	Sandra Day O'Connor David H. Souter Anthony M. Kennedy Ruth Bader Ginsburg Stephen Breyer	John Paul Stevens

The presidential election between George W. Bush and Al Gore was the closest in history and the most controversial. The winner was determined many days after the vote and only through court intervention. The election process and judicial system, however, were both tarnished by claims of political favoritism. While the trial courts of Florida issued rulings that tended to favor Bush, the Florida Supreme Court, and its democratic nominated Justices, uniformly issued rulings in support of the Gore candidacy. The most stinging criticism of political partisanship, however, was levied against the United States Supreme Court when they ruled that the hand recount of votes in Florida violated the Equal Protection Clause of the United States Constitution. *Bush v. Gore*, **No. 00-949, United States Supreme Court (2000).** Whether the Court's image of political neutrality will be tarnished by this controversial ruling remains to be seen. The decision, however, did bring finality to the presidential election but it left Justice Ginsberg to quip that the decision is a "December storm over the U.S. Supreme Court."

A look at the voting records of the Justices however, does not seem to support a critical view of the Court's decision. Seven Justices on the United States Supreme Court agreed that there were constitutional problems with the recount ordered by the Florida Supreme Court that demanded a remedy. The only disagreement among the Court members was the remedy.

Justices Breyer and Ginsberg are the only members of the Court nominated by Democratic presidents. In the 5 to 4 decision, that determined the remedy and the presidential race, these two Justices dissented along with their Republican counterparts of Justices Stevens and Souter. The majority opinion was attributed to Justices Rehnquist, Scalia, Thomas, O'Connor and Kennedy. These specific alliances are consistent with the voting trends identified by the Associated Press for the 1999 - 2000 judicial term and reflect the moderate to conservative leanings of the Court.

For additional reading about the workings of the United States Supreme Court, see *"Gideon's Trumpet"* by Anthony Lewis and *"The Brethren"* by Bob Woodward and Scott Armstrong.

The official web address for the United States Supreme Court is

- **http://www.supremecourt.us.gov**
  This site provides information about our highest court, including biographies of the current Court members, an overview of how the court works, Supreme Court Rules, and Supreme Court decisions.

SECTION 3.15
THE STATE
COURT SYSTEM

We are a nation of states with each having its own court system. While the configuration will vary from state to state, each will have a trial court and at least one appellate court. The state court system in Pennsylvania is provided as an illustration.

The court of original jurisdiction is known as the Court of Common Pleas and is subdivided into the following three divisions: (1) The Trial Court; (2) the Family Court; and Orphan's Court.

The Trial Division will hear both civil and criminal cases. Orphan's Court is concerned with matters involving estates, such as will contests and incompetence hearings. Family Court decides juvenile cases and matters involving the family unit such as divorce, custody and support.

To reduce the backlog of cases, a specialized court has been created to handle small disputes. In Philadelphia, this court is called the Municipal Court. It handles landlord/tenant problems, civil disputes of less than $10,000, criminal cases where the penalty involves less than five years imprisonment, and code violations. In the surrounding counties, district justices who have offices in the various townships throughout the Commonwealth handle these matters.

PENNSYLVANIA STATE
JUDICIAL SYSTEM

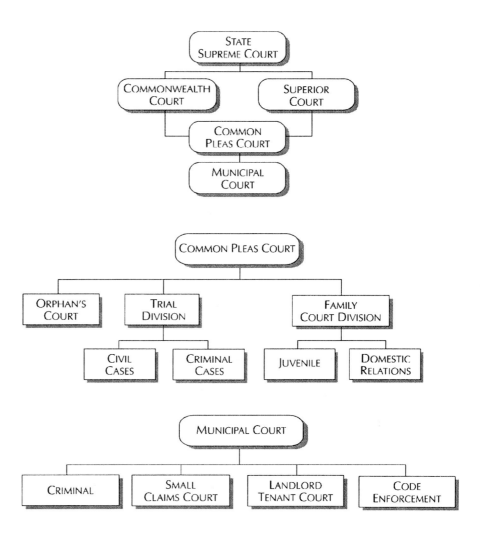

<table>
<tr><td></td><td></td></tr>
</table>

SECTION 3.16
ALTERNATIVE
DISPUTE RESOLUTION

Controversies may be resolved in ways other than by using the state and federal court systems, which may be too time consuming or expensive. Parties may agree to submit to any of a number of alternative methods for resolving their disputes. In considering an alternative dispute resolution mechanism, the parties will focus on factors such as cost, who will represent them, who will arbitrate the dispute, and whether the alternative method will lead to a more helpful or fair resolution.

Arbitration is often used in a commercial setting where both parties agree to have a third party or arbitrator resolve a controversy. When the parties agree to abide by the arbitrator's decision, they are involved in binding arbitration, and the court will enforce the arbitrator's award.

Both parties must agree, however, on the impartial arbitrator. Arbitration proceedings are usually informal, and the parties are not bound by the rules of evidence that control court cases.

Disputes in professional sports between a player and team are generally submitted to arbitration pursuant to a collective bargaining agreement. Some of the issues that an arbitrator is asked to decide, involve salary disputes, disciplinary issues and free agency.

Because of the binding nature of arbitration, the courts will rarely overturn an arbitrator's decision unless there is clear evidence of fraud or gross misconduct. This point is demonstrated in *Sprewell v. Golden State Warrior* where Latrell Sprewell asked the court to overturn an arbitrator's decision concerning his suspension from the National Basketball Association. The player was disciplined after his assault of the head coach for the Golden State Warriors.

LATRELL SPREWELL v. GOLDEN STATE WARRIORS
231 F. 3D 520 (9TH CIR. 2000)

LATRELL F. SPREWELL ("SPREWELL") CHALLENGES the district court's dismissal of his claim against the National Basketball Association ("NBA") and the Golden State Warriors ("the Warriors"). Sprewell raises numerous claims challenging the validity of the punishment meted out by the NBA and the Warriors in response to Sprewell's physical attack on the head coach of the Warriors.

Sprewell joined the NBA in 1992. During Sprewell's tenure with the Warriors, he played under four different head coaches, the last of whom was P.J. Carlesimo. Sprewell's relationship with Carlesimo, quickly deteriorated to the point that both Sprewell and the Warriors openly entertained the possibility of trading Sprewell to another team.

Tensions climaxed on December 1, 1997, during which Carlesimo told Sprewell to pass the ball to a teammate for a quick shot. When Carlesimo subsequently repeated his criticism,

Sprewell slammed the ball down and directed several expletives at Carlesimo who responded with a similar showing of sophistication. Sprewell immediately wrapped his hands around Carlesimo's neck. With his arms fully extended, Sprewell moved Carlesimo backwards, saying "I will kill you." Carlesimo offered no resistance. Sprewell grasped Carlesimo's neck for approximately seven to ten seconds—the time it took for other players and coaches to restrain Sprewell. Sprewell then left the practice floor, saying "trade me, get me out of here, I will kill you," to which Carlesimo countered, "I am here."

After showering, Sprewell returned to the practice facility to again confront Carlesimo. Despite the efforts of two assistant coaches to restrain him, Sprewell was able to approach Carlesimo and throw an overhand punch that grazed Carlesimo's right cheek. Sprewell landed a subsequent blow to Carlesimo's shoulder, but it is uncertain whether it was intentional or the product of Sprewell's attempt to free himself from those restraining him. As Sprewell left the facility, he again told Carlesimo, "I will kill you."

That evening the Warriors suspended Sprewell for a minimum of ten games and expressly reserved its right to terminate Sprewell's contract. Two days later, the Warriors exercised that right and ended Sprewell's reign as a Warrior. The NBA subsequently issued its own one-year suspension of Sprewell.

On December 4, 1997, Sprewell invoked the arbitration provisions of his collective bargaining agreement ("CBA") by filing a grievance challenging both his suspension by the NBA and the Warriors' termination of his contract. The arbitrator found that the dual punishments issued by the NBA and the Warriors were permissible under the CBA, but found that: **(1)** the Warriors' termination of Sprewell's contract was not supported by just cause because, after the Warriors' initial suspension of Sprewell, any residual interest of the Warriors was absorbed by the NBA's investigation of the matter; and **(2)** the NBA's suspension should be limited to the 1997-98 season.

Sprewell filed suit to vacate the arbitration award. Judicial scrutiny of an arbitrator's decision "is extremely limited." *Sheet Metal Workers Int'l Ass'n, Local No. 359 v. Arizona Mechanical & Stainless, Inc.*, **863 F.2d 647 (9th Cir.1988).** The Supreme Court has instructed that "as long as the arbitrator is even arguably construing or applying the contract and acting within the scope of his authority, that a court is convinced he committed serious error does not suffice to overturn his decision." *United Paperworkers Int'l Union v. Misco, Inc.*, **484 U.S. 29 (1987).** We have followed suit in holding that "so far as the arbitrator's decision concerns construction of the contract, the courts have no business overruling him, because their interpretation of the contract is different than his." *San Francisco-Oakland Newspaper Guild v. Tribune Pub. Co.*, **407 F.2d 1327 (9th Cir. 1969).**

Notwithstanding the foregoing, we have identified four instances in which the vacatur of an arbitration award is warranted: **(1)** when the award does not draw its essence from the collective bargaining agreement; **(2)** when the arbitrator exceeds the scope of the issues submitted; **(3)** when the award runs counter to public policy; and **(4)** when the award is procured by fraud. Sprewell seeks refuge under each of the four exceptions.

Sprewell contends that the arbitrator's approval of Sprewell's "multiple punishments" did not draw its essence from the CBA. The thrust of Sprewell's argument is that the arbitrator improperly ascribed a conjunctive meaning to the word "or" in the CBA provision that subjects players "to disciplinary action for just cause by his Team or by the Commissioner." Sprewell alleges that by failing to read the word "or" in the disjunctive, the arbitrator not only discarded the "plain and unambiguous" language of the CBA, but actually rewrote it.

We have held that an arbitration award will only be set aside for failing to draw its essence from the contract in "those egregious cases in which a court determines that the arbitrator's award ignored the plain language of the contract." *Stead Motors of Walnut Creek v. Automotive Machinists Lodge No. 1173*, **886 F.2d 1200 (9th Cir. 1989).** This is not such a case. The arbitrator explained in detail the logic underlying his conclusion, including why he read the word "or" in the conjunctive rather than the disjunctive.

Sprewell argues that the arbitrator "exceeded the scope of his authority" because he was required either to uphold or to reject the suspension in its entirety. The Supreme Court has held that an arbitrator should be given substantial latitude in fashioning a remedy under a Collective Bargaining Agreement. Accordingly, we reject Sprewell's contention that the arbitrator exceeded the scope of his authority.

Sprewell alleges that the arbitration award should be vacated on the ground that it contravenes California's public policy against race-discrimination. The crux of Sprewell's argument is that by upholding the dual punishments issued by the NBA and the Warriors, the arbitrator simultaneously spread the virus of racial animus plaguing those penalties. The arbitrator held that Sprewell's punishments were wholly justified by the language of the CBA and by virtue of the uniquely egregious nature of Sprewell's misconduct. Therefore, Sprewell has failed to demonstrate that the public policy of California militates against the enforcement of the arbitration award.

Finally, Sprewell claims that the NBA and the Warriors tainted the arbitration process by introducing false statements and doctored pictures of Carlesimo's injuries. This claim can be dismissed under the rule that "where the fraud is brought to the attention of the arbitrator, a disappointed party will not be given a second bite at the apple." Sprewell's fraud claim was ruled upon by the arbitrator. Thus, we do not find it necessary to revisit this issue.

For the reasons outlined above, we affirm the district court's dismissal of Sprewell's claims against the NBA and the Warriors.

The American Arbitration Association is the largest full-service ADR provider and has been involved in resolving disputes since 1926 in a wide range of business related problems including employment, technology, healthcare, financial services, and international trade. According to the American Arbitration Association, nearly 500 companies and 5 million employees use the services of this organization to resolve work place conflicts. This not-for-profit, public service organization, handled more than 140 thousand cases in 1999. To learn more about the American Arbitration Association and to obtain the rules and procedures for this type of process, visit their site at: **http://www.adr.org.**

Mediation is used primarily in disputes between labor and management, but also is suited to disputes between neighbors and family members. Mediation is different from arbitration because it is advisory in nature. A mediator makes recommendations to the parties in order to aid them in solving their differences. Successful mediation will keep the parties out of court. Mediation is gaining popularity in divorce cases in helping the parties work out their differences.

In 1947, Congress created the Federal Mediation and Conciliation Service in order to promote and establish stable labor-management relations. This national agency is involved in mediating labor disputes as well as contract negotiations between employers and unions in both the public, private, and federal sectors. The web address for this national organization is: **http://www.fmcs.gov.**

Private judging is used when both sides are constrained by time and can afford to hire a private judge, usually a retired judge. Private judging proceeds as a normal trial would be conducted.

Non-binding or **mini-trials** are another form of private dispute resolution in which the parties may or may not be represented by a lawyer. Usually, the parties submit their case to a panel of experts and a neutral advisor, who aids both sides. The panel and advisor suggest the likely outcome if the case were to go to court. This method is helpful for business disputes involving long processes of fact-finding.

Neighborhood Justice Centers derive from a program initiated in the 1970s. The centers receive their cases from local police or magistrates' offices. The cases usually involve neighborhood or family disputes, in which the two sides represent themselves before a panel of local residents. The aim is to avoid having the disputes escalate to the point where the criminal court system takes over.

SECTION 3.17
INTERPRETATION
OF AN NFL
PLAYER'S CONTRACT

PROBLEM THREE—B

HODGE, DODGE AND LODGE
ATTORNEYS AT LAW
MEMORANDUM

To: All Law Clerks

From: Gregory Olan Dodge

Re: Hodge v. The Stallions

Tony Hodge has another problem. I fear that Tony's shooting may be the beginning of a future filled with problems—that is, legal problems. My annoyance at having a niece in constant trouble seems comical now that I have both kids to defend. At least now I appreciate the wisdom of the law firm's hiring committee. It is clear that the firm needed a number of law clerks for the sole purpose of handling the Hodge's family problems.

Tony's most recent dilemma concerns his football contract. He has several disputes with the team regarding their imposition of certain sanctions pursuant to the terms of his contract. At a minimum, the Stallions want to suspend Tony without pay for one month. They are also considering an injunction to prohibit his racing activities, permanent suspension from the game, and possible termination of his contract. As you can now appreciate, this is a serious matter. Your performance thus far, however, indicates that you should be able to handle this matter. Please don't disappoint me.

The Stallions allege three violations of the contract. The first one relates to paragraph three of the contract. The team learned that Tony spends a considerable amount of time at the ATCO Raceway. Their concern is not his love, as a spectator, of this daredevil sport. Rather, they worry because Tony is a regular participant in the races. The club requested that Tony voluntarily stop drag racing, but he refused. As he asserts, "They pay me to **play** the game. They don't have the right to run my life off the field." The Stallions have threatened to enjoin this activity if my nephew refuses to voluntarily stop drag racing.

The other two disputes relate directly to the shooting incident of Christopher. Because Tony is a professional athlete, this minor transgression received considerable publicity. Consequently, the club was not pleased (to put it mildly). The Stallions claim his conduct was not in keeping with the good character and image required of professional football players. The team wants to suspend Tony without pay for one month. They maintain that the contract allows for this penalty. Tony feels this charge is ridiculous, and can't understand why he was even arrested.

Unfortunately, there is more to Tony's problem. His arrest for shooting Christopher was more complicated than you know. Tony was almost charged with a drug offense. Tony submitted to a urine analysis, which revealed the use of marijuana. Luckily, there was insufficient evidence to meet the statutory requirements. He was severely admonished by the police concerning any future drug arrests. But the drug issue was otherwise forgotten. Tony still claims he never smoked pot. According to him the results reflect his exposure to Kathy and her "druggie" friends. The night before his arrest, Tony had been in the basement rec room watching a video when her group invaded the scene. Normally, he went to his room when Kathy and her friends were around. Tony hated the drug scene, and was even more bothered by smoke-filled rooms. This night, however, he was too engrossed in his film to leave (and complaining would have been a futile gesture). Somehow the NFL learned of the positive results of the drug test revealing the use of marijuana. The League, however, is not interested in Tony's explanation. As far as they are concerned, drug use is cause for indefinite suspension and possible termination of the contract.

At this point in time, neither the Stallions nor the League have taken any affirmative action. Tony did not take these threats seriously until I explained that these were not unfounded threats. Attached is a copy of Tony's players contract. Please read the contract and provide a memorandum analyzing the following questions. According to the terms of the contract:

1. Does the Club or League have the authority to stop Tony from racing? What language in the document would support an injunction? Why would the Club or League be able to regulate Tony's conduct when he's not playing football?

2. Does the Club or League have the power to suspend Tony for one month without pay because he shot his neighbor? What other remedies are available to the Club or League if they wish to sanction Tony? What recourse is available to Tony to dispute the sanctions? In other words, where should Tony go to challenge the Club's assertions?

3. Can the NFL suspend Tony? Can the League terminate his contract? What recourse is available to Tony to challenge the **League's** sanctions? Which portion(s) of the contract support your answer?

NFL PLAYER CONTRACT

THIS CONTRACT is between **Anthony Hodge**, hereinafter "Player," and the **Playwell Football Association**, a Maryland corporation, hereinafter "Club," operating under the name of the "**Stallions**" as a member of the National Football League, hereinafter, "League."

In consideration of the promises made by each to the other, Player and Club agree as follows:

1. **TERM.** This contract covers three football seasons, and will begin on the date of execution or August 1, whichever is later, and end on July 31, unless extended, terminated, or renewed as specified elsewhere in this contract.

2. **EMPLOYMENT AND SERVICES.** Club employs Player as a skilled football player. Player accepts such employment. He agrees to give his best efforts and loyalty to the Club, and to conduct himself on and off the field with appropriate recognition of the fact that the success of professional football depends largely on public respect for and approval of those associated with the game. Player will report promptly for and participate fully in Club's official pre-season training camp, all Club meetings and practice sessions, and all pre-season, regular season and post-season football games scheduled for or by club. If invited, Player will practice for and play in any all-star football game sponsored by the League. Player will not participate in any football game not sponsored by the League unless the game is first approved by the League.

3. **OTHER ACTIVITIES.** Without prior written consent of the Club, Player will not play football or engage in activities related to football otherwise than for Club or engage in any activity other than football which may involve a significant risk or personal injury. Player represents that he has special, exceptional and unique knowledge, skill, ability, and experience as a football player, the loss of which cannot be estimated with any certainty and cannot be fairly or adequately compensated by damages. Player therefore agrees

that Club will have the right, in addition to any other right which Club may possess, to enjoin Player by appropriate proceedings from playing football or engaging in football-related activities other than for Club, or from engaging in any activity other than football which may involve a significant risk of personal injury.

4. **PUBLICITY.** Player grants to Club and League, separately and together, the authority to use his name and picture for publicity and promotional purposes in newspapers, magazines, motion pictures, game programs and roster manuals, broadcasts and telecasts, and all other publicity and advertising media, provided such publicity and promotion does not in itself constitute an endorsement by Player of a commercial product. Player will cooperate with the news media, and will participate upon request in reasonable promotional activities of Club and the League.

5. **COMPENSATION.** For performance of Player's services and all other promises of Player, Club will pay Player a yearly salary of $450,000.00 payable as provided in Paragraph 6; such earned performance bonuses as may be called for in Paragraph 24 of or any attachment to this contract; Player's necessary traveling expenses from his residence to training camp; Player's reasonable board and lodging expenses during pre-season training and in connection with playing pre-season, regular-season, and post-season football games outside Club's home city; Player's necessary traveling expenses to and from pre-season, regular season, and post-season football games outside Club's home city; Player's necessary traveling expenses to his residence if this contract is terminated by Club; and such additional compensation, benefits and reimbursement of expenses as may be called for in any collective bargaining agreement in existence during the term of this contract. (For purposes of this contract, a collective bargaining agreement will be deemed to be "in existence" during its stated term or during any period for which the parties to that agreement agree to extend it.)

6. **PAYMENT.** Unless this contract or any collective bargaining agreement in existence during the term of this contract specifically provides otherwise, Player will be paid as follows: If Player has not previously reported to any NFL club's official pre-season training camp in any year, he will be paid 100% of his yearly salary under this contract in equal weekly or bi-weekly installments over the course of the regular season period, commencing with the first regular season game played by club. If Player has previously reported to any NFL club's official pre-season training camp in any year, he will be paid 10% of his yearly salary under this contract in equal weekly installments over the course of the pre-season pe-

riod, commencing with the end of the first week of Club's official pre-season training camp as designated for Player and ending one week prior to the first regular season game played by Club, and 90%; of his yearly salary in equal weekly or bi-weekly installments over the course of the regular season period, commencing with the first regular season gamed played by Club. If this contract is executed or Player is activated after the start of Club's official pre-season training camp, the yearly salary payable to Player will be reduced proportionately and Player will be paid the weekly or bi-weekly portions of his yearly salary becoming due and payable after he his activated. If this contract is terminated after the start of Club's official pre-season training camp, the yearly salary payable to Player will be reduced proportionately and Player will be paid the weekly or bi-weekly portions of his yearly salary having become due and payable up to the time of termination (prorated daily if termination occurs before one week prior to the first regular season game played by Club).

a. The club agrees to give player a signing bonus of $50,000.00 at the time of the execution of this contract.

b. Player shall receive an additional bonus of $50,000.00 each time player is selected to play in an All-Star football game.

c. Player shall receive an additional compensation of $100.00 for each point he scores during a regular season and playoff game.

7. **DEDUCTIONS.** Any advance made to Player will be repaid to Club, and any properly levied Club fine or Commissioner fine against Player will be paid, in cash on demand or by means of deductions from payments coming due to the Player under this contract, the amount of such deductions to be determined by Club unless this contract specially provides otherwise.

8. **PHYSICAL CONDITION.** Player represents to Club that he is and will maintain himself in excellent physical condition. Player will undergo a complete physical examination by the Club physician upon Club request, during which physical examination Player agrees to make full and complete disclosure of any physical or mental condition known to him which might impair his performance under this contract and to respond fully and in good faith when questioned by the Club physician about such condition. If Player fails to establish or maintain his excellent physical condition to the satisfaction of the Club physician, or make the required full and complete disclosure and good faith responses to the Club physician, then Club may terminate this contract.

9. **INJURY.** If Player is injured in the performance of his services under this contract and promptly reports such injury to the Club physician or trainer, then Player will receive such medical and hospital care during the term of this contract as the Club physician may deem necessary, and, in accordance with Club's practice, will continue to receive his yearly salary for so long, during the season of injury only and for no subsequent period, as Player is physically unable to perform the services required of him by this contract because of such injury. If Player's injury in the performance of his services under this contract results in his death, the unpaid balance of his yearly salary for the season of injury will be paid to his stated beneficiary, or in the absence of a stated beneficiary, to his estate.

10. **WORKMEN'S COMPENSATION.** Any compensation paid to Player under this contract or under any collective bargaining agreement in existence during the term of this contract for a period during which he is entitled to workmen's compensation benefits by reason of temporary total, permanent total, temporary partial, or permanent partial disability will be deemed an advance payment of workmen's compensation benefits due Player, and Club will be entitled to be reimbursed the amount of such payment out of any award of workmen's compensation.

11. **SKILL, PERFORMANCE AND CONDUCT.** Player understands that he is competing with other players for a position on Club's roster within the applicable player limits. If at any time, in the sole judgment of Club, Player's skill or performance has been unsatisfactory as compared with that of other players competing for positions on Club's roster, or if Player has engaged in personal conduct reasonably judged by Club to adversely affect or reflect on Club, then Club may terminate this contract.

12. **TERMINATION.** The rights of termination set forth in this contract will be in addition to any other rights of termination allowed either party by law. Termination will be effective upon the giving of written notice, except that Player's death, other than as a result of injury incurred in the performance of his services under this contract, will automatically terminate this contract. If this contract is terminated by Club and either Player or Club so request, Player will promptly undergo a complete physical examination by the Club physician.

13. **INJURY GRIEVANCE.** Unless a collective bargaining agreement in existence at the time of termination of this contract by Club provides otherwise, the following injury grievance procedure will apply: If Player believes that at the time of termination of this contract by Club he was physically unable to perform the services required of him by this contract because of any injury incurred in the performance of his services under this contract, Player may, within a reasonably brief time after examination by the Club physician, submit at his own expense to examination by a physician of his choice. If the opinion of Player's physician with respect to his physical ability to perform the services required of him by this contract is contrary to that of the Club's physician, the dispute will be submitted within a reasonable time to final and binding arbitration by an arbitrator selected by Club and Player, if they are unable to agree, the selection shall be made by the League Commissioner on application by either party.

14. **RULES.** Player will comply with and be bound by all reasonable Club rules and regulations in effect during the term of this contract which are not inconsistent with the provisions of this contract or of any collective bargaining agreement in existence during the term of this contract. Player's attention is also called to the fact that the League functions with certain rules and procedures expressive of its operation as a joint venture among its member clubs and that these rules and practices may affect Player's relationship to the League and its member clubs independently of the provisions of this contract.

15. **INTEGRITY OF GAME.** Player recognizes the detriment to the League and professional football that would result from impairment of public confidence in the honest and orderly conduct of NFL games or the integrity and good character of NFL players. Player therefore acknowledges his awareness that if he accepts a bribe or agrees to throw or fix an NFL game; bets on an NFL game; knowingly associates with gamblers or gambling activity; uses or provides other players with stimulants or other drugs for the purpose of attempting to enhance on-field performance; or is guilty of any other form of conduct reasonably judged by the League Commission to be detrimental to the League or professional football, the Commissioner will have the right, but only after giving Player the opportunity for a hearing at which he may be represented by counsel of his choice, to fine Player in a reasonable amount; to suspend Player for a period certain or indefinitely; and/or to terminate this contract.

16. **EXTENSION.** If Player becomes a member of the Armed Forces of the United States or any other country, or retires from professional football as an active player, or otherwise fails or refuses to perform his services under this contract, then this contract will be tolled between the date of Player's induction into the Armed Forces, or his retirement, or his failure or refusal to perform, and the later date of his return to professional football. During the period this contract is tolled, Player will not be entitled to any compensation or benefits. On Player's return to professional football, the term of this contract will be extended for a period of time equal to the number of seasons (to the nearest multiple of one) remaining at the time the contract was tolled. The right of renewal, if any, contained in this contract will remain in effect until the end of any such extended term.

17. **RENEWAL.** Unless this contract specially provides otherwise, Club may, by sending written notice to Player on or before the February 1 expiration date referred to in Paragraph 1, renew this contract for a period of one year. The terms and conditions for the renewal year will be the same as those provided in this contract for the last preceding year, except that there will be no further right of renewal in Club and, unless this contract specially provides otherwise, the rate of compensation for the renewal year will be 110% of the rate of compensation provided in this contract for the last preceding year. The phrase "rate of compensation" as used above means yearly salary, including deferred compensation, and any performance bonus, but, excluding any signing or reporting bonus. In order for Player to receive 100% of any performance bonus under this contract he must meet the previously established conditions of that bonus during the renewal year.

18. **ASSIGNMENT.** Unless this contract specially provides otherwise, Club may assign this contract and Player's services under this contract to any successor to Club's franchise or to any other Club in the League. Player will report to the assignee club promptly upon being informed of the assignment of his contract and will faithfully perform his services under this contract. The assignee club will pay Player's necessary traveling expenses in reporting to it and will faithfully perform this contract with Player.

19. **FILING.** This contract will be valid and binding upon Player and Club immediately upon execution. A copy of this contract, including any attachment to it, will be filed by Club with the League Commissioner within 10 days after execution. The Commissioner

will have the right to disapprove this contract on reasonable grounds, including but not limited to an attempt by the parties to abridge or impair the rights of any other club, uncertainty or incompleteness in expression of the parties' respective rights and obligations, or conflict between the terms of this contract and any collective bargaining agreement then in existence. Approval will be automatic unless, within 10 days after receipt of this contract in his office, the Commissioner notifies the parties either of disapproval or of extension of this 10-day period for purposes of investigation or clarification pending his decision. On the receipt of notice of disapproval and termination, both parties will be relieved of their respective rights and obligations under this contract.

20. **DISPUTES.** Any dispute between Player and Club involving the interpretation or application of any provision of this contract will be submitted to final and binding arbitration in accordance with the procedure called for in any collective bargaining agreement in existence at the time the event giving rise to any such dispute occurs. If no collective bargaining agreement is in existence at such time, the dispute will be submitted within a reasonable time to the league Commissioner for final and binding arbitration by him, except as provided otherwise in Paragraph 13 of this contract.

21. **NOTICE.** Any notice, request, approval or consent under this contract will be sufficiently given if in writing and delivered in person or mailed (certified or first class) by one party to the other at the address set forth in this contract or to such other address as the recipient may subsequently have furnished in writing to the sender.

22. **OTHER AGREEMENTS.** This contract, including any attachment to it, sets forth the entire agreement between Player and Club and cannot be modified or supplemented orally. Player and Club represent that no other agreement, oral or written, except as attached to or specifically incorporated in this contract, exists between them. The provisions of this contract will govern the relationship between Player and Club unless there are conflicting provisions in any collective bargaining agreement in existence during the term of this contract, in which case the provisions of the collective bargaining agreement will take precedence over conflicting provisions of this contract relating to the rights or obligations of either party.

23. **LAW.** This contract is made under and shall be governed by the laws of the State of Maryland.

24. SPECIAL PROVISIONS.

a. Club agrees to provide player with private lodging whenever the team travels to play an away game.

b. Club agrees to provide player with five season tickets to each home game.

THIS CONTRACT is executed in five (5) copies. Player acknowledges that before signing this contract he was given the opportunity to seek advice from or be represented by persons of his own selection.

Anthony Hodge   (SEAL)   *John Young*   (SEAL)

PLAYER   **THE STALLIONS**
                                    PRESIDENT

ANSWER SHEET
PROBLEM THREE—B

Name   **Please Print Clearly**

1. Does the club have the authority to stop Tony from racing? What language in the document would support an injunction? Why would the NFL be able to regulate Tony's conduct when he's not playing football?

_____

_____

_____

_____

_____

_____

_____

_____

_____

_____

_____

_____

_____

_____

_____

_____

_____

_____

2. Does the Club have the power to suspend Tony for one month without pay because he shot his neighbor? What recourse is available
   to Tony to dispute the Club's sanctions? In other words, where
   should Tony go to challenge the Club's assertions?

   _____

   _____

   _____

   _____

   _____

   _____

   _____

   _____

   _____

3. Can the NFL suspend Tony and can the League terminate his contract? What recourse is available to Tony to challenge the League's
   sanctions? Which portion(s) of the contract support your answer?

   _____

   _____

   _____

   _____

   _____

   _____

   _____

   _____

   _____

   _____

SECTION 3.18
PROBLEM CASES

1. Francis Thomas received an envelope at his New Jersey home with a return address from the Philadelphia Chamber of Commerce. Upon opening the letter, he discovered two tickets to a Philadelphia 76ers game. Mr. Thomas could not believe his good fortune and took his son to the contest at the First Union Center. During the second period, the Sheriff tapped Thomas on the shoulder and served him with a lawsuit concerning a motor vehicle accident that had happened one year earlier in New Jersey. Does the Philadelphia Court have jurisdiction over this New Jersey resident since Thomas was served with the lawsuit within its boundaries? See: *M. H. Eastburn v. Saul Turnoff*, **147 A.2d 353 (Pa. 1959).**

2. Robert DeLuca had a long history of being involved in violent crimes. During his criminal trial for extortion, the trial judge empaneled an anonymous jury in order to safeguard the panel members' identity and to prevent jury tampering. Spectators were also screened and had to produce identification before being allowed into the courtroom. DeLuca claimed that his Sixth Amendment right to a public trial were violated by the judge's unusual actions. Do you agree? *United States v. Robert DeLuca,* **96-1173, (1ˢᵗ Cir. Ct. 1998).**

3. A franchise agreement between Charles Jones and General Nutrition Companies, Inc. required that all disputes concerning the agreement be litigated in a Pennsylvania venue. Jones operated a GNC store in California. Following a dispute, he sued GNC in his home state since that is where Jones' store is located, the contracts were entered into in California and the majority of witnesses are in that state. GNC requested a change of venue so that the case could be removed to Pennsylvania based upon the forum selection clause in the contract even though California does not favor this type of clause. Where should the case be heard? *Charles Jones v. GNC Franchising, Inc.,* **CV-98-10611-DMT (9ᵗʰ Cir. Ct. 2000).**

4. Beer Across America sold beer to a minor via the Internet. The liquor was shipped from the store's location in Illinois to the child's home in Alabama. After the parents returned home from vacation, they discover the beer in the refrigerator. This prompted the parents to file a suit in Alabama against the Illinois company for the unlawful sale of liquor to a minor. Beer Across America was not registered to do business in Alabama, it owned no property within the state and it did not advertise with the local media. Is a passive Internet site, which acts as an electronic billboard for the posting of information which may be accessed from any where in the world, sufficient to confer jurisdiction over a non-resident defendant for doing business in Alabama? *Lynda Butler v. Beer Across America,* **83 F. Supp. 2d 1261 (2000).**

SECTION 3.19
INTERNET REFERENCES

To learn more information about the court system and the jury selection process, see the following sites:

A. *The Jury Process*

- **www.fija.org**
  This is the site for the Fully Informed Jury Association, a nonprofit educational association devoted to providing information about jury duty, including a citizen's guide to jury duty, and frequently asked questions about jury duty.

- **http://www.edwright.com/voir_dire_intro.html**
  Tips on the voir dire process are offered on this site maintained by an attorney.

- **http://www.geocities.com/heartland/7394/lysander.html**
  A historical justification for trial by jury is presented in this article.

B. *The Court*

- **www.law.emory.edu/fedcts/**
  Federal Court decision from 1995 through the present are located at this site.

- **http://law.about.com/newsissues/law/library/courts b1899_toc.htm**
  This site provides a general discussion on the federal court system.

- **www.uscourts.gov/faq.html**
  This Federal Judiciary Homepage provides answers to frequently asked questions about the federal court system.

- **http://www.supremecourtus.gov**
  The Supreme Court's official site is contained at this address and contain copies of the court's opinions, court rules, and other general information about the Supreme Court of the United States.

- **http://vls.law.vill.edu/locator**
  Villanova University School of Law maintains this web site which provides access to federal court decisions from the district court to the United States Supreme Court as well discussions from the courts of the various states.

- **www.aopc.org/index/ujs/courtswork.htm**
  An overview of the Pennsylvania's court system may be found at this address.

- **http://www.mcsc.dni.us**
  The National Center for State Courts is an independent, non-profit organization dedicated to the improvement of state courts. The site provides the web address for the state and county courts, the Federal Circuit Courts and various international tribunals.

- **http://oyez.nwu.edu**
  Northwestern University maintains a multimedia data base and virtual tour of the Unites State Supreme Court at this address.

CHAPTER 4

DUE PROCESS

"No law perfectly suits the convenience of every member of the community; the only consideration is, whether upon the whole it be profitable to the greater part."

Levi
"History of Rome," c.10 B.C.
"The Quotable Lawyer" Facts on File, 1986

Part of the Fifth Amendment of the United States Constitution states that no person shall be deprived of life, liberty, or property without **due process** of law. This guarantee is designed to insure that the government acts fairly with members of society.

Due process consists of two parts:

1. Substantive due process; and

2. Procedural due process.

In order to understand these two concepts, one must first ascertain the meaning of substantive law and procedural law.

Substantive law is the "actual law." It defines the duties and rights of members of society. The Motor Vehicle Code is an example of substantive law. It provides for the proper operation of motor vehicles and prohibits such conduct as speeding, reckless driving, or proceeding through a red light. It is only by the enforcement of the Motor Vehicle Code that the roads are made safer for the public to transverse.

Procedural law is the way that the substantive law is made, enforced, and administered. For example, the Motor Vehicle Code is enforced by issuing an errant driver a traffic ticket and requiring the offender to appear in court to answer the charges.

This Chapter will present an overview of the due process guarantee with an emphasis on legislation and the elements of a fair hearing.

**SECTION 4.2
LEGISLATION**

Article I, Section 1 of the United States Constitution provides that "All legislative powers herein granted shall be vested in a Congress of the United States, which shall consist of a Senate and House of Representatives."

The United States Senate is composed of 100 members. Two senators are elected from each state for six-year terms. The House of Representatives is composed of 435 members elected every two years from among the 50 states, according to population. The legislature meets in two-year periods called Congress.

The chief function of Congress is the making of laws. In addition, the Senate has the function of consenting to treaties and to certain nominations by the President.

The work of Congress is initiated by the introduction of a proposal in one of four principle forms. These are: the bill, the joint resolution, the concurrent resolution, and the simple resolution. A **bill** is the form used for most legislation. Bills may originate in either the House of Representatives or the Senate. A bill originating in the House of Representatives is designated by the letters "H.R." followed by a number. A Senate bill is designated by the letter "S." followed by its number.

Any member of the legislature may introduce a bill while Congress is in session by simply placing it in the "hopper" located at the side of the clerk's desk in the House Chamber. The bill is then assigned to a committee that has jurisdiction over the subject matter of the bill.

One of the most important phases of the congressional process is the action taken by the committee. That is where the most intense consideration is given to the proposed measures and where citizens are given an opportunity to be heard.

If a bill is of sufficient importance, and particularly if it is controversial, the committee will usually set a date for public hearings. Each committee is required to make public announcement of the date, place, and subject matter of any hearing to be conducted by the committee. Witnesses may testify at the hearing either voluntarily or at the request or summons of the committee. A vote of the committee is taken to determine whether it will issue a favorable report or "table" the bill. Committee reports are a valuable element of the legislative history of a law. They are used by courts, executive departments, agencies, and the public, as a source of information regarding the purpose and meaning of the law.

When a committee gives a bill a favorable report, the house in which the proposed legislation originated votes on the bill. If that house passes the bill, the other house then considers it. A bill that is agreed to by both bodies becomes the law if the President signs it. A bill also becomes law when the President fails to return it with objections to the House in which it originated within ten days. The President may veto a bill that he does not want to enact into law. However, two-thirds of the members in each house can vote to override the veto. In that event, the bill becomes law.

State and Federal laws are called statutes. Local laws are called ordinances. *See*: Willett, "How Our Laws Are Made," H.R. Doc. No. 99-158, 99 Cong., 2d Sess. (1986). To learn more about the activities of Congress, visit the official web sites of the House of Representatives and the Senate. Those addresses are: **http://www.house.gov** and **http://www.senate.gov.**

SECTION 4.3
SUBSTANTIVE
DUE PROCESS

Substantive due process requires that the law itself be fundamentally fair. This means that the legislation must be capable of serving a legitimate public interest, and the law cannot be vague. One who does not believe that the law satisfies these requirements may challenge the legislation in court.

Examine the following cases to ascertain if the laws are constitutional:

A state legislator is unhappy with the damage to property that is taking place on college campuses especially in the dorms. He believes that the majority of trouble-makers are the kids with long hair who have nothing better to do but drink and deface school property. To curb the transgressions of these disruptive youths, the legislator introduces a bill requiring any student with long hair who attends a state related institution to pay an additional $100 in tuition. The state representative believes that this assessment will help defray the cost of damage done to school property by the responsible parties. A student with long hair refuses to pay the extra tuition and claims that his substantive due process rights are being violated. The issue presented is whether the law is capable of serving a legitimate public interest. Just because an individual has long hair does not mean that he will be disruptive. The law is also vague since the statute is silent as to what constitutes "long hair." Does the law apply to women as well as men? The standard to be applied is not what the individual who introduced the bill thinks but whether the average person would think that the law is sensible and capable of serving a public interest. This statute is clearly unconstitutional.

There has been a great deal of publicity and public debate over the right to die and assisted suicide in the terminally ill. Before his incarceration, Dr. Jack Kevorkian led the crusade in providing technical assistance to critically ill people who wished to die with dignity. Other members of society, however, believe that suicide under any circumstance is morally and legally wrong. Most states have laws that impose criminal penalties against anyone who aids a person in a suicide attempt. Several physicians who treat terminally ill patients challenged the state of Washington's prohibition against assisted suicide as a violation of one's substantive due process rights. If a terminally ill person wishes to end his or her life, does that individual have the constitutional right to die with dignity? This was the issue presented to the Supreme Court in *Washington v. Glucksberg*.

STATE OF WASHINGTON v. HAROLD GLUCKSBERG, M.D.
117 S. Ct. 2258 (1997)

THE QUESTION PRESENTED IN THIS CASE is whether Washington's prohibition against "causing" or "aiding" a suicide offends the Fourteenth Amendment to the United States Constitution. We hold that it does not.

Washington law provides: "A person is guilty of promoting a suicide attempt when he knowingly causes or aids another person to attempt suicide." "Promoting a suicide attempt" is a felony, punishable by up to five years' imprisonment and up to $10,000.

Harold Glucksberg, M. D., Abigail Halperin, M. D., Thomas A. Preston, M. D., and Peter Shalit, M. D., are physicians who practice in Washington. These doctors occasionally treat terminally ill, suffering patients, and declare that they would assist these patients in ending their lives if not for Washington's assisted-suicide ban.

The plaintiffs asserted "the existence of a liberty interest protected by the Fourteenth Amendment which extends to a personal choice by a mentally competent, terminally ill adult to commit physician-assisted suicide." Though deeply rooted, the States' assisted-suicide bans have in recent years been reexamined and, generally, reaffirmed. Because of advances in medicine and technology, Americans today are increasingly likely to die in institutions, from chronic illnesses. Public concern and democratic action are therefore sharply focused on how best to protect dignity and independence at the end of life, with the result that there have been many significant changes in state laws and in the attitudes these laws reflect. Many States,

for example, now permit "living wills," surrogate health-care decision making, and the withdrawal or refusal of life-sustaining medical treatment. At the same time, however, voters and legislators continue for the most part to reaffirm their States' prohibitions on assisting suicide.

The States are currently engaged in serious, thoughtful examinations of physician-assisted suicide and other similar issues. Attitudes toward suicide itself have changed, but our laws have consistently condemned, and continue to prohibit, assisted suicide. Despite changes in medical technology and notwithstanding an increased emphasis on the importance of end-of-life decision making, we have not retreated from this prohibition. ("The States—indeed, all civilized nations—demonstrate their commitment to life by treating homicide as a serious crime. Moreover, the majority of States in this country have laws imposing criminal penalties on one who assists another to commit suicide.") Indeed, opposition to and condemnation of suicide—and, therefore, of assisting suicide—are consistent and enduring themes of our philosophical, legal, and cultural heritages.

More specifically, for over 700 years, the Anglo-American common-law tradition has punished or otherwise disapproved of both suicide and assisting suicide.

We have not retreated from this prohibition. Against this backdrop of history, tradition, and practice, we now turn to respondents' constitutional claim.

The Due Process Clause guarantees more than fair process, and the "liberty" it protects includes more than the absence of physical restraint. The Clause also provides heightened protection against government interference with certain fundamental rights and liberty interests. *Reno v. Flores,* **507 U.S. 292 (1993).** We have also assumed, and strongly suggested, that the Due Process Clause protects the traditional right to refuse unwanted life saving medical treatment.

We now inquire whether this asserted right has any place in our Nation's traditions. Here we are confronted with a consistent and almost universal tradition that has long rejected the asserted right, and continues explicitly to reject it today, even for terminally ill, mentally competent adults. To hold for respondents, we would have to reverse centuries of legal doctrine and practice, and strike down the considered policy choice of almost every State.

Respondents contend, however, that the liberty interest they assert is consistent with this Court's substantive-due-process line of cases, if not with this Nation's history and practice. According to respondents, our liberty jurisprudence, and the broad, individualistic principles it reflects, protects the "liberty of competent, terminally ill adults to make end-of-life decisions free of undue government interference." The question presented in this case, however, is whether the protections of the Due Process Clause include a right to commit suicide with another's assistance.

The history of the law's treatment of assisted suicide in this country has been and continues to be one of the rejection of nearly all efforts to permit it. That being the case, our decisions lead us to conclude that the asserted "right" to assistance in committing suicide is not a fundamental liberty interest protected by the Due Process Clause. The Constitution also requires, however, that Washington's assisted-suicide ban be rationally related to legitimate government interests. This requirement is unquestionably met here. As the court below recognized, Washington's assisted-suicide ban implicates a number of state interests.

First, Washington has an "unqualified interest in the preservation of human life." The State's prohibition on assisted suicide, like all homicide laws, both reflects and advances its commitment to this interest.

Those who attempt suicide—terminally ill or not—often suffer from depression or other mental disorders. Research indicates, however, that many people who request physician-assisted suicide withdraw that request if their depression and pain are treated. Thus, legal physician-assisted suicide could make it more difficult for the State to protect depressed or mentally ill persons, or those who are suffering from untreated pain, from suicidal impulses.

Next, the State has an interest in protecting vulnerable groups—including the poor, the elderly, and disabled persons—from abuse, neglect, and mistakes. We have recognized, however, the real risk of subtle coercion and undue influence in end-of-life situations. The risk of harm is greatest for the many individuals in our society whose autonomy and well-being are already compromised by poverty, lack of access to good medical care, advanced age, or membership in a stigmatized social group." If physician-assisted suicide were permitted, many might resort to it to spare their families the substantial financial burden of end-of-life health-care costs.

We therefore hold that the Washington law does not violate the Fourteenth Amendment, either on its face or "as applied to competent, terminally ill adults who wish to hasten their deaths by obtaining medication prescribed by their doctors."

Throughout the Nation, Americans are engaged in an earnest and profound debate about the morality, legality, and practicality of physician-assisted suicide. Our holding permits this debate to continue, as it should in a democratic society.

Drunk driving is a major problem in our society. There are countless horror stories of innocent people who are seriously injured or killed as the result of individuals who get behind the wheel of a car while intoxicated. Society has become intolerant of these selfish drivers and judges are imposing stiffer penalties for these infractions. In fact, a number of state legislatures have imposed mandatory sentencing for "Driving under the Influence of Drugs or Alcohol." The City of New York has taken a radical step in their efforts to penalize those individuals who drink and drive. The City has adopted a tough law that provides for the forfeiture of one's motor vehicle upon arrest by the police for drunk driving. This law has been challenged as being violative of Due Process because it authorizes the police to take and retain a vehicle without a hearing. The constitutionality of this law is the subject of the following case.

GRINBERG V. POLICE COMMISSIONER SAFIR
SUPREME COURT, NEW YORK COUNTY, NEW YORK (1999)

ON FEBRUARY 20, 1999, Police Commissioner Safir announced that the City would apply the Property Clerk Forfeiture Law to vehicles operated by individuals arrested for Driving While Intoxicated. On February 21, 1999, the police stopped and arrested petitioner for DWI. The arresting officer concluded that petitioner was intoxicated based on the strong smell of alcohol, watery and bloodshot eyes, and coordination tests. A breathalyzer indicated 0.11 per cent blood alcohol content, over the 0.10 per cent intoxication threshold. Officers took petitioner's 1988 Acura for forfeiture.

New York City Administrative Code Section 14-140 defines the status of property by its nexus to crime and declares the City's right to hold it. *Administrative Code § 14-140(4)(b)* directs that certain property, including that "suspected of being used as a means of committing crime or employed in or furtherance of crime…shall be given…into the custody" of the Police Department property clerk. The law provides that anyone who used such property shall not be deemed the lawful claimant. The City's forfeiture procedures permit the property clerk to decline to return property if there is "reasonable cause to believe that [it]….was the instrumentality of a crime…." The property clerk then must "cause a civil forfeiture proceeding or other similar civil proceeding to be initiated" within 25 days of a claimant's demand.

Petitioner alleges that the new City policy violates the Due Process clause of the constitution because it authorizes the police to take and retain a vehicle without a seizure hearing.

The Due Process Clause guarantees that, absent extraordinary circumstances, "individuals must receive notice and an opportunity to be heard before the Government deprives them of their property." *U.S. v. James Daniel Good Real Property*, **510 U.S. 43.** Forfeiture actions inherently may present such extraordinary circumstances. A pre-hearing seizure of an instrumentality for forfeiture comports with due process when:

> the seizure has been necessary to secure an important governmental or general public interest. Second, there has been a special need for very prompt action. Third, the State has kept strict control over its monopoly of legitimate force: the person initiating the seizure has been a government official responsible for determining, under the standards of a narrowly drawn statute, that it was necessary and justified in the particular instance.

Immediate seizure of a drunk driver's automobile upon arrest is necessary because the arrestee is legally and physically incapable of driving. Pre-seizure notice and hearing might prevent police from effecting forfeiture. A car is property that could be removed to another jurisdiction, destroyed, or concealed, if advance warning of confiscation was given.

The seizure is simultaneous with a DWI arrest for which the police must have probable cause. The arresting officer evaluates an offense committed in his or her presence. Indicia of alcohol consumption and objective tests confirming the presence of alcohol, minimize the risk of erroneous deprivation.

While the City's DWI policy prevents accused drunk drivers from using property before a determination in the criminal action, the City's interest in deterring drunk driving and ensuring enforceability of a subsequent forfeiture order, clearly outweighs the private interest affected.

Petitioner argues that the City's retention of his car, without a hearing, for several months prior to conclusion of the forfeiture action, violates due process.

Due process requires a meaningful adversary proceeding at a meaningful time. Whether the delay between a seizure and the initiation of judicial proceedings violates due process is judged by the standards for determining a constitutional speedy trial violation. The factors include: "length of delay, reason for the delay, the defendant's assertion of his right, and prejudice to the defendant." *Barker v. Wingo*, **407 U.S. 514, 530, 92 S.Ct. 2182, 33 L.Ed.2d 101.**

Retention prevents the vehicle from being used for repeated illegal activity. An automobile is an integral part of DWI; it poses the threat of being used as an "instrumentality of death" should the crime be repeated. Just as there is a strong public interest in withholding a non-contraband murder weapon from a homicide defendant, there is a strong public interest in withholding a car from a DWI defendant.

Petitioner has not met his burden of demonstrating that the City DWI forfeiture policy is unconstitutional. Accordingly it is ADJUDGED that the petition is denied and the proceeding is dismissed.

Drug testing in the work place is a common occurrence. The test is no longer limited to college, professional or Olympic athletes. Rather, 40% of the working population is subjected to drug testing and marijuana is the illegal substance that surfaces in the majority of positive tests results. Employers are in favor of drug testing because of the financial implications of absenteeism, low productivity, injuries and theft. Workers are concerned about the accuracy of the test results. For instance, a false positive test result can occur with something as simple as a person eating a poppy seed bagel which may suggest opium use.

When drug testing is part of the collective bargaining agreement, employee concerns can be minimized though the negotiation process. Ardent criticism of drug testing is more apt to occur when the test is unilaterally imposed on members of the work force. This can happen when the legislature mandates drug testing of a particular work group. Such legislation usually triggers a constitutional challenge to the drug testing program on a variety of grounds such as invasion of privacy, due process and unlawful search and seizure.

The earliest legislative mandated drug testing program focused on railroad employees, who were involved in train accidents. The courts have upheld that legislation because of the need to protect the public against alcohol and drug abuse among transit workers. Random drug testing of student athletes has also been upheld in order to protect the welfare of children who might be susceptible to the physical, emotional and social damage of drug abuse.

In *O'Neill v. Lawson,* the court had to decide the legality of a random drug testing program for elected officials. Since no evidence was presented to show that there was any history or pattern of drug abuse among elected officials or that they occupied safety sensitive positions, the court found the law unconstitutional.

PHILLIP O'NEILL V. STATE OF LOUISIANA
197 F.3D 1169 (5TH CIR. 1999)

THE LOUISIANA LEGISLATURE ENACTED *Section 1116.1* of the Louisiana Revised Statutes which provided that the State Board of Ethics ("the Board") would implement random drug testing of elected officials.

Section 1116.1 declares that "the state has a compelling interest in establishing a requirement that all elected officials demonstrate that they do not use illegal drugs, without the necessity of showing any measure of individualized suspicion." The statute calls for the development and implementation of a scheme for conducting random drug testing of elected officials. The program requires selected officials to submit to drug screening at a laboratory approved by the Board.

Initial positive test results are released only to the elected official and an individual designated by the Board to receive such information, but the Board itself may obtain results should a second, confirmatory test also suggest the presence of illegal drugs. Finally, the statute forbids any elected official from either testing positive for drugs or refusing to submit to a drug screen when requested to do so.

Plaintiff O'Neill is the elected Justice of the Peace for Jefferson Parish, Louisiana and he challenged the constitutionality of Section 1116.1. His complaint requests an injunction against implementation of drug testing.

In recent years, when evaluating the constitutionality of suspicion less drug tests, the Court has continued to require the existence of "special needs". The Court's struggle to give some concreteness to this concept is perhaps nowhere more evident than in cases involving Fourth Amendment challenges to drug testing laws (as violations of the law against unlawful search and seizures).

The clash between drug testing and the Fourth Amendment is a recent phenomenon, with its genesis in the rise of drug abuse in this country during recent decades. The scourge of drug abuse naturally provoked attempts to control the problem. One of these approaches involved urinalysis of particular employees to ensure that they were not abusing drugs.

The Supreme Court's first significant treatment of the issue occurred in *Skinner v. Railway Labor Executives' Ass'n.*, **489 U.S. 602 (1989).** In that case, the Court examined whether Federal Railroad Administration regulations mandating blood and urine tests of employees involved in accidents, and authorizing them for those who violated certain safety rules, passed constitutional muster. After determining that the collection and analysis of urine samples implicated reasonable societal expectations of privacy and amounted to a search. The majority emphasized that the Fourth Amendment only prohibited unreasonable searches and seizures.

After recognizing that urine testing implicated reasonable expectations of privacy, the focus shifted to whether the government possessed a special need to conduct the screens. In *Skinner,* the Court held that where the intrusion was minimal, a search might be reasonable even without individualized suspicion.

The *Skinner* Court determined that there existed a history of alcohol and drug abuse among railway employees, giving rise to a legitimate government interest in preventing accidents caused by employees' use of such substances. The Court found that these factors, coupled with the pervasive regulation that is characteristic of the railroad industry, led to the conclusion that the government's compelling interest in safety and the individual's diminished expectation of privacy in the railroad context permitted urine testing, even without any showing of individualized suspicion.

The Supreme Court confronted these issues again in *Vernonia School Dist. v. Acton,* **515 U.S. 646 (1995).** In that case, an Oregon student challenged a local school district's policy of requiring student athletes to undergo random urinalysis for the detection of drugs as a condition of participation in school athletic programs.

The majority concurred that drugs were a significant presence at the school and that athletes' use of drugs and their status as role models for other students exacerbated this problem. The Court located a safety issue in the concern for the welfare of children, who might be particularly susceptible to physical, emotional, and social damage from drug abuse. Like the railway employees in *Skinner,* the students in

Vernonia possessed a diminished expectation of privacy, due primarily to the in loco parentis role played by school officials. Indeed, "students within the school environment have a lesser expectation of privacy than members of the population generally," and "[l]egitimate privacy expectations are even less with regard to student athletes." In view of these factors, the majority concluded that the school district's policy was constitutional.

Skinner and *Vernonia* revealed some common considerations the Court found persuasive in deciding whether to uphold a particular drug testing scheme. In both cases, it seemed that the majority opinions identified a history of drug abuse, a fairly immediate safety concern, and a diminished expectation of privacy as justifications for bestowing the Court's constitutional blessing on the programs at issue.

This Court will now turn its attention to the statute challenged in this case. Section 1116.1 clearly states its intention to authorize drug testing "without the necessity of showing any measure of individualized suspicion." The state acknowledges the absence of any history or pattern of drug abuse among elected officials.

While it is true, that the lack of an existing pattern of abuse is not by itself sufficient to strike down a drug testing statute, other considerations in conjunction with this one are fatal to Section 1116.1.

Elected officials do not occupy safety sensitive positions within the meaning of its drug testing jurisprudence. What is left then, is the diminished expectation of privacy characteristic of all public officials. The purpose of Section 1116.1 is largely symbolic. Despite the laudable intentions of the legislature in trying to present an example for the public, the Supreme Court has stated unequivocally that symbolism alone is insufficient to justify suspicionless searches in violation of the Fourth Amendment.

In summary, this Court concludes that Louisiana has failed to carry their burden in demonstrating that "special needs" beyond the normal needs of law enforcement exist, such that an exception to the rule requiring individualized suspicion is warranted. For this reason, Louisiana's proposed scheme of random, suspicionless drug testing is an unconstitutional search in violation of the Fourth Amendment.

QUESTIONS FOR DISCUSSION:

Are the following laws constitutional?

1. In order to prevent the sexual harassment of women walking pass construction sites, a city passes an "anti-ogling" law for its employees. Looking at someone for more than nine seconds in a leering manner is considered "ogling" and illegal. First time violators face verbal warnings and repeat offenders can be fired.

2. A beach town enacts an ordinance that prohibits a person who is not physically fit from wearing a bikini on a public beach. The penalty is removal from the beach and a $200.00 fine.

3. A city passes a parental responsibility ordinance that makes parents liable for offenses committed by their children under 18. The

law makes failing to supervise a minor a civil offense. First time offenders receive a warning. Repeat offenders may be fined as much as $1,000 and be compelled to attend eight-week "parenting courses" approved by the court. In addition, parents must pay for property damage caused by their children.

4. In order to slow down Chicago's increasing murder rate among gang members, the city enacts a law that allows police officers to order the dispersal of individuals whom the officers reasonably believe are street gang members remaining in a public place with no apparent purpose. Those who do not promptly obey the order to move can be arrested.

5. To regulate the flow of sexual explicit materials to children, Congress passes a law that bans the transmission of "indecent" materials across the Internet to minors.

Consider the following two cases and determine whether the laws violate a person's substantive due process rights:

1. In California, a pregnant woman was given a $271 traffic ticket for allegedly driving by herself in the car-pool lane on her way to work. Although the passenger's seat was empty, she argued that the law is vague so that an unborn baby should be counted as a second person. To counter this argument, the government argued that the driver might have violated other laws. In California, it is illegal for two people to sit behind the wheel at the same time, and its illegal for two people to share a single seat belt.

2. In Ohio, two Amish hunters were fined $50 for refusing to wear bright orange safety clothing. They argued that it is against the Amish religion to wear bright colors so that the law violates their religious beliefs. Another common problem in the Amish community is resistance to putting triangular red-and-orange "Slow Moving Vehicle" signs on their horse-drawn buggies. Does the state's interest in the safety of the citizens outweigh the Amish community's freedom to practice their religion?

SECTION 4.4
THE DRAFTING OF
A STATUTE

The drafting of a statute is not an easy task. The problems of society are complex, and the legislature must deal with issues ranging from trash collection to nuclear energy. It is unrealistic to expect that each member of the legislature is an expert in every field of proposed legislation. They must rely upon others for guidance and are subjected to pressures from their peers, constituents, and special interest groups. This requires a constant balancing of personal beliefs against the wishes of others when considering proposed legislation.

In drafting a law, it is a primary goal to avoid using ambiguous words and to make a statute as clear as possible. Unfortunately, this cannot always be done. It is impossible to envision every problem or predict how future events will affect the legislation. For instance, definitions that once seemed obvious become subject to attack as technology changes.

Examine the word, "motor vehicle." As automobiles became the favored mode of transportation, statutes were adopted requiring "motor vehicles" used for the transportation of people to be registered with the state. Cars, buses, and trucks are obviously within the contemplation of the legislation but would airplanes, jet skis, or mopeds be covered?

Hodge, Dodge and Lodge has assisted the State Legislature in drafting various bills over the years. The firm has retrieved one of its old files for your review. The matter involves an anti-graffiti statute. The facts that led up to the passage of the statute, the legislative debate, and the actual legislation is included. When this material is read as a whole, it is possible to gain a better appreciation of how compromises are made to insure passage of a law and how the pieces of the puzzle are put together to produce the legislation.

**SECTION 4.5
SAMPLE STATUTE**

The Senate Committee on Law and Order was assigned the task of drafting a statute in response to Senator Bowman's call for legislation to combat Pennsylvania's graffiti problem. Actually, Estelle Hodge instigated the action. Senator Bowman had been notorious as a youngster for his logo, "Kool Bow," which appeared on nearly every bridge, bus, and train throughout Philadelphia and its surrounding areas. While Bowman was not overly concerned with this issue, he knew that when Estelle got hooked on a cause it was easier to placate her than to resist her incessant pestering.

Estelle Hodge took up this cause after discovering six foot tall letters, spelling out "Kool Bowman, Jr.," spray painted on the side of her suburban home. This incident made Estelle cognizant of the significant degree of defacement to property, which literally covered most of the town. Everywhere she went—the ladies' room, the schoolyard, public transportation—Estelle noticed graffiti. She was incensed. Estelle called the Philadelphia Anti-Graffiti League and found out their view on this subject. Estelle also hired a team of investigators to learn more about graffiti and its causes. This investigation revealed immediate information regarding the culprits. It seems that kids under the age of 18 are the primary offenders, and the tools of their trade consist of cans of spray paint and indelible markers.

The Senate Committee learned of Mrs. Hodge's interest in the project and invited her to speak in response to many of the Senators' questions. The group wanted to learn more about the problem before drafting any form of legislation. The following are excerpts from this session:

MRS. HODGE: Ladies and gentlemen, it's imperative that you enact legislation to combat this problem. Graffiti is disgraceful. Our youths' destructive behavior has gone unpunished for entirely too long.

SENATOR BUTEN: Ma'am. Respectfully, I must disagree. The problem is not lack of legislation. The Crimes Code contains laws prohibiting defacement to property and vandalism. The problem stems, not from deficiencies within our penal code, but rather from the difficulty in apprehending the culprits. Generally, this type of vandalism occurs at night and only when the area is deserted.

MRS. HODGE: Then we need preventive measures. You will have to outlaw the sale of paint.

SENATOR SEARS: We can't make the sale of paint illegal. There are many legitimate uses for the product.

SENATOR BUTEN: Wait a minute, John. Perhaps Mrs. Hodge has a point. We don't need to make all sales of paint illegal. The studies reveal that this is a particular problem among teenagers. Therefore, all we need to do is to prevent them from gaining access to the needed materials. If we make it illegal for retailers to sell paint to minors, we will be able to control the problem without effecting legitimate users.

MRS. HODGE: Senator that's a great idea. Your solution will force parents to supervise their children. Kids who have legitimate need for paint will still be able to use paint. They will just need their parents to authorize the purchase.

SENATOR GLOSS: Will this law affect all types of paint? Isn't that overly broad?

MRS. HODGE: My investigators found that 99% of graffiti was accomplished with the use of spray paint containers and indelible markers. The kids need to be able to write their messages quickly, noticeably, and permanently. That is why they use spray paint and indelible markers.

SENATOR EARL: We also need to discuss how we want to define minors. Mrs. Hodge's studies reveal that 15 and 16-year-olds predominantly perpetrate the crimes. Nevertheless, 17-year-olds still commit a significant portion of these acts—approximately 20%.

SENATOR BUTEN: Then we must make it illegal for a retail establishment to sell these materials to anyone under 18 years of age that is not accompanied by a parent. Clearly, we do not want to regulate the 18 to 21-year-old age group. This is not an issue dealing with the sale of alcohol. We could never withstand the criticism from these young adults who have voting privileges. The law should also contain a provision punishing any child who uses false identification to prove majority. We are all aware of the problem with false credentials that kids use to purchase liquor.

SENATOR EARL: The only remaining issue is the penalty. I suggest we impose a fine of between $50 and $300. These amounts should be minimal enough as to not punish the shopkeeper too severely. Yet, the amount should provide sufficient sting to encourage sellers to take action to prevent the minor's easy access to these materials. Also, by giving judges discretion as to the amount of the fine, they will be able to crack down on those shopkeepers who continually refuse to cooperate in this effort to combat the problem. In fact, we should also allow up to 90 days of imprisonment at the judges' discretion.

Following a spirited debate, the Senate Committee on Law and Order drafted *Bill No. 5205* and forwarded it to the legislature for consideration.

The legislature considered the issue and agreed that remedial measures had to be implemented to stop the defacement of property by the use of spray paint and indelible markers. A number of lawmakers rightfully concluded that it would be inappropriate to totally ban the sale of spray paint and convinced their colleagues that *Bill No. 5205* offered a good compromise to the problem.

Several modifications to the proposed legislation were made to clarify certain provisions and to insure final passage. The Bill was then voted on and easily passed. The governor signed the legislation into law with an effective date of one hundred and eighty (180) days after final passage.

The anti-graffiti statute is as follows:

Section 9-617. Sale of Spray Paint Containers and Indelible Markers:

WHEREAS, There is widespread use of spray paint and indelible markers in the permanent defacement of public and private property; and,

WHEREAS, The marring of public and private property has contributed to the blight and degradation of neighborhoods and public places; and,

WHEREAS, The easy application and ready accessibility to spray paint and indelible markers facilitates its misuse and hinders enforcement agencies from preventing persons from defacing public and private property or apprehending those committing the offensive conduct; and

WHEREAS, A substantial portion of the defacement of public and private property has been caused by minors using spray paint containers and indelible markers, obtained both legally and illegally; now, therefore,

1. **Definitions**

   a. Indelible Marker. Any felt tip marker, china marker or similar device that is not water soluble and which has a flat or angled writing surface one-half inch or greater.

   b. Minor—Any person under the age of eighteen (18) years.

   c. Person—Any retail establishment.

2. **Prohibited Conduct**

   a. No person shall sell or offer for sale, transfer or offer to transfer any spray paint container or indelible marker unless such spray paint container or indelible marker is held for sale or transfer in an enclosed device which is constructed to prevent removal of the merchandise except by authorized attendants or is stored, out of sight, in such a way as to prevent free access to the merchandise by the public.

   b. No person shall sell or otherwise transfer any spray paint container or indelible marker to a minor, unless said minor is accompanied by parent or legal guardian at time of purchase or transfer.

   c. No minor shall, at the time of purchase of items specified in Section 9-617(2)(b), knowingly furnish fraudulent evidence of majority including, but not limited to, a motor vehicle operator's license, a registration certificate issued under the Federal Selective Service Act, an identification card issued to a member of the Armed Forces, or any document issued by a federal, state, county or municipal government.

3. **Penalties**

   a. Any person who violates the provisions of Section 9-617(2)(a) shall be subject to a fine or penalty not less than fifty ($50.00) dollars nor more than three hundred ($300.00) dollars, plus a minimum of fifty ($50.00) dollars for each day the violation continues and/or imprisonment not exceeding ninety (90) days.

   b. Any person who violates the provisions of Section 9-617(2)(b) or any minor who violates the provisions of Section 9-617(2)(c) shall be subject to a fine or penalty not less than fifty ($50.00) dollars nor more than three hundred ($300.00) dollars and/or imprisonment not exceeding ninety (90) days.

SECTION 4.6

PROBLEM FOUR—A

HODGE, DODGE AND LODGE
ATTORNEYS AT LAW
MEMORANDUM

To: All Law Clerks

From: Gregory Olan Dodge

Re: Drafting of Legislation to Prohibit the Stalking of People by Photographers

---

Congress is considering the adoption of a bill to prohibit paparazzi from stalking famous people in order to sell pictures to the tabloid magazines. Many support the legislation in light of the death of Representative Sonny Bono, who was the primary advocate of this legislation, and the general annoyance of movie stars, athletes, and national celebrities by these photographers.

Estelle Hodge, however, has made the issue a personal one. While Estelle understands the desire of fans to learn more about their favorite stars, she believes that celebrities should be able to have some private moments especially when they take reasonable steps to protect their privacy. After all, famous people should not be prisoners in their own homes. They must have access to public facilities such as shops and restaurants.

To maintain my good relationship with members of Congress, I promised them that I would write a draft of this legislation for their review and ultimate approval. One Senator, however, told me that she was troubled by the constitutionality of this proposed law and informed Estelle of her concerns. For instance, the Senator thought the bill could criminalize routine newsgathering. The Senator also wanted to know who would be covered under the law and how the phrase "reasonable expectation of privacy" would be defined since that is the term that Estelle keeps discussing in her lobbying efforts.

A number of celebrities wrote letters in support of the legislation. Arnold Schwarzenegger, George Clooney, Sean Penn and Madonna have had problems with the press. One female celebrity complained about an incident in which a photographer tried to bungy jump into her penthouse in order to take a picture of her infant son. Another celebrity complained about a group of photographers who followed him into the restroom in order to take a picture of him while in a compromising position. In a short time, Estelle had accumulated a lot of support for her mission on the local, national and international levels. In fact, Estelle has turned the tables by arming a group of supporters with cameras so they can follow the paparazzi around in order to take pictures of the photographers in restaurants and other public places.

The tabloids are upset about Estelle's picketing and lobbying efforts. The media explained that they have the right to take pictures of celebrities because the stars are public figures. They further explained that the general public wanted to know anything and everything about their favorite celebrities. Fans interest ranged from learning about a star's favorite color to learning what flavor ice cream he or she likes. In light of the public's curiosity, the paparazzi believe they are doing a public service whenever they take "candid" pictures of famous people—when they least expected a camera. Besides, the photographers assert that celebrities know that being famous entails an encroachment into their private lives.

The paparazzi also claim that Estelle's proposed bill is unconstitutional because it will be too vague. For instance, Estelle wants to target photographers who take pictures for profit and would exempt from prosecution a lunatic fan who follows a celebrity. They claim that this distinction makes no sense. After all, the paparazzi do not want to hurt the celebrities while lunatic fans have actually stalked their favorite stars thereby presenting an actual and real danger to the celebrities.

The task of drafting the bill has been assigned to you but you should keep several goals in mind. Estelle vehemently maintains that people have a constitutional guarantee to be left alone especially when one takes extra steps in order to protect his or her privacy. Estelle also mentioned that the law should target photographers who sell pictures to tabloid magazines.

Please write a draft of the law and focus on the following three aspects:

1. Definitions. Who should be covered under the legislation and how should the phrase "reasonable expectation of privacy" be defined? This section needs careful attention to detail in order to prevent a constitutional challenge on the basis of vagueness.

2. Define what conduct is prohibited. As I mentioned before, Estelle believes that photographers should be prevented from taking pictures of an individual when he or she has a reasonable expectation of privacy.

3. What penalties should be imposed for violating the statute? Should the penalty be criminal in nature or should the remedy be civil in which case the aggrieved person can collect money damages?

I have prepared the following outline for your use in drafting the legislation:

1. Definitions

2. Prohibited Conduct

3. Penalty

SECTION 4.7
PROCEDURAL
DUE PROCESS

Q. *What do Jeffrey Dahmer, Mike Tyson, the Oklahoma City bombing defendants, the officers in the Rodney King beating trial, Gary Heidnik and Charles Manson have in common?*

A. Their trials all raised issues as to whether they could obtain a fair and impartial hearing as guaranteed by the Constitution.

Procedural due process guarantees that before a person's rights can be determined, he or she must be given a fair hearing. A fair hearing consists of three elements:

1. Notice of the proceeding;

2. Opportunity to be heard; and

3. An impartial tribunal.

The first element necessary to insure a fair hearing is proper notice. Just imagine if you went home and found a certified letter from th court informing you for the first time that you were tried and cc victed of burglary the week before. To insure that this does not occu a party must receive some type of notification of the pending litiga on.

In a civil action, the defendant is given a copy of the lawsuit. In a c inal case, the defendant is arrested and informed of the charges agai him.

Each party must be given the opportunity to be heard. This accomplished by allowing the litigants to be present at trial and to articipate in the proceeding. They may sit with counsel during all ases of the trial and assist in presenting or attacking the evidence. I not uncommon to see a litigant pass a note to counsel during the al or to speak to the attorney in whispered tones.

Can a party be denied the right to be present durir the trial without violating the tenets of due process? Yes! The co has the superior right to make sure that the trial progresses in an derly fashion. Unruly parties can and will be excluded from the c troom. A number of infamous cases can be cited which involved ruptive behavior by litigants, attorneys or spectators. One such c involved the Chicago Seven. This criminal proceeding dealt with e prosecution of seven flamboyant individuals who were charged ith conspiring to incite a riot during the 1968 Democratic National nvention. The defendants disrupted the proceedings by shouting v garities, singing songs from the witness stand, eating jelly beans, rea ng comic books, reciting Hari Krishna Mantra, and showing up for e court session wearing judicial robes. The court held the defenda s in contempt and ordered them to be restrained and gagged for po ns of the proceedings.

The trial of Charles Manson for the murder of actress, Sharon Tate, also involved disruptive behavior, which resulted in the defendants being removed from the courtroom. Manson threatened the judge during the trial several times and on one occasion leaped toward the judge wielding a pencil. At another point, Manson and three co-defendants disrupted the trial by singing and chanting. To avoid a mistrial, the judge removed the defendants from the courtroom and placed them in a separate room where they were permitted to listen to the testimony through a sound system.

Finally, a fair hearing requires the right to be tried by an impartial tribunal. Because of the extensive media coverage provided unusual or notorious cases, the defendant's right to a fair trial is frequently an issue. How can a defendant receive a fair trial when most of the prospective jurors have already heard about the case and have formed an opinion as to innocence or guilt?

The Court must exercise great care to minimize outside influences that may improperly affect the verdict. Measures to insure a fair trial range from issuing a gag order in order to control the dissemination of information to moving the trial to another location where the case is not so well known.

The Fugitive, is a movie loosely based upon the murder trial of Dr. Sam Shepard, who was convicted of the bludgeoned death of his pregnant wife in the upstairs bedroom of their home. The case ended up before the United States Supreme Court on the issue of whether Dr. Shepard received a fair trial because of the massive, pervasive and prejudicial publicity that attended his prosecution.

During the murder investigation, the news media published a number of stories which emphasized the evidence that intended to incriminate Shepard and they pointed out discrepancies in the doctor's statements to the authorities. One editorial asked, "Why don't police quiz top suspect," with a demand that Dr. Shepard be taken to police headquarters. Another editorial stated, "Why isn't Sam Shepard in Jail?" During the trial, which took place two weeks before the General Election, the chief prosecutor was a candidate for Common Pleas Court judge, and the trial judge was a candidate to succeed himself. The newspapers published the names and addresses of all potential jurors and a radio station was permitted to set up broadcasting facilities next to the jury room. When Dr. Shepard was brought into the court room before each session, he was surrounded by reporters and extensively photographed for the newspapers and television. During deliberations, the sequestered jury was allowed to make telephone calls with out any type of supervision.

In considering whether Dr. Shepard's procedural due process rights were violated, the Supreme Court noted that the extensive newspaper, radio and television coverage of the criminal trial, together with the physical arrangements in the courtroom for the news media, deprived Shepard of the judicial serenity and calm to which he was entitled. The Justices noted that the theory of our legal system, is that the conclusion to be reached in a case will be induced only by the evidence and arguments in open court, and not by any outside influences, whether by private talk or public print. The carnival atmosphere could have been avoided since the court room and courthouse were subject to the control of the trial judge. The court should have adopted stricter rules governing the use of the courtroom by reporters and efforts should have been initiated to control the release of leads, information and gossip to the press. The Supreme Court concluded that the trial court did not protect Dr. Shepard from the inherently prejudicial publicity which saturated the community, and the jurist failed to control the disruptive influences in the court room. Due process requires that the accused receive a trial by an impartial jury free from outside influences. This did not occur in the Sam Shepard criminal trial.

In Philadelphia, the trial of Gary Heidnik for the brutal murders and torture of several mentally handicapped women could not proceed until an impartial jury was empaneled. The case was so gruesome and shocking in detail that it received daily press coverage. Very few citizens in Philadelphia were unaware of the killings.

Of the 180 potential jurors called, all had heard about Mr. Heidnik and 124 had already predetermined his guilt or innocence based upon the press coverage. The presiding judge agreed with the defense about the prejudicial affect of the pre-trial publicity and noted that, "It was impossible to get a fair and impartial jury in Philadelphia because this case was turned into nothing short of a freak show." The judge considered moving the trial to Pittsburgh. Instead, a panel of jurors from Pittsburgh were selected and brought to Philadelphia for the trial. In this way, the court balanced the right of the public to know what was going on in the Gary Heidnik case with the defendant's right to have a fair and impartial tribunal.

In Jeffrey Dahmer's murder trial, defense lawyers questioned whether their client could obtain a fair trial given the widespread publicity surrounding the gruesome nature of the murders. Dahmer was accused of killing 17 people and storing their remains in his apartment. His lawyers asked that jurors be selected from outside Milwaukee, where the media focus would be less intense. The court denied this request citing the worldwide publicity given to the case.

Smith, the nephew of Sen. Edward Kennedy, was acquitted in 1991 of raping a woman he met at a Palm Beach bar. But defense lawyers and prosecutors both worried that extensive pre-trial publicity—including clips on TV magazine shows like "A Current Affair"—would bias jurors. Eventually, the judge allowed the attorneys to question each potential juror about the effect of pre-trial publicity.

Although the judge allowed it in the Smith case, questioning of jurors about pre-trial publicity is not required. Earlier in 1991, the U.S. Supreme Court ruled in *Mu'Min v. Virginia,* **111 S. Ct. 1899,** that the Sixth Amendment's right to be tried by an "impartial jury" does not mean that potential jurors are obligated to divulge what and how much they know about the case as long as they promised to be fair.

A current controversy in jury selection involves the racial makeup of the jury. Nowhere was that more prominent than in the trial of four white Los Angeles police officers accused of beating Rodney King, an African American. At the request of the defendants, the trial was moved from Los Angeles, which has a 13 percent black population, to suburban Simi Valley, where the black population is 2 percent. The officers were then acquitted of all but one of 11 criminal charges by a jury in a California State court. The jury was composed of 10 whites, one Hispanic and one Asian American. The outcry after the verdict led to angry mob violence. The officers were later tried in federal court and two were convicted of violating King's civil rights. As a result of the rioting in Los Angeles, Florida nervously sought to move the trial of a Miami police officer accused of fatally shooting an African American motorcyclist and his passenger. The first trial of Officer William Lozano ended in a conviction on manslaughter charges, but an appeals court reversed the verdict, saying that the jurors may have feared that an acquittal would spark rioting in Miami, just as it did in Los Angeles in the King case.

Lozano's trial was moved several times between Orlando and Tallahassee. Ultimately, a jury in Orlando acquitted Lozano of the charges.

In a personal injury case, can a severally disfigured plaintiff be excluded from the courtroom because the defendant does not believe he can obtain a fair trial? Will the jury be sympathetic because of the plaintiff's disfigurement and award damages regardless of the liability of the defendant? This is the issue in *Cary v. Oneok.*

ERIC CARY V. ONEOK, INC.
940 P.2D 201 (OK. 1997)

SUMMERS, Vice Chief Justice.

THE QUESTION IS WHETHER IT WAS ERROR to exclude a badly burned child from his trial because of his physical appearance. We hold that it was, and reverse.

Eric Cary is a boy who was severely burned when the water heater in the garage of his home exploded. He was trapped in the garage until rescued by his mother, and suffers from permanent disfigurement. At the time of the incident he was almost three years old. His mother brought this suit on his behalf alleging negligence on the part of the defendant Oneok in inspecting and lighting the water heater.

Prior to trial Oneok presented a motion asking that Eric, then six and one-half years old, be kept out of the court room fearing that the jury would be sympathetic to plaintiff because of his disfigurement. The trial court ordered that Eric be excluded from the trial.

Plaintiff asserts that the Constitution requires that a party be permitted to attend his own civil trial. He continues by pointing out that children younger than six have been permitted to testify in trials. In this case plaintiff was the only eyewitness to the incident. Regardless of whether he was to testify, Eric's counsel asserts that his presence would be of aid to his attorney by showing the jury the actual person whose life has been affected. He asserts that a jury may respond differently when faced with the person who suffered the harm.

Oneok asserts that Eric's appearance would serve no legitimate purpose, and would inflame the passions of the jury. Oneok argues that the Constitution does not guarantee an individual's right to be present during the trial of his or her case. It contends that his mother's presence during the trial protected the injured child's rights, as she was his mother and legal representative. Oneok also surmises that Eric would have been of no assistance at trial due to his young age at the time of the incident and his cloudy recollection of the events.

Courts differ in their approach to this question. Some courts hold that the right to attend trial is an absolute right, arising out of state or federal constitutional provisions. In *Helminski v. Ayerst Laboratories*, **766 F.2d 208 (6th Cir.1985)**, the Circuit Court observed that although the Due Process clause does not give a civil litigant the absolute right to be present personally during his trial, due process is offended if he is excluded arbitrarily or in the absence of extreme circumstances. It went on to conclude that a plaintiffs physical appearance alone does not warrant his expulsion.

Others, without relying on constitutional provisions, hold that absent an overwhelming reason to the contrary, a party has a right to attend the trial of his lawsuit. *Mason v. Moore*, **226 A.D.2d 993, 641 N.Y.S.2d 195 (N.Y.S.Ct.1996)**.

Regardless of their approach, courts agree on two points: **(1)** The ideals behind due process and a fair trial permit a party to be present in the courtroom absent extreme conditions and **(2)** the possibility of juror sympathy alone is not juror prejudice, and is insufficient to exclude a party from the courtroom. It also appears that a party's physical condition alone does not warrant exclusion.

Oklahoma has never held, nor do we so hold here, that a party's right to be present in the courtroom is absolute. We can contemplate situations in which the disruptive behavior of a party would necessitate the party's exclusion from the courtroom, and a trial may proceed after a party has voluntarily waived the right to be present. However, we find no authority for the proposition that a party may be excluded solely by reason of his disfigurement. Absent a voluntary waiver we hold that only in the case of extreme circumstances may a party be excluded from the proceedings.

A party's physical appearance cannot be the sole basis for exclusion from the courtroom, and does not amount to an "extreme circumstance" permitting exclusion. In the present case the plaintiff was excluded because he was a party to the lawsuit, and due to his appearance the judge feared that the jury would be overly sympathetic. If Eric had been merely an observer and not a party, he would have been permitted in the courtroom. It is impermissible that he is kept from observing and participating in the proceedings solely because of his status as a party who was burned and is thus physically scarred.

We agree that a fundamental cornerstone of due process is an impartial jury. *Agee v. Gant*, **412 P.2d 155, 162 (Okla.1966).** We do not agree with Oneok's assumption that the likelihood of jury sympathy is the equivalent of prejudice, and amounts to a denial of due process. A juror's sympathetic feeling toward a party does not necessarily lead to the conclusion that the jury will disregard the law to reach a verdict based on sympathy alone.

Based on the record before the trial court and before us on review, we conclude that Eric was entitled to attend his own trial, and his exclusion requires reversal. The opinion of the Court of Appeals is vacated, the judgment for the Defendant is reversed, and the cause is remanded to the trial court for further proceedings.

Violence in schools is an unfortunate reality in today's society. Incidents range from threats and assaults to multiple killings. Since the tragic occurrence at Columbine High, schools have adopted a "no-tolerance" or "get tough" policy" on violence. Metal detectors have been installed at schools, police have conducted simulations of assaults in order to effectively deal with future incidents and students have been expelled if found in possession of a weapon. In fact, one educational institution threatened to suspend a grade school student because he carried a nail clipper to class.

Several incidents have arisen where students have used the internet to post inappropriate or threatening messages involving classmates or teachers. Because of the "no tolerance" policy, these transgressions have been dealt with swiftly and the punishment is usually expulsion. Procedural due process, however, still requires that the pupil be afforded a fair hearing before a final decision may be rendered concerning the student's punishment. In *J.S., a minor v. Bethlehem Area School District,* an eighth grade student created a web-site which contained several pages of derogatory or threatening comments concerning an algebra teacher. The child was expelled from school following a disciplinary hearing and suit was instituted in order to determine whether the eighth grader was provided with a fair hearing consistent with the requirements of procedural due process.

J.S., A MINOR V. BETHLEHEM AREA SCHOOL DISTRICT
757 A.2D 412 (PA. CMWLTH. 2000)

J.S. (STUDENT), APPEALS THE ORDER OF THE COURT that affirmed the decision of the Bethlehem Area School District (School District) to permanently expel J.S. from its schools.

Student was in the eighth grade at Nitschmann Middle School. Student created a web-site on his home computer. The web-site, titled "Teacher Sux," consisted of several web pages that made derogatory comments about Student's algebra teacher, Mrs. Fulmer, and Nitschmann Principal, Mr. Kartsotis.

Prior to accessing the web-site, a visitor had to agree to a disclaimer. The disclaimer indicated, that the visitor was not a member of the School District's faculty or administration and that the visitor did not intend to disclose the identity of the web-site creator or intend to cause trouble for that individual.

Through an anonymous e-mail, a Nitschmann instructor learned of the web-site and promptly reported it to the principal who then convened a faculty meeting and contacted the local police authorities. The Federal Bureau of Investigation was also contacted. Both agencies conducted investigations and were able to identify Student as the creator of the web-site.

On or about July 30, 1998, the School District sent Appellants a letter articulating its intent to suspend Student for a period of three days. The letter alleged that Student violated School District policy through three Level III offenses: threat to a teacher, harassment of a teacher and principal and, disrespect to a teacher and principal. After a hearing on the suspension, the School District opted to extend the suspension period to ten days, effective the beginning of the 1998-99 school year. Shortly thereafter, the School District commenced expulsion proceedings against Student.

Expulsion hearings were conducted on August 19 and 26, 1998. By that time, however, Parents had enrolled Student in an out-of-state school for the 1998-99 school year and thus, Student was unable to attend the August 26, 1998 hearing.

On August 31, 1998, the School District issued the following "Findings of Fact," in relevant part:

- The Web page regarding Mrs. Fulmer stated: "Why Should She Die?" *(Take a look at the diagram and the reasons I gave, then give me $20.00 to help pay for the hitman.)*

- Another Web page has a diagram of Mrs. Fulmer with her head cut off and blood dripping from her neck.

- After viewing the Web page, [Mrs. Fulmer] was frightened, fearing someone would try to kill her.

Based upon its findings, the School District concluded that **1)** Student's statement "Why Should [Mrs. Fulmer] die?…give me $20 to help pay for the hitman" constituted a threat to a teacher and was perceived by Mrs. Fulmer and others as a threat, **2)** the statements regarding Mrs. Fulmer constituted harassment of a teacher, **3)** the statements constituted disrespect to a teacher resulting in actual harm to the health, safety and welfare of the school community, **4)** the School District Code of Conduct prohibited such student conduct and **5),** the statements caused actual physical harm to Mrs. Fulmer, as well other students and teachers. Consequently, the School District voted to permanently expel Student from its schools.

The Department of Education's regulations provide that certain due process requirements are to be observed with regard to formal hearings. They include:

(i) Notification of the charges shall be sent to the student's parents by certified mail.

(ii) Sufficient notice of the time and place of the hearing must be given.

(iii) The student has the right to be represented by counsel.

(iv) The student has the right to request that any such witnesses appear in person and answer questions or be cross-examined.

(v) The student has the right to testify and present witnesses on his own behalf.

Appellants complain that Student was denied the right to have counsel of his choice present at the hearing and the right to a continuance until such time as Student could be present to confront the witnesses against him. We make short shrift of these arguments.

Student was indeed afforded the right to counsel and was represented at the expulsion hearings. Appellants maintain, however, that Student was denied the right to counsel inasmuch as the School District refused to grant a continuance so that Student could obtain additional counsel that was more experienced in First Amendment issues. We conclude that where Appellants affirmatively represented that they were represented by counsel, the School District was under no legal obligation to delay its hearings so that Appellants could "counsel-shop."

In addition, the School District did not deny Student the right to face the witnesses against him. Student attended the August 19, 1998 expulsion hearing, but the hearing ran rather late into the evening. The School District offered to continue the hearing until the next evening; however, Student's father was unavailable.

The next meeting date available was August 26, 1998, a week later. Student did not attend the hearing because his Parents chose to enroll him in another school prior to the expulsion hearings. Appellants contend that the expulsion hearing should have been postponed until Student was available to attend, which would have been Student's Thanksgiving break. There is no right to a three-month continuance, especially given the fact that all of the School District's witnesses against Student were subject to cross-examination by counsel.

Interesting, Appellants' argument that the School District erred in refusing to grant a continuance is seemingly inconsistent with its argument that the School District denied Student's right to a speedy hearing. Appellants complain that Mr. Kartsotis learned of the web-site in May of 1998, but that no action was taken against Student until August. However, the School District accepted Mr. Kartsotis' explanation that no school action was taken against Student until the local authorities and the FBI completed their investigations.

Mr. Kartsotis could not anticipate whether Student would be otherwise held accountable for his actions until the authorities completed their investigations. Accountability through another forum might have influenced the School District's decision of whether to seek expulsion. In our view, the School District proceeded cautiously and took the more prudent course of action by not pursuing the matter until all the facts became available to it. Moreover, Appellants did not demonstrate that they suffered any prejudice as a result of the minimal delay in the proceedings. Indeed, Appellants were provided with ample opportunity to defend against the action and formulate a response, which included enrolling Student in another school district.

Accordingly, we conclude that the trial court was correct in its determination that Student's constitutional rights were not violated.

QUESTIONS FOR DISCUSSION:

1. How important is the racial makeup of a jury? If it is important, what should the justice system do to make sure a defendant receives a fair trial by an "impartial" jury?

2. It is often said that a defendant must be tried by a jury of peers, but there's nothing in the Constitution that requires it. Should there be? What is a "peer?"

3. Should individuals not be allowed to be excused from jury duty regardless of the reason so that the litigants obtain a cross section of the population?

4. What is the best way to handle a disruptive party in the courtroom so that due process is not violated?

5. Should the government be required to buy the defendant clothes for a trial so that the jury does not see the defendant in prison garb?

SECTION 4.8
KATHY HODGE
AND HER UNFAIR
CRIMINAL TRIAL

PROBLEM FOUR—B

HODGE, DODGE AND LODGE
ATTORNEYS AT LAW
MEMORANDUM

To: All Law Clerks

From: Gregory Olan Dodge

Re: Kathy Hodge And Her Unfair Criminal Trial—Procedural Due Process

Kathy's latest problem involves her recent drug conviction. After reading the National Enquirer's recent exposé on the criminal justice system, Kathy is convinced that her conviction should be reversed. Kathy claims she did not receive a fair and impartial trial, as guaranteed by the Constitution. She believes her Due Process rights were violated.

Kathy was arrested for possession of drugs after running a stop sign. Officer O'Brien had been keeping his eye on Kathy, so he was right on the scene when she failed to stop. Needless to say, Kathy was quite annoyed. She had a baggy filled with marijuana on the seat beside her and cocaine hidden in the gym bag in her trunk. Somehow O'Brien caught a glimpse of the baggy when he peered through her window while examining her license. His subsequent search of the car uncovered an ounce of marijuana and a kilo of cocaine.

Kathy was arrested for possession of marijuana and cocaine. Pursuant to Title 35 of the Pennsylvania Statutes *Section 780-113 (16),* she was convicted and is awaiting sentencing. Not surprisingly, the trial was a nightmare. From the moment of her arrest, Kathy was belligerent, disruptive, and uncontrollable. On the way into the courtroom, she attempted to run away from the police escorts. When they recaptured her, a struggle ensued with Kathy biting and kicking the officers. It took four armed men to eventually contain her. They then had to drag her into the courtroom with her arms handcuffed behind her back and her feet manacled together.

What follows is an excerpt from the courtroom transcript:

THE COURT:	*Ladies and Gentlemen of the jury, you should know that the defendant has been escorted into this courtroom in handcuffs and manacles because she refused to enter peacefully and of her own volition. You must not look upon these restraints as indicating in any way that she is guilty of the crime charged. I remind you that you must presume the defendant is innocent until the government proves otherwise. Ms. Hodge, the restraints will be removed if you agree to remain peaceably within the courtroom.*
HODGE:	I will cooperate, Your Honor.
THE COURT:	*Remove the restraints.*

Kathy was cooperative for the initial stages of the trial. Actually, there was no further trouble until Kathy took the stand. She exploded when the Judge granted the government's objection to strike one of my questions. At this point, Kathy grabbed a book from along side the witness box and hurled it at the judge. The court had Kathy removed from the witness stand and handcuffed to her chair.

THE COURT:	*Ms. Hodge, you will remain handcuffed to your seat until I have adequate assurances that you will control yourself.*
HODGE:	You're not giving me a fair trial.
THE COURT:	*Ladies and Gentlemen of the jury, please pay no attention to the defendant.*
HODGE:	Pay attention to everything that's prejudicial. I can't get a fair trial. You're not giving my attorney half a chance.
THE COURT:	*You will be bound and gagged if you continue. Now be quiet!*

HODGE:	I will not sit here quietly while you railroad me into jail. I know O'Brien paid you off!
THE COURT:	*You will be bound and gagged with one more outburst. Be quiet or you will be very sorry you ever set foot in this courtroom!*

At that point, Kathy proclaimed her constitutional right to freedom of speech and started to recite the Pledge of Allegiance. She was finally quieted when the bailiff taped her mouth shut. The gag was removed after Kathy promised to contain herself. It was only used for a few minutes.

Kathy claims that the gagging, handcuffing and manacling offended her Due Process rights to a fair and impartial trial. Her position was that the sight of her in these restraints prejudiced the jury. She insists that we appeal her conviction. I am not entirely convinced that Kathy's case is as clear-cut as she presents it. My partner, Mr. Lodge, researched the issue and found two cases—**Commonwealth v. Cruz** and **State v. Lee**. Please read the cases and answer the questions presented discussing whether the firm should handle Kathy's appeal. Your answers should address the following questions:

1. According to rules set forth in **State v. Lee**, is it permissible for the judge to merely gag Kathy rather than have her removed from the courtroom as the judge did in **State v. Lee?**

2. What are the pros and cons of the alternative disciplinary measures enumerated in **State v. Lee?** What do you think some of the considerations should be in determining which approach is the best to use against a disruptive defendant?

3. How does the approach taken to control Kathy compare with the approaches taken in **Lee** and **Cruz?**

4. Even if you do not agree with the approach used by the court, did Kathy's trial comply with the demands of Due Process?

COMMONWEALTH OF PENNSYLVANIA V. CRUZ
311 A.2D 692 (PA. 1973)

CRUZ CONTENDS HE IS ENTITLED TO A NEW TRIAL because of the prejudicial effect of being seen handcuffed in the courtroom by members of the jury.

Appellant was tried with a co-defendant on the charge of possession of marijuana. The jury found the appellant guilty and the co-defendant not guilty.

The record reveals that appellant was hand-cuffed when the court recessed for the day while a portion of the jury was still in the jury box and on the following morning he was brought into the courtroom while handcuffed.

The early Common Law recognized that a defendant in a criminal trial had the right to appear in a court free of restraint. "The prisoner must be brought to the bar without irons and all matter of shackles or bonds unless there be danger of escape…" 2 **Hale's Pleas of the Crown**, 219 (1678). Such has been the rule in this country from the time that issue was first discussed.

Under ordinary circumstances a defendant's freedom from handcuffs, shackles or manacles is an important component of a fair and impartial trial, and restraints should not be employed except to prevent him from escaping or injuring others, and to maintain a quiet and peaceable trial.

In *State v. Roberts*, 86 N.J. Super. 159, 206 A.2d 200, 205 (1965), defendant was compelled to appear before the jury with his feet and hands shackled, the court stated: "In any case where the trial judge, in the exercise of sound discretion, determines that the defendant must be handcuffed or shackled, it is of the essence that he instruct the jury in the clearest and most emphatic terms [which the Judge did not do in the instant case] that it give such restraint no consideration whatever in assessing the proofs and determining guilt. This is the least that can be done toward insuring a fair trial. It may be doubted whether any jury, even with the best of cautionary instructions, can ever dismiss from its mind that the accused has appeared before it in handcuffs or chains. His being restrained must carry obvious implications even to the most fair-minded of juries. Unless the situation is so exceptional as to call for shackles, the trial court should instead arrange for additional guards in the courtroom for the pro-tection of all present and the prevention of any disorder or escape."

Furthermore, the ABA Project on Standards for Criminal Justice, Trial by Jury, Approved Draft (1968) suggests:

"[A]s confusion or embarrassment of the person and jury prejudice can result from wearing the clothing of a convict or prisoner just as it can from the wearing of shackles." (In Eaddy, the defendant was brought into court wearing coveralls with the words "County Jail" in large letters across the back).

In *Commonwealth v. Keeler*, **216 Pa.Super. 193 at 195-196, 264 A.2d 407 at 409 (1970)** we held: "A defendant in prison garb gives the appearance of one whom the state regards as deserving to be so attired. It brands him as convicted in the state's eyes It insinuates that the defendant has been arrested not only on the charge being tried but also on other charges for which he is being incarcerated." A clear analogy can be drawn to the appellant being handcuffed in front of the jury and the "prison garb" cases.

The Commonwealth cites *Commonwealth v. Carter*, **219 Pa.Super. 280, 281 A.2d 75 (1971)** in support of its position that a mistrial need not be granted in such a case. That case is inapposite to the appeal. In *Carter*, supra, our court upheld the action of the trial judge in dismissing two jurors who had witnessed the appellant being placed in handcuffs, during a trial recess. The trial judge determined that the dismissed jurors had not discussed the observed event with the other jurors.

Prejudice could have easily been created in the minds of the jurors due to the disparity between the co-defendant and the appellant in that co-defendant appeared in court free of restraints. Furthermore, the record does not indicate appellant was violent while in court, that he conducted himself in an unruly manner, or that he threatened to escape.

For the aforementioned reasons, the judgment of sentence is reversed and the case remanded for a new trial.

STATE OF LOUISIANA V. JAMES LEE
395 SO.2D 700 (LA. 1980)

ON JULY 15, 1977, JAMES ALLEN LEE WAS INDICTED for First Degree Murder. A twelve person jury found the defendant guilty as charged on June 29, 1979. The trial court sentenced the defendant to life imprisonment and the defendant appealed.

The facts incident to the murder are not at issue. The defendant was convicted of shooting Jerry Dennis, the owner of the Shady Oaks Cafe, following an altercation over missing car keys. The defendant turned himself in to police several hours later.

During trial, the defendant persistently interrupted the proceedings by pseudo-Biblical rhetoric and singing the Star Spangled Banner. After numerous warnings by the trial judge, Lee was removed to an adjoining room where he could hear the trial proceedings. After continued outbursts and interruptions from the next room, the defendant was bound and gagged. The jury found him guilty of First Degree Murder.

The defendant urges that the trial court erred in removing the defendant from the courtroom during trial, in overruling defense counsel's objection regarding an alleged inability to communicate effectively with his client, and in having the defendant handcuffed, shackled and gagged. The defendant argues that these measures effectively deprived him of the right to be present during trial, and to confront the witnesses against him.

The selection of prospective jurors as well as the trial proceedings were repeatedly interrupted by defendant's disruptive behavior. He began singing the Star Spangled Banner in front of the prospective jurors. Despite a reprimand and warning from the judge the defendant continued by reciting scripture. The judge initially ordered the defendant removed from the courtroom, but reconsidered and warned both defendant and counsel that he would give Lee another chance but remove him if the behavior continued. After additional outbursts and warnings the defendant was ordered removed to an adjoining room, with the understanding that he would be allowed to return once he agreed to act in an acceptable manner. Arrangements were made for the proceedings to be piped into the adjoining room and an attorney was appointed to sit with the defendant. Jury selection continued and the defendant again began singing the National Anthem, and speaking in a ministerial fashion. Though these outbursts were in the adjoining room, they were loud enough to disrupt proceedings in the courtroom. The defendant at this point had been handcuffed and shackled following an altercation with deputies. The trial judge stated that he had no alternative but to consider gagging the defendant. After some discussion, however, the judge proceeded without having defendant Lee gagged. At some point the defendant was returned to the courtroom only to interrupt the proceedings again by singing the National Anthem. Again the judge warned him that he would be removed and gagged unless he controlled himself. The defendant's disruptive behavior continued throughout the proceedings, and included a prolonged interruption of the state's closing argument. In light of the innumerable interruptions at all stages of the court proceedings it appears that the defendant's arguments objecting to the measures taken by the court are without merit.

In *Illinois v. Allen*, **397 U.S. 337, 90 S.Ct. 1057, 25 L.Ed.2d 353 (1970)** the United States Supreme Court held that "a defendant can lose his right to be present at trial if, after he has been warned by the judge that he will be removed if he continues his disruptive behavior, he nevertheless insists on conducting himself in a manner so disorderly, disruptive, and disrespectful of the court that his trial cannot be carried on with him in the courtroom.

The Court concluded that "trial judges confronted with disruptive, contumacious, stubbornly defiant defendants must be given sufficient discretion to meet the circumstances of each cases." Noting also the absence of a panacea for dealing with disruptive defendants, the court further observed that at least three constitutionally acceptable avenues exist for dealing with a defiant defendant:

   (1) bind and gag him, thereby keeping him present;

   (2) cite him for contempt;

   (3) take him out of the courtroom until he promises to conduct himself properly.

The defendant was given every opportunity to remain in the courtroom without restraint if he conducted himself properly. The handcuffs and shackles were utilized only after the defendant struggled with deputies. The judge saw further outbursts as a security risk and only then allowed the restraints. Considering the incessant outbursts it appears the judge acted with considerable restraint. When the defendant was held in an adjoining room he was able to hear the trial proceedings and was accompanied by a second attorney to relay any messages to lead counsel in the courtroom. This Court has stated that: "We recognize that the use of restraining devices, including manacles, is within the sound discretion of the trial judge. In the absence of a clear showing of abuse of discretion on the part of the trial judge, a conviction will not be disturbed on appeal because of restraint imposed upon defendant." *State v. Burnett*, **337 So.2d 1096 at 1099 (La. 1976).** There was no such abuse of discretion here.

We find these assignments to be without merit.

ANSWER SHEET
PROBLEM FOUR—B

Name _____   **Please Print Clearly**

1. Is it permissible for the judge to merely gag Kathy rather than have her removed from the courtroom?

_____

_____

_____

_____

_____

_____

_____

_____

_____

2. What are the pros and cons of the alternative disciplinary measures discussed in *State v. Lee*? What do you think some of the considerations should be in determining which approach is the best to use against a disruptive defendant?

_____

_____

_____

_____

_____

_____

_____

_____

_____

3. How does the approach taken to control Kathy compare with the approaches taken in **Lee** and **Cruz**?

_____

_____

_____

_____

_____

_____

_____

_____

4. Even if you do not agree with the approach used by the court, did Kathy's trial comply with the demands of Due Process?

_____

_____

_____

_____

_____

_____

_____

_____

_____

SECTION 4.9
PROBLEM CASES

1.   A city passed an ordinance limiting the number of dogs that can be kept at a residential premise to two dogs over the age of six months. A person, who wishes to keep three or four adult dogs at home, must obtain a permit. Holt runs a "stud service" from her house and rescues Newfoundland dogs until homes can be found for them. When the law went into effect, she had twelve adult dogs at her residence. Is this ordinance constitutional? *Mary Holt v. City of Sauk Rapids,* **559 N.W. 2d 444 (Minn. Ct. App. 1997).**

2.   A city passed an ordinance prohibiting the maintenance of a nuisance, and the storage of abandoned or junked motor vehicles, is automatically considered a nuisance. A city inspector found a stove, water heater and car parts on the property owned by Kadash. This individual was then convicted of violating the ordinance. Do the actions of Kadash constitute a nuisance? Is the ordinance constitutional? *George Kadash v. City of Williamsport,* **340 A.2d 617 (Pa. Cmwlth. 1975).**

3.   During Tribblett's criminal trial for robbery, a spectator stood up and began screaming. "He threatened my life. He's going to jail." The individual continued her ravings as she was physically removed from the courtroom. The court admonished the jurors to eliminate the outburst from their minds and to base their verdict solely on the evidence. The attorney for Tribblett moved for mistrial and claimed that his client's procedural due process rights to a fair trial were violated. Do you agree? *Commonwealth of Pennsylvania v. Tribblett,* **363 A.2d 12123 (Pa. Super. 1976).**

4.   Davis was charged with the brutal beating and shooting death of a woman and her two children. The case was the subject of enormous pre-trial publicity, including the fact that Davis had failed a lie detector test, and had a history of violent crime. During the jury selection process, ten out of forty jurors admitted to having prior knowledge about the case. The trial judge, however, refused to allow these jurors to be questioned individually by defense counsel. As a result, the defense was precluded from learning the specific information that the potential jurors had heard or read . Was the right of Davis to a fair and impartial jury violated by the trial court's action? *Allen Davis v. State of Florida,* **473 U.S. 913 (1985).**

5.   Dixon was convicted of attempted robbery. During the course of the crime, he brandished a gun so Dixon was sentenced to an automatic five year imprisonment for the weapon's offence. The state legislative had decided to impose a mandatory sentencing scheme for the use of a firearm when committing a crime in order to protect human life. Dixon challenged the statute as being a violation of his due process rights. Specifically, he argues that the law in-

fringes on his constitutional rights because the legislation has removed the discretion from the judge to sentence a defendant to a shorter term in jail. In other words, the law prohibits a court from imposing a shorter sentence because of mitigating factors such as a first time offender. Does the statute violate Dixon's substantive due process rights? *Commonwealth of Pennsylvania v. Carl Cooke,* **492 A.2d 63 (Pa. Super. 1985).**

SECTION **4.10**
INTERNET REFERENCES

For more information about the topics in this Chapter, see:

A. *The Legislative Process*

- **http://www.loc.gov**
  The Library of Congress maintains a web site which provides access to legislative information, the copyright office, the library and other governmental related functions.

- **http://lcweb.loc.gov/global/legislative/congress.html**
  This is the web site for the Unites States Legislative Branch which provides detailed information about the U.S. Congress, Committees of Congress, Congressional Organizations, and the legislative process.

- **http://thomas.loc.gov**
  This site provides legislative information. An interested party may look up summaries, of the law the status of legislation, text of bills, Committee reports, and other information concerning pending legislation.

B. *Due Process*

- **http://www.wld.com/conbus/weal/wdueproc.htm**
  West Legal Dictionary provides a fairly detailed discussion of Due Process at this internet address.

- **http://encarta.msn.com/find/Concise.asp?ti=(04950000)**
  Encarta Encyclopedia maintains a site that provides a history of the Due Process Clause.

- **http://supreme.findlaw.com/constitution/amendment14**
  Find Law provides an Internet link which contains an in-depth look into the Fourteenth Amendment, including its text, history, and related cases.

- **http://supreme.findlaw.com/constitution/amendment05**
  This web site deals with the Fifth Amendment and provides a detailed listing of the various issues that arise from this Constitutional provision.

CHAPTER 5

TORTS

"That great principle of the common law...declares that it is your duty so to use your own rights as not to cause injury to other people."

Sir Charles Williams
Grey v. North Eastern Rail Co.
48 L.T.R. 905 (1883)
"The Quotable Lawyer"

A **tort** is a private civil wrong committed against another for which the law recognizes an award of money damages. The law of torts establishes standards of conduct for members of society for different types of activities. These standards are created either by statute or by court pronouncement. There are two types of civil wrongs: unintentional and intentional. An unintentional tort is called negligence. An intentional tort is one that the wrongdoer does on purpose and includes such actions as defamation, invasion of privacy, battery, and false imprisonment.

**SECTION 5.2
NEGLIGENCE**

Negligence, generally speaking, is the failure to do what a reasonable person would do under the circumstances. While this definition may seem vague, several principles do emerge. The mere happening of an accident is not negligence. Rather, three elements must be present:

1. A duty must be owed;

2. There must be a breach of that duty; and

3. The negligence must be the proximate cause of the harm.

The plaintiff has the burden of proving by the preponderance of the evidence all three elements. Suppose Joe Hodge is stopped for a traffic light when Peter Christopher loses control of his vehicle and rams the rear of Joe's car. The force of the impact propels Joe forward, and he sustains a whiplash type injury. Is Christopher negligent? Yes. Christopher owed a duty to drive his car carefully and avoid hitting another vehicle. Christopher breached that duty by striking the rear of the Hodge vehicle. Finally, the negligence of Christopher was the proximate cause of Joe's neck injury. Not all cases, however, are so easy to prove, and a more detailed examination of each element of negligence is required.

SECTION 5.3
DUTY OF CARE

Duty of care establishes the type of behavior a person must exhibit in a given situation. The basic rule is that a person must conform to the standard of care of a "reasonable person under the circumstances." This duty can vary from case to case depending upon the age of the actor, the person's expertise, and the specific situation.

Generally, the law does not make a distinction concerning the standard of care of adults of different ages. A 65 year old man will be held to the same standard of care as a person 25 years of age in driving a car. That standard of care is simply the "average driver." A professional, however, is held to a higher standard of care when he or she is engaged in a professional capacity. That person is held to the standard of care of the average professional. For example, a neurosurgeon who makes a mistake during surgery is held to the standard of care of the average neurosurgeon and not to the standard of care of the average person performing surgery.

Children develop differently each year of their lives. There is a vast difference in motor skills between a child of six and a child of twelve. Therefore, minors are held to a different standard than that of the average adult. A minor is held to the standard of care of a child of similar age, intelligence, and experience. The exception to this rule is when a child engages in adult activity such as the driving of a car or the flying of an airplane. In those cases, children are held to the standard of care of the average person.

Not ever case in which a health care practitioner is sued gives rise to a case of malpractice. For instance, a doctor who is involved in a car accident is held to the standard of care of the average driver and not the average doctor driving a car. In *Newland v. Azan*, the court had to consider whether a dentist who sexually assaults a patient can be sued for malpractice since his conduct was unacceptable in the practice of dentistry.

BRENDA NEWLAND v. NOHAUD AZAN, D.D.S.
957 S.W. 2d 377 (Mo. Ct. App. 1997)

BRENDA NEWLAND SOUGHT DENTAL TREATMENT from Dr. Nohaud Azan, a dentist, for a root canal and related dental procedures. Newland alleged that on May 8, 1995, while she was in the dental chair, Dr. Azan sexually assaulted her after giving her several painkiller shots. Newland alleged that Dr. Azan touched her pubic area, kissed her, caressed her cheek and hand, and made sexually suggestive comments. All of these events occurred while Dr. Azan was treating Newland and performing dental services.

Newland filed a petition for professional negligence. Dr. Azan filed a motion for summary judgment (to dismiss the claim).

Newland must show that Dr. Azan's acts fell below the requisite standard of care for a dentist. For a health care worker, the standard of care requires the worker to use the degree of skill and learning ordinarily used under the same or similar circumstances by members of the worker's profession. *Washington v. Barnes Hosp.*, **897 S.W.2d 611, 615 (Mo. banc 1995).** Expert testimony generally must be introduced to establish the standard of care in a medical negligence case. Edward Mosby, D.D.S., an expert witness retained by Newland, testified in his deposition that the behavior of Dr. Azan fell below the standard of care of a practicing dentist. However, Dr. Mosby only testified that Dr. Azan's sexual conduct fell below the standard of care for a dentist. Significantly, he did not testify that Dr. Azan's dental services fell below the requisite standard of care.

This is a case of first impression in Missouri. However, several jurisdictions have decided cases with facts similar to those presented here. In these cases, the issue was whether the dentist's malpractice insurance covered injuries resulting from a sexual assault on a patient that took place while the dentist was performing dental services.

The courts considered whether sexual assault constituted "professional services" rendered by the dentist, for the purpose of determining coverage by the insurance policy. All of the courts found that "professional services" did not include sexual assault. While the insurance coverage issue differs from the issue presented here, we find the reasoning of these cases persuasive in determining whether Dr. Azan's sexual conduct could fall below the standard of care for a dentist.

Whether an act results from a professional service is determined by focusing on the act itself, rather than the place where the act occurred. The fact that an act occurred in a professional's office does not automatically transmute the act into a professional service. Likewise, when there is a complaint of malpractice, attention should focus on the act or service performed rather than the fact that the alleged wrongdoer was a dentist because "the scope of professional services does not include all forms of a medical professional's conduct simply because he or she is a dentist." *Roe v. Federal Ins. Co.*, **587 N.E.2d at 217;** Therefore, the fact that Dr. Azan is a dentist and the sexual conduct took place in his office is not determinative of liability in this case.

There must be some causal connection between the act that caused the harm and the nature of the dentist-patient relationship. That is, it must be a dental act or service that caused the harm, not an act or service that requires no professional skill. Newland's allegations of assault and battery do not describe professional services. Rather, the allegations present "factual issues capable of resolution without application of the standard of care prevalent in the medical community."

Newland does not allege that the actual dental services, including the root canal and related tooth and gum care, were not properly done or performed or that Dr. Azan lacked the skill and learning of a dentist to perform a root canal. Therefore, Newland has failed to show that Dr. Azan's conduct fell below the standard of care for a dentist.

Because we find that Newland failed to show that Dr. Azan's acts fell below the requisite standard of care for a dentist, we find it unnecessary to consider whether she has met the negligence and causation elements of her dental malpractice claim.

The defendant's motion for a partial summary judgment is granted.

Establishing a duty of care is an essential element in every claim for the tort of negligence. This duty can differ depending upon the circumstances. In carrying out the duties of one's trade, a professional is held to a higher standard than an average person and a child is generally held to a lower standard of care than an adult. It is not always possible, however, to establish that a duty of care is owed to a person just because an individual is harmed by the actions or lack of actions of another.

Drug testing in the work place is becoming increasing popular among employers with about 40% of the working force being subjected to drug testing. Whether a person obtains the job or keeps an existing position can hinge on the outcome of the test. If a business refuses to hire a perspective employee based upon the results of a drug-screening test that is improperly labeled or tested, is the laboratory responsible to the aggrieved worker? In other words, if the testing service is hired by the business to perform the drug screening so that no professional relationship exits between the laboratory and the perspective employee, does the drug screening service owe a duty to the job applicant in the event of a lab mistake? This is the issue in the following case.

ROBERT NEY V. AXELROD AND MEDTOX LABORATORIES, INC.
723 A.2D 719 (PA. SUPER. 1999)

ON JULY 31, 1997, ROBERT NEY FILED a negligence action against Appellees Axelrod and Medtox. Axelrod and Medtox had been hired by Ney's prospective employer, Sulkatronic Chemical, Inc., to perform pre-employment drug screening on Ney's urine samples. While Ney had been offered a job at Sulkatronic, the employer required drug screening as a final stage in the employment-hiring process. When Ney's urine samples tested positive for barbiturates, his application for employment was denied.

In his complaint, Ney alleges that Appellees negligently performed the drug screening tests; he asserts that he had never ingested any illegal substances, making it impossible to test "positively." Ney also claims that the Appellees' negligence precluded him from obtaining employment at a significantly higher salary at Sulkatronic than his present job.

The defendants filed motions for summary judgment alleging that they did not owe Ney a duty since they had been hired by Sulkatronic, a third party, to perform the drug screening tests. On May 29, 1998, the trial court granted summary judgment in favor of Appellees. On appeal, Ney presents the following issue for our review:

> Where a prospective employee is damaged by the improper labeling and testing of a urine sample and the results improperly recorded deny him the offered employment position, should not those negligent parties responsible be liable to the prospective employee for their negligence?

Ney claims that as a matter of public policy Appellees owed him a duty of care in handling his urine sample and reading the results of the test. Specifically, Ney asserts that as a result of Appellees' negligence he was denied employment at Sulkatronic and will be detrimentally affected in his pursuit of future employment.

To establish a viable cause of action in negligence, the pleader must aver in his complaint the following elements:

1. A duty, or obligation, recognized by the law, requiring the actor to conform to a certain standard of conduct, for the protection of others against unreasonable risks.

2. A failure on the person's part to conform to the standard required: a breach of the duty.

3. A reasonably close causal connection between the conduct and the resulting injury.

4. Actual loss or damage resulting to the interest of another.

Where a third party has sponsored a medical examination of a person and the person later alleges negligence on the part of the physician who performed the examination, that person cannot succeed on a negligence cause of action. *Tomko v. Marks*, **412 Pa. Super. 54, 602 A.2d 890 (Pa. Super. 1992).** In Tomko, our court held that where there is no therapeutic purpose for medical services provided and no evidence of a resulting professional relationship between the medical provider and the plaintiff, we will impose no duty and, therefore, no resultant liability on the provider.

In the present case, Ney did not contract for Appellees' services or seek or receive medical advice or treatment from Appellees. In fact, it is uncontroverted that the drug screening was performed by Appellees at the behest of Ney's prospective employer that required such testing as a matter of routine procedure for its hiring

process. Accordingly, Ney did not have the required physician-patient relationship based upon a therapeutic purpose that would give rise to a duty on the part of Appellees.

Ney claims that the Appellees' duty to properly perform the drug screening was owed not only to the party with whom it contracted (i.e., Ney's prospective employer), but also to him because of the negative effects it will have upon his future applications for employment.

Based upon the facts of this case, we are not willing to create a theory of liability for negligent doctors or medical laboratories that have contracted with third parties for employment-related testing. Such causes of action do not identify a substantial harm to an identifiable and readily discernible class of plaintiffs such that we feel compelled to create liability based on a public policy rationale

Furthermore, we are reticent to lend credence to future plaintiffs' claims that they have suffered a "loss of employment advancement or opportunity" in such a situation where a plaintiff has not passed the final stages in a hiring process, and, therefore, is not even an "employee." In fact, "it has always been the rule that an employer may be selective about the persons he employs as long as he does not unlawfully discriminate among the applicants." *Philadelphia Electric Co. v. English*, **68 Pa. Commw. 212, 448 A.2d 701 at 708.** As such, our decision today upholds the principles underlying this Commonwealth's "employment-at-will" doctrine and freedom in employment-related decisions.

Accordingly, the trial court properly granted summary judgment because it is clear that Appellees are entitled to judgment as a matter of law. Order affirmed.

Does the law impose a duty upon a person to go to the aid of another in trouble? The cases are well documented of people who turn their back on victims of crimes, the injured and sick. This conduct is morally reprehensible but is it actionable in a civil lawsuit? Generally, there is no legal duty to aid or protect another.

The law, however, does require a person who harms another or places another in peril to go to that individual's assistance. A legal duty is also imposed in those cases where a special relationship exists between the parties. For example, a parent must go to the aid of a child, a spouse must help the other spouse, and an employer must protect an employee.

Must a physician stop and render emergency aid to the victim of a car accident? Despite the doctor's specialized training, the answer is no. Physicians are reluctant to become involved because of the fear of being sued for malpractice. To encourage health care professionals to render emergency help many states have passed "Good Samaritan" statutes, which impose liability only in the event of gross misconduct.

The following Pennsylvania law is an example:

8331. MEDICAL GOOD SAMARITAN CIVIL IMMUNITY.

a.   **General rule**—Any physician or any other practitioner of the healing arts or any registered nurse, licensed by any state, who happens by chance upon the scene of an emergency or who is present when an emergency occurs and who, in good faith, renders emergency care at the scene of the emergency, shall not be liable for any civil damages as a result of any acts or omissions by such physician or practitioner or registered nurse in rendering the emergency care, except any acts or omissions intentionally designed to harm or any grossly negligent acts or omissions which result in harm to the person receiving emergency care.

This limited immunity also extends to a lay person rendering emergency aid if that individual possesses a current certificate evidencing the successful completion of a course in first aid or basic life support sponsored by the American National Red Cross or a similar organization. A lay person will not enjoy the protection of the Good Samaritan statute if the emergency aid extends beyond one's specialized training. For instance, a person trained in CPR cannot perform open-heart surgery or administer intravenous drugs to regulate the rhythm of the heart.

WILLIAM FRIELDS V. ST. JOSEPH'S HOSPITAL AND MEDICAL CENTER
305 N. J. SUPER. 244 (1997)

PLAINTIFF APPEALS FROM ORDERS granting summary judgment in favor of defendants St. Joseph's Hospital (Hospital) and the City of Paterson (City). The motion judge ruled that the mobile intensive care unit personnel from the Hospital and the emergency medical technicians from the City who responded to plaintiff's call for assistance were immune from liability pursuant to statute. We affirm.

On September 15, 1990, William T. Frields (Billy) arrived at his father's residence in Paterson. Soon thereafter, Billy reported to his father that he felt dizzy and collapsed on the kitchen floor. His father noticed that his son's breathing was irregular and instructed one of his daughters to call an ambulance. Mr. Frields attempted to assist his son's breathing and massaged his back until emergency personnel arrived.

A Mobile Intensive Care Unit (MICU) from the Hospital and an Emergency Medical Technician (EMT) team from the City arrived in response to Fried's call. The MICU team noted that Billy had vomited and was incontinent before their arrival. Believing that Billy exhibited signs of a drug overdose, the MICU personnel administered 2mg of Narcan to counteract the effect of any narcotic. Soon thereafter, Billy "woke up."

It is undisputed that when Billy became responsive he resisted mightily the efforts of the emergency personnel to subdue him and to transfer him to an ambulance. Several men, including a police officer on the scene, were required to restrain him. Once restrained, the emergency personnel were able to transport him to the ambulance. Billy arrived at the Hospital between 7:50 and 7:55 p.m. He died at 9:02 p.m. An autopsy revealed that he died from a subarachnoid hemorrhage.

Mr. Frields filed a wrongful death and survival action against the Hospital and the City based on the actions of the Hospital and City emergency personnel on September 15, 1990. He complained that the emergency personnel used excessive force in their attempt to restrain his son. The motion judge dismissed the complaint on the ground that the emergency personnel were immune from liability pursuant to the terms of the Good Samaritan Act.

The Legislature has granted qualified immunity to a wide range of persons who provide medical assistance in emergency situations. Volunteers and paid professionals who respond to a medical emergency and render treatment are immunized. This statute is commonly known as the Good Samaritan Act. It provides that any individual, including licensed health care professionals, or any member of a volunteer first aid or rescue quad who in *good faith* renders medical care at the scene of an accident or emergency to a victim is immune from damages in a civil action as a result of any act or omission by the person rendering the medical care.

It is undisputed that the Hospital personnel were members of a mobile intensive care unit and that the City personnel qualify as EMT-intermediates. Therefore, the inquiry is whether they acted in good faith.

"Good faith" has been defined as "honesty of purpose and integrity of conduct without knowledge, either actual or sufficient to demand inquiry, that the conduct is wrong." *Marley v. Borough of Palmyra,* **193 N.J.Super. 271, 294, 473 A.2d 554 (Law Div.1983).** Summary judgment, however, is appropriate when the employee demonstrates that his/her actions "were objectively reasonable or that [he] performed them with subjective good faith." *Canico v. Hurtado*, **144 N.J. 361, 365, 676 A.2d 1083 (1996).** This test recognizes that even a person who acted negligently is entitled to a qualified immunity, if he acted in an objectively reasonable manner.

Applying these principles to the proofs offered by plaintiff and drawing all reasonable inferences in favor of plaintiff, we are satisfied that plaintiff presents proofs that the emergency personnel may have acted negligently; however, any negligence does not strip them of their immunity. Plaintiff contends that the emergency personnel used excessive force to restrain his son. He contends that his son could have been restrained sooner and with less force, if he had

been sedated. His expert, Dr. Steven M. Lomazow, supports this claim.

Plaintiff's expert does no more than state a case for paramedic or emergency personnel negligence. Coupled with his concession that the emergency personnel could not be expected to diagnose a subarachnoid hemorrhage in the field, plaintiff has failed to present any facts which create a genuine issue of material fact that defendants' employees did not act in an objectively reasonable manner. Accordingly, the City personnel were immune, and the Hospital employees were immune and summary judgment in favor of defendants was appropriate.

Affirmed.

Generally, a person does not owe a duty to go to the aid of another who is in a position of peril. There are exceptions to this rule such as when the person causes the harm or when there is a special relationship between the parties. Will liability attach, however, if a Good Samaritan is prevented by a third person from rendering emergency medical help to an ill person? Will the third person be responsible to the injured party when no duty existed to help the ill party in the first place? This is the issue in *Barnes v. Dungan.*

SHARON BARNES v. EARL DUGAN
90 N.Y.S.2D 338 (N.Y. 1999)

THIS IS AN APPEAL FROM AN ORDER of the Supreme Court, which denied defendant's motions to dismiss the complaint for failure to state a cause of action.

Sharon L. Barnes was an employee at defendant Peace Plantation Animal Sanctuary in October 1996 when she suffered a heart attack while on duty. Co-worker Jodi Seeley, certified to perform cardiopulmonary resuscitation, immediately re-

sponded and offered to resuscitate decedent but was prohibited from doing so by defendant Earl Dungan, her supervisor at Peace Plantation. Plaintiff (decedent's husband) contends that had Seeley been permitted to perform CPR, decedent would have survived the heart attack.

Plaintiff commenced this action alleging an intentional interference with lifesaving medical assistance. Prior to answering, defendant moved to dismiss the complaint pursuant to alleging that no legal duty existed which required them to render emergency medical assistance.

Notably, the complaint alleges that defendants affirmatively prevented Seeley, a co-employee, from administering CPR as opposed to a failure to provide or procure emergency medical assistance. Upon that basis, plaintiff contends that there existed a legal duty to refrain from interfering with Seeley, a third party, who was willing and able to render necessary medical assistance. The *Restatement of Torts* so defines that duty: "One who intentionally prevents a third person from giving to another aid necessary to prevent physical harm to him, is subject to liability for physical harm caused to the other by the absence of the aid which he has prevented the third person from giving."

Although no New York court has been directly confronted with this issue and we make no comment as to whether the allegations, taken as true, will ultimately be proven, we acknowledge the standard enunciated by *Riggs v. Colis* **(107 Idaho 1028, 695 P.2d 413),** which addressed this issue in a motion for summary judgment. There, in analyzing whether there was a breach of the aforementioned duty when the defendant prevented a bystander from providing emergency aid to the plaintiff while she was under attack, the court instructed that a viable claim must show "the necessary fact situation of three parties—the victim, a rescuer, and one who prevents or interferes with the rescuer—and the aid must have been actually prevented."

Here, notwithstanding the fact that both Dungan and Seeley were both employees of the Peace Plantation at the time that Dungan ordered Seeley not to render aid to the decedent, we find that an analysis of the claim based upon the *Riggs v. Colis* standard, Seeley may be found to have volunteered emergency medical thereby constituting the "rescuer" who was prevented or interfered with by Dungan from rendering needed medical aid to the decedent.

Accordingly, we affirm Supreme Court's order.

SECTION 5.4
HODGE v. FEELGOOD

PROBLEM FIVE—A

HODGE, DODGE AND LODGE
ATTORNEYS AT LAW
MEMORANDUM

To: Part-Time Law Clerks

From: Gregory Olan Dodge

Re: Estelle Hodge v. Dr. Donald Feelgood

Estelle Hodge wants to sue her neighbor, Dr. Feelgood. These are the facts:

A few weeks ago, Estelle Hodge went with her club to watch the crew races along the Schuylkill River. It was a perfect day for a picnic by the river. The women were dressed for the occasion in new outfits. Estelle still stood apart from the others, however, since her brightly colored hat was really something special. The only thing possibly outdoing the outfits was the food. Four Seasons catered the function and presented a magnificent display of salads, fruits and light pastries. In short, everything was in place for a great afternoon.

Everyone was enjoying themselves until midway through the race. For some unknown reason, Estelle decided to approach the bank of the Schuylkill. As she peered into the water, someone bumped Estelle, and she fell head first into the slimy river. As Estelle was bobbing up and down in the water-gasping for air-two of her companions ran to get help. One lady went to find the race officials, while the other screamed for a police officer. The rest of the crowd stood passively by and counted, in unison, the number of times Estelle surfaced.

At this time, Dr. Feelgood happened to be jogging along the bank of the river. When he heard the commotion, he stopped running to find out what was going on and to see if he could help. When he learned that a woman was drowning, Dr. Feelgood immediately went to her rescue. He jumped into the river, but Estelle was no longer visible. All that remained was her hat marking the spot where she went under water. Dr. Feelgood found the limp body and pulled Estelle to the surface of the water. As he started to drag her to shore, he realized for the first time that the drowning woman was Estelle. So he let her go. Dr. Feelgood swam away leaving Estelle to drown.

A few seconds later, the rescue squad arrived and quickly retrieved Estelle from the water. Once on land, they performed CPR. Eventually, things settled down. Estelle was emotionally distraught, but otherwise healthy.

Estelle claims that the doctor's aborted rescue effort caused her to suffer severe emotional trauma. The partial rescue, she claims, was more upsetting than the near drowning. Please read *Miller v. Arnal Corp.* and let me know if Estelle can successfully sue Dr. Feelgood. Your answer should include a discussion of the following questions: Does everyone have a duty to aid others in an emergency if they are capable of doing so? Even if Dr. Feelgood doesn't have a duty to help Estelle, does the fact that he started to rescue her affect his liability? Once someone starts to help, must they always continue the rescue effort? According to **Miller** what considerations are involved? How do these standards apply here?

CLINT MILLER V. ARNAL CORPORATION
129 ARIZ. 484 (1981)

O'CONNOR, Presiding Judge.

THIS IS AN APPEAL FROM A DENIAL OF A MOTION for a new trial following a jury verdict against the plaintiff and in favor of the defendant in an action alleging that the defendant willfully, negligently, and unreasonably terminated a rescue effort to assist the plaintiff.

The plaintiff, Clint Miller, and five companions hiked on Humphrey's Peak in the mountains near Flagstaff, Arizona, in December 1972. The group assembled for the hike in the parking lot of the Snow Bowl ski area and camped out overnight. The next morning, they began their hike and set up camp for the night of December 31 in a ravine at an elevation of approximately 11,200 to 11,500 feet. During the night a severe storm developed, with high winds, blowing snow and extremely low temperatures. Much of the group's shelter and equipment was lost or destroyed in the storm. The following morning, four members of the group including Douglas Richard, decided to descend the mountain and to return to the Snow Bowl and try to obtain assistance for Mr. Miller and another companion, Allison Clay. Mr. Miller had suffered from exposure and frostbite during the preceding night and he did not want to attempt to walk down the mountain. Ms. Clay decided to remain with Mr. Miller. The four who left the campsite arrived at the Snow Bowl lodge at approximately 1:45 p.m. on January 1, 1973. They contacted Danny Rich, the assistant Director of the ski patrol and an employee of the Snow Bowl, which was owned and operated by defendant, Arnal Corporation. Rich asked several other ski patrolmen whether they wanted to volunteer for the rescue attempt and told them to begin gathering their equipment

and warm clothing. He also telephoned the Coconino County Sheriff's Office to obtain assistance from their search and rescue unit. Richard told Rich that the plaintiff and Ms. Clay were camped somewhere near the top of the chair lift, indicating what he believed to be the general area on a map Rich showed him. In fact, the plaintiffs' location was a substantial distance farther around the mountain. Rich planned to use the ski chair lift to ascend the mountain, and then traverse on skis over to the stranded hikers. However, another storm was developing and the wind was blowing so hard that the chair life had been shut off. Rich asked his supervisor, Dave Kuntzleman, the defendant corporation's mountain manager, to start the ski lift for the rescue party to ascend. Kuntzleman refused on the ground that it was too dangerous in the existing high winds and he thought the chair lift cable might derail, and also because he wanted the ski patrol to remain on duty to protect skiers on Snow Bowl property. In making his decision, Kuntzleman testified that he was aware the hikers could suffer serious harm or death if they were forced to spend another night on the mountain. An argument ensued between Rich and Kuntzleman, but Kuntzleman refused to start the lift.

The Coconino County Sheriff's search and rescue party did not arrive at the Snow Bowl until approximately 5:30 p.m. Efforts were made to reach the two stranded hikers but the rescuers did not reach them until early morning on January 2. The storm during the night of January 1 was more severe than on the previous night. On arrival, the rescuers found Miller in serious condition with hypothermia and frostbite. Ms. Clay had frozen to death. As a result of his exposure, Mr. Miller lost all ten toes, other portions of both feet, and all fingers of his right hand.

Plaintiff contends that the jury instruction was improper. He claims he was put in a worse position by appellee's termination of a rescue attempt by its own ski patrol and the jury should have been allowed to compensate him for his loss of the chance of being rescued by the ski patrol. While he concedes that the law presently imposes no liability upon those who stand idly by and fail to rescue a stranger who is in danger, he distinguishes this situation by citing to **Restatement (Second) of Torts** Section 323, which reads:

> One who undertakes, gratuitously or for consideration, to render services to another which he should recognize as necessary for the protection of the other's person or things, is subject to liability to the other for physical harm resulting from his failure to exercise reasonable care to perform his undertaking, if:
>
> 1. his failure to exercise such care increases the risk of such harm, or
>
> 2. the harm is suffered because of the other's reliance upon the undertaking.

W. Prosser, "Handbook of the Law of Torts" Section 56 at 341-42 (4th ed. 1971) explains the general rule as follows:

> Thus far the difficulties of setting any standards of unselfish service to fellow man, and of making any workable rule to cover possible situations where fifty people might fail to rescue one, has limited any tendency to depart from the rule to cases where some special relation between the parties has afforded a justification for the creation of a duty, without any question of setting up a rule of universal application. Absent a spe-

cial relationship between the parties, the law imposes no duty to aid another. Some exceptions where a duty is imposed include the requirement that a carrier take reasonable affirmative steps to aid a passenger in peril, that an innkeeper aid his guest, and that a ship save a seaman who has fallen overboard. There is now respectable authority imposing the same duty upon a shopkeeper to his business visitor, upon a host to his social guest, upon a jailer to his prisoner, and upon a school to its pupil. There are undoubtedly other relations calling for the same conclusion.

Thus, the law seems to favor no liability for failure to aid another unless there is some special relationship between the parties which justifies the imposition of such a duty. However, once a rescuer gratuitously begins to render aid, he assumes certain obligations, and must act according to certain reasonable standards of care. According to "Restatement (Second) of Torts" Section 323, comment (c), this does not mean that the rescue service cannot be terminated once begun.

> The fact that the actor gratuitously starts in to aid another does not necessarily require him to continue his services. He is not required to continue them indefinitely, or even until he has done everything in his power to aid and protect the other. The actor may normally abandon his efforts at any time unless by giving the aid, he has put the other in a worse position than he was in before the actor attempted to aid him. His motives in discontinuing the services are immaterial. It is not necessary for him to justify his failure to continue the services by proving a privilege to do so, based upon his private concerns which would suffer from the continuance of

the service. He may without liability discontinue the services through mere caprice, or because of personal dislike or enmity toward the other.

Where, however, the actor's assistance has put the other in a worse position than he was in before, either because the actual danger of harm to the other has been increased by the partial performance, or because the other, in reliance upon the undertaking, has been induced to forego other opportunities of obtaining assistance, the actor is not free to discontinue his services where a reasonable man would not do so. He will then be required to exercise reasonable care to terminate his services in such a manner that there is no unreasonable risk of harm to the other, or to continue them until they can be so terminated.

There is no evidence that plaintiff relied on any rescue undertaking by defendant in the sense that he chose rescue by the ski patrol over any other available alternative. Plaintiff's companions did not rely on defendant by choosing not to pursue other possible avenues of rescue on his behalf. Defendant's employee Rich telephoned the county search and rescue unit almost immediately after plaintiff's companions arrived at the lodge. The county unit then began organizing equipment and personnel for its rescue attempt. The evidence shows that the county's rescue efforts were not delayed, discouraged, or prevented by any act of the defendant's.

Plaintiff urges us to hold the law in the jurisdiction to be that a rescue effort, once begun in any manner and in any degree whatsoever, may not thereafter be abandoned or terminated if it would leave the other person with an unreasonable risk of serious harm, even though there has been no reliance on the rescue effort and the extent of the risk has not been increased. We decline to so hold. As discussed above, there is no duty to rescue an endangered stranger. Thus, there is no basis upon which to hold defendant liable. The corporation cannot be held liable for interfering with another rescue attempt simply because it chose to abandon its own rescue attempt.

The order of the trial court is affirmed.

What duty does an owner or possessor of land owe to a person who comes upon the premises? The answer will depend on whether the individual is a trespasser, licensee, or business visitor.

A **trespasser** is one who comes upon the premises of another without consent and with no legal right to be on the property. For instance, a burglar is a trespasser. The only obligation a land owner or possessor of property owes to a trespasser is to avoid injuring the person through willful and wanton misconduct. Suppose Joe Hodge fills his pool with piranha to keep trespassers out of the water. Will Joe be liable if someone climbs over the fence, dives into the water and is attacked by the man-eating fish? According to *Katco v. Briney*, the answer is yes. The conduct of Joe Hodge is willful and wanton.

A **licensee** is a person who comes on the property of another with the owner's consent or with the legal right to be on the land. The most common type of licensee is a social guest or a person walking on the sidewalk. The owner or possessor of land is liable to a licensee for a defect on the property that the owner or possessor of land knew of or should have known of, and guest is not liable to discover. For example, if the owner of a house is having the basement steps repaired and fails to warn the licensee of the repairs, the owner is liable if the guest falls. On the other hand, a thief who breaks into the same house and falls down the basement steps will not collect damages from the homeowner since the failure to warn the thief is not willful and wanton misconduct.

A **business visitor** is one who enters the premises for a business purpose. A person who goes to a department store to shop is a business visitor. In these circumstances, the landowner or possessor of land is liable for a defect that he knew of or should have known of, and the visitor is not liable to discover. While this standard seems to be the same as that owed to a licensee, the difference is that the business establishment owes a duty to make a reasonable inspection of the premises to make sure it is safe for the business visitor.

Businesses open to the public, such as department stores, theaters, and food markets are particularly susceptible to having debris strewn on the floor. The proprietor of such a business must maintain the premises in a reasonable safe condition. The mere fact that a harmful condition may exist on the property, however, does not establish negligence on the part of the store owner. The injured patron must prove that the dangerous condition existed for such a sufficient period of time that a reasonable inspection would have discovered the problem. For instance, a puddle of milk on the floor of a supermarket that is partially dried, filled with foot prints, and contains shopping cart wheel marks, would establish constructive notice on the part of the merchant of the dangerous situation. After all, this condition could only occur after a lengthy passage of time. On the other hand, a puddle of white milk that was not created by the actions of the merchant and is not soiled in anyway, would indicate a very recent spill for which the supermarket will have no liability. Not all cases are this clear. Consider the following case in which a fan slipped on refuse while walking near a souvenir stand at Yankees Stadium. The issue is whether or not the Yankees had actual or constructive notice of the dangerous condition.

ANNA GIAMBRONE V. NEW YORK YANKEES
581 N.Y.S. 2D 756 (N.Y. 1992)

ANNA GIAMBRONE ALLEGES THAT SHE SLIPPED and fell on refuse while walking near refreshment and souvenir stands in Yankee Stadium. Although an accident report, made that same day by Yankee's employees and signed by Giambrone, indicated that she slipped on a piece of paper, both at her examination before trial and in her affidavit in opposition to the Yankee's motion for summary judgment, plaintiff stated that she slipped on a paper cup and a frankfurter which, upon examination, appeared to be crushed and dirty.

The Yankees moved for summary judgment, contending that there is no evidence that it had notice of the debris on which plaintiff fell. In support of its position, defendant relies on *Gordon v. American Museum of Natural History,* 67 N.Y. 2d 836, which held that, where the plaintiff slipped on wax paper from a concession stand located between two tiers of steps, neither a general awareness of litter in area nor the fact that plaintiff observed other papers on other steps approximately 10 minutes before his fall was sufficient to establish notice of the particular piece of paper on which plaintiff slipped.

Giambrone argues that the instant case is distinguishable in that, unlike the plaintiff in Gordon, she described the debris on which she

fell as crushed and dirty, suggesting that it had been there for a substantial period of time. Moreover, plaintiff indicated that the litter in the area had not been removed since the seventh inning. Giambrone argues, together with evidence that only 14 persons were assigned to clean the entire arena during game time, suggests that the debris was permitted to remain on the ground for a substantial period and raises a triable issue of fact regarding the Yankee's notice of the condition.

Summary judgment was properly denied. The general rule is that for a landlord to be held liable for a defective condition upon the premises, he must have actual or constructive notice of the condition for such a period of time that, in the exercise of reasonable care, he should have corrected it. Where the defendant causes or permits a temporary slippery condition to exist, there may be liability—which issue is or the jury to decide. Where the record contains some evidence tending to show that defendant had constructive notice of a dangerous condition which allegedly caused injuries to its customer, a prima facie case is made out. Only where the record is "palpably insufficient" to establish actual or constructive notice that the condition existed for a sufficient period to afford the defendant, in the exercise of reasonable care, an opportunity to discover and correct it can it be said that there is no factual issue to submit to the trier of fact. Thus, where the plaintiff alleged that he tripped on a piece of paper, the case should not have been submitted to a jury on the theory of actual or constructive notice where the trial record contained no evidence that anyone, including plaintiff, observed the piece of white paper prior to the accident.

In this case, Giambrone alleges that she observed litter on the walkway in the vicinity of a refreshment stand during the seventh inning and that the condition of the area remained unchanged at the time she fell which, was "several innings" later. This matter is factually similar to *Kelsey v. Port Auth. of New York and New Jersey*, in which the plaintiff "testified that she saw cigarette butts, paper cups and wetness on two steps of the stairway the first time she descended, but on her second descent some 15 or 20 minutes later, she stepped on something that slipped, causing her fall" **(383 N.Y. S.2d 347).** This court concluded that, "[a]lthough`plaintiff was unable to specify the precise condition which caused her fall," the jury could reasonably infer that the condition present when she first descended the stairway remained unchanged for 15 or 20 minutes was the proximate cause of the fall.

The record in this case is sufficient to raise an issue which respect to the Yankees' constructive notice of the defective condition alleged to have caused Giambrone's injury, requiring its submission to the trier of fact. In this regard, any asserted inconsistency in Giambrone's account of events and the accident report bearing her signature, together with the question of her comprehension of written English, merely present issues of fact for resolution at trial.

THOMAS A. WHELAN V. CLARENCE E. VAN NATTA
382 S.W. 2D 205 (KY. CT. APP. 1964)

MONTGOMERY, J.

THOMAS A. WHELAN SUED CLARENCE E. VAN NATTA, doing business as Van Natta Grocery, for damages resulting from injuries sustained when Whelan fell into an open stair well in the floor of Van Natta's grocery. Whelan appeals from a judgment in favor of Van Natta. He contends that he was an invitee on the premises and was entitled to be warned of the danger and that he was not contributorily negligent.

At about 8 a.m. on March 20, 1961, appellant arrived at the store to purchase cigarettes. He had traded there regularly for the past ten years. Appellant made his purchase and then inquired of appellee about a box for his son. Appellee was busy behind the counter. He replied, "Go back in the back room. You will find some back there."

Appellant went to the rear of the store and opened the door to the storage room. The room was dark so appellant paused to allow his eyes to become accustomed to the darkness. He testified that he did not see a light cord and did not look for one. There was a light in the room but it was so situated that if turned on it might not have illuminated the stair well. Across the room and above the stair well there was a window, through which little light filtered because of paint or dirt.

After appellant's eyes had adjusted to the darkness, he saw a box. On reaching down to pick it up, he discovered it was full. Appellant then walked about twelve or fifteen feet toward the window and fell into an unseen stair well, sustaining his injuries.

The stairwell was located beyond a large walk-in refrigerator as appellant approached it. The opening extended a foot or two beyond the refrigerator and into the ten or twelve-foot corridor or walkway leading past the refrigerator.

Appellant said that he never before had been in the storage room. Appellee testified that appellant had been in the room on two or three occasions; that he did not warn appellant of the existence of the stair well; that the storage room light had been on that morning when he had opened the safe located in the room; and that he could not say whether the light was still on at the time of appellant's fall.

The trial court held that appellant was a licensee at the time of his fall to whom appellee owed no duty to provide a safe place, save and except to have abstained from doing any intentional or willful act endangering his safety or knowingly letting appellant run upon a hidden peril. Appellant contends that he entered the store on business with appellee and thus had the status of an invitee and that he still occupied this status when he fell and was injured. The question is: "Did the status of appellant change from invitee to licensee after he made his purchase and went into the storage room to obtain the box?" The status of appellant determines the degree of responsibility of appellee.

Pertinent discussion of the scope of the invitation is contained in "Torts, Restatement of the Law," Second, as follows:

> "The possessor of land is subject to liability to another as an invitee only for harm sustained while he is on the land within the scope of his invitation. Thus an invitee ceases to be an invitee after the expiration of a reasonable time within which to accomplish the purpose

for which he is invited to enter, or to remain. Whether at the expiration of that time he becomes a trespasser or a licensee will depend upon whether the possessor does or does not consent to his remaining on the land.

Likewise, the visitor has the status of an invitee only while he is on the part of the land to which his invitation extends, or in other words, the part of the land upon which the possessor gives him reason to believe that his presence is desired for the purpose for which he has come. In determining the area included within the invitation, the purpose for which the land is held open, or the particular business purpose for which the invitation is extended, is of great importance.

If the invitee goes outside of the area of his invitation, he becomes a trespasser or a licensee, depending upon whether he goes there without the consent of the possessor, or with such consent. Thus one who goes into a shop which occupies part of a building, the rest of which is used as the possessor's residence, is a trespasser if he goes into the residential part of the premises without the shopkeeper's consent; but he is a licensee if the shopkeeper permits him to go to the bathroom, or invites him to pay a social call."

Lerman Brothers v. Lewis, **277 Ky, 334, 126 S.W.2d 461,** is an example of the principle stated as applied to similar facts. There, a customer who went into the store for the purpose of doing some shopping and, with permission, proceeded to an alteration room reserved for employees in search of a particular saleswoman and who, upon entering therein, fell down a stairway, was held to be a licensee who was required to take the premises as she found them, and, hence, the storekeeper was not liable for her injuries.

Judgment for the defendant affirmed.

The courts have been confronted with a great number of cases involving people who drive under the influence of alcohol or drugs and cause accidents. Bars and restaurants that serve alcohol to people who are visibly intoxicated are held liable to those who are injured as the result of a drunk driver. The legislature has imposed this duty under a statute known as the *Dram Shop Act*.

In *Brandjord v. Hopper,* the court had to decide the novel issue of whether a group of friends, who drank together at a tailgate party, owed a duty to an injured pedestrian to prevent the drunk driver from operating his automobile. The incident occurred outside of Veterans Stadium following a Philadelphia Eagles versus Dallas Cowboys football games.

Basically, the court found that a passenger does not owe a duty to a third-person when the driver of the vehicle is intoxicated even if the driver and passenger participated in the joint purchase and consumption of alcohol.

MICHAEL BRANDJORD v. THOMAS HOPPER
688 A.2D 721 (PA. SUPER. 1997)

ON OCTOBER 23, 1988, MICHAEL BRANDJORD was struck and seriously injured by a vehicle operated by James Punch. The uncontested facts reveal that Mr. Punch, together with Charles Costello, William Campbell, and Thomas Hopper, attended a football game between the Philadelphia Eagles and the Dallas Cowboys at Veterans Stadium ("the Vet"). Appellees arrived at the former JFK parking lot located on 11th Street at approximately 11:30 a.m. Upon arrival, they engaged in the tradition of "tailgating," enjoying food and consuming several 12 ounce cans of beer which they had purchased together. The atmosphere was very convivial. After approximately ninety minutes of "tailgating," Punch, Costello, Campbell, and Hopper entered the Vet. One of the group brought in a container, which he had filled with beer, planning on continuing consumption throughout the game. Punch, however, did not sit with Campbell or Costello during the game.

The game was very competitive, but in the end the Eagles defeated their hated rivals, the Cowboys. The game ended around 4:00 p.m., at which time Punch, Campbell, Costello, and Hopper reconvened at Punch's van. All were extremely excited that the Eagles had won. To celebrate the win and to avoid the heavy traffic clogging the roads around the stadium, the group decided to engage in post-game "tailgating." At around 6:00 p.m., because the traffic had subsided, the group decided to go home. Punch pulled his van out of the JFK parking lot, heading south on 11th Street. As Mr. Brandjord attempted to cross the southbound lane of 11th Street, he was struck by the van driven by Punch. Mr. Brandjord suffered serious personal injuries.

Mr. Brandjord filed suit against the three passengers alleging that they owed Brandjord a duty not to permit Punch to drive because they knew Punch was intoxicated.

Do motor vehicle passengers who plan and participate in the joint purchase and consumption of large quantities of alcoholic beverages along with [the] driver and further plan to attend crowded social events during the consumption of the alcohol, have a duty to persons within the ambit of danger created by the driver operating under the influence of alcohol?

In order to hold a defendant liable for injuries sustained by a plaintiff, it must be shown that the defendant breached a duty of obligation recognized by the law which required him to conform to a certain standard of conduct for protection of persons such as the plaintiff.

The Brandjords assert that Campbell and Costello, passengers in Punch's van, owed a duty to Mr. Brandjord and breached that duty by consuming alcohol with Punch and then failing to take reasonable steps to prevent him from driving. The Brandjords explain that this duty should be recognized because it would force passengers to designate a driver or otherwise face potential liability for the actions of their driver if he or she were intoxicated.

A passenger does not owe a duty to a third-person where the driver of the vehicle is intoxicated, particularly when passengers and the driver merely participate in the joint procurement and ingestion of alcohol, absent the existence of a special relationship, joint enterprise, joint venture or a right to control the vehicle. To impose a duty on a passenger making him liable to others for what the driver chooses to do is inappropriate; such a rule assumes, incorrectly, that a passenger somehow shares in the management of the vehicle and the driver is amenable to the passenger's influence. Moreover, the passengers may not be aware of the amount of alcohol consumed by the driver. Adults cannot be charged with the supervision of other adults merely because they arrived and departed together.

In the present case, there are no facts to support finding the appellees responsible of any circumstance other than the mere participation in the procurement and ingestion of alcoholic beverages. Because liability cannot be premised upon mere participation by passengers in the procurement and ingestion of alcoholic beverages with a driver, we conclude that there was no issue of any material fact. Appellees, Campbell and Costello, therefore, were entitled to summary judgment.

SECTION 5.5
BREACH OF DUTY

The second element of a negligence action is quite simple. If a duty is owed, and a person fails to fulfill that obligation, a **breach of duty** has occurred. For example, a property owner owes a duty to a business visitor to make the property safe. This includes the obligation to inspect the premises on a reasonable basis. If a department store does not inspect its facility, and a business visitor is injured because a broken bottle is not cleaned up, the store owner has breached its duty of care.

SECTION 5.6
PROXIMATE CAUSE

Proximate cause requires that there be a reasonable connection between the negligence of the defendant and the harm suffered by the plaintiff. The fact that a party is careless and another suffers an injury is not by itself enough to impose liability. Rather, the negligent conduct must be a substantial factor in causing the harm. For instance, a surgeon who leaves an instrument in a patient's abdomen following surgery has obviously breached the duty of exercising reasonable medical care. The patient's need for additional surgery to remove the medical instrument would be directly related to the doctor's malpractice.

The driver of a car traveling 90 m.p.h. down the opposite side of the road is negligent. Suddenly, a wheel from an airplane flying overhead falls off and kills the passenger in the speeding automobile. While the driver of the car is operating the vehicle in a negligent fashion, that negligence is not the proximate cause of the passenger's death. The falling wheel from the airplane is the substantial factor in causing the harm.

In *Brown v. Philadelphia College of Osteopathic Medicine,* the court had to decide whether an erroneous diagnosis of a venereal disease by a physician was the proximate cause of the termination of the plaintiffs' marriage or whether the marriage ended because of the unfaithfulness by one of the martial partners.

YVETTE BROWN V. PHILADELPHIA COLLEGE OF OSTEOPATHIC MEDICINE
760 A.2D 863 (PA. SUPER. 2000)

IN THIS NEGLIGENCE ACTION, we are called upon to determine whether an erroneous syphilis diagnosis was the proximate cause of the breakdown of a marriage, physical violence and loss of employment. Philadelphia College of Osteopathic Medicine ("PCOM") sought a new trial following the entry of judgment against it. PCOM argues that Appellees failed to prove a causal connection between its alleged negligence and the "remote and unforeseeable consequences and injuries" for which they claim damages.

Yvette Brown delivered the couple's second child at PCOM on August 29, 1991. Soon after her delivery, the child was given a blood test to detect congenital syphilis. Mrs. Brown testified that a PCOM physician told her the test results revealed that her daughter had syphilis. The physician further told Mrs. Brown that the baby only could have contracted the disease from her. When her husband arrived at the hospital, she confronted him with the diagnosis and questioned whether he had been unfaithful to her. Mr. Brown admitted to an affair with a co-worker.

After the baby was released from the hospital, the Browns requested that she be tested again for syphilis. They then learned that the child did not have syphilis nor did a test performed on Mr. Brown reveal that he had syphilis.

Central to the Browns' damage claim was an episode in November 1991. Mrs. Brown was a police officer and the incident began when she received a telephone call at her home from her male partner on the police force. According to Mrs. Brown, upon hearing a man's voice on the line, Mr. Brown became suspicious and "snatched the phone out of the wall and hit me several times." Mrs. Brown then retrieved her service revolver and pursued Mr. Brown out of the house. She described the incident that followed: "I went outside and I fired the gun after him. But the gun I fired…all the bullets hit the car."

Both of the Browns were arrested and Mrs. Brown was discharged from the Philadelphia police force for conduct unbecoming an officer. The Browns separated after this incident.

The Browns filed suit against PCOM alleging 'that as a "direct and proximate result of the negligence of PCOM," Mrs. Brown suffered "severe physical and psychological damage" and "loss and/or impairment of her earnings ." At the conclusion of the trial, the jury awarded $500,000 in damages to Mrs. Brown and $10,000 to Mr. Brown.

PCOM's argues that Appellees "failed to prove causation between the alleged negligence of PCOM and the alleged remote and unforeseeable consequences and injuries."

It is not sufficient that a negligent act may be viewed to have been one of the happenings in the series of events leading up to an injury. A finding of proximate cause turns upon "whether the law will extend the responsibility for the negligent conduct to the consequences which have in fact occurred…."

The law will not support a finding of proximate cause if, as in the present case, the negligence was so remote that as a matter of law, the actor cannot be held legally responsible for the harm which subsequently occurred. To determine proximate cause, "the question is whether the defendant's conduct was a 'substantial factor' in producing the injury." *Vattimo v. Lower Bucks Hosp., Inc.,* **465 A.2d 1231 Pa. (1983).**

It is abundantly clear that factors other than the negligence of PCOM had a far greater effect in producing the harm complained of by the Browns. Mr. Brown conducted an extramarital affair and confessed this to his wife. It is this affair and his confession to it, together with Mr. Brown's suspicions that his wife was having an affair herself, not the false diagnosis of syphilis, that had the greatest effect in bringing about the marital discord and eventual breakdown for which the couple seeks compensation. Therefore, the actions of PCOM are not a substantial factor in bringing about these alleged damages. Accordingly, we are constrained to reverse the judgment of the court.

**SECTION 5.7
DEFENSES TO A
NEGLIGENCE ACTION**

Even though a defendant is negligent, an injured party's own conduct may preclude recovery. Two defenses to a negligence action are **contributory negligence** and **assumption of the risk**.

Contributory negligence is the failure of the plaintiff to act as a reasonable person under the circumstances. A driver who fails to stop for a red light is negligent. While the operator of the vehicle with the green light has the right of way, that driver may not blindly proceed through the intersection without first looking to the left and right. If the two vehicles collide, and neither driver looked for the other, they are both negligent. Since the individual who went through the red light bears the bulk of the liability, can the other motorist collect damages? No. A plaintiff may not recover if he or she has any degree of contributory negligence even if that fault is 1% of the responsibility for the accident.

Some states find this principle too harsh and have adopted a modified concept called **comparative negligence**. Basically, as long as the plaintiff's negligence is not greater than that of the defendant, the plaintiff may recover damages but the verdict will be reduced by the percentage of the plaintiff's negligence. In other words, if the plaintiff is found to be 30% at fault and the verdict is $10,000, the award will be reduced to $7,000.

If the plaintiff and defendant are found to be equally at fault, the plaintiff will receive one-half of the verdict since the plaintiff's negligence is not greater than that of the other responsible party. If the plaintiff, however, is found to be 51% at fault, the claimant will receive nothing since his negligence is greater than that of the defendant.

Pedestrians do not always have the luxury or ability to walk on a sidewalk adjacent to the street. A number of property owners are not required to maintain sidewalks for pedestrian use. This is especially true in rural areas. This fact forces automobiles and walkers to compete for the same space on the open road. A person who stubbornly shares the middle of the road with passing cars is comparatively negligent. A reasonable person does not walk in the middle of the street with on coming traffic. Is a pedestrian, however, who walks on the shoulder of a road comparatively negligent if that individual is struck by a car when no sidewalk is available for use? This is the issue in *Zangrando v. Sipula,* where Zangrando was walking along the berm of the road with her two dogs when one of the animals was struck by a passing vehicle. The driver of the car argued that he should not be responsible for the dog's veterinary bills under the doctrine of comparative negligence. The court was unimpressed with this assertion since no evidence existed that the dog's owner veered off of the berm of the road and into the street with her canines. The decision is noteworthy because of the court's literary use of rhyme in expressing its opinion.

JULIA ZANGRANDO V. JAN SIPULA
756 A.2D 73 (PA. SUPER. 2000)

Appellee and two little dogs were walking down the street,
tending to business as they went, but soon they were to meet;

Appellant, who this wintry day was driving toward the pair;
their mistress reined them to a stop along the thoroughfare.

Angel and Autumn were their names, one white, one apricot;
to walk beside her on a leash was their happy lifelong lot.

The poodles waited for the car, and watched as it drew near,
thinking there was nothing to cause them fear,

For often cars would pass them by, but this was no wayfarer -
the car begin to veer toward them and caution turned to terror.

To appellee this was nothing short of an unmitigated disaster;
the wingless Angel had taken flight and ascended quickly past her.

In this brace of miniature poodles, neither one wide nor tall,
'twas Angel who took the fall.

The impact could have killed the pup but Angel would survive;
a doctor of the veterinary kept the dog alive.

The bill for Angel's treatment was anything but small,
and appellee felt that appellant should pay it all,

So she filed this civil action in county court,
seeking eleven hundred, fifty-five dollars for the nearly fatal tort.

The car driver says that appellee was standing in the road,
in blatant violation of the Motor Vehicle Code;

So comparative negligence, the trial court should have found,
precluding his obligation to pay for damaging the tiny hound.

Appellant points to Code Section 3544,
which provides that pedestrians are required to do more,

Than choose just any path while they are going down street's way;
one must walk to the left, and off the road he should stay.

Appellee was toward the left side curb, and just about as far
as she could be from the roadway and the car.

We find that being on the berm, when she could do no more,
does not make a violation of Section 3544.

We find no negligence in staying off the neighbor's grass;
the road was fifteen feet in width, with room to safely pass.

Even if the poodle strained to reach the leashes' end,
appellant veered toward Angel, testimony we may not amend.

For everyone who finds the needs of their beloved pet
makes them walk within the confines of their street, and yet

They cannot be fair game for cars that drive that very street
And cars will always win the ties, when pedestrian and auto meet.

Be it interstate or neighborhood, drivers get no free shot
at things they may encounter, whether in the street or not.

So while counsel raises issues that are worthy and well taken,
in the end we find the effort to apply them here's mistaken.

We must conclude the issues raised do not warrant a new trial
and all that we may offer now is this respectful rhymed denial.

The second defense to a negligence action is **assumption of the risk.** If the plaintiff knows of the danger but yet voluntarily exposes himself to the harm, the plaintiff will be barred from recovery. For example, if a person jumps over an open manhole instead of walking around it, he will have assumed the risk of injury if he falls into the hole.

JOHN BOWSER v. THE HERSHEY BASEBALL ASSOCIATION
516 A.2D 61 (PA. SUPER. 1986)

THE HERSHEY BASEBALL ASSOCIATION is an association organized to provide a summer baseball program for youths and adults in Dauphin County. John B. Bowser, the plaintiff, was a former baseball player and coach. It was determined that the association should field a "teener" team which would compete in a larger league. The tryouts were held. Bowser and four other members of the association conducted them. During batting practice, the batters positioned themselves behind home plate and approximately five feet from the backstop so as to eliminate the need for a catcher. Except for the pitcher, the batter and the "on-deck batter," the candidates for the team were scattered about the infield and outfield to field the balls hit by the batter. Most of the adults who were serving as coaches and evaluators were standing along the right side of the diamond, near the players' bench, in order to observe the batters and the fielders.

Bowser kept track of the roster and called players in from the field to bat. During most of the tryouts, he had been located behind the backstop. After about two hours, however, he moved to the vicinity of the players' bench, where the group of coaches and evaluators were standing. After standing in that area for a minute or so, Bowser turned toward the outfield to call in two more players. As he turned back toward the batter, he was struck in the eye by a batted ball.

At the completion of the plaintiffs' testimony on liability, the court granted the association's motion for a compulsory nonsuit on the grounds that as a matter of law, Bowser had assumed the risk of being struck by a batted ball.

When Bowser agreed to participate on the field during the baseball tryouts, he voluntarily exposed himself to the risks inherent in baseball. One of the risks inherent in baseball is being hit by a batted ball. See: *Jones v. Three Rivers Management Corp.*, **483 Pa. 75, 394 A.2d 546 (1978)**. Having voluntarily exposed himself to the risk of being hit by a batted ball, Bowser cannot recover from the sponsor of the baseball event for injuries caused by this very risk.

Earlier decisions which reached this result relied upon the doctrine of voluntary assumption of the risk. These decisions held that by attending a baseball game, a plaintiff knowingly accepted and assumed he reasonable risks inherent in the game. See: *Iervolino v. Pittsburgh Athletic Co.*, **212 Pa.Super. 330, 243 A.2d 490 (1968)**; *Schentzel v. Philadelphia National League Club*, **173 Pa.Super. 179, 96 A.2d 181 (1953)**. More recently, the rationale adopted by the courts for this rule is that persons conducting the activity have no duty to warn or protect participants against risks, which are common, frequent, expected and inherent in the activity itself. See: *Jones v. Three Rivers Management Corp.*, **supra, 483 Pa. at 85, 394 A.2d at 551.** Thus, persons conducting an event are not negligent for failing to warn or protect a participant against risks, which are inherent in the activity. It is beyond cavil that those who position themselves on or near the field of play while a baseball event is in progress are charged with anticipating, as inherent to the sport of baseball, the risk of being struck by a batted ball.

Bowser argues, however, that baseball tryouts are different than a baseball game and that the risk of being struck by a batted ball is not inherent therein. We reject this argument. Hitting is an essential element of baseball; batting practice is as common as the game itself; and the risk of being struck by a batted ball is even greater than in a regulation game, for during batting practice more than one ball is frequently in use. These facts are matters of common knowledge. When appellant participated on the field during tryouts, which involved batting practice, he was aware of and accepted the risk of being struck by a batted ball. There was no requirement that warnings be given or that special precautions be taken to protect him from batted balls. The rule was not altered in any way because there was no catcher and the batter was standing behind home plate and immediately in front of a stationary backstop.

Order affirmed.

Over the years, a number of lawsuits have been filed for injuries to spectators at sporting events who are hit by flying objects such as baseballs or hockey pucks. This type of claim is generally unsuccessful because the risks are well known and inherent to the event. Most people who attend baseball games are aware that foul balls are hit into the stands on a regular basis. The allure of catching one of these errant balls is also part of the fun of attending the game.

To reinforce the awareness of the danger for purpose of assumption of the risk, the reverse side of an event ticket will contain a warning concerning the danger of flying objects leaving the playing field. The awareness of this danger is reinforced when the announcer repeats the warning over the public address system both before and during the game. For instance, the hockey ticket provided by the Philadelphia Flyers provides on the reverse side:

> Pucks flying into spectator areas can cause serious injury. Be alert when in spectator areas, including after the stoppage of play. If injured, notify an usher for directions to medical station. Ticket holder assumes all risks and dangers of personal injury and all other hazards arising from or related in any way to the event for which this ticket is issued, whether occurring prior to, during or after the event, including, specifically (but not exclusively), the danger of being injured by hockey pucks and sticks, and other spectators or players or by thrown objects. Ticket Holder agrees that the Spectrum Arena Limited Partners, the National Hockey League, Comcast - Spectacor, L.P., the Philadelphia Flyers, the playing teams, the players and the officers, employees and agents of each are expressively released by Ticket Holder from claims arising from or in any way related to the foregoing causes...

Before the games, the Flyers announcer also warns fans about the danger of pucks leaving the playing surface and that fans should be vigilant of this risk at all times.

Does a fan, however, assume the risk of injury when she is injured while other fans wildly chase a foul baseball that goes into the stands or by a football that sails over the end zone net and into the seats? In other words, should the management of a stadium be liable for failing to protect a fan from the unruly actions of people who will do anything, including knocking people over, in their pursuit of a souvenir ball? This is the issue in the following case.

MITCHELL TELEGA V. SECURITY BUREAU, INC.
719 A.2D 372 (PA. SUPER. 1998)

APPELLANTS, MITCHELL AND KAREN TELEGA, appeal from the Order of the Allegheny County Court of Common Pleas granting summary judgment in favor of Appellee, Security Bureau, Inc. For the reasons set forth below, we reverse.

Mitchell Telega and his wife, Karen, attended a Pittsburgh Steelers football game at Three Rivers Stadium in Pittsburgh on December 6, 1992. For approximately two years, the Telegas were season ticket holders whose seats were located in Section 41, the pie-shaped end-zone section of the stadium behind the Steelers' goalpost. During the last quarter of the December 6th game, the Steelers' kicker attempted a field goal. The football was catapulted through the uprights of the goalpost, over the stadium net designed to catch it, and into the stands. Mr. Telega, who saw the ball coming his way, stood up in front of his assigned seat, extended his arms, and cleanly fielded the football. When he attempted to sit down, Mr. Telega was thrust from his seat and trampled face first into the cement aisle by aggressive fans who stripped him of the souvenir ball. Mr. Telega suffered numerous injuries from this attack, including facial lacerations, a sprained shoulder and arm resulting in extensive physical therapy, and a broken nose that required surgery.

Prior to this incident, the Telegas and other patrons seated in the end zone section of the stadium lodged complaints with the stadium's Guest Relations Office and security personnel concerning the lack of security and crowd control in their seating area during field goal and extra point attempts. They often complained that the football regularly clears the catch net, lands in the stands, and causes a disturbance among the fans, resulting in a danger to the welfare of the patrons seated in their section. It is undisputed that Appellee, Security Bureau, Inc., was responsible for providing security services at the Stadium during home games.

Appellants filed a complaint asserting a cause of action in negligence against Security Bureau, Inc. alleging that the defendants breached a duty of care owed to Mr. Telega by, failing to supervise security guards at the Stadium and failing to regulate crowd control in the end-zone seating area.

In *Jones v. Three Rivers Management Corp.*, 483 Pa. 75, 394 A.2d 546 (1978), the trial court determined that because "the risk of injury was obvious, reasonably foreseeable and voluntarily assumed by [Mr. Telega]," Appellee owed him no legal duty. We disagree.

Our courts have long refused to grant recovery for injuries sustained by amusement patrons, which were caused by a risk inherent in the activity in question. For example, our Supreme Court granted judgment in favor of a movie theatre where the patron alleged only that his injury was caused by the lighting conditions ordinarily utilized in the exhibition of motion pictures. *Beck v. Stanley Co. of America*, 355 Pa. 608, 615, 50 A.2d 306, 310 (1947). The Court has also denied recovery where a spectator at a stockcar race track was struck by one of the racing vehicles while he was standing in the unprotected "pit" area of the track; the patron admitted that his presence in the pit area was unauthorized and that collisions in this area were common. *Shula v. Warren*, 395 Pa. 428, 434-35, 150 A.2d 341, 345 (1959).

The question before this Court is whether a spectator will be held to assume as inherent in the game the risk of being attacked by displaced fans if he catches a soaring football. We believe not.

Although this type of unruly, improper fan conduct may have occurred in Mr. Telega's section of the stadium before, being trampled by displaced fans is not a risk inherent in or so ordinary a part of the spectator sport of football such that it is certain to occur at any and every stadium in the Commonwealth. The trial court's reliance on Mr. Telega's prior knowledge of such "fan upheaval" and his report of this dangerous behavior to management and security personnel is an attempt improperly to shift the focus of the inquiry from the risks inherent in the game of football itself to an examination of other risks which may be present in a particular football stadium. By creating the notion that "if it happened before, it must be customary," the trial court concludes that if a spectator is injured at a football game, and had prior knowledge of the risk of injury, the risk is automatically an inherent part of the spectator sport and recovery is barred. This broad-sweeping extension inappropriately attributes to Mr. Telega the responsibility to ensure his own safety and protect himself from the behavior of aggressive fans despite the presence of Appellee whose primary obligation it was to regulate crowd control. Indeed, such an interpretation would permit amusement facility operators to avoid liability for "universally prevalent negligent conditions," and all duty to protect against any risk within the facility. This approach is clearly undesirable and defies the well-established principles of negligence.

The risk involved here is unlike the risk of being struck by an errant puck while a spectator at a hockey game, falling down or being bumped by other skaters at a roller skating rink, or being hit by a batted ball during baseball tryouts. Contrary to the instant matter, these cases involve risks that are inherent in the activity itself and are specific to the activity at any appropriate venue. They are, therefore, as a matter of law, risks assumed by the spectators and participants who patronize the amusement facilities. It is not a matter of universal knowledge that an onslaught of displaced fans is a common, frequent or expected occurrence to someone catching a souvenir football. Therefore, it cannot be said that the injuries suffered by Mr. Telega resulted from a risk that any spectator would be held to anticipate and against which an amusement facility has no duty to protect. Certainly this matter would compel a different result had Mr. Telega been injured by the aerial football itself rather than the displaced fans intent on obtaining it.

Therefore, the trial court committed an error of law and we must reverse.

While children who commit negligent acts are afforded a degree of protection by the courts, is a person who injuries another while insane offered a similar protection from liability? This is the issue in *Delahanty v. Hinkley*. Generally, an insane person will remain liable for his or her torts. The courts believe that where one of two innocent people suffers a loss, the risk should remain with the one who caused the loss rather than upon the other who had no part in producing it and could not have avoided the problem.

THOMAS DELAHANTY V. JOHN HINKLEY, JR.
799 F. SUPP. 184 (D. D.C. 1992)

THIS CASE IS BEFORE THE COURT for compensatory damages on defendant's Motion for Summary Judgment on the issue of liability for damages. After giving careful consideration to the motion, the Court concludes for reasons set out below that the motion must be denied.

Defendant contends that while he was in a deluded and psychotic state of mind, he fired at the President of the United States of America. Plaintiffs, who were near the President were struck by bullets fired by the defendant. The criminal case was tried before a federal jury and the defendant was found not guilty by reason ·of insanity on all counts. *See: United States v. John W. Hinkley, Jr.* On the basis of this verdict and a subsequent evaluation and report on Mr. Hinckley's mental condition, defendant was involuntarily committed to St. Elizabeth's Hospital. Defendant asserts that these events require a finding of summary judgment in his favor since they demonstrate that he was legally insane at the time of the shootings. In accordance with this argument defendant contends that the historical rule in this jurisdiction, requiring that an insane actor be held liable for compensation to the victims of his torts, should be rejected by this Court.

An insane person is liable for compensatory damages for his torts where express malice or evil intent is not a necessary element of the tort. *Aetna Casualty and Surety Co. v. Porter (D. D.C. 1960)*, 181 F.Supp. at 88. The primary purpose of such a rule is to compensate the victims for their loss. Defendant urges the Court to reject this well established rule.

While the Court acknowledges that commentators have criticized the common law rule, the fact remains that "courts in this country almost invariably say in the broadest terms that an insane person is liable for his torts." *Williams v. Kearbey*, 13 Kan. App.2d 564, 775 P.2d 670 (1989). Moreover, there are modern justifications for such a rule. See: *Splane, Tort Liability of the Mentally Ill in Negligence Actions*, 93 Yale L.J. 153,163 (1983) (using the objective standard to determine primary negligence helps minimize the burden on the community from deinstitutionalization, helps foster community acceptance of the mentally ill, and encourages the mentally ill to become self-sufficient responsible members of the community).

Defendant relies on *Fitzgerald v. Lawhorn*, 29 Conn.Supp. 511, 294 A.2d 338 (1972) in which the court was not willing to accept the majority view that insane persons are liable for their torts because "it appears to be an outdated point of view." However, Fitzgerald has been overruled in *Polmatier v. Russ*, 206 Conn. 229, 537 A.2d 468 (1988). In that case the court held that "the majority rule is consistent with the settled common-law rule that where one of two innocent persons must suffer loss from an act done, it is just that it should fall on the one who caused the loss rather than upon the other who had no agency in producing it and could not by any means have avoided it.

In view of the foregoing discussion, the Court will deny defendant's motion for summary judgment in its entirety.

SECTION 5.8
IMPUTED NEGLIGENCE

Imputed negligence or vicarious liability means that because of a special relationship that exits between the parties one person can be held liable for the negligence of the other. The classic example of such a relationship is that of employer and employee. Even though the employer has done nothing wrong, it will be responsible for the torts of its employees committed within the scope of the employment. For example, a bus company will be liable for an accident caused by the negligence of a bus driver. However, the bus company will generally not be liable for the assault of a customer by a bus driver since an assault is beyond the scope of the employment.

An employer will also not be liable for the torts of an **independent contractor**. An independent contractor is one who undertakes to perform the act requested on his own and is not subject to the control of an employer. If a professional sports team charters an airplane to fly the team to its next game, the airline is an independent contractor and not an employee of the sports franchise. The team exercises no control over how to fly the plane and the team would not be liable for the torts of the pilot if the plane crashes even though it hired the airline.

JAMES DeFULIO v. SPECTAGUARD, INC.
FEBRUARY TERM, 1990 #6199 (C.P. PHILA, 1990)

GOLDMAN, J.

ON MAY 16, 1988, PLAINTIFF JAMES DeFULIO was climbing a fence to enter Veteran's Stadium (the Stadium) to see a Pink Floyd concert. He did not have a ticket. As Plaintiff neared the top of the fence he was climbing, he used his hand to gasp the ledge of concrete platform above him. Testimony revealed that a security guard who was standing on the platform stepped on Plaintiff's hand causing him to fall 15 feet to a concrete concourse and fracture both ankles.

Plaintiff brought the instant suit against Spectaguard, Inc. (Spectaguard) and Electric Factory Concerts, Inc. (Electric Factory) alleging that they were vicariously liable for the guard's actions.

Spectaguard employed the security guard in question and one of the guards duties was to prevent people who did not have tickets from entering the Stadium. In turn, Spectaguard was employed by Electric Factory who had leased the stadium from the City of Philadelphia for the concert and was under the terms of the lease, under an obligation to provide security and ushering services at the concert. Following a trial, the jury found in favor of Plaintiff in the amount of $165,000 and against Spectaguard and Electric Factory.

Defendants argued that there was no evidence that the guard's contact with Plaintiff was within the course and scope of his employment and that the issue should not have been presented to the jury.

Under the doctrine of respondeat superior, the negligence of an employee may be imputed to the employer. *Fitzgerald v. McCutcheon*, **410 A.2d 1270 (Pa.Super. Ct. 1979)**. However, before an employer will be held liable for an employee's actions, it must be determined that the employee's actions occurred within the course and scope of his employment. Pennsylvania courts have adopted the Restatement (Second) of Agency Section 228 in determining whether an employee's conduct is done within the scope of employment:

1. Conduct of a servant is within the scope of employment if, but only if:

    a. it is of the kind he is employed to perform;

    b. it occurs substantially within the authorized time and space limits;

    c. it is actuated, at least in part, by a purpose to serve the master, and

    d. if force is intentionally used by the servant, the use of force is not unexpected by the master.

Defendants conceded that the guard's conduct occurred within the authorized time and space and that it was "arguably actuated by a purpose to serve his employer." However, Defendants argue that there was no evidence that the guard's conduct was of the kind he was employed to perform. Further, Defendants argued that there was no evidence that the force used by the guard (in stepping on Plaintiff's fingers) was "not unexpected" by Spectaguard. In support thereof, Defendants pointed to the testimony of Lewis Bostic, Spectaguard's Risk Manager. Mr. Bostic testified that "[i]t would be contrary to every instruction our people are given" to remove Plaintiff from the fence as he described and that "there's no way they [guards] would grab or touch anybody climbing up that fence."

Pennsylvania Courts have addressed the issue of whether an employee's action is unexpected by the employer and not of the kind he is employed to perform.

It is, in general sufficient to make the master responsible that he gave to the servant an authority, or made it his duty to act in respect to the business in which he was engaged when the wrong was committed, and that the act complained of was done in the course of his employment. The master in that case will be deemed to have consented to and authorized the act of the servant, and he will not be excused from liability, although the servant abused his authority, or was reckless in the performance of his duty, or inflict an unnecessary injury in executing his master's orders. The master who puts the servant in a place of trust or responsibility, or commits to him the management of his business or the care of his property, is justly held responsible when the servant, through lack of judgment or discretion, or from infirmity or temper, or under the influence of passion aroused by the circumstances and the occasion, goes beyond the strict line of his duty or authority and inflicts an unjustifiable injury upon another.

The law, as applied to the facts of the instant case, supported the jury's finding that the guard's actions occurred within the scope of his employment. First, there was evidence that the guard's conduct was of the kind he was employed to perform. Specifically, the guard was employed, in part, and authorized by Spectaguard to make contact with and prevent entry to the Concert by people who did not have tickets. Since Plaintiff was climbing the Stadium's fence, it surely appeared obvious to the guard that Plaintiff was the sort of person that Spectaguard paid its employees to make contact with and keep out of the concert. Secondly, the conduct in question occurred within the authorized time and space limits. Without question, it occurred at the concert and on stadium grounds. Thirdly, the guard's actions served the purpose of Spectaguard by preventing an individual whom did not have a ticket from entering the stadium. Finally, regarding the force employed, Spectaguard's incident report from the night in question evidenced the fact that guards ejected people from the concert including people who did not have tickets and who climbed the fences surrounding the Stadium. The guard showed a lack of judgment but such conduct does not necessarily extinguish an employer's liability. Under the instant circumstances it was within the province of the jury to determine whether the guard's conduct was not unexpected by Spectaguard and whether Spectaguard and Electric Factory could he held liable for the tortuous conduct of the guard.

Defendants' request is denied.

SECTION 5.9
JOE HODGE
V. THE STALLIONS

PROBLEM FIVE—B

HODGE, DODGE AND LODGE
ATTORNEYS AT LAW
MEMORANDUM

To: All Law Clerks

FROM: Gregory Olan Dodge

RE: Joe Hodge v. The Stallions

For Joe Hodge's birthday, his son ordered a "Press Pass" for his father to attend the Stallions home opening football game. Joe was ecstatic since he never saw Tony play in a live professional football game. Joe stood on the sidelines next to the Stallions' bench and told everyone that his son was the place-kicker. As a special treat, Tony had arranged for some of the Stallions' cheerleaders to give his father a birthday cheer. During the beginning of the second quarter, the cheerleaders started to chant Joe's name. Joe turned away from the field to see who was calling his name and noticed the cheerleaders lined up behind him.

At this point in time, the cheerleaders started to sing "Happy Birthday." Joe Hodge was speechless. Unfortunately, the game was still being played and the Stallions' 250-pound fullback caught a pass and was pushed out of bounds. The player's momentum carried him into Joe who still had his back to the field. Mr. Hodge was violently knocked to the ground and broke his right leg in three places.

We have been retained by Joe to file suit against the Stallions for negligence in not protecting him against being hit as he stood on the sidelines. Joe contends the team should not have issued a sideline pass if it was dangerous for an individual to stand on the sidelines. I am sure the Stallions will argue that Joe assumed the risk of being injured. Would a person normally assume the risk of being hurt by a football player when the spectator is standing ten yards off the field? Based upon *Lowe v.*

California League of Professional Baseball, can Joe prevail in a suit against the Stallions since Joe's was watching the cheerleaders at the time he was hurt? Are the Stallions responsible for the actions of their cheerleaders in diverting Joe's attention from the game? The team will argue that the Cheerleaders exceeded their duties by engaging in a private cheer. Please refer to *DeFulio v. Spetaguard, Inc.,* which is set forth immediately before this problem, in order to ascertain whether the cheerleaders were acting within the scope of their employment with the Stallions.

JOHN LOWE V. CALIFORNIA PROFESSIONAL BASEBALL
56 CAL. APP. 4TH 112 (1997)

JOHN LOWE WAS SERIOUSLY INJURED when struck on the left side of his face by a foul ball while attending a professional baseball game. The game was being played at "The Epicenter," home field of the Rancho Cucamonga Quakes, Class "A," minor league baseball team.

The Quakes, at their home games, feature a mascot who goes by the name of "Tremor." He is a caricature of a dinosaur, standing seven feet tall with a tail, which protrudes out from the costume. Tremor was performing his antics in the stands just along the left field foul line. Tremor was behind plaintiff and had been touching him with his (Tremor's) tail. Plaintiff was thereby distracted and turned toward Tremor. In the next moment, just as plaintiff returned his attention to the playing field, he was struck by a foul ball before he could react to it.

Very serious injuries resulted from the impact. As a result, the underlying action was commenced against the California League of Professional Baseball and Valley Baseball Club, Inc., which does business as the Quakes (defendants). The case was resolved in the trial court by summary judgment entered in favor of defendants.

Defendants were able to persuade the trial court, under the doctrine of primary assumption of the risk. *Knight v. Jewett,* **3 Cal. 4th 296, 834 P.2d 696 (1992),** that defendants owed no duty to plaintiff, as a spectator, to protect him from foul balls. Such rationalization was faulty. Under *Knight,* defendants had a duty not to increase the inherent risks to which spectators at professional baseball games are regularly exposed and which they assume. As a result, a triable issue of fact remained, namely whether the Quakes' mascot cavorting in the stands and distracting plaintiff's attention, while the game was in progress, constituted a breach of that duty, i.e., constituted negligence in the form of increasing the inherent risk to plaintiff of being struck by a foul ball.

Thus, the trial court improperly granted the defendant's motion for summary judgment and it must be reversed accordingly.

In the action, filed after his injury, plaintiff's complaint was styled in a single count, a refreshing example of clear and concise pleading. The key charging allegations were contained in two paragraphs:

1. On said date and some time after the stated time and after the seventh inning, 'Tremor' the Quake's mascot, came up into the stadium in the area where plaintiff and his group were seated. Tremor was accompanied by an usher as he performed antics and entertained the crowd. Tremor is a person who wears a dinosaur costume with a long protruding tail. As John Lowe sat in his assigned seat, he was facing forward and looking toward the playing field when suddenly, and without warning or his consent, his right shoulder was touched by the tail of Tremor's costume. As he turned to his right to see who, or what, was touching him, baseball play had resumed and a batted ball, believed to be a foul ball, hit the plaintiff on the left side of his face breaking multiple facial bones.

2. The Left Terrace Section, where the plaintiff was seated with his group, is located northwesterly of the left field foul ball territory, and in the direct line of foul balls passing west of the third base line. Tremor's antics and interference, while the baseball game was in play, prevented the plaintiff from being able to protect himself from any batted ball and foreseeably increased the risks to John Lowe over and above those inherent in the sport.

These deposition excerpts provide an insight into how plaintiff was injured:

Q. *Where was the mascot at the time that the foul ball was hit?*

A. **Directly behind me.**

Q. *How long had the mascot been directly behind you at the time you were hit?*

A. **I would say probably two minutes.**

Q. *Was the mascot standing in the same place for that long?*

A. **He was moving around back and forth. But whatever he was doing, he was doing it directly behind my seat.**

Q. *So he was at the row or in the row behind your row?*

A. **Our row of seats backed up to an aisle. He was standing in the aisle directly behind my seat.**

Q . *And at the time that you were hit, the mascot was standing behind your row of seats in the aisle?*

A. **Yes.**

Q. *Did any part of the mascot's costume or person touch you before you were hit?*

A. **Yes.**

Q. *And what or how were you touched by this mascot?*

A. **With his tail.**

Q. *When did that occur in relationship to when you were hit by the ball?*

A. **Well, during that approximate two-minute span he was doing his act. And I felt this bam, bam, bam, on the back of my head and shoulders, and I turned around to see what he was doing.**

Q. *You felt something on your shoulders?*

A. **Right.**

Q. *How do you know it was the tail that tapped you on the shoulder?*

A. **I turned around and looked.**

Q. *And when you turned around and looked, what did you see?*

A. **Well, I noticed that he was doing his antics to the crowd that was in the immediate area. And I saw that as he was turning his body, his tail was hitting me.**

Q. Is that something that you actually saw or is that something that you assumed that the tail was hitting you?

A. No, I saw the tail. I could see the tail hitting me.

Q. All right. Were you annoyed by the mascot's tail tapping you on the shoulder?

A. Initially, no, but as it continued, it was a little bothersome.

Q. Where were you looking at the moment the ball was hit?

A. I had just turned my head towards the field as the ball arrived.

Q. And in terms of timing, was it almost instantaneous that you turned your head to the field and got hit?

A. Yes.

Q. Where were you looking immediately before you turned your head toward the field?

A. Up at Tremor.

Q. And at that time you were looking at Tremor immediately before turning your head back to the field and getting hit, was the reason that you were looking at Tremor that his tail had just tapped you on the shoulder again and you turned around and looked?

A. Yes.

The dispositive issue in this case then is whether the mascot's antics and their resulting distraction of the plaintiff operated to increase the inherent risks assumed by a spectator at a baseball game. In this regard, it is well established that defendants generally do have a duty to use due care not to increase the risks to a participant over and above those inherent in the sport." *Knight v. Jewett*, **supra, 3 Cal. 4th 296, 315-316.** The rule is no different in instances involving spectators.

The key inquiry here is whether the risk which led to plaintiff's injury involved some feature or aspect of the game which is inevitable or unavoidable in the actual playing of the game. In the first instance, foul balls hit into the spectators' area clearly create a risk of injury. If such foul balls were to be eliminated, it would be impossible to play the game. Thus, foul balls represent an inherent risk to spectators attending baseball games. Under *Knight*, such risk is assumed. Can the same thing be said about the antics of the mascot? We think not. Actually, the declaration of the person who dressed up as Tremor, recounted that there were occasional games played when he was not there. In view of this testimony, as a matter of law, we hold that the antics of the mascot are not an essential or integral part of the playing of a baseball game. In short, the game can be played in the absence of such antics. Moreover, whether such antics increased the inherent risk to plaintiff is an issue of fact to be resolved at trial.

We note further, under the holding in *Neinstein v. Los Angeles Dodgers*, **185 Cal. App. 3d 176,** absent any distraction by the mascot, that plaintiff could have assumed the risk. Justice Compton, writing in Neinstein, observed that the plaintiff "voluntarily elected to sit in a seat which was clearly unprotected by any form of screening.. She was sufficiently warned of the risk by common knowledge of the nature of the sport.. The Dodgers were under no duty to do anything further to protect her from the hazard."

However, in *Neinstein*, there was no mascot bothering the plaintiff and thus distracting her attention from the playing field. Thus, *Neinstein* is readily distinguishable.

The same can be said of the *Clapman* case decided by the Court of Appeals of New York. In that case, a spectator at Yankee Stadium was struck by a foul ball. He contended that a vendor moving in front of him obscured his view. As to this contention, the court said "respondents had no duty to insure that vendors moving about the stadium did not interfere with *Clapman's* **479 N.Y.S.2d 515.** That is not this case. In *Clapman*, the plaintiff at all times was facing the field of play. Here, plaintiff, because of the distraction, had turned away. This presents a substantially different set of facts, recognized at once by anyone who has ever attended a professional baseball game.

Based upon the foregoing analysis, we hold that the trial court improperly granted the motion for summary judgment.

ANSWER SHEET
PROBLEM FIVE—B

Name   **Please Print Clearly**

1. Did Joe Hodge assume the risk of his injuries? Explain your answer.

2. Will the Stallions be held liable for the actions of the cheerleaders?

_____

_____

_____

_____

_____

_____

_____

_____

_____

_____

_____

_____

_____

_____

_____

_____

_____

_____

_____

_____

_____

_____

Generally, parents are not held vicariously liable for the torts of their children unless a parent is directly at fault or if the child is acting as the agent of the parent at the time of the harm. For instance, a parent will be held liable if he or she leaves a loaded gun on the table and a young child shoots someone with the weapon. Liability attaches because the parent is a fault in leaving the gun unattended and not because of the parental relationship.

Some states have passed laws to hold parents liable for the torts of their children in specific instances. The following statute is the law in Pennsylvania:

23 PA. C.S.A. SECTION 5502 —LIABILITY OF PARENTS

Any parent whose child is found liable or is adjudged guilty by a court...of a tortuous act shall be liable to the person who suffers the injury to the extent set forth in this chapter.

23 PA. C.S.A. SECTION 5503—ESTABLISHING LIABILITY IN CRIMINAL PROCEEDINGS

In any criminal proceeding against a child...the court shall ascertain the amount sufficient to fully reimburse any person who has suffered injury because of the tortuous act of a child and direct the parents to make payment in the amount not to exceed the limitations set forth in section 5505.

23 PA. C.S.A. SECTION 5505—MONETARY LIMITS OF LIABILITY

Liability of the parents under this Chapter shall be limited to:

1. The sum of $1,000 for injuries suffered by any one person as a result of the tortuous act or continuous series of tortuous acts.

2. The sum of $2,500 regardless of the number of persons who suffer injury as a result of one tortuous act or continuous series of tortuous acts.

A number of incidents have occurred in which children have committed violent acts against others including the multiple shootings of classmates. Can parents be held liable for the acts of their children who have aggressive tendencies under a theory of negligent supervision? This is the issue in *Kilgore v. Synder.*

JASON KILGORE V. BRANDON SNYDER
NO. 1996 - C- 148 (NORTHAMPTON CT. PA. 1997)

THE COMPLAINT ARISES FROM AN ALLEGED assault on a minor, Jason Kilgore, by Brandon Snyder, teenage son of the moving defendants. It is averred that the three minor defendants surrounded Jason (while) Snyder and Dorsey hit him in the face knocking him unconscious. Jason sustained serious and permanent injuries and was in the hospital in the intensive care treatment unit for five days. The complaint against Merritt Snyder and Joanne Snyder, (the parents of Brandon Snyder) asserts that they were negligent in failing to recognize their son's dangerous violent propensities, failing to warn others of the propensities and failing to control their son to prevent him from acting in a violent fashion.

The parents of Brandon Snyder move for summary judgment (to dismiss them from the case) contending that they owed no duty to act to prevent the alleged assault.

In *Condel v. Savo*, **350 Pa. 350 (1944)**, the Supreme Court wrote:

> At common law, the mere relation of parent and child imposes upon the parent no liability for the torts of the child, but the parents may be liable where the act of the child is done as the agent of the parents or where the negligence of the parents makes the injury possible. The injury committed by the child must have been the natural and probable consequence of the parents' negligent act and ought reasonable to have been foreseen as likely to flow from such negligent act.

Further, the Court added:

Mere knowledge by the parents of the child's mischievous and reckless disposition is not enough to make them liable for the torts of the child, but their liability arises from (their) failure to exercise the control which they have over their child, when they know, or in the exercise of due care should know, that injury to another is a natural and probable consequence, for such failure to act and restrain the child amounts to an approval and sanctions of, or consent to, (the child's) acts by the parents.

In *Condel v. Savo*, the Pennsylvania Supreme Court held that a complaint was sufficient to charge the parents with negligence given express averments that the defendants' minor son was in the "habit" of assaulting smaller children, that the defendants knew of such habit, allowed him to continue to assault small children, and encouraged the boy by resenting any resistance or admonition made by the parents of his victims. It was further expressly averred the defendant parents had been notified of "many similar" vicious and unlawful attacks on little children, (and they) failed and neglected to exercise reasonable care so to control (their son) as to prevent him from intentionally harming others and from so conducting himself to create an unreasonable risk of bodily harm..."

A second source of law is ***Restatement of Torts 2nd Section 316*** which provides as follows:

Duty of Parent to Control Conduct of Child.

> A parent is under a duty to exercise reasonable care so to control his minor child as to prevent it from intentionally harming others or from so conducting itself as

to create an unreasonable risk of bodily harm to them, if the parent (a) knows or has reason to know that he has the ability to control his child, and (b) knows or should know of the necessity and opportunity for exercising such control.

While under *Condel v. Savo*, supra, a parent is liable if he fails to control a child who has displayed a "habit" or "vicious propensity" for tortious conduct, the *Restatement of Torts 2nd Section 316* provides a broader theory of liability. There is no requirement of exhibition of "vicious propensity" by a child as a precondition of parental liability for a child's tort. All that is needed to establish a negligence cause of action against a parent for a child's act is an act or omission of the parent in controlling the child which (the parent) knows or ought to know creates unreasonable risk of harm to another. Or course, knowledge or reason to know of a child's special or peculiar "propensities" is a factor in determining the parents duty in the circumstances.

In the instant case the plaintiffs have offered evidence that two years before the assault on plaintiff, Brandon Snyder assaulted another minor by striking him in the face so severally that the boy had to go to the hospital emergency room for treatment. Brandon was suspended from school for the attack. Both parents were aware of the prior assault.

Also, the youth's baseball coach stated that (Brandon) had a reputation as a "wise guy", and that his parents defended him when he was reprimanded by the coaching staff. A neighbor (also) reported that Brandon has loud parties while his mother is away, uses foul language and that the mother fails to put a stop to drinking parties on weekends when she is at work.

Parent are not responsible for the delinquent acts of their minor children merely because of the parental relationship. Nor is every delinquent act of a child reasonable foreseeable because the child has previously acted in a delinquent or incorrigible way. However, when a minor commits a serious delinquent act, the parents are alerted and should reasonably foresee a recurrence of the same kind of misconduct. When a minor commits a serious delinquent act, parents share responsibility for a *repeat* of the misconduct unless they have acted reasonably to prevent a recurrence. On a prior occasion Brandon Snyder struck another youth in the face repeatedly; this is not a mere playground scuffle. It is now averred that he committed the same kind of delinquent act sending Jason Kilgore to the intensive care unit for five days and causing serious permanent injury. It is a proper subject of inquiry in this action for compensation as to what, if anything, the parents of Brandon Snyder did after the first assault to prevent a recurrence. A parent's ability to monitor and physically control a child diminishes as the child grows into a teenager. Parents cannot be expected to restrain a child as they would a vicious animal; however, there are reasonable responses available. For example, did they reprimand him, discipline him, deprive him of privileges, threaten loss of privileges if there was a recurrence, obtain professional counseling, and monitor his associations?

The defendants' motion for a summary judgment is denied.

SECTION 5.10
INTENTIONAL TORTS

When the wrongdoer purposely sets out to harm another, that conduct gives rise to an intentional tort. Theories of liability include actions for a battery, assault, invasion of privacy, defamation, infliction of emotional distress, and false imprisonment.

Intentional torts are treated more seriously by the courts and verdicts frequently include awards of both compensatory and punitive damages.

SECTION 5.11
INFLICTION OF
EMOTIONAL DISTRESS

A person who by extreme and outrageous conduct intentionally or recklessly causes severe emotional distress to another is liable to that person for any bodily harm that may result from the emotional distress. The outrageous conduct must go beyond the bounds of normal decency and be considered as intolerable in a civilized community.

LAVON ANKERS v. DENNIS RODMAN
995 F SUPP.132 (D.C. UTAH 1997)

LAVON ANKERS WAS EMPLOYED at the Delta Center in Salt Lake City as an usher during basketball games. On May 5, 1994, the Utah Jazz basketball team was hosting the San Antonio Spurs in a nationally televised game. Dennis Rodman was employed as a player for the Spurs. Plaintiff was standing in her assigned courtside area.

At the beginning of the fourth quarter of play, defendant attempted to gain possession of a loose ball without going out of bounds. However, he was unable to do so and left the court to retrieve the ball. He walked past plaintiff, then turned around and started to walk back to the court. As he passed plaintiff again, he placed his hand on plaintiff's buttocks and pinched her.

Roman's conduct was witnessed by spectators present at the game as well as a national television audience. The television broadcast, although not revealing the actual touching of plaintiff's buttocks showed Rodman coming up behind plaintiff and plaintiff's reaction to defendant's apparent touch.

Plaintiff brought suit for intentional infliction of emotional distress. Ankers contends that, as a result of defendant's behavior, she "was and continues to be greatly humiliated, shamed, embarrassed" and has "endured great mental suffering." Moreover, plaintiff alleges defendant's touching constituted "outrageous conduct" such that she has "suffered and continues to suffer severe and extreme emotional distress." Defendant asserts the conduct plaintiff attributes to him is not sufficiently outrageous for plaintiff to state such a claim.

The elements of intentional infliction of emotional distress require that plaintiff show **(a)** that the defendant intentionally engaged in some conduct toward the plaintiff considered outrageous and intolerable in that it offends the generally accepted standards of decency and morality **(b)** with the purpose of inflicting emotional distress or where any reasonable person would have known that such would result, and **(c)** that severe emotional distress resulted as a direct result of the defendant's conduct.

The burden of proving "outrageous conduct" is a heavy one as liability exists only where the conduct is "atrocious, and utterly intolerable in a civilized community." Moreover, for a plaintiff to prevail, the case must be one in which the recitation of the facts to an average member of the community would arouse his resentment against the actor, and lead him to exclaim, "Outrageous!" As the **Restatement of Torts** explains:

> The liability clearly does not extend to mere insults, indignities, threats, annoyances, petty oppressions, or other trivialities. The rough edges of our society are still in need of a good deal of filing down, and in the meantime plaintiffs must necessarily be expected and required to be hardened to a certain amount of rough language, and to occasional acts that are definitely inconsiderate and unkind. There is no occasion for the law to intervene in every case where some one's feelings are hurt.

Utah cases analyzing the tort of intentional infliction of emotional distress have found merit only in extreme situations.

Defendant argues that, while the alleged pinch, which lasted for a moment only, may have been rude, inappropriate or offensive, it does not rise to the level such that a reasonable jury could find it outrageous, atrocious, or utterly intolerable in civilized society.

Plaintiff counters initially that defendant's conduct was outrageous because of its context; it occurred not only in front of spectators at the Delta Center, but in front of a national television audience as well. Moreover, plaintiff suggests the impact of defendant's conduct was greatly magnified because defendant was the center of attention. Plaintiff first notes defendant is Dennis Rodman, a basketball player known for his controversial behavior. Plaintiff further argues that, because defendant had the ball, the eyes of the audience were upon him at the time of the alleged touching. Finally, plaintiff states Madonna, defendant's girlfriend at the time, was present.

The court agrees with defendant that reasonable minds would not differ in concluding that defendant's alleged pinch does not constitute atrocious or utterly intolerable behavior. Rather, in the court's opinion, the alleged conduct constitutes an insult, indignity, or act which is definitely inconsiderate and unkind but which does not rise to a level warranting imposition of liability. Therefore, the court concludes defendant's alleged conduct is not outrageous so as to support a claim for intentional infliction of emotional distress.

SECTION 5.12
ASSAULT AND BATTERY

A **battery** is the intentional touching of the body of another or an object closely associated with the body in an offensive or harmful manner. Mere recklessness or negligence on the part of the actor is insufficient. The tortfeasor must in fact have intended to cause the harm.

An offensive touching is as objectionable as a harmful touching. For example, the uninvited touching of the body of another or an unappreciated kiss is as actionable as a punch in the mouth. There are times, however, when an intentional touching will not be deemed a battery. A person who engages in sport or play impliedly consents to the usual touching associated with that sport. For instance, professional football is a violent sport in which players frequently are injured because of the severity of the impact. If a star running back is injured while being tackled by five members of the opposing team, he can not sue the opposing players since the tackle is part of the game. The Cincinnati Bengals, however, were required to defend a lawsuit brought by a Denver Bronco who was intentionally hit in the back of the head by a Cincinnati player following an intercepted pass. The court ruled that the general customs of football do not approve the intentional punching or striking of other players. *Jack Hackbart v. Cincinnati Bengals, Inc.,* **601 F.2d 516 (1979).**

Professional boxing is a violent and vicious sport in which one of the primary objects is to knock out the opponent as quickly as possible. Head butts are occasionally landed during a match and are part of the fight. The biting of Evander Holyfield's ear by Mike Tyson during their heavyweight bout, however, was not a usual touching of the sport and would constitute a battery.

A consensual touching may be a battery if the consent was procured by fraud. For example, a party who touched the arms and legs of a woman on the fraudulent misrepresentation that he was a doctor was responsible for a battery.

MARGARET ANDREWS V. RICHARD PETERS
330 S.E. 2D 638 (CT. APP. N.C. 1985)

THE FACTS, BRIEFLY STATED, are as follows. The plaintiff, Margaret H. Andrews, was injured when her co-employee, August Richard Peters, III, walked up behind her at work and tapped the back of her right knee with the front of his right knee, causing her knee to buckle. Andrews lost her balance, fell to the floor, and dislocated her right kneecap. Andrews instituted this action against Peters for intentional assault and battery. She sought compensation for medical expenses, loss of income, pain and suffering, permanent disability, and punitive damages.

The trial judge submitted the case to the jury on the theory of battery. The jury entered a verdict in favor of Andrews on liability and awarded her $7,500 in damages. Andrews filed a motion for a new trial on the issue of damages, alleging that the inadequate verdict was the product of passion or prejudice and that the evidence was insufficient to support the verdict. The trial court granted Andrews' motion and Peters appealed.

Peters alleges that there is no evidence that he intended to injure Andrews. As summarized in Peters' brief:

> [Peters] testified that he did not intend to be rude or offensive in tapping [Andrews] behind her knees. He stated that the same thing had only moments before been done to him by a co-worker

and that it struck him as fun. He stated that he tried to catch [Andrews] to prevent her from striking the floor, that he was shocked by what had happened, and that he immediately apologized to [Andrews] and attempted to help her. Peters' contention ignores the nature of the intent required for an intentional tort action.

The intent with which tort liability is concerned is not necessarily a hostile intent, or a desire to do any harm. Rather it is an intent to bring about a result which will invade the interests of another in a way that the law forbids. The defendant may be liable although intending nothing more than a good-natured practical joke, or honestly believing that the act would not injure the plaintiff, or even though seeking the plaintiff's own good. **W. Prosser and W. Keeton**, The Law of Torts (5th ed. 1984). For example, liability for the intentional tort of bat-

tery hinges on the defendant's intent to cause a harmful or offensive contact. Significantly, [t]he defendant's liability extends, as in most other cases of intentional torts, to consequences which the defendant did not intend, and could not reasonably have foreseen, upon the obvious basis that it is better for unexpected losses to fall upon the intentional wrongdoer than upon the innocent victim. **Prosser and Keeton**, supra, Sec. 9, at 40. Peters does not deny that he intended to tap Andrews behind the knee. Although tapping Andrews' knee was arguably not in and of itself a harmful contact, it easily qualifies as an offensive contact. "A bodily contact is offensive if it offends a reasonable sense of personal dignity." **Restatement**, Section 19. There is no evidence of consent to the touching. We hold that the trial court did not err in denying Peters' motions for a directed verdict. Vacated and remanded for further proceedings consistent with this decision.

An **assault** is an act intended to put another in fear of an immediate battery. To commit an assault, it is not necessary that the tortfeasor actually intend to cause an offensive or harmful touching upon the body of another. Rather it is sufficient that the person intends to cause only a fear of such contact. Pointing a gun at a person and saying, "I am going to kill you" is an assault. However, a gunman who points his weapon at another with the warning, "I would kill you on the spot if this gun didn't make so much noise" has not committed an assault. The victim has not been placed in fear of an immediate touching.

STATE OF MONTANA V. MICHAEL ROULLIER
977 P.2D 970 (MONT. 1999)

ON SEPTEMBER 5, 1996, OFFICER JOHN STEVENS of the Polson Police Department responded to a domestic disturbance report at Allison Salmon's apartment. Salmon called the police after she had a fight with her boyfriend and roommate, Michael Roullier. Roullier had broken a window and an aquarium during the dispute, and then left the apartment prior to Stevens' arrival. Stevens noted the damage, and in the process also noticed a number of snake cages to which were attached "Caution: Venomous snake" warnings.

A short time after Stevens left, Roullier returned to the apartment, where he broke a door and appeared very upset. Salmon testified that she thought Roullier was suicidal. Roullier grabbed a snake from a cage and left the apartment, at which point Salmon again called the police. Stevens and his partner, Officer Tina Schlalie, returned to the apartment building and chased Roullier back into the apartment.

Inside the apartment, the officers found Roullier holding the snake, with one hand on the snake's head. Stevens, who was approximately six feet away from Roullier, told him to put the snake down, but Roullier refused. Roullier told the officers to get out of his way because he wanted to leave the apartment. Roullier advanced toward the officers while motioning with the snake's head, and told them that "if this snake bites you, you're dead." The officers backed up, but refused to let Roullier leave and told him again to put the snake down. Stevens testified at trial that he "thought [Roullier] was going to try to attack me with the snake," and that he feared serious bodily injury from the snake.

Schlalie prepared to hit the snake's head with her baton, but Roullier drew the snake close to his body. Stevens then threatened to use his pepper spray on Roullier. Roullier said, "If you spray me, then I will let it bite me and I will be dead." He continued to hold the snake's head to his arm as if he was going to let it bite him, while the officers repeated their requests that he put the snake down. Roullier eventually threw the snake behind him toward the cages and was handcuffed by the officers. He told them how to handle the snake and how to return it to its cage. The officers later learned that the snake was a Rhinoceros Viper, which is a very toxic African snake.

Roullier was charged with assault based on his alleged threatened use of the snake against Stevens. Roullier was convicted and ordered by the court to serve a five year sentence. *Section 45-5-202(2)(b)* of the *Montana Code* states that "[a] person commits the offense of assault if the person purposely or knowingly causes reasonable apprehension of serious bodily injury in another by use of a weapon."

Roullier contends that the State failed to prove that he actually "used" the snake to cause Stevens apprehension of serious bodily injury. Rather, he contends that the State's evidence only proved that he was in possession of the snake, and that possession alone is insufficient to prove use.

The record establishes that when the officers entered the apartment, they were confronted by Roullier with the snake in his arms. Roullier continued to hold the snake after repeated orders from the officers to put the snake down.

The record also shows that Roullier told the officers that a bite from the snake would be deadly, and that he advanced toward the officers with the snake extended in an effort to persuade them to move out of his way and permit him to leave the apartment. Furthermore, Stevens testified that he feared Roullier was going to attack him with the snake and that he would be seriously injured by the snake. Despite the failed nature of his attempts to get by the officers, and the fact that the snake did not bite either Roullier or the officers, there was sufficient evidence in the record from which a jury could find that Roullier's manipulation of the snake amounted to much more than mere possession, and that its use knowingly caused Stevens reasonable apprehension of serious bodily injury. Accordingly, we affirm the jury's verdict.

SECTION 5.13
INVASION OF PRIVACY

A person has the right to be left alone. An unwarranted intrusion upon this right constitutes the tort of **invasion of privacy**. Wiretapping of a neighbor's telephone, calling a divorced spouse every fifteen minutes, or disclosing private embarrassing facts about another are actionable wrongs.

Truth is not a defense to an invasion of privacy. For example, disclosing at a party that the host was a prostitute twenty years earlier is highly offensive and a private matter. Even though the information is true, that fact would not protect the disclosing party form liability.

As the age of technology continues to expand, serious questions have developed as to what is private in the workplace. Increasingly, employers are monitoring phones, using hidden cameras, and reading an employee's e-mail. In fact, some of the nation's largest and most respected companies have been sued for intruding into employee love affairs.

For example, IBM gave an employee a choice between her lover and her job. Since her lover worked for a competitor, IBM supervisors figured they had good reason to fire her. A court said they were wrong.

In the following case of *Harms v. Miami Daily News*, the court had to decide whether a newspaper violated the plaintiff's rights of privacy when it published her work telephone number in a story about sexy voices. She received numerous calls at work from people who wanted to hear her voice.

LOUISE HARMS v. MIAMI DAILY NEWS
127 SO.2D 715 (FLA. 1961)

HORTON, Chief Judge.

THE DEFENDANT NEWSPAPER, in an article written by defendant Rau, published the following statement: "Wanna hear a sexy telephone voice? Call _____ and ask for Louise."

The plaintiff, Louise Cook Harms, filed a complaint wherein she alleged that she was the "Louise" referred to and that the telephone number was that of the business office in which she is employed.

The complaint alleged:

> "Prior to the above publication Plaintiff has cherished and held precious the right to keep private her personal life, and her rights to be left alone, free from unwarranted, undesired and unsought after publicity.

> The above publication caused the Plaintiff to be flooded with many hundreds of telephone calls by various and sundry persons seeking to talk to and listen to the Plaintiff.

> The publication was an unwarranted invasion of the Plaintiff's rights to be let alone, free from unwarranted publicity and to be protected from a wrongful intrusion into her life, which has outraged her and caused her mental suffering, shame and humiliation."

> The trial court granted a motion to dismiss and entered judgment for the defendant. The question here is whether or not the complaint stated a cause of action.

The right of privacy is defined as the right of an individual to be let alone and to live a life free from unwarranted publicity. The right of privacy has its limitations. Society has its rights. The right of privacy must be accommodated to freedom of speech and of the press and to the right of the general public to the dissemination of information.

The right of privacy does not forbid the publication of information that is of public benefit, and the right does not exist as to persons and events in which the public has a rightful interest. *Reed v. Real Detective Pub. Co.*, **162 P.2d 133,** and *Barber v. Time, Inc.*, **159 S.W.2d 291.** The two principal limitations placed on the right of privacy are publication of public records and publication of matters of legitimate or public interest.

The right of privacy is relative to the customs of the time and place, and it is determined by the norm of the ordinary man. The protection afforded by the law to this right must be restricted to "ordinary sensibilities," and cannot extend to supersensitiveness or agoraphobia. In order to constitute an invasion of the right of privacy, an act must be of such a nature as a reasonable man can see might and probably would cause mental distress and injury to anyone possessed of ordinary feelings and intelligence, situated in like circumstances as the complainant; and this question is to some extent one of law."

At some point the public interest in obtaining information becomes dominant over the individual's desire for privacy. It has been said that the truth may be spoken, written, or printed about all matters of a public nature, as well as matters of a private nature in which the public has a legitimate interest. However, the phrase "public or general interest," in this connection, does not mean mere curiosity.

A person who, by his accomplishments, fame, or mode of life, or by adopting a profession or calling which gives he public a legitimate interest in his doings, his affairs and his character, may be said to have become a public personage, and he thereby relinquishes at least a part of his right of privacy.

The appellees argue that Harms should be considered as engaging in public affairs or public life to the extent that public interest drawn upon her or her "telephone voice." This is so merely because Harms was employed in a business office and the fact that she was called upon to answer the telephone in connection with her employment.

It would not appear that employment in a business office would render Harms a public personage. This is especially true since the appellee Rau's statements were not directed to news or information about the business office.

Reversed and remanded.

The tort of invasion of privacy may arise in a variety of situations, including:

- Unwarranted publicity;

- Intrusion into a person's private life;

- Disclosure of a private embarrassing fact; and

- Use of a person's name or likeness for another's financial gain.

As noted in *Harms v. Miami Daily News*, invasion of privacy is defined as the right of an individual to be left alone and to lead a life that is free from unwarranted publicity. This right, however, has its limitations. The right of privacy does not forbid the use of information that is of public benefit nor does it extend to information which the public has the right to know.

Based upon these concepts, the life of a public figure, such as a politician, actor, musician or athlete, is newsworthy so great latitude is afforded concerning disclosures of personal information about these individuals.

Over the years, a number of cases have arisen where the name, voice or likeness of a well-known person is used to promote a commercial venture without the celebrity's permission. This type of exploitation gives rise to the tort of invasion of privacy, which claim may be advanced by alleging; **(1)** the defendant's use of the plaintiff's identity; **(2)** the use of the plaintiff's name or likeness for the defendant's benefit; **(3)** the lack of consent to use the plaintiff's name or likeness; and **(4)** a resulting injury.

Cheers reined as one of the top television programs for many years. This show was memorable because of the colorful cast of characters whose dysfunctional lives unfolded on television while they sat around the bar talking about their problems. Two of the featured characters were Norm and Cliff, whose roles were played by George Wendt and John Ratzenberger.

The bar's image in providing a fun gathering place, "where everybody knows your name," has resulted in a number of pubs being opened at airports modeled after the Cheers set. As part of the motif, animatronic, robotic figures of Norm and Cliff were installed without the permission of the actors. The robots' physical likeness to Wendt and Ratzenberger, prompted the actors to file suit for invasion of privacy claiming that their likenesses are being used for another's financial gain. The Court's opinion on the merits of this lawsuit is set forth below.

GEORGE WENDT V. HOST INTERNATIONAL, INC.
117 F. 3ʳᴰ 1427 (9ᵀᴴ CIR. 1997)

ACTORS GEORGE WENDT AND JOHN RATZENBERGER appeal the district court's grant of summary judgment in favor of Host International, Inc. ("Host") and Paramount Pictures Corporation (Paramount), dismissing their action for violation of California's common law right of publicity. We reverse.

Wendt and Ratzenberger argue that the district erred in dismissing their action because they have raised issues of material fact as to whether Host violated their trademark and publicity rights by creating animatronic robotic figures (the "robots") based upon their likenesses without their permission and placing these robots in airport bars modeled upon the set from the television show Cheers.

California recognizes a common law right of privacy that includes protection against appropriation for the defendant's advantage of the plaintiff's name or likeness. *Eastwood v. Super. Ct. for Los Angeles County,* **198 Cal. Rptr. 342 (Cal. Ct. App. 1983).** The right to be protected against such appropriations is also referred to as the "right of publicity." A common law cause of action for appropriation of name or likeness may be pleaded by alleging (1) the defendant's use of the plaintiff's identity; (2) the appropriation of plaintiff's name or likeness to defendant's advantage, commercially or otherwise; (3) lack of consent; and (4) resulting injury.

The so-called right of publicity means that the reaction of the public to name and likeness, which may be fortuitous or which may be managed and planned, endows the name and likeness of the person involved with commercially exploitable opportunities. The protection of name and likeness from unwarranted intrusion or exploitation is the heart of the law of privacy. *Lugosi v. Universal Pictures,* **603 P.2d 425, 431 (1979).**

Appellees argue that the figures appropriate only the identities of the characters Norm and Cliff, to which Paramount owns the copyrights, and not the identities of Wendt and Ratzenberger, who merely portrayed those characters on television and who retain no licensing rights to them. They argue that appellants may not claim an appropriation of identity by relying upon indicia, such as the Cheers Bar set, that are the property of, or licensee of, a copyright owner. *Sinatra v. Goodyear Tire & Rubber Co.,* **435 F.2d 711, 716 (9th Cir.1970).**

Appellants freely concede that they retain no rights to the characters Norm and Cliff; they argue that the figures, named "Bob" and "Hank," are not related to Paramount's copyright of the creative elements of the characters Norm and Cliff. They argue that it is the physical likeness to Wendt and Ratzenberger, not Paramount's characters, that has commercial value to Host.

While it is true that appellants' fame arose in large part through their participation in Cheers, an actor or actress does not lose the right to control the commercial exploitation of his or her likeness by portraying a fictional character.

Appellants have raised genuine issues of material fact concerning the degree to which the figures look like them. Because they have done so, appellants have also raised triable issues of fact as to whether or not appellees sought to appropriate their likenesses for their own advantage and whether they succeeded in doing so. The ultimate issue for the jury to decide is whether the defendants are commercially exploiting the likeness of the figures to Wendt and Ratzenberger intending to engender profits to their enterprises. See: Eastwood, 198 Cal.Rptr. at 349 ("The first step toward selling a product or service is to attract the consumer's attention"). We therefore reverse the grant of summary judgment in favor of Host and Paramount on the common law right of publicity claim.

REVERSED and REMANDED.

SECTION 5.14 DEFAMATION	A statement is **defamatory** if it is false and tends to harm the reputation of another or to lower him in the estimation of the community. There are two categories of defamation: **libel and slander.**

Libel involves the publication of defamatory matter by written or printed words. **Slander**, on the other hand, is a defamatory communication that is verbal or oral in nature. Merely saying something defamatory to the aggrieved party is insufficient regardless of the false nature of the communication. In order for the defamatory comment to be actionable, it must be conveyed to a third person.

In the case of defamation, the truth of the matter communicated is an absolute defense. If the defendant can prove that what was said or written was true, a suit for defamation will fail.

Jack Kevorkian, M.D. v. American Medical Association
602 N.W. 2d 233 (Mich. App. 1999)

Jack Kevorkian, possibly the best known and most controversial proponent of assisted suicide, filed suit against defendant alleging that he had been defamed. Specifically, plaintiff claimed that the general counsel of the AMA, published a letter stating that plaintiff "perverts the idea of the caring and committed physician," "serves merely as a reckless instrument of death," "poses a great threat to the public," and engages in "criminal practices." Plaintiff further alleged that the AMA's executive vice president issued a news release alleging, "continued killings" and "criminal activities" by plaintiff and that the AMA's vice president for professional standards, published false and defamatory statements to the media calling plaintiff "a killer."

A communication is defamatory if it tends to so harm the reputation of another as to lower an individual's reputation in the community or deter third persons from associating or dealing with that individual. However, not all defamatory statements are actionable. For example, the United States Supreme Court has rejected the idea that all statements of opinion are protected, and has directed that the defamatory statement must be provable as false to be actionable.

The Supreme Court has also determined that defamatory statements must, in order to be actionable, state actual facts about a plaintiff, thereby protecting statements which, although factual on their face and false, could not reasonably be interpreted as stating actual facts about the plaintiff. Generally included as such protected speech are parodies, political cartoons and satires. However, it is also clear that two completely conflicting statements can "state actual facts" about an individual. In other words, plaintiff's acts of assisted suicide, for ex-

ample, can be described as murder or mercy, and any reasonable person could understand that both *or neither* could be taken as stating actual facts about plaintiff.

Statements, which are not protected and therefore are actionable, include false statements of fact, i.e., those which state actual facts but are objectively provable as false, and direct accusations or inferences of criminal conduct. Language, which accuses or strongly implies that someone is involved in illegal conduct, crosses the line dividing strongly worded opinion from accusation of a crime. Indeed, this Court has stated that an accusation of the commission of a crime is defamatory per se, meaning that special harm need not be proved.

Where a defendant's statements are not protected by the First Amendment, a plaintiff can establish a defamation claim by showing **(1)** a false and defamatory statement concerning the plaintiff, **(2)** an unprivileged publication to a third party, **(3)** fault amounting at least to negligence on the part of the publisher, and **(4)** either actionability of the statement irrespective of special harm (defamation per se) or the existence of special harm caused by the publication (defamation per quod. Where a public figure is involved in a defamation case, the public figure must prove by clear and convincing evidence that the publication was a defamatory falsehood, and that it was made with actual malice, i.e., with knowledge of falsity or with reckless disregard for the truth.

In this case, there is no dispute that plaintiff is a public figure. Indeed, more than most in recent memory, plaintiff "voluntarily exposed himself to the risk of defamation by injecting himself into public controversy." Additionally, the parties do not dispute that the issue of assisted suicide is a matter of public concern. Therefore, we must accord maximum protection to defendants' speech about plaintiff, with "special solicitude" for their speech on a matter of such urgent public concern.

However, even without that maximum protection and special solicitude, we hold as a matter of law that the alleged defamatory statements, taken individually or together, taken in or out of context so harm plaintiff's reputation as to lower that reputation in the community or to deter third persons from associating with him. We find that, as to the issue of assisted suicide, plaintiff is virtually "libel proof," which has been defined as "a rather loose-woven legal conception of the federal courts." *Brooks v. American Broadcasting Co*, **932 F 2d 495, 500 (CA 6, 1991).** In Brooks, the Court further defined the concept as follows: "[I]n those instances where an allegedly libelous statement cannot realistically cause impairment of reputation because the person's reputation is already so low—the claim should be dismissed so that the costs of defending against the claim of libel, which can themselves impair vigorous freedom of expression, will be avoided. "

In light of our conclusion that the implication that plaintiff is a murderer, which arises from the statements forming the basis of plaintiff's complaint, is not defamatory as to plaintiff. We decline plaintiff's invitation to hold as a matter of law that all accusations of criminal activity are automatically defamatory

Even if we were to conclude that defendants' statements are defamatory, state objectively verifiable facts about plaintiff and are provable as false, we would find that as to this highly public plaintiff, the statements also are necessarily subjective and could also be reasonably understood as not stating actual facts. They are either nonactionable rhetorical hyperbole or must be accorded the special solicitude reserved for protected opinion.

Plaintiff's very celebrity or notoriety derives exclusively from his participation in a national debate over the propriety of 'assisted suicide'— whether it is more akin to an act of mercy or to an act of homicide. Having exercised his leadership on behalf of one side of this debate, and having contributed substantially to the awareness of the American people of this debate, it is now more than a little disingenuous for plaintiff to accuse those on the opposite side of this debate of defamation. Such alleged defamation is nothing more than the fact that defendants are in disagreement with plaintiff's position: they would characterize plaintiff's conduct differently than plaintiff would characterize it. Where an alleged defamatory statement, occurring in the course of a public debate initiated or perpetuated by plaintiff himself, is focused precisely on a matter lying at the heart of the debate, it is hard to understand how the tort law could be implicated. Indeed, it is hard to imagine anything that could more effectively chill legitimate public debate.

Reversed and remanded for entry of judgment for defendants.

Even though a communication is false, an action for defamation will only be successful if the statement actually harms the reputation of another so as to lower the individual in the estimation of the community or to deter others from associating or dealing with that person. Therefore, an individual who believes that he has been defamed must be readily identifiable by and associated with the statement. This creates a problem when a class of people are the subject of the false statement. For instance, if a newspaper publishes an article that the students at a particular college are unruly drunks and bores, the individual students at the school will fail in a defamation action since they are not sufficiently identified in the article.

TEXAS BEEF GROUP V. OPRAH WINFREY
11 F. SUPP. 2D 858 (M.D. TEXAS 1998)

ON MARCH 20, 1996, BRITISH HEALTH Minister Stephen Dorrell announced that a committee of scientists had linked a deadly, degenerative brain disease in cattle known as Bovine Spongiform Encephalopathy (BSE) with a fatal human disorder known as Creutzfeldt-Jakob Disease (CJD). Minister Dorrell announced that consumption of beef was "the most likely explanation" for this new variant, which is characterized by the formation of holes in the brain creating a sponge-like appearance of brain tissue. It is always fatal.

BSE is commonly referred to as "Mad Cow Disease." It was first diagnosed in cattle herds in Great Britain in 1986. BSE is an infectious neurological disorder of cattle whose rapid spread in some countries is believed to have caused by the feeding of certain infected cattle and sheep tissues to cattle in the form of "ruminant" derived protein supplements. Cattle are ruminant animals.

On March 22, 1996, two days after the British announcement, the Animal & Plant Health Inspection Service of the United States Department of Agriculture called an emergency meet-

ing to explain the information coming out of Great Britain on Mad Cow Disease and to answer questions.

On April 2 and 3, 1996, the World Health Organization convened a two-day session to discuss Mad Cow Disease and issued a report stating, in part: "All countries should ban the use of ruminant tissues in ruminant feed."

On April 8, 1996, representatives from the Centers for Disease Control and Prevention, the National Institutes of Health, the Food and Drug Administration, the USDA, and the United States Department of Defense held a meeting to share information about the British announcement of the suspected link between BSE and the new variant of CJD in Britain.

On April 16, 1996, The Oprah Winfrey Show broadcast a program entitled "Dangerous Food" which included a segment on Mad Cow Disease. The show was taped on April 11, 1996. It was then edited to fit within a 42 minute and 30 second timeframe.

The show began with a discussion of Mad Cow Disease in England. A guest for this segment was Beryl Rimmer, from England, whose granddaughter was in a coma suffering from a form of CJD. Ms. Rimmer believed that her granddaughter contracted CJD from eating a hamburger tainted by Mad Cow Disease. She was critical of what she believed has been a cover-up by the British government of the link between Mad Cow Disease and CJD.

The second segment considered the question, "Could it happen here?" Guests in connection with that segment included... Defendant Howard Lyman, a former cattle rancher-turned-vegetarian who is executive director of the Humane Society's Eating With Conscience campaign. Lyman stated that the United States is at risk of an outbreak similar to that in England, if the practice continued. The program did not mention Texas or name any of the Plaintiffs.

The Plaintiffs are cattlemen operating in the Panhandle of Texas. Plaintiffs claim that the "Dangerous Food" show was "nothing more than a 'scary story', falsely suggesting that U.S. beef is highly dangerous because of Mad Cow Disease and that a horrible epidemic worse than Aids could occur from eating U.S. beef." Plaintiffs claim that Defendant Lyman is "a vegetarian activist and lobbyist, with an agenda to wipe out the U.S. Beef industry..." Plaintiffs contend that the April 16, 1996, broadcast of The Oprah Winfrey Show caused beef markets to "immediately" crash and that they were damaged thereby.

A defamation claim requires proof that the defendant in question published to a third person... a false statement of defamatory fact that was "of and concerning" the Plaintiff in question with the required degree of fault which proximately caused damage to the reputation of the Plaintiff in question. *Rosenblatt v. Baer*, **383 U.S. 75, 81, 86 S.Ct. 669, 673, 15 L.Ed.2d 597 (1966).**

The Court held in *Rosenblatt* that the jury could not find liability without evidence that the published statement "was made specifically of and concerning" the plaintiff. Texas law imposes the same "of and concerning" standard before a plaintiff can state a defamation claim "the settled law requires that the false statement point to the plaintiff and to no one else."

Texas law on defamation is: "A libel is a defamation expressed in written or other graphic form that tends to blacken the memory of the dead or that tends to injure a living person's reputation and thereby exposes the person to public hatred, contempt or ridicule, or financial injury or to impeach any person's honesty, integrity, virtue, or reputation or to publish the natural defects of anyone and thereby expose the person to public hatred, ridicule, or financial injury." The action for defamation is to protect the personal reputation of the injured party.

Even if a statement on the program could be construed to meet the definition of defamation, it cannot meet the "of and concerning" requirement. None of the Plaintiffs were mentioned by name on the April 16, 1996 Oprah Winfrey Show. Plaintiff Paul Engler testified that the statements made were about him "as well as the rest of the cattle feeding industry." Engler also testified that there are "about a million" cattlemen in the United States and that the states of Kansas and Colorado have feeding operations similar to Cactus Feeders in Texas.

The Texas Court of Appeals has held that an individual may not recover damages for defamation of a group or class in excess of 740 persons of which he is a member. Therefore, Plaintiffs have failed as a matter of law to meet their burden of establishing the "of and concerning" element of the defamation cause of action.

Accordingly, the Court grants Defendant's Motion for Judgment as a matter of law made at the close of Plaintiffs' case on the defamation claim.

SECTION 5.15
FALSE IMPRISONMENT

False Imprisonment is the unlawful detention of a person against his or her will. The tort is defined as the intentional and wrongful infliction of confinement against a person's will. The confinement may result from acts or words which the person fears to disregard. By implication, it is required that a person being detained be aware of the confinement and that the actor intended to confine the victim.

For example, a person detained in a department store who has been falsely accused of stealing merchandise may sue the store for false imprisonment if the business establishment acted without just cause in its actions.

CHRISTOPER VINCENT v. CHARLES BARKLEY
644 N.E. 2D 650 (ILL. APP. 1996)

PLAINTIFF CHRISTOPHER VINCENT seeks his day in court after a tough night in a Chicago bar.

This complaint was brought against Jayson Williams and Charles Barkley. Vincent alleged that Williams hit him over the head with a beer mug while they were out "socializing." Williams asserted the defense of self-defense.

Vincent further claimed that Williams and Barkley falsely accused Vincent of threatening Williams with a knife. Vincent was arrested and charged with aggravated assault. The case was stricken when Williams and Barkley failed to appear in court. Based on these facts, Vincent sought recovery for false imprisonment.

Vincent alleged that Williams and Barkley conspired together to fabricate a fictitious story about Vincent threatening Williams with a knife. This story, Vincent said, was a cover-up for Williams' unprovoked attack on the plaintiff. When the police came to the bar to investigate a report of a fight, Williams and Barkley, in furtherance of their plot, informed the police of this fictitious threat. Based upon this information, Vincent was arrested, charged with aggravated battery,

and confined in jail for approximately twelve hours before he was released on bail.

To state a cause of action for false imprisonment, the plaintiff must allege that his personal liberty was unreasonably or unlawfully restrained against his will and that defendants caused or procured the restraint. An unlawful arrest by an officer, caused or procured by a private person, is the same as an arrest by the private person. For liability to attach to the private person, however, the arresting officer must have relied solely on the information given to him by the private party when making the arrest.

It is clear to us that Vincent's complaint, on its face, states a cause of action for false imprisonment. Defendants argue that the trial court, by taking judicial notice of the police report that had been attached to plaintiff's prior complaint (but later withdrawn), could find that the officer did not arrest Vincent based solely on information given by them. This report indicated that two female witnesses gave the investigating police officers the "same info" given by the defendants.

This police report is not a "source of indisputable accuracy." It is an inadmissible hearsay document of unproved verity.

But even if judicial notice of this document were taken, it would not negate Vincent's allegation that defendants caused or procured his arrest. The report merely indicates that two other witnesses gave the police the "same info" given by defendants. The report does not say whether the witnesses' statements were based on direct observation of the incident or exactly what information they corroborated. This hearsay report, vague and general, should not be a substitute for direct, testimonial evidence.

For these reasons, the plaintiff's factual allegation that defendants, in conspiracy with one another, falsely and maliciously caused or procured his arrest are sufficient to withstand the motion.

SECTION 5.16
PRODUCTS LIABILITY

One of the more significant legal developments in recent times has been the adoption of **Section 402A of the Restatement (2nd) of Torts**. More commonly known as product liability, or strict liability, the law holds sellers of defective products liable for the harm caused to the user, consumer, or his property. This is the case even though the seller has exercised all possible care in the preparation and sale of the product.

The law of products liability has developed in response to society's changing attitude towards the relationship between the seller of a product and the consumer. Basically, the courts have abandoned the principle of caveat emptor and have made the supplier of a product a virtual guarantor of its safety. This insures that manufacturers who places a defective product in the market place will be responsible for the costs of injuries resulting from the defect rather than by the injured person who is powerless to protect himself.

The law of product liability provides that:

1. One who sells any product in a defective condition unreasonably dangerous to the user or consumer or to his property is subject to liability for physical harm thereby caused to the ultimate user or consumer, or to his property, if

   a. the seller is engaged in the business of selling such a product, and

   b. it is expected to and does reach the user or consumer without substantial change in the condition in which it is sold.

2. The rule stated in Subsection (1) applies although

   a. the seller has exercised all possible care in the preparation and sale of his product, and

   b. the user or consumer has not bought the product from or entered into any contractual relation with the seller.

STEPHEN PAVLIK V. LANE LIMITED/TOBACCO EXPORTERS INTERNATIONAL
135 F.3D 876 (3RD CIR. PA. 1998)

ON APRIL 10, 1994, AT ABOUT 2:30 A.M., plaintiff George Pavlik was asleep on his sofa when he was awakened by the sound of his twenty-year-old son, Stephen, arriving home after having spent the evening with his sister and friends. Shortly thereafter, Mr. Pavlik heard a loud "thud" coming from an upstairs room. When he investigated this unusual sound, Pavlik found Stephen lying on the floor of his bedroom, gasping for breath. Pavlik immediately called the police and began to perform CPR. Paramedics soon arrived and unsuccessfully attempted to revive Stephen. He was pronounced dead later that morning.

The coroner listed the cause of Stephen's death as cardiac dysrhythmia complicating abusive hydrocarbon inhalation. It is uncontroverted that this was the result of Stephen's intentional inhalation of butane gas. At the time of his death, a canister of Zeus brand butane was found atop Stephen's bedroom bureau. Warning language on the back panel of the Zeus can reads:

DO NOT BREATHE SPRAY
KEEP OUT OF REACH OF CHILDREN

Shortly after Stephen's death, Mr. and Mrs. Pavlik searched their son's room and found seven more cans of butane hidden under Stephen's underwear in a drawer of the bureau. Five of these cans were Zeus brand butane, and the other two bore the Clipper brand name. The back panel of the Clipper can warns in part:

CAUTION

KEEP OUT OF REACH OF CHILDREN

DELIBERATELY INHALING THE
CONTENTS MAY BE HARMFUL
OR EVEN FATAL.

Plaintiff filed the present lawsuit against Lane, the United States distributor of Zeus brand butane, alleging strict product liability for failure to warn.

The Pennsylvania Supreme Court, has adopted *Section 402A of the Restatement (Second) of Torts*, which imposes strict liability on the purveyor of a product in a defective condition "unreasonably dangerous to the user or consumer." Under **Section 402A**, an otherwise properly designed product may still be "defective" if the product is distributed without sufficient warnings to apprise the ultimate user of the latent dangers in the product. See *Davis v. Berwind Corp.*, **547 Pa. 260, 690 A.2d 186, 190 (Pa.1997).**

To recover under § 402A, a plaintiff must establish: **(1)** that the product was defective; **(2)** that the defect was a proximate cause of the plaintiff's injuries; and **(3)** that the defect causing the injury existed at the time the product left the seller's hands. In the context of a failure to warn case, to satisfy the second prong, the plaintiff must establish that it was the total lack or insufficiency of a warning that was a cause-in-fact of the injuries.

In a failure to warn case, we focus our analysis on the additional precautions that might have been taken by the end user had the allegedly defective warning been different.

There is evidence in the record indicating that Stephen Pavlik's mother, who passed away approximately one year after Stephen's death, knew that her son had inhaled butane on at least two prior occasions, once in 1992 and again in 1994. The coroner's certificate of identification, for example, states that Mrs. Pavlik had caught

Stephen inhaling butane about two years before his death, though she believed that he had since stopped. Stephen's sister, Theresa, also testified that Mrs. Pavlik had caught Stephen "doing something that's not right" with two cans of butane sometime in 1992, and that Mrs. Pavlik had told Stephen that if he continued, he would be thrown out of the house.

This evidence, however, is not uncontroverted. Theresa Pavlik consistently testified that Mrs. Pavlik did not know specifically what Stephen was doing with the cans of butane when the alleged 1992 incident occurred.

It is tempting to superimpose upon the record our own street-wise assumption that everyone knows the dangers (and warning signs) of butane abuse. But, as judges, we cannot do so. While it appears that Mrs. Pavlik gave some warning to Stephen, it is uncertain what the content of that warning was. Next, since the content of Mrs. Pavlik's warning is unclear, we cannot conclusively determine whether it was adequate to put Stephen on notice of the full extent of the risk of bodily injury, posed by butane inhalation.

The defendants also argue that Stephen had the type of adequate prior knowledge of the danger at hand because he had read the warnings on the Clipper and Zeus cans prior to his fatal inhalation.

We have serious doubts that the Zeus warning sufficiently warns users of the potentially fatal consequences of butane inhalation, and we are not convinced of its adequacy under § 402A. More specifically, the *"DO NOT BREATHE SPRAY"* warning appears to give the user no notice of the serious nature of the danger posed by inhalation, intentional or otherwise, and no other language on the Zeus can does so. Yet, we similarly cannot find that such a directive is inadequate as a matter of law, and so we must leave the question for the jury.

The twist in this case is that the defendants have also made the adequacy of the Clipper warning a central issue by virtue of their proximate cause analysis. The Clipper warning states, in small capital letters on the back panel of the can, *"Deliberately inhaling the contents may be harmful or even fatal."*

The inadequacies of the Clipper warning alleged by plaintiff are both substantive (i.e. the warning does not adequately describe the danger posed) and communicative (i.e. the warning does not command the attention of the user). Plaintiff primarily relies upon a report by E. Patrick McGuire, who is offered as a warnings expert. McGuire concludes that the Clipper warning is defective for the following reasons:

1. The inhalant danger is not listed on the front panel of the can, despite the fact that this is one of the "primary biological hazards associated with the foreseeable use of the product;"

2. The warning fails to specifically warn of the dangers of concentrating the product, i.e. the prohibitions about breathing the "contents" of the can are misleading such that some readers "will interpret this admonition to mean that a harmful dosage level is only inhaled;"

3. The warning is set in conditional language, as opposed to stating that inhalation is "likely" to produce a fatal reaction.

McGuire's opinion raises genuine issues of fact about the adequacy of the Clipper warning. On a substantive level, we can reasonably infer from McGuire's second and third critiques that even if Stephen Pavlik had read the Clipper warning, he would not have adequately been fully warned of the danger of bodily harm posed by butane inhalation.

But even if the warning was substantively sound, that might not be enough, for the case law suggests that factors such as the placement and size of warning labels should also be considered.

A manufacturer may be liable for failure to adequately warn where its warning is not prominent, and not calculated to attract the user's attention to the true nature of the danger due to its position, size, or coloring of its lettering.

We could also conclude from McGuire's testimony that the Clipper warning was insufficient to "catch the attention" of Stephen Pavlik. As McGuire noted in his report, the Clipper warning is listed on the back panel of the can. It is printed in relatively small type, of the same font, color, and size as the instructions for use. Indeed, we note that against the bright yellow label background, the non-highlighted, black text of the warning, in which the admonitions about avoiding extreme temperatures, flammability, and keeping the product away from children, run directly into the warning about inhalation, may appear as a blur to the average user.

Thus, drawing all inferences from the record in plaintiff's favor, we find that there is a genuine issue of material fact whether the Clipper warning was sufficient to catch Stephen Pavlik's attention.

As we have explained, the record is not unequivocal as to Stephen Pavlik's knowledge of the dangers posed by butane inhalation and his likely course of conduct. In sum, although a jury may not find enough evidence here to find for Pavlik at trial, he has introduced at least enough to create a genuine issue of material fact precluding summary judgment.

QUESTIONS FOR DISCUSSION:

1. Should a manufacturer of a microwave be strictly liable for failing to warn a consumer that a cat should not be dried in the appliance?

2. Should a manufacturer of a lawnmower be strictly liable when a person is injured when he uses a lawnmower to trim his hedges?

SECTION 5.17
REVIEW CASES

1. Hustler Magazine featured a "parody" of an advertisement for Campari Liqueur entitled "Jerry Falwell talks about his first time." While the parody was modeled after an actual Campari advertising campaign, the Hustler ad clearly played to the sexual double entendre of the subject, "first times." Copying the layout of the Campari ads, Hustler's editors chose this conservative religious official as their featured celebrity and drafted an alleged "interview" in which Falwell states that his "first time" was during a drunken incestuous rendezvous with his mother in an outhouse. Falwell sued Hustler Magazine for defamation and infliction of emotional distress. Hustler defended the claim on the basis of the First Amendment and the fact that Falwell is a public figure. Who should win the case? *Hustler Magazine v. Jerry Falwell*, **No. 87-1278 (U.S. 1986).**

2. Dustin Hoffman is a highly successful and recognizable motion picture actor. He has a strong policy of not endorsing commercial products for fear that he will be perceived in a negative way which would suggest that his career is in the decline. Los Angeles Magazine published a photograph of Hoffman as he appeared in the movie "Toostie," and, through computer software, altered the photograph to make it appear as though the actor was wearing a contemporary silk gown designed by Richard Tyler and high healed shoes created by Ralph Lauren. Underneath the picture contained the quote: "Dustin Hoffman isn't a drag in a butter-colored silk gown by Richard Tyler and Ralph Lauren heals." Hoffman sued the magazine for invasion of privacy for their commercial use of his name and likeness in a commercial venture. Is the magazine liable for the altered photograph of the actor or is it merely a parody for which no liability will attach? *Dustin Hoffman v. Capital City/ABC, Inc.*, 33 F. Supp. 2d 867 (1999).

3. Schick and his father were playing golf along with two other people. Schick teed off from the 16th hole, followed by two other golfers including his father. Subsequently, Verloito teed off and sliced his drive into the woods on the right, but the ball did not go out of bounds. Schick and his father then walked to their golf cart in front of the tee, assuming that Verloito would play his second shot from the woods. Instead, the golfer unexpectedly hit a second shot from the tee striking Schick in the face. Did Schick assume the risk of his injuries for being hit by a ball on the golf course? *Jeffrey Schick v. John Verloito*, 744 A.2d 219 (N.J. Super. 2000).

4. Linda Matarazzo attended an Aerosmith concert at Madison Square Garden. She was injured during the concert by an unknown patron who struck her in the nose as she attempted to return to her seat. Matarazzo sued Aerosmith on the grounds that the group's music encourages violence and their concerts attract "crazies" who are particularly drawn to this type of message. Warner Brothers Records was also sued under the theory that Warner Brothers willfully, intentionally, and deliberately aided and abetted Aerosmith in attracting such "crazies" to their concerts by promoting and selling records and tapes of the group's music. Should Aerosmith and Warner Brothers be responsible for the injuries sustained by the plaintiff? *Linda Matarazzo v. Aerosmith Productions, Inc.* 1989 W.L. 140322 (S.D. N.Y. 1989).

5. Debbie Tay had been a frequent guest on the Howard Stern show before her death at the age of 28. She was a topless dancer whose claim of having had sexual encounters with females from outer space earned her the nickname of "Space Lesbian." Tay was cre-

mated and her ashes were given by the family to her friend, Chaunce Hayden, who appeared on the Stern Radio Show with a box containing some of the remains. Stern played prior video clips of Tay's appearances on the program and then shook and rattled the box containing the decedent's remains. Stern even handled some of the bone fragments. These actions prompted a lawsuit by Tay's next of kin against Stern for infliction of emotional distress. Can the family hold Howard Stern responsible for the way he handled the decedent's ashes on his television show? *Jeffrey Roach v. Howard Stern,* 653 N.Y.S. 2d 532 (S. Ct. 1996).

6. Fisher and Segal composed the classic '50s' tune, "When Sunny Gets Blue." Rich Dees requested permission to use part of the composition in order to create a comedic version of the song but permission was refused. A few months later, Dees released a comedy tape entitled "Put It Where the Moon Don't Shine." One cut on the release was, "When Sonny Sniff's Glue." The parody was an obvious take-off on the composers' song and copied the first six of the composition's thirty-eight bars of music - its recognizable main theme. In addition, the remake changed the opening lyrics from "When Sunny gets blue, her eyes get gray and cloudy, then the rain begins to fall," to "When Sonny sniffs glue, her eyes get red and bulgy, then her hair begins to fall." The composers sued Dees for defamation claiming the new version of the song associated the composition with obscene, indecent and offensive words." Will Dees be responsible for the parody? *Marvin Fisher v. Rick Dees,* 794 F.2d 432 (9th Cir. 1986).

SECTION 5.18
INTERNET REFERENCE

For more information about the topics in this Chapter, see the following Internet sites:

- **http://www.lawguru.com/auto.html**
  For information on automobile accidents.

- **http://www.ljx.com/practice/negligence/index.html**
  This site discusses news related to the law of torts.

- **http://www.itslegal.com/infonet/injury/injurymain.html**
  Answers to frequently asked questions about tort law, including transportation accidents, injuries to property, medical malpractice, and defamation are provided at this address.

- **http://www.prairielaw.com/articles/article.asp?channelid= 22&articleid=1371**
  A general overview of the law of personal injury is located at this web address.

- **http://www.lectlaw.com/tmed.html**
  This site offers practical information about medical malpractice, civil litigation, and standards of care.

- **http://www.ashcraftandgerel.com**
  A law firm, which specializes in tort law, has created a web address that provides general information about the subject, and maintains a library of articles on the law of torts, including materials on medical malpractice and automobile accident litigation.

- **http://www.legalaidman.com**
  Practical information about personal injury claims, including what to do after an accident and the litigation process, is offered at this website.

- **http://encarta.msn.com/index/conciseindex/17/0170400.htm**
  Encarta Encyclopedia provides an overview of the law of negligence at this address, including the burden of proof in a civil case.

CHAPTER 6

CIVIL PROCEDURE

We belong to a litigious society whose members think nothing of instituting suit over every conceivable problem that one can imagine. "You'll be hearing from my lawyer" seems to be the battle cry of the day. Cases range from tragic plane crashes involving the loss of many lives to matters involving trivial sums of money to soothe the indignation of an aggrieved party.

The multitude and complexity of lawsuits requires the implementation of rules to govern the course of civil litigation from start to end. These pronouncements are called the Rules of Civil Procedure and will vary in formality depending upon the type of legal proceeding. The Rules governing a matter before Small Claims Court or People's Court will be very informal since litigants are encouraged to represent themselves. In more serious matters, the Rules are formal and quite detailed. Time deadlines are imposed for all phases of the litigation process and failure to comply with the Rules can result in sanctions such as a case being dismissed.

Civil litigation consists of three phases:

1. the Pleadings; 2. Discovery; and 3. the Trial.

The Pleadings consist of the initial papers filed with the court setting forth the relief requested by the plaintiff and the defenses of the parties being sued. These documents include such papers as the Complaint, Answer, New Matter or Affirmative Defenses, and Counterclaim. The pleadings establish the boundaries of the lawsuit since matters not asserted are generally waived. For instance, the defense of the Statute of Limitations must be raised at this time. Discovery allows each party to find out more information about the opponent's case. It is during this stage of the litigation that witnesses can be questioned under oath and counsel can obtain copies of the exhibits that will be used by the opponent at the time of trial. In addition, medical or psychological examinations of a party may be ordered if relevant to the case.

The final stage of litigation is the trial itself. It is at this judicial proceeding that questions of fact and credibility will be decided, and a verdict will be rendered. The trial is very formal in its presentation, and Rules of Evidence determine the admissibility and sequence of witnesses.

SECTION 6.2
PETER CHRISTOPHER
V. JOSEPH HODGE

As you know, we represent Joseph Hodge and his family in a variety of legal matters. Gregory Dodge, a senior partner in the firm, has recently completed a most unusual trial in a suit brought by Peter Christopher against Joseph Hodge for serious personal injury. The jury is presently deciding the outcome of that suit. Dodge needs your assistance to ascertain whether his client received a fair trial. All relevant documents have been provided for your review and include the pleadings, discovery and trial transcript.

A member of the firm will go over the documents with you so you can obtain a better appreciation for the significance of each item. This is the only way that you will be able to provide Mr. Dodge with a meaningful analysis of the problem. His concerns are addressed in a memo that accompanies the trial transcript. Mr. Dodge is under a lot of pressure to win this case since a loss would mean the financial ruin of our best client, Joseph Hodge. Your anticipated help is most appreciated.

SECTION 6.3
FACTS

Harry, the Hodge family's pet gorilla, attacked and seriously injured Peter Christopher on September 3. Peter now suffers the loss of his left leg. Along with other less severe bite wounds, the animal inflicted this injury by mauling Peter's leg. The incident occurred on Sunday of the Labor Day holiday weekend. The temperature was in the mid 90's which combined with the 85% humidity level made the heat unbearable. Both the Hodge family and their neighbor, Peter Christopher, were outside attempting to relax by their swimming pools.

Later in the afternoon, the Hodges went inside to eat and Harry fell asleep by the portion of the fence which bordered Christopher's property. The smell of the animal next to his property aggravated Christopher who was intoxicated at this point in time. The neighbor poked the animal with a pole. He had hoped to awaken Harry and relocate him to the opposite side of the yard. Instead, Christopher angered Harry so much that the animal became vicious and attacked him.

Christopher was seriously injured and his leg had to be amputated because of the deep nature of the wound and an infection that set in. Christopher has filed suit over the attack claiming that Joe was negligent in keeping the gorilla in his back yard and in failing to take the necessary measures to prevent a wild animal from attacking a person.

SECTION 6.4
FEE ARRANGEMENTS

Individuals can hire attorneys under a variety of fee arrangements. These include a fixed price, a per hour billing, a retainer and a contingent fee agreement.

In a limited number of cases, an attorney knows exactly how much time will be involved in the handling of a matter and can quote a specific price. These matters include a simple uncontested divorce, the drafting of a will, or the incorporation of a business. Most cases are handled on a per hour basis. An attorney will charge only for the actual time expended on the handling of a case. The per hour fee will vary depending upon the sophistication of the problem and expertise of the attorney. The average range will vary between $90 and $300 per hour. All client contact is recorded and the client is billed for that time. This includes telephone conferences and the writing of letters on a client's behalf. Anyone who retains an attorney on a per hour basis should ask for an itemized bill setting forth the time spent by the attorney on the case by date and service rendered. These statements should be sent on a periodic basis such as a month or two months apart.

Personal injury matters are frequently handled by plaintiff's counsel on a contingent fee basis. This means that the attorney will take a percentage of the recovery as the legal fee. If counsel is unsuccessful in recovering money for a claimant, no legal fee is due and owing the attorney. The contingent fee agreement will vary in percentage from one-third to 50 percent of the recovery. The average arrangement is 40 percent but some firms will offer a staggered rate depending upon the amount of work expended to create the settlement. For instance, if a case is settled before suit, an attorney may take 30 percent of the recovery, if the settlement is achieved after the institution of suit, the percentage may increase to 35 percent and if the case is tried, the fee will increase to 40 percent.

SECTION 6.5 CONTINGENT FEE AGREEMENT

In the case of *Peter Christopher v. Joseph Hodge,* Peter Christopher signed a contingent fee agreement. The following is a sample of that document and provides for a one-third recovery from the gross settlement.

> *The undersigned hereby constitutes and appoints the law firm of Smith and Dunkum, P. C., as his attorney to prosecute all causes of action on account of an accident or incident which occurred on September 3, involving Harry, the gorilla.*

> *I hereby agree that the compensation of my attorney for services shall be determined as follows:*

> *Out of whatever sum which is secured by either my said attorney or by me from the defendants, or from anyone else, either by way of voluntary payment, settlement or verdict, my said attorney, for and in consideration of the professional services rendered in the investigation and general conduct of the said case or claim, including the institution of suit, if necessary, shall retain or be entitled to forty percent (40%) of the gross amount of any recovery.*

> *I understand and agree that my attorney is under no obligation to represent or continue to represent me on any appeal from an adverse verdict or deci-*

sion. I reserve the right to decide on the acceptability of any settlement offer that may be made and to decide whether an appeal from an adverse verdict or decision will be taken. Should no money be recovered by verdict or settlement by either my attorney, or by me, my said attorney is to have no claim against me of any kind for services rendered by him.

Peter Christopher

_____ (SEAL)

Peter H. Christopher

SECTION 6.6
HOURLY BILL

Joseph Hodge is being defended on a per hour basis. The time expended on his case is recorded daily on a timelog broken down into six-minute intervals. For instance, one-tenth of an hour or ".1" is the equivalent of six minutes.

THE FOLLOWING IS A SAMPLE BILL.

HODGE, DODGE AND LODGE
1515 MARKET STREET, 6TH FL.
PHILADELPHIA, PA 19100

Joseph A. Hodge
39 Royal Court
Rydal, Pennsylvania 19000   **Invoice:** 1010101
                                   Page: 1

RE: *Christopher v. Hodge*

For Professional Services Rendered:

Date	Description of Service	Hours	Rate Per Hour
1/5	Conference with client	0.5	$125
1/5	Letter to opposing counsel	0.3	$125
1/7	Legal research	3.0	$125
1/9	Phone conference with oppos. counsel	0.5	$125
1/9	Review of medical records	2.0	$125
1/9	Letter to client	0.3	$125

Total Hours: 6.60

Total Amount of Bill: *$825.00*

What happens when a client hires a lawyer on a contingent fee basis and then fires that lawyer before the case begins? Is the attorney still entitled to the full fee even though he is no longer working on the file? The courts generally award the discharged attorney a fee based on the value of services rendered to the date of discharge, or in legal terms, on a "quantum meruit" basis. Quantum Meruit is an equitable remedy that provides for a form of restitution. A case is made out when one person has been unjustly enriched at the expense of another.

Some states, such as New Jersey and New York, regulate the percentage that an attorney may charge to handle a contingency fee case. Pennsylvania on the other hand, does have a restriction on the amount that can be charged by an attorney unless the case involves a minor or a worker's compensation claim. In a lawsuit in which Hulk Hogan was a party, an attorney in New York tried to change the fee arrangement from one-third to one-half on the eve of trial. The court was very critical of this action and refused to allow the increased fee.

BELZER V. TERRY BOLLEA, A/K/A HULK HOGAN
571 N.Y.S. 2D 365 (N.Y. 1990)

THIS CASE HAVING BEEN SETTLED on the eve of trial, plaintiff's attorney has made application to this court to approve additional compensation of 50% of the recovery, instead of the normal one-third contingency fee, for the "angst, aggravation and life's blood which this case caused."

The attorney's application for additional compensation was supported by the client. He stated that while a one-third contingency retainer was initially agreed upon, as the trial approached, he had agreed to increase the attorneys' contingent compensation to 50%. The client's supporting affidavit spoke in glowing terms of the dedication and devotion of his attorneys. However, after the attorneys had submitted the formal application for the additional fees, the plaintiff, in a letter to the court, stated that despite his prior supporting affidavit, he in fact objected to the increased compensation requested by his attorneys, and had agreed to the higher fee only under duress and upon his attorneys' threats to withdraw from the action before trial. In view of the inestimable benefits the attorney claims to have achieved for his client, he charges his client is a "paradigm of ingratitude." Well might he mutter, as did King Lear, "Ingratitude, thou marble-hearted fiend!"

The purpose of the rules fixing contingent fees in personal injury actions is to prevent attorneys from exacting unconscionable fees even though there appears to be agreement by the client. The function of the courts "to keep the house of the law in order does not hinge upon whether clients, worn down by injuries, delay, financial need and counsel holding the purse strings of settlement, knowing little about law or lawyers, have the stamina to resist." It was in recognition of the possibility that clients might readily agree to fee arrangements which courts considered unconscionable, and to prevent the attorney from making himself the equal partner of the injured party by taking 50% of the recovery, that the Appellate Division undertook to regulate the amounts which could be charged.

The contingent fee rules which govern attorneys in actions involving personal injury, no matter what the agreement between the attorney and client may be, are now embodied in **22 NYCRR**

603.7 (e). Subdivision (e) (1) provides that fees in excess of those contained in the schedule of fees "shall constitute the exaction of unreasonable and unconscionable compensation", unless they have been authorized by a written order of the court. **Subdivision (e) (2)** then sets forth the schedule of presumptively reasonable fees.

Two alternatives are presented. Under schedule A, a sliding scale of permissible recovery is set running from 50% of the first $ 1,000 to 25% of sums over $ 25,000. Alternatively, the compensation may be fixed pursuant to schedule B, which calls for a flat percentage not exceeding 33 1/3% of the sum recovered.

In this action, the original retainer agreement did provide for charges in excess of the permitted contingency fees because it called for a contingent fee of 33 1/3% of the gross proceeds "or whatever the Firm's straight time billing charges would have been, whichever is greater."

An attorney may handle a case on the basis of a flat retainer, on the basis of charges for time incurred, or on a contingency. If there is a contingency agreement, the attorney cannot exceed the permitted percentages by providing for alternatives which would result in even higher compensation. The contingent fee is permitted because the attorney takes the risk of recovering nothing at all. If the agreement pro-

vides for the certainty of recovery in any event, the risk which justifies the contingency fee is removed, especially if there can be a recovery on a time billing basis should that turn out to be more remunerative.

The attorney here claims that on the basis of straight time charges, including over 50 hours for the preparation of an assault complaint, the value of the firm's services was well above what a one-third contingent fee would permit. But an attorney cannot have it both ways. If he fixes a one-third contingent retainer, his ultimate fee is tied in with the client's recovery, for better or for worse. He takes the risk of a loss if the ultimate recovery is too low, but he may have a windfall if the recovery is much greater. The essence of a contingent fee is risk — shared risk. Sometimes the attorney wins, sometimes he loses, sometimes he breaks even.

Pursuant to these rules, the court will treat any provision of the agreement which calls for compensation greater than 33 1/3% a nullity, and whether the client in fact agreed or disagreed to additional fees, and no matter how sterling the representation may have been to the time of trial, the court concludes that there is no authority for the award of additional compensation. The application of the attorneys is therefore denied.

SECTION 6.7
SERVICE OF PROCESS

Procedural due process requires that a defendant be notified of the legal proceeding. In a criminal case, this occurs when the defendant is arrested or indicted. In a civil matter, the defendant is served with a copy of the Complaint. This is usually accomplished by a designated officer of the court, such as the Sheriff, who personally hands a copy of the lawsuit to the defendant. Frequently, the Sheriff attempts personal service only to find the defendant not at home. Is the Sheriff mandated to continue to search for the individual, or can this judicial officer serve another person such as a spouse or business partner?

The rules of court allow service of a legal document upon one other than the defendant as long as the service is reasonably calculated to notify a person that he or she is the subject of a claim. For example, Pennsylvania Rule of Civil Procedure 402 sets forth the various ways that a lawsuit may be served on the defendant. Basically, the litigant must be handed a copy of the legal document personally, or the Sheriff

may serve an adult member of the household of the defendant at the residence.

THE FOLLOWING IS THE TEXT OF THE RULE:

RULE 402. MANNER OF SERVICE
ACCEPTANCE OF SERVICE

a. Original process may be served:

1. by handing a copy to the defendant; or

2. by handing a copy

   (i).   at the residence of the defendant to an adult member of the family with whom he resides; but if no adult member of the family is found, then to an adult person in charge of such residence; or

   (ii). at the residence of the defendant to the clerk or manager of the hotel, inn, apartment house, boarding house or other place of lodging at which he resides; or

   (iii). at any office or usual place of business of the defendant to his agent or to the person for the time being in charge thereof.

Based upon Rule 402, which of the following situations constitute proper service over Joseph Hodge in the case of *Peter Christopher v. Joseph Hodge:*

1. The Sheriff serves Estelle, Joe's wife, at their home;

2. The Sheriff serves Kathy, Joe's 16-year-old daughter at the household;

3. The Sheriff hands the Complaint to a painter who is painting the Hodge's home;

4. The Sheriff proceeds to the supermarket a block away from the Hodge household and serves Estelle in the store as she is buying a watermelon;

5. The Sheriff serves Tony, while he is attending a Philadelphia Flyers game at the First Union Center;

6. The Sheriff hands the Complaint to the mailman who gives it to Joe with the other mail while making the daily mail delivery to Joe's home or

A copy of the Sheriff's Return of Service is attached showing that the Sheriff personally served Joseph Hodge with the Complaint on November 12 at 9:00 a.m. The document was handed to the defendant at his home at 39 Royal Court, Rydal, Pennsylvania.

SHERIFF'S RETURN OF SERVICE- PHILADELPHIA CO.	COURT TERM AND NUMBER OCTOBER TERM - NO. 555	
TO BE COMPLETED BY ATTORNEY	SHERIFF'S NUMBER 365	
PLAINTIFF(S) PETER H. CHRISTOPHER	COST $110.00	MILEAGE 35
DEFENDANT(S) JOSEPH A. HODGE	DISTRICT ☐ SUMMONS ☐ COMPLAINT ☐ OTHER _____	

SERVE AT
    37 Royal Court
    Rydal, PA 19000
	TYPE OF ACTION
	
	              CIVIL	

SPECIAL INSTRUCTIONS		

TO BE COMPLETED BY SHERIFF

Served and made known to _____ Joseph A. Hodge _____ , Defendant(s)

on the ___12___ day of ___November___ 19_____ at ___9___ o'clock ___A.M.___

at ___37 Royal Court, Rydal, PA 19000___ Street, county of Philadelphia

Commonwealth of Pennsylvania, in the manner described below:
☐ Defendant(s) personally served.
☐ Adult family member with whom said Defendant(s) reside(s). Relationship is _____
☐ Adult in charge of Defendant's residence who refused to give name or relationship
☐ Agent or person in charge of Defendant's office or usual place of business
☐ _____ and officer of said Defendant company
☐ Other _____

SHERIFF RALPH C. PASSIO III

By _____

DEPUTY SHERIFF

What happens if the defendant is lured into the jurisdiction through fraud or deceit solely for purposes of serving that individual with the lawsuit? Will this type of conducted be allowed? This is the issue presented in *Hotlen v. Middour.*

ARTHUR HOTLEN v. CHARLES MIDDOUR
404 PA. 351 (1961)

DEFENDANT, G. CHARLES MIDDOUR, is a manufacturer of aluminum storm windows and doors. His factory and principal place of business is in Waynesboro, Franklin County, Pennsylvania. Defendant does no business in Philadelphia and except for passing through on a train has been in Philadelphia only twice in the past five years. Plaintiff, Arthur M. Hotlen, (trading under the name of Easy Aluminum Products Company), has since 1959 sold Middour's products. Hotlen's place of business is in Philadelphia.

The present controversy arose over a transaction between plaintiff (Hotlen) and one Sidney Smith, who was doing business under the name Apex Window Company. Smith had ordered a number of window frames from Hotlen. Hotlen had then ordered the frames from Middour.

While Middour was in the process of constructing the frames, and after some of them had been made, Hotlen notified him not to make shipment since Smith had not paid him (Hotlen). A number of telephone calls between Hotlen and Middour ensued. Plaintiff (Hotlen) told defendant that Smith would make payment only to defendant and that defendant would have to come to Philadelphia to discuss the deal and receive payment. It was finally agreed that defendant would come to Philadelphia on September 7, 1960, to meet plaintiff and Smith and that a telephone call confirming this meeting would be made on September 6. On September 6, the prothonotary of the Court of Common Pleas of Philadelphia County issued a writ of summons against defendant. At 7:28 that evening defendant, as previously agreed, called plaintiff and at that time plaintiff told him that they would meet Smith on the sidewalk in front of Bookbinders Restaurant in Philadelphia at noon the next day, September 7.

Defendant arrived at the appointed place at noon and was met by plaintiff. Plaintiff greeted him and thereupon excused himself. A deputy sheriff then approached defendant, identified himself and handed defendant the summons, which came as a surprise and a shock to defendant. Defendant had no other business in Philadelphia nor did he do business here; and Smith never appeared or testified for plaintiff.

The general rule is as follows:

"Personal service of process, if procured by fraud, trickery, or artifice is not sufficient to give a court jurisdiction over the person thus served, and service will be set aside upon proper application."

Relief is accorded in such cases not because, by reason of the fraud, the court did not get jurisdiction of the person of the defendant by the service, but on the ground that the court will not exercise its jurisdiction in favor of one who has obtained service of his summons by unlawful means. Thus, if a person resident outside the jurisdiction of the court and the reach of its process is inveigled, enticed, or induced, by any false representation, deceitful contrivance, or wrongful device for which the plaintiff is responsible, to come within the jurisdiction of the court for the purpose of obtaining service of process on him in an action brought against him in such court, process served upon him through such improper means is invalid, and upon proof of such fact the court will, on motion, set it aside: The American Jurisprudence text is supported by *Eastburn v. Turnoff*, **394 Pa. 316, 319-320, 147 A.2d 353.**

It is clear to us from the record that plaintiff tricked, lured and inveigled defendant into

Philadelphia County for the purpose of serving him with process and that the pretended meeting with Smith was a sham to conceal plaintiff's real purpose.

Order reversed with directions to enter an order sustaining defendant's preliminary objections and dismissing the complaint.

SECTION 6.8
THE PLEADINGS

The purpose of the pleadings is to place the parties on notice of the claim, to set forth the theories of liability and defenses, and to establish the boundaries of the litigation. In other words, if the plaintiff asserts that the defendant was negligent in the operation of a car, he can not allege that the defendant intentionally ran him off the road at trial. Likewise, if the defendant has a defense to the lawsuit, it must be asserted at this time or it will be waived.

The plaintiff initiates a lawsuit by filing a complaint with the Clerk of the Court or Prothonotary. This pleading is like a short story and sets forth the plaintiff's theory of liability against the defendant as well the damages the claimant maintains that he or she is entitled to receive.

The complaint will generally follow the following outline:

1. It will identify the parties to the lawsuit and set forth their addresses;

2. It will set forth the facts in a light most favorable to the plaintiff;

3. It will identify the theory of liability such as negligence or invasion of privacy;

4. It will list the damages and/or injuries; and

5. It will conclude by asking for a dollar amount.

Regardless of the merits of the *complaint*, the defendant must file a response to the lawsuit within a specified number of days. Generally, the response is called the *answer* and the defendant must admit or deny each paragraph of the complaint. The defendant is also required to assert his or her defenses at this time, such as the statute of limitations or assumption of the risk. This is done in a pleading called *new matter* or *affirmative defenses*.

If the defendant has a cause of action against the plaintiff, it may be raised as a *counterclaim*. In the alternative, the defendant can simply file a separate lawsuit against the plaintiff.

If a pleading is defective, a party may file *Preliminary Objections* and the matter will be referred to a judge for a ruling.

HODGE, DODGE and LODGE   Attorney for Defendant
1515 Market Street, 6th Fl.   Joseph Hodge
Philadelphia, PA 19100
By: Gregory Olan Dodge
I.D. No. 99923

PETER H. CHRISTOPHER	: **COURT OF COMMON PLEAS**
35 Royal Court	: **CIVIL TRIAL DIVISION**
Rydal, PA 19000	:
	:
v.	: **PHILADELPHIA COUNTY**
	:
JOSEPH A. HODGE	:
37 Royal Court	:
Rydal, PA 19000	: **OCTOBER TERM NO. 555**

ANSWER OF JOSEPH HODGE TO THE COMPLAINT OF PETER H. CHRISTOPHER

1-2. Admitted.

3.   Admitted. However, the backyard was enclosed by a five-foot high fence.

4-5. Denied. Said paragraphs call for a conclusion of law.

6.   Denied. The plaintiff's injuries were the result of his own misconduct.

7-10. Denied. Said paragraphs call for conclusions of law to which no responsive pleading is needed. Furthermore, after reasonable investigation, plaintiff lacks knowledge or information sufficient to form a belief as to the truth of these averments.

NEW MATTER

11. Plaintiff has failed to state a cause of action.

12. Plaintiff's claim is barred by the provisions of the Comparative Negligence Act.

13. Plaintiff's claim is barred by the doctrine of Assumption of the Risk.

COUNTERCLAIM OF JOSEPH HODGE, AS LEGAL GUARDIAN FOR HARRY THE GORILLA AGAINST PETER CHRISTOPHER

14. On or about September 3, Joseph Hodge was the owner and legal guardian of a gorilla named Harry which was kept in the backyard.

15. On the aforesaid date, Peter Christopher trespassed on the property of Hodge and willfully and wantonly attacked Harry with a metal pole thereby causing the gorilla to sustain serious and permanent injuries.

16. Solely by reason of the aforesaid occurrence, Harry sustained a cervical sprain and strain, bruises and contusions about the body, and was made to undergo great pain, mental anguish and agony from which he has suffered, and may, and probably will in the future, continue to suffer.

17. Solely by reason of the aforesaid occurrence, Joseph Hodge has, and will in the future, be obliged to expend various sums of money for veterinarian care and medicine, in an endeavor to treat and cure Harry.

WHEREFORE, Joseph Hodge, on behalf of Harry Hodge, claims damages from Peter Christopher in an amount in excess of $50,000.00.

HODGE, DODGE & LODGE

Gregory Olan Dodge
_____
Gregory Olan Dodge, Esquire
Attorney for Joseph Hodge, as an
Individual and as Guardian for
Harry the Gorilla

HODGE, DODGE AND LODGE
ATTORNEYS AT LAW
MEMORANDUM

To: All Law Clerks

FROM: Gregory Olan Dodge

RE: Hodge v. Johnson

While Tony Hodge was home during the off season, he decided to visit Temple University in order to see some of his friends. While he was stopped at a red light facing southbound on Broad Street at its intersection with Montgomery Avenue, Tony's Corvette was struck in the rear by a car being driven by Jim Johnson.

Apparently, Johnson was so intent on changing the radio station on his stereo that he did not see Tony's car stopped in front of him. While Tony was not hurt, his new Corvette sustained $3,000.00 in property damage. Tony has also learned that it will take two weeks to fix his car and he will have to rent another vehicle in order to get around. A substitute car will cost $420.

I want to file a Complaint against Johnson for the property damage that he caused to Tony's car. Please prepare the pleading so that we can file it with the Court of Common Pleas in Philadelphia County. As you know, Tony lives at 37 Royal Court, Rydal, Pennsylvania. Mr. Johnson resides at 805 Broadway in Philadelphia. You are to follow the form of the Complaint involving Peter Christopher, which is described in *Section 6.8*. The cause of action should be based on allegations of negligence. Your document should set forth in detail what Johnson did wrong.

Section **6.10**
Discovery

Between the time that a lawsuit is filed and the case proceeds to trial, the litigants will engage in discovery. This process allows an attorney to learn more about an opponent's case by the orderly exchange of information between counsel.

The tools of discovery may be classified as follows:

1. Interrogatories

2. Request for Production of Documents

3. Depositions

4. Submission to a Medical Examination

5. Request for Admissions

Interrogatories are written questions submitted to an opponent that must be answered in writing under oath. This tool is used so frequently by attorneys that forms have been created for specific kinds of cases. For example, form Interrogatories exist for personal injury cases involving medical malpractice, car accidents and products liability. Since the issues are generally the same, standard questions may be utilized in various cases. When the circumstances warrant, specific questions can be crafted to cover any situation.

A **Deposition** is the oral questioning of a person under oath in which everything that is said is recorded by a stenographer. Depositions are informal in nature and can take place in a courthouse or in an attorney's office. Anyone with knowledge about a case can be deposed.

A **Request for Production of Documents** requires an attorney to turn over to opposing counsel a copy of the file. While an attorney's work product and mental impressions are exempt, statements of witnesses, photographs, records, and medical reports must be exchanged.

A party may be required to submit to a **physical or mental examination** if relevant. For example, if a plaintiff institutes suit for personal injury, a defendant has the right to have the claimant examined by a doctor of the defendant's own choice.

Request for Admissions are used to narrow the issue for trial. A litigant can ask an opponent to admit certain facts about the case. If the information is admitted, then it does not have to be proven at the time of trial. For example, a defendant may ask a plaintiff to admit that the claimant had a previous back injury. If the fact is admitted, the defendant will not have to produce the medical records about the previous back injury at trial.

The following is a copy of the Interrogatories propounded by the attorneys for Joseph Hodge and sent to Peter Christopher. You will see that the questions are quite broad but they allow opposing counsel to obtain a basic understanding of the claim as well as learning background information about the opponent.

HODGE, DODGE and LODGE   Attorney for Defendant
1515 Market Street, 6th Fl.   Joseph A. Hodge
Philadelphia, PA 19100
BY: Gregory Olan Dodge, Esq.
I.D. No. 99923

PETER H. CHRISTOPHER	:	**COURT OF COMMON PLEAS**
35 Royal Court	:	
Rydal, PA 19000	:	
	:	
v.	:	**PHILADELPHIA COUNTY**
	:	
JOSEPH A. HODGE	:	
37 Royal Court	:	
Rydal, PA 19000	:	**OCTOBER TERM NO. 555**

INTERROGATORIES ADDRESSED TO THE PLAINTIFF

I. PERSONAL BACKGROUND

1. **What was (a) your residence address at the time of the incident giving rise to this lawsuit and (b) what is your present residence address?**

   a. *35 Royal Court, Rydal, PA 19000*

   b. *Same as above.*

2. **What is your date of birth?**

   April 1, 1965.

3. **What is your social security number?**

   653-11-0058

4. **What was your marital status at the time of incident giving rise to this lawsuit and what is your present marital status?**

   Single

II. EMPLOYMENT

(To be answered only if the person responding to interrogatories was employed at time of accident giving rise to this lawsuit)

1. **Did you, as a result of the incident giving rise to this lawsuit, lose any earning capacity, lose any time from your occupation or business or employment or lose any wages or emoluments from your occupation or employment?**

   Yes.

2. **If, as a result of the incident giving rise to this lawsuit, you lost any time from any occupation or employment, please state what your occupation or employment was at the time of the incident.**

   At the time of the incident, I did freelance work in surveillance and investigation.

3. **If, as a result of the incident giving rise to this lawsuit, you lost any time from any occupation or employment, please state the full name and address of your employer (a) at the time of the incident giving rise to this lawsuit and (b) at the present time.**

   Self-employed.

4. **If, as a result of this incident giving rise to this lawsuit, you lost any time from any occupation or employment, what were the dates for which you experienced such income loss?**

   Six months after accident.

   I have also had to decline future employment with the government of Santa Domingo which would have begun January 1 and continued indefinitely.

5. **If, as a result of the incident giving rise to this lawsuit, you lost any time from any occupation or employment, (a) what was your average gross income received per pay period within one month prior to the accident and (b) how frequently were you paid?**

   a. My average gross income per month was $25,000.00.

   b. I was paid weekly.

6. **If, as a result of the incident giving rise to this lawsuit, you lost any time from any occupation or employment, please state the total earnings you received from your occupation or employment for the twelve months prior to the incident giving rise to this lawsuit.**

   $273,000.00.

7. **At the time that you returned to work, what tasks, if any, were you unable to perform as well as immediately prior to the incident giving rise to this lawsuit?**

   I have not been able to do any work since the incident, and I do not anticipate being able to return to work doing undercover surveillance.

III. INCIDENT FACTS

1. **In the eight-hour period immediately preceding the accident, did you consume or ingest any alcohol, drug, narcotic, sedative, tranquilizer, or form of medication?**

   Yes.

2. **If the answer to the preceding interrogatory is in the affirmative, state the type of item consumed, the quantity consumed, and the time or times of day said items were consumed.**

   I had few beers but can't recall the exact amount.

3. **Did you do anything to provoke the gorilla?**

   I prodded him a few times with a metal pole.

4. **Were you on your own property at the time of the attack?**

   No.

5. **If the answer to the previous interrogatory is in the negative, (a) on whose property were you? (B) why?**

   (a) *I was on the Hodge's property.*

   (b) *I was trying to move the animal away from my property because of the noise and smell that were coming from the animal thereby disrupting the piece and enjoyment of my property.*

6. **What is the name and address of any person *who* saw all or any part of the incident giving rise to this lawsuit?**

   There were no witnesses.

7. **Describe how the incident occurred.**

   I was trying to get the gorilla to move to the other side of the yard. I tapped him with one of my pool tools to awaken him. He was a wild animal from the moment he opened his eyes. Before I could get away from him, he had hold of my leg in his mouth. I could feel his huge teeth bearing down upon my skin. I screamed and kicked, but my cries were useless. His jaw ripped my leg in two. I don't remember anything after that. I am told that I passed out, and that after hearing my screams the Hodges rescued me from further injury.

IV. Personal Injuries

1. **Did you suffer any personal injuries as a result of the incident giving rise to this lawsuit, including, but not limited to physical, emotional or mental injuries?**

   Yes.

2. **If the answer to the preceding interrogatory is in the affirmative, what injuries did you sustain?**

   Amputation of the left leg below the left knee cap, multiple bruises and abrasions, scarring and post traumatic concussions.

3. **Have you ever been involved in any kind of accident or occurrence before or after the incident upon which this lawsuit is based affecting any part or function of your body claimed in this lawsuit?**

   No.

4. **Did you ever suffer any injuries, sickness, or disease or abnormality of any kind prior to the accident or occurrence giving rise to this lawsuit which involved any part or function of the body claimed in this suit to have been injured?**

   No.

5. **As of this date, have you received any bill or charges for any medical treatment received by you for injuries sustained in the accident giving rise to this lawsuit?**

   Yes.

6. **What is the name, address and dates of treatment, nature of treatment, and charge for each hospital, clinic, nursing home, or other institution which provided you medical attention for injuries sustained as a result of the incident giving rise to this lawsuit?**

   Temple University Hospital

9/3	*Emergency Room*	*$ 4,500*
9/3	*Operating Room*	*8,400*
9/3 - 9/14	*Patient Room*	*15,700*
9/3	*Telephone*	*110*
9/3 - 9/14	*Medicines*	*920*
		$ 39,630

7. **What is the name, address and date of treatment, nature of treatment, and charge relative to each doctor, or therapist who examined you or treated you for injuries arising out of the incident giving rise to this lawsuit?**

Dr. Donald Feelgood
39 Royal Court
Rydal, PA 19000

9/3	*Surgery*	*6,300.00*
9/18	*Examination*	*75.00*
10/18	*Examination*	*75.00*
		$ 6,450.00

Dr. Sylvia Sleeper
1820 Broad Street
Suite 4
Jenkintown, PA 18000

9/3	*Anesthesia*	**$ 1,270.00**

Dr. Wanda Walker
238 Park Avenue, Suite 150
Cherry Hill, NJ 08804

9/8 - 14	*Physical therapy in hospital, daily care)*	*$ 1,050.00*
9/15 - 10/15	*Physical therapy (at home, daily care)*	*3,000.00*
10/15 - 11/15	*Physical therapy (maintenance program)*	*1,800.00*

Dr. Albert Abrams
10 Garden Lane
Huntington Valley, PA 15000

9/15	*Psychotherapy (in hospital)*	*$150.00*
9/22	*Psychotherapy*	*150.00*
10/2	*Psychotherapy*	*150.00*
10/7	*Psychotherapy*	*150.00*
10/14	*Psychotherapy*	*150.00*
10/6	*Psychotherapy*	*150.00*
10/18 - 20	*Psychotherapy*	*450.00*
10/28	*Psychotherapy*	*50.00*
11/2 - 4	*Psychotherapy*	*450.00*
11/10	*Psychotherapy*	*150.00*
11/15	*Psychotherapy*	*150.00*
		$ 2,400.00

8. Do you claim that any medical treatment or expense may be required in the future in regard to any injuries sustained in this accident?

Yes.

9. If the answer to the preceding interrogatory is in the affirmative, state the injury which would require such medical treatment or expense in the nature of the future treatment that might be required.

My amputated leg will require my undergoing continued physical therapy until at least march and the fitting of an artificial leg.

10. What is your present physical condition as compared with your condition immediately prior to the incident giving rise to this lawsuit?

I am now lame whereas I used to have normal use of both of my legs.

11. If you have not fully recovered from all of the injuries sustained in the incident giving rise to this lawsuit, describe any and all pains, ailments, complaints, injuries, or disabilities that you presently have as a result of the incident giving rise to this lawsuit.

I have recurrent throbbing in my left leg and walk with a limp. I cannot walk, run, jump, or engage in any other physical activity requiring the use of two legs. I am also extremely depressed and often suicidal over my disfigurement.

12. Did you wear or use any prosthetic device or appliance such as a cane, crutches, medical braces, casts, corsets or elastic bandage as the result of the incident giving rise to this lawsuit?

Yes.

13. If the answer to the preceding interrogatory is in the affirmative, what was the name of the device used, its cost, and the dates which you used it?

I have an artificial limb, and also use medical braces. These devices cost, respectively, $9,800.00 and $479.00. I have used them continuously since September 8.

SMITH AND DUNKUM   HODGE, DODGE and LODGE

Peter Smith   *Gregory Olan Dodge*
_____   _____
Peter Smith, *Esquire*   **Gregory Olan Dodge,** *Esquire*
Attorney for Plaintiff   Attorney for Defendant

HODGE, DODGE and LODGE 1515 Market Street, 6th Fl. Philadelphia, PA 19100 (BY: Gregory O. Dodge, Esq. I.D. No. 99923	Attorney for Defendant Joseph A. Hodge

PETER H. CHRISTOPHER 35 Royal Court Rydal, PA 19000	: COURT OF COMMON PLEAS : CIVIL TRIAL DIVISION : :
v.	: PHILADELPHIA COUNTY :
JOSEPH A. HODGE 37 Royal Court Rydal, PA 19000	: : : OCTOBER TERM NO. 555

REQUEST TO PRODUCE

To: *Peter Smith, Esquire*   Attorney for *Peter H. Christopher*

You are directed to produce at 9:00 a.m. on November 1, for purposes of inspection and copying at the offices of Hodge, Dodge and Lodge, 1515 Market Street, 6th. Fl., Philadelphia, PA 19100, or such other site in the City of Philadelphia as you may designate in writing filed of record and served on all other counsel the items listed below:

1. All documents concerning the manner in which the accident occurred including but not limited to statements of witnesses.

2. All documents concerning the injuries sustained by any party to this action.

3. All bills, reports, and records, from any and all physicians, hospitals, or other health care providers concerning the injuries sustained from the accident or occurrence by any person other than the party serving this request.

4. Any and all reports, writings, memoranda, Xeroxed cards and/or other writings, lists compilations concerning this action or its subject matter.

Gregory Olan Dodge

GREGORY OLAN DODGE, ESQUIRE
Attorney for Joseph A. Hodge

SECTION 6.11
SUBPOENA

A subpoena is a Court Order directing a person to appear in court or at another designated location to provide testimony in a court proceeding. Failure to obey the subpoena can result in a recalcitrant witness being held in *contempt of court*. It is through this process that parties are able to compel witnesses to testify in judicial proceedings so that the facts may best be presented to the finder of fact. Subpoenas are used both at the time of trial and through the pre-trial process of discovery.

There is nothing magical about the form itself. Subpoenas are generally purchased from the Clerk of the Court and kept in the attorney's office until needed in a case. They are pre-signed by the court and the attorney merely fills in the appropriate biographical information on the document to identify the witness. A representative of the attorney's office such as a private investigator personally serves the subpoena upon the witness. A witness is entitled to a modest fee for his or her appearance which compensation should be tendered at the time that the subpoena is served. Never ignore a subpoena since it carries with it the contempt powers of the court. If a problem exists with the date for the witness' testimony, one should contact the attorney whose name is listed at the bottom of the document to see if the date can be changed.

SUBPOENA NO.

Commonwealth of Pennsylvania
County of Philadelphia

95 0046141

In the matter of:

COURT OF COMMON PLEAS

PETER H. CHRISTOPHER
(Plaintiff)   (Demandante)

OCTOBER _____ Term, 19____

vs.

No. _____ 555 _____

JOSEPH A. HODGE
(Defendant)   (Demandado)

Subpoena

To: DONALD FEELGOOD, M.D.
(Name of Witness)   (Nombre del Testigo)

1. YOU ARE ORDERED BY THE COURT TO COME TO *(El tribunal le ordena que venga a)*
COURTROOM 302 _____, AT PHILADELPHIA, PENNSYLVANIA ON *(en Filadelfia,*
Pennsylvania el) ___ DECEMBER 15 ___, AT *(a las)* ___9:00___ O'CLOCK ___A.___ M., TO
TESTIFY ON BEHALF OF *(para atestiguar a favor de)* _____ PLAINTIFF _____ IN THE
ABOVE CASE, AND TO REMAIN UNTIL EXCUSED *(en el caso arriba mencionado y permanecer hasta que le autoricen irse)*.

2. AND BRING WITH YOU THE FOLLOWING *(Y traer con usted lo siguiente)*:
ALL MEDICAL RECORDS OF THE PLAINTIFF

NOTICE	AVISO
If you fail to attend or to produce the documents or things required by this subpoena, you may be subject to the sanctions authorized by Rule 234.5 of the Pennsylvania Rules of Civil Procedure, including but not limited to costs, attorney fees and imprisonment.	Si usted falla en comparecer o producir los documentos o cosas requeridas por esta cita, usted estara sujeto a las sanciones autorizadas por la regla 234.5 de las reglas de procedimiento civil de Pensilvania, incluyendo pero no limitado a los costos, remuneracion de abogados y encarcelamiento.

INQUIRIES CONCERNING THIS SUBPOENA SHOULD BE ADDRESSED TO *(Las preguntas que tenga acerca de esta Citacion deben ser dirigidas a)*:
ISSUED BY:
MARY DUNKUM, ESQUIRE
(Attorney)   (Abogado/Abogada)
ADDRESS *(Direccion)* ___ One Logan Square, 40ᵗʰ Fl., Philadelphia, PA
TELEPHONE NO. *(No. de Telefono)* 555-8989
ATTORNEY *(Abogado ID #)* 689950
BY THE COURT *(Por El Tribunal)*

PRO _____ (Clerk) *William Langelotti*

10-200 (Rev. 1*/94)

While the court has great discretion in being able to hold a party in contempt, the imposition of sanctions must be fair. A finding of criminal contempt will be sustained when the Court finds (1) misconduct; (2) in the presence of the court; (3) committed with the intent to obstruct the proceeding; and (4) that obstructs the administration of justice. Samples of contemptuous behavior include cases where the defendant removed his clothing down to his underwear, and persisted in arguing with the judge, where the defendant told a judge to go to hell, and where the defendant failed to return to the courtroom for the afternoon trial session. *Commonwealth v. Odom*, **764 A.2d 53 (Pa. Super. 2000).**

Consider the case of ***U.S. v. Flynt*** in which Larry Flynt was imprisoned for his disruptive behavior. His outbursts were prompted by Flynt's desire to obtain a continuance of his case in order to mount a defense based upon his mental condition. If a person lacks the necessary mens rea to understand that his conduct is inappropriate, can he or she be held in contempt?

UNITED STATES OF AMERICA V. LARRY FLYNT
756 F.2D 1352 (NINTH CIR. 1985)

LARRY FLYNT APPEALS FROM FIVE JUDGMENTS of criminal contempt entered by Judge Manuel Real. Because we conclude that the denial of appellant's motion for a continuance constituted abuses of the trial court's discretion, we reverse appellant's convictions.

On December 12, 1983, Flynt appeared before Magistrate James W. McMahon for arraignment on charges of flag desecration and unlawful wearing of a Purple Heart. Flynt, who is paralyzed and confined to a wheelchair, had worn an American flag as a diaper and pinned the Purple Heart to his shirt when he appeared at the courthouse in connection with an earlier unrelated contempt proceeding. During his arraignment, Flynt made a series of insulting, abusive, and obscene remarks to Magistrate McMahon.

The dialogue in which appellant and the Magistrate engaged was as follows:

THE MAGISTRATE: Mr. Flynt, if you tell me that you do not understand that you have the right to have an attorney represent you, I am going to be obliged, in order to protect your rights, to appoint an attorney to represent you.

THE DEFENDANT: *Don't do me any favors, your Honor. I mean, you are the madam, and over here (indicating) is another whore and this guy who says he is my attorney is a street walker.*

THE MAGISTRATE: Mr. Flynt, I expect you to behave yourself here.

THE DEFENDANT: *Then you might as well put my ass in jail. Now, I am trying to be nice to you, god damn it. Now, are you going to let me read my arraignment and plea or are you going to put me in jail again? What the f... is going on here?*

THE MAGISTRATE: All right. I am going to appoint Mr. Isaacman to represent you.

THE DEFENDANT: *Then take my ass to jail,— because I—*

THE MAGISTRATE: All right.

THE DEFENDANT: *—refuse to go through this bullshit.*

THE MAGISTRATE: All right, would you proceed with the arraignment?

THE DEFENDANT: *You dumb, ignorant mother f...... Now, I am telling you; you are not going to get away with this.*

THE MAGISTRATE: Proceed with the arraignment.

THE DEFENDANT: *There are [sic] no f...... way you are going to get away with it. You are denying me my counsel of my choice. You are just as dumb as that god damn Burger up there on the Supreme Court, and I am ready to stay in jail until hell freezes over or until I have the attorney of my choice. You god damn, no good, 14 karat piece of shit, you. Just cause you got on that robe, you don't have any god damn right to abuse the Constitution that you are supposed to be upholding.*

Magistrate McMahon issued an Order to Show Cause why Flynt should not be held in contempt and ordered Flynt to appear before Chief Judge Real. Flynt's counsel informed the court that Flynt's defense would consist of a showing that he lacked the requisite mental capacity to commit contempt. He argued that Flynt's incarceration prevented him from submitting to psychiatric examinations by psychiatrists of his own choosing. He then requested a thirty-day continuance in order to allow Flynt to obtain expert witnesses.

Judge Real granted a one-day continuance to allow Flynt to obtain his desired counsel. The next day Flynt again appeared before Judge Real and renewed his motion for a thirty-day continuance in order to obtain psychiatric evaluations relevant to his defense. Judge Real again denied the motion for a continuance and began the hearing immediately.

Flynt's defense consisted of testimony from seven non-expert witnesses, including himself and his bodyguard, concerning his mental and emotional conditions on the date of the alleged offense. In the course of Flynt's direct examination, he was asked to state reasons for his outbursts before the Magistrate. He responded with a series of epithets directed toward the judiciary in general. Judge Real called a recess and ordered Flynt gagged. When the hearing resumed, Judge Real admonished Flynt that any further outbursts would result in contempt citations. He then ordered removal of the gag and Flynt resumed his testimony.

The following exchange (then) took place between appellant and the court:

FLYNT: *I move that you call the U.S. marshal to the stand that was present when I took the drugs, when I was flung on the floor by an inmate, and when I was kicked, when I was smacked. I want the U.S. marshal called, I also want the guard called that tipped me off that this asshole was sending me to Springfield.*

THE MARSHALL: *Open up the door.*

THE COURT: No, that is all right. He's got the responsibility. That is going to cost you 30 days, Mr. Flynt.

THE DEFENDANT: *Hey, you know what punishment-- is. Well, you don't give a...*

THE COURT: Mr. Flynt, you just keep that up.

THE DEFENDANT: *Give me life without parole you foul mother- f...*

THE COURT: That is another 30.

THE DEFENDANT: *I want you—give me more. You chicken-shit son-of-a-bitch.*

THE COURT: That is another 30 days.

THE DEFENDANT: *Give me more.*

There can be no question that the type of conduct in which Flynt engaged cannot be tolerated in a courtroom. There are a number of measures that may be taken to bring such conduct to an immediate end. Punishment, including a term of incarceration, may be imposed, if appropriate procedures are followed. However, the issue before us is not whether Flynt engaged in the conduct with which he is charged. The issue is not even whether Flynt actually had the mental capacity to commit the offense of contempt. Rather the issues presented here are procedural ones that raise questions of essential fairness. No matter how opprobrious the offense, every person is entitled to have his guilt or innocence determined in a manner that complies with our rules, laws and Constitution.

In defense to the charge of contempt, Flynt proposed to offer evidence that he lacked the requisite capacity to commit contempt. To this end, appellant was entitled to call psychiatric witnesses of his own choosing who, after examining appellant, could testify as to his mental state. However, appellant remained incarcerated in the Medical Center in Springfield, Missouri until three days prior to the hearing and was not examined by any such prospective witnesses. Subsequently, upon the court's grant of a one-day continuance rather than the thirty-day continuance requested by appellant, appellant's counsel advised the court that he had obtained three expert witnesses but that while all three had agreed to examine appel-

lant and testify to their conclusions, they were unable to perform adequate evaluations within the time constraints imposed by the district court.

It should have been apparent from the nature of Flynt's defense, from his erratic behavior, and from the other evidence before the district court that the testimony would be relevant. In our view, the continuance, if granted, clearly would have served a useful purpose.

It is clear that appellant's sole defense to the contempt charge was that he lacked the requisite mental capacity to commit the offense. It is equally clear that he could not establish this defense without the testimony of expert witnesses. Although he had identified his expert witnesses, they had not had an opportunity to examine him and, therefore, were not in a position to testify. Thus, the result of the court's refusal to grant a continuance "was to deprive the accused of the only testimony potentially effective to his defense." *United States v. Fessel,* **531 F.2d 1275, 1280 (5th Cir.1976).**

There are no mechanical tests for deciding when a denial of a continuance warrants reversal. Here, appellant has established that he suffered prejudice as a result of the district court's decision to deny the continuance. Hence, we find that the district court abused its discretion in denying the continuance and we reverse the conviction that was based on appellant's conduct before Magistrate McMahon.

SECTION 6.12
RULES OF EVIDENCE[1]

Cases are tried by the presentation of evidence. Witnesses are called and questioned by the attorneys. The finder of fact will listen to the testimony and decide who is telling the truth.

Rules of Evidence have been established to govern the way an attorney may examine a witness or ask a question. These Rules are complex and attempt to cover a wide range of possible situations arising in all types of trials.

The following is an overview of some of the Rules of Evidence. It has been prepared by the staff of the Law Education and Participation (LEAP) Program at Temple University School of Law for use in High School Mock Trial Competitions. LEAP organizes the program in conjunction with the National Institute for Citizen Education in the Law of Washington, D.C.

EXAMINATION OF WITNESSES

A witness is questioned on direct examination when he or she is called by an attorney to prove the client's side of the case. A witness who testifies on direct examination may not be asked a "leading question" by the attorney who calls that witness. A leading question is one that suggests to the witness the answer desired. For example, the question, "Isn't it true that you last saw Mrs. Jones on January 1st?" is leading. The correct way to phrase the inquiry is, "When did you last see Mrs. Jones?" A question on direct examination should be designed to obtain a short narrative answer.

An exception to the leading question rule exists if an attorney calls the opponent as a witness, or a witness is shown to be "hostile." The Court may allow the attorney to ask leading questions under these circumstances. The purpose of this exception is to prevent a hostile witness from avoiding direct, non-leading, questions.

Hearsay testimony is generally prohibited in court. Hearsay is an out of court statement made by someone other than the witness, to prove the truth of the facts contained in the statement. An example of hearsay is when Mr. Smith testifies that "Joe told me that Harry was wearing a light blue coat." The opposing attorney can object when Smith says, "Joe told me…," indicating that the witness is relying upon what someone else said. To be objectionable, the answer would also have to be relevant to the case that Harry was wearing a blue coat. The Court, however, may allow the hearsay statement if Joe is the opposing party and the out of court statement made by Joe was against his interest.

There are a number of exceptions to the hearsay rule. One of the more unusual exceptions deals with a **dying declaration.** If the decedent has been the victim of a crime, is critically wounded and identifies the culprit on his deathbed, the identification will be allowed in the criminal trial even though the statement is hearsay. The idea behind the rule is that a person is not going to lie just before death. A dying declaration will be admissible even though the statement is hearsay, if **(1)** the victim identifies his attacker, **(2)** the victim believes he is going to die, **(3)** death is imminent, and **(4)** death actually occurs.

Opinion testimony is an expression of non-factual conclusions. Generally a "lay witness" can only testify as to observed facts and those areas of "opinion" that the Court would consider to be within the general knowledge of the witness. For example, a person may testify as to the speed of a car if the witness has had some experience in driving or observing cars travelling at the speed concerned. Opinion testimony, however, may be given by an expert witness. An expert is a person who can be "qualified" as having specialized knowledge in a given field because of professional credentials and/or experience acceptable to the Court. In the alternative, the attorneys for each side can agree or "stipulate" that a witness is an expert.

Relevant evidence is testimony or an exhibit that helps establish a fact which is controverted or necessary to prove one's side of the case. The Court usually allows an attorney to obtain "background information" from an important witness. For example, an attorney may ask the witness about his age, family, or work experience even though it is not relevant to the central issue of the case. The opposing attorney is granted leeway in questioning the witness to explore the truthfulness of the person's direct testimony, including omitted facts, bias or prejudice.

Not all evidence that may shed light on an issue, however, will be allowed into evidence. In Federal court, the trial judge is also required to examine the prejudicial effect of the proffered evidence. If the probability of the evidence in establishing a fact is substantially outweighed by negative factors, such as confusion of the issue, unfair prejudice, or misleading the jury, the admissibility of the evidence will be denied.

The safety of the American public from a terrorist attack was rudely shattered in 1995 when a several thousand pound bomb, secreted in a Ryder truck, destroyed the federal courthouse in Oklahoma City. Timothy McVeigh was convicted of the crime, which killed or injured hundreds of people. The apparent motive for this act of terrorism was to seek revenge for the incident at Waco, which McVeigh believed was planned by the FBI at the Federal building in question.

During his criminal trial, McVeigh wanted to introduce testimony identifying other radicals who could have destroyed the Federal building. The court refused to allow this proffered evidence on the basis of relevancy. The judge felt that this defense was too speculative and its probative value was outweighed by the prejudicial nature of the testimony.

UNITED STATES OF AMERICA v. TIMOTHY McVEIGH
CASE #97-1287 (10ᵀᴴ CIR. 1998)

TIMOTHY J. McVEIGH WAS CONVICTED, and sentenced to death as the result of the bombing of the Alfred P. Murrah Federal Building in Oklahoma City, Oklahoma, that resulted in the deaths of 168 people. McVeigh appeals his conviction on the grounds that the court erred by excluding evidence that someone else may have been guilty.

At 9:02 in the morning of April 19, 1995, a massive explosion tore apart the Murrah Building, killing a total of 168 people and injuring hundreds more. Fifteen children in a day care center visible from the front of the building, and four children visiting the building, were included among the victims. Eight federal law enforcement officials also lost their lives. The explosion, felt and heard six miles away, tore a gaping hole into the front of the Murrah Building and covered the streets with glass, debris, rocks, and chunks of concrete.

Just 77 minutes after the blast, Oklahoma State Trooper Hanger stopped the Mercury driven by McVeigh because the car had no license tags. The stop was just before the exit for Billings, Oklahoma, precisely 77.9 miles north of the Murrah Building. If McVeigh had left the Murrah Building right after the bombing, he would have arrived at the Billings exit around 10:17 a.m., the approximate time of the stop. An FBI test found that McVeigh's clothing contained explosives residue associated with the materials used in the construction of the bomb.

McVeigh challenges the court's decision to exclude evidence that McVeigh argues would suggest that persons connected with a white-supremacist, anti-government organization in Stillwell, Oklahoma, known as "Elohim City," were involved in the conspiracy to destroy the Murrah Building. McVeigh contends that the court abused its discretion when it excluded as "not sufficiently relevant" the proffered testimony from Carol Howe, an undercover government informant at Elohim City.

Howe allegedly would have testified that during her trips to Elohim City, she met Dennis Mahon, one of Elohim City's leaders, and that Mahon was a violent opponent of the federal government. Howe would have testified that Mahon instructed her in the preparation of napalm and had shown her various bomb components. Mahon also discussed the availability of the explosive Semtex, as well as his experience in building and exploding a 500-pound ammonium nitrate bomb under a truck.

Howe's proffered testimony also promised to discuss Andreas Strassmeir, another leader at Elohim City, who allegedly discussed acquiring bomb components. Howe was to testify that Mahon and Strassmeir had discussed targeting a federal building in either Oklahoma City or Tulsa. Howe also was to testify about the appearance at Elohim City in the spring of 1995 of James Ellison, who had developed plans to bomb the Murrah Building in 1983 before he was imprisoned on unrelated charges.

After hearing the proffer, the court ruled, "Well, we've had a number of disclosures concerning Mahon, Strassmeir, Elohim City and now some additional information from Carol Howe. But my ruling is that it's excluded, not sufficiently relevant to be admissible."

Under the **Federal Rules of Evidence,** "[a]ll relevant evidence is admissible," subject to the limitations provided by the **Federal Rules.** Thus, the threshold to admissibility is relevance.

Rule 401 which provides that evidence is relevant if it has "any tendency to make the existence of any fact that is of consequence to the determination of the action more probable or less probable than it would be without the evidence."

Even though evidence may meet the relevancy standard of **Rule 401,** a court still may exclude it on the grounds that its probative value – the evidence's probability of establishing a fact of consequence – is "substantially outweighed" by certain negative factors. **Fed. R. Evid. 403.** Those factors include "unfair prejudice," "confusion of the issues," and "misleading the jury."

In the course of weighing probative value and adverse dangers, courts must be sensitive to the special problems presented by "alternative perpetrator" evidence. Although there is no doubt that a defendant has a right to attempt to establish his innocence by showing that someone else did the crime, a defendant still must show that his proffered evidence on the alleged alternative perpetrator is sufficient to show a nexus between the crime charged and the asserted "alternative perpetrator." *Matthews v. Price*, 83 F.3d 328 (10th Cir. 1996). It is not sufficient for a defendant merely to offer up unsupported speculation that another person may have done the crime. Such speculative blaming intensifies the grave risk of jury confusion, and it invites the jury to render its findings based on emotion or prejudice.

Finally, after identifying the degree of probative value and adverse danger, courts exclude relevant evidence if the adverse dangers "substantially outweigh" the probative value. **Fed. R. Evid. 403.**

Even if we assume that the proffered evidence had some marginal relevance, the Howe testimony cannot survive the balancing under **Rule 403.** We conclude that the probative value of such proffered testimony was slight because of its highly generalized and speculative nature. The fact that another group held similar anti-government views as did McVeigh and that some of its members expressed vague threats to bomb a variety of potential targets in Oklahoma, possibly including a federal building in Oklahoma City, says very little about whether this group actually bombed the Murrah Building. That others shared McVeigh's political views is a slender reed upon which to vault the dangers of unfair prejudice and jury confusion. Finally, there was no evidence that would establish a probative nexus between the alleged Elohim City conspiracy and the bombing of the Murrah Building.

In the face of the speculative value of Howe's testimony, we must confront the very real dangers of unfair prejudice and confusion of the issues. The Howe testimony presented a great threat of "confusion of the issues" because it would have forced the government to attempt to disprove the nebulous allegation that Elohim City was involved in the bombing. This side trial would have led the jury astray, turning the focus away from whether McVeigh – the only person whose actions were on trial – bombed the Murrah Building. It also presented a threat of "unfair prejudice" as it would invite the jury to blame absent, unrepresented individuals and groups for whom there often may be strong underlying emotional responses.

Thus, the district court did not err in excluding this testimony and the defendant's conviction is hereby upheld.

Cross examination is the questioning of the other side's witnesses. An attorney on cross examination may ask leading questions. For example, an attorney may ask: "Isn't it true Mr. Jones, that you were wearing a light blue jacket on the night of January 1st?" Questions that permit a witness on cross examination to explain the answer are usually avoided.

The Court should restrict the subject areas on cross examination to those matters raised by direct testimony. However, the court does allow some leeway. Attacking the truthfulness of a witness may be attempted on cross examination if the witness has been convicted of crimes of dishonesty.

Questioning by the court may occur at any point. These questions, however, should only clarify points that are unclear. The judge should not attempt to prove any part of either side's case.

INTRODUCING EXHIBITS

Physical evidence, if relevant, can be introduced by either attorney when presenting one's case, or during cross examination.

An attorney must follow a specified procedure when introducing exhibits into court. The attorney will ask the judge: "Your Honor, I request that this document be marked as P-1 (if it is a Plaintiff's exhibit) or "D-1" (if it is a Defendant's exhibit). The Exhibit will then be marked by the clerk of the court and will be shown to opposing counsel so that he or she knows what is being discussed. The document is then **authenticated.** This is done by showing the exhibit to the witness and asking, "Mr. Jones can you identify this exhibit for the Court?" The witness should briefly explain the exhibit and attest to its accuracy.

After the document is shown to the judge and the witness is questioned about the exhibit, the attorney formally offers the exhibit into the record. This is done by the attorney saying, "Your Honor, I offer this exhibit into evidence."

One should note that if an exhibit is authenticated, questions can be asked about its contents even if the document is never offered into the record. Also, the exhibit can be offered into evidence at the conclusion of the attorney's case but before the attorney "rests."

Opposing counsel can always object to the exhibit being offered into evidence if it is not relevant or if it has not been properly authenticated. An opposing attorney can also offer the exhibit into evidence.

OBJECTIONS

Objections are made by counsel when it is felt that the opposing attorney is violating the Rules of Evidence. Objections may be made for a number of reasons. The manner in which these objections are made are outlined below.

Leading Questions: "Your Honor, I object to counsel's leading the witness." A leading question is only objectionable if asked by the counsel on direct examination, not on cross.

Irrelevant Evidence: "I object your Honor, the question is not relevant to the facts in this case." This objection is used sparingly because opposing counsel usually does not care if the opponent is not getting to the important facts.

Non-responsive: "Your Honor, the witness is not answering the question asked." This objection may be used when the witness is not answering the questions presented.

Hearsay: "Objection Your Honor. Counsel is asking for hearsay testimony." If the witness provides an answer that is based on hearsay, the attorney can ask the court to strike the answer from the record.

Beyond the scope of direct: "Your Honor, I object. Counsel is asking about matters that were not raised on direct examination." This objection is used to limit overly broad cross examination.

An attorney may object to testimony that violates a confidential communication. In striving to protect the confidentiality of certain communications, the court allows for privileged communication in four situations:

1. attorney-client privilege,
2. doctor-patient privilege,
3. priest-penitent privilege, and
4. husband-wife privilege.

In these situations, a party to the conversation can not be forced to testify in court against the other party to the communication.

In *Emerich v. Emerich,* the court had to decide whether a mental health care professional can be held liable if he or she does not affirmatively disclose a confidential communication made by a patient which reveals that the patient plans on harming another person.

EMERICH V. PHILADELPHIA CENTER FOR HUMAN DEVELOPMENT, INC.
720A.2D 1032 (PA. 1999)

THIS ADMITTEDLY TRAGIC MATTER ARISES from the murder of Teresa Hausler, by her former boyfriend, Gad Joseph ("Joseph"). At the time of the murder, Joseph was being treated for mental illness and drug problems.

A detailed recitation of the facts is necessary to analyze the important issue before us. The factual allegations raised in the complaint are as follows.

Ms. Hausler and Joseph were cohabiting in Philadelphia. For a substantial period of time, both Ms. Hausler and Joseph had been receiving mental health treatment at the Philadelphia Center for Human Development.

Joseph was diagnosed as suffering drug and alcohol problems, and explosive and schizoaffective personality disorders. He also had a history of physically and verbally abusing Ms. Hausler and a history of other violent propensities. Joseph often threatened to murder Ms. Hausler and suffered from homicidal ideations.

Several weeks prior to June 27, 1991, Ms. Hausler ended her relationship with Joseph, and moved from their Philadelphia residence. Angered by Ms. Hausler's decision to terminate their relationship, Joseph had indicated during several therapy sessions at the Center that he wanted to harm Ms. Hausler.

On the morning of June 27, 1991, Joseph telephoned his counselor, Mr. Scuderi, and advised him that he was going to kill Ms. Hausler. Mr. Scuderi immediately scheduled and carried out a therapy session with Joseph. During the therapy session, Joseph told Mr. Scuderi that his irritation with Ms. Hausler was becoming worse because that day she was returning to their apartment to get her clothing and that he

was going to kill her if he found her removing her clothing from their residence.

Mr. Scuderi recommended that Joseph voluntarily commit himself to a psychiatric hospital. Joseph refused; however, he stated that he was in control and would not hurt Ms. Hausler. The therapy session ended, and Joseph was permitted to leave the Center "based solely upon his assurances that he would not harm" Ms. Hausler.

Mr. Scuderi received a telephone call from Ms. Hausler informing him that she was in Philadelphia en route to retrieve her clothing from their apartment, located at 6924 Large Street. Ms. Hausler inquired as to Joseph's whereabouts. Mr. Scuderi instructed Ms. Hausler not to go to the apartment. In what ultimately became a fatal decision, Ms. Hausler ignored Mr. Scuderi's instructions and went to the residence where she was fatally shot by Joseph.

Joseph was subsequently arrested and convicted of the murder of Ms. Hausler. Based upon these facts, Appellant filed wrongful death and survival actions, alleging, that Appellees negligently failed to properly warn Ms. Hausler, and others including her family, friends and the police, since Joseph presented a clear and present danger of harm to her.

We must determine if a mental health care professional owes a duty to warn a third party of a patient's threat of harm to that third party. Supported by the wisdom of decisions from other jurisdictions, we determine that a mental health care professional owes a duty to warn a third party of threats of harm against that third party.

As a general rule, there is no duty to control the conduct of a third party to protect another from harm. However, an exception to the general rule has been recognized where a defendant stands in some special relationship with either the person whose conduct needs to be controlled or in a relationship with the intended victim of the conduct, which gives to the intended victim a right to protection.

The vast majority of courts that have considered the issue have concluded that the relationship between a mental health care professional and his patient constitutes a special relationship which imposes upon the professional an affirmative duty to protect a third party against harm. Thus, the concept of a duty to protect by warning has met with virtually universal approval.

It is axiomatic that important policy considerations exist regarding the public's interest in safety from immediate and serious, if not deadly, harm. Countervailing policies regarding the treatment of mental health patients, specifically recognition of the difficulty in predicting violent behavior, the importance of confidential communications between therapist and patient, and the policy that patients be placed in the least restrictive environment must be acknowledged. We believe, however, that the societal interests in the protection of this Commonwealth's citizens from harm mandates the finding of a duty to warn. Simply stated, it is reasonable to impose a duty on a mental health professional to warn a third party of an immediate, known and serious risk of potentially lethal harm.

Having determined that a mental health professional has a duty to protect by warning a third party of potential harm, we must further consider under what circumstances such a duty arises. We are extremely sensitive to the conundrum a mental health care professional faces regarding the competing concerns of productive therapy, confidentiality and other aspects of the patient's well being, as well as an interest in public safety. In light of these valid concerns, we find

that the circumstances in which a duty to warn a third party arises is extremely limited.

First, the predicate for a duty to warn is the existence of a specific and immediate threat of serious bodily injury that has been communicated to the professional. Moreover, the duty to warn will only arise where the threat is made against a specifically identified or readily identifiable victim. Thus, we believe that a duty to warn arises only where a specific and immediate threat of serious bodily injury has been conveyed by the patient to the professional regarding a specifically identified or readily identifiable victim.

A duty to warn would not require a mental health professional to violate therapist-patient confidentiality. Rather, the therapist-patient privilege, as interpreted by the State Board of Psychology, embraces the concept. Therefore, the privilege clearly does not prohibit a duty to warn.

Where a patient threatens to inflict serious bodily harm to another person or to himself or herself and there is a reasonable probability that the patient may carry out the threat, the physician should take reasonable precautions for the protection of the intended victim, including notification of law enforcement authorities.

It is clear that the law regarding privileged communications between patient and mental health care professional is not violated by, and does not prohibit, a finding of a duty on the part of a mental health professional to warn an intended victim of a patient's threats of serious bodily harm. As succinctly stated by the court, "The protective privilege ends where the public peril begins." *Tarasoff v. Regents of the Univ. of California, 17 Cal.3d 425 (Cal. 1976).*

In summary, we find that in Pennsylvania, based upon the special relationship between a mental health professional and his patient, when the patient has communicated to the professional a specific and immediate threat of serious bodily injury against a specifically identified or readily identifiable third party and when the professional, determines, or should determine under the standards of the mental health profession, that his patient presents a serious danger of violence to the third party, then the professional bears a duty to exercise reasonable care to protect by warning the third party against such danger.

For the foregoing reasons, we affirm the judgment of the Superior Court.

Throughout the trial of a case, both sides have the opportunity of calling witnesses and presenting evidence. Since the plaintiff in a civil case has the burden of proof, that party will go first in the presentation of the evidence. In a civil case, the burden of proof is by the preponderance of the evidence. In other words, the plaintiff must tip the scale in his or her favor in order to win.

The court in *Se-Ling Hosiery, Inc. v. Margulies*, **70 A.2d 854 (Pa. 1950)** explained the meaning of a preponderance of the evidence with the following illustration:

> If we visualize evidence as something weighed in an ordinary balance scale, and if the evidence plaintiff authors in support of his claim is so much more weighed in probative value then the evidence offered in opposition to it that it tips the scales on the side of the plaintiff, the latter has proved his claim by a fair weight of the evidence.

To put this burden of proof in perspective, it should be compared to the burden of proof in a criminal case which requires the government to prove each element of the crime beyond a reasonable doubt. This more difficult burden of proof has been defined as follows:

> The defendant is presumed to be innocent and the burden is upon the Commonwealth to prove his guilt beyond a reasonable doubt. A reasonable doubt cannot be a doubt fancied or conjured up in the minds of the jury to escape an unpleasant verdict; it must be a honest doubt arising out of the evidence itself, the kind of a doubt that would restrain a reasonable person from acting in a matter of importance to himself. *Commonwealth v. Donough*, **103 A.2d 694 (Pa. 1954).**

The purpose of discovery is to assist the litigants by making them aware of the various witnesses who will testify and the evidence that each side will present at trial. These pre-trial disclosures allow the attorneys to plan their strategies and to prevent surprise. What happens, however, if an attorney learns the identify of a new witness during trial? The court will not automatically allow the presentation of this new evidence because of the prejudice that may be imposed on the other side. The trial judge has several ways of handling this surprise situation. The witness may be prevented from testifying, a mistrial may be declared or the judge may allow a brief intermission so that the other side may conduct an investigation of the new information, including the taking of the person's deposition.

The Mike Tyson rape trial of a beauty contestant in Indianapolis presented this problem. Several days into the prosecution of the case, the defense learned of the identity of several new witnesses, who claimed that they saw the victim and boxer enter the hotel shortly before the alleged incident. Defense counsel notified the district attorney of this new information a few days later, but the court refused to allow the witnesses to be called at trial because of the several days delay in the disclosure of the new witnesses.

MIKE TYSON V. STATE OF INDIANA
619 N.E. 2D 276 (IND. APP. 1993)

TYSON WAS CHARGED WITH RAPE, criminal deviate conduct, and confinement. The confinement charge was dismissed during trial; the jury convicted Tyson of the remaining charges.

Tyson argues the trial court erred when it refused to permit him to call as witnesses certain women who came forward during the course of the trial.

Prior to trial, the court ordered that "the Defendant shall disclose to the State of Indiana the names, addresses and phone numbers of all witnesses whose testimony will be relevant specifically to the issue of whether the victim consented to sexual intercourse with Tyson.

Jury selection began on Monday; the State began presenting its case on Thursday. In the afternoon of Thursday, a secretary from Black Expo contacted the office of James Voyles, one of Tyson's trial attorneys, and told an associate that three women had come forward claiming to have information regarding the Tyson case.

The associate spoke to one of the woman by telephone, midday Friday, and had a face-to-face interview with two of the women, Carla Martin and Pam Lawrence, on Friday evening.

Immediately after his interview, the associate met with Tyson's trial attorneys, Voyles and Heard, and told them what he had learned. Voyles and Heard decided to inspect the limousine to determine whether Ms. Martin and Ms. Lawrence could have seen through the windows as they claimed. After viewing the limousine on Saturday evening, they concluded that it was possible to see through the tinted windows. Voyles and Heard also decided to personally interview Martin and Lawrence, which they did on Sunday. After that interview, Voyles contacted the Prosecutor and gave him the names of Martin and Lawrence, along with a summary of the information the women claimed to have.

On the following Monday, Tyson filed a motion in which he sought leave to call Martin and

Lawrence as witnesses. A hearing on the motion was held on Tuesday, after which the court denied the motion.

The trial court ordered disclosure of witnesses whom Tyson reasonable anticipated would testify by December 18, 1991. The names of Martin, and Lawrence could not have been disclosed by that date in as much as Tyson was unaware of their existence until January 30, 1992. However, the purposes of pretrial discovery are to promote justice and prevent unfair surprise. These purposes would be frustrated if there was not a continuing duty upon the parties to disclose the identity of newly discovery potential witnesses as soon as reasonably possible; a party could circumvent disclosure merely by failing to diligently discover potential witnesses until after discovery was closed. Thus, the issue is whether Tyson violated his duty to disclose the identity of the women as soon as reasonably possible.

The trial began on Monday. The office of one of Tyson's trial attorneys was contacted and an associate was told about Martin and Lawrence on Thursday, the day the State began presenting its case-in-chief. The prosecution team was first notified of their existence late in the afternoon on Sunday.

Tyson argues the delay was unavoidable because members of the trial team met with the women as soon as possible and the defense was not obliged to interview these witnesses earlier than it did or to reveal their existence before interviewing them, and making a decision whether it would or might use them. This argument overlooks the fact that an attorney from defense counsel's law firm spoke by telephone with one of the women on Friday around noon, and interviewed Martin and Lawrence on Friday evening before meeting with the trial team to apprise them of what he had learned. Therefore, the trial court reasonably concluded that, at that point, the State should have been notified of the existence of the women and their potential testimony.

The trial court did not abuse its discretion in prohibiting the testimony since the delay was excessive; the associate had interviewed Martin and Lawrence at some length and made a judgment regarding the relevance of the information they possessed and their credibility two days before the State was notified. Judgment affirmed.

SECTION 6.13 **EXECUTION**	Following the verdict and the court's disposition of post trial motions, the plaintiff will move to have the verdict reduced to a judgment. If no appeal is taken, the aggrieved party is entitled to enforce the judgment. If the defendant will not voluntarily satisfy the award, the plaintiff may seek the help of the Sheriff in seizing the assets of the opponent and selling them at Sheriff's sale. For instance, a home owned by the defendant may be sold at Sheriff's sale and money in a bank account can be attached in order to satisfy the judgment. Even property that is transferred to a third person in order to make the defendant judgment proof, may been seized as a transfer to defraud a creditor.

The mere fact that a plaintiff secures a judgment, however, does not mean that the aggrieved will recover the amount owed. If the defendant is judgment proof, or has no assets, the victorious litigant will collect no money. Certain types of property may also be exempt from execution depending upon the jurisdiction. For instance, some states will not disturb property that is owned by a husband and wife if the judgment is against only one of the marital partners. A debtor's interest in a pension fund or life insurance policy are also safe from seizure. A judgment, however, is valid for a number of years so a plaintiff may be able to seize assets that a debtor accumulates several years after the entry of the judgment.

SECTION 6.14
TRIAL MEMO

PROBLEM SIX—B

HODGE, DODGE AND LODGE
ATTORNEYS AT LAW
MEMORANDUM

To: All Law Clerks

From: Gregory Dodge

Re: Christopher v. Hodge

I have just returned from the trial of Joe Hodge for the attack of Peter Christopher by the family's pet gorilla. The jury is still out deliberating. I ordered an expedited copy of the trial transcript since I plan on appealing the case if we lose. I don't believe we received a fair trial but will admit that I am biased and angry.

Please read the trial transcript so that we can talk about the case. I want your honest assessment of what happened. Be prepared to discuss the following questions:

1. Who should win the case?

2. Were the court's evidentiary rulings correct?

3. Was the court correct in refusing to allow my surprise witness to appear in court?

In The Court of Common Pleas

First Judicial District of Pennsylvania

Civil Trial Division

PETER H. CHRISTOPHER	: October Term
	:
v.	:
	:
JOSEPH A. HODGE	: No. 555

Trial Transcript

Before The Honorable Anna Brady

Courtroom 903
City Hall
Philadelphia, Pennsylvania

APPEARANCES:

Smith and Dunkum P.C.	Hodge, Dodge and Lodge, P.C.
BY: Mary Dunkum, Esquire	BY: Gregory Dodge, Esquire
One Logan Square East, 10th. Fl.	1515 Market Street, 6th. Fl.
Philadelphia, PA 19100	Philadelphia, PA 19100
COUNSEL FOR THE PLAINTIFF	COUNSEL FOR THE DEFENDANT

COURT OFFICER: OYEZ! OYEZ! All persons who stand bound by recognizance or otherwise having to do business before the Honorable Judge of this Court of Common Pleas may at present appear and they shall be heard. The Honorable Judge Anna Brady presiding. God save this Commonwealth and this Honorable Court.

THE COURT: *Ladies and gentlemen of the jury, you have been sworn and this case is ready to proceed. Counsel for the parties will each speak to you and tell you what they intend to prove. Ms. Dunkum, you may proceed.*

OPENING STATEMENT OF MS. DUNKUM Members of the jury, good morning. My name is Mary Dunkum, and I represent the plaintiff, Peter Christopher, in this matter.

What comes to mind when I hear the words "man's best friend," are images of Lassie walking side by side with his owner as a loyal and steadfast companion. What we ask of you today, members of the jury, is to consider whether one man's choice in best friends is another man's worst enemy. In this case, a wild gorilla named Harry was kept in the backyard by the defendant Joseph Hodge as a family pet. On September 3 to be exact, the solitude of Peter Christopher's backyard was shattered by ferocious and wild sounds coming from this gorilla.

MR. HODGE: That is not true. Harry was not bothering anybody!

THE COURT: *Mr. Hodge you will refrain from such outbursts or I will hold you in contempt.*

MS. DUNKUM: Thank you, Your Honor, may I proceed.

THE COURT: *You may.*

It was on this day that my client Peter Christopher was attacked by this vicious gorilla . . .

MR. HODGE: That's a lie! My pet is not vicious.

MS. DUNKUM: Your Honor!

THE COURT: *Mr. Hodge you have been warned once. One more time and I will hold you in contempt. Do I make myself clear!*

MR. HODGE: Yes. I'm sorry your Honor.

THE COURT: *Ladies and Gentlemen of the jury, please disregard that last outburst. Ms. Dunkum, you may proceed.*

As I was saying, the vicious attack by the defendant's so called pet caused Peter Christopher's left leg to be amputated. Now members of the jury, he was not attacked by this gorilla in a zoo or in the wild, he was attacked in his very own backyard.

If keeping a gorilla as a family pet was not bad enough, we will prove that Mr. Hodge gave this ape alcoholic beverages in order to quiet him down. The ape eventually fell asleep against the fence abutting my client's yard and was making loud noises. Cautiously, Mr. Christopher nudged the gorilla through the fence with a pole to move the ape to the other side of the yard. The gorilla awakened in a frenzy and pulled Peter over the fence into the defendant's backyard and mauled him. My client suffered a devastating injury as a result of this unfortunate incident. Mr. Christopher lost part of his left leg.

Christopher will tell you of the terrifying events of the brutal attack and the agony he felt as the animal's powerful jaws ripped his leg in pieces. He will tell you of the devastating effect the attack had on his life including the loss of his business and life's pleasures.

You will hear from the doctor who performed the emergency surgery on my client's left leg. He will explain the severity of Pete Christopher's injuries and the heroic efforts that were undertaken to stabilize Mr. Christopher. Unfortunately, these efforts could not prevent the amputation of a part of the leg.

Members of the jury, at the conclusion of the evidence you will find that Joseph Hodge, through his wanton negligence, caused the plaintiff to be attacked by this wild and vicious gorilla and we will request that you award Mr. Christopher a sum of money that will compensate him for his loss. *Thank you.*

THE COURT: *Does defense counsel wish to make a statement?*

MR. DODGE: Yes, indeed, Your Honor.

THE COURT: *You may proceed, Mr. Dodge.*

OPENING STATEMENT BY MR. DODGE

Good morning. My name is Gregory Dodge and I represent the defendant, Joseph Hodge. Members of the jury, there are two sides to every story. I admit that what happened to Peter Christopher is a tragedy. However, the accident was not caused by Joe Hodge's negligence. Rather, Peter Christopher's injury was the result of his own misconduct while under the influence of intoxicants. Peter Christopher provoked and taunted the animal. While intoxicated, he climbed over a fence into the Hodge's yard and attacked the sleeping gorilla with a long pole. Maybe the Hodge family's choice of pets was unique, but Peter Christopher took his life in his own hands by taunting the animal.

You will hear from Joe Hodge, who will speak about his unique family pet who never harmed anyone. He will tell you of his relationship with this lovable creature that Christopher battered with a pole and will explain the physical and emotional injuries sustained by Harry.

At the close of the evidence, we are sure you will find for the defendant, and it is in your fair judgement that Joe Hodge places his confidence. Thank you.

THE COURT: *Ms. Dunkum, are you prepared to present your first witness?*

MS. DUNKUM: Yes, Your Honor, I call Peter Christopher.

DIRECT TESTIMONY OF PETER CHRISTOPHER BY MS. DUNKUM

Q. **Please state your name for the record.**

A. *My name is Peter Christopher that's C H R I S T O P H E R.*

Q. **And Mr. Christopher where do you live?**

A. *35 Royal Court, Rydal, Pennsylvania.*

Q. **When were you born?**

A. *April 1, 1965*

Q. **Are your married?**

A. *No, I'm not.*

Q. **And what do you do for a living?**

A. *I used to be a private investigator and undercover surveillance specialist. Presently, I am unemployed.*

Q. **Mr. Christopher turning your attention to September 3, can you tell the jury what happened that day?**

A. *Well, it was Sunday of labor day weekend. The Hodges, who live next door to me, had finally stopped their partying. But their pet gorilla was laying close to my property asleep, snoring loudly, and it was driving me crazy. Anyway, I was trying to get the gorilla to move to the other side of the yard where the smell of the animal would not be so offensive. So, I gently tapped him with a pole to awaken him. He was wild from the moment he opened his eyes. The ape grabbed me and pulled me by the hair over the fence into the Hodges' back yard. Before I could get away from him, Harry had a hold of my leg in his mouth. I could feel his sharp teeth bearing down on my skin and I screamed but no one heard me. I don't remember anything after that.*

Q. **What do you remember next?**

A. *I awakened in the hospital. Dr. Feelgood was with me, and part of my leg had been amputated. I couldn't believe it. I'd never be able to walk normally again.*

Q. **Have you been able to work since this accident?**

A. *I lost my job and my investigative service went bankrupt.*

Q. **Are you getting any physical therapy or treatment?**

A. *Yes, I am.*

Q. **Mr. Christopher how long will this treatment last?**

A. *Well, I go to physical therapy three times a week and this should continue indefinitely.*

Q. **Mr. Christopher, are there any activities that you can no longer perform?**

MR. DODGE: Objection - irrelevant.

THE COURT: *I'll allow it.*

A. *Well, I can't run, dance, or do anything which involves the use of two legs.*

Q. **No further questions.**

THE COURT: *Any cross examinations Mr. Dodge?*

MR. HODGE: Ask him about the pole!

THE COURT: *The court will come to order! You're going to have to advise your client Mr. Dodge, to control himself if he is to remain in this courtroom. You may proceed with your cross-examination at this time.*

CROSS EXAMINATION OF PETER CHRISTOPHER BY MR. DODGE

Q. **Mr. Christopher did you dance or run in races before the accident?**

A. *Well, no, but it was always an ambition of mine.*

Q. **Now Mr. Christopher where were you when you "tapped" the gorilla?**

A. *I was in my backyard.*

Q. **You were aware that the gorilla was next to the fence, weren't you sir?**

A. *Sure, he was making so much noise and he smelled.*

Q. **And you were also aware that gorillas are not like other domestic animals, aren't you?**

A. *Absolutely. Hodge should never had had such a vicious animal as a pet.*

Q. **Now, Mr. Christopher, you did more than just jab the gorilla, didn't you?**

MS. DUNKUM: Objection - leading.

THE COURT: *Overruled. You may answer.*

A. *I told you I just wanted to move the gorilla away from my property.*

Q. **You hit the gorilla with a pole, didn't you Mr. Christopher?**

A. *(Witness does not answer).*

Q. **Your Honor, the witness is not responding to the question.**

THE COURT: *You'll have to answer Mr. Christopher.*

A. *Well, yes, I tapped the ape to wake him.*

Q. Mr. Christopher you were intoxicated weren't you?

A. I had a few beers. It was a beautiful day.

Q. You had more than just a few beers, isn't that right?

MS. DUNKUM: Objection. Your Honor, defense counsel is obviously not paying attention. The witness has answered his question.

THE COURT: *Sustained, the witness has responded to your question.*

Q. Don't you have a distillery in your basement, sir?

MS. DUNKUM: Objection, your Honor. Irrelevant and prejudicial.

THE COURT: I'll allow it.

A. No sir. I do not.

MR. DODGE: No further questions.

THE COURT: *Is there any redirect?*

MS. DUNKUM: *Yes, your Honor, just one question.*

REDIRECT EXAMINATION OF PETER CHRISTOPHER BY MS. DUNKUM

Q. Mr. Christopher, tell the jury what you did with the pole.

A. I attempted to push the gorilla away from the fence so he would move to the other side of the property. I didn't try to attack the gorilla.

MS. DUNKUM: Thank you.

THE COURT: *Ms. Dunkum, please call your next witness.*

MS. DUNKUM: I call Dr. Feelgood.

DIRECT EXAMINATION OF DR. FEELGOOD BY MS. DUNKUM

Q. Please state your name for the record.

A. My name is Donald Feelgood.

Q. Where did you attend undergraduate school?

A. University of Massachusetts.

Q. And where did you attend medical school?

A. The University of Grenada.

Q. When did you graduate?

A. In 1985.

Q. **And what did you do after that?**

A. *I had a residency at Cook County Memorial Hospital in Chicago.*

Q. **Where do you practice now?**

A. *I am a surgeon at Temple Hospital.*

MR. DODGE: We will stipulate that the doctor is qualified to practice medicine.

THE COURT: *Very well. Ms. Dunkum, please proceed to the incident in question.*

Q. **Dr. Feelgood, turning your attention to September 3, did you treat the plaintiff, Peter Christopher?**

A. *Yes, I did. I saw him in the emergency room and we had to perform emergency surgery.*

Q. **Can you tell us the nature of that surgery?**

A. *Yes, he had massive abrasions, contusions, and lacerations on his entire left side. Looked like someone took a rake and . . .*

MR. DODGE: Objection. The doctor is speculating.

THE COURT: *Sustained.*

A. *Oh, sorry. Anyway, upon further examination, we discovered that the area below his knee was severely damaged, and we had to amputate. We were lucky to be able to do surgery below the knee and not take the whole leg.*

Q. **So for the record, this was the left leg.**

A. *Left leg.*

Q. **Doctor, were these injuries the result of a vicious gorilla attack?**

MR. DODGE: Objection. Leading and asking for an opinion.

THE COURT: *Sustained.*

MR. DODGE: Thank you very much.

THE COURT: *You'll have to rephrase that counselor.*

Q. **Dr. Feelgood, upon examining the plaintiff were you able to discover the cause of these injuries?**

A. *Yes, they appeared to be the work of an animal attack.*

Q. **Doctor in your opinion, was there any possible alternative to the amputation of the leg?**

A. *No, absolutely not! As I said, we were lucky to save the upper portion of the leg.*

Q. **Have you seen and treated the patient since September 3?**

A. *Yes. Four times to fit him with a prosthesis.*

Q. **Dr. Feelgood, what, if anything, did the ambulance driver say to you when they brought the plaintiff into the hospital on September 3?**

MR. DODGE: Objection - hearsay.

THE COURT: *Sustained.*

Q. **Dr. Feelgood can you state with a reasonable degree of medical certainty the cause of the injury and amputation?**

A. *Sure. Considering the way the leg was mauled, it was clear that a large animal had attacked the patient.*

MS. DUNKUM: Thank you, Dr. Feelgood.

CROSS EXAMINATION
OF DR. FEELGOOD
BY MR. DODGE

Q. **Dr. Feelgood, isn't it true that the plaintiff's wounds are healing well?**

A. *Surprisingly, yes.*

Q. **You also fitted him with an artificial limb, didn't you?**

A. *Yes.*

Q. **Dr. Feelgood, the plaintiff can walk pretty well with that artificial limb, can't he?**

A. *Yes, he can.*

Q. **Doctor, when you operated on the plaintiff's knee, you knew that he had been drinking, didn't you?**

MS. DUNKUM: Objection, your Honor, improper foundation.

THE COURT: *You'll have to rephrase that counselor.*

MR. DODGE: Yes, your Honor.

Q. **Did you test Mr. Christopher's blood before the operation?**

A. *Standard procedure.*

Q. Did you check to see if there was any alcohol in his system?

A. *Yes. It's important before surgery to test the blood for any drugs or alcohol that may complicate the anesthesia.*

Q. So for the record, you did run a test?

A. *Yes.*

Q. Doctor, what did you learn, if anything, from the blood analysis?

A. *There was a clear indication that there was alcohol in his system.*

Q. In fact, he was intoxicated wasn't he?

A. *That is not for me to say.*

Q. Wasn't the plaintiff's blood alcohol level .25?

A. *Yes.*

Q. Legally intoxicated?

A. *Yes, by legal standards.*

Q. Doctor, did you prescribe medication to the plaintiff before the surgery?

A. *No.*

Q. Did you find medication in his system?

A. *Yes.*

Ms. DUNKUM: Objection.

THE COURT: *Overruled.*

Q. So you found medication in his system?

A. *Yes.*

Q. Cocaine?

A. *No.*

Ms. DUNKUM: Objection, your Honor.

Q. Amphetamines?

Ms. DUNKUM: Objection.

Q. Glue?

MS. DUNKUM: Objection, your Honor, please. These questions are ir-
                relevant!

THE COURT: *Sustained.*

Q. Marijuana?

THE COURT: *Mr. Dodge, the objection was sustained.*

MR. DODGE: Thank you, your Honor.

Q. Now, doctor, you live in the plaintiff's neighborhood, don't you?

   A. Yes.

Q. Have you heard anything about his reputation.

MS. DUNKUM: Objection. This is irrelevant and hearsay.

THE COURT: *You may answer.*

   *A. Dr. Feelgood: I know of his reputation first hand. I have seen some of
    the things Christopher has done personally. Well, he's a regular at the
    local precinct where I am the police surgeon. Always getting into trouble.*

**Q. Isn't it true that you treated the plaintiff three months ago for a
torn cartilage in the knee?**

MS. DUNKUM: Objection. The question is irrelevant.

MR. DODGE: It is relevant. This man had a pre-existing knee injury.

THE COURT: *Overruled. I recognize that a torn cartilage is not the same as
                an amputation but it does show a pre-existing problem to the
                leg in question. I will allow the question. Doctor, answer the
                question.*

   *A. Yes, he hurt his knee about a month before the attack when he feel in a
    hole.*

**Q. Dr. Feelgood, are you currently being sued by my client for mal-
practice?**

MS. DUNKUM: Objection. Irrelevant and immaterial.

MR. DODGE: It is relevant. It shows that he could be biased against
                Joseph Hodge.

THE COURT: Overruled.

   A. I don't see what relevance that claim has to this case.

Q. I don't care what you see, doctor, I ask the questions.

MS. DUNKUM: Objection. Counsel is badgering the witness.

THE COURT: Overruled.

Q. Dr. Feelgood, aren't you being sued by Joe Hodge and his family for medical malpractice?

A. *I don't see what my personal life has to do with this.*

Q. Well, Dr. Feelgood, we contend that you are biased. That's what your personal life has to do with this. So answer the question!

A. *Well, one of his kids ran into me with his bike.*

Q. Doctor, aren't you being sued for medical malpractice by Joe Hodge?

A. *I haven't seen any legal papers.*

Q. Doctor, didn't you receive a letter from me telling you that the Hodge family was suing you for malpractice?

A. *Yes.*

Q. Thank you. No further questions.

THE COURT: Redirect?

MS. DUNKUM: No further questions.

THE COURT: The witness is excused.

MS. DUNKUM: That is plaintiff's case and we rest.

THE COURT: *Will the defense call its first witness?*

MR. DODGE: *Certainly, your Honor. The defense calls Joseph Hodge.*

DIRECT EXAMINATION OF JOSEPH HODGE BY MR. DODGE

Q. Please state your name for the record.

A. *Joseph Hodge.*

Q. Now Joe where do you live?

A. *Next to Mr. Christopher. He has caused my family nothing but problems since he moved into the neighborhood.*

MS. DUNKUM: Objection, your Honor! Will you please instruct Mr. Dodge to control his client.

THE COURT: *Sustained. Mr. Hodge just answer the questions. Members of the jury, please disregard Mr. Hodge's outburst. Proceed counselor.*

Q. Mr. Hodge, answer the question.

A. I live at 37 Royal Court, Rydal, Pennsylvania.

Q. When were you born?

A. June 10, 1947.

Q. Are you married?

A. Yes

Q. Do you have any children?

A. I have four children: Anthony, Kathy, Brad and Gregory.

Q. Joe, what do you do for a living?

A. Well, times were tough for the Hodge family for a long while and . . .

THE COURT: *Mr. Hodge, just answer the question!*

Q. Joe, you may answer.

A. I own my own construction company and I make over $25,000 a month.

MS. DUNKUM: Objection, your Honor. His salary is irrelevant.

MR. HODGE: $25,000 a month is a lot of money.

MS. DUNKUM: Your Honor, please!

MR. DODGE: I apologize for my client and ask that the court reporter strike his comments about his salary from the record.

THE COURT: *It will remain counselor. I want a record of your client's outbursts because I am going to hold him in contempt the next time he says anything out-of-line. I sincerely advise you to control Mr. Hodge before he is physically removed from this courtroom and placed in jail. He is his own worst enemy. Do I make myself clear?*

MR. DODGE: I move for a mistrial. Your comments are prejudicial to my client and are denying him a fair trial.

THE COURT: *Mr. Dodge, spare me. I have been very tolerant of your client's continued outbursts. Now move on!*

Q. Joe, do you own a dog?

A. No, I don't have any dogs.

Q. How about a cat?

A. No cats either.

Q. Do you have a gorilla?

A. *Well, yes as a matter of fact I do have a gorilla named Harry.*

Q. Mr. Hodge, will you please tell the court why you bought the gorilla?

A. *I love my kids, and they love the circus. I would take them to the circus any time I could. Well the kids fell in love with Harry and so did I. The circus went bankrupt, and we decided to buy Harry and give him a real home. We've kept him in the backyard ever since.*

Q. Has Harry ever been violent before the incident on September 3?

A. *He wouldn't hurt a fly. Christopher provoked the incident.*

MR. DUNKUM: Objection. I ask that the last reference to my client be stricken from the record.

THE COURT: *The jury will disregard that last remark.*

Q. Turning your attention to September 3, did anything unusual happen that day?

A. *Well, it was labor day weekend and we were relaxing around the pool. Harry was very restless that day, but he finally fell asleep. We then went into the house to eat lunch.*

Q. Then what happened?

A. *All of a sudden, we heard shouts coming from our yard. I ran outside to see what was wrong, and I saw peter Christopher in my backyard with that pole, passed out. Poor Harry was lying face down with blood all over him. I told Estelle to get an ambulance for Christopher.*

Q. So Harry was injured, Mr. Hodge?

A. *Harry had several wounds which had to be stitched by a veterinarian at the University of Pennsylvania Emergency Animal Clinic.*

Q. Mr. Hodge, how did Mr. Christopher get in your backyard?

A. *He must have climbed over the fence.*

MS. DUNKUM: Objection—speculation.

THE COURT: *Mr. Hodge, did you see the plaintiff climb over the fence?*

A. *No.*

THE COURT: *Objection sustained.*

Q. How high is the fence?

   A. *Five feet.*

Q. How long have you had Harry, Mr. Hodge?

   A. *Two years.*

Q. Has Harry ever hurt anyone before?

   A. *No. Harry is afraid of his own shadow.*

Q. And how long were you and Mr. Christopher neighbors before this incident occurred?

   A. *Six months.*

Q. Has Mr. Christopher ever complained to you about Harry?

   A. *Never.*

Q. Was Harry treated for injuries as the result of this incident?

   A. *Yes. He was tested for rabies and was quarantined for one week.*

Q. Did you incur any expenses to treat Harry?

   A. *Yes. I paid $1,000.*

CROSS EXAMINATION OF JOSEPH HODGE BY MS. DUNKUM

Q. Did Harry have a license?

   A. *Of course not. Harry is not a dog so he is not required to be registered.*

Q. You stated that the blood you saw was that of the gorilla, is that right?

   A. *Yes, that's right.*

Q. Was Harry treated for any injuries Mr. Hodge.

   A. *Yes, back and neck injuries.*

Q. Now, Mr. Hodge, wouldn't you agree that a back injury is much different than a puncture wound?

   A. *Yes, I guess so.*

Q. Wasn't the blood from Peter Christopher and not the gorilla?

   A. *I don't know. All I know is that the blood was on Harry's fur.*

Q. The blood was from Peter's leg, wasn't it?

   A. *I guess, but I am not certain since Harry was also bleeding.*

Q. Isn't it true, Mr. Hodge, you enjoy getting Harry drunk?

A. *No. I do not enjoy getting the gorilla drunk. That would be bad for his health.*

Q. Didn't Harry attack your son Tony at one time or have physical contact with Tony?

MR. DODGE: Objection, your Honor. What does counsel mean by physical contact?

THE COURT: *Rephrase your question counselor.*

Q. Didn't the gorilla a have physical confrontation with your son?

A. *Yes, but they were just wrestling. They had a great time. Harry never hurt my son.*

Q. Mr. Hodge, isn't it true that my client, Mr. Christopher, was a little more than passed out when you went outside?

A. *Well, he was bleeding.*

Q. Bleeding! Mr. Hodge didn't the gorilla have Peter Christopher's leg in his mouth when you saw him?

MR. DODGE: Objection, your Honor.

THE COURT: *Overruled. Answer the question.*

A. *Yes, my wife called the ambulance right away and I . . .*

Q. Just answer the question, Mr. Hodge.

A. *Yes. Harry had Christopher's leg in his mouth.*

Q. No further questions.

THE COURT: *Any redirect, counselor?*

MR. DODGE: Yes, your Honor.

REDIRECT OF JOSEPH
HODGE BY MR. DODGE

Q. What did you do when you went outside?

A. *I wrapped Peter Christopher's leg in a towel to stop the bleeding and my wife called the ambulance.*

Q. Now, Mr. Hodge, did you ever let Harry out of the backyard?

A. *Never. I was worried that strangers would be afraid of Harry just because he was a gorilla.*

Q. And has Harry ever hurt anyone before?

A. No.

Q. No further questions. Thank you.

THE COURT:	*The defense may call its next witness.*
MR. DODGE:	May I have a minute to confer with my client?
THE COURT:	*You may. We will recess for 10 minutes.*
MR. DODGE:	Your Honor, we have one more witness who is waiting in the hall.
MS. DUNKUM:	Your Honor, the plaintiff is unaware of any other witnesses relevant to this case and demands an offer of proof.
THE COURT:	*Is this a fact witness or an eyewitness?*
MR. DODGE:	An eyewitness, Your Honor.
MS. DUNKUM:	Please note my objection. I was never informed of an eyewitness to the incident.
MR. DODGE:	The witness is not a surprise. In fact, he played a very important part in the incident.
THE COURT:	*Very well, in the interest of justice we will allow him to testify today.*
MS. DUNKUM:	Oh my God! Your Honor, Hodge is leading a gorilla into the courtroom. Your Honor, please help! Please!
THE COURT:	*Mr. Hodge, remove that animal from this courtroom immediately. Mr. Dodge, what is the meaning of this stunt? I am very close to holding you in contempt of Court.*
MR. DODGE:	Your Honor, we wish to show that Harry's a very unique and gentle gorilla.
MS. DUNKUM:	Your Honor, the defense is obviously grasping at straws.
THE COURT:	*Counselors, stop arguing and approach the bench immediately, and I mean now!*
MR. DODGE:	The jury is entitled to meet Harry and judge for themselves as to whether he is a wild and vicious animal. Harry is like a little baby and would never hurt anyone unless provoked. If the jury could merely see Harry and Joe together, they would have a better understanding of this case. You are depriving my client of that oppor-

tunity. In addition, Harry was hurt in the incident and can't walk properly.

MS. DUNKUM: This request is outrageous and is being done solely to inflame the passions of the jury. The ape is dangerous and a security threat.

MR. DODGE: Your Honor, I would like to make a formal offer of proof. I believe there is precedent for what I am trying to do. Dogs are routinely used by the police in drug searches. These animals have been trained to sniff out drugs in luggage or in a car. These actions by the dog have been used to establish probable cause that drugs are present and are routinely allowed into evidence as long as the dog has a history of providing reputable information. Gorillas and the "Great Ape" species are genetically very similar to humans. Some evolutionists believe that man evolved from Great Apes. Doctors have even transplanted the hearts of apes into humans. In fact, human DNA and chimpanzee DNA are more than 98% identical. Animal research demonstrates that gorillas can be taught sign language and develop a vocabulary of over 300 words. Professor David McCord of Drake University Law School has written a paper on this very issue. Professor McCord advances the idea that apes should be treated like a human witness and the court should focus on four testimonial capacities: perception, memory, sincerity and communication. I have a copy of the article for your review. It is entitled "Can Apes Testify," and the paper is located at **http://www.law.umich.edu/ thayer/mccape.htm.** Gorillas are much more intelligent that dogs. If police testimony concerning searches by dogs for drugs is allowed into evidence, I should be allowed to at least show Joe's pet gorilla to the jury.

THE COURT: *I have to agree with Ms. Dunkum. A gorilla has no place in a courtroom and the prejudicial affect of this stunt outweighs the probative value of the evidence.*

THE COURT: *You will both return to your seats and make closing arguments.*

CLOSING ARGUMENT
BY MS. DUNKUM

Ladies and gentlemen of the jury, this case is quite simple. Is it reasonable to keep a wild, vicious gorilla in one's backyard? To make matters worse, the owner of that gorilla then decides to provide the animal with liquor in order to quiet the so called pet down. Are these actions normal? The law is clear. One who keeps a non-domesticated animal, like a gorilla, on his property is absolutely liable to anyone injured by that animal. The only defense is if the injured party assumed the risk of injury. Do you really believe that Peter thought that he would lose his leg by gently nudging the gorilla with a pole from his own backyard to move the beast away from the fence. I think not! The only real issue in this case is how much money should Peter be awarded for the loss of his leg. In making this calculation, remember the massive jaws of the gorilla as they crushed through the plaintiff's leg, ripping flesh from bone. Remember that Peter must go through each day of the rest of his life without a limb. He can't run, play sports or do the things that we each take for granted. Just think how your life would be affected if you lost a leg.

Peter carries both physical and emotional scars with him. Everyone can see the stump of what was once a leg. Few people, however, can see the torment, the emotional burden, that plagues my client. No one will hire him and his investigative business went bankrupt. This incident has cost him and will continue to cost Mr. Christopher a lot of money. Members of the jury, I ask that you please award my client a sum of money that will reimburse him for his past and future losses and will send a clear signal to others like Joe Hodge that we will no longer tolerate the selfish conduct of people who display disrespect for their neighbors. Thank you.

CLOSING ARGUMENT
BY MR. DODGE

Members of the jury, we are all sorry that Peter Christopher lost his leg. However, this is a court and your duty is to assess liability based upon the law and not pity. I must admit that keeping a gorilla as a pet is a bit eccentric. But, do you really believe that Joe would do anything to jeopardize his family's safety? Harry is a docile and tame animal who was kept enclosed in the backyard. Peter got hurt through his own fault.

The plaintiff incited the incident by attacking the sleeping gorilla with a pole. Wouldn't it have been easier if Christopher had merely telephoned Joe and asked him to move Harry? The plaintiff has taken great pain during the trial to tell you how he was in his own yard when the gorilla attacked him. How then did Peter end up in Joe's backyard? Did the gorilla jump the fence, attack the plaintiff and then throw the plaintiff's limp body back into Joe's yard? I think not. I suggest that Peter, with pole in hand, climbed over the fence to teach Harry a lesson. By engaging in such conduct, Peter assumed the risk of the attack and must take full responsibility for the consequences.

The loss of a limb is a serious injury but Peter was fitted with an artificial limb and is able to move about freely. There are many jobs available to him. In fact, there is a professional baseball player who has only one arm. It is all a question of motivation. Peter doesn't have the motivation because he wants to exact his pound of flesh through this lawsuit. Don't be fooled by his actions.

Not only should you find against Christopher, but you should award Joe money for the injuries sustained by Harry. The animal was asleep minding his own business when he was violently struck with a metal pole. It is about time that we recognize that animals have rights, and a money judgment in favor of Harry will make more people aware of this fact. Thank you for your patience in this most unusual case.

CHARGE OF THE COURT

I must admit that this is the most unusual case that I have heard during my tenure as a judge. I will not summarize the testimony since the trial was short. You are to be guided by your own recollection of the evidence. Issues of credibility have arisen during the trial. You are to be guided in deciding whom to believe by your own common sense and life's experiences.

As for the law, one who keeps a non-domesticated animal on his property is liable to another who is injured by that animal. A gorilla is a non-domesticated animal no matter how cute or playful that animal appears to be, and the owner is liable for any harm inflicted by that creature. On the other hand, one who subjectively knows of a danger, but yet still voluntarily exposes himself to that risk is barred from recovery.

You must decide where Peter Christopher was located when he hit the gorilla with the pole. Was he in his own backyard and stuck the pole through the fence, or did he assume the risk of the attack by climbing over the fence into the backyard of his neighbor to confront the gorilla? In the latter case, the plaintiff is barred from recovery.

If you find in favor of the plaintiff, then you must award a sum of money to compensate him for his injuries and losses. In other words, you want to award a sum of money that will return the plaintiff to the condition he was in before the incident even occurred. Your award will include compensation for medical expenses, lost past and future wages, and pain and suffering.

The plaintiff has the burden of proof in this matter. He must prove his case by the preponderance of the evidence. This means that in order for the plaintiff to win, you must place all of the credible evidence on a scale and the scale must tip in favor of the plaintiff no matter how slight for the plaintiff to recover damages. If the scales are even or tip in favor of the defendant, then you must find in favor of the defendant. In addition, it is only after the scales tip in favor of the plaintiff that you can even consider the issue of damage.

If you find that Joe Hodge is not responsible for the injuries suffered by Peter Christopher, then you will return with a verdict for the defense. In that event, you may consider an award of damages to Joe Hodge for the injuries to the gorilla.

Please return to the jury room and decide upon a verdict.

ANSWER SHEET
PROBLEM SIX—B

Name   **Please Print Clearly**

1. Who should win the case? Please explain your answer.

_____

_____

_____

_____

_____

_____

_____

_____

_____

_____

_____

_____

_____

_____

_____

_____

_____

_____

_____

_____

2. Were the court's evidentiary rulings correct?

_____

_____

_____

_____

_____

_____

_____

_____

_____

3. Was the court correct in refusing to allow Harry, the Gorilla, to appear in court?

_____

_____

_____

_____

_____

_____

_____

_____

_____

SECTION 6.15 REVIEW CASES

1. Miller was found lying face down in the street and bleeding profusely. A police officer asked Miller who shot him, and Miller identified Griffin as his assailant. At the time of trial, the District Attorney calls the police officer to introduce into evidence the statement made by Miller before he died in order to prove that Griffin committed the crime. Is this hearsay statement admissible? *Commonwealth of Pennsylvania v. Aaron Griffin*, **453 Pa. Super. 657 (1996).**

2. Mathis was arrested in a stolen van. He testified that while hitchhiking from Georgia to Tennessee to attend a Rod Stewart concert, he was given a ride by an unknown person who fled when the van was stopped by the police. In rebuttal to this testify, a state witness testified that his firm represented Rod Stewart in obtaining theatrical bookings; that he had checked the company's records and they revealed that Rod Stewart was in New Mexico on the day in question. The testimony was objected to as an alleged violation of the best evidence rule. Should this testimony have been excluded on that basis? *Mathis v. The State of Georgia*, **228 S.E. 2d 228 (Ga. App. 1976).**

3. During the trial over an automobile accident, a witness for the plaintiff was asked to estimate how fast the defendant's car was going before the accident. The defense objected on the basis that the answer would constitute opinion evidence which can only be expressed by an expert witness. Can a witness, who has no specialized technical or scientific knowledge, testify as to the speed of a motor vehicle? *Dugan v. Arthurs*, **79 A.2d 626 (Pa. 1911).**

4. Haight was accused of committing burglary by moving electrical equipment from a property. At the time of trial, the prosecution was allowed to introduce into evidence the fact that Haight was unemployed and on welfare at the time of the crime. The Commonwealth argued that this evidence was relevant to show a motive for the burglary, namely a desire for money. Was this line of questioning relevant to establish a motive for burglary? *Commonwealth of Pennsylvania v. Haight*, **31 A.2d 357 (Pa. Super. 1984).**

5. Following the imposition of sentence on a robbery charge, Williams decided to express his dissatisfaction with the court's punishment. He did so by (1) raising his middle finger, and (2) stating, "F _ _ k You." The Judge ordered Williams returned to the court room, at which time the judge found Williams guilty of two counts of contempt and imposed two consecutive sentences of six month for each of the offensive acts. Was it proper to find Williams in contempt of court for his voicing displeasure over the sentence? Was it proper for the court to find him responsible for two separate acts of contempt over the one incident? *Commonwealth of Pennsylvania v. Walter Williams*, **753 A.2d 856 (Pa. Super. 2000).**

SECTION **6.16**
INTERNET REFERENCES

For more information on the topics in this Chapter, see the following Internet sites:

- **http://www.findlaw.com/oltopics/29litigation/index.html**
  This site contains government documents, journals, newsletters and articles on litigation.

- **http://www.law.cornell.edu/rules/fre/overview.html**
  Cornell School of Law provides a listing of the Rules of Evidence for both criminal and civil proceedings in Federal Court.

- **ww.pa-bar.org**
  This is the site for the Pennsylvania Bar Association, which includes news and information about litigation in that state.

- **www.abanet.org**
  The American Bar Association sponsors this website that provides answers to frequently asked litigation questions and offers general public resources.

- **www.brobeck.com/docs/deposition.htm**
  General information about depositions and tips on how to handle a deposition can be located at this address.

- **www.pennlegal.com/index.html**
  This site contains the Pennsylvania Rules of Evidence.

- **www.law.umich.edu/thayer**
  The University of Michigan Law School maintains this site which is dedicated to evidentiary issues and offers news and articles related to evidence.

- **www.megalaw.com/index.php3?content=research/rules/parules.html**
  This site provides access to the Pennsylvania courts and lists the rules of the court for this state.

- **www.litigationlaw.com**
  Recent news concerning litigation matters may be accessed at this address.

- **www.courttv.com**
  Court Television Network maintains a library of various courtroom materials involving well known cases.

Footnotes   1. Reprinted with permission from **Simplified Rules of Evidence,** by Temple University School of Law and the Law Education and Participation (LEAP) program.

CHAPTER 7

CRIMINAL LAW AND PROCEDURE

"The real significance of crime is in its being a breach of faith with the community of mankind."

Joseph Conrad
Lord Jim, 1900

As a general rule, an individual can engage in any type of conduct that he or she wishes unless the law specifically prohibits it. The legislature will intercede whenever necessary to regulate and prohibit conduct that society deems inappropriate.

A crime is an offense against society or the state that violates a penal law and carries a possible punishment of imprisonment. Different crimes number in the thousands and specific definitions will vary from jurisdiction to jurisdiction.

This section will provide a general definition for some of the better known crimes as they evolved over the years.

HOMICIDE

A **homicide** is a killing of another human. There are three types of homicide:

1. justifiable;

2. excusable; and

3. criminal.

A **justifiable homicide** is a killing in self-defense or an execution carried out by court order. An **excusable homicide** is a killing by accident or mistake where the wrongdoer does not have any criminal culpability. A child who is unintentionally killed when he darts in front of a car is an example. **Criminal homicide** is the unlawful killing of another and includes murder and manslaughter. Murder is further divided into three classes and manslaughter consists of both voluntary and involuntary manslaughter.

First Degree Murder is the unlawful killing of another with malice aforethought and the specific intent to kill. This homicide is commonly referred to as premeditated murder and involves a killing by such things as torture, poisoning or lying in wait. It is this element of a premeditated and deliberate killing that distinguishes first degree murder from all other types of criminal homicide. Specific intent to kill may also be inferred from the surrounding circumstances, such as the use of a deadly weapon upon a vital part of the victim's body.

Malice aforethought describes conduct that exhibits a wanton disregard for the safety of others. This legal term of art has been defined by the courts to include not only ill-will towards a person, but a wickedness of disposition, hardness of heart and recklessness of consequences. In other words, malice aforethought includes such things as discharging a gun into a crowd, throwing a rock off the top of a building or punching another in the face.

How much time must elapse in order to establish premeditation or specific intent to kill? There is no exact time requirement. Instead, premeditation may be proven by a person's words or conduct. For instance, premeditation may be inferred by the intentional use of a deadly weapon upon a vital part of the body. A contract killing or assassination are simple examples of this principle.

COMMONWEALTH OF PENNSYLVANIA V. DAVID SATTAZAHN
763 A.2D 359 (PA. 2000)

ON JANUARY 22, 1999, A JURY CONVICTED David Sattazahn of first-degree murder in the slaying of Richard Boyer and sentenced him to death. This is a direct appeal of this verdict.

On April 12, 1987, Sattazahn and his accomplice, Jeffrey Hammer hid in a cleared wooded area waiting to rob Boyer, who was the manager of the Heidelberg Family Restaurant. They had watched Boyer for several weekends and determined that Sunday would be the busiest day in the restaurant. At closing, Sattazahn and Hammer confronted Boyer in the parking lot. Hammer carried a .41 caliber revolver and Sattazahn had a .22 caliber Ruger semiautomatic pistol. With these guns drawn, the pair attempted to rob Boyer of the bank deposit bag with the day's receipts, but Boyer threw the bag toward the roof of the restaurant. While Sattazahn told Boyer to get the bag, Boyer did

not comply and began to run away. Both Sattazahn and Hammer fired shots and Boyer fell to the ground. The two men then grabbed the bank deposit bag and fled.

Because this is a direct appeal death penalty case, we conduct an independent review of the sufficiency of the evidence supporting the jury's verdict of guilt on the charge of first-degree murder.

To find a defendant guilty of first-degree murder, a jury must find that the Commonwealth has proven that he or she unlawfully killed a human being, and did so in an intentional, deliberate and premeditated manner. It is the element of a willful, premeditated and deliberate intent to kill that distinguishes first-degree murder from all other criminal homicide. Specific intent to kill may be inferred from the defendant's use of a deadly weapon upon a vital party of the victim's body.

With this standard in mind, we have reviewed the evidence and have found it sufficient to support the jury's verdict. At trial, the Commonwealth presented the testimony of the accomplice, who testified as to the details of the crime as recited in the fact portion above. Hammer's testimony was confirmed by an autopsy that revealed that Boyer suffered two gunshot wounds in the lower back and one each in the left shoulder, the lower face and the back of the head. All wounds were consistent with being caused by a .22 caliber bullet, the caliber gun that Hammer attributed to Sattazahn, and which a gun shop owner testified that Sattazahn purchased. Moreover, the .22 and the two slugs recovered from Boyer's body, and the five cartridges found at the scene, were identified as being fired from Sattazahn's gun.

A review of the record indicates that the facts were more than sufficient to support the conviction.

QUESTIONS FOR DISCUSSION:

1. Dudley, Stephens and another sailor were cast adrift in a small boat following a storm with no food or water. Dudley and Stephens discussed sacrificing one of the three so that the remaining two could survive. The two sailors then killed the decedent and fed upon his body for nourishment. The survivors were tried for first degree murder even though all three would have died of starvation. The decedent was chosen because he would have expired first because of his frail and deteriorating health. Are Dudely and Stephens guilty of first degree murder? *Regina v. Dudley and Stephens*, **14 Q.B.D. 273 (1884).**

2. Ms. Carrol was selected to attend an electronic's school for nine days. His wife greeted the news with a violent argument. Prior to his departure, and at the request of his wife, Carrol put a loaded 22 caliber pistol on the window sill, at the head of the common bed. Later than evening, the parties engaged in another protracted argument. Carrol's wife proceeded to follow her husband into the bedroom as they continued to argue. Carrol remembered the gun on the window sill, so he grabbed the pistol, and spontaneously shot his wife twice in the back of the head. Is this a case of premeditated murder? *Commonwealth v. Carrol*, **194 A.2d 911 (Pa. 1963).**

3. In the book and movie Alive, a plane carrying 15 members of the Uruguay national rugby team crashed in the Andes Mountains. The survivors ate the flesh of their dead friends in order to stay alive until they were rescued. How does this case differ from *Regina v. Dudley and Stephens?*

The penalty for first degree murder in Pennsylvania is death or life imprisonment. The decision is for the jury to decide by use of the following penalty determination sheet. To impose the death penalty, the jury must find that the aggravating circumstances behind the murder outweigh the mitigating circumstances.

FIRST DEGREE MURDER VERDICT
PENALTY DETERMINATION SHEET

We, the jury, empaneled in the above entitled case, having heretofore determined that the defendant, is guilty of murder of the first degree, do hereby find:

AGGRAVATING CIRCUMSTANCE(S)	CHECK YES
The victim was a fireman, peace officer or public servant concerned in official detention who was killed in the performance of his duties.	( )
The defendant paid or was paid by another person or had contracted to pay or be paid by another person or has conspired to pay or be paid by another person for the killing of the victim.	(X)
The victim was being held by the defendant for ransom or reward, or as a shield or hostage.	( )
The death of the victim occurred while the defendant was engaged in the hijacking of an aircraft.	( )
The victim was a prosecution witness to a murder or other felony committed by the defendant and was killed for the purpose of preventing his testimony against the defendant in any grand jury or criminal proceeding involving such offenses.	(X)
The defendant committed a killing while in the perpetration of a felony.	( )
In the commission of the offense the defendant knowingly created a grave risk of death to another person in addition to the victim of the offense.	( )
The offense was committed by means of torture.	(X)
The defendant has a significant history of felony convictions involving the use of threat of violence to the person.	(X)

MITIGATING CIRCUMSTANCE(S)	CHECK YES
The defendant has been convicted of another Federal or State offense, committed either before or at the time of the offense at issue, for which a sentence of life imprisonment or death was impossible or the defendant was undergoing a sentence of life imprisonment for any reason at the time of the commission of the offense.	( )
The defendant has no significant history of prior criminal convictions.	( )
The defendant was under the influence of extreme mental or emotional disturbance	( )
The capacity of the defendant to appreciate the criminality of his conduct or to conform his conduct to the requirements of law was substantially impaired.	( )
The age of the defendant at the time of the crime.	( )
The defendant acted under extreme duress, although not such duress as to constitute a defense to prosecution under Section 309 (relating to duress), or acted under the substantial domination of another.	( )
The victim was a participant in the defendant's homicidal conduct or consented to the homicidal acts.	( )
The defendant's participation in the homicidal act was relatively minor.	( )
Any other evidence of mitigation concerning the character and record of the defendant and the circumstances of his offense.	( )

The aggravating circumstance(s) outweigh the mitigating circumstance(s).

YES (X)   **NO ( )**

We the jury render the following sentencing verdict:

Death (X)   **Life Imprisonment ( )**

Renee De Simone , **Foreperson**

Renee De Simone

Second Degree Murder or **felony murder** is the unintentional killing of another committed during the commission of a felony. For instance, Jones sets fire to a building unaware that the owner is inside. The fire rages out of control and the owner is killed. Since the owner died during the commission of a felony, Jones is guilty of felony murder even though he did not know the owner was inside the building.

Is it a defense to felony murder that the killing was an accident or unintentional?

COMMONWEALTH OF PENNSYLVANIA V. EVANS
494 A.2D 383 (PA. SUPER. 1985)

THIS IS AN APPEAL FROM A SECOND DEGREE murder and robbery convictions.

As a 68 year old man approached his parked Cadillac in a shopping center, two accomplices forced him at the point of a sawed-off shotgun into the back seat of the Cadillac and proceeded to follow Evans, who was driving a Volkswagen. Evans and his accomplices drove through Fairmount Park where they took the victim's wallet before releasing him. The complaint of the victim was recorded by a radio dispatcher:

Caller: I was coming out of the Acme and I walked to my car and these guys were waiting for me.

Radio: And what happened?

Caller: They put me, I can't talk, I have a heart condition.

Radio: Yeah, well just ...

Caller: They put me in the car, cleaned me out. They had a sawed-off shotgun on me.

Radio: Just try, try to relax if you can.

Caller: Okay.

Radio: Do you have any medication that you could be taking or anything?

Caller: Yeah, I got a nitro.

Radio: You got it with you?

Caller: Yeah, I took one.

Radio: Okay.

Caller: I'm having a little trouble breathing.

Radio: You are?

Caller: Yeah, I'm having…yeah, here they are now.

Radio: All right, tell them about your breathing.

Shortly after the police arrived, they rushed the victim to a nearby hospital where he died within four hours as a result of cardiac arrest.

Evans argues that since the death of the victim from cardiac arrest was not foreseeable, the homicide could rise no higher than third degree murder. "A criminal homicide constitutes murder of the second degree when it is committed while defendant was engaged, as a principal or an accomplice, in the perpetration of a felony." **18 Pa. C.S. § 2502(b).** While it is true that the tort liability concept of proximate cause has no proper place in prosecutions for criminal homicide, if the wound inflicted by the accused is not itself mortal, and a subsequent event is found to be the immediate cause of death, the accused does not escape legal liability if his act started an unbroken chain of causation leading to the death. The legal cause of death is thus sufficiently proven if the criminal behavior is shown to have been a direct and substantial factor in bringing about the death. Death must, of course, be the consequence of the felony, and not merely a coincidence.

The evidence was clearly sufficient to convict appellant of second degree murder. The Commonwealth introduced testimony of a forensic pathologist who opined:

The cause of death was due to the arteriosclerotic heart disease, the heart disease I described which was aggravated by the robbery and kidnapping. The manner of death was homicide.

The statute defining second degree murder does not require that a homicide be foreseeable; rather, it is only necessary that the accused engaged in conduct, as a principal or an accomplice, in the perpetration of a felony. It cannot be denied that the felonious conduct of Evans not only "started an unbroken chain of causation", but also was a "direct and substantial factor" in bringing about the death of the victim. The trial court's decision is affirmed.

The penalty for a second-degree murder in Pennsylvania is life in prison.

Third Degree Murder is the killing of another with malice aforethought but with no specific intent to kill and not occurring during the commission of a felony. For example, in a situation where an individual is shot in the foot and dies as a result of medical complications, that action will give rise to third degree murder. The shooting is evidence of malice but no specific intent to kill existed.

COMMONWEALTH OF PENNSYLVANIA V. JOHN KLING
731 A.2D 145 (PA. SUPER. 1999)

JOHN KLING WAS DRIVING HIS RED CHRYSLER Conquest near McConnellsburg when he noticed a black Camaro in his rear view mirror. The Camaro took off and both automobiles began racing up a curvy mountain road known as ScruB Ridge. At speeds in excess of 80 M.P.H., both vehicles reached the crest of Scrub Ridge, and with Kling in the lead, the improvident competitors began descending the mountain road.

The first downside mile from the top of Scrub Ridge is riddled with eight substantial curves

and five cautionary speed signs. Nevertheless, Kling maintained his excessive speeds, pulling away from the Camaro and disappearing into the blind curves.

Approaching the eighth major curve on the downslope, Kling swung into the no-passing zone and blew past two pickup trucks traveling in front of him. He then headed into the sharp double curve at nearly 70 M.P.H., crossed the centerline again, and struck a vehicle driven by Helen Mellott. The collision killed Ms. Mellott instantly.

Third degree murder occurs when a person commits a killing, which is neither intentional nor committed during the perpetration of a felony, but contains the requisite malice. Malice exists where there is a wickedness of disposition, hardness of heart, cruelty, recklessness of consequences, and a mind regardless of social duty, although a particular person may not be intended to be injured. Where malice is based on a reckless disregard of consequences, it is not sufficient to show mere recklessness; rather, it must be shown the defendant consciously disregarded an unjustified and extremely high risk that his actions might cause death or serious bodily injury. A defendant must display a conscious disregard for almost certain death or injury such that it is tantamount to an actual desire to injure or kill; at the very least, the conduct must be such that one could reasonably anticipate serious bodily injury would likely and logically result.

In view of this heightened mens rea motor vehicle crashes seldom give rise to proof of the malice needed to sustain a conviction for third degree murder.

Kling was deliberately racing his high-powered car at speeds of 75-80 M.P.H. on a two and one-half mile stretch of a curvy mountain road. He was familiar with this road, having traveled it two to three times per week for over a year prior to the crash. He passed five cautionary signs warning him to slow down around the treacherous curves. In spite of these warnings, Kling proceeded at high rates of speed and, cutting the curves in order to negotiate the road. Without a doubt, the aggregate of these circumstances plainly warned Kling his conduct was nearly certain to result in disaster. Nevertheless, he consciously disregarded this awareness and continued his race for eight-tenths of a mile after running people off the road. Illegally passing two pick-up trucks, sustaining his reckless and malicious conduct, Kling sped into a dangerous double blind curve where he smashed into the victim killing an innocent person.

Kling chose to play Russian roulette with the other drivers on Scrub Ridge. By speeding through the curves, he pulled the trigger four or five times with one near miss; on the last pull, however, he killed a person. This conduct exhibited the sustained recklessness, in the face of warnings, necessary to prove a knowing and conscious disregard that death or serious bodily injury was reasonably certain to occur. We therefore uphold Kling's convictions for third degree murder.

Voluntary Manslaughter is the intentional killing of another committed in the heat of passion and as a result of provocation.

Certain types of conduct can provoke a reasonable person to act without consideration for his or her actions. Provocation has been recognized in cases where one spouse finds the partner in bed with another person or if the assailant learns that a spouse or child has been the victim of a sexual attack.

Is a person guilty of voluntary manslaughter or first-degree murder if she kills a woman with whom her husband was having an affair?

FLORENCE SCROGGS v. STATE OF GEORGIA
93 S.E.2d 583 (Ga. App. 1956)

TOWNSEND, J.

ON CHRISTMAS EVE, THE DEFENDANT Florence Scroggs called a taxi and instructed the driver to "go over about town and to turn down a dirt road to look for a car." After locating the car, she then instructed the driver to turn on to a four-lane highway to follow the car. The defendant left the taxi and paid the driver at a restaurant on the highway. The car which had preceded them to this place contained the defendant's husband and the deceased woman, Effie Adams, who had driven up to the restaurant in the defendant's husband's car. They parked in front where they were sitting side by side. They were there approximately three minutes when the defendant came up to the car and fired a number of bullets into it, one of which entered Effie Adams' spine, causing her death. The defendant then left and went home. When the police arrived some time later, she informed them she had done the killing.

At trial, the defendant put up a number of witnesses who testified as to her good character and as to the bad character of the deceased for lack of virtue and chastity. She further made a statement from which it appeared that the deceased, immediately after being released from prison, began coming to the place she and her husband operated to drink beer; that she was always drinking; that she would attempt to hug and kiss defendant's husband who at first repulsed her advances; that she continued sending people there to tell him to come to her; that the defendant warned her to leave her husband alone; that three weeks before the night of the shooting, the defendant's husband announced he was going over to see Effie Adams and did so; that he returned drunk and muddy; that on that afternoon he went out ostensibly to a barber shop, but returned and said, "I had to carry Effie home"; that he then informed the defendant he was not going to take her to their family's home as planned for Christmas; that he was buying her no god damned groceries, she could starve to death; that he was going to get some beer and he and Effie were going off, and he then left. Several cases of beer were found in the automobile of the defendant's husband after the homicide.

If a wife kills another woman to prevent sexual relations between such other woman and her husband, and if the killing, although apparently necessary to prevent adultery, was actually done by the defendant under a violent and sudden impulse of passion, the offense is that of voluntary manslaughter. Although a jury is not required to give any weight whatever to the defendant's statement, so much of the statement of this defendant is corroborated by undisputed evidence independent thereof as to require the reasonable and logical conclusion that sexual relations in violation of the marital rights of the defendant were planned between the defendant's husband and the victim.

The evidence is sufficient to support the theory, that the killing was necessary to prevent decedent from committing adultery with defendant's husband, and that the defendant acted in the sudden heat of passion.

Involuntary Manslaughter is the unintentional killing of another, which is the result of outrageous conduct or gross negligence. For example, an intoxicated driver who causes an accident and kills another person is guilty of this crime.

COMMONWEALTH OF PENNSYLVANIA V. HICKS
201 A.2D 294 (PA. 1964)

THE OFFENSE OF INVOLUNTARY MANSLAUGHTER consists of the killing of another person without malice and unintentionally, but in doing some unlawful act not amounting to a felony, or in negligently doing some lawful act. Where the act in itself is not unlawful, to make it criminal, the negligence must be such a departure from prudent conduct as to evidence a disregard of human life or an indifference to consequences. Reckless driving upon the highway is such a departure from prudent conduct.

A review of the evidence in a light most favorable to the verdict establishes the following:

Arthur Gilmore, an eyewitness, testified that at 7:15 p.m. on March 4, 1963, Harry Yeager, a pedestrian was struck by a 1955 or 1956 Chrystler or Plymouth car which was being driven south on 17th Street. The accident occurred at the intersection of 17th Street and Columbia Avenue, in Philadelphia. Mr. Gilmore described the car as being black with a red top. He estimated the speed of the car at fifty miles per hour as the light turned amber. The light was red as the car passed through the intersection. The front of the car struck Yeager, who was crossing the street, throwing his body eleven feet into the air and a distance of thirty feet. He further testified that the driver stopped for a few seconds but made no move to leave the car or render assistance to Yeager. When Gilmore called to the driver to halt, the driver turned off his lights and "took off," throwing a lot of smoke.

It is our conclusion that the evidence is sufficient to support the verdict of involuntary manslaughter.

RAPE

Rape is the unlawful carnal knowledge of a woman by another through force or the threat of force and without consent. The crime does not require the assailant to complete the act of sexual intercourse. Rape merely requires penetration, no matter how slight.

Is it a defense to the crime of rape that the assailant believed the victim had consented to his sexual advances? This is the issue in *Commonwealth v. Farmer.*

COMMONWEALTH OF PENNSYLVANIA V. JAMES FARMER
758 A.2D 173 (PA. SUPER. 2000)

JAMES FARMER APPEALS HIS CONVICTIONS FOR RAPE.

Farmer and the victim were among several people at the CYS bowling club in Erie, Pennsylvania. The victim was at the club with her sister, Judith Freeman, and her friend, Patricia Wydro. The women bowled from 6:15 p.m. until 9:00 p.m. During that time, the victim consumed two or three alcoholic drinks. After bowling, the women proceeded to the bar and met with a male friend. Farmer was also in the bar with friends. The victim and Farmer were unacquainted to this point.

Farmer began having a conversation with Ms. Freeman and Ms. Wydro, who were conversing with other friends. At some point, Ms. Freeman went over to the victim and pointed out Farmer's resemblance to a relative. Soon after, Farmer told his friends that he was leaving and the victim indicated that she was tired and wanted to go home. Farmer and the victim subsequently had sexual relations in his car in the parking lot.

The court below found that as the victim left the bowling alley, Farmer grabbed her shoulders, physically pushed her backwards and pushed her to his vehicle. Once inside the vehicle, he grabbed her head and used his body to hold her down as she pushed in resistance, including pushing a bowling ball at him but she was unable to runaway from him.

Farmer then had sex with the victim. Following the encounter, she returned to the bowling alley, where several people described her as "hysterical, distraught and disheveled." She recounted the incident and someone called the police. She was taken to a hospital and had a post-rape medical examination. Farmer claimed that the encounter was consensual.

Framer argues that trial counsel was ineffective for failing to request a jury instruction regarding a reasonable mistake as to consent. He claims that *Commonwealth v. Fischer*, **721 A.2d 1111 (Pa. Super. 1998)**, "sent a clear signal that Pennsylvania law was ready to require a charge as to defendant's mental state when at issue."

We look to *Commonwealth v. Williams*, **294 Pa. Super 93 (1982)**, as the Court relied on it in Fischer. In Williams, the defendant argued that the trial judge should have instructed the jury that if (he) reasonably believed that the victim had consented to his sexual advances so that this would constitute a defense to rape. If the element of the defendant's belief, as to the victim's state of mind is to be established as a defense to the crime of rape, then it should be done by the legislature which has the power to define crimes and offenses. We refuse to create such a defense.

Judgment of sentence affirmed.

How would you answer the following questions?

1. Is it rape if a woman in a darkened room has sexual relations with a man who pretends to be her husband?

2. Can a husband rape his wife?

3. Can a woman rape a man?

4. Can a man rape another man?

Often, the elements of rape are not easily determined. Courts have struggled with two major questions in recent years: **(1) what constitutes force?** and **(2) did the woman consent?** These are especially difficult questions in instances of date rape and where the woman has been psychologically coerced into having sex.

Is consent present if a woman has the presence of mind to plead that her attacker wears a condom? Consider that many rape crisis counselors urge women to do whatever they must to survive. In 1992, a grand jury in Texas refused to indict an accused rapist because his victim pleaded with him to use a condom so that she wouldn't get AIDS. According to interviews in newspapers and on TV, the grand jury had interpreted the woman's request as amounting to consent. The case met with a public outcry, and eventually the accused rapist was tried and convicted of sexually assaulting his neighbor. According to testimony at the trial, the assailant broke into his neighbor's apartment and threatened her with a knife.

But what kind of behavior amounts to a threat, and how "reasonable" must the woman have been in resisting the sexual act? In *Commonwealth v. Rhodes*, **510 A.2d 1217 (Pa. 1986)**, the Pennsylvania Supreme Court held that force implies more than just physical force; it may also include psychological coercion as well. Before that ruling, rape convictions were not upheld when, for example, the assailant threatened his victim with sending her back to a juvenile detention center if she didn't comply with his sexual advances, *Commonwealth v. Mlinarich*, **498 A.2d 395 (Pa. Super. 1985)**, and when a father told his daughter that the Bible commanded her to have sex with him. *Commonwealth v. Biggs*, **467 A.2d 31 (Pa. Super. 1983)**.

The rape laws in Pennsylvania have dramatically changed in recent times, largely in response to *Commonwealth v. Berkowitz*, **641 A.2d 1161 (Pa. 1994)**. In *Berkowitz*, a female college student, who had been drinking, claimed that another student raped her after she entered his dormitory room looking for a mutual friend. The victim testified that although he did not shove her or apply any force, she continued to say "no" throughout the encounter. The Pennsylvania Supreme Court, in a controversial decision, found that although the victim established her lack of consent, she did not establish a threat of force or psychological coercion, which is a necessary requirement for rape. The court remanded the case for trial on the charge of indecent assault, which is a misdemeanor as opposed to rape, which is a felony.

In reaching this decision, the court cited the following testimony in noting that the victim's testimony was devoid of any statements which clearly or adequately described the use of force or threat of force:

> In response to defense counsel's question, "Is it possible that when Berkowitz lifted your bra and shirt you took no physical action to discourage him," the complainant replied, "It's possible." When asked, "is it possible that Berkowitz was not making any physical contact with you...aside from attempting to untie the knot [in the drawstrings of complainant's sweatpants]," she answered, "It's possible." She testified that "He put me down on the bed. It was kind of like he didn't throw me on the bed. It's hard to explain, it was kind of like a push but not, I can't explain what I'm trying to say." She concluded that "it wasn't much" in reference to whether she bounced on the bed, and further detailed that their movement to the bed "wasn't slow like a romantic kind of thing, but it wasn't a fast shove either. It was kind of in the middle." She agreed that Berkowitz's hands were not restraining her in any manner during the actual penetration, and that the weight of his body on top of her was the only force applied. She testified that at no time did Berkowitz verbally threaten her. The complainant did testify that she sought to leave the room, and said "no" throughout the encounter. As to the complainant's desire to leave the room, the record clearly demonstrates that the door could be unlocked easily from the inside, that she was aware of this fact, but that she never attempted to go to the door or unlock it.
>
> As to the complainant's testimony that she stated "no" throughout the encounter, we point out that, while such an allegation would be relevant to the issue of consent, it is not relevant to the issue of force.

Criticism over the decision that "no doesn't mean no," prompted the Pennsylvania legislature to amended the rape statute by creating a new offense to encompass "Berkowitz" situations. Section 3124 now makes "sexual assault" a felony of the second degree when a person "engages in sexual intercourse or deviate sexual intercourse with a complainant **without the complainant's consent**." The result of this legislation is that in Pennsylvania "no" now means "no."

The legislature further amended the rape statute to afford greater protection to victims by prohibiting sexual conduct "where the complainant is unconscious or the person knows that complainant is unaware that sexual intercourse is occurring. Rape also exists where the person has substantially impaired the complainant's power to control his or her conduct by employing, without the knowledge of the complainant, drugs or intoxicants. There have been a number of cases in which women have been raped after a drug has been placed in a victim's drink without her knowledge, rendering the victim unconscious.

The following is the new rape statute in Pennsylvania:

> *A person commits a felony of the first degree when he or she engages in sexual intercourse with a complainant:*

1. By forcible compulsion.

2. By threat of forcible compulsion that would prevent resistance by a person of reasonable resolution.

3. Who is unconscious or where the person knows that the complainant is unaware that the sexual intercourse is occurring.

4. Where the person has substantially impaired the complainant's power to appraise or control his or her conduct by administering or employing, without the knowledge of the complainant, drugs, intoxicants or other means for the purpose of preventing resistance.

5. Who suffers from a mental disability which renders the complainant incapable of consent.

6. Who is less than 13 years of age.

The Pennsylvania legislature even addressed the issue of rape between spouses by providing that forcible sex between spouses is now rape.

Is it rape when the victim is "tricked" into consenting to sexual intercourse? Consider the following case where the victim's agreement to intercourse was based upon a belief, fraudulently induced by the defendant, that the sex act was necessary to save her life. The Court ruled that since she was aware of the "nature of the act" her consent was valid and rape did not occur. The Court made the distinction between a case where the victim didn't know the sexual act occurred (fraud in factum) versus a case where the victim consented to intercourse but the consent was obtained through fraud (fraud in the inducement). Fraud in factum is rape, but fraud in the inducement is not.

DANIEL BORO V. SAN MATEO SUPERIOR COURT
210 CAL. RPTR. 122 (CAL. CT. APP. 1985)

DANIEL BORO SEEKS TO RESTRAIN further prosecution of charging him with a violation of Section 261 which defines rape as: "an act of sexual intercourse accomplished with a person not the spouse of the perpetrator…

> where a person is at the time unconscious of the nature of the act and this is known to the accused.

Boro contends that he should have the charge of rape dismissed because complainant, Ms. R., was aware of the "nature of the act." The Attorney General contends that the victim's agreement to intercourse was predicated on a belief-fraudulently induced by Boro, that the sex act was necessary to save her life, and that she was hence unconscious of the nature of the act within the meaning of the statute.

The factual background is as follows: Ms. R., the rape victim, was employed as a clerk at the Holiday Inn in San Francisco. On March 30, she received a telephone call from a person who identified himself as "Dr. Stevens" and said that he worked at Peninsula Hospital.

"Dr. Stevens" told Ms. R. that he had the results of her blood test and that she had contracted a dangerous, highly infectious and perhaps fatal disease; that she could be sued as a result: that the disease came from public toilets; and that she would have to tell him the identity of all her friends who would then have to be contacted in the interest of controlling the spread of the disease.

"Dr. Stevens" further explained that there were only two ways to treat the disease. The first was a painful surgical procedure costing $9,000, and requiring her uninsured hospitalization for six weeks. A second alternative, was to have sexual intercourse with an anonymous donor who had been injected with a serum which would cure the disease. The latter, non-surgical procedure would only cost $4,500. When the victim replied that she lacked sufficient funds the "doctor" suggested that $1,000 would suffice as a down payment. The victim thereupon agreed to the non-surgical alternative and consented to intercourse with the mysterious donor, believing "it was the only choice I had."

After discussing her intention with her work supervisor, the victim proceeded to the Hyatt Hotel as instructed, and contacted "Dr. Stevens" by telephone. He later became furious when he learned Ms. R. had informed her employer of the plan, and threatened to terminate his treatment, finally instructing her to inform her employer she had decided not to go through with the treatment. Ms. R. did so, then went to her bank, withdrew $1,000, checked into another hotel and called "Dr. Stevens" to give him her room number. About a half-hour later the defendant "donor" arrived at her room. When Ms. R. had undressed, the defendant had sexual intercourse with her.

At the time of penetration, it was Ms. R.'s belief that she would die unless she consented to sexual intercourse with the defendant: as she testified, "My life felt threatened, and for that reason and that reason alone did I do it."

Boro was apprehended when the police arrived at the hotel room, having been called by Ms. R.'s supervisor. Boro was identified as "Dr. Stevens" at a police voice lineup by another potential victim of the same scheme.

The People contend that at the time of the intercourse the victim was "unconscious of the nature of the act." Because of Boro's misrepresentation, she believed it was in the nature of a medical treatment and not a simple, ordinary act of sexual intercourse. Boro, on the other hand, stresses that the victim was plainly aware of the nature of the act in which she voluntarily engaged, so that her motivation in doing so is irrelevant.

Our research discloses sparse California authority on the subject. A victim need not be totally and physically unconscious in order for rape to occur. In *People v. Minkowski,* the defendant was a physician who "treated" several victims for menstrual cramps. Each victim testified that she was treated in a position with her back to the doctor, bent over a table, with feet apart, in a dressing gown. And in each case the "treatment" consisted of the defendant first inserting a metal instrument, then substituting an instrument which "felt different"—the victims not realizing that the second instrument was in fact the doctor's penis.

The decision is useful to this analysis, because it exactly illustrates certain tradition rules in the area of our inquiry. Thus, if deception causes a misunderstanding as to the fact that intercourse itself is occurring **(fraud in factum)** there is no legally-recognized consent because the victim did not give consent for sexual intercourse, only some other act. Whereas consent induced by fraud is as effective as any other consent, because the woman consented to have sex and the deception related not to the thing done (the sexual act) but merely to some collateral matter **(fraud in the inducement)**.

The victims in **Minkowski** consented, not to sexual intercourse, but to an act of an altogether different nature, penetration by medical instrument. The consent was to a pathological and not a carnal act, and the mistake was, therefore, **in the factum** and not **merely in the inducement.**

Another relatively common situation is the fraudulent obtaining of intercourse by impersonating a spouse. The courts are not in accord as to whether the crime of rape is thereby committed. Some courts have taken the position that such a misdeed is fraud in the inducement on the theory that the woman consents to exactly what is done (sexual intercourse) and hence there is no rape; other courts, hold such a misdeed to be rape on the theory that it involves **fraud in the factum** since the woman's consent is to an innocent act of marital intercourse while what is actually perpetrated upon her is an act of adultery. Her innocence seems never to have been questioned in such a case and the reason she is not guilty of adultery is because she did not consent to adulterous intercourse.

In California, we have adopted [by statute] the majority view that such **fraud is in the factum** because the wife consents to sexual relations with her husband, not adultery. It is not **fraud in the inducement**, so there is no consent.

Our statute allows for protection when there is fraud on behalf of perpetrating a spouse, but in no other situations. It is clear that the legislature did not intend to protect situations other than those specified. The legislature clearly intended that **fraud in the inducement** not invalidate the consent [in other situations]. Thus, where consent to intercourse is obtained by promises of travel, fame, celebrity and the like—it is not rape.

We note that in this case there is not a shred of evidence that Ms. R. lacked the capacity to appreciate "the nature of the Act," but motivated by a fear of disease, and death, succumbed to Boro's fraudulent representations.

By concluding the act in this case is not rape, does not take away from the heartless cruelty of Boro's scheme, but it is not a violation of Section 261.

The stay of trial shall remain in effect.

STATUTORY RAPE

Statutory rape occurs when a man over the age of 16 has sexual relations with the consent of a girl under 16 who is not his spouse. Because of the tender years of the female, she is presumed incapable of giving a meaningful consent and the man is responsible for statutory rape regardless of his knowledge of her age.

In some states, the required age of the parties will differ. In Pennsylvania, for example, a person is guilty of statutory sexual assault when "that person engages in sexual intercourse with a complainant under the age of 16 years and that person is four or more years older than the complainant and the complainant and that person are not married to each other."

OPEN LEWDNESS

A person commits the crime of **open lewdness** if he or she does any lewd act, which that individual knows is likely to be observed by others who would be affronted or alarmed.

COMMONWEALTH OF PENNSYLVANIA V. MENDOZA
79 WESTMORELAND COUNTY, PENNSYLVANIA 35 (1996)

THIS MATTER IS BEFORE THE COURT as the result of the defendant's Pre-trial Motion challenging the sufficiency of the evidence related to two counts of open lewdness.

At No. 2727 C 1995, the defendant is charged with one count of open lewdness. This involved an incident that occurred on July 6, 1995, when the defendant lifted her top exposing her breasts to two other females standing in a yard next to her house. Nancy Lackey was waiting on the steps of her home for the woman that delivered her newspaper, Dorene Holzapfel. Ms. Holzapfel arrived at approximately 7:00 a.m. They engaged in short conversation. Ms. Holzapfel then told Ms. Lackey that her neighbor was looking out of her window. Ms. Lackey responded that the neighbor always does that when Ms. Lackey gets company. Ms. Holzapfel

then made the statement to the defendant, "why don't you take a picture?" After this was said the defendant lifted the top of her clothing and exposed her breasts to the two females for a very short time.

At No. 2828 C 1995 the prosecution charges that over a period of months, from November 1994 through July of 1995, the defendant would regularly get undressed in front of a window of her home which did not have curtains or blinds to prevent the conduct from being seen. This window was located on the side of the house of the defendant and it faced the side of the house of the complainants. There were brief occasions when the defendant was totally nude and other occasions when she was in various stages of undressing. The defendant's conduct was observed by the complainants from their darkened bathroom looking into the defendant's bedroom. There is no evidence that the defendant was aware that the complainants were observing this conduct. The defense has introduced into evidence a video tape recording of several instances, over a number of months, of the complained of conduct. This videotape was made by the complainants to provide examples of the conduct complained. This tape shows the defendant in what appears to be her bedroom, on various occasions at night when she appears to be undressing to go to bed. At no time, on any of the occasions shown on the tape, did the defendant stand for any extended period of time in front of the window. Rather, the defendant was in continuous motion while getting undressed and for the most part was not in view. It did not appear, as a result of viewing the tape, that the defendant was even aware that someone was watching her at the time.

The issue for this court to determine is whether evidence of these types of conduct was sufficient to establish a prima facie case of open lewdness. Section 5901 of the Pennsylvania Crimes Code defines the crime of open lewdness as follows: "A person commits a misdemeanor if he does any lewd act which he knows is likely to be observed by others who would be affronted or alarmed." At common law the crime was defined as an act of gross and open indecency which tends to corrupt the morals of the community. Even though the language of the statute does differ in some respects from the common law definition, there is no difference in meaning. *Commonwealth v. Williams*, **574 A.2d 1161 (Pa. Super. 1990);** *Commonwealth v. Heinbaugh*, **354 A.2d 244 (Pa. 1976)** Further, the Model Penal Code, Tentative Draft describes lewd conduct as the "...gross flouting of community standards in respect to sexuality or nudity in public." Given these guidelines, it is not surprising to find that all of the reported Pennsylvania cases on open lewdness involved public masturbation or public displays of genitalia. Thus, it would appear that the purpose of the statute is to discourage public conduct, which is lewd or lascivious. Section 5901 does not proscribe all conduct that might be described as bizarre, or offensive, or distasteful, or as a breach of etiquette. It extends to conduct that, **(1)** involves public nudity or public sexuality and **(2)** represents a gross departure from community standards as to rise to the level of criminal liability.

There is no reported Pennsylvania case where conduct that amounts to a person undressing and getting ready for bed and passing briefly in front of a window nude or partially nude is guilty of conduct which represents a gross departure from accepted community standards and therefore criminal.

Concerning the described conduct of the defendant on July 6, 1995, given the surrounding circumstances, this likewise does not rise to the level of open lewdness. The act of the defendant briefly exposing her breasts to two other females occurred in the context of a neighborhood feud and in response to a comment made by one of the persons observing the defendant. It may have been an act of scorn, contempt, insolence and antagonism, but it was not lewd. This can hardly be said to be conduct that was intended to flout community standards with respect to sexuality or nudity in public.

BURGLARY

At common law, **burglary** was the breaking and entering of a building at night with the intent of committing a felony. Since the purpose of this crime is to allow people to be secure in their homes, should it matter whether the offense occurred during the day or night? The modern definition of burglary is that a person is guilty of the crime if he enters a building or occupied structure with the intent to commit a crime unless the premises are at the time open to the public. The distinction of committing the crime between the day or night has been eliminated as well as the requirement of a breaking and entering.

Burglary is a crime in and of itself and does not require the substantive offense to be committed by the criminal. If a person breaks into a home to steal a rare painting, but the painting is no longer there, the individual is still guilty of burglary.

Can a person be convicted of burglarizing his own home? That is the issue in the following case.

COMMONWEALTH OF PENNSYLVANIA V. ABDUL MAJEED
694 A.2D 336 (PA. 1997)

APPELLANT MARRIED HIS WIFE IN **1982** and they had seven children together. Mrs. Majeed also had a daughter, Khadijah, before the marriage. The couple separated in 1992. Mrs. Majeed and the children continued to reside at 1312 Wood Street, in Pittsburgh, while Appellant relocated. Appellant, however, is the exclusive owner of the home.

In March of 1993, Mrs. Majeed petitioned the Court for an order pursuant to the **Protection from Abuse Act**. By consent of the parties, the court entered an order that provided:

Defendant is completely excluded from the Plaintiff's residence at 1312 Wood Street. Defendant shall have no right or privilege to enter or be present on the premises.

Five days after entry of the Order, Appellant went to 1312 Wood Street. When he arrived, his stepdaughter, Khadijah, was standing at a bus stop near the house. Appellant grabbed her arm and led her to the door of the house. Appellant revealed to her that he had a gun and asked her to unlock the door. When Khadijah replied that she did not have a key, Appellant kicked in the door. Khadijah testified that Appellant forced her to commit a sexual act.

While he was in the house, the police arrived. When an officer entered Khadijah's bedroom, Appellant sprang from the closet with a semiautomatic pistol in hand.

A jury found Appellant guilty of burglary and simple assault. We granted allocatur to decide whether an individual can be convicted of burglarizing a home he owns after entering the premises in violation of an Abuse Order.

A person is guilty of burglary if he enters a building or occupied structure, with intent to commit a crime therein, unless the premises are at the time open to the public or the actor is licensed or privileged to enter.

Although Appellant owned 1312 Wood Street, when he entered into the consent order, he voluntarily relinquished any license or privilege he had to enter the premises and granted Mrs. Majeed exclusive possession of it. His very method of entry — kicking in the door further evidences that his license or privilege to enter the premises had expired. Because Appellant was not licensed or privileged to enter the home, the lower court properly upheld his conviction for burglary.

The purpose of the **Protection from Abuse Act** is to prevent domestic violence, and to promote the security of the home. Here, Appellant voluntarily agreed to refrain from entering their home. Thus, the court and the parties, specifically intended the Abuse Order to protect Mrs. Majeed and her children from exactly the type of conduct Appellant committed. He forcibly entered the home with the intent to commit a crime. Moreover, his unlawful entry facilitated his harassment of Khadijah.

For the foregoing reasons, we affirm the order of the lower court.

How would you answer the following questions?

1. If a person breaks into a car to steal the radio, is this burglary?

2. If a person enters a mobile home to assault occupant, is this burglary?

3. If a person enters a department store while it is open in order to steal a coat, is this burglary?

LARCENY

Larceny is the taking and carrying away of property of another without consent and with the intention of depriving the other of the goods permanently.

Because of the difficulty in distinguishing larceny from embezzlement and other theft related crimes, the offenses have been consolidated into the crime of theft.

ROBBERY

Robbery consists of all of the elements of larceny with the additional requirement that the taking be accomplished by force or the threat of force.

The force needed to accomplish a pick-pocket is not of the type ordinarily required for robbery. If a weapon is used, however, the crime will be considered robbery. For instance, a purse snatch in which the victim is knocked to the ground is robbery.

RECEIVING STOLEN PROPERTY

A person commits the crime of **receiving stolen property** if he intentionally obtains or disposes of property of another knowing that it has been stolen, or believing that it has probably been stolen.

This crime is aimed at penalizing those who take possession of stolen merchandise. The court will look at the circumstances behind the transaction to decide the criminal intent of the person who obtained the goods.

COMMONWEALTH OF PENNYLVANIA V. MATTHEWS
632 A.2D 570 (PA. SUPER. 1993)

WILLIAM MURPHY DISCOVERED THAT HIS HOME had been burglarized. Among the items taken were the keys to his automobile. The car had also been stolen.

A few days later, Officer Bush spotted Matthews driving the stolen car. Bush asked Matthews to produce his driver's license and owner's registration. Matthews was unable to produce either. The officer then informed Matthews that the vehicle had been reported stolen.

At trial, Matthews testified that he had rented the car from Charles Lewis in exchange for two "rocks" of crack cocaine. Matthews testified that he needed the car in order to perform a plumbing job at the home of Edward Thorton, and, at the time he was stopped by Officer Bush, he was on his way to return the car to Charles Lewis.

It is undisputed that the vehicle showed no physical manifestations of theft, such as signs of forced entry, broken ignition system or obliterated vehicle identification number.

In order to obtain a conviction for receiving stolen property, the Commonwealth must prove beyond a reasonable doubt that the property was stolen, the defendant was in possession of the property and the defendant knew the property was stolen or had reason to believe the property was stolen.

A permissible inference of guilty knowledge may be drawn from the unexplained possession of recently stolen goods. The mere possession of stolen property, however, is insufficient to permit an inference of guilty knowledge. There must be additional evidence, circumstantial or direct, which would indicate that the defendant knew or had reason to know that the property was stolen.

In this case, we find that the evidence presented by the Commonwealth was insufficient to establish that Matthews knew or had reason to believe that the vehicle in question had been stolen. Matthews was cooperative with the police; the car showed no physical signs that it had been stolen; and, Matthews offered an explanation for his possession of the vehicle at trial which was consistent with his statement to police at the time of his arrest. Accordingly, we reverse the judgment of sentence for receiving stolen property.

CONSPIRACY

Conspiracy is an agreement between two or more people to commit a crime or to do a lawful act in an unlawful manner. Two individuals, who plan and carry out a bank robbery, have clearly committed the offense of conspiracy. Does a conspiracy arise, however, when the parties agree to rob the bank but take no further action? A mere agreement to commit a crime is not enough. The courts require the co-conspirators to perform an overt act or to take some type of positive action in further of the illegal agreement.

The following case deals with a civil conspiracy involving Jean Claude Van Damme.

TARA LEBLANC v. JEAN CLAUDE VAN DAMME
1994 WL 144 271 (E.D. LA. 1994)

PLAINTIFF TARA LEBLANC CLAIMS that she and her boyfriend, defendant Carey Crone, were joined by Jean Claude Van Damme and Darcy Lapiere for dinner in the New Orleans French Quarter. After dinner, the four went to several bars before going to the Windsor Court Hotel. After checking into the hotel, Crone and LeBlanc went to their suite, while Van Damme and LaPiere went to the adjoining suite. Plaintiff claims that she got into bed, and Crone went into the bathroom. Van Damme and LaPiere, who were both nude, came through the adjoining door and got into bed with LeBlanc. Crone joined the three in bed, she claims. Plaintiff argues that it was obvious that Crone knew of the "plan" that was unfolding.

LeBlanc claims that Van Damme began "touching, groping, and fondling" her. Van Damme physically forced LeBlanc to perform oral sex on him, she claims. LeBlanc claims that she resisted then pretended to pass out. She avers that Van Damme became angry when she pretended to pass out, and the three defendants left the room.

As part of her claim, LeBlanc asserts that Van Damme, LaPiere and Crone conspired to lure her into "the sexual trap" at the hotel. She alleges that the three placed her at ease by going on a double date that evening before returning to the hotel. The three planned to overwhelm plaintiff and force her into group sex, she alleges.

Crone and LaPiere ask the court to dismiss the conspiracy claim because plaintiff makes a vague and conclusory allegation that fails to assert any facts against Crone and LaPiere regarding their participation in the alleged assault.

LeBlanc, argues that the facts provided in the complaint are sufficient to sustain her conspiracy claim because she alleges that Van Damme, Crone and LaPiere agreed to commit a series of tortuous acts against her. Specifically, she claims that the defendants acted together to allow LaPiere and Van Damme to enter the room through the normally locked door. The three got into bed with LeBlanc and attempted to engage in group sex, she claims.

Louisiana law provides that he who conspires with another person to commit an intentional or willful act is answerable, with that person, for the damage caused by such act. La. Civ. Code Ann. Art. 2324(A).

Louisiana courts interpret the article as creating liability for acts performed pursuant to a conspiracy which causes injury or damage to a plaintiff. To recover, a plaintiff must prove that an agreement existed to commit an illegal or tortuous act that resulted in plaintiff's injury.

Circumstantial evidence is often the only available evidence in proving a conspiracy because conspirators rarely formulate their plans in ways susceptible of proof by direct evidence.

Here, plaintiff's allegations support a conspiracy claim by averring that the three defendants planned to engage her in group sex by having Van Damme and LaPiere come into her bed nude and uninvited. The court finds that plaintiff alleges sufficient facts to withstand the motion to dismiss but makes no comment about final determination of the claim.

IT IS ORDERED that the motion to dismiss the conspiracy claim against defendants Carey Crone and Darcy LaPiere is DENIED.

SECTION 7.2
DEFENSES TO A CRIME

An alleged criminal act may be considered excusable or justified under the appropriate circumstances. Defenses in this category include **self-defense** and actions in defense of others. The law recognizes the right of a person unlawfully attacked to use reasonable force in self-defense. However, only a person who reasonably believes there is imminent danger of bodily harm can use a reasonable amount of force under the circumstances.

Some defenses to a crime rest on the defendant's assertion that he or she lacked criminal responsibility for the criminal act. As a general rule, **intoxication** is not a defense unless it negates a specific mental state, such as specific intent to kill, which is required to prove the crime. Some defendants invoke the defense of **insanity** as demonstrating lack of criminal responsibility. Insanity rests on the theory that people who suffer from a mental disease or defect should not be convicted if they fail to appreciate that what they are doing is wrong or if they don't know the difference between right and wrong. The insanity defense only applies if the accused was insane at the time of the crime. Insanity during or after the trial does not affect criminal liability.

In many states, there are at least four possible verdicts: guilty, innocent, no contest and not guilty by reason of insanity. Not guilty by reason of insanity results in the automatic commitment to a mental institution. Recently, states have created a new verdict: guilty but mentally ill. This option arose from the shooting of President Reagan by John Hinkley. The assailant shot the President in order to impress actress, Jodie Foster who he became infatuated with from the movie, **Taxi Driver**. Pennsylvania has adopted the verdict of guilty but mentally ill, which means that a jury, which returns with such a verdict, is saying that the defendant has criminal responsibility for his actions but it is acknowledged that the defendant suffers from a mental problem.

The following explanation of the insanity defense was offered in *Commonwealth v. Bowers*:

> The verdict of not guilty by reason of legal insanity labels a defendant as a sick person rather than a bad person. It signifies that in the eyes of the law that person, because of mental abnormality at the time of the crime, does not deserve to be blamed and treated as a criminal for what he did.

> The verdict of guilty but mentally ill labels a defendant as both bad and sick. It means that in the law's eyes that person at the time of the crime was not so mentally abnormal as to be relieved from blame and criminal punishment for what he did, but that he was abnormal enough to make a prime candidate for special therapeutic treatment.

Defendants found guilty but mentally ill will be sent to a hospital or mental institution for treatment and will then be transferred to prison after they have recovered.

SECTION 7.3
POLICE INVESTIGATION

When a crime is reported, the police conduct an investigation to ascertain more facts about the case and to learn the identity of the perpetrator of the crime.

While justice demands that the culprit be apprehended, the government must not violate the constitutional rights of the suspect in their zest to solve the crime. Over the years, the police have developed a number of tools and procedures to help identify the criminal. Suspects will be questioned and search warrants will be issued. Several of these police methods are discussed in the following subsections.

SECTION 7.4
POLICE SKETCH

During the initial meeting with the victim or witnesses, the identity of the assailant will be a focal point of the investigation. When possible, a sketch of the assailant is made by a police artist or detective through the use of an identification kit.

The sketch on the previous page is an example of a drawing made by the use of a kit. The unit consists of hundreds of plastic overlays that show different parts and shapes of the face.

The artist will put the sketch together with the assistance of the witness and is able to quickly change the shape of the nose, eyes or mouth to try and create an accurate representation of the accused.

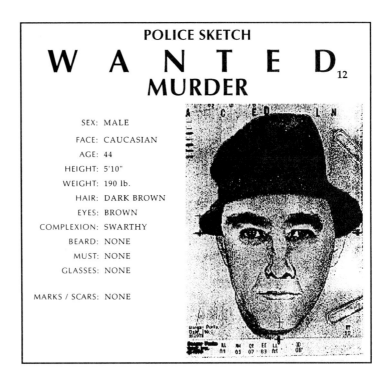

POLICE SKETCH

W A N T E D₁₂

MURDER

SEX: MALE
FACE: CAUCASIAN
AGE: 44
HEIGHT: 5'10"
WEIGHT: 190 lb.
HAIR: DARK BROWN
EYES: BROWN
COMPLEXION: SWARTHY
BEARD: NONE
MUST: NONE
GLASSES: NONE

MARKS / SCARS: NONE

**SECTION 7.5
THE POLYGRAPH**

The police will frequently ask suspects and complainants to submit to a polygraph or "lie detector" examination. No one can be forced to take the test and the results are generally not admissible in court since the polygraph is subject to error.

POLYGRAPH EXAMINATION REPORT

The machine fits into a small case and consists of devices to measure skin temperature, blood pressure and respiration. The person to be tested is told of the questions that will be asked in advance of the examination. The test is then administered with the questions being repeated and the responses recorded on graph paper.

The scientific community remains divided over the accuracy of the lie detector. The advocates of the test praise the machine's ability to detect deception with an accuracy rate of at least 85%. The critics of the polygraph place the accuracy of the test at less than 50%. For the most part, state and federal courts continue to question the validity of the polygraph and the results of the test are not admitted into court as accurate scientific evidence.

POLYGRAPH EXAMINATION REPORT

ABINGTON TOWNSHIP POLICE DEPARTMENT

POLYGRAPH EXAMINATION REPORT   PRIVILEGED AND CONFIDENTIAL

PART "A" (To be completed by Detective requesting examination)

Department NARCOTICS   Requesting Detective JOHN O'BRIEN
Case Number 89-5325   Date submitted JUNE 10,
Person to be examined KATHY HODGE   Age 16 Sex F
Address 505 SWAMP ROAD   House phone 555-2199
Date/time requested June 10   - 3:00 P.M Work phone
Nature of crime POSSESSION OF DRUGS

(Do not write below this line)

PART "B"

Polygraph examination approved by _George Steele_   Date June 10
                    APD Detective Supervisor

PART "C"   REPORT

On June 10 _Kathy Hodge_ voluntarily came to the Polygraph
Suite for a Polygraph examination. The main issue under consideration was whether
or not SHE   was telling the truth when SHE claimed that SHE
DIDN'T KNOW DRUGS WERE IN HER CAR   .
Before THE pre-test interview KATHY HODGE voluntarily signed a permission
form stating that SHE was taking the examination of HER own free will.

[N/A] In the Polygraph recordings there were _____ indications of truthfulness [ ]
when _____ answered the four pertinent test questions.

[N/A] In the Polygraph recordings there were _____ indications of lying [ ]
when _____ answered the four pertinent test questions.

[N/A] During the testing procedure _____ stated to the Polygraphist
that _____ was lying about _____ involvement in the issue under consideration. [ ]

[X] Throughout this persons tests, there were reactions that could not be analyzed, [X]
therefore the Polygraphist could not form any opinion and it is the recommendation of the Polygraphist that KATHY HODGE be given the opportunity
of taking a re-examination.

[N/A] Person failed to show   [ ] Person refused during examination

Respectfully submitted,
Kenneth J. Clark
Kenneth J. Clark, Polygraphist.

In **United States v. Scheffer,** the Supreme Court was asked to decide whether an individual, who had passed his polygraph examination concerning his use of drugs but had tested positive on his urine analysis, could use the test results of the lie detector in the defense of his case. In excluding the polygraph evidence, the Court reconfirmed the inadmissibility of the test results because of the lack of uniform scientific opinion concerning the validity of the test.

UNITED STATES OF AMERICA V. EDWARD SCHEFFER
118 S. CT. 1261 (1999)

THIS CASE PRESENTS THE QUESTION whether Military Rule of Evidence 707, which makes polygraph evidence inadmissible in court-martial proceedings, unconstitutionally abridges the right of accused members of the military to present a defense. We hold that it does not.

In March 1992, respondent Edward Scheffer, an airman stationed at March Air Force Base in California, volunteered to work as an informant on drug investigations for the Air Force Office of Special Investigations (OSI). His OSI supervisors advised him that, from time to time during the course of his undercover work, they would ask him to submit to drug testing and polygraph examinations. In early April, one of the OSI agents supervising respondent requested that he submit to a urine test. Shortly after providing the urine sample, but before the results of the test were known, respondent agreed to take a polygraph test administered by an OSI examiner. In the opinion of the examiner, the test "indicated no deception" when respondent denied using drugs since joining the Air Force.

On April 30, Scheffer unaccountably failed to appear for work and could not be found on the base. He was absent without leave until May 13, when an Iowa State patrolman arrested him following a routine traffic stop and held him for return to the base. OSI agents later learned that respondent's urinalysis revealed the presence of methamphetamine.

Scheffer was tried by general court-martial on charges of using methamphetamine, failing to go to his appointed place of duty, wrongfully absenting himself from the base for 13 days, and, with respect to an unrelated matter, uttering 17 insufficient funds checks. He testified at trial on his own behalf, relying upon an "innocent ingestion" theory and denying that he had knowingly used drugs while working for OSI. On cross-examination, the prosecution attempted to impeach respondent with inconsistencies between his trial testimony and earlier statements he had made to OSI.

Scheffer sought to introduce the polygraph evidence in support of his testimony that he did not knowingly use drugs. The military judge denied the motion, relying on Military Rule of Evidence 707, which provides, in relevant part:

> (a) Notwithstanding any other provision of law, the results of a polygraph examination, the opinion of a polygraph examiner, or any reference to an offer to take, failure to take, or taking of a polygraph examination, shall not be admitted into evidence.

The military judge determined that Rule 707 was constitutional because the President may, through the Rules of Evidence, determine that credibility is not an area in which a fact finder needs help, and the polygraph is not a process that has sufficient scientific acceptability to be relevant.

Scheffer was convicted on all counts and was sentenced to a bad-conduct discharge, confinement for 30 months, total forfeiture of all pay and allowances, and reduction to the lowest enlisted grade.

A defendant's right to present relevant evidence is not unlimited, but rather is subject to reasonable restrictions. A defendant's interest in presenting such evidence may thus bow to accommodate other legitimate interests in the criminal trial process. As a result, state and federal rulemakers have broad latitude under the Constitution to establish rules excluding evidence from criminal trials. Such rules do not abridge an accused's right to present a defense so long as they are not "arbitrary" or "disproportionate to the purposes they are designed to serve." Moreover, we have found the exclusion of evidence to be unconstitutionally arbitrary or disproportionate only where it has infringed upon a weighty interest of the accused.

Rule 707 serves several legitimate interests in the criminal trial process. These interests include ensuring that only reliable evidence is introduced at trial, preserving the jury's role in determining credibility, and avoiding litigation that is collateral to the primary purpose of the trial.

State and federal governments unquestionably have a legitimate interest in ensuring that reliable evidence is presented to the trier of fact in a criminal trial. Indeed, the exclusion of unreliable evidence is a principal objective of many evidentiary rules.

The contentions of Scheffer notwithstanding, there are simply no consensus that polygraph evidence is reliable. To this day, the scientific community remains extremely polarized about the reliability of polygraph techniques. Some studies have concluded that polygraph tests overall are accurate and reliable. See, e.g., S. Abrams, *The Complete Polygraph Handbook* 190-191 (1968) (reporting the overall accuracy rate from laboratory studies involving the common "control question technique" polygraph to be "in the range of 87 percent"). Others have found that polygraph tests assess truthfulness significantly less accurately- that scientific field studies suggest the accuracy rate of the "control question technique" polygraph is "little better than could be obtained by the toss of a coin," that is, 50 percent. See Iacono & Lykken, *The Scientific Status of Research on Polygraph Techniques: The Case Against Polygraph Tests,* in 1 Modern Scientific Evidence, supra, § 14-5.3, p. 629.

This lack of scientific consensus is reflected in the disagreement among state and federal courts concerning both the admissibility and the reliability of polygraph evidence. Although some Federal Courts of Appeal have abandoned the per se rule excluding polygraph evidence, leaving its admission or exclusion to the discretion of district courts, at least one Federal Circuit has recently reaffirmed its per se ban, and another recently noted that it has "not decided whether polygraphs has reached a sufficient state of reliability to be admissible." Most States maintain per se rules excluding polygraph evidence. New Mexico is unique in making polygraph evidence generally admissible without the prior stipulation of the parties and without significant restriction. Whatever their approach, state and federal courts continue to express doubt about whether such evidence is reliable.

The approach taken by the President in adopting Rule 707--excluding polygraph evidence in all military trials--is a rational and proportional means of advancing the legitimate interest in barring unreliable evidence. Although the degree of reliability of polygraph evidence may depend upon a variety of identifiable factors, there is simply no way to know in a particular case whether a polygraph examiner's conclusion is accurate, because certain doubts and uncertainties plague even the best polygraph exams. Individual jurisdictions therefore may reasonably reach differing conclusions as to whether polygraph evidence should be admitted. We cannot say, then, that presented with such widespread uncertainty, the President acted arbitrarily or disproportionately in promulgating a rule excluding all polygraph evidence.

For the foregoing reasons, Military Rule of Evidence 707 does not unconstitutionally abridge the right to present a defense. The judgment of the Court of Appeals is reversed.

SECTION 7.6
QUESTIONING
OF A SUSPECT

Part of the Fifth Amendment provides that no person shall be compelled in any criminal case to be a witness against himself. This fundamental guarantee is the basis for the Miranda Warnings. If a person is the subject of **custodial interrogation**, the police must inform the suspect that he or she has the right to remain silent and that a lawyer can be present during the questioning.

The form on the following page is used by the police to help prove in court that the suspect was provided with the Miranda Warnings.

How broad is the Fifth Amendment right against self-incrimination? The courts have ruled that this guarantee does not protect an individual from being fingerprinted or photographed since the procedures are not testimony.

ABINGTON TOWNSHIP POLICE DEPARTMENT

1166 OLD YORK ROAD

ABINGTON, PENNSYLVANIA 19001

CONSTITUTIONAL RIGHTS   CASE # 01-4322

We have a duty to explain to you and to warn you that you have the following legal rights

A. You have a right to remain silent and do not have to say anything at all.

B. Anything you say can and will be used against you in court.

C. You have a right to talk to a lawyer of your own choice before we ask you any questions, and also to have a lawyer here with you while we ask you questions.

D. If you cannot afford to hire a lawyer, and you want one, we will see that you have a lawyer provided to you, free of charge, before we ask you any questions.

E. If you are willing to give us a statement, you have a right to stop any time you wish.

1. Q. Do you understand that you have a right to keep silent and do not have to say anything at all?
    A.   YES

2. Q. Do you understand that anything you say can and will be used against you?
    A.   YES

3. Q. Do you want to remain silent?
    A.   NO

4. Q. Do you understand that you have a right to talk with a lawyer before we ask you any questions?
    A.   YES

5. Q. Do you understand that if you cannot afford to hire a lawyer and you want one, we will not ask you any questions until a lawyer is appointed for you free of charge?
    A.   SURE

6. Q. Do you want to talk with a lawyer at this time, or to have a lawyer with you while we ask you questions?
    A.   NO

7. Q. Are you willing to answer questions of your own free will without force or fear, and without any threats or promises having been made to you?
    A. YES

DATE: JUNE 9,

TIME: 11:30 P.M.

OFFICER: John O'Brien

BADGE: 342

SIGNED:

SIGNED:
(parent or guardian)

WITNESS:

COMMONWEALTH OF PENNSYLVANIA V. GRAHAM
703 A.2D 510 (PA. SUPER. 1997)

IN THIS APPEAL WE DECIDE WHETHER A PROVISION of the Motor Vehicle Code is constitutional that permits the Commonwealth to introduce into evidence the fact that a defendant refused to be tested for alcohol or drugs where the defendant is charged with driving under the influence. We conclude that the statutory provision is constitutional and affirm the judgment of sentence.

The fatal automobile accident occurred on August 2, 1994. On that evening, appellant was driving northbound on Interstate 95, weaving back and forth between lanes at an estimated speed of seventy miles per hour. As appellant made one of his abrupt lane changes, his vehicle collided with another northbound vehicle. His vehicle was then hurled over the median barrier into the southbound lane, crashing into several other cars. Several persons were seriously injured, and one person was killed.

After the accident, Lieutenant Mingacci and Sergeant Stieber of the highway patrol noticed that appellant was agitated, had glassy, bloodshot eyes, was acting disoriented, had difficulty standing and had a strong odor of alcohol on his breath. Believing that appellant may have been driving while under the influence of alcohol or a controlled substance, Sergeant Stieber radioed Lieutenant Nestle, a specialist in administering field sobriety tests, and requested that he report to the scene.

When Lieutenant Nestle arrived, he requested that appellant submit to a field sobriety test. Once appellant assented, Lieutenant Nestle administered the "one leg stand" and the "walk and turn" tests, neither of which appellant could successfully complete. Appellant was then transported to police headquarters where Officer Waerig told appellant that the rights provided by *Miranda v. Arizona,* **384 U.S. 436, 86 S.Ct. 1602, (1966),** do not apply to chemical testing, and if the accused refuses to consent, his driver's license will be suspended for one year. Appellant agreed to submit to the breathalyzer test.

The results of the breathalyzer test revealed that the alcohol level of appellant's blood was within the legal limit. However, due to appellant's erratic conduct, Officer Waerig believed that appellant was under the influence of a controlled substance in addition to alcohol. Officer Waerig then requested that appellant submit to a blood test and appellant consented to the blood test. An analysis of appellant's blood revealed the presence of cocaine metabolite, marijuana and marijuana metabolite.

After a (non-jury) trial, appellant was found guilty of homicide by vehicle while driving under the influence of alcohol or a controlled substance, and WAS sentenced to an aggregate term of fifteen to thirty years in prison. This appeal followed.

Appellant argues that the results of his blood test should not have been admitted at trial. He maintains that his consent to the blood test was invalid because the officer coerced him to incriminate himself in violation of his Fifth Amendment rights. He asserts that he consented to the test only because he was afraid of the inferences the fact finders would draw if they learned he refused to take the blood test. He contends that such consent deprived him of his right not to incriminate himself.

Although appellant acknowledges that the Motor Vehicle Code permits a defendant's refusal to submit to chemical testing to be introduced at trial, appellant argues that this provision is unconstitutional because it attaches a penalty to his exercise of a constitutional right.

The United States Supreme Court has made it clear that a defendant does not have a constitutional right to refuse blood tests. *Schmerber v. California*, 384 U.S. 757, 86 S.Ct. 1826, 16 L.Ed.2d 908 (1966). While blood test evidence may be "an incriminating product of compulsion," such evidence in no way implicates an accused's *testimonial* capacities and therefore, its admission does not offend the privilege against self incrimination embodied in the Fifth Amendment. The Court noted that the Fifth Amendment privilege relates to testimony or communication from an accused. The privilege does not prevent the police from using the accused's body or blood as physical evidence when it is material.

Taking this analysis another step, the United States Supreme Court has further reasoned "that since submission to a blood test could itself be compelled, ... a State's decision to permit a suspect to refuse to take the test but then to comment upon that refusal at trial [does] not 'compel' the suspect to incriminate himself and hence (does) not violate the privilege." *Pennsylvania v. Muniz*, 496 U.S. 582, 110 S.Ct. 2638, (1990). Because it is clear that appellant had no constitutional right to refuse the blood test, the Motor Vehicle Code does not burden appellant's constitutional rights by allowing evidence of his refusal to consent to be admitted at trial. As such, a defendant's consent to a blood test after being informed that his refusal could be admitted at trial, is valid and not coerced.

SECTION 7.7 **COMMONWEALTH** **v. CHRISTOPHER**	**HODGE, DODGE AND LODGE** **ATTORNEYS AT LAW** **MEMORNDUM**

PROBLEM SEVEN

TO: Part-Time Law Clerk #3

FROM: Gregory Olan Dodge

RE: Commonwealth v. Peter Christopher
           In Court Identification

As you may recall, Kathy's behavioral problems began after she was assaulted in the school gym. Kathy often stayed at school after volleyball practice to workout in the weight room. Usually the wrestling team was there with her. However, this one night it so happened that the team was away at a meet.

Kathy was so busy exercising that she didn't notice the presence of her attacker—at least not until it was too late. Kathy first realized that she wasn't alone when she looked up and saw a shark staring back at her. When she looked again, she realized it was a guy with a tatoo of a shark on his left shoulder. The strange thing was that he was wearing a ski mask. Before she had time to realize what was happening, she was assaulted and her pocketbook was stolen.

Kathy was troubled by the incident. She could not stop thinking about the tattoo since Joe's daughter knew she had seen it before. To her shock and amazement, Kathy soon realized that she knew her assailant. It was her next door neighbor, Peter Christopher. He had a tattoo of a shark on his shoulder and he intensely disliked the family.

Peter Christopher was arrested by the police and pleaded not guilty to the charges. During the second day of his criminal trial, the District Attorney requested Peter Christopher to stand before the jury and remove his shirt so the panel could ascertain if the defendant had a tattoo of a shark on his shoulder. The defense vigorously objected to this in-court identification claiming that it would violate Christopher's Fifth Amendment rights against self-incrimination. The issue before the court concerns these identifying marks on the defendent's shoulder. The Fifth Amendment guarantees that no person shall be compelled to testify against himself. According to *Morgan v. State*, can the District Attorney compel Christopher to remove his shirt to show the jury his tattoo? Why would this type of in court identification violate (or not violate) the Constitution?

GLENMORE MORGAN v. STATE OF MARYLAND
558 A.2D 1226 (MD. APP. 1989)

WE ARE CALLED UPON TO DECIDE whether requiring a defendant to don an article of clothing in the courtroom in front of the jury so that the jury may see if the article of clothing fits violates his privilege against self-incrimination under the 5th Amendment.

In the case before us, Glenmore Morgan, defendant, was charged with possession of cocaine with intent to distribute, possession of cocaine and possession of controlled paraphernalia. During a jury trial, the court required the defendant to put on a jacket seized by officers of the Montgomery County Police Department pursuant to a search warrant.

At the time the search warrant was executed, defendant and two other men were present in the living room of the residence. After the two other men retrieved their coats, Morgan queried, "What about my jacket?" When asked by the police if a jacket located on the loveseat in the living room was his, Morgan hesitated before responding, "No." Police search of the jacket revealed a small quantity of cocaine, a beeper, keys to the residence and a key to a safe in the kitchen. During a search of the safe, the police discovered bottles of inositol powder, several baggies, razor blades, measuring spoons, a box containing a grinder, and twenty-three grams of cocaine. Morgan was convicted on all charges.

The Fifth Amendment of the United States Constitution provides: "No person... shall be compelled in any criminal case to be a witness against himself." Defendant contends that the court's order requiring him to put on the jacket in front of the jury violated his constitutional right against compelled self-incrimination.

The Court of Appeals in *Andrews v. State* upheld a trial court order restraining Andrews from shaving his head or facial hair until the conclusion of this trial. Purportedly, he had changed his appearance immediately after the crime in question by shaving his head and beard. The trial court order was designed to prevent the defendant from defeating "legitimate avenues of identification" by disguising his appearance.

In *Schmerber v. California,* **384 U.S. 757 (1966),** the Supreme Court stated that the privilege against compelled self-incrimination "protects an accused only from being compelled to testify against himself or otherwise provide the State with evidence of a testimonial or communicative nature..." Requiring a defendant to put on an article of clothing, simply does not constitute an act compelling a testimonial or communicative response. The fact that an article of clothing fits may give rise to a inference of ownership, which under the facts of any given case could be incrimination, is not a communicative response from the defendant.

By granting the prosecutor's request to order the defendant to don the coat in the presence of the jury, the trial court compelled the defendant to disclose nothing of his personal knowledge. This is not communication within the meaning of the Fifth Amendment. Moreover, it is of no consequence that the defendant declined to take the stand to testify on his own behalf; his physical display simply does not constitute "testimony."

In this case, the trial court order requiring defendant to don a coat, which admittedly contained incriminatory evidence, to determine whether it fit him did not constitute a compulsion to elicit communicative or testimonial evidence from the defendant.

Judgment affirmed.

**ANSWER SHEET
PROBLEM SEVEN**

_____

Name   **Please Print Clearly**

1. According to _Morgan v. State,_ can the District Attorney compel
    Christopher to remove his shirt to show the jury his tattoo? Explain
    your answer.

_____

_____

_____

_____

_____

_____

_____

_____

_____

_____

_____

_____

_____

_____

_____

_____

_____

_____

_____

_____

2. Why would this type of in court identification violate or not violate Christopher's constitutional rights? Explain your answer.

_____

_____

_____

_____

_____

_____

_____

_____

_____

_____

_____

_____

_____

_____

_____

_____

_____

_____

_____

_____

SECTION 7.8
SEARCH AND SEIZURE

The Fourth Amendment prohibits unlawful search and seizure and provides that all warrants shall be issued upon probable cause. A judge following a hearing issues warrants. A government official, such as a police officer, will appear before the court and provide the necessary information to establish probable cause. If a warrant is issued, it will be specific as to location and evidence that is the subject of the search.

The general test to determine if a warrant is needed by the police to conduct a lawful search and seizure is to ascertain whether the person had a reasonable expectation of privacy. If the individual enjoyed a reasonable expectation of privacy, a warrant must be obtained before the search can be undertaken. For example, people have an expectation of privacy while at home, but would a man have such an expectation if he were walking down the street holding a shotgun? Obviously, the police can confiscate the weapon without the need of a search warrant.

Commonwealth v. Thomas involves a search by law enforcement officials for drugs. A police officer climbed the fire escape of an apartment building in order to search the roof for drugs. The court found that the search was valid since the roof is not within the tenant's possession or control nor did the tenant have a reasonable expectation of privacy to that common area.

COMMONWEALTH OF PENNSYLVANIA V. THOMAS
698 A.2D 85 (PA. SUPER. 1997)

TAMILIA, Judge:

THIS IS AN APPEAL FROM THE JUDGMENT of sentence imposed following appellant's convictions of manufacture and possession of a controlled substance.

Appellant was charged with the above crimes after Pittsburgh police officers received information from a confidential informant and a telephone complaint that marijuana was growing on the roof of the apartment building at 5738 Howe Street by an actor known as "Chris." The telephone complaint further informed the officers that the roof could be reached either by using the fire escape or by confronting the residents of the top-floor apartment and requesting access to the roof. Acting on that information, the officers located the described apartment building. Without first attempting to obtain a search warrant, Officer Hildebrand scaled the fire escape and climbed onto the roof. He observed a freestanding rooftop apartment situated in the center of the roof and walked its perimeter. Once he had taken two turns around the corners of the apartment, he noticed a bridgewalk connected to the roof of the adjacent building and a small garden partially enclosed by a wall located a few feet from the door of appellant's apartment. The officer stated the garden contained at least two varieties of plants, a few of which had red and yellow flow-

ers on them. Officer Hildebrand did not approach the plants to determine if the flowers were real or artificial but stated, in any event, that he knew some of the plants were marijuana. The officers left the scene after approximately 30 minutes and during that time saw no one use or attempt to use the fire escape. Subsequently, a search warrant was obtained based upon an affidavit of probable cause, which incorporated the information supplied by the confidential informant, the telephone complaint and the results of Officer Hildebrand's investigation of the rooftop garden. The police executed the search warrant, seized the marijuana plants, drug paraphernalia and weapons, and took appellant's statement that the plants were his and that his roommates were not involved in any illegal activity.

On appeal, appellant makes several arguments. First, he argues the findings of fact and conclusions of law were unsupported by the record. Specifically, appellant asserts as error the suppression court's finding that Officer Hildebrand's investigation of the rooftop garden was constitutional because the fire escape that the officer used to scale the apartment building was open to the public and used on a daily basis by tenants of the adjacent apartment building in order to enter and exit their residence. Second, the search warrant was invalid because it contained tainted information obtained by the above mentioned "warrantless search."

In the instant case, we conclude the suppression court judge's finding that the fire escape was used on a daily basis for ingress and egress is not supported by the record. Nevertheless, because Officer Hildebrand observed the marijuana plants from his position on the fire escape route of the apartment buildings, the legal conclusion that the evidence should not be suppressed was a reasonable one. That is, the officer did not stray from the path that the residents of appellant's apartment or the adjacent building would have taken during an emergency. No Fourth Amendment protection is afforded appellant with respect to fire escapes and common hallways of an apartment building where he has no possessory interests. *Commonwealth v. Boykin,* **246 Pa. Super. 154, 157, 369 A.2d 857, 859 (1977).** The fire escape entrance used by the police was a door from the common hallway. While a tenant may have the right to use both hall and fire escape, neither is a part of the (leased) premises under his possession or control." Assuming appellant had a subjective expectation of privacy in the rooftop area outside of his apartment, no reasonable expectation of privacy on the part of appellant was invaded by the officer's conduct. The observation of the plants, made from a lawful vantage point outside of any protected area, was not a search, regardless of whether the evidence in open view was located in a protected or unprotected area. *Commonwealth v. Carelli,* **377 Pa. Super. 117, 546 A.2d 1185 (1988).** Accordingly, Officer Hildebrand's investigation of the rooftop garden was constitutional, the subsequent search warrant issued on a probable cause affidavit that included the results of the officer's investigation was constitutional.

Judgment of sentence affirmed.

There are a number of exceptions, however, to this general rule. The police are not required to obtain a search warrant in the following situations:

1. **Plain View:** If the subject of the search is readily observable, there is no reasonable expectation of privacy. For instance, if marijuana is growing in one's backyard and is visible from the sidewalk, the police do not need a search warrant to seize the plants. An improper search, however, will occur if the police peer into a basement window, and with the aid of a flashlight uncover contraband since the homeowner would have a reasonable expectation of privacy against this type of intrusion.

2. **Emergency:** If the time delay in obtaining the warrant will defeat the ends of justice, the police can engage in the search without the warrant. Car searches generally fall within this exception since vehicles are mobile and can avoid the police by merely driving away. If the vehicle is towed to the police station and impounded, a search warrant will have to be obtained in order to conduct a lawful search. The emergency situation is no longer present since the car is in the possession of the authorities.

3. **Search Incident to an Arrest:** Police officers can search a defendant and the area within that person's immediate reach for weapons. This exception was established to protect the public from possible harm.

4. **Hot Pursuit:** If the police are pursuing a suspect who is fleeing the scene of a crime, they may make a reasonable search of the area looking for the suspect.

5. **Consent:** The police are not required to obtain a search warrant when a suspect consents to a search. The consent, however, must be freely and voluntarily given, and not be coerced by law enforcement officials. Certain third parties may also consent to a search. For instance, parents may allow the police to search a child's room and a school principal is authorized to allow the police to search student lockers at the educational institution. While a roommate may allow the police to search the common areas in an apartment, a landlord does not have the authority to allow the police to search the leased premises without a search warrant.

6. **Search Incident to a General Police Measure:** Border and custom searches are allowed to prevent the entry of illegal aliens and contraband. Customs agents can check everyone's luggage regardless of the existence of probable cause. Other examples include searches of passengers at the airport and individuals can be required to pass through a metal detector before being allowed to enter a courtroom. Both of these measures are designed to protect the safety of the public. The police, however, may not selectively discriminate against a particular racial group under the auspices of conducting a search incident to a general police measure. For example, the police may not stop young Afro-American males on the New Jersey Turnpike merely because the individual may match a racial profile.

7. **Stop and Frisk:** Police officers may conduct "pat-down" searches when there is probable cause to believe that a crime is about to occur and the suspect may possess a weapon. If the police find contraband during the "pat-down" that is instantly recognizable, by feel, it may be seized without a warrant. This seizure is called "plain feel." This exception has the potential for abuse, so courts generally require that the officers present very specific facts that lead to a conclusion of probable cause.

COMMONWEALTH OF PENNSYLVANIA V. FINK
700 A.2D 447 (PA. SUPER. 1997)

CAVANAUGH, Judge.

The facts as aptly stated by the trial court are as follows:

OFFICER GARY WHITEMAN WAS DISPATCHED to 747 West Fourth Street, Williamsport, ("747") at 3:44 a.m. on April 30, 1995, in response to a report of a woman at that address "screaming for the police." Officer Linn entered the front door of 747, a multi-unit rooming house with rooms on three floors, which faces north onto Fourth Street. Once inside, Officer Linn radioed that there was a white male exiting the south door, which goes out toward Mifflin Place.

When first seen, the white male was still on the property of 747, approximately thirty feet from the back door. Officer Whiteman explained to the Defendant that the call was received from within 747, from an unknown origin, and that "[a]ll we know is there is a woman screaming for help." Officer Whiteman explained to the Defendant that due to the nature of the call, he would like to pat him down for officer safety.

After receiving the Defendant's consent, Officer Whiteman conducted an exterior soft patdown. In doing so, he felt an object within the exterior jacket pocket, which he believed to be a marijuana pipe. After removing the object and discovering that it was in fact a marijuana pipe, Officer Whiteman secured the Defendant and conducted a more thorough search of his person, finding a bag containing marijuana and some rolling papers.

Our independent review of the facts leads us to conclude that there existed a reasonable, suspicion that criminal activity was afoot. Appellant was the only white male, Officer Whiteman saw just after Officer Linn radioed that a white male

had exited the south door of the building from where the screams came. Moreover, Officer Whiteman first observed this white male, still on the property of 747, approximately thirty feet from the back door, only five to ten seconds after hearing Officer Linn's radio communication. These factors, coupled with the fact that the incident occurred in the early morning hours, in an area well known for criminal activity, are more than sufficient to establish reasonable suspicion justifying Officer Whiteman's stop of appellant.

Appellant contends that, assuming the officer had a legal right to conduct a pat-down search, he did not have the right to reach into appellant's pocket and seize the pipe, the rolling papers and the marijuana. We agree. Similar to the well-established plain view doctrine, this court now recognizes the seizure of non-threatening contraband detected by an officer's "plain feel" during a pat-down for weapons if: **(1)** the officer is lawfully in a position to detect the presence of contraband, **(2)** the incriminating nature of the contraband is immediately apparent and, **(3)** the officer has a lawful right of access to the object.

After our thorough review, we find the trial court's conclusion, that the seizure of the pipe, rolling papers and marijuana from appellant was based on probable cause, is not supported by the record. Only where the *"incriminating nature of the contraband is immediately apparent"* can an officer seize non-threatening contraband during a pat down for weapons. "Immediately apparent" means that the officer conducting the frisk readily perceives, without further search, that what he is feeling is contraband.

At the suppression hearing, Officer Whiteman testified that the object in appellant's pocket felt "like a pipe, a regular smoking pipe without the stem." On cross-examination at trial, Officer Whiteman responded to the question whether "these same pipes can be used to smoke legitimate non-controlled substances as well" by stating that they "can be used to smoke just about anything, yes."

Officer Whiteman readily admitted that the nature of the pipe was not necessarily illegal. Based on this testimony, we disagree with the trial court's conclusion that the incriminating nature of the pipe was immediately apparent. Not only do we find Officer Whiteman's testimony to be lacking the requisite certainty of the incriminating nature of the object, we find it questionable that he was able to feel the precise "texture" and the refined shape of this object through appellant's clothing to such a degree that it was "immediately apparent" to him that what he felt was a pipe, let alone a pipe used to smoke marijuana.

In sum, we hold that, although Officer Whiteman had the reasonable suspicion necessary to initially stop appellant and the consent of appellant to conduct a pat-down search of his person, he did not have probable cause to seize the marijuana pipe, marijuana and rolling papers from appellant's pocket.

While police officers have considerable latitude in stopping cars and searching the interior when probable cause exits, the Pennsylvania Superior Court recently held that police lack the authority to stop motor vehicles solely because their drivers or front-seat passengers are not wearing seat belts. In *Commonwealth v. Henderson*, the court ruled that evidence gained as a result of a motor vehicle stop effectuated solely because of the failure to use seat belts should have been suppressed because the state's mandatory seat belt law does not give police the authority to stop a car based on that safety violation.

When police or law enforcement officers enter a home pursuant to a lawful search warrant and damage the home in the process, the government cannot generally be compelled to compensate the owner for damages, even if the owner is innocent. In Sacramento, California, the owner of a convenience store spent $275,000 to clean up after police bombarded the store with tear gas to flush out a robbery suspect. The California Supreme Court in *Customer Co. v. City of Sacramento* refused to award damages, and said that while it may appear fair to require the government to compensate innocent persons for damage resulting from routine efforts to enforce criminal laws, the theory of inverse condemnation (saying police caused damaged that was an unconstitutional taking of property) was not designed for such a purpose. The court suggested the store owner seek compensation under a statutorily authorized program to aid crime victims.

SECTION 7.9
THE PROGRESS OF
A STATE CRIMINAL CASE[1]

1. **The Obligations of Crime Victims and Witnesses**. A victim or witness to a crime is expected to report the crime to the police, and to testify in court about what happened. The police will take a statement and file a *criminal complaint*, which is a statement of facts about the crime and later becomes the basis of the formal charges against the accused. After the complaint is drafted, a judge will issue a warrant for the offender's arrest or a summons commanding the accused to appear for a preliminary hearing.

STATE CRIMINAL PROCEDURE

CRIME REPORTED

POLICE INVESTIGATION

ARREST

PRELIMINARY ARRAIGNMENT

PRELIMINARY HEARING

ARRAIGNMENT

TRIAL

PRE-SENTENCE INVESTIGATION

SENTENCING

2. **Preliminary Arraignment**. In cases where the offender is arrested he or she, now called the *defendant*, appears within hours for a preliminary arraignment, which is held before the district justice in the district where the offense occurred or at the Roundhouse if the crime occurred in Philadelphia. It is not necessary that a victim appear for the preliminary arraignment.

    One of the purposes of this hearing is to set *bail*. Bail is a means of insuring that the defendant will continue to appear at scheduled court appearances. In setting bail, the judge considers such factors as the seriousness of the crime, the circumstances of the defendant, his age, employment status, etc., and whether the accused is likely to flee if released. Bail may take several forms, but usually involves the use of money or property of the defendant or someone on his behalf along with the promise of the defendant to remain available. If the defendant fails to appear for a scheduled court appearance, the court may issue a bench warrant for the defendant's arrest and order revocation or forfeiture of bail.

    The preliminary arraignment is also held to advise the defendant of Constitutionally guaranteed rights and to set a date for preliminary hearing, usually scheduled within three to ten days. At the end of the preliminary arraignment the defendant is released on bail or placed under confinement.

3. **Preliminary Hearing.** This hearing is held before the District Justice or a Municipal Court Judge in Philadelphia, and is usually the First Hearing at which the victim or witness will be called to appear. The purpose of the hearing is to determine whether there is probable cause that the defendant committed the offense or offenses charged. A police officer or prosecutor asks questions of witnesses and sometimes the defendant. Counsel for the defendant may conduct cross-examination. It is important to remember that this hearing is not to determine guilt, only whether it is more likely than not that the defendant committed the crime charged. If the Judge determines that the defendant probably committed the offense, the case is bound over for further proceedings in the Court of Common Pleas. If no probable cause has been established, the defendant is released and the case is over.

4. **Arraignment**. When a case is bound over to Common Pleas Court, the records and transcripts from the earlier proceedings are sent from the District Justice to the appropriate county court house. There, the Court Clerk amasses a file and the District Attorney draws up an *information*, which is a formal list of charges against the defendant. This process takes several weeks. Then, usually within ten days after the information is filed, an arraignment is held.

The purposes of arraignment are to insure the defendant's awareness of the formal charges against him, to determine whether he has a lawyer, to establish time periods for the filing of various motions and to set a date for a trial. An arraignment is very informal, often conducted without the defendant being present, since he or she may forego or "waive" formal notice of the charges in the information. The presence of a victim or witness is not necessary at the arraignment.

5. **Trial**. After thirty days have passed from arraignment, the case may be scheduled for trial. Once a specific date, time and courtroom are assigned, the defendant is notified and witness subpoenas are dispatched in the mail. A witness should receive a subpoena to appear in court about a month before trial. Unless the case is *continued*, or postponed to a later date, the case is called before the court at the designated time.

    Many cases are resolved prior to trial. Often the defendant decides to plead guilty. When this happens, or when the case is postponed, the witness should be contacted by the Witness Assistance Clerk from the District Attorney's Office and be informed that his or her presence for the date listed in the subpoena will be unnecessary.

    When a case does proceed to trial, the trial may take place before a judge and jury or just before a judge. In jury trials, the jury decides factual questions based on the evidence and on the law as provided by the judge. In other words, the jury decides what actually happened on the occasion in question and then renders a decision on the defendant's guilt or innocence. This is called the *verdict*. In non-jury or *bench* trials the judge decides both factual and legal questions.

    Trials consist of several phases. After a jury is picked, the prosecution, which in Pennsylvania is called the *Commonwealth*, makes an *opening statement*. The purpose of this statement is for the prosecutor to describe what the evidence will prove. The defense makes its opening statement either right after the Commonwealth's or at the beginning of the defense case. After opening statements the Commonwealth presents its *case in chief*. That is, the prosecutor calls witnesses and puts on evidence aimed at establishing the defendant's guilt. This is the phase at which a witness will testify if needed. After the prosecution concludes, or *rests*, the case for the defense is presented. After all the evidence has been heard, each side is permitted to make a *closing speech* to the jury. In these speeches, the attorneys argue to the jury how and why the evidence supports their view or theory of the case, asking respectively for verdicts of guilt and innocence. Afterwards, the judge *charges* the jury, explaining what law they must consider in reaching a verdict. The jury deliberates until it reaches a verdict. Once a decision of guilt or innocence is made, the verdict is announced 'and the court makes it final by pronouncing a *judgment* on the verdict. The trial is now concluded.

6. **Sentencing.** In cases where the defendant pleads guilty, sentencing is usually immediately imposed by the court. In other cases a future date for sentencing is set by the court. Sometimes the court orders the filing of a *pre-sentence investigation report.* The purpose of the report is to advise the court of the circumstances of the defendant which could affect the type of sentence to be imposed. The Commonwealth and the defense may ask for punishment of greater or lesser severity. The court considers these arguments, the contents of the pre-sentence investigation report, as well as any input made by the victim, and then pronounces sentence on the defendant. Sentencing may call for fines, imprisonment, or both. In addition the defendant is required to pay court costs and, whenever feasible, to make restitution to victims for lost or damaged property or other financial losses. The sentence is carried out by the offices of parole or probation.

SECTION 7.10 THE PROGRESS OF A CRIMINAL CASE IN FEDERAL COURT

An arrest may be initiated following a grand jury presentment or by a complaint and warrant.

The Fifth Amendment of the Constitution guarantees that "no person shall be held to answer for a capital, or otherwise infamous crime unless by presentment or indictment by a grand jury…" The grand jury indictment is utilized to determine that probable cause exists that a crime has been committed and that the target of the investigation probably did commit the crime. A grand jury consists of twenty-three people and a majority vote is required to indict. The proceedings are conducted in secret and a witness does not have the right to have counsel present.

Following indictment, a bench warrant is issued for the arrest of the suspects, and they are brought before a Federal Magistrate for an Initial Appearance.

Federal prosecutions can also be initiated by a complaint and warrant. This method is used where immediate arrest is necessary because of fear of flight of the suspect. The complaint is prepared by the United States Attorney with the assistance of a Federal law enforcement agent who narrates the facts of the case. A judge then examines the document and a Federal agent must be present to attest to its veracity. By issuing the warrant, the Court determines that probable cause exists for arrest.

Federal arrestees are often detained in local detention centers where cells are reserved and paid for by the Federal Government. An Initial Hearing is held promptly after the defendant's arrest. If a defendant is arrested on a weekend, he will be brought in for the Initial Hearing on the next business day following his arrest. At the Initial Hearing, bail is set, the defendant is advised of his rights, and legal counsel appointed if the defendant has none.

FEDERAL CRIMINAL PROCEDURE

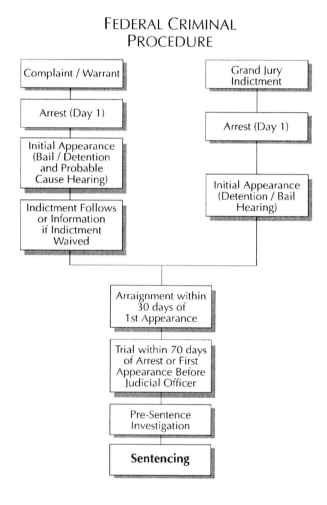

If the arrest was effected pursuant to a grand jury indictment, the case proceeds to arraignment where the charges are read, pleas are entered and a trial date is selected. If the arrest is made pursuant to the complaint and warrant procedure, a grand jury indictment will follow unless waived and replaced with an information (formal list of charges). The arraignment follows in either case within thirty days of the arrest and the trial occurs within 70 days of the initial appearance. This is required by the Speedy Trial Act. Fewer cases go to trial in the Federal system since 95% of Federal criminal cases are resolved through guilty pleas.

SECTION 7.11
THE GRAND JURY[2]

The grand jury determines whether there is probable cause to believe that a crime was committed and that a specific person or persons committed it. If the grand jury finds probable cause to exist, then it will return a written statement of the charges called an "indictment." After that, the accused will go to trial.

The grand jury normally hears only that evidence presented by an attorney for the government which tends to show the commission of a crime. The grand jury must determine from this evidence, and usually without hearing evidence for the defense, whether a person should be tried for a serious federal crime, referred to in the Bill of Rights as an "infamous crime." An infamous crime is one which may be punished by imprisonment for more than one year. As a general rule, no one can be prosecuted for a serious crime unless the grand jury decides that the evidence it has heard so requires. In this way, the grand jury operates both as a "sword," authorizing the government's prosecution of suspected criminals, and also as a "shield," protecting citizens from unwarranted or inappropriate prosecutions. A person may, however, waive grand jury proceedings and agree to be prosecuted by a written charge of crime called an **information**.

The major portion of the grand jury's work is concerned with evidence brought to its attention by an attorney for the government. The grand jury may consider additional matters otherwise brought to its attention, but should consult with the United States Attorney or the court before undertaking a formal investigation of such matters. This is necessary because the grand jury has no investigation staff, and legal assistance will be necessary in the event an indictment is voted.

It should be borne in mind that a federal grand jury can take action upon federal crimes that have been committed within the district in which it has been impaneled. Furthermore, a federal grand jury is not authorized to investigate situations involving the conduct of individuals, public officials, agencies or institutions that the grand jury believes is subject to mere criticism rather than a violation of federal criminal statutes. Its concern must be devoted solely to ascertaining whether there is probable cause to believe that a federal crime has been committed and to report accordingly to the court.

The following are examples of Criminal Complaints on the federal and state levels. ***United States v. Pickett*** involves an Indiana man who brandished, and fired a 38 caliber revolver outside of the White House just a few days after George W. Bush assumed office. The second complaint is from the State of Michigan and deals with rap star, Eminem. The charges stem from an incident outside of a nightclub that occurred when a man allegedly tried to kiss the wife of the rapper. The recording artist was charged with assault and carrying a concealed deadly weapon.

UNITED STATES DISTRICT COURT
For the District of Columbia

UNITED STATES OF AMERICA	:	CRIMINAL COMPLAINT
	:	
V.	:	
	:	
ROBERT W. PICKETT	:	
DOB: 3/20/53	:	CASE NUMBER
PDID	:	

I, Timothy J. Moser, Officer with the United States Park Police being duly sworn states the following is true and correct to the best of my knowledge and belief.

On February 7. 2001 at approximately 11:24 hours a white male, later identified as Robert W. Pickett, DOB 3/20/53, SOC 314-50-9438, Tyler Avenue Evansville, Indiana, approached the south fence line of the White House located in the 1600 block of E. Street N.W. Washington D.C. and brandished a loaded 38 caliber Braztech revolver with serial number RH72326.

United States Secret Service Uniform Division (USSSUD) became aware of the armed suspect and sent uniformed officers to the area. One USSUD officer witnessed a shot fired. Later investigation revealed two shots were discharged. The officers were easily identified in police issued uniforms. Once in the area, uniformed officers engaged PICKETT. The USSSUD uniformed officers ordered PICKETT to drop his weapon, and he refused to comply with their orders. PICKETT then pointed his weapon at uniformed USSSUD Emergency Response Team (ERT) Officers located in the bushes, which were approximately 15 yards from his location at the fence line.

It was at this point, while Pickett's gun was still pointed in the direction of the ERT officers that a member of the USSSUD ERT, located on the south lawn heard the suspect's gun click and fearing for the safety of his team members and others, fired his service weapon once, striking and wounding PICKETT.

Said acts by Robert Pickett were done in violation of Title 18 United States Code, Section 111(a)(b).

Timothy J. Moser, Officer

Timothy J. Moser, Officer
United States Park Police

February 9, 2001

STATE OF MICHIGAN 37A JUDICIAL DISTRICT 16TH JUDICIAL CIRCUIT	COMPLAINT FELONY	DISTRICT CIRCUIT	CASE NO. 251803
District Court OFU- MI		Circuit Court OFU-MI	

THE PEOPLE OF THE STATE OF MICHIGAN v.	Defendant's name MARSHALL BRUCE MATHERS W/M	Victim or complainant JOHN GUERRA	
		Complaining witness DET. THOMAS RANDALL	
Co-defendant(s)		Date: On or about 06-04-2000	
City/Twp./Village WARREN	County in Michigan Wacomb	Defendant CTN 50-00006717-01	Defendant SID	Defendant DOB 10/17/1972
Witnesses		Defendant DON M362585098800MI	

OFFICER IN CHARGE DET. THOMAS RANDALL

APA WILLIAM A HARDING (P28342)

STATE OF MICHIGAN, COUNTY OF   Wacomb

The complaining witness says that on the date and at the location described, the defendant, contrary to law,

COUNT 1   Defendant(s) 01 ASSAULT W/ DANGEROUS WEAPON
did make an assault upon John Guerra with a dangerous weapon, to-wit: pistol, but without intending to commit the crime of murder or to inflict great bodily harm less than the crime of murder; contrary to MCL 750.82; MSA 28.77. (750.82).

COUNT 2   Defendant(s) 01 WEAPONS - CARRYING CONCEALED
did carry a dangerous weapon, to wit: pistol, whether concealed or otherwise in a vehicle operated or occupied by said defendant, to wit: automobile; contrary to MCL 750.227; MSA 28.424. (750.227)
FELONY: 5 Years or $2,500.00

Warrant authorized on _____ by:
            Date

Prosecuting official _____

☐ Security for costs posted

The complaining witness asks that defendant be apprehended and dealt with according to law.

Det. Thomas Randall

Complaining witness signature

Subscribed and sworn to before me on_____

_____
Judge/Magistrate/Clerk

At the completion of a criminal trial, the fact finder my return with a variety of verdicts including **(1)** Innocent; **(2)** Guilty; **(3)** Not Guilty by Reason of Insanity; and **(4)** Guilty but Insane.

The verdicts of innocent and guilty are easy to understand. If the defendant is found innocent, the case is over and the accused may not be prosecuted again for the same crime. This result will not change even if new evidence is found. Double jeopardy mandates this result. If the defendant is found guilty, the case proceeds to the sentencing phase.

The verdicts of not guilty by reason of insanity and guilty but insane are much less common. A person will be found not guilty by reason of insanity if he or she does not know the difference between right and wrong because of a defective thought process caused by mental illness. If a jury concludes that a person is insane at the time of the crime, the defendant will be sent to a mental institution instead of prison. Once the individual regains his sanity, he will be released from the mental facility. On the other hand, a person who suffers from a significant mental disorder that is not severe enough to cause the person to be classified as criminally insane may be found guilty but insane. In that event, the defendant will be sent to a mental institution for treatment and will then serve time in jail. The following case is an example of a defendant who was found guilty but insane.

COMMONWEALTH OF PENNSYLVANIA V. JOHN DUPONT
730 A.2D 970 (PA. SUPER. 1999)

JOHN E. DUPONT APPEALS FROM JUDGMENT of sentence imposed after a jury found him guilty, but mentally ill, of third degree murder. We affirm the judgment of sentence.

Prior to his arrest in January 1996, appellant resided on an 800-acre estate known as "Foxcatcher Farm" located in Delaware County. For many years appellant operated a wrestling training facility on the premises, and provided housing on the estate to some of the wrestlers who trained at his facility and were members of "Team Foxcatcher," a wrestling team founded by appellant.

People who knew appellant noticed a change in his behavior and emotional state around the time of his mother's death in 1988. Appellant became extremely security conscious and hired a security firm in 1993 to provide protection on the estate. Despite the firm's efforts implementing extensive security measures, appellant exhibited paranoid fear on several occasions that he was being spied upon and that his life was in danger. During 1993, for example, appellant installed razor wire in the walls of his home to prevent persons from hiding within the walls; he also had excavators dig on his property to search for underground tunnels he believed to lead to his home. In spite of his unusual behavior, however, appellant continued to manage his facility and maintain the daily operations.

Over time appellant developed close relationships with some of the wrestlers at his facility, and came to dislike others. He began to exhibit animosity toward David Schultz, a successful wrestler and also one of the facility's wrestling coaches, sometime in 1995. On the afternoon of January 16, 1996, appellant went to the residence of Mr. Schultz accompanied by one of the estate security consultants, Patrick Goodale. Mr. Schultz was working on his car, but greeted appellant on his arrival. Appellant asked Mr. Schultz, "You got a problem with me?" and shot him three times with a .44 Magnum revolver. He also pointed the weapon at Mr. Goodale and toward Mr. Schultz' wife who was in the house. Appellant then fled in his vehicle to his mansion, reloaded and locked up his weapon, and refused to surrender to police. During the two-day standoff, which followed, appellant spoke with his attorney on numerous occasions. He was finally apprehended on January 28, 1996 when he left the mansion to attempt a repair of the heating system.

At trial, appellant did not dispute that he shot Mr. Schultz, but put forth a defense of insanity. Following the guilty but *mentally ill* verdicts, he was sentenced on May 13, 1997 to a term of imprisonment of thirteen to thirty years on the murder conviction. This appeal followed.

(In addition to other claimed errors) appellant challenges the constitutionality of the application of the Pennsylvania statutes relating to "Guilty but *mentally ill*" and "Not guilty by reason of *insanity*." Those provisions, in relevant part, are as follows.

§ 314. Guilty but mentally ill

General rule—A person who timely offers a defense of insanity may be found "guilty but mentally ill" at trial if the trier of facts finds, beyond a reasonable doubt, that the person is guilty of an offense, was *mentally ill* at the time of the commission of the offense and was not legally insane at the time of the commission of the offense.

(c) Definitions.

"Mentally ill." One who as a result of mental disease or defect lacks substantial capacity either to appreciate the wrongfulness of his conduct or to conform his conduct to the requirements of the law.

§ 315. Insanity

General rule—The mental soundness of an actor engaged in conduct charged to constitute an offense shall only be a defense to the charged offense when the actor proves by a preponderance of evidence that the actor was legally insane at the time of the commission of the offense.

Definition—For purposes of this section, the phrase "legally insane" means that, at the time of the commission of the offense, the actor was laboring under such a defect of reason, from disease of the mind, as not to know the nature and quality of the act or, if the actor did know the quality of the act, that he did not know that what he was doing was wrong.

…With respect to the mental illness issue, Appellant contends (among other things) that he has been subjected to cruel and unusual punishment based on the verdict, because he has been imprisoned as a result of his mental illness. Appellant reiterates that he could be considered "insane"… under statutes of other jurisdictions. Appellant was found guilty but *mentally ill* based on application of Pennsylvania law. The jury did not determine him to be legally insane. There is no prohibition in the Constitution against punishment simply because the law in other jurisdictions differs and might yield another penalty. This argument is without merit.

The sentencing phase of a trial does not usually take place immediately upon conviction. Rather, there is a short delay between the trail and the penalty phase of the case. This allows time for post-trial motions and a background check.

Most courts have discretion in the punishment that may be imposed, and conduct a pre-sentence investigation. This investigation includes a search for prior convictions and a medical or psychiatric exam. Punishment can range from incarceration to probation.

To curb crime resulting from the actions of repeat offenders, New Jersey enacted into law a bill that would jail three-time violent offenders for life. The legislation sets up a two-tiered system in which offenders committing first-degree crimes of murder, aggravated manslaughter, kidnapping, sexual assault, armed robbery, and carjacking, qualify for a mandatory life term. Three-time violent offenders sentenced to life under the bill could not seek parole until they had served 35 years of their sentence and reached the age of 70. Then they would have to convince the parole board that they are no longer a threat to society before being released. Those who commit three crimes classified as less violent offenses, would serve extended prison sentences under terms of the bill.

In what could be considered the most unusual sentence, a Cincinnati judge who convicted a man of domestic violence ordered him to marry the girlfriend he punched in the mouth within nine months or risk jail under a harsh sentence. Believing that marriage would generate mutual respect for the couple, the judge felt that "traditional American values" would curb the behavior after the abuser testified he wanted to marry the victim. The judge later dropped the order saying "it was an ill-conceived idea on my part that I now wish I had never made."

The Eighth Amendment prohibits cruel and unusual punishment. Controversy over punishment has arisen in a variety of contexts including the ordering of castration for sex offenders, public whippings, and overcrowding in jails. Much debate has arisen in recent times over Megan's law. This law requires the police to notify any community in which a convicted sex offender goes to live.

The death penalty has been the subject of many constitutional challenges over the years. While it was once considered cruel and unusual punishment, the death penalty is currently recognized as an acceptable remedy. Nevertheless, the courts have become very critical of death by electrocution. In those states that retain the death penalty, more and more jurisdictions are moving to death by lethal injection because of humanitarian considerations.

JIMMY GLASS V. STATE OF LOUISIANA
471 U.S. 1080 (1984)

BRENNAN, J., dissenting

JIMMY GLASS HAS BEEN CONDEMNED to death by electrocution—"that is, causing to pass through the body of the person convicted, a current of electricity of sufficient intensity to cause death, and the application and continuance of such current through the body of the person convicted until such person is dead." Glass contends that electrocution causes the infliction of unnecessary pain and suffering and does not comport with evolving standards of decency, and therefore, violates the Eight and Fourteenth Amendments. The Supreme Court of Louisiana rejected his claim under established principles of law and observed that the claim is wholly lacking in medical and scientific merit.

Eighth Amendment claims must be evaluated, "in the light of contemporary human knowledge," rather than in reliance on century-old factual premises that may no longer be accurate. "Thus courts can consider, through a "discriminating evaluation" of all available evidence, whether a particular means of carrying out the death penalty is "barbaric" and unnecessary in light of currently available alternatives.

What are the objective factors by which courts should evaluate the constitutionality of a challenged method of punishment? First and foremost, the Eighth Amendment prohibits "the unnecessary and wanton infliction of pain." Thus in explaining the obvious unconstitutionality of such ancient practices as disemboweling while alive, drawing and quartering, public dissection burning alive at the stake, crucifixion, and breaking at the wheel, the Court has emphasized that the Eighth Amendment forbids "inhuman and barbarous" methods of execution that go beyond "the mere extinguishment

of life" and cause "torture or a lingering deathly." It is beyond debate that the Amendment proscribes all forms of "unnecessary cruelty" that cause gratuitous "terror, pain, or disgrace."

This is because the Eighth Amendment requires that, as much as humanly possible, a chosen method of execution minimize the risk of unnecessary pain, violence, and mutilation. If a method of execution does not satisfy these criteria, if it causes "torture or a lingering death" in a significant number of cases, then unnecessary cruelty inheres in that method of execution and the method violates the Cruel and Unusual Punishment Clause.

There is considerable empirical evidence and eyewitness testimony, however, which if correct, would appeal to demonstrate that electrocution violates every one of the principles set forth above. This evidence suggests that death by electrical current is extremely violent and inflicts pain and indignities far beyond the "mere extinguishment of life." Witnesses routinely report that, when the switch is thrown, the condemned prisoner "cringes," "leaps," and "fights the straps with amazing strength." The hands turn red, then white, cords of the neck stand out like steel bands." The prisoner's limbs, fingers, toes, and face are severely contorted. The force of the electrical current is so powerful that the prisoner's eyeballs sometimes pop out and rest on his cheeks. The prisoner often defecates, urinates, and vomits blood and drool. The body turns bright red as its temperature rises, the prisoner's flesh sears and his skin stretches to the point of breaking. Sometimes the prisoner catches on fire, particularly if he perspires excessively. Witnesses hear a loud and sustained sound like bacon frying ...In the meantime, the prisoner almost literally boils: the temperature in the brain itself approaches the boiling point of water, and when the post-electrocution autopsy is performed, the liver is so hot that doctors have said it cannot be touched by the human hand. The body is frequently badly burned and disfigured.

Whether because of shoddy technology and poorly trained personnel, or because of the inherent differences in the "physiological resistance" of condemned prisoners to electrical current, it is an inescapable fact that the 95-year history of electrocution in this country has been characterized by repeated failures swiftly to execute and the resulting need to send recurrent charges into condemned prisoners to ensure their deaths. The very first electrocution required multiple attempts before death resulted, and our cultural lore is filled with examples of attempted electrocutions that had to be restaged when it was discovered that the condemned "tenaciously clung to life."

Here is one eyewitness account of Alabama's electrocution of John Louis Evans:

> "At 8:30 p.m. the first jolt of 1900 volts of electricity passed through Mr. Evans' body. It lasted thirty seconds. Sparks and flames erupted from the electrode tied to Mr. Evans' left leg. His body slammed against the straps holding him in the electric chair and his fist clenched permanently. The electrode apparently burst from the strap holding it in place. A large puff of greyish smoke and sparks poured out from under the hood that covered his face. An overpowering stench of burnt flesh and clothing began pervading the witness room. Two doctors examined Evans and declared he was not dead. The electrode on the left leg was refastened. At 8:30 p.m. Mr. Evans was administered a second jolt of electricity. The stench of burning flesh

was nauseating. More smoke emanated from his leg and head. Again, the doctors examined Mr. Evans. The doctors reported that his heart was still beating, and that he was still alive.

> "At that time, I asked the prison commissioner, who was communicating on an open telephone line to Governor George Wallace to grant clemency on the grounds that Mr. Evans was being subjected to cruel and unusual punishment. The request was denied.

> At 8:40 p.m., a third charge of electricity, thirty seconds in duration, was passed through Mr. Evans' body. At 8:44, the doctors pronounced him dead. The execution of John Evans took fourteen minutes."

Thus, there is considerable evidence suggesting that death by electrocution causes far more than the "mere extinguishment of life." This evidence, if correct, would raise a substantial question whether electrocution violates the Eighth Amendment in several respects. First, electrocution appears to inflict "unnecessary and wanton . . . pain" and cruelty, and to cause "torture or a lingering death" in at least a significant number of cases. Second, the physical violence and mutilation that accompany this method of execution would seem to violate the basic "dignity of man." Finally, even if electrocution does not invariably produce pain and indignities, the apparent century-long pattern of "abortive attempts" and lingering deaths suggests that this method of execution carries an unconstitutionally high risk of causing such atrocities. These features of electrocution seem so inherent as to render it, per se cruel and unusual and therefore, forbidden by the Eighth Amendment.

Moreover, commentators and medical experts have urged that other currently available means of execution—particularly forms of lethal gas and barbiturates—accomplish the purpose of extinguishing life in a swifter, less violent, and more humane manner. Several state legislatures have abandoned electrocution in favor of lethal injection for these very reasons.

For me, arguments about the "humanity" and "dignity" of any method of officially sponsored executions are a constitutional contradiction in terms. Moreover, there is significant evidence that executions by lethal gas—at least as administered in the gas chambers—and barbiturates—at least as administered through lethal injections—carry their own risks of pain, indignity, and prolonged suffering. But having concluded that the death penalty in the abstract is consistent with the "evolving standards of decency that mark the progress of a maturing society," courts cannot now avoid the Eighth Amendment's proscription of "the unnecessary and wanton infliction of pain" in carrying out that penalty simply by relying on 19th-century precedents that appear to have rested on inaccurate factual assumptions and that no longer embody the meaning of the Amendment. For the reasons set forth above, there is an evermore urgent question whether electrocution is in fact a "humane method for extinguishing human life or is, instead, nothing less than the contemporary technological equivalent of burning people at the stake.

Much publicity was generated concerning the case of a 35 year old, female school teacher who had sexual intercourse with a 13 year old student whom she taught. Her sexual encounters with the child lead, to not one, but two pregnancies. The teacher was convicted of a sex offense involving a child and was sent to prison when she failed to honor a court order directing her to stay away from the student. In addition to her imprisonment, the woman was ordered to have no in-person contact with her biological children while they were minors in the absence of an adult supervisor. This sentence was appealed by the former teacher as a violation of her constitutional rights. In *State of Washington v. Mary Letourneau,* the appellate court ruled that the state failed to demonstrate that prohibiting Letourneau from unsupervised, in-person contact with her children was reasonably necessary in order to protect them from of sexual molestation by their mother.

STATE OF WASHINGTON V. MARY LETOURNEAU
997 P.2D 436; 2000 (WASH. APP. 2000)

MARY LETOURNEAU PLEADED GUILTY to two counts of second degree rape of a child. The trial court sentenced her to 89 months of confinement but suspended the sentence on various conditions. The court ordered that Letourneau have no con-tact with the child. This sentence was revoked some 3 months later, after Letourneau was discovered in the company of the victim. Letourneau was then sent to prison and the trial court directed that in-person contact with minor children, including Letourneau's own biological minor children, be supervised by a person who is approved by the Department of Corrections or by the court.

In early 1997, the King County Department of Public Safety received information that Letourneau — a 35 year-old sixth grade teacher and mother of four children — was having sexual intercourse with V.F., a 13-year-old student at the school where she taught. After investigation, the State charged Letourneau with second degree rape of a child. She pleaded guilty and the court ordering Letourneau to confinement in the county jail for 180 days and suspending the remainder of the confinement, conditioned upon her compliance with the sentence.

Less than 2 weeks after Letourneau's release from jail, Police Officer Harris discovered Letourneau alone in her car with V.F. The court found that Letourneau had violated the terms of her sentence by having unsupervised contact with the victim, and ordered her to serve 89 months in the Department of Corrections.

The court then entered an order which stated: "In-person contact with minor children including defendant's natural children, shall be supervised by an adult approved by the Department of Corrections or this Court.

Meanwhile, in May of 1997, Letourneau had given birth to her fifth child. In October of 1998, Letourneau gave birth to her sixth child. Each of these children was fathered by the victim, V.F.

Letourneau challenges the provision in her sentence that prohibits her from unsupervised in-person contact with her biological minor children after she is released from prison, contending that this prohibition is unconstitutional.

The fundamental right at issue is Letourneau's right to raise her children without State interference. The State contends that the compelling interest that justifies interference with a fundamental liberty is the State's interest in preventing harm to Letourneau's children. Courts have recognized prevention of harm to children to be a compelling state interest. Thus, we must determine whether the record supports the proposition that prohibiting Letourneau from unsupervised in-person contact with her minor children after she is released from prison is reasonably necessary to prevent harm to her children — specifically, whether the restriction is reasonably necessary to prevent Letourneau from sexually molesting her own children.

Letourneau has two sons and four daughters. The record contains no evidence of past molestation of any of these children. One evaluator opined that Letourneau posed a danger of harm to her own children. "If she were in a parenting role, it is inevitable she would 'mold' her children's minds based on her distortions as she did with her victim, causing them to see wrong as right - harmful as harmless - ignoble as noble - inappropriate as appropriate. Sexual offenders who sexually assault children should not be in a position of power over children or other vulnerable persons." Two other evaluators recommended that the best interests of Letourneau's children be determined after the appointment of suitable guardians investigate and report to the court regarding the children's needs.

We conclude that the State failed to demonstrate that prohibiting Letourneau from unsupervised in-person contact with her children is reasonably necessary to protect those children from the harm of sexual molestation by their mother. Letourneau is not a pedophile. Children of sex offenders are entitled to the same protection from being molested by the offender as all other children in society. The Legislature has authorized courts to require offenders who are convicted of a felony sex offense to comply with terms and conditions of community placement imposed by the Department of Corrections relating to contact between the sex offender and a minor victim or a child of similar age or circumstance as a previous victim. But this does not mean that the court or the Department has the authority to place restrictions upon an offender's contact with his or her own biological children who are not of similar age as a previous victim, where the restriction is not necessary to protect the offender's biological children from the harm of sexual molestation. The general observation that many offenders who molest children unrelated to them later molest their own biological children, without more, is an insufficient basis for State interference with fundamental parenting rights. There must be an affirmative showing that the offender is a pedophile or that the offender otherwise poses the danger of sexual molestation of his or her own biological children to justify such State intervention. Nothing in this record rises to that level. We strike the provision from Letourneau's sentence that restricts unsupervised, in-person contact with her biological minor children following her release from total confinement.

SECTION 7.13
PROBLEM CASES

1. Three packages containing more that $500,000 fell out of the back of an armored truck. Morant, an individual walking down the street, retrieved and carried away the bags. The money was not returned immediately nor were the police notified that the money had been located. A couple of days later, the armored truck company posted a $75,0000 reward and Morant came forward with the money in order to claim the reward. Has this individual committed the crime of theft by retaining the money until a reward was posted?

2. Anthony Saduk filled a muzzleloader rifle with gun powder, cigarette butts, and paper-towel wadding. As a practical joke, he shot the gun in the direction of his roommate but three of the cigarette butts penetrated his friend's chest causing death. Since Saduk had no intention of hurting his friend, and was merely carrying out a practical joke, did he have the necessary intent to be found guilty of any type of criminal homicide?

3. The police suspected that Gindlesperger was growing marijuana in his basement. An officer aimed a thermal detection device at the home from the street in order to measure the heat emissions coming from the defendant's house. The temperature of the home was felt to be consistent with marijuana production activities. Did the warrantless search of the house, with a thermal detection device, constitute an unlawful search and seizure? *Commonwealth of Pennsylvania v. Gregory Gindlesperger,* **706 A.2d 1316 (Pa. Super. 1997).**

4. The police set up a road block as part of a program to interdict drunk drivers. Schavello, who was driving towards the road block, made a legal U-turn in order to avoid police contact. He was then stopped by the police a short distance away and alcohol was de-

tected on his breath. Schavello failed a field sobriety test and was arrested for driving under the influence of alcohol. Is the avoiding of a road block sufficient probable cause to stop a motor vehicle when it makes a U-turn without any further suspicion by the police of illegal activity? *Commonwealth of Pennsylvania v. Schavello,* **734 A.2d 386 (Pa. 1999).**

5.   The manager of an apartment building was making yearly repairs and maintenance inspections. The date of these inspections were posted throughout the building. During his examination of one of the units, the manager observed drugs on the kitchen table and immediately contacted the police. The manager then lead the officers into the apartment with a pass key. The police observed five plastic bags containing crack cocaine on the kitchen table. Based upon their observations, one officer left the apartment in order to obtain a Search Warrant. The other officer remained behind and arrested Davis when he entered the apartment. The lease agreement provided that, "Landlords and anyone allowed by the landlord, may enter the leased unit after first notifying tenant." Was the entry by the police into the apartment without a search warrant legal? *Commonwealth of Pennsylvania v. Curtis Davis,* **743 A.2d 946 (Pa. Super. 1999).**

6.   Booth disregarded a stop sign while he was driving and collided with the car of Nancy Boehm. She was 32 weeks pregnant at the time and lost the fetus as a result of the trauma. Booth's alcohol level was .12 and he was charged with involuntary manslaughter or homicide by vehicle. The Motor Vehicle Code provides that any person, who unintentionally causes the death of another individual as the result of driving under the influence of alcohol or controlled substances has committed the crime of voluntarily manslaughter. Is an unborn fetus, a person for the purposes of involuntarily manslaughter? *Commonwealth of Pennsylvania v. Jeffrey Booth,* **2001 WL 166998 (Pa. 2001).**

The following Internet references provide a good starting places to find information on criminal law and crime-related topics:

SECTION 7.14
INTERNET REFERENCES

To learn more information about the topics in this chapter see the following internet references:

A. Criminal Law

- **www.crimelibrary.com**
  The Crime Library has assembled various stories about famous criminal cases, classic crime stories, mass and serial murders, as well as terrorists, spies, and assassins at this location.

- **www.talkjustice.com**
  A person is able to post messages at this location about the criminal justice system and can access Cybrary, an online library which provides 12,000 links to different web sites relating to criminal justice.

- **http://www.law.indiana.edu/law/crimlaw.html**
  This site from Indiana University School of Law-Bloomington allows a user to downloads short speeches about different aspects of criminal law, such as double jeopardy and being called as a witness.

- **http://jec.unm.edu/training/tofc_IT.htm**
  The Judicial Education Center, offers interactive training on different criminal topics, such as hearsay, search warrants, and sentencing. Through a series of multiple-choice questions, the reader will learn why the answer chosen is correct or incorrect.

- **www.thebestdefense.com**
  Information about specific crimes and the process of a criminal case is offered at this criminal law firm's web site.

- **http://raperecovery.terrashare.com**
  The Rape Recovery Help Line and Information Page is located at this site.

- **www.softport-co.com/safety/home.html**
  The Los Angeles County Sheriff presents an article on how to prevent a home burglary at this location.

- **www.Nashville.Net/~police/risk**
  The Nashville Police Department maintains a site which allows the reader to assesses his or her risk of being the victim of a crime.

- **http://www.usdoj.gov.**
  United States Department of Justice. For information on criminal justice programs and initiatives, as well as other information on the United States criminal justice system, go to the U.S. Department of Justice's home page.

- **http://www.ncjrs.org**
  The Justice Information Center provides information on criminal and juvenile justice throughout the world at this address.

- **http://www.fbi.gov**
  The Federal Bureau of Investigation's site provides information and statistics on crime, including concerning FBI investigations, international crime, wiretapping, electronic surveillance, and economic espionage.

- **http://www/aclu.org/issues.criminal/hmcj.html**
  The American Civil Liberties Union offers information on the protection of a person's constitutional rights within the criminal justice system at this address.

B. *The Polygraph*

- **www.polygraph.org**
  This site by the American Polygraph Association offers a variety of information on the lie detector.

- **www.truthorlie.com**
  This site provides answers to frequently asked questions about the polygraph test.

- **http://truth.idbsu.edu/polygraph/polylaw.html**
  Court cases and opinions relating to the polygraph are listed at this address.

C. *Miranda Warnings*

- **http://acquittal.com/your_miranda_rights.htm**
  A general explanation of the Miranda Warnings is contained at this location.

- **www.courttv.com/legalhelp/lawguide/criminal/91.html**
  This site provides general information about the Miranda Warnings and its history.

D. *Search and Seizure*

- **http://supreme.findlaw.com/constitution/amendment04/**
  The Constitutional Law Center provides a variety of information relating to the law of search and seizure at this site, including the history, cases, and statutes concerning this Amendment.

- **www.dcd.uscourts.gov:80/frcrp-index.html**
  This site contains the Federal Rules of Criminal Procedure.

E. *Grand Jury*

- **http://archive.abcnews.go.com/sections/us/DailyNews clinton_jury.html**
  ABC News has created this link to explain the inner workings of the grand jury System.

- **www.udayton.edu/~grandjur**
  This site explains how the Federal and State Grand Jury systems work.

F. *Sentencing*

- **http://pcs.la.psu.edu/welcome.htm**
  The Pennsylvania Commission on Sentencing maintains this site devoted to sentencing.

- **www.sentencing.org**
  This is the site for the Coalition for Federal Sentencing Reform, and provides articles, history, and links to relevant sites.

Footnotes

1. This summary has been partially reproduced from the "Victim's Rights Handbook" written by the District Attorneys' Office of both Bucks and Montgomery Counties and has been reproduced with their permission.

2. This has been reprinted in part from a manual entitled "Handbook for Federal Grand Jurors," published by the Administrative Office of the United States Supreme Court. Washington, D.C. 20544.

CHAPTER 8

CONTRACTS

A **contract** is the voluntary exchange of promises between two or more people that creates a legal obligation, which is enforceable in court. While most agreements are informal in nature, parties do enter into formal written contracts. In either case, the elements of a valid contract are the same. While the terms may vary from bargain to bargain, five essential elements must be present. They are:

1. offer
2. acceptance
3. consideration
4. capacity
5. legality

When a party fails to honor the terms of the bargain, a breach of contract has occurred, and the breaching party may be found liable for damages. The penalty may range from nothing, to substantial money damages.

A contract may dictate the consequences in the event of a breach of the agreement. This is referred to as **liquidated damages**. The contract may also specify how the dispute is to be resolved. For example, a contract may provide for binding arbitration or leave the parties to the traditional remedies in court, but specify where the suit must be filed.

Contracts may be characterized in several different ways. The agreement may be classified as a bilateral or unilateral contract, depending on the number of promises involved. Contracts may be expressed or implied, depending on the expression of the promises. Contracts may also be classified as valid, void, voidable, or unenforceable, depending on their validity and enforceability.

UNILATERAL AND BILATERAL CONTRACTS

Although contracts involve at least two parties, not all contracts involve two promises. When one makes a promise in exchange for an act, the basis for a **unilateral contract** is formed. For example, the promise of a reward for the return of a lost ring forms the basis for a unilateral contract. Many people may search for the object, but only the person who returns the ring will receive the money.

A **bilateral contract** is created when the parties exchange mutual promises. For example, if Joe Hodge promises to sell his pet gorilla to the Zoo for $1,000, and the Zoo promises to buy "Harry" for $1,000, a bilateral contract is formed at that moment in time. Both the buyer and seller are bound by their promises and are under a legal obligation to perform. If Joe subsequently changes his mind because he can't part with "Harry," the Zoo may sue for damages for the loss of the bargain.

Can a person sue a date who stands that individual up for a date? Is this the type of agreement that gives rise to a contract, or is it merely a social agreement that has moral significance but no legal significance? A high school student from Lower Burrell, Pennsylvania did sue her date when he was a no-show for her senior prom. The school district requires all out-of-town prom dates to agree in writing to stay at the dance and to see the student home afterwards. The judge ruled that there was a breach of contract and awarded $548 for the dress and court costs.

When there is doubt as to the type of promise made, courts generally construe the agreement as bilateral. An offer by a homeowner to pay a real estate agent a commission, if and when the Realtor finds a buyer for the property, is a unilateral contract. If the Realtor finds a buyer willing to purchase the land, but the seller changes his mind, is the agent entitled to the commission?

JUDD REALTY, INC. V. FRANK TEDESCO
400 A.2D 952 (R.I. 1979)

WEISBERGER, Justice.

THIS IS AN APPEAL FROM A JUDGMENT dismissing with prejudice the plaintiff's complaint in an action to recover a commission under a real estate brokerage agreement.

On November 19, 1973, defendant, Frank Tedesco, signed a document entitled "EXCLUSIVE AGENTS CONTRACT," which agreement had been provided by the president of Plaintiff Corporation, Judd Realty, Inc. This agreement reads as follows:

"EXCLUSIVE AGENTS CONTRACT
Date November 18, 1973 between Judd

Realty Inc. and Frank Tedesco. You may list my property described on the opposite side hereof and sell same for the following price $25,000.

In consideration of the agreement to afford me the facilities of your office, I hereby constitute you as agent with EXCLUSIVE RIGHTS TO SELL for 6 months from this date.

Should a **purchaser** be found during the life of this agreement by me; by you or by any other person (or, if within sixty days thereafter it shall be sold to a customer to whose attention it has been brought, previous to expiration of this agreement) I will pay you a commission of 8% of the price received.

[signed] Frank Tedesco, Owner(s)"

Pursuant to this agreement plaintiff was permitted to list for the price of $25,000 the subject lot.

At trial, plaintiff's president, who also acted as a broker for the Plaintiff Corporation, testified that she attempted to find buyers during the 6-month period following November 18, 1973. She testified that approximately a week before the agreement expired, she presented to defendant a purchase and sale agreement signed by a prospective purchaser. The broker testified that the purchase and sale agreement was accompanied by a check for $1,000, dated May 10, 1974. She also testified that defendant stated that he did not have time to read the instrument when it was presented, because his mother was ill in the hospital. The broker testified that defendant did not get back to her as promised, and that finally she reached him at home within days thereafter.

The defendant testified that he received a purchase and sale agreement containing a $25,000 sale price 2 days before the brokerage agreement expired. Further, he stated that he was busy at the time, that the broker did not contact him as promised until the day after the agreement expired, and that when she finally reached him, he told her he did not want to sell "under those conditions." The defendant sold the property in July 1974 to another party for $23,000 and plaintiff instituted suit to recover the commission on the uncompleted sale.

The defendant moved to dismiss the complaint on the ground that plaintiff had not sustained its burden of proof. The trial justice granted the motion and construed the word "purchaser" to mean "someone who actually purchases the property." The trial justice reasoned that the commission was earned only if someone actually purchased the property within the contract time.

We conclude that the trial justice erred as a matter of law in construing the word "purchaser" in the brokerage agreement to mean "someone who actually purchases the property." The defendant's arguments are based on the premise that the term "purchaser" was ambiguous and that a question of fact regarding its meaning was presented. Quite simply, we do not believe that the word "purchaser" was ambiguous.

It is well settled that a broker has sufficiently performed and is entitled to compensation under a brokerage contract when the broker has produced a prospective purchaser who is ready, willing, and able to purchase at the price and terms of the seller. This general rule applies where no contract delineates what constitutes performance thereunder. In the present case the brokerage agreement contains no language indicating any intention of the parties to depart from the aforementioned general rule. Accordingly, we hold that the trial justice erred as a matter of law in construing the term "purchaser."

We also believe that the trial justice erred as a matter of law in determining that the brokerage contract was "illusory" because plaintiff undertook to do nothing under the contract. Brokerage agreements may be either bilateral or unilateral in nature. **Williston** distinguishes unilateral and bilateral contracts as follows:

> "An offer for a unilateral contract generally requires an act on the part of the offeree to make a binding contract. This act is consideration for the promise contained in the offer and doing it with intent to accept without more will create a contract. On the other hand, an offer for a bilateral contract requires a promise from the offeree in order that there may be a binding contract."

Corbin also contrasts unilateral contracts with bilateral contracts in respect to brokerage agreements:

> "The most commonly recurring case is one in which the owner employs a broker to find a purchaser able and willing to buy, on terms stated in advance by the owner, and in which the owner promises to pay a specified commission for the service. This is an offer by the owner, the broker's power of acceptance to be exercised by the actual rendition of the requested service. Here the only contemplated contract between the owner and the broker is a unilateral contract—a promise to pay a commission for services rendered.
>
> Cases are very numerous in which the owner, after the broker has fully performed the requested service, fails to make conveyance to the purchaser and refuses to pay the commission. Such a refusal is not the revocation of an offer; it is the breach of the fully consummated unilateral contract to pay for services rendered. If the requested service is merely the production of a purchaser able and willing to buy on definitely stated terms, the broker has a right to his commission even though the owner at once refuses to accept the purchaser's offer."

An offer to pay a commission to a broker upon production of a purchaser is an offer to enter into a unilateral contract and the offer is for an act to be performed. The owner promises to pay a commission for the services rendered of producing a purchaser. We conclude that plaintiff demonstrated a right to relief under the theory of performance under a unilateral contract.

We recognize the principle generally expressed, that the broker has the burden of proving by a fair preponderance of the evidence that he produced a purchaser ready, willing and able to buy on the seller's terms. In this case, however, the trial justice improperly interpreted the brokerage agreement and never determined whether plaintiff met the burden of proof under the aforementioned standard.

The case is remanded to the Superior court for proceedings consistent with this opinion.

EXPRESS AND IMPLIED CONTRACTS

An **express contract** is formed when the parties specifically manifest their agreement in direct terms. The words may be either written or spoken. A real estate lease or bank loan are examples of express contracts in writing. These types of agreements are normally comprehensive and of considerable length. Nevertheless, express contracts may be made orally and be extremely brief. For example, if a person offers to sell this textbook to another student for $20.00, and the buyer answers "I accept," an express contract has been formed.

The promises made by each party do not have to be expressly stated to form a contract. They may be inferred from the surrounding circumstances. These contracts are **implied-in-fact** because it is reasonable to infer that the parties intended to create a contract by their conduct. For example, it is reasonable to infer that a person who picks up and eats a banana in a grocery store intends to purchase the fruit for the price stated. Would the terms of an employment manual, however, create a contract implied-in-fact?

Another type of implied contract is one **implied-in-law** or quasi contract. The court to prevent unjust enrichment imposes an implied-in-law contract. For instance, if Dr. Feelgood renders emergency aid to an unconscious victim of a motor vehicle accident brought to the hospital by the police, he should be compensated for his services. The court will reject the argument of the patient that he didn't agree to pay for the services.

VALID, VOID, VOIDABLE, AND UNENFORCEABLE CONTRACTS

Contracts may be classified in terms of their validity and enforceability. A contract is **valid** when it satisfies all of the requirements of a binding and enforceable agreement. Either party to the agreement can enforce a valid contract. An agreement is **voidable** if one of the parties has the legal right to withdraw from the contract without any liability. For example, a contract with a child is voidable since the minor lacks the capacity to enter into the agreement, and the child has the sole option to cancel the agreement.

A **void** contract lacks one or more of the essential elements of a valid contract and can be attacked by either party to the agreement. Examples of void contracts would include an agreement to perform an illegal act or a contract, which lacks consideration.

A contract is **unenforceable** when it satisfies the requirements of a valid contract but will not be enforced by the courts. For instance, a contract for the sale of land must be in writing to be enforceable. The courts, therefore, will not enforce an oral promise to transfer realty.

Since we enter into many contracts on a daily basis, most of these agreements are informal, oral in nature and constitute enforceable contracts. In ascertaining the intent of the parties to an oral contract, one must consider not only the language used in forming the oral agreement, but also the circumstances surrounding the making of the arrangements, the motives of the parties, and the purposes which the parties sought to accomplish. The major problem with this type of agreement is proving the existence of the arrangement. When a dispute arises over an oral contract, the courts are required to assess the credibility of the parties in trying to ascertain the thoughts of the litigants since they are not spelled out in writing. *Eadie v. Worldwide Wrestling Federation* required the court to ascertain the financial terms of an alleged oral agreement between a promoter and two wrestlers known as "Ax" and "Smash" of the tag team "Demolition."

WILLIAM EADIE V. WORLD WRESTLING FEDERATION
1997 U.S. DIST. LEXIS 7670 (CT. D. 1997)

THIS CASE PROVIDES AN INTERESTING GLIMPSE into the world of professional wrestling. This lawsuit arise out of defendants' alleged misappropriation and commercial exploitation of the plaintiff's ideas for two fictional wrestling characters, known as "Ax" and "Smash" of a wrestling tag team called "Demolition."

WWF wrestling features two or more professional wrestlers, often appearing as fictional characters in outlandish costumes, who demonstrate their wrestling skills and abilities in the context of a simulated wrestling match. All of the personnel appearing in WWF wrestling matches are performing in designated roles, including the wrestlers themselves, the managers who attend them, and the officials, such as referees and timekeepers. These wrestling matches are roughly scripted or formatted so that the winner of each match is predetermined. Professional wrestling is a form of staged entertainment, not a contest to win like a sport.

William Eadie entered into his first booking agreement with Titan Sports on January 6, 1984. The agreement provided for Eadie to appear and wrestle professionally as "The Masked Superstar" for the year 1984. Eadie claims that he terminated this agreement at the end of 1984. Indeed, the contract stated that it would terminate on December 31, 1984, unless extended for an additional period of time at the sole discretion of Promoter. In January 1985, Eadie entered into a written agreement with New Japan Pro-Wrestling of Tokyo to wrestle as "The Masked Superstar" for that Japanese promoter.

In 1986, Eadie returned to wrestle for Titan as "The Super Machine" along with Andre the Giant as members of the tag team known as

"The Machines." Neither party has produced a booking agreement for Eadie's appearing as "The Super Machine" and, based on events that later transpired wherein Titan tried to resurrect the 1984 Masked Superstar agreement, one could reasonably infer that there never was a booking agreement for "The Super Machine."

Randy Colley, another wrestler, states that in 1986 he approached Vincent K. McMahon about a new character, a "Demolition type of character." The extent of Eadie's involvement with the initial development of the "Demolition" characters is not set forth in detail. Regardless, it is undisputed that Titan was able to develop dolls, videos, and other concession items based on these characters for which it collected significant sums of money.

Eadie contends that McMahon promised him that they were going to be the main event and that an oral contract was formed between the parties regarding the compensation for the development and portrayal of these new professional wrestling characters.

Defendants counter that there never was an oral contract; and that the original booking agreement controlled the relationships of the parties, vis-à-vis these new characters.

Eadie continued to wrestle as "Ax" of "Demolition" from January, 1987, until part of 1990, he alleges that he did so without a contract. He states that he was repeatedly promised compensation by McMahon in addition to the monies he actually received for his personal appearances and as royalties for the merchandising materials, but that these promises never materialized. Defendants state that Eadie received domestic earnings, including royalties, of $776,508 and Canadian earnings of $99,811 for the period 1987 to 1991.

In May, 1990, Eadie became ill and McMahon replaced Eadie with another wrestler. Eadie claims that on May 26, 1990, he had a telephone conversation with McMahon who promised him that if he should become disabled from wrestling, Titan would employ Eadie as an agent for life at a starting salary of $125,000, which was part of the bargain for his trading his interest in the "Demolition" characters that he had helped to develop.

A representative of Titan asked Eadie to sign an "amendment" to his 1984 booking agreement. Eadie refused to sign the document. In his opinion, the 1984 contract had been terminated. On June 26, 1990, a representative of Titan threatened Eadie that if he did not sign the agreement, he would be terminated. Because of these threats, Eadie states that he signed the amendment, which provided:

> This letter will serve as an amendment to your contract. It acknowledges that effective September 1, 1987, you began wrestling for "The World Wrestling Federation" under the ring name of "Ax"/ "Demolition," which name was created and developed by Titan, and that all rights granted to Titan under your contract dated January 6, 1984 as extended, including all terms and conditions therein, are and will remain in force and effect.

Eadie asserts that defendants McMahon and Titan breached an oral contract with him relating to the compensation he was to be paid for allowing defendants to commercially exploit the "Demolition" characters that he had developed.

Titan contends that the 1984 booking agreement governed the contractual relationship between it and Eadie. Eadie counters that the 1984 booking agreement pertained solely to his portrayal

of the character "The Masked Superstar" and was not intended to create a contractual relationship beyond December 31, 1984. As evidence that his 1984 agreement was terminated, he asserts that he wrestled as "The Masked Superstar" for various other promoters and that Titan did nothing to try to stop him. When he returned to Titan, he did so as "The Super Machine," under compensation terms different than in 1984. He states that as "Ax" he worked for Titan pursuant to an oral contract between the parties. Therefore, he claims his oral agreement with defendants, not the 1984 booking agreement, controlled the relationship between the parties.

In ascertaining the intent of the parties to a contract, the courts have considered not only the language used in the contract but also the circumstances surrounding the making of the contract, the motives of the parties, and the purposes which the parties sought to accomplish. The circumstances surrounding the making of the original booking agreement do not support the conclusion urged by defendants that the parties intended the original booking agreement to remain in effect or to cover other wrestling characters.

Further, the 1984 agreement provided that Eadie waived all rights to any income, such as royalties from any promotional products. But Titan paid Eadie substantial royalties for "Ax" of "Demolition." Thus, the parties' course of dealings over the intervening years belies defendants' claim that the 1984 agreement controlled their relationship.

Titan invokes the 1990 "amendment" to argue that the 1984 agreement controlled the parties' relationship during all of the intervening years, but genuine issues of material fact exist as to whether Eadie was fraudulently induced to sign that amendment at a time when he and Titan thought that his wrestling career might be coming to an end. The timing of the amendment is more than a little suspicious. One can reasonably infer that Titan was concerned about protecting its rights to the "Demolition" characters and was attempting to get a "headlock" on Eadie by forcing him to sign this amendment in an effort to protect its continued stream of income from the "Demolition" characters.

The court finds that any contractual obligations between the parties arose as a result of an oral contract between Titan and Eadie under which the parties performed for over three years, if not longer. The precise terms of this contract are factual issues to be resolved by a jury. Defendants' motion for summary judgment will be denied.

SECTION 8.3 THE ELEMENTS OF A CONTRACT	In determining whether there is a mutual agreement between the parties to enter into a contract, the primary test is one of **intent**. The intention of the parties is determined not only from their words, but also from their conduct and the surrounding circumstances. In ascertaining the intent of the parties, the courts will apply an objective standard. What would a reasonable person conclude about a party's intent to contract? An offer made in jest or while intoxicated cannot be taken seriously by the other party.

JOHN LEONARD V. PEPSICO, INC.
UNITED STATES DISTRICT COURT, 210 F. 3RD 88 (S.D. N.Y. 2000)

THIS CASE ARISES OUT OF A PROMOTIONAL campaign conducted by defendant, the distributor of the soft drinks Pepsi and Diet Pepsi. The promotion entitled "Pepsi Stuff," encouraged consumers to collect "Pepsi Points" and redeem these points for merchandise featuring the Pepsi logo. Plaintiff saw the Pepsi Stuff commercial that he contends constituted an offer of a Harrier Jet.

Because whether the television commercial constituted an offer is the central question in this case, the Court will describe the commercial in detail. The commercial opens upon an idyllic, suburban morning, where the chirping of birds in sun-dappled trees welcomes a paperboy on his morning route. As the newspaper hits the stoop of a conventional two-story house, the tattoo of a military drum introduces the subtitle, "MONDAY 7:58 AM." The stirring strains of a martial air mark the appearance of a well-coifed teenager preparing to leave for school, dressed in a shirt emblazoned with the Pepsi logo, a red-white-and-blue ball. While the teenager confidently preens, the military drumroll again sounds as the subtitle "T-SHIRT 75 PEPSI POINTS" scrolls across the screen. Bursting from his room, the teenager strides down the hallway wearing leather jacket. The drumroll sounds again, as the subtitle "LEATHER JACKET 1450 PEPSI POINTS" appears. The teenager opens the door of his house and, unfazed by the glare of the early morning sunshine, puts on a pair of sunglasses. The drumroll then accompanies the subtitle "SHADES 175 PEPSI POINTS." A voiceover then intones, "Introducing the new Pepsi Stuff catalog," as the camera focuses on the cover of the catalog.

The scene then shifts to three young boys sitting in front of a high school building. The boy in the middle is intent on his Pepsi Stuff Catalog, while the boys on either side are each drinking Pepsi. The three boys gaze in awe at an object-rushing overhead, as the military march builds to a crescendo. The Harrier Jet is not yet visible, but the observer senses the presence of a mighty plane as the extreme winds generated by its flight create a paper maelstrom in a classroom devoted to an otherwise dull physics lesson. Finally, the Harrier Jet swings into view and lands by the side of the school building, next to a bicycle rack. Several students run for cover, and the velocity of the wind strips one hapless faculty member down to his underwear. While the faculty member is being deprived of his dignity, the voiceover announces: "Now the more Pepsi you drink, the more great stuff you're gonna get."

The teenager opens the cockpit of the fighter and can be seen, helmetless, holding a Pepsi. "[L]ooking very pleased with himself," the teenager exclaims, "Sure beats the bus," and chortles. The military drumroll sounds a final time, as the following words appear: "HARRIER FIGHTER 7,000,000 PEPSI POINTS." A few seconds later, the following appears in more stylized script: "Drink Pepsi--Get Stuff." With that message, the music and the commercial end with a triumphant flourish.

Inspired by this commercial, plaintiff set out to obtain a Harrier Jet. Plaintiff consulted the Pepsi Stuff Catalog. The Catalog specifies the number of Pepsi Points required to obtain promotional merchandise. The Catalog includes an Order Form, which lists, on one side, fifty-three items of Pepsi Stuff merchandise redeemable for Pepsi Points. Conspicuously absent from the Order Form is any entry or description of a Harrier Jet.

The rear foldout pages of the Catalog contain directions for redeeming Pepsi Points for merchandise. The Catalog notes that in the event that a consumer lacks enough Pepsi Points to obtain a desired item, additional Pepsi Points may be purchased for ten cents each; however, at least fifteen original Pepsi Points must accompany each order.

Although plaintiff initially set out to collect 7,000,000 Pepsi Points by consuming Pepsi products, it soon became clear to him that he "would not be able to buy (let alone drink) enough Pepsi to collect the necessary Pepsi Points fast enough." Reevaluating his strategy, plaintiff "focused for the first time on the packaging materials in the Pepsi Stuff promotion," and realized that buying Pepsi Points would be a more promising option. Through acquaintances, plaintiff ultimately raised about $700,000.

On or about March 27, 1996, plaintiff submitted an Order Form, fifteen original Pepsi Points, and a check for $700,008.50.

On or about May 7, 1996, defendant's fulfillment house rejected plaintiff's submission and returned the check, explaining that:

> The item that you have requested is not part of the Pepsi Stuff collection. It is not included in the catalogue or on the order form, and only catalogue merchandise can be redeemed under this program. The Harrier jet in the Pepsi commercial is fanciful and is simply included to create a humorous and entertaining ad. We apologize for any misunderstanding or confusion that you may have experienced and are enclosing some free product coupons for your use.

The general rule is that an advertisement does not constitute an offer. Advertisements and order forms are "mere notices and solicitations for offers which create no power of acceptance in the recipient." Under these principles, plaintiff's letter of March 27, 1996, with the Order Form and the appropriate number of Pepsi Points, constituted the offer. There would be no enforceable contract until defendant accepted the Order Form and cashed the check.

Plaintiff's understanding of the commercial as an offer must also be rejected because the Court finds that no objective person could reasonably have concluded that the commercial actually offered consumers a Harrier Jet.

In evaluating the commercial, the Court must not consider defendant's subjective intent in making the commercial, or plaintiff's subjective view of what the commercial offered, but what an objective, reasonable person would have understood the commercial to convey.

If it is clear that an offer was not serious, then no offer has been made:

> What kind of act creates a power of acceptance and is therefore an offer? It must be an expression of will or intention. It must be an act that leads the offeree reasonably to conclude that a power to create a contract is conferred. This applies to the content of the power as well as to the fact of its existence. It is on this ground that we must exclude invitations to deal or acts of mere preliminary negotiation, and acts evidently done in jest or without intent to create legal relations.

Plaintiff's insistence that the commercial appears to be a serious offer requires the Court to explain why the commercial is funny.

First, the commercial suggests that use of the advertised product will transform what, for most youth, can be a fairly routine and ordinary experience. The military tattoo and stirring martial music, as well as the use of subtitles in a Courier font that scroll terse messages across the screen, such as "MONDAY 7:58 AM," evoke military and espionage thrillers. The implication of the commercial is that Pepsi Stuff merchandise will inject drama and moment into hitherto unexceptional lives. A reasonable viewer would understand such advertisements as mere puffery, not as statements of fact.

Second, the youth featured in the commercial is a highly improbable pilot, one who could barely be trusted with the keys to his parents' car, much less the prize aircraft of the United States Marine Corps.

Third, the notion of traveling to school in a Harrier Jet is an exaggerated adolescent fantasy.

Fourth, the number of Pepsi Points the commercial mentions as required to "purchase" the jet is 7,000,000. To amass that number of points, one would have to drink 7,000,000 Pepsis (or roughly 190 Pepsis a day for the next hundred years--an unlikely possibility), or one would have to purchase approximately $700,000 worth of Pepsi Points. The cost of a Harrier Jet is roughly $23 million dollars, a fact of which plaintiff was aware when he set out to gather the amount he believed necessary to accept the alleged offer. Even if an objective, reasonable person were not aware of this fact, he would conclude that purchasing a fighter plane for $700,000 is a deal too good to be true.

In sum, there are two reasons why plaintiff's demand cannot prevail as a matter of law. First, the commercial was merely an advertisement, not an offer. Second, the tongue-in-cheek attitude of the commercial would not cause a reasonable person to conclude that a soft drink company would be giving away fighter planes as part of a promotion.

SECTION 8.4
OFFER

An **offer** is a proposal by one party (offeror) to the other (offeree) manifesting an intention to enter into a valid contract. An offer has three requirements. It must be (1) a definite proposal, (2) made with the intent to contract and (3) be communicated to the party for whom the offer is intended.

For a proposal to be definite, its terms may not be vague or indefinite. The offer should identify the subject matter of the transaction, the quantity, and the price of the object. If Joe Hodge informs the Zoo that he is interested in selling his pet gorilla, and a Zoo official replies, "We accept," a contract is not formed since the parties failed to specify the price and other elements of the deal.

Prize contests are a common marketing tool used to entice the public to purchase a product, such as a magazine subscription. If the contestant fulfills the terms of the offer, may the promoter withdraw the prize before it is awarded? The promoter of a prize contest makes the offer, and if before the offer is withdrawn, another person acts upon it, the promoter is bound to perform his promise. *Pacitti v. Macy's East, Inc.* involved a talent search for Broadway's new "Annie". Following a series of auditions, Pacitti won the starring role in the musical and embarked on a pre-Broadway tour. Three weeks before the show was to open in New York, the young actress was replaced. Suit was filed against Macy's in an attempt to enforce the terms of their advertisement, which according to the plaintiff, required the winner of the audition to be awarded the starring role of "Annie" on Broadway. Pacitti claims that she accepted the offer by winning the competition so that a binding contract was formed concerning the prize-winning contest.

STELLA PACITTI v. MACY'S EAST, INC.
193 F.3D 766 (3RD CIR. 1999)

STELLA AND JOSEPH PACITTI, on behalf of their daughter, Joanna Pacitti ("plaintiffs"), appeal the District Court's granting of summary judgment in favor of Macy's East, Inc. ("Macy's) arising from Macy's role as promoter and host of "Macy's Search for Broadway's New 'Annie'" (the "Search").

In May 1996, the producers of "Annie" and Macy's, a retail department store chain, entered into an agreement under which Macy's agreed to sponsor the "Annie 20th Anniversary Talent Search." Specifically, Macy's agreed to promote the event and to host the auditions. The producers agreed to select one finalist from each regional store to compete in a final audition in New York City. The producers also agreed to offer the winner "a contract for that role to appear in the 20th Anniversary Production of Annie ... subject to the standard Actors' Equity Production Contract guidelines. Macy's publicized the Search in newspapers and in its stores. All of the promotional materials referred to the event as "Macy's Search for Broadway's New Annie". Plaintiffs learned of the Search from an advertisement in the Philadelphia Inquirer that stated, in pertinent part:

> If you are a girl between 7 and 12 years old, the starring role in this 20th Anniversary Broadway production and national tour could be yours! Just get your hands on an application...and bring it to the audition at Macy's King of Prussia store.... Annie's director/lyricist will pick the lucky actress for final callbacks ...at Macy's Herald Square. Annie goes on the road this fall and opens on Broadway in the Spring of 1997.

In June 1996, Joanna, and her mother picked up an application. The application form announced:

> Annie, America's most beloved musical and Macy's, the world's largest store, are conducting a talent show for a new "Annie" to star in the 20th Anniversary Broadway production and national Tour of Annie....

The reverse side of the form contained the "Official Rules [of] Macy's Search for Broadway's New 'Annie'" and provided in relevant part:

> All determinations made by the Producer or their designated judges are being made at their sole discretion and each such determination is final.

Unlike Macy's contract with the producers, neither the official rules nor any of the promotional materials included a provision informing the participants that the winner of the Search would receive only the opportunity to enter into a standards actors' equity contract with the producers. Joanna and her mother signed the official rules and proceeded to the initial audi-

tions at the King of Prussia store. Macy's publicized the event by placing balloons, signs, pins and other promotional material advertising "Macy's Search for Broadway's New 'Annie'" throughout the store. After auditioning hundreds of "Annie" hopefuls, the producers selected Joanna as the regional finalist. In a press release, Macy's announced Joanna's success to the public: "One in Ten She'll Be a Star!!! Macy's Brings Local Girl One Step Closer Towards Tomorrow to Become Broadway's New Annie."

Joanna and her mother traveled to New York City for the "Annie-Off-Final Call Back". After auditioning for two days, the producers selected Joanna to star as "Annie". Again, Macy's announced Joanna's success to the public, referring to her as "Broadway's New 'Annie'."

Joanne and her mother met with the producers and signed an Actors' Equity Association Standard Production Contract. Consistent with the Actors' Equity Association's rules governing production contracts, the producers retained the right to replace Joanna with another actor at any time as long as they paid her salary through the term of her contract.

For nearly a four-month period, Joanna performed the role of "Annie" in the production's national tour. Joanna appeared in over 100 performance in six cities. Approximately three weeks before the scheduled Broadway opening, the producers informed Joanna that her "service [would] no longer be needed," and she was replaced by her understudy.

On March 21, 1997, plaintiffs filed suit against Macy's alleging *(among other things)* breach of contract. In particular, plaintiffs alleged that Macy's failed to deliver the prize it had offered, i.e., the starring role of "Annie" on Broadway, and that Macy's knew it could not award this prize but promoted its ability to do so nonetheless.

Macy's moved for summary judgment, contending that it did not deprive Joanna of any prize she had been promised and that her rights were limited by the terms of her contract with the producers. Macy's proffered its contract with the producers, which specified that the successful contestant would receive only the opportunity to enter into a standard actors' equity contract with the producer.

The District Court granted summary judgment in favor of Macy's and concluded that the contract was unambiguous and capable of only one reasonable interpretation—i.e., that Macy's offered only an audition for the opportunity to enter into a standard actors' equity contract with the producers.

Under the law of Pennsylvania, [t]he promoter of a [prize-winning] contest, by making public the conditions and rules of the contest, makes an offer, and if before the offer is withdrawn another person acts upon it, the promoter is bound to perform his promise. The offer to award a prize results in an enforceable contract if the offeree performs the required action before the offer is withdrawn. Here, the parties entered into an enforceable contract. Macy's offered girls the opportunity of becoming "Broadway's New 'Annie'" by participating in and winning the auditions, and Joanna participated in and won the auditions. Therefore, the dispute in this appeal relates to the parties' interpretation of that contract and, in particular, to the question whether the District Court properly found that the contract is unambiguous.

A contract is ambiguous if it is capable of more than one reasonable interpretation. In determining whether a contract is ambiguous, the court "assumes the intent of the parties to an instrument is embodied in the writing itself, and when the words are clear and unambiguous the intent is to be discovered only from the express language of the agreement.

We conclude that the District Court erred in determining that the contract was capable of only one reasonable interpretation. Plaintiffs' interpretation —Macy's offered the prize of performing as "Annie" on Broadway for at least some period — is a reasonable alternative to that of the District Court. The official rules and promotional materials referred to the promotion as "Macy's Search for Broadway's New 'Annie'." The official rules provided that the producers and Macy's were "conducting a talent search for the new 'Annie' to star in the 20th Anniversary Broadway production," and the advertisement in the Philadelphia Inquirer promised that "[t]he starring role in the 20th Anniversary Broadway Production and National Tour could be yours!" From these assertions, one reasonably could conclude that Macy's offered the winner of the Search the prize of starring as "Annie" on Broadway.

Moreover, it is not unreasonable to conclude that Macy's had the ability to offer the winner of the Search the starring role on Broadway. The official rules provided that:

> Annie, America's most beloved musical, and Macy's, the world's largest store, are conducting a talent search for a new "Annie" to star in the 20th Anniversary Broadway production and national Tour of Annie....

The passage suggests that Macy's and the producers jointly promoted and hosted the Search. It does not indicate that any relative imbalance of authority in favor of the producers. Further, Macy's at no point revealed that the winner of the search would receive only the opportunity to sign a standard actor's equity contract with the producers. Therefore, we conclude that it was reasonable for plaintiffs to believe that Macy's offered the starring role of "Annie" on Broadway.

For these reasons, we hold that the contractual language is ambiguous, and its interpretation should be left to the fact finder for resolution.

The second element of a valid offer is that the party making the offer intends to contract. Phrases such as, "Are you interested" or "Would you give me" are merely words to make an offer. Terms such as "I bid" or "My lowest price is" evidence a present intention to contract and are words of an offer.

The final element of an offer is that it must be communicated to the offeree. In other words, the offeree must know of the offer to accept it. The mere fact that the offeree consents to identical terms, does not create a contract if the offeree did not know of the offer. Suppose a person returns a lost puppy to its owner unaware that the owner has posted a reward. The Good Samaritan will not be entitled to the reward. There has been no communication of the offer.

Once a valid offer has been made, how long does that offer remain open? A rejection or counter offer by the buyer terminates an offer. If in response to a $1,000 offer to sell a car, the buyer tenders $500, the original offer is terminated. An offer may also be revoked at any time before its acceptance, and an offer may terminate by its own terms. If a party is given five days to make a decision, the offer automatically terminates at the end of that period. An offer may also terminate if the subject matter of the bargain is destroyed before acceptance, if one of the parties dies, or if the proposal contract is deemed illegal.

SECTION 8.5
ACCEPTANCE

An **acceptance** is an agreement by the offeree to be bound by the terms of the offer. Like the offer, the acceptance must be (1) made with the intent to contract, (2) be communicated to the offeror, and (3) be unconditional. An acceptance may occur by the return of a promise, the performance of an act, or by any other method of acceptance that is stated in the offer. In a bilateral contract, an offer to sell a car for $1,000 is accepted by the promise of the buyer to pay $1,000. In a unilateral contract, the offer is accepted by the performance of an act. For example, the individual who returns the lost item with knowledge of the reward has accepted the offer and is entitled to the money.

Is the mistaken deposit of a check by the offeror an acceptance of an offer? This is the issue in *Crouch v. Marrs* in which the court ruled that the acceptance and endorsement of the check accompanying the offer to purchase constitutes an acceptance of the offer.

FRANK KNOX V. MARRS
430 P.2D 204 (KAN. 1967)

HATCHER, Commissioner:

THIS WAS AN ACTION TO ENJOIN interference with plaintiff's right of ingress and egress to land on which was located a building he was attempting to salvage. The result of the action was to have the title to the building determined. Judgment was rendered against plaintiff and he has appealed.

An old silica processing plant was owned by the Purex Corporation. On February 26, 1964, the plaintiff, Crouch, wrote to the Purex Corporation asking for their lowest price if they were interested in selling the building and its contents. The letter read in part:

> "I would be interested in buying the old building that housed the plant and what other items that are still left. The items that are still left are: two crushers, furnace and the elevator is about all that is left."

On March 4, 1964, Crouch received a letter of reply from Purex Corporation signed by Frank Knox which stated:

> "We will sell this building and the equipment in and about that building for a total of $500."

On March 19, 1964, Crouch wrote to Frank Knox, Purex Corporation, stating that the building was in "pretty bad condition" and asking "would you consider taking $300.00 for what is left?" This letter was not answered.

Later, on April 16, 1964, Crouch addressed another letter to Frank Knox, Purex Corporation, which read:

> "I guess we will try the building for the amount you quoted, $500. I am sending you a personal check for this amount."

On April 17, 1964, the Purex Corporation, through Frank Knox, wrote a letter to Martin Asche which stated:

> "In answer to your inquiry about our property approximately six miles north of Meade, Kansas, we will sell for $500.00 the mine building and whatever machinery and equipment which remains in or about that building. If this price is acceptable we will be pleased to receive a cashier's check to cover."

On April 24, 1964, Asche wrote a letter accepting the offer of April 17.

On April 27, 1964, Frank Knox sent Crouch the following telegram:

> "Your counter offer received April 23 is unacceptable. Your check mistakenly deposited by Purex will be recovered and returned to you or Purex check will be issued to you if your check cannot be located."

There followed a letter dated May 16, 1964, which read:

> "This is a follow-up to our telegram to you of April 27, advising you that your check which we received on April 23 was not acceptable, but that it had been deposited by mistake. Since we were unable to recover your check, we herewith enclose our check for $500 to reimburse you.
>
> We wish to explain, that the reason we could not accept your counter-offer of $500 for the mine building and machinery at Meade, Kansas was because we

had received and accepted an offer from another party prior to receipt of yours on April 23."

In the meantime Martin Asche had entered into a contract to sell the building to Roy Marrs for $500.

Crouch commenced salvage of the building but Roy Marrs put a lock on the gate and would not allow Crouch to enter.

Crouch then brought an action to enjoin Marrs from interfering with his salvage operations. Marrs answered alleging that he had purchased the building from Asche.

The trial court decreed that no contract came into existence between plaintiff Crouch and the Purex Corporation; that Asche had purchased the building and equipment and sold the building to Marrs.

Appellant contends that on the basis of the prior negotiations, the acceptance and endorsing appellant's check by the Purex Corporation constituted the formation of a contract of sale.

The appellee contends that the appellant's check was cashed through inadvertence or an error in office procedure and under such circumstances the casing of the check did not constitute an acceptance of appellant's offer. The difficulty with this contention is that there was no evidence of any character as to why the check was cashed. Neither would the error void the contract unless mutual mistake was pleaded. The question is whether the endorsing and depositing appellant's check constituted an acceptance of his offer to buy? We think it did. The depositing of a check accompanying an offer to purchase is not necessarily acceptance of payment. The giving of a check which does not clear is no payment.

The endorsing and depositing of a check constitutes an acceptance of the offer to buy which accompanies it because the act itself indicates acceptance. An offer may be accepted by performing a specified act as well as by an affirmative answer. Also, where the offeree exercised dominion over the thing offered him—in this instance the check—such exercise constitutes an acceptance of the offer. The rule is well stated in *Autographic Register Co. v. Philip Hano Co.*, **198 F.2d 208**, where it was said:

> "* * * However, a finding of positive intention to accept an offer is not always necessary to the creation of a contract. It is elementary that an offer may be accepted by performing or refraining from performing a specified act as well as by an affirmative answer and it is stated in Restatement, Contracts, Section 72(2) as the general rule that 'Where the offeree exercises dominion over things which are offered to him, such exercise of dominion in the absence of other circumstance showing a contrary intention is an acceptance.'"

We are forced to conclude that the acceptance and endorsement of the check accompanying the offer to purchase the property in controversy constituted an acceptance of the offer.

The judgment is reversed with instructions to the district court to quiet plaintiff's title to the building and equipment in controversy against the defendants and enjoin them from interfering with plaintiff's ingress and egress for the purpose of salvaging the property.

Suppose you receive in the mail an unsolicited compact disc of your favorite rock group from a mail order house. The CD is accompanied with a letter that says if you don't want the record, merely return it to the sender. You have never done business with the mail order house before so you throw the letter away and keep the CD. Are you responsible to pay for it? The mail order house argues that by keeping the disc and not returning it to the company, you have accepted the offer.

Generally, silence or inaction on the part of the offeree is not considered an effective acceptance. In addition, pursuant to the Postal Reorganization Act and various state statutes, an unsolicited product received in the mail is a "gift."

Silence may constitute an acceptance, however, if the offeree remains silent with the intent to accept the offer or where a prior course of dealings between the parties has treated silence as an acceptance. A party who has contracted with a record club to accept a compact disc on approval every month, may not sit back and keep the goods without paying for them.

Like the offer itself, an acceptance is valid only when it has been communicated to the offeror. Generally, the offer will dictate the medium, manner, and time by which the offer is to be accepted. The amount of time the offeree has to communicate the acceptance is generally as long as the offer remains open. If the offer does not specify the medium to be used, it is assumed that the acceptance is to be communicated by the same or similar medium as the offer.

This can create a problem if the parties are using the mail because of the time delay between dispatch of the acceptance and its receipt by the offeror. The courts have resolved the problem by making the acceptance of the offer effective on dispatch. In other words, acceptance of the offer takes place as soon as it is mailed and not when it is received by the offeror. Revocation of an offer is effective on receipt.

LAWRENCE PRIBIL v. BERTHA RUTHER
262 N.W. 2D 460 (NEB. 1978)

BOSLAUGH, Justice.

THIS IS AN APPEAL IN AN ACTION for specific performance of a real estate contract. The defendant Bertha Ruther owns a quarter section of land in Holt County, Nebraska. The defendant listed this property for sale with John Thor, a real estate broker, on January 20, 1976.

On April 12, 1976, the plaintiff Lawrence Pribil executed a written offer to purchase the property for $68,000. The offer to purchase was on a form known as a Uniform Purchase Agreement, which included a space for a written acceptance of the offer. The defendant and her husband signed the acceptance on the same day and handed an executed copy of the agreement to Thor for delivery to the plaintiff.

Thor returned to his office and asked an office employee, Mrs. Kasebaum, to send a copy of the agreement to the plaintiff. Mrs. Kasebaum wrote a letter to the plaintiff, dated April 14, 1976, with a copy of the agreement enclosed, which was sent to the plaintiff by certified mail. The letter was postmarked "April 15, 1976 P.M." and was received by the plaintiff on April 16, 1976.

The defendant became dissatisfied with the transaction the day after she had signed the acceptance. The defendant testified that she called the plaintiff's home at about 5 p.m., on April 13, 1976, and told the plaintiff's wife that she, the defendant, would not sell the property. The plaintiff's wife testified this conversation did not take place until some 10 days later, near the end of April 1976.

The defendant further testified that she called Thor the next morning, April 14, 1976, and said that she was going to "terminate the contract." According to Thor this conversation took place at 11:42 a.m., on April 15, 1976. Thor testified that immediately after receiving the call from the defendant he called the plaintiff and told the plaintiff that the defendant was not going to sell the farm.

The principal issue in this case is whether the defendant had effectively rejected the plaintiff's offer and revoked her acceptance of the offer before the acceptance had been communicated to the plaintiff. The trial court found that an executed copy of the purchase agreement had been sent to the plaintiff by the defendant's agent on or before April 15, 1976, and that the plaintiff was entitled to a decree of specific performance. The defendant and her husband have appealed.

An express contract is proved by evidence of a definite offer and unconditional acceptance. Where the offer requires a promise on the part of the offeree, a communicated acceptance is essential. The signing of the acceptance on the Uniform Purchase Agreement by the defendant did not make the contract effective. It was necessary that there be some communication of the acceptance to the plaintiff. There must be some irrevocable element such as depositing the acceptance in the mail so that it is placed beyond the power or control of the sender before the acceptance becomes effective and the contract is made. Delivery to the agent of the defendant was not delivery to the plaintiff and did not put the acceptance beyond the control of the defendant.

The plaintiff contends that the deposit of the acceptance in the mail satisfied the requirement that the acceptance be communicated. Where transmission by mail is authorized, the deposit of the signed agreement in the mail with the proper address and postage will complete the contract. The difficulty in this case is that there is no evidence that the acceptance was deposited in the mail before Thor called the plaintiff and informed him that the defendant would not sell the property.

The evidence is that Thor handed the purchase agreement to Mrs. Kasebaum with instructions to send a copy to the plaintiff. Mrs. Kasebaum did not testify. Thor testified, "I can't testify when she mailed it, except by reading the postmarks on the envelope and the return receipts." The postmark indicates only that the postage was canceled sometime during the afternoon of April 15, 1976. The telephone call from the defendant was received at 11:42 a.m. The call from Thor to the plaintiff was made immediately afterward.

If we assume that transmission by mail was authorized in this case, there is no evidence to show that the acceptance was deposited in the mail before the defendant's call to Thor, and

Thor's call to the plaintiff notifying him that the defendant had rejected his offer. The evidence does not show that the acceptance was communicated to the plaintiff and thus became effective before the defendant changed her mind and rejected the offer.

The judgment of the District Court is reversed and the cause remanded with directions to dismiss.

SECTION 8.6
CONSIDERATION

Consideration is what each party gives up in return for the act or promise received. This is called the **Quid Pro Quo.** Two elements must be present. It must appear that both parties intend to incur legal rights and liabilities and the bargained for exchange must have legal value. For example, if a person purchases a slice of pizza from a vendor for $2.00, what is the consideration? The vendor is giving up a slice of pizza. In exchange, the merchant is receiving $2.00. The consumer is giving up $2.00 and will receive a piece of pizza in return. This is a bargained for exchange or a *Quid Pro Quo* that is supported by consideration on both sides. If the merchant only has one slice of pizza left and you offer the vendor $20.00 for it in order to outbid three other customers, is the contract valid since the consideration is unequal? Yes. The value of the bargain does not have to be equal as long as fraud or undue influence is not present.

Not all individuals or businesses have sufficient credit to obtain a loan or merchandise on credit. Occasionally, a third person will be required to guarantee the obligation of the borrower in the event of a default. For instance, a college student may not have a sufficient credit history in order to finance the purchase a new car so the credit company will request that a parent co-sign the loan obligation.

A co-signer may be considered either a surety or guarantor depending upon the financial arrangement required by the lender. The primary difference between the two types of agreements is that a surety is primarily liable for the debt as though he or she borrowed the money. A guarantor is only secondarily liable. In other words, the creditor will look to the guarantor only after the debtor has defaulted and the creditor is unsuccessful in recovering the money from the borrower.

Is the promise by the third party to be the responsible for the debt of another supported by consideration? This is the issue in *Arnold Fashion, L.P. v. Celeb Sales, Inc.* which dealt with a licensing agreement entered into by Arnold Fashion for the sale of clothing under the celebrity names of Roseanna and Tom Arnold. A third party was asked to guarantee the royalty payments due to the Arnolds. When the debtor defaulted, the guarantor was called upon to make the royalty payment.

ARNOLD FASHION, L.P., v. CELEB SALES, INC.
172 F. 3D 875 (9TH CIR. 1999)

CELEB SALES, INC., AND STANLEY WARNER APPEAL the court's judgment in an action brought by Arnold Fashion, L.P. because Celeb Sales had failed to make a royalty payment, which Warner had guaranteed.

Celeb Sales entered into two written licensing agreements (the "Sublicense Agreements") with Arnold Fashion for the sale of clothing lines under the celebrity names of Roseanne and Tom Arnold. The Sublicense Agreements provided for a minimum of $1,000,000 in advance royalty payments, to be paid in four $250,000 installments. Celeb Sales made the first payment, but failed to make the second payment when it was due.

Rather than terminate the Sublicense Agreements, Arnold Fashion subsequently agreed to extend the date of payment for the second installment (the "Modification Agreement"). In consideration for that modification, Warner executed a written guaranty of Celeb Sales' obligation to make the second payment (the "Guaranty Agreement"). Celeb Sales failed to meet the extended deadline, and Warner did not honor his guaranty. Accordingly, Arnold Fashion instituted this action, claiming breach of the Sublicense, Modification, and Guaranty

Warner argues that the court erred in ruling that sufficient consideration was provided for the Guaranty Agreement. He contends that the following assurances, allegedly promised by Arnold Fashion, were required as consideration for the contract: that the Arnolds would participate in a fashion show for the new clothing line; that there would be a two-page spread in the National Enquirer promoting the new clothing line; and that the Arnolds would no longer be involved in any further adverse publicity.

However, Warner provides no concrete evidence that these alleged promises were ever made or that they served as consideration for the guaranty. None of these promises were put in writing, and the only consideration to which the Modification and Guaranty Agreements refer is Arnold Fashion's extension of the payment deadline for the second royalty advance. See Cal. Civ. Code Section 2792 where a suretyship obligation is entered into at the same time with the original obligation, or with the acceptance of the later by the creditor, and forms with that obligation a part of the consideration to him, no other consideration need exist.

Warner requests that this court permit him to submit extrinsic evidence so that a jury can determine whether those alleged oral promises were required as consideration for the guaranty. However, such a determination is unnecessary, for the deadline extension provided was sufficient and "material" consideration to sustain the Guaranty Agreement.

For the foregoing reason, the district court's rulings are affirmed.

Suppose a friend promises to give you $500 in celebration of your 21st birthday but fails to deliver the gift as promised. Will the court enforce the promise? No! A gift is not supported by consideration. The party promising the gift has not incurred any liability for the promise nor has the person with the birthday given up anything of value for the promise.

When a couple becomes engaged, the man frequently gives the woman an engagement ring. What happens if the marriage does not take place? Is the ring returned to the man under the theory that the ring was a conditional gift based upon the marriage taking place or is the woman allowed to keep the ring? Please review the following problem involving Tony Hodge and his broken engagement.

SECTION 8.7
TONY HODGE AND THE
ENGAGEMENT RING

PROBLEM EIGHT —A

HODGE, DODGE AND LODGE
ATTORNEYS AT LAW
MEMORANDUM

To: All Law Clerks

From: Gregory Olan Dodge

Re: Tony Hodge v. Lillian Winter

During the off-season, Tony Hodge, the field goal kicker for the Stallions, reluctantly returned to his apartment in the Philadelphia area where he became restless and lonely. Being stuck in his apartment without his teammates and friends, caused Tony to miss his favorite nightspots in Chicago, Dallas and New York. One evening, the football player decided to visit the new club in town which had developed a reputation as providing gourmet food. While eating his meal, Tony struck up a conversation with Lil Winter, an exotic dancer, who was also eating dinner before the start of the show.

As the night club was closing, Tony invited Lil to Dave and Buster's for some late night entertainment. The couple hit it off instantly and found that they had much in common. Following a three-week romance in which Tony saw Lil every night, he asked her to marry him. Lil accepted on the spot. They spent the rest of the night talking and planning their future together. When the jewelry store opened the next morning, Tony and Lil were their first customers. Tony had just received an endorsement check from a car dealer in the Stallions' hometown. Less than an hour later, Tony had purchased a 2-karat flawless diamond ring in antique platinum setting for $18,000.

Overjoyed by his new found love, Tony also took Lil to a car dealer where he replaced her 1985 Ford hatchback with a new Mustang convertible. The new car would provide Ms. Winter with dependable transportation to visit him during the season.

Unfortunately, two months later, Tony's luck and Lil's love ran out. She told Tony that their romance was over. Things were moving too quickly and Lil wasn't ready to give up her career as a dancer. Once Tony got over the initial shock and disappointment, he realized that he had just spent over $50,000 and had nothing to show for it. Tony asked Lil to return the ring and the car, but she refused, claiming that they were gifts. Broken hearted and defeated, Tony came to see me. He said the only reason he bought the items for Lil was that he wanted his girlfriend to be happy. He insisted that his purchases were not outright gifts, but given in anticipation of their marriage. Since Lil canceled the wedding, Tony insisted that she should have to give the ring and the car back.

Please read the case of *Lindh v. Surman*, and answer these questions:

1. Does Lil get to keep the ring?
2. Who gets to keep the car?
3. What role does fault have in determining which items are to be returned?

ROGER LINDH V. JANIS SURMAN
702 A.2D 560 (PA. SUPER.1997)

THIS APPEAL REQUIRES RESOLUTION of the novel question whether the law of Pennsylvania should permit retention of an engagement ring or its value by the donee, (the person receiving the gift) after the donor (the person giving the gift) of the ring breaks their engagement. The facts follow.

Rodger Lindh (Rodger) asked appellant Janis Surman (Janis) to marry him on August 24, 1993. Janis accepted his proposal and Rodger gave Janis a diamond engagement ring worth approximately $21,000. Unfortunately, Rodger experienced misgivings about the impending marriage and requested the ring's return in October of 1993. Janis returned the ring. However, Janis and Rodger subsequently reconciled, and once again planned to marry. Rodger again gave the diamond ring to Janis and Janis wore it. Janis began to make wedding plans.

On March 20, 1994, Rodger unexpectedly informed Janis that he no longer loved her and broke their engagement. Janis questioned Rodger, but he was unable or unwilling to explain or to seek counseling regarding his decision. Rodger requested that Janis return the ring, but Janis refused. Litigation ensued. Rodger filed a civil action to recover the ring or its value.

The trial court found no case directly on point. The court discovered, however, that other states had addressed the issue, and although the majority of states followed the so-called *fault rule*, an increasing number of jurisdictions were adopting a *no-fault rule*. The no-fault jurisdictions hold that absent an agreement to the contrary, the ring is returned to the donor regardless of the circumstances surrounding the engagement's termination. The trial court ruled that the no-fault engagement rule *should be followed* in Pennsylvania as well.

Both Janis and Rodger agree that Pennsylvania follows the law of conditional gifts in engagement ring matters. They disagree over what condition renders the gift complete. Janis' position is that the conditional gift of an engagement ring is incident to the engagement itself. The condition attached to the gift is her agreement to marry Rodger. The condition of the gift thus satisfied, she should be entitled to retain the ring.

For his part, Rodger contends that his gift of the engagement ring to Janis was conditioned upon the marriage rather than her agreement to marry him. Because the condition, marriage, never took place, Rodger contends the trial court's award of the ring to him should be affirmed. We agree.

The law of conditional gifts is set forth in the Restatement of Restitution. With particular interest we note that engagement rings are treated differently from *other wedding* and/or engagement gifts:

GIFTS MADE IN RELIANCE ON A RELATION.

A person who has conferred a benefit upon another, manifesting that he does not expect compensation therefor, is not entitled to restitution merely because his expectation that an existing relation will continue or that a future relation will come into existence is not realized, unless the conferring of the benefit is conditioned thereon.

COMMENT:

(b) Conditional gifts.

The gift may be conditional upon the continuance or creation of a relation, and if conditional, the donor is entitled to its return if the relation terminates or is not entered into. The condition may be stated in specific words or it may be inferred from the circumstances. Likewise, as in the case of engagement and wedding gifts, justice may require the creation of a *condition* although the donor had no such condition in mind.

(c) Wedding and engagement gifts.

Gifts made in the hope that a marriage or contract of marriage will result are not recoverable, in the absence of fraud. Gifts made in anticipation of marriage are not ordinarily expressed to be conditional and, although there is an engagement to marry, if the marriage fails to occur without the fault of the donee, normally the gift cannot be recovered. If, however, the donee obtained the gift fraudulently or if the gift was made for a purpose which could be achieved only by the marriage, a donor who is not himself at fault is entitled to restitution if the marriage does not take place, even if the gift was of money. If there is an engagement to marry and the donee, having received the gift without fraud, later wrongfully breaks the promise of marriage, the donor is entitled to restitution if the gift is an engagement ring, a family heirloom or other similar thing intimately connected with the marriage, but not if the gift is one of money intended to be used by the donee before the marriage.

In addition, the Reporter's Notes to this section recognize that many jurisdictions utilize a fault analysis in resolving engagement ring cases, and that this analysis is inconsistent with the law of conditional gifts.

The engagement ring cases, where universally the plaintiff has been allowed to recover upon the breaking of the promise by the defendant, can rest either upon the ground that the giving of the ring is connected with the consideration, although this seems to be a very low ground upon which to rest it, or that the ring is given as a symbol to be worn only during the continuance of the relation between the parties. If it were a truly conditional gift, it would be immaterial whether the donor or the donee broke the engagement....

We now turn to Pennsylvania cases, which apply the law of conditional gifts in antenuptial gift contests. We believe these cases make clear that in this Commonwealth, engagement rings 'are *conditional gifts.*

An early case, ***Ruehling v. Hornung*, 98 Pa.Super. 535 (1930),** reflects the Restatement's characterization of an engagement ring as a *conditional gift*. In Ruehling, the donor in contemplation of marriage presented his fiancée with a diamond ring, a diamond wristwatch, and a medallion. The question of who broke the engagement was in dispute and the donee refused to return the three items. In analyzing the status of the three gifts, this court set forth:

[t]he contention of [the donor] appellant is that gifts to a person to whom the donor is engaged to be married, made in contemplation of marriage, are conditional; and that if the donee breaks the engagement the gifts or their value may be recovered by the donor.

We find no case in this State directly bearing on this question, but in (a law treaties) it is stated: 'A gift to a person to whom the donor is engaged to be married, made in contemplation of marriage, although absolute in form, is conditional; and upon breach of the marriage engagement by the donee the property may be recovered by the donor. But if the gift is made simply for the purpose of introducing the donor to the donee's acquaintance and to gain her favor, the property is not recoverable, although marriage does not ensue. So where a Christmas present is made by a man to his fiancée, it becomes her property and the subsequent breaking of the engagement does not entitle him to recover it back.'

Following a review of case law from other jurisdictions, the court stated:

It will be observed that in each of the cases above cited, in which the court permitted a recovery of the property by the donor, there was a breach of the promise of marriage by the donee. In the case at bar no such breach was proved. It does not appear whether the engagement was broken by plaintiff or whether it was dissolved by mutual consent. It follows that in order to permit a recovery by plaintiff, it would be necessary to hold that the gifts were subject to the implied condition that they would be returned by the donee to the donor whenever the engagement was dissolved. Under such a rule the marriage would be a necessary prerequisite to the passing of an absolute title to a Christmas gift made in such circumstances. *We are unwilling to go that far, except as to the engagement ring.* Such a ring is given as a pledge or symbol of the contract to marry. We think that it is always given subject to the implied condition that if the marriage does not take place either because of the death, or a disability recognized by the law on the part of, either party, or by breach of the contract by the donee, or its dissolution by mutual consent, the gift shall be returned. It only becomes the absolute property of the recipient if the marriage takes place. Good sense usually secures the return of the ring. Our conclusion is that plaintiff's evidence in respect to the engagement ring was sufficient to take the case to the jury. As to the other articles involved the evidence was insufficient.

Hence, as far back as 1929, this court has adhered to the law of *conditional gifts* with respect to engagement rings. The retention of the gift is subject to the implied condition that marriage takes place and absent that occurrence, for whatever reason, it is impossible for the gift to become complete.

The law of conditional gifts has also been followed by courts of this Commonwealth in *Stanger v. Epler,* **382 Pa. 411, 115 A.2d 197 (1955)** (denying donor's claim for one-half interest in bank account established by him and donee prior to marriage; distinguishing conditional gift analysis which returned gift to donor in *Ruehling* on the basis gift was an engagement ring).

Janis, while recognizing the above authority nevertheless distinguishes it either on its facts or because there is no appellate case which clearly sets forth what should happen to the engagement ring if the donor breaks the engagement. However, we believe that this question is answered by the law of conditional gifts. As set forth in the Restatement of Restitution, if the engagement ring is a conditional gift, as Pennsylvania law has consistently held, then it is immaterial who breaks the engagement. Contrary to Janis' contention, the gift of the engagement ring, without more, is conditioned upon the marriage taking place and the ring must be returned to the donor if that condition does not occur.

Pennsylvania jurisprudence merely follows basic principles of restitution found in gift law in awarding antenuptial property. While Rodger, the donor in this case, proposed marriage, the marriage between Rodger and Janis did not occur. Thus, we find the gift of the ring to Janis at the time of their betrothal was subject to an *implied condition* requiring its return if the marriage did not take place.

After careful analysis, we affirm the order of the trial court which denied Janis post-trial relief and awarded judgment in Rodger's favor.

**ANSWER SHEET
PROBLEM EIGHT— A**

Name   **Please Print Clearly**

1. Who is entitled to the ring? Explain your answer.

_____

_____

_____

_____

_____

_____

_____

_____

_____

_____

_____

_____

_____

_____

_____

_____

_____

2. Who is entitled to the car? Explain your answer?

_____

_____

_____

_____

_____

_____

_____

_____

_____

3. What role does fault have in decided who is entitled to the items?

_____

_____

_____

_____

_____

_____

_____

_____

_____

_____

_____

SECTION 8.8
CAPACITY

The courts will usually not disturb a contract freely entered into by parties of similar bargaining strength. Nevertheless, when one of the parties does not have the **capacity** to fully understand the ramifications of the contractual obligation, mutual assent to bargain is lacking. The law provides protection to certain groups deemed to lack the capacity to contract. They include children, insane people, and intoxicated individuals.

Contracts of a minor are voidable at the child's election. This means that the minor may disaffirm the contract, but the adult is bound by the agreement. In order to disaffirm, the child does not have to return the adult to the status quo. The minor only has to return what is left of that purchased or received. In addition, a minor may ratify a contract upon reaching majority. Ratification occurs when a child reaches maturity and expresses an intention to be bound by the agreement or fails to disaffirm the contract. For instance, a child who continues to drive a car that he purchased as a minor after reaching majority will be found to have ratified the contract.

A minor because of public policy considerations may not disaffirm certain types of contracts. These include contracts for necessities such as food and shelter, contracts with colleges or the armed forces, and agreements of minors involved in a business.

Insane individuals, like minors, lack the capacity to enter into binding contracts. Individuals are considered **insane** when they are unable to understand the nature and consequences of their acts at the time they enter into an agreement. Mere psychological or emotional problems are not enough. It is also irrelevant whether mental illness, mental retardation, senility, alcohol, or drug abuse causes the insanity. The only requirement is that the individual must be incompetent at the time of entering into the contract.

A contract entered into by one who has previously been adjudged incompetent by a court is void. An adjudication by the court of incompetency is notice to the world that the person lacks capacity to contract. Contracts entered into by persons claiming to be insane, but not adjudged insane by the court, are voidable. In the latter situation, it is the responsibility of the person claiming to be incompetent to prove that he or she was insane at the time of contracting.

Unlike a child, an incompetent can't disaffirm the contract unless he can return the parties to the status quo. The exception to this rule is if the other party knows of the disability but still enters into the contract. In that event, the incompetent merely has to return what is left and does not have to return the parties to the status quo.

SECTION 8.9
LEGALITY

The law requires that the purpose and subject matter of an agreement be legal in order for the contract to be valid. A contract is **illegal** if its performance is criminal, tortious, or against public policy.

Illegal contracts are void and not enforceable in court. Neither party may sue for performance or damages even if they have partially or fully performed the act or promise specified in the agreement. Courts will simply leave the parties where it finds them. For example, the court will not enforce a gambling debt between two friends over a football game.

Over the years, there have been scattered reports of friends or co-workers who have pooled their funds and purchased a winning lottery ticket. Are these types of agreements enforceable if the party holding the winning ticket refuses to honor the arrangement? In *Dickerson v. Deno,* the court had to decide if this type of agreement constituted an illegal gambling contract.

TONDA DICKERSON v. SANDRA DENO
770 SO. 2D 62 (ALA. 2000)

THE PLAINTIFFS AND THE DEFENDANT Tonda Dickerson were employees at the Waffle House restaurant in Alabama. Edward Seward was a regular customer of the Waffle House. On several occasions Seward would travel to Florida and purchase lottery tickets and upon his return would give the tickets to various friends and family members, including the employees of the Waffle House.

A drawing for the Florida lottery was scheduled for Saturday night, March 6, 1999. During the week before that drawing, Seward traveled to Florida and purchased several lottery tickets. He placed each individual ticket in a separate envelope and wrote the name of the intended recipient on the outside of the envelope. Seward presented the plaintiffs Deno, Tisdale, and Adams each with an envelope containing one lottery ticket. The numbers on these lottery tickets did not match the numbers drawn in the March 6 drawing.

On the day after the drawing had already been concluded, Seward presented a ticket to the plaintiff Fairley, and he also presented the defendant Dickerson with a ticket. Farley's numbers on her ticket did not match the winning numbers. Subsequently, Dickerson opened her envelope and determined that the numbers on her ticket matched the winning numbers drawn in the lottery the night before. The ticket won a prize of approximately $5 million.

The plaintiffs sued Dickerson, alleging that they and Dickerson had orally contracted with each other that if any one of them should win, then the winner would share any lottery winnings with the other ticket recipients.

Dickerson averred that any oral agreement made by the parties was a gambling contract and could not be enforced under Alabama law. Section 8-1-150 provides that "all contracts founded in whole or in part on a gambling consideration are void."

The plaintiffs concede that Section 8-1-150 seeks to prohibit the enforcement of any payment for actual wagering or gambling, or on games of chance, but they argue that the oral agreement in this case is not void, because, "an agreement to share proceeds from a legal winning lottery ticket is simply not a wager between the parties to the agreement in the State of Alabama." They cite several cases they contend support their argument that the oral agreement was not founded on a gambling consideration.

Dickerson points out that in the cases cited by the plaintiffs, the courts relied heavily on the fact that the parties did not gamble among themselves, but, rather, jointly gambled with a foreign lottery. In her concluding argument, Dickerson says:

> Every case cited by Plaintiffs on the gambling issue, without exception, is a case in which the parties were joint owners of lottery tickets, even as Plaintiffs concede that the parties to this suit were not joint owners of the tickets, but were instead owners of individual tickets. Plaintiffs could only be entitled to a share of the winning tickets by virtue of their alleged side agreement with each other to hedge their bets, made in Ala-

bama, not as a result of an ownership interest in the winning ticket.

We agree with Dickerson that the facts in this case show that there was no agreement to jointly purchase or to jointly hold the lottery tickets. Each lottery ticket was purchased by Seward in Florida and was presented by him to one or the other of the parties, separately. The alleged oral contract in this case was an exchange of promises to share winnings from the parties' individually owned lottery tickets upon the happening of the uncertain event that the numbers drawn in the Florida lottery matched the numbers on one of the tickets held by the five individuals. Consequently, the agreement between the parties was nothing more than an attempt by each of the five lottery-ticket holders to increase his or her odds of winning some portion of the Florida lottery. Stated differently, the agreement, according to the plaintiffs' own evidence, was that Dickerson would pay the plaintiffs a sum of money upon the happening of an uncertain event over which no party had control, that is, upon Dickerson's ticket winning the Florida lottery. Consequently, we conclude that the agreement here was founded on a gambling consideration and was, therefore, void. Judgment is rendered in favor of the defendant, Dickerson.

SECTION 8.10
ESTELLE HODGE v. TRI-COUNTY GOLF CLUB

PROBLEM EIGHT—B

HODGE, DODGE AND LODGE
ATTORNEYS AT LAW
M E M O R A N D U M

To: All Law Clerks

From: Gregory Olan Dodge

Re: Tri-County Golf Course

Just when I think I have seen it all, along comes the Hodge family. Estelle Hodge has a rather interesting problem. She agreed to play in a charity golf tournament at Tri-County Golf Club. To encourage golfers to join the event, a Mercedes was offered to anyone who hit a hole in one on the 8th hole. Estelle stepped up to the tee and hit her shot straight and true. The ball landed on the green and headed directly to the cup. When the golf ball was less than one inch away from the hole, the most amazing thing happened. A frog was hiding in the cup but became scared when he heard all of the noise. The frog jumped out of the hole just as the ball was about to drop in, brushing the ball aside. Everyone looked around in amazement. Because the golf course was in a wooded area surrounded by water, Tri-County had many animals on its property, but this was the first time that a frog had interfered with a golf shot. Estelle demanded her prize and the golf course officials consulted with the tournament judge. This individual just happened to Dr. Feelgood who promptly denied Estelle's claim to the prize. Since the ball did not go into the hole, Feelgood said the shot did not fulfill the terms of the offer. Feelgood then disallowed the shot because of frog interference and directed Estelle to shoot the ball over.

Joe's wife wishes to sue the golf course in order to claim the prize. I have looked at the tournament's entry form that Estelle signed when she made her $500.00 donation to play in the event. That form notes that, "Disputes concerning the winner of the tournament, the scoring of any round, or other issues involving a specific shot will be determined solely by the appointed judge whose decisions are final in all matters relating to the event." The signs promoting the tournament advertised that any person who shoots a hole in one on the designated hole will be awarded a new Mercedes.

Estelle claims that the only reason she is being denied the car is because of Dr. Feelgood's bias against the family. After all, she says, the doctor is being sued by my husband for malpractice.

I have found one case that deals with the awarding of a disputed prize in a contest. Please read *Giunto v. Florida Panthers*, and let me know whether you think we will be successful in a claim against the golf course.

RANDI GIUNTO V. FLORIDA PANTHERS HOCKEY CLUB, LTD.
745 S. 2D 1020 (FLA. APP. 1999)

GIUNTO COMPLETED A SWEEPSTAKES APPLICATION for the "Coca-Cola/Blockbuster/ Florida Panthers Sweepstakes." The application contained contest rules (the "Entry Form Rules"). Pursuant to the Entry Form Rules, ten persons would be chosen to receive free tickets to one of ten different Florida Panthers home games. At the game, the ticket winner would be given a chance to win $1,000,000 by shooting a hockey puck across the ice "into and through a special small goal." Mr. Giunto was selected as one of the persons to have a try at the $1,000,000 prize.

Giunto appeared at the Florida Panthers game for his attempt at the prize. Just prior to his attempt, Mr. Giunto signed a Spectator Agreement to Participate ("SAP"). Included on the SAP was the requirement that in order for the contestant to win, the puck had to "pass completely through" the goal.

The target in this case was a piece of plywood placed in front of the hockey goal. At the bottom of the plywood sheet, a small slot had been created, somewhat larger than the hockey puck.

From a position of 118 feet from the hockey goal, Giunto took the contest shot. A videotape shows that the puck hit the corner of the small slot and rebounded from side to side. It did not go completely through the opening, but came to rest just slightly within the slot. A contest judge declared that the shot was unsuccessful.

Giunto sued the Sponsors for breach of contract alleging that he had successfully made the goal. Giunto contended that the controlling contest requirement was that the puck pass "into and through" the goal; that the SAP requirement that the puck pass "completely through" the goal was a nullity; and that "into and through" was satisfied if any part of the puck entered the opening, even if the puck did not pass completely through the opening.

The Sponsors claimed that Mr. Giunto's claims were barred because the contest judge had made the determination that Mr. Giunto did not successfully make the shot. The Entry Form Rules provided, "By participating in this sweepstakes, entrants agree to abide by and be bound by these official rules and the decisions of the judges, which are final in all matters relating to this sweepstakes." By submitting the application containing the Entry Form Rules, Mr. Giunto agreed to abide by the decision of the judges.

Other jurisdictions have held that "when a contestant agrees to be bound by the decisions of a tournament director or an awards committee, such decisions are final and binding on contestants absent evidence of fraud, gross mistake, or lack of good faith." *National Amateur Bowlers, Inc. v. Tassos*, 715 F.Supp. 323 (D. Kan. 1989) (holding that decisions of the tournament committee would be final, unless there was "fraud, intentional or gross mistake, or lack of good faith").

The contest judge determined that Mr. Giunto had not successfully made the hockey shot. There was neither pleading nor proof of fraud, gross mistake, or lack of good faith. When the puck entered the plywood slot but did not pass completely through it, the contest judge was required to decide whether Mr. Giunto had won under the contest rules. The judge's decision was binding on Mr. Giunto.

As to the question of whether the puck had to pass "into and through," or "completely through" the opening, Mr. Giunto signed the SAP which stated, "I understand that the Official Rules are as follows: The puck must pass completely through the target template." This document clearly informed Mr. Giunto, before he took his contest shot, that the judges would interpret "into and through" to mean "completely through" in order to win. The contest judge's ruling was in accordance with that interpretation.

Dissent:

The unilateral offer in this case represents the ultimate in a "contract of adhesion." It is the rule that any ambiguities or conflicts, within or between agreements, must be resolved against the draft persons. The applicable requirement was not that the puck "pass completely through" the goal, as provided in the Spectator Agreement to Participate, but only the lesser one, that it go "into and through" it, as stated in the first contract.

The same legal reasoning applies to the terms of the contract that "the decisions of the judges ... are final in all matters relating to this sweepstakes" upon which the majority so heavily relies. That provision should be entirely disregarded because it conflicts with the Spectator Agreement, which contains no such term. Even if this is not the case, the judge's decision clause is wholly invalid and unenforceable, because the omnipotent, omniscient judge turned out to be one, Declan Bolger, who is the Director of Promotions of the Florida Panthers. The rule that no person may be a judge in her own case, precludes the defendant's reliance on what amounts to their own denial of their own responsibility.

ANSWER SHEET
PROBLEM EIGHT—B

Name   **Please Print Clearly**

1. What arguments can we advance on behalf of Estelle as to why she should be awarded the prize?

_____

_____

_____

_____

_____

_____

_____

_____

_____

2. What arguments will be raised by the golf club?

_____

_____

_____

_____

_____

_____

_____

_____

_____

3. Based upon the Florida Panthers case, who should win? Please explain your answer so that I may inform Estelle of her legal rights.

_____

_____

_____

_____

_____

_____

_____

_____

_____

_____

_____

_____

_____

_____

_____

_____

_____

_____

_____

_____

_____

SECTION 8.11
PROBLEM CASES

1. Story promised his nephew $5,000 if he would refrain from drinking liquor, using tobacco, swearing, or playing cards until he became 21 years of age. The nephew fulfilled the terms of this promise and requested the money upon becoming 21. This request was refused on the basis that the contract lacked of consideration. Did the nephew provide legal consideration for the promise so that he may be awarded the money? *Hamer v. Sidway,* 27 N.E. 25 (N.Y. 1891).

2. Pemerton, accepted an invitation to appear on "The Jerry Springer Show." In exchange, she received airfare from Tennessee and her expenses were paid for two days in Chicago. Prior to the show's taping, she signed a document entitled "Jerry Springer Consent and Release" which provided that any dispute arising out of her appearance on the show would be resolved by binding arbitration with the American Arbitration Association. Pemerton sued Springer in state court for the injuries she received when her arch enemy burst from behind the scenes and beat Pemerton about the head and shoulders during the taping. Pemerton claims that Springer promised not to invite her assailant to the studio. Pemerton asserts that the Release does not cover the assault. She claims that it merely covers disputes arising out of the production of the show. Does the Arbitration agreement cover this claim for person injury? *Tracy Pemerton v. Jerry Springer,* 1995 W.L. 579465 (N.D. Ill. 1995).

3. Following the murder of Gianni Versace in front of his South Beach home, the FBI offered a reward leading to the "arrest and conviction of Andrew Cunanin." A dock attendant at a marina saw an individual who fit Cunanin's description on a nearby house boat. He notified the authorities and the FBI surrounded the house boat containing Cunanin. Following a volley of gun shots, Cunanin was found dead inside the vessel. Since Cunanin was never brought to trial, is the dock worker entitled to the reward since he did not provide information leading to the "arrest and conviction" of the fugitive?

4. Turilli operates the Jessie James Museum and contends that the man, buried as Jessie James in 1882, was an imposter. He claims that Jessie James lived for many years thereafter under the alias of J. Frank Doulton. Turilli offered a $10,000 reward "to anyone who could prove me wrong." The widow of the desperado's son, maintained that Jessie James was shot and killed by Robert Ford who pleaded guilty to the murder. Ms. James submitted affidavits to Turilli which noted that **(1)** the James Family Bible recited the death of Jessie James in 1882; **(2)** the outlaw's mother often stated that she identified the body of her son; **(3)** a boyhood neighbor of Jessie James swore that he went to the James home right after the shooting and

identified the body; and **(4)** Jessie James' own son declared that when he was seven years old, he heard the fatal shot and saw his father die in his mother's arms. Has the daughter-in-law of Jessie James presented sufficient evidence to fulfill the terms of the offer? *Stella James v. Lou Turilli*, **473 S.W. 2d 757 (Mo. App. 1971).**

5. Great Entertainment Merchandise (GEM) purchases the merchandising rights from performing artists before they go on tour. Vince Neal of Motley Crue, entered into negotiations with GEM to transfer his merchandising rights to the manufacturer in order for GEM to produce various memorabilia for the upcoming concert tour. In anticipation of the licensing agreement, Neal incorporated a "loan out" company. This type of entity is standard in the music industry so that artists can take advantage of certain tax incentives. Neal then transferred his merchandising rights to the "loan out" company, who in turn, assigned those rights to GEM. GEM paid $1 million to the company based upon 800,000 paid concert attendees. Neal also entered into a contract with GEM agreeing to use his best abilities to discharge the obligations undertaken by the artist. The actual attendance was well below the projected numbers. Therefore, GEM requested that Neal pay back part of the money on the basis that the separate agreement signed by the musician was a guarantee agreement. Neal counters that the clause merely guaranteed that he would use his best efforts to perform for 800,000 attendees. Is Neal responsible to pay back the money on the basis that he guaranteed the obligations of the "loan out" company? *Great Entertainment Merchandising, Inc. v. Vince Neal*, **1996 U.S. Dist. Lexis 8973 (N.Y. 1996).**

6. At the start of his employment with Douglas and Lowmenson, Anderson was given an employee handbook which described a progressive disciplinary policy. After three years on the job, Anderson was fired because a box of company pencils was found in his pickup truck. Anderson sued the employer for breach of contract claiming that they did not follow the progressive disciplinary policies outlined in the handbook for unauthorized possession of company property. These progressive discipline policies merely required a written notice for the first offense. May an at-will employee be discharged at any time or is an employer bound by the terms of the employee handbook? *Terry Anderson v. Douglas & Lowmenson Company*, **540 N.W. 2d 277 (Ia. 1995).**

SECTION 8.12
INTERNET REFERENCES

The following Internet references offer more information on contract law, including breach of contract and remedies.

- **http://www.law.cornell.edu/topics/contracts.html**
  Legal Information Institute. This gives a good overview of contract law with federal and state materials and recent Supreme Court decisions.

- **http://www.loc.gov/**
  Library of Congress. This site provides online links to an extensive menu of topics concerning contract law. This site contains documents, photos, movies and sound recordings of American history.

- **http://www.uchastings.edu/plri/fall94/whipple.html**
  This reference provides a link to a research project on the nature and enforceability of electronic contracts.

- **http://www.ira-wg.com/library/contract.html**
  This site provides an overview of contract law.

- **www.wld.com/conbus/weal/wcontra1.htm**
  A discussion of the different types of contracts is contained at this site.

- **www.ilrg.com/forms.html**
  This site shows different kinds of contracts.

CHAPTER 9

PROPERTY LAW

BY: BARBARA SCHNELLER, ESQ.

"Land is, like any other possession, by natural right wholly in the power of its present owner; and may be sold, given or bequeathed, absolutely or conditionally. But natural law would avail little without the protection of the law."

Samuel Johnson

SECTION 9.1
INTRODUCTION

Property includes everything that may be owned, either as **real property** or **personal property**. Real property consists of the land going from the center of the earth to the heavens and everything permanently attached to the land. Personal property includes such things as a car, books, clothes, and furniture as well as bank accounts, stocks, bonds, patents and copyrights. Property law defines and enforces the rights and responsibilities that accompany ownership.

SECTION 9.2
OWNERSHIP

Ownership has often been viewed as a bundle of rights. Owners have certain rights with respect to their property: they may use it, prevent others from using it, lend it to someone else, sell it, give it away, or destroy it. **Title** is the right of ownership. A person who has title to property has all of the rights of ownership. But the idea of title, in a legal context, is more abstract. Courts are often asked to determine who among several contenders has ownership rights to a given piece of property. With respect to real property, a **quiet title** action is used for this purpose. The court listens to the facts presented by everyone who has a claim to the real property and decides who the owner is, i.e., who has title.

It is customary to use **documents of title** to prove ownership, for example, title to a car; a "deed" to a house; or a "bill of sale" for merchandise.

A. Concurrent Ownership

Concurrent or joint ownership occurs when ownership to property is shared and two or more people hold title. The most common forms of concurrent ownership are **tenancy in common** and **joint tenancy with the right of survivorship**. Both forms of concurrent ownership give the co-owners essentially equal rights to the property. Each owner, however, has given up the right of exclusivity, meaning one owner cannot prevent his co-owner(s) from using the property.

The difference between tenancy in common and joint tenancy has to do with what happens when one co-owner dies. In a tenancy in common, if one co-owner dies, his share will pass to his heirs. In a joint tenancy, the right of survivorship means that if one co-owner dies, his share will pass to the surviving co-owner. Thus, if Joe Hodge and Peter Christopher have a joint bank account as tenants in common, either of them may make deposits or withdraw funds. If Joe dies, his share will pass to his heirs, usually the family, and Peter will keep his one-half share. If, on the other hand, Joe and Peter are joint tenants with the right of survivorship, and Joe dies, his share will pass to Peter and now Peter will be the sole owner of the bank account. When property is owned concurrently as joint tenants with the right of survivorship the co-owners give up their individual right to "alienate," or dispose of, the property as they wish at the time of their death. The property is automatically transferred to the survivor.

It is sometimes unclear whether the property is owned as a joint tenancy or as a tenancy in common. When a dispute arises over the form of ownership, courts scrupulously examine the document of title to determine what types of ownership the co-tenants specified or, if the language is ambiguous, what they intended. In Pennsylvania, the issue is determined by a statute, which provides that unless the owners clearly state that the co-tenancy is a "joint tenancy with the right of survivorship," it will be considered a tenancy in common.

As the following case shows, the court's decision on how to classify ownership may be crucial in determining how much a creditor can force a debtor to repay.

UNIVERSITY OF MONTANA V. MARK COE
704 P.2D 1029 (MONTANA 1985)

THIS CASE INVOLVES AN EXECUTION on a bank account to recover student loans under the National Direct Student Loan Program.

The appellant, Mark D. Coe, a former Montana University student, took out a series of student loans under the National Direct Student Loan Program, amounting to $6,437.30. For these loans he was required to sign, through the University, a promisor note pursuant to the National Direct Student Loan Program of the United States. He defaulted on the loans and when later requested, made only one payment of $20. The University, respondent herein, brought suit and obtained a partial summary judgement in the sum of $6,437.30.

Through one of several executions, the University levied against the joint checking account of Mark Coe at the First Bank-Western Montana,

Missoula. The savings account was in the name of "Tammerly or Mark D. Coe," which at the time of execution had a balance of $3,179.23. Tammerly Coe requested the Bank not to release the funds, claiming that the funds did not belong to Mark Coe, bur rather belonged to her and to Jordan Coe, brother to Tammerly and Mark.

Tammerly Coe and her brother, Jordan contend that they deposited the money in the bank and that their brother, Mark, deposited no funds whatsoever. However, one of the exhibits presented to the District Court was a copy of the signature card of the account which listed the names of Tammerly Coe or Mark D. Coe, along with their addresses, which stated that Mark was "the owner of a joint checking account with his sister." Jordan Coe did not sign this account, nor does his name appear on the signature card though he claims he owns $2,000 of the funds in the account. Jordan alleges he gave that amount to Tammerly for safe keeping on his behalf. Tammerly claims the remainder of the funds, less the $2,000 deposited by her brother Jordan, belong to her and that Mark Coe, as previously noted, never made a deposit.

This case is one of first impression addressing the question of whether a joint bank account is subject to execution on a judgment against only one joint depositor, and if so, to what extent. The District Court concluded that the entire account was subject to execution.

The appellants argue that the District Court erred for two reasons. The first reason was that the sole issue that the court was to decide, was who owned the money in the account. Based upon that determination, the court was to decide what amount was subject to execution.

In Montana's cases involving third parties, one joint owner is truly an owner with an unquestionable right to withdraw the entire funds. It is only where one joint tenant seeks to take advantage of the other without third party rights

being affected, that this Court has allowed evidence beyond the joint account signature card and its legal consequences.

In the instant case such third party rights are the primary consideration and therefore no extrinsic evidence was admissible. Mark Coe, Tammerly Coe and Jordan Coe all admit in their affidavit that Mark was an owner of the joint account.

The second issue considers whether the joint account is distinguished from a traditional common law fractional share, and a creditor of one depositor can execute on the whole account. The statutes that control in this matter cover the property and ownership therefore and ownership of joint bank accounts in Montana. They provide as follows:

"Property defined-ownership. The ownership of a thing is the right of one or more persons to possess and use it to the exclusion of others. In this code, the thing of which there may be ownership is called property."

Section 32-1-422 concerning ownership of joint bank accounts in Montana, provides in pertinent part:

"When a deposit has been made or shall hereafter be made in any bank transacting business in this state in the names of two or more persons, payable to either or payable to either or the survivor, or any survivor, such deposit, or any part thereof, or any interest or dividend thereon, may be paid to any of said persons whether the other or others be living or not."

Section 70-1-306 provides: The ownership of property by several persons is either of:

1. "joint interests;
2. partnership interests;
3. interests in common."

In consideration of the controlling issues in this case, the question is whether this is a joint account under our statutory and case law, or a tenancy in common with no survivor. This Court in *Ivins v. Hardy*, **179 P.2d 745,** held that a tenancy in common is created whenever the instrument bringing an estate of two or more persons into existence does not specifically state that the estate created is other than a "tenancy in common." The facts situation concerning the signing of the signature card in *Casagranda v. Donahue*, and the facts situation in this case are different. The card signed in the joint account in **Casagranda** specifically said:

> "The undersigned hereby open an account in your bank as joint tenants and not as tenants in common, and, upon the death of either or any of us, all monies then in this account shall be paid to the survivor or survivors as his, her, or their individual property. All monies hereafter deposited in this account shall likewise be joint tenants and not tenants in common. You are hereby directed to honor checks or orders on this account signed by either or any of us, or survivors of either or any of us."

Under the facts situation in **Casagranda**, we held that the savings account became the individual property of respondent upon the decedent's death. Right of survivorship, which is an essential characteristic of any joint tenancy, cannot be defeated by the executrix of decedent's estate, and any attempt to satisfy the general devises in a will.

In the case at bar the signature card signed by Tammerly D. Coe or Mark D. Coe noted:

"The signature of each person authorized to sign on this account appears on the reverse side of this card and signifies agreement that the account is subject to all applicable rules of this bank now existing or hereafter adopted. I acknowledge receipt of a copy of the Bank's Rules and Regulations Governing Bank Accounts."

The reverse side of the signature card had the following notated at the bottom:

"The undersigned depositor, whose bank account is described on the reverse side, hereby appoints the person(s) whose specimen signature(s) appears above, agent(s) of the undersigned with respect to said bank account with the authority specified in the Bank's posted General Rules and Regulations Governing Bank Accounts."

We find that the major distinguishing characteristic of a joint tenancy as opposed to a tenancy in common is a right of the survivor of each of the co-tenants. We hold, under the facts of this case, that this is a tenancy in common and that the creditor, University of Montana, is entitled to one-half, not the total amount levied against the account currently being held by the Clerk of the Court of the Fourth Judicial District.

The judgment of the District Court is modified and remanded with direction to comply with the provisions of this opinion.

**Hodge, Dodge and Lodge
Attorneys at Law
Memorandum**

To: All Law Clerks

From: Gregory Olan Dodge

Re: Joe's Bank Account

Joe Hodge and his neighbor, Donald Feelgood, decided to open a joint checking account with their golf partner, Osgood Huntington, so that they could put away their golf bets.

Feelgood and Osgood told Joe they would go to the local bank and open the account. They signed the papers saying that all three are joint tenants of the account. Joe didn't sign the bank card because he was unavailable, but the good doctor assured Joe he would be in it. So Joe deposited $500,000 he won from his latest visit to Atlantic City.

Osgood decided he would give A.C. a try, too, since he always envied Joe's luck. He entered a casino, dropped his first quarter in the slot, and drew three cherries, collecting $1 million on his first shot. Immediately, he had the casino wire the money to the joint account. Unfortunately, Osgood wasn't so lucky driving home: He was killed when a casino bus on the Atlantic City Expressway totaled his car at 3 in the morning.

The next day, Joe heard about Osgood's death and he was very upset by the tragic news. Unfortunately, Joe received more bad news when he received a phone call from a woman with whom Joe had an extramarital relationship one year earlier. She told Mr. Hodge that he was the father of a beautiful baby boy. Because the woman needed to support the child in a certain life style, she was forced to file an action against Joe for support. Since Joe failed to appear at the hearing, the court agreed to the tune of $750,000. Joe wrote a check from the joint account he held with Donald and the late Osgood to pay his support obligation. Joe used this secret account so that Estelle wouldn't learn about this latest indiscretion.

When Dr. Feelgood got wind of this, he sued to prevent Joe from withdrawing the money from the account. Feelgood's lawyer claims that since Joe never signed the account, he is not a co-tenant. And, even if he is, the suit claims, he is only a tenant in common, and thus entitled only to $500,000—a third of the account balance.

We think Joe may be a joint tenant with right of survivorship, thus entitling him to $750,000—half of the $1.5 million. Our claim is that the trio intended for the account to be a joint tenancy with right of survivorship. Therefore, upon his death, Osgood's share would have passed to the survivors of the account instead of going to Osgood's heirs. Consider *University of Montana v. Coe* when arriving at your answers to the following questions:

1. Do we have a good case? Why or why not?
2. How does Pennsylvania law apply to this case?
3. What are the advantage and disadvantage of a tenancy in common?
4. What value do you think a joint tenancy with rights of survivorship serves?

ANSWER SHEET
PROBLEM NINE

Name   Please Print Clearly

1. Do we have a good case? Why or why not?

_____

_____

_____

_____

_____

_____

_____

_____

_____

2. How does Pennsylvania law apply to this case?

_____

_____

_____

_____

_____

_____

_____

_____

_____

3. What are the advantages and disadvantages of a tenancy in common?

_____

_____

_____

_____

_____

_____

_____

_____

4. What value do you think a joint tenancy with right of survivorship serves?

_____

_____

_____

_____

_____

_____

_____

_____

B. Other Kinds of Concurrent Ownership

There are special forms of co-ownership for married couples. Most states recognize a **tenancy by the entirety**, which is similar to a joint tenancy because it carries the right of survivorship. It differs from a joint tenancy, however, in that neither spouse can convey his or her interest in the property. In other words, each spouse owns a 100 percent interest in the property. Community property laws apply in several western states. As with a tenancy by the entirety, neither spouse can convey separately his or her interest during life. In some states community property will pass to the surviving spouse if one dies, in others the deceased spouse's interest will pass to his or her heirs. Both a tenancy by the entirety and community property rights will be terminated or severed by a divorce. This property is automatically transferred to a tenancy in common with each owning a half interest. These forms of co-ownership apply to both real and personal property.

NANCY FAZEKAS v. GEORGE FAZEKAS
737 A.2D 1262 (PA. SUPER. 1999)

GEORGE FAZEKAS AND NANCY FAZEKAS were married in 1970 and separated in 1986. On July 15, 1986, wife filed for divorce. Thereafter, a dispute arose over the proceeds of a bar husband and wife sold to Thomas Mangol. As a result of the dispute, $10,000 was placed in escrow with the Prothonotary of Armstrong County. The escrow amount, which was held by husband and wife in the entireties, represented mortgage payments made by Mangol. Wife acknowledges she also may have received additional payments from Mangol that were not part of the escrow funds. Husband died on September 22, 1996, while still married to wife. Because the escrow funds were held by the entireties with husband, wife sought a court Order directing the Prothonotary to pay the funds to her. Her husband's estate opposed such an Order on the basis that wife's receipt of mortgage payments that were not included in the escrow funds, to the exclusion of husband, operated to sever the entireties

estate and converted the escrow funds into joint property. As a result, the estate argued one-half of the escrow funds should be distributed to husband's estate. The court dismissed the pending divorce action and directed payment of the escrow funds to wife. This appeal followed.

The estate argues that wife's receipt of mortgage funds to the exclusion of her husband operated to sever the entireties estate and convert it into an estate of joint ownership whereby husband and wife were each entitled to one-half of the escrow amount.

Our analysis begins with well-established legal principles. A tenancy by the entireties is a form of co-ownership of real or personal property by husband and wife, with its essential characteristic being that each spouse is seized of the whole or the entirety and not of a share or divisible part. When one spouse dies, the surviving spouse takes no new estate; rather, the only change is in the properties of the legal entity holding the estate. For the duration of the entireties estate, either spouse has the presumptive power to act for both, so long as both spouses share the proceeds and neither spouse may appropriate property for his or her own use, to the exclusion of the other spouse, without the consent of the other spouse.

With specific reference to this case, it is well-established that severance of an entireties estate may be achieved only through divorce, a joint conveyance or mutual agreement, either express or implied; a tenancy by the entireties cannot be severed or conveyed away by the independent action of one spouse.

Two elements must be present in order for a court to find that an implied mutual agreement has severed a tenancy by the entireties. First, a misappropriation by one spouse must occur (the offer); second, the other spouse must file suit for an accounting, division or other appropriate relief (the acceptance). It is a two-part test of an offer, consisting of a misappropriation, and an acceptance, consisting of the filing of an action to partition [or other remedy that must be shown.)

Applying this standard to the instant facts, we reiterate wife's concession that she may have received mortgage funds from Mangol and that those funds were retained to the exclusion of husband. This receipt of funds may well have been an implied offer by wife to destroy the tenancy by the entireties. There is no evidence, however, that husband ever filed an action seeking any type of relief at any time prior to his death in 1996. As a result, husband took no ac-

tion that would constitute an acceptance of wife's offer to destroy the entireties estate, despite the fact that he lived for approximately four to five years after wife made her implied offer by receiving mortgage funds from Mangol.

Apparently recognizing that half of the two-part test for severance has not been met, the estate argues that "the time has come to allow the estate of a spouse who has been harmed by misappropriation of marital funds to bring an action for a severance of the entireties' property to prevent injustice on the part of the surviving wrongdoer." In making this argument, the estate is apparently urging us to abandon the acceptance requirement and to permit severance where only an offer is made by one spouse. If we were to endorse this argument, we would necessarily destroy the time-honored principle that a tenancy by the entireties may not be altered by the unilateral action of one spouse. By requiring the joint action necessary for both offer and acceptance, our holding strikes a balance between protection of the wronged spouse's interest in the diverted funds and maintenance of the unity underlying a tenancy by the entireties. We decline the estate's invitation to disturb that balance.

Finally, we note that application of the two-part test standard is not altered by the fact that husband is now deceased. As the Supreme Court has noted, the essential issue in the case is the status of the entireties estate at the time of [the spouse's] death. Here, at the time of husband's death, the tenancy by the entireties had not been severed. As a result, wife was entitled to all funds held in escrow by the Prothonotary of Armstrong County.

C. Encumbrances

As a sole owner or as a co-owner it is possible to give up one or more of the rights of ownership. In real property law, this is called an **encumbrance**. An encumbrance is any right or interest that someone has in another's property. For example, if a homeowner rents her house, she has given the tenant the rights of possession and use. The title to the real property is encumbered: he still owns the house but he no longer has all of the rights of ownership because she has given some to the tenant for the term of the lease.

A bailment is the delivery of personal property by the owner to another person usually for a particular purpose. For example, a bailment is created when a person parks in a public lot and gives the keys to the parking attendant. The owner retains title and expects and has the right to receive the property back. While the bailment is occurring, however, the owner has given up the right to possess and use the property. His rights of ownership have been lessened and his title is encumbered.

SECTION 9.4
PERSONAL PROPERTY

Various legal terms are used to describe items of personal property. **Chattel**, an old English word for cattle, has come to mean all forms of personal property: animate (living), inanimate, tangible or intangible. Tangible personal property refers to physical objects. Personal property that is both tangible and movable is called a **good**. An automobile is an example. Intangible property gives the owner a right rather than a physical object of independent value. For example, the owner of a share of stock in a company has certain rights, such as the right to receive dividends and the right to vote for the corporation's officers. But there is no physical object that goes with it, aside from the stock certificate that says the investor owns a share of the corporation. Other forms of intangible personal property include bank accounts, patents, trademarks, and copyrights.

SECTION 9.5
ACQUIRING TITLE TO
PERSONAL PROPERTY

Personal property may be acquired by purchase, gift, production or possession. The most common way to acquire ownership of personal property is to purchase it. A purchase is the transfer of title from one owner to another for payment or compensation. State law governs the purchase and sale of goods. The states have adopted part or all of Article 2 of the Uniform Commercial Code, a lengthy catalog that details the rights and responsibilities of the sellers and buyers of goods. Federal and state laws, including the Securities Exchange Act and Articles 3 and 4 of the Uniform Commercial Code regulate the purchase and sale of intangibles.

Personal property may also be acquired by gift, a transfer of title to property without payment or compensation. A gift may be made **inter vivos**, while the donor is alive, or it may take effect upon death under the terms of a will or the laws of inheritance. There are three requirements for an inter vivos gift to be valid: **(1)** the donor must intend to make a gift of the property; **(2)** the donor must deliver the property to the donee; and **(3)** the donee must accept the property. If the gift is valid, all the rights of ownership pass from the donor to the donee.

Personal property may also be acquired by production. A person who takes scraps of material and creates a quilt owns the quilt because she has created or produced it by her labor. Similarly, the author of a book owns the copyrights to the book because she produced it. She may, however, transfer those rights to a publisher in order to have the book published.

Possession is another means of acquiring personal property. Historically, if one captured or killed a wild animal he acquired title to the animal. If, however, he captured or killed the animal while he was trespassing on someone else's property, the owner of the land would acquire title to the animal. Today, state game statutes typically provide that the state owns and retains title to the wild animals captured or killed within its borders unless the animal was hunted or trapped pursuant to state laws regulating hunting, trapping and fishing.

If personal property has been abandoned by its owner, title may be acquired by anyone who finds it. Abandoned property is that which has been discarded and the owner has no intention of claiming it. Abandoned property also includes property that was lost and its owner has given up all attempts to find it. An example would be a broken television set, put out for trash by its owner that is picked up and repaired by a teenager. The teenager now has title to the television. As with wild animals, if the abandoned property was discovered while the finder was trespassing, the landowner will acquire title to the property. An exception to this rule protecting the rights of landowners is the doctrine of "treasure-trove." Treasure trove is money, gold, silver or bullion that has been found buried in the earth or hidden in a private place. If the owner of the treasure-trove is unknown, the finder will acquire title as against the owner of the land where it is found.

If property has been lost or mislaid, however, the person who lost or misplaced it retains title. Lost property is that which the owner has involuntarily and accidentally parted with and does not know where to find it. If someone finds lost property he does not acquire title to it as against its rightful owner. The finder will, however, have better title to it than anyone other than the rightful owner. For example, the finder of a wallet that contains identification must return it or be guilty of the tort of conversion. If the wallet contains no identification but the owner learns that the wallet has been found and requests that it returned, the finder must do so.

Most states, however, have statutes that govern lost property. These statutes typically provide that if a finder of lost property turns it over to the appropriate authority and the loss is advertised, then the finder will acquire title to the property. This is the case even against the original owner if its rightful owner does not claim the property within a specified period of time.

Mislaid property has been voluntarily and intentionally placed somewhere by the owner and then forgotten. For example, someone leaves a textbook in the back seat of a friend's car and can't remember where he left it. The friend does not acquire title to the book but becomes an involuntary bailee and has a duty to take care of the book for the owner.

SECTION 9.6
BAILMENTS

A bailment occurs when the owner of an item of personal property gives possession of the item to someone else, usually for a particular purpose. The owner is called the **bailor**, the person in possession is the **bailee**. The bailor continues to have title to the property but has given some of the rights of ownership, possession and use, to the bailee. Bailments can be placed into three categories: **(1)** for the sole benefit of the bailor, e.g., when someone takes care of a friend's dog as a favor; or a friend forgets her gloves at another's house; **(2)** for the sole benefit of the bailee, e.g., when someone lends his car to a friend so he or she can get to work; and **(3)** for the mutual benefit of the bailor and the bailee, e.g., renting a car, taking clothes to the cleaner, shipping a package. Mutual benefit bailments are the most common. Typically one party receives monetary compensation for supplying a good or service to the other.

All forms of bailments have three elements: **(1)** the item is personal property; **(2)** the property is delivered into the possession of another; **(3)** the property is delivered pursuant to an agreement, which may be either express or implied.

Although the rights and responsibilities of the bailor and bailee may be specified in the agreement, there are certain rights and duties implied by law. The bailee has the rights to temporarily possess and use the property for the purposes of the agreement. In addition, the bailee has a right of compensation. Usually the amount of compensation will be expressed in the agreement. For example, if a customer takes a jacket to the cleaners, the shop owner will be entitled to the cost of providing the cleaning service. Even if the amount of compensation is not expressly agreed upon, the bailee will have the right to receive a reasonable amount if it is a mutual benefit bailment. If the bailor does not pay the bailee's compensation, the bailee may retain possession of the item until the bill is paid. This is called a **bailee's lien**. Thus, the cleaner can keep the jacket until the bill is paid.

A bailee also has certain duties with respect to the item. The bailee has the duty to take reasonable care of the item. If the bailee fails to take reasonable care of the property entrusted to him, he will be liable for damages. The bailee also has the duty to return the item at the end of the bailment.

If there is an express agreement between parties the bailee can limit his liability either by a set dollar amount or by type of risk. For example, when you take film to be developed, it is common for the developer to limit its liability to replacing the film if your film is lost or destroyed. This type of limitation of liability is generally valid if it is conspicuous and the bailor has notice of limitation.

A bailor also has certain rights and responsibilities with respect to the bailment. The bailor has the right to have the property returned in the same condition or as altered pursuant to the terms of the agreement. Any service provided by the bailee must be performed in a workman-like manner. The bailor is responsible to notify the bailee of any known or discoverable defects in the property. If the bailor fails to do so, she will be responsible for any injuries that result. For example, someone rents a car and the brakes are not working properly. If the renter is injured in an accident because of the defective brakes, the car rental company will be liable for the injuries because it did not give notice of a defect that it should have discovered.

Municipalities, businesses and property owners have become very protective of their parking areas. Many have contracts with a towing service to remove any vehicle which has been parked in a spot without authorization. What kind of bailment arises when a car is towed to a storage facility because it was illegally parked and is damaged while in the possession of the bailor or towing company? That is the issue in *Hadfield v. Gilcrest.*

MARK HADFIELD v. SAM GILCHRIST
538 S.E.2D 268 (S.C. 2000)

GILCHRIST OWNS A MOTOR VEHICLE towing service and maintains a storage facility for the retention of the towed vehicles. Gilchrist operates under a license issued by the City of Charleston.

Hadfield went to retrieve his 1988 Lincoln Continental from the parking spot where his wife parked the vehicle. The parking spot was on private property owned by Allen Saffer.

Hadfield's wife parked the vehicle on Saffer's property without permission. The vehicle was not in the parking spot when Hadfield arrived as Saffer had called Gilchrist to have the vehicle removed.

Gilchrist towed Hadfield's car to his storage facility. Gilchrist maintained a chain link fence around the storage area, and had an employee on the lot around the clock. The employees' duties included periodically leaving the office to check on the storage area which was some distance away from the office.

Hadfield called to retrieve his vehicle, but was informed he would have to wait until the next morning and pay towing and storage fees. Upon Hadfield's arrival to pick up his car, he paid the fees. When he went to the storage area to collect his vehicle, Hadfield discovered the vehicle had been extensively vandalized. The vandals entered the storage area by cutting a hole in the fence. They vandalized between six and eight vehicles on the lot that night.

Hadfield's attempts to persuade Gilchrist to pay for the damages were futile. Hadfield left the vehicle on Gilchrist's lot as he could not afford to repair it. After more than 60 days elapsed, Hadfield sold the vehicle for $1,000.00.

A bailment is created by the delivery of personal property by one person to another in trust for a specific purpose, pursuant to an express or implied contract to fulfill that trust. Bailment has been defined as the delivery of a chattel for some express or particular purpose upon a contract, that, after the purpose has been fulfilled, then the chattel shall be redelivered to the bailor, or otherwise dealt with according to his directions.

Bailments are generally classified as being for **(1)** the sole benefit of the bailor; **(2)** the sole benefit of the bailee; or **(3)** the mutual benefit of both. Bailments which benefit only one of the parties, the first and second classifications, are often described as gratuitous.

A gratuitous bailment is one in which the transfer of possession or use of the bailed property is without compensation. For instance, a gratuitous bailment arises if the bailment is undertaken as a personal favor. A gratuitous bailee acts without expectation of reward or compensation. To show the bailment was for the sole benefit of the bailor, the bailee must establish that it was not expecting compensation.

By contrast, a bailment for the mutual benefit of the parties arises when one party takes the personal property of another into his or her care or custody in exchange for payment or other benefit.

Although a bailment is ordinarily created by the agreement of the parties, the agreement of the parties may be implied or constructive, and the bailment may arise by operation of law. Such a constructive bailment arises when one person has lawfully acquired possession of another's personal property, other than by virtue of a bailment contract, and holds it under such circumstances that the law imposes on the recipient of the property the obligation to keep it safely and redeliver it to the owner. A constructive bailment may occur even in the absence of the voluntary delivery and acceptance of the property which is usually necessary to create a bailment relationship.

Gilchrist argues he towed the vehicle pursuant to the **Charleston Municipal Ordinances,** and the ordinances are for the sole benefit of the vehicle owners. Accordingly, he contends, the relationship created is a gratuitous bailment. We disagree.

The vehicle owned by Hadfield was plucked by Gilchrist from the private property of Saffer. Gilchrist acted pursuant to the licensing authority under the city ordinance. We conclude a constructive bailment, for the mutual benefit of Hadfield and Gilchrist, was created.

After finding a bailment for mutual benefit exists in this case, we must determine whether Hadfield is entitled to damages.

The degree of care required of a bailee for mutual benefit is defined as ordinary care, or due care, or the degree of care which would be exercised by a person of ordinary care in the protection of his own property.

The burden of proof in this case rests first upon the bailor, Hadfield, to prove a prima facie case. He must show: 1) the goods were delivered to the bailee in good condition; and 2) they were lost or returned in a damaged condition. When the bailor, Hadfield, has so proven, the burden is then shifted to the bailee, Gilchrist, to show that he has used ordinary care in the good's storage and safekeeping.

Hadfield testified regarding the "nice" condition of his vehicle prior to it being towed, and the damage to his vehicle, and the other vehicles on the lot. Thus, Hadfield made out his prima facie case. The burden then shifted to Gilchrist to show that he used ordinary care in protecting the vehicle while in his care.

Gilchrist impounded the cars in a storage lot surrounded by a chain link fence. The person on duty spent time in the office and only visited the storage lot to check on it. The vandal cut a hole in the fence and broke into six to eight cars on the night in question. The fact the guard was not on duty at the impound lot and, considering the only other security for the vehicles was the chain link fence, the trial judge could have concluded Gilchrist failed to exercise ordinary care.

We rule that where a city ordinance is utilized as the legal justification for taking possession of a vehicle on private property, the entity lawfully acquiring possession of the property becomes a constructive bailee as a matter of law. We find a constructive bailment, for the mutual benefit of Hadfield and Gilchrist, was created. We also conclude the burden of proof in a constructive bailment case rests first upon a bailor to prove a prima facie case and, once so proven, the burden shifts to the bailee to show the use of ordinary care in the storage and safekeeping of the property. Accordingly, the order of the lower court is affirmed in favor of the plaintiff and he is awarded $4,030 in damages.

SECTION 9.7
REAL PROPERTY

Real property is land and everything attached to the land. Thus, the owner of a parcel of real estate owns the land itself, any minerals such as oil, ore, or gems located under the ground, the air space above the land, and the buildings, plants and trees attached to the land. Ownership comprises the bundle of rights that allows someone to possess, use, exclude others, encumber or alienate the real estate. There might be a sole owner or there may be co-owners who share these rights of ownership.

The purchase of a home has certain inherent problems. Disputes frequently arise as to what was included in the sale. When the buyers inspected the home, a crystal chandelier hung in the foyer. At the time of settlement, the chandelier has been replaced by a plastic fixture. The seller refuses to give the buyer the chandelier claiming that it is a family heirloom worth several thousand dollars. The buyer maintains that the fixture was part of the realty since it was on display at the time the home was inspected. Who is correct? The answer will depend on whether the item is real or personal property.

The word **estate** is used in real property law to refer to the extent of a person's interests or rights in the property. There are several types of estates; the most common is the fee simple absolute. Its name derives from the same root as "fief" or "feudalism" because the concept of fee land ownership descends from the feudal system. Originally, the term denoted land that was held by a "free holder" in exchange for certain rights or duties paid to the superior lord. In fact, the property system used today—estates in land, eminent domain, alienability, and tenancy—evolved from the feudal system in England and France.

The fee simple absolute estate is the most complete form of ownership of real property. It includes the rights to possess, use, exclude others, encumber and alienate the property. It is not, however, totally unrestricted ownership because the government retains certain rights in privately owned property.

For example, the government has the right to regulate an owner's use of the property through zoning laws, which prescribe which areas of a community may be used for residential, commercial or industrial purposes. Although the owner of the land owns the airspace above it, the United States government has passed various statutes that allow the public to use that airspace for air traffic and commerce.

The government also has the right to tax real property. Typically each parcel of property is taxed based on its value. If the owner does not pay the tax, the government will place a tax lien on the property. The tax lien is a form of encumbrance that allows the government to have the property sold at a sheriff's sale to satisfy the unpaid tax bill.

Finally, the government has the right of eminent domain, the right to take private property for a public purpose. However, the Fifth and Fourteenth Amendments to the United States Constitution require the government to pay just compensation to the private property owner whose land is taken by eminent domain.

Other than the fee simple absolute, there are lesser estates in which the owner of the real property does not have all of the rights of ownership. These include the **fee simple defeasible** and the **life estate**. The fee simple defeasible estate, also known as a conditional or qualified fee, conveys all the rights of ownership so long as the owner complies with a certain condition. For example, if an owner gives her real estate to her church to be used for church purposes, the church receives all of the rights of ownership but the use of the property is restricted to church purposes. If the church attempts to use the property for any other purpose or attempts to alienate the property, the real estate will revert to the original owner or her legal heirs if she is no longer living. The owner, therefore, is said to retain a **reversionary interest** in the property.

A life estate conveys an ownership interest, which is limited to the life of the person holding it. The holder of the life estate has all the rights of possession, use and exclusivity. When that person dies, the estate reverts to the original owner or his heirs or other grantees. They hold the future interest in the property, called the **remainder**.

The remaindermen have the right to receive the property without diminution in value. This right imposes a duty on the life tenant not to allow or commit waste, the deterioration, destruction or material alteration of the property. Waste may include cutting timber for more than household purposes, removing subsurface minerals, and not maintaining the property. If the life tenant commits waste, the remaindermen may seek an injunction to prevent the wasteful conduct.

A leasehold estate is commonly called a **lease**. As mentioned earlier, a lease is an encumbrance upon the property: the landlord is the owner of the property and he has a fee simple absolute estate. But the landlord has given to the tenant the rights to possess and use the property exclusively.

SECTION 9.9 LEASEHOLD ESTATES

The right and responsibilities of the **lessor** (landlord) and the **lessee** (tenant) are usually specified by a written lease agreement. Even in the absence of a written lease, the law provides certain rights and responsibilities. The tenant receives the rights to exclusively possess and use the real estate by the landlord's covenant of quiet enjoyment. In other words, the landlord promises that he will not disturb the tenant's possession and use of the property. If the landlord, or anyone working for the landlord, unreasonably disturbs the tenant's enjoyment of the property, the tenant will have the right to sue for damages or the lessee may elect to terminate the lease under the doctrine of constructive eviction. A constructive eviction occurs whenever the landlord breaches his duties to the extent that the tenant's use and possession of the premises is impossible or extremely difficult. A landlord may enter the premises for reasonable purposes, such as to do maintenance and repair, but many leases require the landlord to give the tenant notice of such entry unless there is an emergency.

A residential tenant also has the right to insist that the premises are fit for human habitation. This right is contained in the landlord's **implied warranty of habitability**, which the law requires to be a part of all residential leases. This warranty, however, does not apply to leases of property for commercial purposes. Lack of heat during winter months, no hot or cold running water, a substantial leak in the roof or pest infestation to the extent it may injure the health of the residents are examples of defects which render the premises uninhabitable. If the premises are not habitable a constructive eviction has occurred.

Many states have passed statutes that provide additional remedies for a breach of the warranty of habitability. These remedies include the withholding of rent and placing the money into an escrow account, or repairing the defect and deducting the cost of the repair from rent. Before engaging in these self-help remedies, the tenant is usually required to give the landlord notice of the problem and an opportunity to repair it. In addition, many local housing ordinances provide that a violation of building and housing codes constitutes a breach of the warranty of habitability.

TERRI JOHNSON v. SCANDIA ASSOCIATES, INC.
717 N.E.2D 24 (IND. 1999)

SOME INDIANA CASES HAVE RECOGNIZED that a warranty of habitability may be implied in a residential lease, giving rise to damages for breach of contract upon appropriate proof. In this appeal, we recognize for the first time that such a warranty may be implied in some leases and explore the conditions under which it may be held to exist.

Scandia Associates, Inc., owns and operates an apartment complex through agent Oxford Management, Co. Terri Johnson sued Scandia and Oxford after suffering physical injuries caused by an electric shock she received when simultaneously touching two kitchen appliances while cooking in her apartment.

We begin our analysis by reviewing the common law development of the warranty of habitability in Indiana. Some describe the changes in landlord-tenant law from the late 1960's onward as a "revolution." Influenced by commentary, the civil rights movement, the "war on poverty," and the exposure of harsh conditions in urban slums, some courts expanded residential tenants bundle of rights.

Indiana has been part of this movement. This Court first imported a warranty of habitability into conveyances of real property when we adopted the opinion in *Theis v. Heuer,* 280 N.E.2d 300 (Ind. 1972). There, the plaintiffs sued the builder-vendor of their new home because substantial defects caused property damage, rendering the house uninhabitable, and deprived them of the benefit of their bargain.

We overruled the doctrine of caveat emptor, holding that a warranty of fitness for habitation may be implied in a builder-vendor's sale of a new house to the first purchaser.

Then, in *Barnes v. Mac Brown & Co.,* Inc. 342 N.E.2d 619 (Ind. 1976), we extended the protection of the implied warranty to subsequent purchases of the house, but limited its scope to latent or hidden defects.

Asked whether a warranty of habitability is implied in the residential leasehold contract, we hold that a landlord could be found liable to his tenant on a breach of implied warranty, at least where there was a housing code and city inspectors had cited the landlord with multiple violations.

A warranty is a promise relating to past or existing fact that incorporates a commitment by the promisor that he will be responsible if the facts are not as manifested. Habitability means reasonably fit for occupation as a dwelling. Thus, when a landlord warrants habitability, the warranty is an affirmative declaration of the apartment's fitness for habitation, that is, as a dwelling place.

When a landlord enters a lease agreement with her tenant, she voluntarily confers certain rights upon the tenant, such as possession and quiet enjoyment for a specific term. She does this in consideration of the tenant's promise to pay rent, not to waste the property, and not to "hold-over" beyond the term. The landlord agrees to this legal relationship after balancing the costs and benefits, and the same is true for the tenant.

Defining a warranty of habitability broadly as a tenant's right to be free from injury might have many effects. A broad definition might cause landlords to increase maintenance of properties, at least where doing so would still produce an economic return. It would undoubtedly prompt landlords to purchase additional insurance, spreading the risk of harm more broadly.

Potential negative outcomes also could flow from a warranty rule on injury—because high standards of upkeep could be discouraged by shifting the risk of liability, and thus economic incentive, from the landlord to the insurer. A contractual right could diminish a tenant's incentive to report or repair defects by eliminating the economic risk of contributory negligence. All of these outcomes would increase the risk of harm to tenants, residents, and guests.

In light of these considerations, we conclude that a warranty of habitability is a landlord's promise to convey to a tenant an apartment suitable for living, and breach of which promise occurs when a landlord fails to tender a suitable apartment.

Even though an implied warranty of habitability is not imposed by law on every residential lease contract, it may be implied in fact in the agreement between landlord and tenant. Contracts and covenants implied in fact arise from the course of dealing between the parties and may be evidenced by acts done in the course of performance or by ordinary practices in the trade.

Johnson does not identify any state or local law as the source of the warranty she pleads as implied in her contract. Moreover, she has not identified any facts demonstrating that a warranty of habitability was either express or implied-in-fact in the agreement.

When a landlord warrants his property to be suitable for living and then breaches that promise by conveying an unsuitable apartment, the tenant's remedy may take several forms, including conveyance of a suitable property, rescission and reformation of the agreement while the tenant retains possession, recision of the contract, or damages at law. The thread tying the remedy to the breach is the nature of the promise: at an agreed rental price, the landlord will convey to the tenant an apartment he warrants as suitable for living.

Consequential damages may be awarded on a breach of contract claim when the non-breaching party's loss flows naturally and probably from the breach and was contemplated by the parties when the contract was made. Thus, to claim consequential damages the tenant must show the parties intended to compensate for personal injury losses caused by the apartment's unfitness. The tenant may prove the promise to compensate personal injury by showing its expression as a contract term or by pointing to evidence showing it to be implied in the agreement.

Johnson complains that her apartment was not suitable for living because its fixtures unexpectedly released an electric current and, second, that her injuries were foresee ably caused by the breaching condition. She does not allege whether the defect was present at the time of entry or arose after taking possession, nor does she have any contention about giving Scandia notice of the defect.

Johnson pleads no facts which, if true, tend to show that the agreement formed with Scandia gives a warranty of habitability. Her failure to plead a factual basis showing that Scandia actually extended the warranty as part of the lease agreement results in a failure to state a valid claim that the warranty was breached.

Indiana's law governing the landlord-tenant relationship has developed a warranty of habitability. The warranty derives from the agreement between the tenant and the landlord and may be express or implied. The existence of an implied warranty may be proven through evidence of the parties' course of dealing or performance and by evidence of ordinary practices in the trade. Where the warranty is express, consequential damages for injury to the person may be available as a remedy. Where the warranty is implied-in-fact, however, consequential damages may not be awarded because personal injury is outside the parties' contemplation. Johnson's complaint does not aver facts tending to show that Scandia warranted the apartment's habitability or that her injury was reasonably foreseeable within a warranty of habitability.

For these reasons, we affirm the trial court and find in favor of the defendants.

The tenant's rights to use and possession, however, are not unlimited. The tenant may not create a nuisance that would interfere with other tenants' rights of quiet enjoyment. The tenant also has a duty not to commit waste by abusing, destroying or altering the premises. If the tenant causes a problem that renders the premises uninhabitable, it will be the tenant's responsibility to repair it.

The primary right of the landlord is to receive rent; if the tenant does not pay it the landlord may evict him. Most states require the landlord to give the tenant notice (frequently 30 days) to vacate the premises. If the tenant does not move out, the landlord may sue. If the tenant has no defense, such as breach of the implied warranty of habitability, the court will order the tenant to vacate the premises within a reasonable time (e.g., 10-30 days). If the tenant still refuses to move out, the landlord may request that the sheriff forcibly remove the tenant from the premises.

The tenant has a corresponding duty to pay rent for the entire term of the lease, which means that if the tenant leaves before the term has expired, she is still responsible to pay the rent unless the landlord is able to lease the premises to someone else. The landlord has a duty to mitigate damages by attempting to lease the property; if he is unable to find a suitable new tenant, however, the original tenant will be liable for the rent until the end of the lease term.

In a residential lease the landlord has a duty to maintain and repair the premises pursuant to the warranty of habitability. If a defective condition renders the premises unfit for human habitation and causes an injury to the tenant or a guest, the landlord will be liable.

The law imposes upon the landlord a duty to maintain common areas in a reasonably safe condition. A common area is used by some or all tenants and remains under the control of the landlord — sidewalks, parking lots, entrance ways, halls, stairs and elevators. If a tenant or guest is injured in a common area because the landlord has failed to maintain it in a safe condition, the landlord is liable for negligence. Some written leases contain an exculpatory clause, which provides that the landlord is not liable for injuries sustained upon the leased premises, whether due to the landlord's negligence or some other cause. Exculpatory clauses are not enforceable in residential leases because they violate the public policy that people need a safe place to live. In commercial leases exculpatory clauses may be enforceable if the tenant is aware of and knowingly agrees to the clause.

BRENDA DEAN V. RICHARD GRUBER
978 S.W.2D 501 (MO. APP. 1998)

ON NOVEMBER 15, 1993, MS. DEAN FELL and sustained injuries while walking down the driveway at 5139 Swope Parkway. At the time, she was visiting her sister, Cynthia Gorman. Ms. Dean claims that her fall was caused, by a loose handrail.

Approximately four months prior to Ms. Dean's fall, Ms. Gorman rented the single-family dwelling from Mr. Gruber. The lease was a verbal month-to-month agreement. Gorman states that the only entrance to the premises was the driveway and, because of the condition of the driveway, the lack of lighting at night, and the slope of the driveway, it was necessary to use the handrail to enter and exit the residence. Gorman also states that she noticed that the handrail was loose shortly after moving in, and reported the problem, to Gruber's employees, but that no repairs were made. Additionally, Ms. Gorman stated that at the time of the verbal rental agreement, she and Gruber agreed that all repairs would be made by the landlord. Gruber's employees were at the house to repair the plumbing, a toilet, a screen door, and a clogged basement drain.

Gruber stated that he was not aware that the hand railing was loose or in a dangerous condition until after Dean's fall, and that "at no time during the tenancy of Cynthia E. Gorman did she report...any dangerous condition of the hand railing, driveway or lighting, of which plaintiff complains" and at no time did he "promise Gorman to fix or repair any reported dangerous condition of the hand railing."

The general rule is that a landlord does not owe a duty to his tenant, and is not liable for personal injuries, received by a tenant or by a tenant's invitee, caused by dangerous conditions of the premises. Exceptions to the rule include: **(1)** when the landlord had knowledge of a dangerous condition, which condition is not discoverable by the tenant, and the landlord fails to make disclosure; **(2)** when the injury occurs in a common area; and **(3)** when a landlord is responsible for making repairs, but negligently fails to do so. The tenant argues that exceptions two and three are applicable here.

First, with respect to the common area exception, Dean argues that the driveway, where the fall occurred, is a common area subject to Gruber's control. Common areas have been defined as areas which are used by more than one tenant such as parking lots, sidewalks and steps as common use areas. If the area is solely used by one tenant, it is not a common area. A landlord is not ordinarily liable for injuries resulting from a defective condition in part of the premises not reserved by the landlord for the common use of two or more tenants, but which are demised to a particular tenant.

This was a single-family home with a driveway which is for the exclusive use of the tenant of the homeowner and her invitees. The driveway was not a common area used by more than one tenant. Thus, the common area exception to the general rule of landlord non-liability is inapplicable.

Next, Dean contends that Gruber maintained control of the premises such that he was responsible for making repairs. A landlord is under no obligation to a tenant to repair unless there is a contract which creates a duty to repair. However, where the landlord retains partial control over the leased premises for the purpose of making repairs, the landlord is then obligated to make such repairs and to keep the premises in a reasonably safe condition for the intended use.

The dispositive inquiry in cases where the tenant claims that the landlord assumed the responsibility of making repairs to the premises, is whether the landlord did retain control of the particular portion of the premises under consideration. This is because the foundation of the landlord's duty is based upon his retention of control.

The possession or control which must be shown in order to make a landlord liable is not to be found merely in the obligation of the landlord to make repairs or the right to enter the premises. There must be some additional fact from which a jury could infer that under the agreement the tenant gave up and surrendered his right to exclusive possession and control and yielded to the landlord some degree or measure of control and dominion over the premises.

Although Dean contends that when she rented the premises from Gruber they agreed that he would make all repairs, such evidence alone does not create a duty. There must be something more from which a jury could infer that under the agreement the tenant gave up and surrendered his right to exclusive possession and control and yielded to the landlord some degree or measure of control and dominion over the premises.

Determination of whether the amount of control a landowner exerts is sufficient to incur liability turns largely on the extent to which the landowner permits the tenant to treat the premises as belonging to the tenant. Viewing all the factual inferences in favor of Dean, there are no facts alleged which would allow a jury to infer Gruber's control of the premises and, in turn, that would demonstrate a duty for him to make repairs. Gruber did not retain a key, or reserve the right to inspect the premises, except with the permission of the tenant. Dean does not present any allegation that Gruber acted on his own initiative with regard to entering the premises or with repairing the premises. The fact that Gruber may have made repairs to the property prior to the injury, does not establish control absent other evidence. There is no assertion of general supervision by Gruber over the premises in order to make the repairs. As a result, the trial court correctly determined that Gruber was entitled to judgment as a matter of law. Judgment affirmed.

SECTION 9.10
ACQUIRING TITLE
TO REAL PROPERTY

There are several ways to acquire title to real property: by gift, adverse possession or purchase. One may acquire title by gift, either inter vivos or testamentary. For an inter vivos gift a deed will be prepared transferring title from the donor to the donee. As with personal property, a valid gift requires that the donor intend to give the property, that the donor delivers it and that the donee accepts it. Because real property cannot be delivered physically, delivery of the deed is a symbolic transfer of possession.

A testamentary gift is one given by a will. For example, a parent may leave property to a child in his or her will. If the owner of real estate dies without a will, the property will be given to the decedent's legal heirs. If there are no legal heirs the property will be transferred to the state under a doctrine called **escheat**, which means that real property lacking an individual competent to inherit will revert to the state.

Title to real property may be acquired by **adverse possession**. Adverse possession requires that the person claiming title to the real estate possess and use it for a statutory period which varies from 5 to 30 years depending on the state. There are five elements required to acquire title by adverse possession; the claimant's use must be: **(1)** adverse or hostile, which means that the claimant is using the property without the owner's permission; **(2)** actual, meaning the claimant is using the real estate in an appropriate fashion; **(3)** open, visible or notorious, which means that the claimant's use of the land is visible to the community to see, it is not secretive; **(4)** exclusive, which means the claimant is asserting the right to exclude others (the land is not being used by the public at large); and **(5)** continuous for the statutory period, meaning that the claimant has continued to use the land for the statutory period without being ejected by the rightful owner.

By far, the most common way to acquire title to real property is to purchase it. The legal process of purchasing a home usually begins when the buyer and the seller enter into an agreement for the purchase and sale of real property.

The agreement specifies how much money is to be paid for the property and when the money is to be paid. In addition, the agreement presumes that the buyer will secure financing. The mortgage contingency clause provides that if the buyer is unable to secure financing, she may terminate the agreement and receive a full refund of any deposit that she has given to the seller or the Realtor, who is the seller's agent. After both parties have signed the agreement, the buyer will apply for a mortgage loan with a bank or mortgage company. If the lender approves the application, it will lend the money to the buyer. The collateral or security for the loan is a mortgage on the real estate purchased by the buyer. A mortgage is a lien that allows the lender to have the property sold at a foreclosure sale if the buyer does not repay the loan.

The agreement normally provides that the seller will convey good and marketable fee simple title to the buyer. A title is marketable if it is free from reasonable doubt as to its validity or if it conveys all the rights of ownership. A title that is encumbered by liens would not be marketable unless the liens were removed.

After the agreement is signed the buyer will usually arrange for a search of the title by a lawyer, or more commonly, by a title insurance company, to be sure that the seller can give a marketable fee simple title. If the seller cannot convey such title, the buyer may terminate the agreement and receive a full refund of his deposit money.

The agreement will specify what items are attached to the property as fixtures and are therefore included in the sale. If any of these items are not to be included in the sale or if there are additional items which are to be included, the parties must state this either in the "Special Clauses" section or by an addendum or rider to the agreement.

A standard agreement will generally provide for remedies in the event the buyer defaults. If the buyer breaks the agreement and refuses to purchase the property for a reason other than buyer's inability to obtain financing or seller's inability to convey marketable title, the seller's most common remedy is to keep the buyer's deposit money as liquidated damages. Liquidated damages are an amount of money agreed upon as damages prior to a breach of the contract. In this case the amount of the buyer's deposit. If the seller breaks the agreement by refusing to convey the property to the buyer, the buyer's usual remedies are either: to seek specific performance, that is sue the seller to convey the property; or to rescind the contract, that is, sue the seller for a return of his deposit and any other money expended to perform his duties under the agreement (such as a loan application fee).

If all goes smoothly after the agreement is signed, the buyer can obtain a mortgage loan and the seller can convey marketable title, the parties will have a closing or settlement, the consummation of the transaction. The buyer will pay the purchase price to the seller and the seller will deliver a deed, which conveys fee simple title to the buyer. Now all of the rights and responsibilities of ownership belong to the buyer.

SECTION 9.11
REVIEW CASES

1. Chavez conveyed his interest in a piece of real estate to himself and his spouse as tenants by the entirety after a lawsuit had been filed against him by Premier Property. Later that year, a judgment was entered against Chavez for $190,000. When Premier learned of the transfer, it moved to set aside the conveyance as being a fraudulent conveyance to defeat the rights of a creditor. Can a debtor transfer property to the other spouse in anticipation of the entry of future judgment in order to defeat the rights of the creditor? *Premier Property Management Inc. v. Claudia Chavez,* **728 N.E. 2d 476 (Ill. 2000).**

2. Bloomfield Club Recreation Association sued the builder of a housing complex for breach of implied warranty of habitability with respect to certain commonly held facilities within their residential development. The builder had created a declaration of covenants agreed to by each homeowner when they purchased their homes, that granted each owner a right of easement to use the common areas, including the club house in the development. The homeowner, however, said the club house was uninhabitable because of defective workmanship. Does the implied warranty of habitability apply to non-residential construction, such as a club house or is it limited to an occupied residence? *Bloomfield Club Recreation Association v. The Hoffman Group, Inc.,* **712 N.E. 2d 330 (Ill. 1999).**

3. Hamilton and Morris were guest at a dinner party where alcoholic beverages were served throughout the evening. Hamilton removed her wrist watch and placed it on the kitchen counter. About midnight, the water in the house went off and Hamilton left kitchen. Morris saw the watch on the counter and picked it up so that it would not be misplaced. Unfortunately, Morris could not remember where she put the watch for safe keeping. Hamilton sued Morris alleging that Morris was the bailee of the watch and that she negligently lost it while it was in her possession. Morris, however, contended that she was a gratuitous bailee and only owed a slight duty of care. Was a bailment created when Morris took possession of the watch? If so, what type of bailment was created and will Morris be responsible for losing the watching? *Andrea Morris v. Marsha Hamilton,* **302 S.E. 2d 51 (Va. 1983).**

4. During his lifetime, the decedent had a romantic relationship with Sharon Clark. During the winter months, they traveled to Florida with a camper. They continued this ritual on an annual basis. The trailer was registered in both of their names. The decedent also maintained a bank account in which he added Clark's name to the account. That account, however, did not have survivorship language on the signature card in the event of the death of Mr. Donahue. How much of the decedent's property is Clark entitled to with respect to the trailer and bank account? *Estate of John Donahue v. Sharon Clark*, **692 N.Y.S. 2d 225 (N.Y. App. 1999).**

5. Rodman was an employee of the Horse Shoe Casino. As an employee, she was required to park her car in an employee's parking lot. One night, her car was stolen from the Casino lot. Employees of the casino were required to park their vehicles in this special lot and they were forbidden to park in the guest parking lot which was much closer to their place of employment. What type of bailment was created and who should win the case? *Robinson Property Group, Ltd. v. Debra Rodman*, **1998 Miss. LEXIS 359 (Miss. 1998).**

SECTION 9.12
INTERNET REFERENCES

For more information on the materials in this Chapter, see the following sites on the Internet:

A. Real Estate

- **http://propertymart.net**
  This company site provides information about real estate, including advertisements about available properties and various related links.

- **www.realtor.com**
  Realtor.com helps prospective home buyers find houses for purchase all over the country. The site also has a reference library relating to real estate matters and offers information about buying, selling, and other important issues regarding real property.

- **www.realestate.com**
  This site discusses home buying, selling, and financing. Specific information is offered on the real estate professional, lending services, appraisers, and service providers.

- **www.vamch.com/reinfo.html**
  This site provides a detailed glossary of real estate and mortgage terms.

- **www.parealtor.org**
  The Pennsylvania Association of Realtors maintains this site devoted to real estate news, consumer information, and updated information regarding real estate legislation.

- **www.legalwiz.com/contract**
  An attorney explains the basics of the real estate contract at this site.

- **http://www.yahoo.com/Government/Law/Property**
  Yahoo's search engine on property law may be located at this address and a person can search through many subjects concerning real estate. For instance, a person can learn about the disposition of property by will.

B. *Intellectual Property*

- **http://www.expresssearch.com/inventor**
  Information about the patent process is offered at this location.

- **www.patentcafe.com**
  This site offers information about patents, including articles, and frequently asked questions on the topic, and discusses other intellectual property issues, such as trademarks and copyrights.

- **http://www.patents.com**
  The law firm of Oppedahl & Larson, LLP, maintains this site which is dedicated to information on intellectual property.

C. *Estate Planning*

- **http://evans-legal.com/dan/**
  Information relating to estate planning is provided at this address, and issues discussed include wills, trusts, and Inheritance Tax.

- **http://www.virginiaweber.com/eplan.htm**
  This site provides answers to frequently asked questions about estate planning.

- **http://www.estateattorney.com/**
  Articles and information about decedent's estate and estate planning is offered at this site maintained by a Pennsylvania estate-planning attorney.

D. Leasing

- **www.pa.landowners.org**
  The Pennsylvania Landowners' Association maintains this site which provides information about the organization and current articles of interest dealing with land that is used for renting to others.

- **http://little.nhlink.net/nhlink/housing/cto/know/kyrr.htm**
  General information about the renting of a property is contained at this location, including a discussion of such issues as eviction, fair housing practices, rent deposits, and terminating a rental agreement.

- **http://www.nolo.com/encyclopedia/articles/ lt/agreement_faq.html**
  Nolo's Legal Encyclopedia provides general information about leases and rental agreements at this address.

- **http://www/ljx.com.practice/landlordtenant/index.html**
  This site provides news, recent articles, cases and statutes relating to landlords.

CHAPTER 10

CYBERLAW

"The Internet is an international network of interconnected computers currently used by approximately 40 million people worldwide."

Reno v. ACLU
117 S. Ct. 2329 (1997)

The internet has had a profound impact on the lives of many people in its short history. Billions of dollars in business are transacted each year through this new technology, and a new communications systems has emerged through e-mail transmissions, instant messages, and websites. By the year 2003, it is projected that Americans will spend over $100 billion dollars for online transactions, and e-commerce will grow to a $1.3 trillion dollar industry. The internet, however, has not been without its legal problems. A number of new legal questions have emerged, such as whether a person may use a photograph found on a website without permission, or whether an individual may download music without paying for it. While the internet may be a new phenomenon, the protection of a person's rights is not. The courts continue to apply traditional principles of property, tort and contract law to a myriad of novel legal issues involving electronic commerce.

The owner of a copyright enjoys a number of valuable property rights, including the exclusive ability to reproduce and distribute copyrighted materials, to display the work publicly, or to create a derivative product, such as the development of a screenplay from a novel. Surprisingly, it is not necessary to register the materials with the United States Copyright Office in order to secure protection. Federal registration merely creates an official record of the copyright. Protection takes effect as soon as the work of authorship is recorded in some fashion–from writing it down on a piece of paper to storing the information on a computer disc. The kinds of literary and artistic endeavors that may be copyrighted encompass such products as books, songs, movies, computer programs, and video games.

The unauthorized distribution of a copyrighted work constitutes an infringement and allows the registered owner of the copyright to seek legal redress, including the recovery of monetary damages, attorneys fees, and court costs. A willful violation of a copyright, such as the "bootlegging" of music for resale, or counterfeiting expensive handbags, may also result in criminal prosecution.

445

The Copyright Act does allow a person to use protected materials without permission under very limited circumstances. This exception is called "fair use" and permits the utilization of a copyrighted work for the restricted purpose of criticism, comment, news reporting, teaching, scholarship, or research. The standard for judging whether the use of a copyrighted work is a "fair use" is based upon the following four factors:

1. The purpose and character of the use, including whether such application is of a commercial nature or is for non-profit educational purposes;

2. The nature of the copyrighted work;

3. The amount and substantiality of the portion used in relation to the copyrighted work as a whole; and

4. The effect of the use upon the potential market for the copyrighted work.

A movie or book review would be an example of "fair use" of copyrighted material. The photocopying of a text book for resale to other students would be a copyright infringement.

Playboy Enterprises, Inc., has achieved a great deal of notoriety for its magazine and product lines, and it has been very aggressive in protecting its name and merchandise from unauthorized use. In fact, several lawsuits have been filed by this adult entertainment company dealing with claims of misappropriation of their property rights through various internet applications.

Playboy Enterprises, Inc. v. George Frena involves a case in which the defendant was accused of infringing on Playboy's copyright to a number of photographs from its magazine. The pictures of Playboy models were posted on the defendant's website for any of the site's paying customers to view and download. Frena admitted that the photographs were copied from Playboy materials, but he asserted the defense of "fair use" in order to negate any copyright violation. While the actual infringement by the defendant was minor in nature, the court found Frena liable for a copyright violation. The federal court judge noted that if this type of conduct became widespread, it would adversely affect Playboy and deny the publisher of considerable revenue.

PLAYBOY ENTERPRISES, INC. V. GEORGE FRENA
839 F. SUPP. 1552 (M.D. FLA. 1993)

GEORGE FRENA OPERATES A COMPUTER bulletin board service, Techs Warehouse BBS ("BBS"), that distributed unauthorized copies of Playboy's copyrighted photographs. For a fee, or to those who purchase certain products from Frena, anyone with an appropriately equipped computer can log onto BBS. Once logged on, subscribers may browse through different BBS directories to look at the pictures. One hundred and seventy of the images that were available on BBS were copies of photographs taken from Playboy's copyrighted materials.

Defendant admits that these materials were displayed on his BBS, that he never obtained authorization from Playboy, and that each of the accessed computer graphic files on BBS is substantially similar to copyrighted Playboy photographs.

The *Copyright Act of 1976* gives copyright owners control over activities of commercial value. The statute provides that:

> ...the owner of a copyright...has the exclusive rights to do and to authorize any of the following: **(1)** to reproduce the copyrighted work in copies...; **(2)** to prepare derivative works based upon the copyrighted work; **(3)** to distribute copies...of the copyrighted work to the public... and **(4)** in the case of...pictorial ...works...to display the copyrighted work publicly.

Engaging in any of these categories without the copyright owner's permission violates the exclusive rights of the copyright owner and constitutes infringement of the copyright, reserved to the copyright owner, and usurpation of that right constitutes infringement. There is no dispute that Defendant Frena supplied a product containing unauthorized copies of a copyrighted work.

Defendant Frena argues that the affirmative defense of "fair use" precludes a finding of copyright infringement. "Fair use" describes limited and useful forms of copying and distribution that are tolerated as exceptions to copyright protection.

The *Copyright Act* mandates four factors which courts shall consider in determining fair use:

> [T]he fair use of a copyrighted work. . . for purposes such as criticism, comment, news reporting, teaching, scholarship or research, is not an infringement of copyright. In determining whether the use made of a work in any particular case is a fair use, the factors to be considered shall include:
>
> 1. the purpose and character of the use, including whether such use is of a commercial nature or is for non-profit educational purposes;
> 2. the nature of the copyrighted work;
> 3. the amount and substantiality of the portion used in relation to the copyrighted work as a whole; and
> 4. the effect of the use upon the potential market for or value of the copyrighted work.

Defendant Frena's use was clearly commercial. BBS was provided to those paying twenty-five dollars ($25) per month or to those who purchased products from Defendant Frena. One who distributes copyrighted material for profit is engaged in a commercial use.

The second factor is the "nature of the copyrighted work." The copyrighted works in this case are in the category of fantasy and entertainment. Therefore, the second factor works against Frena's fair use defense.

Regarding the third factor, the amount and substantiality of the portion of the copyrighted work used, the Supreme Court has directed a qualitative evaluation of the copying of the copyrighted work. That is, a small degree of taking is sufficient to transgress fair use if the copying is the essential part of the copyrighted work.

There is no doubt that the photographs in Playboy magazine are an essential part of the copyrighted work. By pirating the photographs for which Playboy has become famous, Defendant has taken a very important part of Playboy's copyrighted publications.

The fourth factor, the "effect of the use upon the potential market for or value of the copyrighted work," is "undoubtedly the single most important element of fair use, since a proper application of fair use does not impair materially the marketability of the copied work." This factor poses the issue of "whether unrestricted and widespread conduct of the sort engaged in by the defendant would result in a substantially adverse impact on the potential market for or value of the plaintiff's present work." 3 Melville B. Nimmer, *Nimmer on Copyright* § 13.05[A], **at 13.102.61-62 (1993).**

Obviously, if this type of conduct became widespread, it would adversely affect the potential market for the copyrighted work. Such conduct would deny Playboy considerable revenue to which it is entitled for the service it provides.

Defendant Frena infringed Plaintiff's copyrights; specifically, the 170 image files in question in 50 of Plaintiff's copyrighted magazines. The Court finds that the undisputed facts mandate partial summary judgment that Defendant Frena's unauthorized display and distribution of Playboy's copyrighted material is a copyright infringement. Plaintiff's Motion for Partial Summary Judgment is granted.

SECTION 10.3
TRADEMARK INFRINGEMENT

Federal trademark law is regulated by the *Lanham Act* which defines a trademark as a word, name, symbol or slogan which identifies the origins of a product or service from those of a competitor. For instance, "Scotch" is a trademark for tape manufactured by 3M, and "Crest" is a form of toothpaste distributed by Proctor and Gamble. Four interconnected circles is the symbol for Audi automobiles and "You deserve a break today" is a slogan registered to McDonalds. These trademarks are synonymous with a specific product and its reputation in the market place. Only the owner of a trademark may use the name or symbol on the product it was intended to identify.

A trademark infringement occurs when there is a likelihood of confusion as to the source, origin, or sponsorship of a product in a commercial environment. Elements that will be examined in order to determine whether there is a likelihood of confusion between the products include:

1. Product similarity, including sight, sound, and meaning;

2. Strength of the trademark as demonstrated by the amount of consumer recognition and degree of advertising;

3. Evidence of actual confusion among consumers; and

4. Similarities of channels used to market or sell the product.

Pepsi could not market a soda line called "Koka-Kola" and feature a polar bear sipping the soft drink. This would constitute a trademark infringement because of the obvious likelihood of confusion with Coca-Cola. Similarly, a fast-food restaurant specializing in fried chicken could not open a store named Kansas Fried Chicken and feature an elderly gentleman with a beard advertising the product under the banner "KFC."

However, not every reference to a well-known trademark constitutes an infringement. Playboy has created a niche in the world of adult entertainment by featuring a model who is selected as the "Playmate of the Month." At the end of the year, one woman is selected from the group of twelve and is dubbed the "Playmate of the Year." In *Playboy Enterprises, Inc. v. Terri Welles*, the question presented is whether a former "Playmate of the Year" may use this designation on her website without violating Playboy's registered trademark in the phrase.

PLAYBOY ENTERPRISES, INC. v. TERRI WELLES
7 F. SUPP. 2D 1098 (S.D. CAL. 1998)

PLAYBOY ENTERPRISES, INC. (PLAYBOY) FILED a Complaint against Terri Welles, which consists of several causes of action including trademark infringement.

Playboy has two websites. Its free website, **http://www.playboy.com,** has become one of the most popular sites on the Web and is used to promote its magazine, goods, and services. Its other website, the "Playboy Cyber Club," **http://www.cyber.playboy.com,** is devoted to promoting current and former Playboy models.

Playboy owns federally registered trademarks for the terms Playboy, Playmate, Playmate of the Month, and Playmate of the Year. The term Playmate of the Year is sometimes abbreviated "PMOY."

Defendant Welles is a self-employed model who began her modeling career with Playboy magazine in 1980. Ms. Welles appeared on the cover of Playboy magazine and was subsequently featured as the "Playmate of the Month." Ms. Welles received the "Playmate of the Year" award in 1981.

On June 29, 1997, Welles opened a website, **http://www.terriwelles.com,** which includes photographs of herself, a fan-club posting board, and a listing of personal appearances. The domain name for defendant's site is "terriwelles," the heading for the website is "Terri Welles— Playmate of the Year 1981." Each of the pages uses "PMOY '81" as a repeating watermark in the background. Eleven of the fifteen free web pages include a disclaimer, which indicates that the website is not endorsed by Playboy.

Since 1997, defendant has been in contact with plaintiff about the creation of her website. Defendant claims that plaintiff informed her that she could identify herself as the "Playmate of the Year 1981" on her proposed website. According to defendant, Hugh Hefner initially complimented her website and encouraged her use of the title "Playmate of the Year 1981." Mr. Hefner later informed defendant that use of Playboy's trademarks were restricted; instead, he invited defendant to join Playboy's new Cyber Club. Defendant refused this invitation, and Playboy continued to demand that defendant remove the "Playmate of the Year" title from the home page.

Plaintiff has moved to enjoin defendant from using the trademarked term "Playmate of the Year" in the title of her home page.

Plaintiff argues that defendant's use of the Playboy and Playmate trademarks in conjunction with her website is likely to cause confusion, mistake or deception. Specifically, Playboy avers that these alleged infringements are harming it since websurfing consumers are likely to believe that defendant's website is authorized or approved by Playboy when it is not. Defendant contends that her use of the title Playmate of the Year is merely a descriptive use of those terms so as to identify herself to her customers.

It is undisputed that the term Playboy has gained widespread public recognition and is distinctive due to the success and popularity of Playboy magazine and related publications. However, the other trademarks such as Playmate are not only trademarks related to Playboy magazine, but they are titles bestowed upon particular models who appear in that magazine. Much like Academy Award winners, Playboy Playmates are given a title which becomes part of their identity and adds value to their name.

The problem in this case is that the trademarks that defendant uses, and the manner in which she uses them, describe her and identify her. Terri Welles was "Playmate of the Year for 1981."

The "fair use" defense forbids a trademark registrant to appropriate a descriptive term for his exclusive use and so prevent others from accurately describing a characteristic of their goods. Ms. Welles has used the trademark term Playmate of the Year to describe herself. Ms. Welles earned the title of "Playboy Playmate of the Year" in 1981 and has used that title ever since, without objection from Playboy.

It is evident that Ms. Welles has minimized her references to Playboy on her website and has not attempted to trick consumers into believing that they are viewing a website endorsed by Playboy. She does not use Playboy or Playmate in her domain name, she does not use the classic Playboy bunny logo, she inserted disclaimers which clearly state that the website is not endorsed by Playboy, and the font of the Playmate of the Year 1981 title is not recognizable as a Playboy magazine font. Defendant is selling Terri Welles and only Terri Welles on the website. There is no overt attempt to confuse the websurfer into believing that her site is a Playboy-related website.

In **Prestonettes v. Coty, 264 U.S. 359, 368, 44 S.Ct. 350, 68 L.Ed. 731 (1924)**, Justice Holmes noted that "[w]hen the mark is used in a way that does not deceive the public we see no such sanctity in the word as to prevent its being used to tell the truth. It is not taboo." In this case, Ms. Welles has used Playboy's trademarks to identify herself truthfully as the "Playmate of the Year 1981." Such use is not "taboo" under the law. As such, the court denies plaintiff's Motion for a Preliminary Injunction.

Trademarks are categorized according to their inherent distinctiveness and degree of protection afforded by the law. In descending order of importance, these marks are: **(1)** fanciful, **(2)** suggestive, **(3)** descriptive, and **(4)** generic.

A fanciful mark consists of made-up words which serve as a product's brand name, such as Kodak, Sunoco, Cisco, and Pepto-Bismol. Because these marks are inherently distinctive, they receive the greatest protection against infringement.

A suggestive mark requires imagination in order to figure out the nature of the product which the mark represents. Ocean Spray, Handiwipes, Orange Crush, and Chicken of the Sea are examples of words which do not easily disclose the nature of the product which they represent. Through advertising, however, the public is able to associate the mark with a specific product. This category of trademark is also considered inherently distinctive and entitled to protection.

A descriptive mark does not identify the source of the goods. Rather, it describes some feature or characteristic of the product, such as Instant Hot, Quick Print, All Season, or No-Fat. This type of mark will not receive protection unless the term has achieved a secondary meaning. That distinction occurs when the public recognizes a particular mark as an indicator of quality. For instance, Rita's Water Ice has achieved a secondary meaning that everyone associates with water ice, even though Rita is a person's first name which would not normally be protected.

A generic mark enjoys no protection under the *Lanham Act,* since it merely describes a type of product regardless of its source. Examples include shredded wheat, pub, aspirin, cellophane, and orange juice.

It is not always easy to figure out which category is the proper fit for a mark, which frequently forces a party to seek court intervention when a trademark infringement is suspected.

Tsiolis v. Young (a/k/a **Dr. Dre**) provides a good overview of trademark law and offers an explanation of the various types of marks. The facts of the Dr. Dre case deal with use of the name **"Aftermath"** and whether that mark is entitled to trademark protection.

CYRIAKOS TSIOLIS V. ANDRE YOUNG (A/K/A "DR. DRE")
946 F. SUPP. 1344 (N.D. ILL. 1996)

THIS IS AN ACTION FOR TRADEMARK INFRINGEMENT and trademark dilution. It arises out of Defendants' present and threatened use of the name "Aftermath" in connection with his promotion of popular music works.

Tsiolis organized a "heavy metal" musical group in 1985. In 1986, the band members agreed upon a name for the band, "Aftermath". In 1991, Tsiolis obtained a trade name registration for the name "Aftermath."

Defendant Andre Young is a well-known musician and producer of popular music, including music fitting within the genres of rap, hip-hop, and rhythm and blues. He is known in the music world as "Dr. Dre." Dr. Dre either produced or recorded over twenty albums, of which consumers purchased thirty million copies.

Dr. Dre selected the name "Aftermath" because the word signifies both the discontinuation of his relationship with Death Row Records, and the resulting solo venture by Dr. Dre, i.e., the "aftermath" of his separation with Death Row Records. Thereafter, Dr. Dre formed Aftermath Entertainment ("AE").

The first album to be released on the new AE record label is named "Dr. Dre Presents...The Aftermath@.

The word "Aftermath," meaning "the period immediately following a usually ruinous event," Webster's Ninth New Collegiate Dictionary 63 (ed. 1986), is a popular term in the music industry. Between 1984 and 1994, at least eight different songs bore the title "Aftermath" or "The Aftermath." In 1966, the musical group The Rolling Stones released an album entitled "The Aftermath," of which the public bought over a million copies.

A preliminary injunction is an extraordinary remedy, which the court will enter only in extraordinary circumstances. In order to obtain a preliminary injunction, Tsiolis must demonstrate (1) a likelihood that he will prevail on the merits of his claim for relief, (2) an absence of adequate legal, rather than equitable remedies, and (3) that he will suffer irreparable harm without injunctive relief. Should the court find that Tsiolis has established all three above elements, it must then weigh the suggested harm to Tsiolis with the potential injury to defendant.

Tsiolis' federal trademark registration for "Aftermath" is prima facie evidence of the validity of the mark. However, it is well-settled that the presumption of validity may be overcome by a showing that the registered mark is either generic, or, in some cases, descriptive. This is because a registered trademark is not a property right or other legal entitlement, like a copyright or a patent, but merely an identifier of source.

Marks are classified into five categories of increasing distinctiveness: (1) generic, (2) descriptive, (3) suggestive, (4) arbitrary, and (5) fanciful. The level of trademark protection available differs within each mark category. Generic terms receive no trademark protection; descriptive marks are protected only if the mark has achieved A secondary meaning@ in the relevant community; and suggestive, arbitrary, and fanciful marks are deemed inherently distinctive, and thus entitled to full protection.

A **generic term** receives no protection under trademark law. Whether a term is generic is a question "of linguistic usage," If a word appears in a standard dictionary in lower case, "this would be powerful evidence that the term was generic, because nouns and other nominatives listed in dictionaries, save for the occasional proper name, denote kinds rather than specific entities.

On the other hand, **descriptive words**, such as "bubbly" champagne, are terms that "merely describe the ingredients, qualities, or characteristics of an article of trade or a service. Descriptive words are protectable marks only if they have acquired secondary meaning; that is, only if the consuming public would think of the word not as descriptive, but as the name of the product (i.e., "Holiday Inn"). Trademarks that are **fanciful** (i.e., made up, like Kodak or Exxon), arbitrary (e.g., Black & White scotch), or **suggestive** (e.g., Business Week or Coppertone) are protectable in that the use of the mark would almost certainly cause a likelihood of confusion.

The court finds that the term "aftermath" is a term undeserving of trademark protection. In both Webster's Ninth New Collegiate Dictio-

nary and Webster's: New Riverside University Dictionary, the noun "aftermath" appears entirely in lower-case letters. The term is neither fanciful, arbitrary, nor suggestive. Thus, the only two categories within which the word must fit are the generic and descriptive categories.

Whether the term fits into either the generic or descriptive category is a close call, but the court need not make such a determination. Assuming the word "aftermath" is non-generic, and thus descriptive, the word has yet to achieve a "secondary meaning" in the music world. Unlike, The Beatles," the mention of the word "aftermath" in the music community neither connotes a specific band, nor automatically conjures up visions of the heavy metal band in which Tsiolis is a member. Therefore, giving Tsiolis the benefit of the doubt that the word "Aftermath" is descriptive and, not generic, the court nevertheless finds the word +to be undeserved of trademark protection.

Had the court not found the term "Aftermath" to be a mere descriptive term, it would have found that no likelihood of consumer confusion would result from the coexistence of the Band "Aftermath," the Album "The Aftermath," and "Aftermath Entertainment."

Defendants' use of the mark does not interfere with the highly restricted scope of protection afforded Tsiolis' mark. Defendant's markets are wholly different from those of Tsiolis and the Band. Dr. Dre will spend millions to promote the Album and AE, both nationally and internationally, in record stores aimed at the mainstream public. The market in which Dr. Dre, the Album, and AE will permeate is far-reaching. Dr. Dre is a musician with worldwide fame and recognition, and his breakup with Death Row Records only increased the public's awareness of him and his new Album. In short, Defendant's markets are "far removed from those of the trademark holder Tsiolis." Dr. Dre's product, marketing, and consumers, are dissimilar to those of Tsiolis. Thus, the protections afforded the trademark do not interfere with Dr. Dre's use of the word "Aftermath." Because the weak strength of Tsiolis' mark affords the mark very narrow, limited protection, the court finds this factor to weigh in Defendant's favor, as well.

In conclusion, the court denies Tsiolis' motion and, sets the matter for an expedited trial. Tsiolis has not shown that the public, and the Band's fans, will believe that Tsiolis and the Band are affiliated with Defendant or that Tsiolis sold his rights to endorse Defendant and the Album. Moreover, given the narrow protection afforded Tsiolis' mark, it is unlikely that the popularity of Defendant's AE venture and promotion of the Album will result in Tsiolis losing all value of his mark in the Chicago area.

America Online is the world's largest online service, with more than twenty-seven million subscribers who transmit 150 million e-mail messages on a daily basis. For more than ten years, "You've Got Mail" has greeted AOL users whenever a member has a new message. At the same time that this folksy voice is heard, the icon of a yellow envelope emerging from an old-fashioned mailbox appears, which provides the visual notice of a new message.

In 1998, AT&T added e-mail to its AT&T World Net Service with a "You Have Mail" window which, like AOL, included an old-fashioned U.S. mailbox logo. This prompted a lawsuit from AOL for trademark infringement. The court held that the phrase "You've Got Mail" consisted of common English words used as a mark for their ordinary meaning, so that the phrase cannot be appropriated by AOL for their exclusive use. Numerous computer books and other internet providers describe the receipt of e-mail with variations of the "You Have Mail" theme. Therefore, the court reasoned that the words are generic and cannot be protected. The court also found that AOL's "Buddy List" and "Instant Message" designations are generic marks that anyone may use. *America Online, Inc. v. AT&T Corp.*, **64 F. Super. 2d 549 (E.D. Va. 1999).**

The United States Patent and Trademark Office maintains a website that allows a person to conduct an online search of its data bank to see if a name has already been registered. Their address is: **www.uspto.gov.**

SECTION 10.4
DOMAIN NAMES

The name of a business has very important marketing implications and can determine the success or failure of a business venture. With the growing popularity of the internet, companies strive to obtain a domain name or website that is identical to or similar with their product line or business identity. After all, logic dictates that a customer will try to locate a website by logging onto a name that is similar to the name of the company that the customer is seeking to find.

While businesses that do not compete against each other can share variations of a similar name, only one entity can register a specific domain name. For instance, the name "eagles" may refer to a football team, rock group, investigative service, wildlife refuge, or the Boy

Scouts. However, only one of these entities may be assigned the domain name **www.eagles.com.** Therefore, trademark disputes involving domain names have been the source of a great deal of litigation. Much like telephone numbers, internet subscribers register addresses which are used to identify their websites. The internet user may choose any name, so long as it has not been registered by someone else. And much like an area code for a telephone number, each internet address must also have a common denominator. In the case of a domain name, the area code is not a number but a designations such as: .com, .net, .org, .edu, or .gov. These designations are made according to the purposes of the websites and their organizations. For instance, the marker ".edu" is associated with educational endeavors or academic institutions, and ".gov" refers to a governmental affiliation.

Domain names are assigned on a first-come, first-served basis without any type of investigation by the registering company of whether the name violates a prior trademark.

This absence of a monitoring system has encouraged a number of entrepreneurs to register the domain names of well-known companies or individuals in the hope of exacting a financial reward when the trademark owner or famous person wishes to use the name as an internet address. Others purposely register misspellings of a name, anticipating that the site will be frequented by people who incorrectly type the address or who are unaware of how to properly spell the domain name. Since the enterprise is paid by advertisers for each visit or "hit" to the site, this practice can be financially rewarding. This "bad faith" intent to profit from the reputation of another person's name is called "cyberpiracy" or "cybersquatting."

In order to protect businesses and consumers against the improper registration of domain names and to promote the growth of electronic commerce, Congress has enacted the ***Anticybersquatting Consumer Protection Act.*** This legislation makes it difficult for entrepreneurs to lay claim to a domain name that is similar to a well-known person, company, or product line for the purpose of receiving a windfall profit.

Testimony was presented during the Congressional hearings on this piece of legislation to illustrate some of the many abuses that have surfaced involving domain names. For instance, when Mobil and Exxon went public with their proposed merger, an individual registered every possible variation of a resulting domain name, including **"mobil-exxon.com," "exxon-mobil.com,"** and **"mobilexxon.com."** Similarly, a representative of Warner Brothers reported that the company was asked to pay $350,000 for the rights to the domain names of **"warner-bros-records.com"** and **"warnerpictures.com."**

The *Anticybersquatting Consumer Protection Act* prohibits the registration or use of a domain name that is identical to, confusingly similar with, or dilutive of a trademark or name of another with the bad faith intent to profit from the goodwill of that mark. Not only may the cyberpirate lose the ownership of the domain name, but the entrepreneur may be required to pay actual damages to the aggrieved party, such as lost profits, or statutory damages in an amount no less than $1,000 and not exceeding $100,000 per domain name. These damages can increase quickly, to surprisingly high amounts.

One of the major ways in which cybersquatters can profit off of domain names is through online advertisements, which is a thriving business. Advertisers pay between 10 and 25 cents each time an internet user clicks on one of their ads posted on a website, and according to the Internet Advertising Bureau, between 8 and 9 billion dollars was generated in advertising revenues during the year 2000. *Electronics Boutique Holding Corp. v. Zuccarini*, **54 U.S.P.Q. 2d 1705 (E.D. Pa. 2000)** involved a cypersquatter who improperly registered the domain name of "Electronics Boutique" in a variety of misspellings in order to generate advertising revenue from each site visit. Statutory damages in the amount of $500,000 were awarded to the plaintiff in this case, along with legal costs, because of this improper registration.

The Anticybersquatting Consumer Protection Act should send a clear signal to those entrepreneurs who improperly register a domain name that they will be held accountable for their actions.

The *Internet Corporation for Assigned Names and Numbers (ICANN)* a non-profit corporation is recognized by the United States government as the business which coordinates the management of the Internet's domain-name system and IP address numbers. It was created in 1998 by a broad coalition of Internet's business, academic, technical and user communities. All those who register a domain name with this corporation are required to submit disputes to an approved dispute resolution service, or they must file a lawsuit against the domain-name holder in a court of proper jurisdiction. If the parties proceed to arbitration, either side may litigate an adverse determination in court. ICANN is located at **http://www.icann.com.**

The *World Intellectual Property Organization (WIPO)* is the leading dispute resolution service for disagreements arising out of the registration and use of internet domain names. This international organization has rendered hundreds of decisions involving domain names disputes dealing with a number of Fortune 500 companies and celebrity personalities. For instance, Julia Roberts brought a claim against Russell Boyd over his registration of the domain name "**juliaroberts.com,**" and she was successful in obtaining a transfer of the Internet address. The Arbitration Panel found that Boyd had improperly registered not only the domain name of Ms. Roberts, but that of several other famous movie and sport stars as well. *Julia Fiona Roberts v. Russell Boyd,* **WIPO Case No. D2000 - 0210.** Pizza Hut successfully retrieved the name "**pizzahut.org.**" from an entrepreneur who registered the name in bad faith. *Pizza Hut v. R. J. Inc.,* **WIPO Case No. D2000 -0939.** The World Wrestling FedEration was awarded the names of "**www.wwf.com**" and "**www.stonecold.com,**" even though these domain names had been previously registered to Matthew Bessette. The Arbitrators found that the domain names were confusingly similar to the marks "**WWF.com**" and "**stonecold.com.**" *World Wrestling Enterprises, Inc. v. Matthew Bessette,* **WIPO Case No. D2000 - 0256.**

Yet all domain names disputes are not this easy to resolve. In order to obtain a disputed domain name, the complainant must prove three elements:

1. That the disputed domain name is identical or confusingly similar to the trademark or service mark to which it has rights;

2. That the respondent has no rights or legitimate interests with respect to the domain name; and

3. That the disputed domain name has been registered and is being used in bad faith.

What comes to mind when the reader hears the word "sting"–a bee, a wrestler, a woman's basketball team from Charlotte, a junior hockey league team in St. Louis, or an elaborate confidence game involving undercover police? Gordon Sumner is a world-famous musician and recording artist who has used the name "Sting" for more than twenty years. When Sumner went to register the domain name "**sting.com,**" he found that the marker had already been registered, so he filed a claim with WIPO in order to retrieve the name. The Arbitration Panel denied his request, because the mark is not the singer's real name, and the term has various meanings in the English language.

WIPO ARBITRATION AND MEDIATION CENTER
GORDON SUMNER, A/K/A STING V. MICHAEL URVAN
CASE NO. D2000-0596 (2000)

1. The Parties

1.1   The Complainant is Gordon Sumner, professionally known as "Sting", a citizen of the United Kingdom who maintains a residence in the United States. The Respondent is Michael Urvan, of Marietta, Georgia.

2. The Domain Names and Registrar

2.1   The domain name the subject of this Complaint is "sting.com."

2.2   The Registrar of this domain name is Network Solutions, Inc.

3. Factual Background

Complainant's Activities and Trademarks

3.1   In his Complaint, the Complainant asserted he is a world-famous musician, recording and performing artist who has, for over twenty years, rendered high-quality musical services under his name, trademark and service mark STING. The name STING has become synonymous in the minds of the public with the Complainant and his activities in the music industry.

3.2   The Respondent asserted that there are 20 trademark registrations of the word STING in the US, but none of them are registered by the Complainant. The word STING is a common word in the English language, and so registration of it as a domain name is not a violation of the Uniform Policy.

Respondent's Activities

3.3   Until the Respondent was contacted by a representative of the Complainant, the Respondent made no use of the domain name. During February of 2000, and again during May of 2000, the Respondent offered to sell the domain name to the Complainant for $25,000.00.

3.4   In his Response, the Respondent asserted that he has been using the nickname "Sting" publicly on the Internet for at least 8 years. The Respondent registered the domain name in July 1995, approximately 5 years before this dispute was commenced.

4. Parties' Contentions

The Complaint

4.1   The Complainant contends that each of the three elements specified in paragraph 4(a) of the Uniform Policy are applicable to the domain name which is the subject of this dispute.

4.2   In relation to element (i), the Complainant contends that the domain name is identical to the Complainant's unregistered trademark and service mark STING.

4.3   In relation to element (ii), the Complainant contends that the Respondent has no rights or legitimate interests in the domain name in issue.

4.4 In relation to element (iii), the Complainant contends that evidence of bad-faith registration and use is established by the following circumstances. First, the Respondent offered to sell the domain name to the Complainant for $25,000. Secondly, the Respondent has used the domain name to link to the "GunBrokers.com" website, and as such is intentionally attempting to attract, for commercial gain, Internet users to an online location by creating a likelihood of confusion with the STING mark as to source, sponsorship, affiliation, or endorsement. Thirdly, because the Complainant's STING mark has a strong reputation and is world-famous, the Respondent can make no good faith use of the domain name.

The Response

4.5 In relation to element (i), the Respondent admits that he registered that domain name "sting.com," and that the domain name is identical to the STING mark. However, the Respondent challenges the Complainant's claim to owning the STING mark, and exclusively associated with the Complainant and so entitled to protection against dilution. In particular, the Respondent contends that the trademark STING has been the subject of 20 registrations in the United States, none of which have been granted to the Complainant.

4.6 In relation to element (ii), the Respondent contends that his use of the nickname "Sting" on the Internet for at least 8 years has given him a legitimate interest in the domain name.

4.7 In relation to element (iii), the Respondent contends that he did not register the domain name in bad faith. In particular, the Respondent denies the Complainant's contention that the Respondent offered to sell the domain name to the Complainant for a sum greater than out-of-pocket expenses. Rather, the Respondent contends that it was the Complainant, through his attorney, who contacted him in relation to the domain name.

5. Discussion and Findings

Domain Name Identical or Confusingly Similar to Complainant's Mark

5.1 The relevant part of the domain name **"sting.com"** is "sting." This Administrative Panel finds that the domain name is identical to the word STING.

5.2 This Administrative Panel finds, that the Complainant is a world-famous entertainer who is known by the name STING.

5.3 The question that arises is whether being known under a particular name is the same as having rights in that name as a "trademark or service mark." There are a number of cases in which the Panel has treated the name of a famous or widely known person as constituting an unregistered trademark or service mark sufficient for the purposes of paragraph 4(a)(i) (eg. *Julia Fiona Roberts v. Russell Boyd WIPO Case No. D2000-0210).*

5.4 Although it is accepted that the Complainant is world-famous under the name STING, it does not follow that he has rights in STING *as a trademark or service mark.* Unlike the personal name in *Julia Fiona Roberts v. Russell*

Boyd, the personal name in this case is also a common word in the English language, with a number of different meanings.

Domain Name Registered and Used in Bad Faith

5.5   The Complainant has not satisfied this Administrative Panel that the Respondent registered and is using the domain name in bad faith. The Complainant asserted that the Respondent offered to sell the domain name to the Complainant for $25,000, but the Complainant provided no evidence in support of this assertion. The Respondent admitted that he offered to sell the domain name to the Complainant, but only after the Complainant solicited that offer. Although this evidence is *consistent* with the Complainant's contention that the Respondent ac-quired the domain name primarily for the purpose of selling it to the Complainant, this evidence does not *prove* that. This evidence is equally consistent with the Respondent's contention that he acquired the domain name five years ago in good faith.

6. Decision

6.1   This Administrative Panel decides that the Complainant has not proven each of the three elements in paragraph 4(a) of the Uniform Policy in relation to the domain name which is the subject of the Complaint.

6.2   This Administrative Panel denies the request that Network Solutions, Inc., be required either to transfer to the Complainant, Gordon Sumner, p/k/a Sting, or to cancel, the domain name **"sting.com."**

What comes to mind when the reader thinks of the word "Madonna" - a religious icon, the entertainer, or a hospital? Pop star Madonna initiated a claim against Dan Parisi over the right to use the internet address of "Madonna.com." Madonna has used her first name professionally for entertainment purposes for more than twenty years, and she is the owner of a U.S. Trademark Registration for the name. Parisi paid $20,000 to purchase the registration for the disputed domain name and began operating it as a pornographic website. A WIPO Arbitration Panel ordered Parisi to transfer the domain name to Madonna, as it is her real name and has become synonymous in the minds of the public with the singer and her activities in the entertainment field; and the only plausible explanation for Parisi's actions was an intentional effort to trade upon the fame of Madonna's name for commercial gain.

WIPO ARBITRATION AND MEDIATION CENTER
MADONNA CICCONE A/K/A MADONNA v. DON PARISI
AND MADONNA.COM
CASE NO. D2000-0847 (2000)

1. The Parties

The Complainant is Madonna Ciccone, an individual professionally known as Madonna. The Respondent is **"Madonna.com,"** the registrant for the disputed domain name, located in New York or Dan Parisi, the listed contact for the domain name.

2. The Domain Name(s) and Registrar(s)

The disputed domain name is **madonna.com.** The registrar is Network Solutions, Inc.

3. Factual Background

Complainant is the well-known entertainer Madonna. She is the owner of U.S. Trademark Registrations for the mark MADONNA for entertainment services and related goods. She has used her name and mark MADONNA professionally for entertainment services since 1979.

Respondent is in the business of developing websites. On or about May 29, 1998, Respondent, through its business Whitehouse.com, Inc., purchased the registration for the disputed domain name for $20,000. On June 4, 1998, Respondent registered MADONNA as a trademark in Tunisia. On or about June 8, 1998, Respondent began operating an "adult entertainment portal website." The website featured sexually explicit photographs and text, and contained a notice stating "Madonna.com is not affiliated or endorsed by the Catholic Church, Madonna College, Madonna Hospital, or Madonna the singer."

On June 9, 1999, Complainant objected to Respondent's use of the Madonna.com domain name.

The word *"Madonna"* has the current dictionary definition of the Virgin Mary or an artistic depiction of the Virgin Mary, and is used by others as a trademark, trade name, and personal name. After Respondent's receipt of Complainant's objection, it appears that Respondent had communication with Madonna Rehabilitation Hospital regarding the transfer of the domain name to the Hospital.

4. Parties' Contentions

A. Complainant

Complainant contends that the disputed domain name is identical to the registered and common law trademark MADONNA in which she owns rights. She further contends that Respondent obtained and used the disputed domain name with the internet to attract internet users to a pornographic website for commercial gain based on confusion with Complainant's name and mark.

B. Respondent

Respondent does not dispute that the disputed domain name is identical or confusingly similar to Complainant's trademark. Respondent, however, claims that Complainant cannot show a legitimate interest in the domain name because Respondent (a) made demonstrable preparation to use the domain name for a bona fide business purpose; (b) holds a bona fide trademark in the word MADONNA in Tunisia; and (c) has attempted to make bona fide noncommercial use of the name by donating it to the Madonna Rehabilitation Hospital.

5. **Discussion and Findings**

A. **Similarity of the Disputed Domain Name and Complainant's Mark**

Respondent does not dispute that its domain name is identical or confusingly similar to a trademark in which the Complainant has rights.

B. **Lack of Rights or Legitimate Interests in Domain Name**

Complainant has presented evidence tending to show that Respondent lacks any rights or legitimate interest in the domain name. Respondent's claim of rights or legitimate interests is not persuasive.

Respondent contends that its use of the domain name for an adult entertainment website involved prior use of the domain name in connection with a bona fide offering of goods or services. However, Respondent has failed to provide a reasonable explanation for the selection of Madonna as a domain name. We find that name was selected and used by Respondent with the intent to attract for commercial gain Internet users to Respondent's website by trading on the fame of Complainant's mark. We see no other plausible explanation.

C. **Bad Faith Registration and Use**

The only plausible explanation for Respondent's actions appears to be an intentional effort to trade upon the fame of Complainant's name and mark for commercial gain. That purpose is a violation of the Policy as well as U.S. Trademark Law.

6. **Decision**

We find in favor of the Complainant. The disputed domain name is identical or confusingly similar to a trademark in which Complainant has rights; Respondent lacks rights or legitimate interests in the domain name; and the domain name has been registered and used in bad faith. Therefore, we decide that the disputed domain name **madonna.com** should be transferred to the Complainant.

The policy and rules of the World Intellectual Property Organization for domain name disputes, as well as the arbitration decisions rendered by this organization, may be found at: **http://arbiter.wipo.int/ domains/index.html.**

SECTION 10.5
TRADEMARK DILUTION

Trademark infringement provides a clear remedy when someone adopts a name that is confusing similar to a competing product. Can a merchant, however, utilize a well-known name to promote an unrelated product line? Coca-Cola is famous as the leading manufacturer of soft drink products. Enormous sums of money are spent to promote the consumption of this beverage. A clothing manufacturer hoping to cash in on the Coca-Cola name, develops a line of jeans called "Coca-Cola Blue." There is little chance of a consumer confusing the sale of pants with the purchase of a Diet Coke. Nevertheless, Coca-Cola can maintain that its image is being diluted by the sale of an unrelated product that uses the name of Coca-Cola because the clothing line could blur the public's instantaneous recognition of the beverage manufacturer.

This type of problem is remedied by the *Federal Trademark Dilution Act,* which was enacted to protect the owner of a famous mark from dilution regardless of the likelihood of confusion between the products.

In determining whether a name is distinctive and famous, the courts may consider such factors as:

A. The degree of distinctiveness of the mark;

B. The duration and extent of use of the mark;

C. The duration and extent of advertising of the mark;

D. The geographic extent of the trading area in which the mark is used;

E. The channels of trade for the goods or services;

F. The degree of recognition of the mark in the trading areas used by the mark's owner and against whom the injunction is sought;

G. The nature and extent of use of similar marks by third parties; and

H. Whether the mark was registered.

The Toys "R" Us logo has been used since 1960 and has been promoted through a variety of channels both locally and nationally. The company is well-known for its sale of children's toys. An internet site promoting the sale of various sexual devices, however, registered the domain name "adultsrus." While little chance existed for confusion between the toy company and the business selling sexual devices, Toys "R" Us filed suit on the basis of dilution of their famous name. In granting injunctive relief, the court noted that the name "Adults R Us" tarnishes the "R Us" family of marks by associating them with a line of sexual products that are inconsistent with the positive image that Toys "R" Us has worked to maintain.

TOYS "R" US, INC. v. MOHAMMAD AKKAOUI D/B/A ADULTS "R" US
40 U. S. P. Q. 2D 1836 (N.D. CAL. 1996)

PLAINTIFF TOYS "R" US SEEKS A PRELIMINARY injunction against Defendants, all doing business as Adults "R" Us, for trademark dilution. Plaintiffs hold an array of trademarks ending with the phrase "R Us". On August 28, 1996, they learned that Defendants were operating an Internet site and shopping service featuring a variety of sexual devices and clothing under the name "adultsrus." On September 25, 1996, Plaintiffs filed suit in U. S. District Court alleging trademark dilution.

Subject to the principles of equity, the owner of a famous mark is entitled to an injunction "against another person's commercial use in commerce of a mark or trade name, if such use begins after the mark has become famous and causes dilution of the distinctive quality of the mark." *15 U.S.C. § 1125(c)(1).*

When determining whether a mark is famous and distinctive, the Court may consider such factors as:

A. The degree of inherent or acquired distinctiveness of the mark;

B. The duration and extent of use of the mark in connection with the goods or services with which the mark is used;

C. The duration and extent of advertising and publicity of the mark;

D. The geographical extent of the trading area in which the mark is used;

E. The channels of trade for the goods or services with which the mark is used;

F. The degree of recognition of the mark in the trading areas and channels of trade used by the marks' owner and the person against whom the injunction is sought;

G. The nature and extent of use of the same or similar marks by third parties; and

H. Whether the mark was registered under the Act of March 3, 1881, or the Act of February 20, 1905, or on the principal register.

Applying these criteria, the Court finds that the Toys "R" Us family of marks were famous and distinctive before Defendants began identifying themselves as "Adults R Us." Plaintiffs have used the Toys "R" Us trademark continuously since 1960 and the Kids "R" Us mark since 1983, advertising their products through a variety of channels both locally and nationally. Because of Plaintiff's promotional activity and because of the mark's inherent peculiarity, the "R Us" family of marks have acquired a strong degree of distinctiveness. Plaintiffs have registered Toys "R" Us, and a variety of other marks ending in "R Us." Finally, both Plaintiffs and Defendants are using the Internet to advertise their products and services. Toys "R" Us thus qualifies as famous, distinctive marks eligible for protection from dilution under *15 U.S.C. § 1125.*

The statute defines dilution as the "lessening of the capacity of a famous mark to identify and distinguish goods or services, regardless of the presence or absence of *(1)* competition between the owner of the famous mark and other parties, or *(2)* likelihood of confusion, mistake, or deception." *15 U.S.C. § 1127.* In authorizing courts to enjoin dilution, Congress intended "to protect famous marks from subsequent uses that blur the distinctiveness of the mark or tarnish or disparage it." Adults "R" Us tarnishes the "R Us" family of marks by associating them with a line of sexual products that are inconsistent with the image Toys "R" Us has striven to maintain for itself.

Plaintiffs have therefore established a strong likelihood that they will prevail on the merits of their trademark dilution cause of action.

For the foregoing reasons, IT IS HEREBY ORDERED that Defendants shall immediately discontinue using the Internet Website address or domain names **"http://www.adultsrus.com" and "adultsrus.com,"** and Defendants shall also immediately request Network Solutions, Inc. to cancel their **"adultsrus.com"** domain name registration.

SECTION 10.6
E-DEFAMATION

E-mail has clearly established itself as a new and effective method of communicating with other parties. People around the world have created e-mail addresses in order to receive and send messages. The transmission of the communication, however, can only be accomplished by the use of an online service such as America Online, Inc., Comcast, or Prodigy.

Defamatory messages transmitted through the internet occur with some frequency, likely as the result of the impersonal and less formal nature of internet communications. Users often do not practice the same discretion and caution in sending instant messages or e-mails as when composing and mailing letters, and because e-mail messages lack voice contact, they are often less personal than telephone conversations. Web identities and e-mail addresses also provide internet users with a sense of anonymity in message-writing and web chats, which increases the likelihood that inappropriate statements will be made, and because of the ease with which duplicate copies of messages can be sent to others, more people are being exposed to false or inappropriate statements than would normally occur with the mailing of a letter.

A lawsuit for a defamatory e-mail transmission is still based upon established tort principles. The sender of the communication will be responsible if: **(1)** the transmission is false; **(2)** it harms the reputation of another; and **(3)** it is communicated to a third person. Therefore, the liability of the author of the defamatory internet transmission will be no different than if that communication was sent through the mail, posted on a billboard, or written in a newspaper. A more difficult issue concerns the liability of the e-mail service which is used to transmit the defamatory note. Publication of a false statement is a necessary element of a claim for defamation, and only the party or parties who publish the message can be subject to liability. In this way, a newspaper who prints a defamatory story written by a freelance reporter is liable for the false comment just as though it had authored the story itself. An internet service is also legally considered a publisher, since they took part in the distribution of the message. *Zeran v. America Online, Inc.*, 129 3rd 327 (4th Cir. 1997). Yet should an internet service be held equally responsible for a false message because its server is used to transmit the defamatory communication? Unlike a newspaper or telegraph company whose publication of the false material can only occur through the direct participation of a representative of the company, an e-mail provider is similar to a telephone company that exercises no editorial control over the transmission. While newspapers can be responsible as the publisher of a defamatory comment, a telephone company is not liable. The liability of an internet service provider for defamation is the issue in *Lunney v. Prodigy Services Company*. In finding that an Internet service provider has no responsibility for the transmission of a defamatory message, the court concluded that the internet company had not participated in the preparation of the message, exercised any discretion or control over its content, or in any way assumed editorial responsibility.

ALEXANDER LUNNEY v. PRODIGY SERVICES COMPANY
1996 U.S. Dist. LEXIS 17090 (N.D.Calif. 1996)

USURPING THE NAME OF ALEXANDER LUNNEY, an imposter opened a number of accounts with Prodigy Services Company (Prodigy). The imposter posted two vulgar messages in Lunney's name on a Prodigy bulletin board and sent a threatening, profane electronic mail message in Lunney's name to a third person. Lunney has sued Prodigy, asserting that he has been stigmatized by being falsely cast as the author of these messages. The issue is whether Prodigy may be held liable for defamation. For the reasons that follow, we hold that the complaint against Prodigy was properly dismissed.

After opening several membership accounts with Prodigy under slightly different variants of the name Alex or Alexander Lunney, the imposter transmitted an e-mail message, under Lunney's name, to a local scoutmaster. The sub-

ject line of the message read **"How I'm Gonna' Kill U;"** the body was vulgar in the extreme. After receiving the e-mail, the scoutmaster alerted the police and they readily accepted Lunney's innocence in this episode.

Lunney sued Prodigy, claiming that Prodigy was derelict in allowing the accounts to be opened in his name, and was responsible for his having been stigmatized and defamed.

E-mail is the day's evolutionary hybrid of traditional telephone line communications and regular postal service mail. As one commentator explained, "[t]o transmit a message, one must have access to an on-line service's e-mail system and must know the recipient's personal e-mail address." Once this is accomplished, a person may communicate by composing a message in the e-mail computer system and dispatching it telephonically to one or more recipients' electronic mailboxes. A recipient may forward the message or reply in like manner. Commercial on-line services, such as Prodigy, transmit the private e-mail messages but do not exercise any editorial control over them.

Lunney's defamation action is grounded in established tort principles. Although they were fashioned long before the advent of e-mail, these settled doctrines accommodate the technology comfortably.

In *Anderson v. New York Tel. Co.*, this Court was asked to determine whether a telephone company could be held liable as a publisher of a scurrilous message that a third party recorded and made available to the public by inviting anyone interested to dial in and listen (35 N.Y.2d 746, 320 N.E.2d 647). The Court concluding that the telephone company could not be considered a publisher, because in "no sense has it participated in preparing the message, exercised any discretion or control over its communication, or in any way assumed responsibility."

Anderson emphasized the distinction between a telegraph company in which publication may be said to have occurred through the direct participation of agents, and a telephone company, which, as far as content is concerned, plays only a passive role. The *Anderson* doctrine parallels the case before us. Prodigy's role in transmitting e-mail is akin to that of a telephone company, which one neither wants nor expects to superintend the content of its subscribers' conversations. In this respect, an ISP, like a telephone company, is merely a conduit. Thus, we conclude that Prodigy was not a publisher of the e-mail transmitted through its system by a third party.

As distinguished from e-mail communication, there are more complicated legal questions associated with electronic bulletin board messages, owing to the generally greater level of cognizance that their operators can have over them. One commentator defines an electronic bulletin board as "storage media, e.g., computer memories or hard disks, connected to telephone lines via devices known as modems and controlled by a computer." In some instances, an electronic bulletin board could be made to resemble a newspaper's editorial page; in others it may function more like a "chat room." In many respects, an ISP bulletin board may serve much the same purpose as its ancestral version, but uses electronics in place of plywood and thumbtacks.

Lunney argues that because Prodigy, in its membership agreements, reserves for itself broad editorial discretion to screen its bulletin board messages, it should be liable as a publisher of such messages. Prodigy argues that while it reserves the right to screen its bulletin board messages, it is not required to do so, does not normally do so and, therefore, cannot be a publisher of electronic bulletin board messages posted on its system by third parties.

Even if Prodigy "exercised the power to exclude certain vulgarities from the text of certain bulletin board messages," this would not alter its passive character in "the millions of other messages in whose transmission it did not participate," nor would this compel it to guarantee the content of those myriad messages. In this case, Prodigy was not a publisher of the electronic bulletin board messages.

Accordingly, the order of the lower court should be affirmed.

Lunney appealed this adverse determination to the United States Supreme Court, but the Justices refused to hear the appeal. This action by our top judiciary allows the New York appellate court decision to remain in place.

The *Communications Decency Act* was enacted by Congress in 1996 because of its desire to protect interactive computer services from the growing number of lawsuits being filed against internet providers as the result of the improper conduct of its customers. The legislature found that a growing number of Americans rely on this interactive media for an array of educational, political, cultural, and entertainment services. To promote the continued development of the internet, Congress concluded that immunity from suit was needed. As the court noted in *Zeran v. America Online*, **129 F. 3rd 327 (4th Cir. 1997):**

> Congress' purpose in providing immunity was evident. The amount of information communicated via interactive computer services is staggering. The specter of tort liability in an area of such prolific speech would have an obvious chilling effect. It would be impossible for service providers to screen each of their millions of postings for possible problems. Faced with potential liability for each message republished by their services, interactive computer service providers might choose to severely restrict the number and type of messages posted. Congress considered the weight of the speech interests implicated and chose to immunize service providers to avoid any such restrictive effect.

Section 230 of the Communications Decency Act indicates that "no provider or user of an interactive computer service shall be treated as the publisher or speaker of any information provided by another information content provider." In other words, a computer service has no responsibility to an injured party for the transmission of a defamatory message simply because its network is used to transmit the false message.

The protection afforded by this statute is so broad that America Online was found to have no liability for defamatory comments contained in the *Drudge Report,* even though AOL paid Matt Drudge to include his investigative report on its service. The report provides the exclusive writings of this internet journalist with links to many online news sources. America Online was not a passive party to the defamatory transmission. Rather, it actively advertised the Report by issuing a press release which made "clear the kind of material Drudge would provide to AOL subscribers –gossip and rumor –and urged potential subscribers to sign onto AOL in order to obtain the benefits of the Drudge Report." *Blumenthal v. Drudge* **992 F. Supp. 44 (D. D. C. 1998.)**

A second clause in the *Communications Decency Act* provides that no civil liability will attach if the internet service makes a good faith effort to actively police access to obscene, violent, harassing, or otherwise objectionable material on its site. In other words, this provision will protect an internet service provider that wishes to affirmatively oversee or edit information posted on its bulletin board or website service.

EBay is the world's largest online auction company. It was founded in 1995 and has over 18 million registered customers, and according to the company, users of their service transacted over $5 billion in sales in 2000. Online auctions such as eBay are used to sell everything from automobiles to Pez dispensers with an audience that is global in nature. The online auction industry, however, is still relatively new and has experienced some growing pain. According to the Internet Fraud Complaint Center, auctions conducted online account for the largest number of fraud complaints than any other internet service. Since auctioneers charge a fee for their services, a question arises as to whether they should be held accountable if the goods auctioned are not as advertised or counterfeit? In *Stoner v. eBay, Inc.*, a customer filed suit against eBay, claiming that the company reaps massive profits from the sale of bootleg sound recordings which are auctioned over its service. The plaintiff contends that eBay should be held responsible for failing to monitor the products being sold, since the company must know that illicit recordings are being auctioned.

The Court found eBay immune from suit under the *Communications Decency Act*, since it is a provider of an interactive computer service.

RANDALL STONER V. EBAY, INC.
56 U.S.P.Q. 2D 1852 (CAL. SUPER. 2000)

THE QUESTION TO BE DECIDED is whether eBay enjoys immunity under the *Communications Decency Act ("CDA")*, **47 U.S.C. § 230,** for the conduct underlying plaintiff's claims. The Court concludes that eBay is immune from any liability, and therefore, grants defendant's motion for summary judgment.

EBay is an online auction company. Plaintiff claims that eBay "has developed a method of operation that allows it to knowingly reap massive profits from the sale of bootleg and other unauthorized infringing sound recordings."

Defendant's immunity claim is based on **47 U.S.C. §230(c)(1),** which states that "[n]o provider or user of an interactive computer service shall be treated as the publisher or speaker of any information provided by another information content provider." *Section 230* precludes courts from entertaining claims that would place a computer service provider in a publisher's role. "Thus, lawsuits seeking to hold a service provider liable for its exercise of a publisher's traditional editorial functions – such as deciding whether to publish, withdraw, postpone or alter content –are barred." *Zeran v. America Online*, **129 F.3d 327 (4ᵗʰ Cir. 1997).**

Immunity under the *CDA* requires proof of three elements. Defendant must establish **(1)** that eBay is an interactive computer service provider; **(2)** that eBay is not an information content provider with respect to the disputed activity; and **(3)** that plaintiff seeks to hold eBay liable for information originating with a third party user of its services. For purposes of this motion, it is undisputed that eBay is an interactive computer service provider. Additionally, eBay has satisfied its burden of establishing that it is not an information content provider. The descriptions of the goods auctioned over the eBay service are created entirely by the sellers. EBay is not responsible for the creation or development of information relating to any of the products for which it provides auction services. EBay, therefore, is not an information content provider with respect to the description of auctioned goods.

Plaintiff contends that eBay's services constitute more than mere publication of product descriptions prepared by others, and are instead independent acts of eBay in furtherance of illegal sales. Therefore, plaintiff claims, this suit does not seek to hold eBay responsible for the publication of information provided by others, but for eBay's own participation in selling contraband musical recordings.

Despite plaintiff's attempt to characterize eBay as an active participant in the sale of products auctioned over its service, plaintiff is still seeking to hold eBay responsible for informing prospective purchasers that illegal recordings may be purchased–information that originates with the third party sellers who use the computer service. EBay provides an interactive computer service by which sellers of goods and services describe over the Internet the products that they wish to sell, and sell them to the person who agrees, by submitting a bid through eBay's website in accordance with the rules of the service, to pay the highest price for the product. EBay provides interactive computer services for which it charges a fee just as America Online provides interactive services for which it charges a fee. EBay does not select items to be auctioned, does not inspect or come into possession of those items at any time, does not describe the items to prospective bidders, and does not determine the minimum price which the seller will accept for the item.

EBay has over 4 million listings on its website, with approximately 275,000 listings in the music category alone. Many of these products may be contraband, and however many it might be possible for defendant to identify as such, Congress intended to remove any legal obligation of interactive computer service providers to attempt to identify or monitor the sale of such products. While such a service may be aware that a fraction of the large volume of data exchanged over its facilities involves unlawful activity, the threat of liability for failing to monitor effectively would, in the judgment of Congress, deter companies such as eBay from making their service available as widely and as freely as possible.

Accordingly, defendant's motion for summary judgment must be **GRANTED.**

The eBay website contains a User Agreement which describes the terms and conditions applicable to a person's use of the company's services. In order to make the public aware of their role in auctions and to reduce their liability for products auctioned on the eBay site, the following disclaimer is posted on their website:

> Our site acts as the venue for sellers to list items (or, as appropriate, solicit offers to buy) and buyers to bid on items. We are not involved in the actual transaction between buyers and sellers. As a result, we have no control over the quality, safety, or legality of the items advertised, the truth or accuracy of the listings, the ability of sellers to sell items or the ability of buyers to buy items. We cannot ensure that a buyer or seller will actually complete a transaction.

> …Because we are not involved in the actual transaction between buyers and sellers, in the event that you have a dispute with one or more users, you release eBay. . . from claims, demands and damages. . . of every kind and nature, known and unknown, suspected and unsuspected, disclosed and undisclosed, arising out of or in any way connected with such disputes.

For a more detailed explanation of eBay's policy, visit their site at: **http://pages.ebay.com/help/community/index.html.**

SECTION 10.7 THE EMBARRASSING INTERNET PHOTOGRAPHS PROBLEM FIFTEEN	HODGE, DODGE AND LODGE ATTORNEYS AT LAW MEMORANDUM

To: All Law Clerks

FROM: Gregory Olan Dodge

RE: Unauthorized transmission of embarrassing photographs

Tony Hodge contacted me on behalf of his teammates about an incident that occurred in the locker room following the Stallions dramatic clinching of the team's first playoff spot in franchise history. With five seconds remaining on the clock, the team lined up in field goal formation at mid-field. When the football was snapped, the field goal holder threw a pass to a wide-open receiver, who walked into the end zone. The other team was in shock as the Stallions erupted in celebration as the players jubilantly ran off the field. Because of the happy occasion, champagne flowed freely in the locker room. The players continued their wild celebration as they showered and talked to the many reporters who had covered the game.

This crazy scene was witnessed by a ten-year-old fan who had won a drawing to be the team's unofficial mascot for the day. Little Bobby Bowen was in awe as he snapped picture after picture of his favorite players with his dad's digital camera. The next day, Bobby wrote an e-mail message about his experience and sent the note to all of his friends, along with the photographs of the players. Embarrassingly, the pictures showed the players in various stages of undress. Things then seemed to get out of hand, and Bobby's uncensored shots of the Stallions were repeatedly copied and e-mailed around town. When Tony learned of this delicate problem, he called for me to put a stop to the showing of the pictures on the Internet. I immediately contacted the various internet service providers, who either ignored me or claimed that there was nothing they could do, since the problem was beyond their control. These responses are unacceptable. Internet service providers are making a lot of money from this new technology, and they should not be allowed to merely shrug their shoulders after learning of this serious problem. I am sure they have the technology to trace the path of the photographs from Bobby's computer and to put a stop to the showing of these embarrassing pictures. They could also send a message to all of their subscribers about the situation with a request to honor the privacy of the players and to delete the photographs. Instead, they have chosen to do nothing.

I would like to file a class action on behalf of the football players against all of the internet service providers whose sites were used to transmit the pictures.

Read *John Doe v. Franco Productions* and let me know the answer to the following questions:

1. What arguments may we make on behalf of the Stallions in order to assert a cause of action against the internet service providers?

2. What defenses will the internet service providers raise to our lawsuit?

3. Who should succeed in winning the case? Please explain your answer so I may know whether the case is worth pursuing. If helpful, you may include materials from the subsection of the book on "Defamation and the Internet."

JOHN DOE V. FRANCO PRODUCTIONS
2000 WL 816779 (N.D. ILL. 2000)

THE PLAINTIFFS WERE INTERCOLLEGIATE athletes who, without their knowledge or consent, were videotaped in various states of undress by hidden cameras in restrooms, locker rooms, or showers. The resulting videotapes were sold by various means, including websites hosted by Genuity.net and TIAC.net that included still images of the Plaintiffs taken from the videotapes. At no time did any of the Plaintiffs authorize the use of their images; in fact, they did not learn of the existence of the videotapes or that they were available for purchase until a newspaper article detailed the operation. They instituted this action to obtain monetary damages and injunctive relief for intrusion into the Plaintiffs' seclusion against the alleged producers and distributors of the videotapes, and against defendants GTE Corporation and GTE Internet (together "GTE"), the respective successors to Genuity.net and TIAC.net. The Court dismissed Plaintiffs' previous complaint, findings that GTE was a service provider and therefore immune from suit under the *Communications Decency Act,* 47 U.S.C. §230 ("CDA"). After the Court granted leave to amend, Plaintiffs filed their amended complaint. They re-alleged their previous claims, this time making their allegations against GTE in their capacity as website host. Presently, GTE moves this court to dismiss the amended complaint against them.

Plaintiffs assert that they are not seeking to hold GTE liable as a publisher or speaker of information provided by another under *§230(c)(1),* thus whatever immunity that section may supply is irrelevant. Rather, Plaintiffs assert that it is seeking to hold GTE liable for their "own conduct" in "knowingly failing to restrict content" under *§230(c)(2). Section 230(c)(2)* provides immunity to those who restrict or enable restric-

tion too objectionable material. Thus, Plaintiffs reason because GTE did not restrict or enable restriction to objectionable material, they are not entitled to immunity under this section. However, what Plaintiffs ignore is that by seeking to hold GTE liable for their decision not to restrict certain content it is seeking to hold them liable in a publisher's capacity. *Section 230(c)(1)* provides, "No provider or user of an interactive computer service shall be treated as the publisher or speaker of any information provided by another information content provider." This "creates a federal immunity to any cause of action that would make service providers liable for information originating with a third-party user of the service...lawsuits seeking to hold a service provider liable for its exercise of a publisher's traditional editorial functions—such as deciding whether to publish, withdraw, postpone or alter content—are barred." See *Zeran v. America Online, Inc.,* **129 F.3d 327, 330 (4th Cir. 1997);** see also *Ben Ezra, Weinstein, and Co. v. America Online, Inc.,* **206 F.3d 980, 985-86 (10th Cir. 2000)** (§230 forbids imposition of liability for exercise of editorial functions.) Thus, because Plaintiffs seek to hold GTE liable for their "own conduct" as publishers, GTE may avail themselves of the *CDA's* immunity in this action under §230(c)(1).

Moreover, Plaintiffs have recast the dismissed claims raised in their previous complaint by alleging that they are bringing the instant suit against GTE in their capacity as "website hosts" rather than service providers. In this capacity as web hosts, Plaintiffs claim that GTE acted as "information content providers" and would, thus, not be immune from suit under the *CDA.* GTE argues that Plaintiffs' amended claims still fail to state a claim because site hosting activities are immunized under the *CDA*.

The Court agrees with the Defendant. The **CDA** creates federal immunity against any cause of action that would hold computer service providers liable for information originating from a third party. Immunity under the **CDA** is not limited to service providers who contain their activity to editorial exercises or those who do not engage in web hosting, but rather, "Congress... provided immunity even where the interactive services provider has an active, even aggressive role in making available content prepared by others." *Blumenthal v. Drudge,* **992 F. Supp. 44, 52 (D.D.C. 1998).**

By offering web hosting services which enable someone to create a web page, GTE is not magically rendered the creator of those web pages. *See 47 U.S.C. (C)(1).*

For the reasons set forth above, the Court grants Defendant GTE's motion to dismiss.

ANSWER SHEET
PROBLEM FIFTEEN

Name   **Please Print Clearly**

1. What arguments my we make on behalf of the Stallions in order to assert a cause of action against the internet service providers?

_____

_____

_____

_____

_____

_____

_____

_____

_____

2. What defense will the internet service providers raise to our lawsuit?

_____

_____

_____

_____

_____

_____

_____

_____

_____

_____

3. Who should succeed in winning the case? Please explain your answer so I may know whether the case is worth pursuing. If helpful, you may include materials from the subsection of the book on "Defamation and the Internet."

SECTION 10.8
E-PRIVACY

The internet has opened new avenues of communication for millions of people. From e-mail transmissions to researching the purchase of a product, this electronic information superhighway has something for everyone. The technology, however, comes with a price–an intrusion into the user's privacy. A personal message sent to a friend can be duplicated with little effort and sent to hundreds of people. The online ordering of a product may result in the disclosure to a third person of personal information, such as a telephone, credit card, or social security number. Visits to the World Wide Web leave a digital trail which can be retrieved by a merchant or marketing service. Even a person's e-mail account at work may be monitored by an employer.

Whether the offending conduct is actionable will frequently depend on whether the intrusion is substantial and highly offensive to a reasonable person or if legislation is in place to prohibit the conduct in question.

People have the right to be left alone and to enjoy their privacy. This principle has its foundation in the Bill of Rights and has long been recognized as a common law tort. *The Restatement (Second) of Torts* defines invasion of privacy as follows:

> One who intentionally intrudes, physically or otherwise, upon the solitude or seclusion of another or his private affairs or concerns, is subject to liability for invasion of his privacy, if the intrusion would be highly offensive to a reasonable person.

Placing a small video camera in the ceiling of the bathroom at work would be a substantial and highly offensive intrusion into a person's privacy. Likewise, repeated and unwarranted telephone calls at all hours of the day and night to a former spouse would be actionable.

This tort will have equal application in the world of electronic commerce when a cause of action arises in one of the following contexts:

1. Misappropriation of a person's name or likeness for another's financial gain;

2. Disclosure of a private embarrassing fact;

3. Publicity that places a person in a false light; and

4. An unreasonable intrusion upon a person's privacy.

The right of privacy specifically protects a person against the commercial exploitation of that individual's name, likeness or image without permission. This tort is sometimes called appropriation. A picture of a couple holding hands in the park which is captured by a photographer cannot be used on the cover of a romance novel without the couple's permission. Likewise, a person's name or likeness may not be commercially exploited merely because that individual is famous. For instance, Bette Midler successfully sued Ford Motor Company for their unauthorized use of a singer who imitated Midler's voice in a commercial in order to promote the sale of a car. The court noted that when a distinctive voice of a professional singer is known and is deliberately imitated in order to sell a product, the seller has misappropriated what is not theirs and has committed the tort of invasion of privacy. *Bette Midler v. Ford Motor Corporation*, 849 F.2d 460 (9th Cir. 1988).

Johnny Carson also won his claim against a portable toilet manufacturer who named their product, "Here's Johnny" after the entertainer's famous introduction. *Jonny Carson v. Here's Johnny Portable Toilets, Inc.* 698 F.2d 83, (6th Cir. 1983).

Howard Stern caused quiet a stir when the shock jock announced his candidacy for Governor of New York. To promote its internet service, a company used a picture of Stern that partially exposed his buttocks in order to encourage people to debate the merits of the candidacy on its electronic bulletin board service. Stern filed suit for invasion of privacy and the court had to determine whether the use of Stern's photograph was related to a legitimate news story, even though the photographs also promoted the defendant's bulletin board service.

HOWARD STERN V. DELPHI INTERNET SERVICE, CORP.
626 N. Y. S. 2D 694 (1995)

This case involves state of the art electronic communication and public figures.

HOWARD, STERN, A CONTROVERSIAL RADIO TALK show celebrity and heavily promoted public figure, announced his candidacy for Governor of New York. Defendant Delphi Internet Service Corporation provides access to paid subscribers to the Internet. Stern brought this lawsuit because his photograph was used without his permission in an advertisement for the online bulletin board service, that Delphi had set up to debate Stern's political candidacy.

Delphi set up on its online electronic bulletin board, a subscriber-participation debate on the merits of Stern's candidacy. A full page advertisement in New York Magazine and the New York Post featured the flamboyant photograph of Stern in leather pants which largely exposed his buttocks. The ad caption read: "Should this man be the next governor of New York?" And it continued: "You've read him. You've seen him. You've been exposed to his Private Parts. Now he's stumping to be governor. Maybe it's time to tell the world exactly what you think. The Internet's the one frontier even the King of (Almost) All Media hasn't conquered. And Delphi's where you get aboard. The online service that 'leads the way in Internet access.' So whether you think Howard-the-Aspiring-Governor should be crowned King of the Empire State, or just greased up and sent face-first down a water slide, don't put a cork in it. Sit down, jack in, and be heard."

Stern alleges that defendant's use of his name and photograph violates the *New York Civil Rights Law* which provides: a person, firm, or corporation that uses for advertising purposes, or for the purposes of trade, the name, portrait or picture of any living person without first having obtained written consent of such person... is subject to injunctive relief and damages.

To state a claim, plaintiff must show that: **(1)** defendant used his name, portrait or picture, **(2)** for purposes of trade or advertising, **(3)** without his written consent. It is undisputed that Delphi used Stern's name and picture without his permission and that both were used "for advertising purposes." Defendant contends, however, that its use of Stern's name and photograph falls within the scope of the "incidental use exception."

Here we are presented with the novel issue of whether Delphi's electronic bulletin board service is to be treated as a news disseminator and whether the incidental use exception is applicable.

Defendant concedes that if the advertisements used plaintiff's name and likeness to advertise products unrelated to news dissemination, plaintiff would have stated a claim for relief. However, since the advertisements were for a service related to news dissemination (in this case plaintiff's very candidacy for public office), defendant argues they are protected by the incidental use exception. Affording protection to an online computer services when they are engaged in traditional news dissemination, such as in this case, is the desirable and required result. Because Stern's name was used by Delphi to elicit public debate on Stern's candidacy, logically the subsequent use of Stern's name and likeness in the advertisement is afforded the same protection as would be afforded a more traditional news disseminator engaged in the advertisement of a newsworthy product.

The Stern candidacy is deemed to be of public interest, namely electoral politics. The fact that the advertisement uses plaintiff's name and photograph to indicate the subject on the computer bulletin board–namely, a debate of Stern's candidacy–clearly brings it within the ambit of the incidental use exception.

Stern's privacy has not been invaded. Stern does not deny that he posed for the photograph in which his backside is exposed, and that he promoted himself as a candidate for governor. Thus, no public purpose would be serviced by permitting Stern to silence Delphi. It is ironic that Stern, a radio talk-show host, seeks to silence the electronic equivalent of a talk show, an online computer bulletin board service.

It is hereby ORDERED that the motion for summary judgment of defendant is granted and the complaint is dismissed.

In 1983, moviegoers were exposed to the fictitious story of a teenage hacker who gained unauthorized access to the country's computerized missile defense system and nearly triggered a nuclear war. *War Games* was entertaining, but given the level of computer technology at the time, its plot was farfetched at best. But unfortunately, this fictional account of breaking into a sophisticated computer system from a remote location has become an unpleasant reality. System security is now a paramount concern, and safeguards to minimize unauthorized access to computer mainframes include the use of passwords, fire walls, and encryption programs.

The *Electronic Communications Privacy Act* provides the primary statutory protection against the interception of electronic communications, including e-mail transmissions. Penalties can be either criminal or civil, and the legislation applies to the improper conduct of both the government and private sectors. Generally, the legislation prohibits **(1)** the intentional interception, use, or disclosure of electronic communications obtained during transmission; and **(2)** the improper accessing of stored electronic communications on a system used by the public. These protections are broad enough to cover hackers as well as disclosures of e-mail messages by a public internet service provider such as America Online or Prodigy to a third party.

Even though a person deletes an e-mail message from the hand drive or relies upon an internet service to automatically delete messages after a certain number of days, a copy of that communication still exists. Internet service providers routinely create a back-up tape of all communications.

This type of stored electronic data can be lawfully reviewed by an internet service provider for such things as marketing or quality assurances purposes. The stored messages, however, may not be disclosed by the internet provider to a third party without a subpoena or search warrant.

The protections afforded by the *Electronic Communications Privacy Act* were found to have been violated when AOL voluntarily disclosed to the Navy the name of a sailor who listed his marital status as "gay" in his screen profile. In issuing an injunction to block the sailor's involuntary discharge, the court noted that the Navy's inquiry directed to an AOL service representative, in order to learn the sailor's identity, was "likely illegal" under the Act. *Timothy McVeigh v. Cohen*, **983 F. Supp. 215 (D.D.C. 1998)**. As the court stated:

> The *ECPA*, enacted by Congress to address privacy concerns on the Internet, allows the government to obtain information from an online service provider– as the Navy did in this instance from AOL–but only if **(1)** it obtains a warrant or **(2)** it gives prior notice to the online subscriber and then issues a subpoena or receives a court order authorizing disclosure of the information in question.

The *Electronic Communications Privacy Act* provides no protection against the disclosure of an electronic message by the recipient of the communication. This type of disclosure must be covered by other principles of law, such as the breach of a confidential relationship or invasion of privacy.

Michael Smyth repeatedly figured he was safe and could talk with impunity while using his employer's e-mail. After all, his employer repeatedly assured the Pillsbury workers that all e-mail messages on the company's electronic communications system could not be intercepted or used against an employee as ground for termination. In response to e-mail messages from his supervisor which Smyth opened on his home computer, Smyth decided to provide his supervisor with some "editorial input" concerning the sales management team. He threatened to "kill the backstabbing bastards" and referred to the planned holiday party as the "Jim Jones Koolaid Affair." These creative efforts of expression were not well received by Pillsbury after they intercepted Smyth's private e-mail messages. The company exercised its own creative efforts of expression when Pillsbury terminated the worker's employment, despite the company's prior assurances of message confidentiality. ***Michael Smyth v. Pillsbury Company, 914 Supp. 97 (E.D. Pa. 1996).***

This case clearly raises the question as to whether an employer can monitor the e-mail accounts of employees without violating invasion of privacy principles. Employers have legitimate reasons for wanting to monitor the electronic communication accounts provided to their employees. Good business practice dictates that the e-mail accounts of workers be reviewed for such things as illegal activity, sexual harassment in the work place, disclosure of trade secrets, productivity and quality control. Employers can even use programs which automatically scan their e-mail systems for violations of company policy, such as the viewing of pornographic materials, online betting or playing the stock market while on company time.

Generally, it is not considered an invasion of privacy for an employer to monitor its e-mail system. The employer's need to regulate its e-mail system takes precedent over privacy interests of the worker. The ***Electronic Communication Privacy Act*** also allows monitoring of employee communications if the electronic communication service is used in the ordinary course of business or if the monitoring takes place with the employee's consent. For instance, growing numbers of businesses are drafting privacy statements informing their employees that the employer reserves the right to review company-supplied e-mail accounts for quality assurance purposes.

What ever happened to Mr. Smyth's suit against Pillsbury in view of the company's repeated assurances of e-mail confidentiality? The court was still unimpressed with the former employee's claim and found that the actions of Pillsbury did not tortiously invade the plaintiff's privacy. The court noted:

> We do not find a reasonable expectation of privacy in e-mail communications voluntarily made by an employee to his supervisor over the company's e-mail system notwithstanding any assurances that such communications would not be intercepted by management. Once plaintiff communicated the alleged unprofessional comments to his supervisor over an e-mail system which was apparently utilized by the entire company, any reasonable expectation of privacy was lost.

> Even if an employee had a reasonable expectation of privacy in the contents of his e-mail communications over the company e-mail system, we do not find that a reasonable person would consider the defendant's interception of these communications to be a substantial and highly offensive invasion of his privacy. The company's interest in preventing inappropriate and unprofessional comments or even illegal activity over its e-mail system outweighs any privacy interest the employee may have in those comments.

The Supreme Court of New Jersey in *Blakey v. Continental Airlines, Inc.*, has now placed employers on notice that business owners may incur financial liability if they fail to monitor a company-sponsored electronic communication system once the employer knows or has reason to know that the system is being used to transmit inappropriate comments.

TAMMY BLAKEY v. CONTINENTAL AIRLINES, INC.
751 A.2D 538 (N.J. 2000)

BLAKEY, A PILOT FOR CONTINENTAL AIRLINES became that airline's first female captain to fly an Airbus. Shortly after qualifying to be a captain, Blakey complained of sexual harassment and a hostile working environment based on conduct and comments directed at her by co-employees. In February 1991, she complained to Continental's management concerning pornographic photo-graphs and vulgar gender-based comments directed at her that appeared in the workplace, specifically in her plane's cockpit and other work areas.

From February to July 1995, a number of Continental's male pilots posted derogatory and insulting remarks about Blakey on the pilots online computer bulletin board called the Crew Members Forum ("Forum"). The Forum is accessible to all Continental pilots and crew member personnel through the Internet provider, CompuServe. Continental requires that pilots and crew "access" the Forum in order to learn their flights schedules and assignments.

Although Continental's management was not permitted to post messages or reply to messages on the Forum, its chief pilots had access to the Forum. Plaintiff asserts that chief pilots are considered management within Continental. Although Continental may have no duty to monitor the Forum, it is possible that a jury could find that Continental had knowledge, either direct or vicarious through managerial employees, of the content of certain messages posted on the Forum.

In December 1995, Blakey filed this complaint against Continental and the pilots alleging defamation, sexual harassment/hostile work environment, business libel, and intentional infliction of emotional distress.

The question is whether the Forum is the equivalent of a cork bulletin board in the pilots' lounge or a work-related place in which pilots and crew members continue a pattern of harassment.

The Court recognized that harassment by a superior that takes place outside of the workplace can be actionable. The fact that the electronic bulletin board may be located outside of the workplace does not mean that an employer may have no duty to correct off-site harassment by co-employees. Conduct that takes place outside of the workplace has a tendency to permeate the workplace.

Plaintiff alleges that she gave notice to Continental by forwarding copies of the offending "threats" to Continental's counsel as notice of the continuing harassment. If such notice was given, Continental's liability will depend on whether the Forum was such an integral part of the workplace, that harassment on the Forum should be regarded as a continuation or extension of the pattern of harassment that existed in the Continental workplace.

Our common experience tells us how important are the extensions of the workplace where the relations among employees are cemented. If an "old boys' network" continued in an after-hours setting, where belittling conduct edges over into harassment, what exactly is the outsider (whether black, Latino, or woman) to do? Keep swallowing the abuse or give up the chance to make the team? We believe that severe or pervasive harassment in a work-related setting that continues a pattern of harassment on the job is sufficiently related to the workplace, that an informed employer who takes no effective measures to stop it "sends the harassed employee the message that the harassment is acceptable and that the management supports the harasser."

Employers may not disregard the posting of offensive messages on company or state agency e-mail systems when the employer is made aware of those messages.

To repeat, employers do not have a duty to monitor private communications of their employees; employers do have a duty to take effective measures to stop co-employee harassment when the employer knows or has reason to know that such harassment is part of a pattern of harassment that is taking place in the workplace and in settings that are related to the workplace.

The matter is remanded to the Law Division for further proceedings in accordance with this opinion.

Section 10.9
e-Contracts

In the course of a day, we enter into a variety of transactions that have legal consequences. Whether it is taking the train to school, buying lunch from a vendor, or purchasing a sweater in a department store, our interactions with others can create binding contracts.

A contract is the voluntary exchange of a promise between two or more people that constitutes a legal obligation that is enforceable in court. These agreements may be contained in a highly technical written document, or they may be casual arrangements which are not reduced to writing. The necessary elements of a valid contract are the same regardless of the formality of the transaction. Each contract must contain the following:

1. **Offer** - An offer is a proposal by one party to another manifesting an intention to enter into a valid contract. The three essential elements of a valid offer are **(a)** intent to contract; **(b)** definiteness of the terms; and **(c)** the offer must be communicated.

2. **Acceptance** - An acceptance in an agreement by the offeree to be bound by the terms of the offer.

3. **Consideration** - Consideration is the bargain for exchange between the parties. While the consideration doesn't have to be economic in nature, it must have legal value, such as the performance of a service, or surrendering a legal right.

4. **Capacity** - The parties to the contract must have the legal capacity to enter into the transaction. This provision is designed to protect those who are incapable of making legal decisions, such as children and the mentally infirm. Such individuals may disaffirm a contract, but the competent party remains legally bound to fulfill the contract's terms. This type of transaction is called a voidable contract.

5. **Legality** - The purpose of the contract must be legal; thus the agreement cannot require the commission of a crime or the performance of a tort.

These traditional principles of contract law have equal application to internet transactions. The only difference with an internet transaction is the introduction of a new set of terms, such as "click-wrap agreements" and "digital signatures."

For instance, the online purchase of a computer printer from Amazon.com is no different than buying a computer printer from the nearest Best Buy electronics store, as the same principles of contract law will apply to both transactions. The offer and acceptance is the agreement to buy the printer, whether it is accomplished by placing the item in an online shopping cart and checking out, or by carrying the printer to the cashier in the store. The consideration, or *quid pro quo*, is the exchange of the printer by the seller for the requested cash price. The contract is perfectly legal, and as long as the buyer is over 18, the parties have the capacity to contract.

Online auctions are becoming an increasing popular way to find unusual or hard-to-locate items. To be a player, however, one must understand how the auction actually works. The key is quite simple and involves the following question: Is the highest bid an offer which the seller can choose to accept or reject, or is the highest bid an acceptance of the seller's offer which forms a binding contract?

Consider the following problem: It is your parents twenty-fifth wedding anniversary, and you want to buy them something special. You find an original Woodstock poster signed by the artist at an online auction site. You make the highest bid for the rock-and-roll memorabilia, but at the end of the auction, the seller refuses to give you the poster. He claims that the poster is worth five times the amount of the bid. Who wins? The resolution depends upon whether the internet auction was "with reserve" or "without reserve." If the online transaction is "without reserve," the seller is required to sell the item, regardless of the final bid price, because the highest bid constitutes the acceptance.

However, if the auction was "with reserve"–meaning that the seller conducted the auction with a specific minimum price in mind–the seller is not obligated to complete the transaction regardless of the bids placed, since the bid was an offer which the seller could accept or reject. Most auctions are "with reserve," and the sale does not take place until the bidding has closed, and the seller accepts the bid. To learn more about the rules for online actions, see: **http://pages.ebay.com/help.**

Computer software may be obtained by downloading the program from the internet or by installing the software from a CD. In each case, the software is accompanied with a license that limits the buyer's remedies in the event that the software does not work properly.

A clickwrap license will accompany the installation of a program from the web. The user is required to click through a series of screens before the program can be successfully installed. These screens contain nonnegotiable terms and conditions imposed by the seller. Most people do not read these materials and merely click "I accept" to the questions, since it is the only way to advance the installation.

A shrinkwrap license receives its name from the fact that computer software bought in a store is packaged in a cellophane shrinkwrap. When the box is opened, the CD is contained in an envelope that includes a printed license. By opening the envelope or by using the software, the buyer agrees to be bound by the terms of the license.

These licenses are generally enforced by the courts even though they favor the software company, limit the buyer's rights in the event of a software problem and are seen by the user for the first time after the software has been purchased.

In *Mortenson v. Timberline Software Corporation*, the Washington Supreme Court had to decide whether to enforce the terms of a shrinkwrap license that limited the buyer's damages to the cost of the software program. Mortenson had used Timberline's software to prepare a construction bid but because the program did not work properly, the bid was almost $2 million dollars lower than it should have been. Mortenson sued the software company to recover its full losses and the limitation on damages contained in the license was asserted by Timberline Software Company as a defense to the suit.

M.A. MORTENSON CO. v. TIMBERLINE SOFTWARE CORP.
998 P.2D 305 (WASH. 2000)

THIS CASE PRESENTS THE ISSUE of whether a limitation on damages enclosed in a "shrinkwrap license" accompanying computer software is enforceable against the purchaser of the licensed software. M.A. Mortenson Company, Inc. (Mortenson), a general construction contractor, purchased licensed computer software from Timberline Software Corporation (Timberline). After Mortenson used the program to prepare a construction bid and discovered the bid was $1.95 million less than it should have been, Mortenson sued Timberline for breach of warranties alleging the software was defective.

All Timberline software is distributed to its users under license. The full text of Timberline's license agreement was set forth on the outside of each diskette pouch and the inside cover of the instruction manuals. The first screen that appears each time the program is used also references the license and states:

NEITHER TIMBERLINE NOR ANYONE ELSE WHO HAS BEEN INVOLVED IN THE CREATION, PRODUCTION OR DELIVERY OF THE PROGRAMS SHALL BE LIABLE TO YOU FOR ANY DAMAGES OF ANY TYPE, INCLUDING BUT NOT LIMITED TO, ANY LOST PROFITS, LOST SAVINGS, LOSS OF ANTICIPATED BENEFITS, OR OTHER INCIDENTAL, OR CONSEQUENTIAL DAMAGES ARISING OUT OF THE USE OR INABILITY TO USE SUCH PROGRAMS, WHETHER ARISING OUT OF CONTRACT, NEGLIGENCE, STRICT TORT, OR UNDER ANY WARRANTY, OR OTHERWISE, EVEN IF TIMBERLINE HAS BEEN ADVISED OF THE POSSIBILITY OF SUCH DAMAGES OR FOR ANY OTHER CLAIM BY ANY OTHER PARTY. TIMBERLINE'S LIABILITY

FOR DAMAGES IN NO EVENT SHALL EXCEED THE LICENSE FEE PAID FOR THE RIGHT TO USE THE PROGRAMS.

Mortenson utilized Timberline's Precision Bid Analysis software to prepare a bid for a project at Harborview Medical Center in Seattle. On the day of the bid, the software allegedly malfunctioned multiple times. After Mortenson was awarded the Harborview Medical Center project, it learned its bid was approximately $1.95 million lower than intended.

Mortenson filed an action alleging breach of express and implied warranties. Timberline moved for summary judgment, arguing the limitation on damages in the licensing agreement barred Mortenson's recovery.

Although no Washington case specifically addresses the type of contract formation at issue, a series of recent cases from other jurisdictions have analyzed shrinkwrap licenses. See *Hill v. Gateway 2000, Inc.,* 105 F.3d 1147 (7th Cir.), cert. denied, **522 U.S. 808 (1997)**; *ProCD, Inc. v. Zeidenberg,* **86 F.3d 1447 (7th Cir. 1996)**.

In *ProCD,* which involved a retail purchase of software, the Seventh Circuit held software shrinkwrap license agreements are a valid form of contracting, and such agreements are enforceable unless objectionable under general contract law, such as the law of unconscionability. *ProCD,* **86 F.3d at 1449-52.** The court stated, "a notice on the outside, terms on the inside, and a right to return the software for a refund if the terms are unacceptable, may be a means of doing business valuable to buyers and sellers alike."

In *Hill,* the customer ordered a computer over the telephone and received the computer in the mail, accompanied by a list of terms to govern if the customer did not return the product within 30 days. The court held the terms of the "accept-or-return" agreement were effective, stating, "competent adults are bound by such documents, read or unread." *Hill,* **105 F.3d at 1149.**

The question in *ProCD* was not whether terms were added to a contract after its formation, but how and when the contract was formed—in particular, whether a vendor may propose that a contract of sale be formed, not in the store or over the phone with the payment of money or a general "send me the product," but after the customer has had a chance to inspect both the item and the terms. *ProCD* answers "yes," for merchants and consumers alike. *Hill,* **105 F.3d at 1150.**

We find the approach of the *ProCD* and *Hill* courts persuasive. We, therefore, hold the terms of the license were part of the contract between Mortenson and Timberline, and Mortenson's use of the software constituted its assent to the agreement, including the license terms. The terms of Timberline's license were either set forth explicitly or referenced in numerous locations.

The terms were included within the shrinkwrap packaging of each copy of the Precision Bid Analysis software; they were present in the manuals accompanying the software; they were included with the protection devices for the software, without which the software could not be used. The fact the software was licensed was also noted on the introductory screen each time the software was used.

We affirm the trial court's order of summary judgment of dismissal.

SECTION 10.10
STATUTE OF FRAUDS

Most agreements do not have to be in writing to be enforced by the courts, and oral agreements can be just as valid as formal written contracts. For instance, most consumer purchases at department stores, supermarkets, or home repair centers are not transacted with signed, written documents; rather, they are informal transactions. The Statute of Frauds, however, requires that certain types of agreements be in writing and be signed by the parties to the contract. This includes contracts for the sale of land, the sale of goods worth more than five hundred dollars, and contracts which cannot be performed in less than one year.

The required writing may be contained in a letter, invoice, telegram, contract or even a faxed transmission which contains one or both signatures of the parties. The signing of the document is also important, since it authenticates the writing and shows the intent of the parties to be bound by the terms of the agreement. In the online environment, however, the correspondence between the parties is electronic and does not generate a paper trail. This presents a problem with e-commerce transactions that must be in writing in order to comply with the Statute of Frauds.

When you purchase items online from a retailer, your order is quickly confirmed by the vendor in an e-mail with a confirmation number and tracking number. But these return messages are not sent as a courtesy. Rather, they represent the seller's attempt to create a written record as evidence of compliance with the Statute of Frauds and to insure the validity of the order.

Because of the importance of electronic commerce, a number of states have passed legislation to validate electronic contracts and signatures. These statutes, however, are not uniform in approach and create uncertainty in the business world.

Congress has remedied the situation by enacting the *Electronic Signatures in Global and National Commerce Act*. The legislation should have a profound impact on internet transactions by making them the equivalent of a signed paper contract. This compliance with the Statute of Frauds is achieved by providing that a signature, contract, or other record relating to a digital transaction may not be denied legal effect solely because it is electronic in nature. Therefore, businesses may now proceed with their online contracts secure in the knowledge that their agreements will be enforced by the courts across the land.

SECTION **10.11**
REVIEW CASES

1. Jcom, Inc. operated a website that catered to the sale of adult entertainment services. The company used the trademark "Barbie's Playhouse" on their website, along with a doll-like figure that resembled the form of a Barbie doll. The address of the website was **"http://www.jcomlive.com/barbie.htm."** Mattel brought suit against JCom., Inc., under the *Lanham Act* for the defendant's violation of the Barbie trademark and under the Federal Trademark Dilution Act. Will Mattel be successful? *Mattel, Inc. v. JCom, Inc.* **1998 U.S. Dist. LEXIS 16195 (S.D. N.Y. 1998).**

2. America Online publishes updated stock quotations on a continual basis. This data is supplied by independent third parties who monitor the various stock exchanges. On several occasions, AOL posted incorrect information concerning the stock price and share value of Ben Ezra, Weinstein & Co., Inc. This prompted a lawsuit by the firm against AOL for defamation and negligence. Is the internet service liable for the posting of the misinformation about the value of the firm's stock, or are they protected by the Communications Decency Act? *Ben Ezra, Weinstein & Co., Inc. v. America Online, Inc.*, **No. 99-2068 (10th Cir. 2000).**

3. An entrepreneur operated a website under the domain name **"www.Painewebber.com."** Visitors to the site would automatically be linked to a pornographic website. Painwebber, Inc., filed an injunction against the website operator to enjoin them from using the internet domain name. Did the website operator violate the Anticybersquatting Consumer Protection Act? *Paine Webber, Inc. v. www.painwebber.com*, **1999 U.S. Dist. LEXIS 6551 (E.D. Va. 1999).**

4. Comedy III Productions has the exclusive right to the exploitation of the trademarks and images of the Three Stooges. But prior to Comedy III's exclusive rights, companies that were affiliated with Robert Walsh possessed a license to sell Three Stooges merchandise. That prior agreement explicitly warned the licensees that they had no right to continue selling Three Stooges products after the expiration of the agreement. Yet following the expiration of that license, a Robert Walsh-controlled company made available for sale on the internet a "Golf With Your Friends Embroidered Golf Shirt," which incorporated the images of the Three Stooges. Does the website advertising of the Three Stooges products by a Walsh-affiliated company violate any rights possessed by Comedy III Productions? Will Comedy III Productions be successful under the Lanham Act for a trademark infringement? *Comedy III Productions, Inc. v. Robert C. Walsh, Jr., et al.*, **1996 U.S. Dist. LEXIS 5710 (S.D. N.Y. 1996).**

5. AOL offers a wide variety of "chatrooms," where its users can converse through messaging. One such chatroom was used by a subscriber to display and sell photographs of an eleven-year-old boy who had engaged in certain sexual acts with the subscriber. While the adult pled guilty to criminal charges, the parents of the minor sought to hold AOL liable for the transmission of the photographs, because their internet chatroom was used. Is AOL responsible for the transmission of the photographs over their system, or are they protected by the Communications Decency Act? *Jane Doe v. America Online, Inc.,* **Case No. 97-25-87 (Fla. Dist. Ct. App. 1999).**

6. Microsoft Network is an online computer service that utilizes a clickwrap license, that prospective members must agree to if they wish to use the MSN internet site. The membership agreement appears on the computer screen in a scrollable window next to two blocks that provide the choices, "I agree" or "I don't agree." The agreement, among other things, requires any user who wishes to bring suit against Microsoft Network to file the claim in the State of Washington. Caspi brought a class-action lawsuit against the internet service provider in New Jersey because of an increase in the membership fees attributable to a change in the service plan. Will Microsoft be successful in having the case dismissed from the New Jersey court because Caspi's choice of jurisdiction violates the clickwrap agreement? *Caspi v. Microsoft Network a/k/a MSN, L.L.C.,* **732 A.2d 528 (N.J. Super. 1999).**

SECTION 10.12
INTERNET REFERENCES

For more information on internet law, see the following sites:

- **http://www.phillipsnizer.com or http://www.perkinscoie.com**
  Both Internet sites provide summaries of court decisions on Cyberlaw. Cases are arranged by issue and the sites are maintained by law firms that specialize in intellectual property.

- **http://www.gigalaw.com**
  This site provides articles on various Internet law issues.

- **http://legal.web.aol.com**
  AOL provides legal information and court opinions on Cyberlaw issues.

- **http://www.jmls.edu/cyber**
  John Marshal Law School maintains a website devoted to Cyberlaw which contains full text of cases and articles on the subject.

Chapter 11

Limitations to Lawsuits

Res Judicata is Latin for "the thing has been decided." When a lawsuit is dismissed on the basis of res judicata, it is because the case has already been litigated and cannot be retried. Res judicata, therefore, insures that the litigants will use their best efforts at trial and that the litigation will conclude at some point in time. This doctrine saves time and expense for the defendant and the court system by avoiding redundant litigation.

Two elements must exist in order for res judicata to apply: **1)** the parties in the second suit must be the same as those who litigated the first case; and **2)** the issue must be the same in each case.

These principles also apply in criminal cases. **Double Jeopardy** refers to the right guaranteed by the Fifth Amendment of the United States Constitution that no person shall be tried twice for the same offense.

The following case deals with whether a party is precluded from litigating a previously adjudicated claim that involves a claim for accidental death benefits under a life insurance policy.

Deborah Ellis v. Amex Life Ins., Co.
211 F. 3rd 935 (Fifth Cir. 2000)

Deborah Ellis appeals from the summary judgment granted to Life Insurance Company of North America. The district court found that Ellis' action was barred by the doctrine of res judicata based on the prior dismissal, as time-barred, of another suit filed by Ellis against Life. We affirm

Ellis claimed that she was improperly denied accidental death benefits due under her mother's insurance policy with Life. Ellis filed the instant suit against Life in Texas state court in 1992 and it was removed to the Eastern District Federal Court of Texas. In December 1992, the case was stayed. In May 1997, Ellis filed a

separate suit with similar allegations in Texas state court. This case was removed to the Northern District Federal Court of Texas. In July 1997, Life moved for summary judgment in the Northern District lawsuit, alleging that it was barred by the statute of limitations. In February 1998, Life's motion was granted and the suit was dismissed with prejudice.

Meanwhile, in September 1997, Ellis moved to lift the stay on the Eastern District Court suit and Life moved for a summary judgment. The district court granted the summary judgment on the ground that the Eastern District suit was barred by res judicata, in light of the previous dismissal of the Northern District Court suit. Ellis appeals.

The preclusive effect of a prior court judgment is controlled by res judicata rules. Res judicata is appropriate if: **1)** the parties to both actions are identical or in privity; **2)** the judgment in the first action is rendered by a court of competent jurisdiction; **3)** the first action concluded with a final judgment on the merits; and **4)** the same claim or cause of action is involved in both suits.

The first and second elements of res judicata are not disputed. Ellis argues that the dismissal of the Northern District suit, as time-barred, was not a decision on the merits for res judicata purposes. We have reject this claim. The dismissal of the Northern District suit was a decision on the merits.

Second, Ellis claims that res judicata is inapplicable because the Eastern District suit was brought prior to the Northern District suit. When two actions are pending which are based on the same claim, or which involve the same issue, it is the final judgment first rendered in one of the actions which becomes conclusive in the other action regardless of which action was first brought.

Finally, Ellis does not appear to renew her argument that the fourth element of res judicata—identity of causes of action—is absent here. Even if this argument is preserved, it is without merit. The district court correctly noted that we apply a transactional test in determining whether two suits involve the same claim, where the critical issue is whether the plaintiff bases the two actions on the same operative facts. As the district court found, both suits arose out of the same transaction: Life's denial of benefits under the mother's insurance policy after her death. Therefore, the district court correctly found that the fourth res judicata requirement was met.

Therefore, we hold that the district court did not err in finding that the dismissal of the Northern District suit should have res judicata effect as to the Eastern District suit. The grant of summary judgment to Life is AFFIRMED.

Section 11.2
Statute of Limitations

The statute of limitations is the time period within which an aggrieved party must institute suit or the claim will be forever barred. The rule is designed to force a plaintiff to act within a specified time so that the party being sued can take the necessary measures to properly defend the action. With the passage of time, people lose track of witnesses and misplace important evidence. By knowing that a lawsuit must be filed by a certain date, a party can rest assured that the matter is no longer of legal significance if the statute of limitations has expired and no suit has been initiated.

Statutes of limitation are established by the legislature and will vary from jurisdiction to jurisdiction. The time periods selected are not magical, but reflect an attempt by the legislature to establish a reasonable date within which a party must file suit. Is justice served by the dismissal of a claim merely because a case is filed one day too late? Ample time exists for the institution of suit and an aggrieved party should not wait until the last minute to seek judicial relief. The statute of limitations are well known and a specific cut-off date must be enforced.

A party is usually aware when an actionable wrong occurs. Loans are to be repaid by a certain date and people know when they are involved in car accidents. The statute of limitations starts to run or "accrues" when the loan is past due or when the collision occurred.

KENNETH BROWN V. WILLIAM COSBY, JR.
433 F. SUPP. 1331 (E.D. PA. 1977)

KENNETH BROWN, FILED SUIT against William (Bill) Cosby, Jr., Jemmin, Inc., a corporation owned primarily by Cosby, Filmation Associates, and Lou Schimer and Norm Prescott, the two principals in Filmation.

Brown alleges that defendants Cosby, Jemmin, Schimer, Prescott, and Filmation have breached written and oral contracts in which they agreed **(1)** to pay him a "fair share" of the profits derived from the commercial exploitation of cartoon characters he created; **(2)** to utilize his services exclusively in the preparation of artwork necessary for the commercial presentation of the characters; and **(3)** to have Brown retained as a consultant by firms developing or selling in any form the characters created by him.

Plaintiff and Cosby were childhood friends who grew up together. In September 1970, Cosby contacted plaintiff and asked him to create cartoon characters representing mutual childhood friends whom Cosby had adapted into his comedy routine. With some of the ideas coming from Cosby, plaintiff developed various characters who are known by such names as **"Fat Albert," "Old Weird Harold," "Mush Mouth," "Crying Charlie,"** and **"Dumb Donald."** Plaintiff developed the Characters on paper over the next several months receiving $250 per week from Jemmin to support himself. Plaintiff's un-

derstanding with Cosby and Jemmin was that initially he would keep his costs and salary very low for developing the Characters, but that he would receive substantial benefits from the development of the Characters at a later date.

Plaintiff, at the request of Cosby and Jemmin, delivered samples of the Characters to Schimer, Prescott and Filmation, who promised to hire plaintiff as a consultant for the development of a television show for children using the Characters. After receiving the Characters, these defendants refused to communicate with plaintiff, but on January 19, 1971 Cosby and Jemmin requested plaintiff to, and he did, sign a letter agreement. The agreement provided that plaintiff was to be employed as an independent contractor to produce a series of comic strips to be published by Jemmin. Plaintiff was to receive a flat salary plus a percentage of receipts above certain amounts derived from syndication of the series. In the event that the series were published in comic book form, Jemmin agreed to negotiate with plaintiff in good faith as to additional compensation.

Proximate to the time the agreement was entered into between the parties, Cosby, Schimer and Prescott promised plaintiff, as he understood, that he would participate in any other forms of commercial exploitation of the Characters, to wit, that he would receive no less than 25% of the profits generated by the Characters as his "fair share."

Pursuant to the letter agreement, plaintiff developed the Characters into comic strip form, delivered the first set of drawings and received the initial $5,000 due under the agreement. In April 1971 plaintiff informed Cosby that he could not continue to meet deadlines and pay helpers on the money he was receiving. Cosby thereupon paid plaintiff $1,500. By the end of April 1971, the comic strip finals of the Characters were delivered to Jemmin, Cosby, Schimer and Publisher. Cosby and Jemmin continued to urge plaintiff to keep working and to keep his development costs for the Characters low. They repeatedly stated that plaintiff would get his "fair share."

On June 27, 1971, Jemmin forwarded a new letter agreement to plaintiff for his signature. The proposed agreement would terminate the previous letter agreement of January 19, 1971. It provided that plaintiff was to receive the sum of $1,600, that no other compensation was due him under the previous agreement, and that Jemmin was the owner of all "results and proceeds" of plaintiff's services rendered under the previous agreement. Plaintiff refused to sign the proposed letter agreement.

After the breakdown in relations, defendants participated in the production of a television show entitled "Fat Albert" using characters which are identical or similar to the Characters created by plaintiff. Plaintiff's Characters have also been commercially exploited by defendants for films, books and a variety of novelty products. The commercial exploitation of the Characters has resulted in very substantial profits for the defendants.

The Complaint alleges both breach of the January 1971 letter agreement and breach of the oral contract modifying and supplementing the written agreement. Defendants assert that since the breach of the written agreement occurred at the time or soon after the proposed termination agreement of June 27, 1971 was forwarded to plaintiff, any claim for breach of the written agreement is barred by California's four-year statute of limitations. They further argue that the oral modification of the contract was a promise to hire plaintiff as a consultant for the development of a television show utilizing the Characters, that this agreement was also breached on or about June 27, 1971 when defendants failed to hire plaintiff as a consultant, and, therefore, plaintiff's claim for breach of the oral agreement is barred by California's two-year statute of limitations governing a cause of action for breach of an oral contract.

Plaintiff does not dispute that the written agreement standing alone would be barred by the four-year limitations statute. He contends that the letter agreement "was orally modified by defendant, Cosby, and others to indicate that plaintiff was to get his 'fair share' not only of the profits to be generated from the comic strip, but also of all other forms of commercial exploitation of the characters

The obligation is to pay a fair share of the profits from use of the plaintiff's idea. The breach occurred when there was a failure to pay a fair share of the first profits earned. Case law suggests that this should start the limitations period for recovering all future profits. Moreover, the behavior of the defendants was such that the first breach by them was clear notice to plaintiff that they intended to breach the entire contract.

The use of plaintiff's Characters substantially destroyed their value to him. Once defendants appropriated plaintiff's Characters for use in the television series, plaintiff was unable to sell them as characters with different names and personalities. Brown could have sued for his share of the profits, for an accounting of any future profits, and/or for an injunction to prohibit future exploitation of the Characters without some assurance that Brown would receive his "fair share."

Permitting Brown to delay suit until after defendants had found a highly profitable market for the Characters would allow him to rest on his rights, shifting to defendant the risk and expense attendant upon commercial exploitation of his idea, and then to assert his claim only when that exploitation had yielded a net profit.

The first failure of defendants to pay plaintiff a "fair share" of the profits from any commercial exploitation of the Characters would give rise a cause of action for breach of the contract and would, therefore, start the running of the statute of limitations. At the time defendants first failed to account to plaintiff for his "fair share" of profits, cause of action, and that cause of action started the running of the limitations period. Plaintiff's memorandum states that there has been a commercial exploitation of his Characters since 1972 or 1973, and that he has not participated in the profits. Plaintiff sues on an admittedly oral contract, thus the two year limitations period is applicable. The instant suit was not filed until October 28, 1976, more than two years after plaintiff's cause of action for breach of the oral contract accrued. Plaintiff's claims for breach of contract are, therefore, time barred.

SECTION 11.3
HODGE V. FEELGOOD

PROBLEM ELEVEN

HODGE, DODGE AND LODGE
ATTORNEYS AT LAW
MEMORANDUM

To: Part-Time Law Clerk #3

From: Gregory Olan Dodge

Re: Hodge v. Feelgood
           Statute of Limitations - Medical Malpractice

Joe Hodge is here to see you. He was clearly the victim of medical malpractice. However, Joe's claim may be time-barred by the statute of limitations. Pennsylvania has a two-year time limitation on bringing tort actions. While Joe did not discover his tort claim until a few months ago, the surgeon's act of negligence actually occurred over two years ago. Thus, you need to ascertain when the statute began to run. Does it start when one discovers his injury, when the tort occurred, or at some other time? You will need more information in order to assess the situation so the following summary is provided.

Joe's problems stem back to the evening of December 31, 1998. Joe and Estelle were celebrating New Year's eve with some of their friends. It was a tradition among the friends to spend a relaxing evening at one of their homes. Each couple prepared one course of an elaborately planned gourmet dinner. This particular night will never be forgotten because Joe almost died. While eating an exotic Thai-style dish, something got caught in his throat. Luckily, Dr. Feelgood was a member of this social gathering. It was not until Joe had turned blue from lack of oxygen that one of the women realized there was a problem, and screamed for help. Dr. Feelgood instantly knew what to do. A quick maneuver seemed to dislodge whatever was choking Joe. Joe began to breathe again but Dr. Feelgood wasn't satisfied that Joe was out of danger. Joe's breathing was still somewhat strained. After several minutes of observation, the doctor told Joe to go to the hospital. Once there, Dr. Feelgood suggested exploratory surgery to determine the nature of the problem. As it turned out, the surgery was needed. A chicken bone was lodged in Joe's stomach and had perforated his esophagus.

The operation was successfully completed just after midnight. It was certainly a memorable way to begin 1999.

Joe's post-surgical recovery was uneventful. At his six-month checkup, it appeared that he was in perfect health. But in December of 1999, almost one year after surgery, Joe began to experience stomach problems. He had mild aches and pains in his lower abdomen. At first, Feelgood wasn't concerned. This type of discomfort was common after major surgery. He prescribed medication to alleviate the pain. Joe's symptoms, however, continued on a sporadic basis over the next six months. Joe then decided to make another appointment with his doctor. Though he was only experiencing minor discomfort, the symptoms were persistent enough to warrant further examination. In June of 2000, Dr. Feelgood saw Joe and immediately ordered x-rays. These tests revealed the cause of Joe's discomfort. A surgical sponge had been left in his stomach during the operation. Joe was livid. He had to undergo additional surgery to remove the sponge. Dr. Feelgood performed this in July of 2000 for free.

Because Joe has stopped talking to Dr. Feelgood, a great deal of animosity between the neighbors has arisen since the surgery. Mr. Hodge wants to institute suit against Dr. Feelgood for medical malpractice. Assume that the date is now January 2002.

You have been given this assignment because of your expertise on the case of *Bayless v. Philadelphia National League Club.* According to that case, when does the Pennsylvania statute of limitations begin to run? Should we take Joe's case, or does the two-year statute bar it? Please explain your answer in no more than two pages.

PATRICK BAYLESS V. PHILADELPHIA NATIONAL LEAGUE CLUB A/K/A THE PHILLIES
579 F.2D 37 (3RD CIR. 1978)

THIS DIVERSITY ACTION PRESENTS THE QUESTION whether the Pennsylvania two-year statute of limitations bars an action by one who did not discover the cause of his injury within the two-year period. Because there exist genuine issues of material fact as to when the limitations period began to run, we reverse the summary judgment granted the defendant.

The facts, considered in the light most favorable to the plaintiff, are as follows. Upon his graduation from high school in 1966, Patrick Bayless was hired as a baseball pitcher by the defendant Philadelphia National League Club, popularly known as the Philadelphia Phillies. In May of 1971, while playing on a Phillies' minor league team, Bayless began to experience severe pain in the lumbar-sacral area of his back and in his right leg. He complained to the team trainer and physician who treated him by administering massive doses of the pain-killing drugs, Decadron, Xylocaine, and Butazolidin. He claims to have been compelled to pitch while in a drug-induced stuporous condition. Bayless's pitching performance deteriorated. On August 12, 1971, the Phillies gave him his unconditional release.

Within thirty days, Bayless collapsed; an emergency laminectomy was performed. Nonetheless, he continued to suffer pain in his back. In September of 1971, Bayless began to exhibit erratic behavior and to suffer from severe depression. He was thereafter confined in state mental institutions on numerous occasions and has been diagnosed as a paranoid schizophrenic. He alleges that this condition was triggered by the drugs he was administered. He seeks damages from the Phillies for injuries associated with his back condition and for the mental illness he has suffered.

On October 15, 1976, more than five years after ingesting the drugs but, or so he claims, less than two years from the time that he discovered that it was the drugs that caused his mental illness, he filed this action. The defendant moved for summary judgment on the grounds that the action was barred by the Pennsylvania statute of limitations.

The district court ruled that Bayless's claims arising out of his back condition and those involving his mental illness were both governed by Pennsylvania's two-year limitations period for personal injuries, but it treated the two claims separately. It held that the cause of action based upon the back injuries arose no later than September 12, 1971, the date on which Bayless underwent the emergency laminectomy. It was then that Bayless knew of his back injury, and the district court held this was more than two years prior to filing the present suit. Thus, the court held that this claim was time-barred. Bayless does not challenge this aspect of the trial court's ruling on appeal.

With respect to the claim for mental illness, the trial court ruled that the limitations period began to run "when plaintiff knew or reasonably should have discovered the extent of his mental illness." The court ruled that this occurred no later than January 23, 1973, the date on which Bayless was discharged from Napa State Hospital diagnosed, according to hospital records, as a paranoid schizophrenic. In other words, the court held that the limitations period began to run when Bayless learned that he suffered from a mental illness. Accordingly, the court held that this claim was barred as well.

The Pennsylvania statute of limitations for personal injuries reads, in relevant part:

> Every suit hereafter brought to recover damages for injury wrongfully done to the person, in case where the injury does not result in death, must be brought within two years from the time when the injury was done and not afterwards;

Our task is to decide when the limitations period commences to run. The court below held that it runs from the moment that the injury is known to the plaintiff, in this case, from the moment he knew of his mental illness. We hold that the rule in Pennsylvania is that the limitations period begins to run from the time that the plaintiff knows or reasonably should know the cause of his injury.

Analysis begins with the case of *Ayers v. Morgan*, **397 Pa. 282, 154 A.2d 788 (1959).** Plaintiff Ayers underwent surgery for an ulcer in 1948. He was discharged within two week but he continued to suffer pains in his abdomen. In January of 1957, he returned to the hospital for tests. At that point it was determined that the surgeon who had performed surgery nine years earlier had left a sponge in his body. Defendant raised the statute of limitations as a bar; the trial court granted summary judgment in its favor. The Pennsylvania Supreme Court reversed, holding that the statue of limitations did not begin to run until Ayers knew, or by the exercise of reasonable diligence, could have learned of the presence of the foreign substance within his body. Because Ayers had averred that he did not become aware of the sponge until January 1957, and he had filed suit within two years of that date, the Court held that he was entitled to go to trial on his claims.

In *Irrera v. Southeastern Pennsylvania Transportation Authority*, **231 Pa. Super. 508, 331 A.2d 705 (1974),** plaintiff suffered a fall due to a hole in a street surface. Pennsylvania law required that a notice of claim be filed within six months. Plaintiff gave notice more than six months after the accident, but within six months after ascertaining that the defendant was responsible for road maintenance. The court equated the notice statute with a statute of limitations. After discussing *Ayers* and *Daniels v. Beryllium Corp.*, **227 F. Supp. 591 (E.D. Pa. 1964),** it stated:

> From these cases it appears that the rule that best manifests the legislature's intent . . . is that time begins to run on the date of injury unless, because of fraud or concealment by the authority, or *in spite reasonable diligence by the claimant, knowledge of the negligence or its causes cannot be discovered until after the six month period.*

Because there was no evidence in the record to suggest that plaintiff could not have learned of the defendant's responsibility had she exercised reasonable diligence, summary judgment in defendant's favor was affirmed.

The *Daniels* case, which was cited with approval in *Irrera*, stands directly for the proposition that the statute of limitations does not begin to run until the plaintiff, in the exercise of reasonable diligence, could have discovered that his injury was caused by the defendant. In *Daniels*, plaintiff brought suit for beryllium poisoning caused by contamination of the atmosphere by defendant's manufacturing plant. Plaintiff first became ill in 1943, but her illness was not diagnosed as beryllium poisoning until 1953, and she did not bring suit until 1958. The court held that the statute began to run not when her symptoms first appeared, and not when the diagnosis was made, but rather when plaintiff should have known the causal connection between her illness and defendant's activities. This was deemed to be a jury question. Judge Higginbotham, now a member of this Court, had earlier interpreted Pennsylvania law in this matter in a wrongful death action. In *Gemignani v. Philadelphia Phillies National League Baseball Club, Inc.,* **287 F. Supp. 465 (E.D. Pa. 1967),** the deceased, like Bayless, played for the Phillies. In 1959, an examination by one of the Phillies' team physicians revealed a symptomatic blood condition. Nevertheless, the deceased was not treated, nor was he informed of his malady. In August 1960, he was hospitalized because of a serious kidney problem. He died as a result of uremic kidneys on September 3, 1960. On August 31, 1962, plaintiff instituted suit on the theory that the Phillies' failure to treat or to advise the deceased more than two years earlier permitted his condition to develop into one which was terminal.

Notwithstanding that the defendant's allegedly wrongful acts or omissions occurred in 1959, more than two years before suit was filed, the court ruled that the action was not time-barred. It framed the dispositive issue as follows; whether the statute of limitations begins to run from the date on which the plaintiff knows facts from which, through the exercise of reasonable diligence, he could learn the cause of the injury; or whether the statute begins to run from the time the plaintiff, through the exercise of reasonable diligence, should have learned both the facts in question and that those facts bore some causative relationship to the injury. The court opted for the later view:

> It is true that in *Byers v. Bacon,* **250 Pa. 564, 95 A. 711 (1915);** *Smith v. Bell Telephone Co.,* **397 Pa. 134, 153 A.2d 477 (1959);** *Ayers v. Morgan,* **397 Pa. 282, 154 A.2d 788 (1959),** the courts spoke in

terms of discovery of facts. However, it is also clear from reading those cases that discovery of the causative facts necessarily gave us, simultaneously to discovery of the causative relationship. Moreover, it would require the most narrow reading of the language of those cases and the ignoring of the policy basis thereof to fail to recognize that "discovery of the cause of harm" must comprehend discovery of both the facts or occurrences and also discovery of reason to believe that those facts might bear a causative relationship to the harm.

Because the record was devoid of any evidence that prior to August 31, 1960, plaintiff reasonably suspected or should have reasonably suspected that the examination, the facts which it revealed, and the failure of the Phillies to either treat the condition or to inform the deceased's family about it were causally connected to the deceased's terminal illness, the suit was deemed timely.

We think that *Gemignani* accurately states the law of Pennsylvania. If common sense and reason dictate that the limitation period is not to run at least until a plaintiff knows that he has been hurt, then it should not run until he can reasonably determine what or who hurt him. Ordinarily, the two events will occur simultaneously, but this need not always be so. There are cases where one knows of an injury, but not its cause. This may be such a case.

The record here shows that Bayless began to develop symptoms of mental illness in September of 1971. His condition became so serious that he was institutionalized as early as 1972. According to the record, however, the first suggestion that Bayless's mental condition might have been caused by his ingestion of pain-killing drugs is a Neurology Clinic Consultation Report, dated January 15, 1973, prepared by a physician one week prior to Bayless's release from the Napa State Hospital in California. This report states in part, "One thought to keep in mind could be a toxic reaction to some of the drugs such as Butazolidin which does at times cause rather severe mental disturbances." The report, on its face, is titled, "Confidential Patient Information." There is nothing in the record to suggest that its contents were disclosed to the plaintiff or that the report was made available to him. In any event, under the circumstances of this case, the question when Bayless knew or should have known that his mental illness resulted from the Phillies' treatment of his back complaint is for the jury.

The order of the district court granting summary judgment to the defendant will therefore be reversed and the case will be remanded for further proceedings.

**ANSWER SHEET
PROBLEM ELEVEN**

Name   **Please Print Clearly**

1. According to **Bayless**, when does the statute of limitations begin to run?

2. Should we take Joe's case, or does the two-year statute bar it?

_____

_____

_____

_____

_____

_____

_____

_____

_____

_____

_____

_____

_____

_____

_____

_____

_____

_____

_____

_____

_____

_____

_____

_____

_____

SECTION 11.4
IMMUNITY FROM SUIT

In a bizarre twist of fate, a convicted murderer who had bludgeoned his aunt to death and spent ten years in a mental institution for sexually assaulting an eleven year old girl, was hired as a special police officer by the City of Scranton. Clothed with the official authority of a badge and gun, he sexually assaulted and killed two boys. Suit was filed against a variety of governmental entities for the deaths of the teenagers. Without even considering the merits of the claim, the case was dismissed by the court on the basis of immunity of the government from suit. *Freach v. Commonwealth*, 370 A.2d 1163 (Pa. 1977).

Part of the fabric of our common law is the recognition that certain entities are immune from suit. Those who traditionally enjoyed protection under the law may be classified as follows:

1. sovereign or governmental immunity;
2. judicial immunity;
3. charitable immunity;
4. intra-family immunity; and
5. immunity by contract.

Charitable immunity and intra-family immunity are out-dated concepts and the majority of jurisdictions have abolished this type of immunity or have severely limited its application. Sovereign immunity and immunity by contract are complex topics which are still recognized by the courts and warrant a further discussion.

SECTION 11.5
SOVEREIGN IMMUNITY

Sovereign immunity means, "the king can do no wrong." In application, this ancient English concept prohibits suits against any level of the government unless the sovereign gives its expressed consent to the litigation. As Justice Holmes stated, "A Sovereign is exempt from suit... on the logical and practical ground that there can be no legal right as against the authority that makes the law on which the right depends." *Kawananakoa v. Polyblank*, 205 U.S. 349 (1907).

The justification for sovereign immunity is that:
1. such liability would open a floodgate of litigation;
2. governmental bodies have no available funds to pay damage awards; and
3. public policy favors the idea that it is better that one individual bear the burden of the loss than the public be inconvenienced.

It is not hard to imagine the injustices done over the years to unsuspecting plaintiffs who are denied "a day in court" simply because the government happens to be the wrongdoer. While the courts are reluctant to bar an aggrieved party from pursuing a claim, sovereign immunity is constitutional and recognized by the courts.

Has the government ever given its consent to be sued? In 1946, Congress enacted the Federal Torts Claim Act whereby the federal government agreed to be responsible for the wrongful conduct of its employees committed within the scope of the employment to the same extent as a private individual would be responsible for a "negligent or other wrongful act or omission." Actions by federal employees that constitute intentional torts or discretionary acts are still exempt.

In those sectors of the government that have not passed legislation on the issue of immunity, the courts make a distinction between functions that are "governmental" and those which are "proprietary." Governmental functions are those tasks which can be performed adequately only by the governmental unit and are immune from suit. Examples include the police department, fire department and public schools. Proprietary functions are these activities which are performed by the government but can be delivered just as well by the private sector. These functions include rubbish collection and the providing of utilities. Suit against the governmental unit for these activities are allowed.

In those states or municipalities that have passed legislation on the topic, one must examine the terms of the specific law to see when suit has been authorized. For example, Pennsylvania has enacted legislation on both the state and local levels.

The Commonwealth of Pennsylvania has voted to retain its immunity for the torts of its officers and employees in all cases except nine areas. These areas of liability may be summarized as follows:

1. vehicle liability;
2. medical/professional liability;
3. improper care, custody or control of personal property;
4. dangerous conditions related to Commonwealth real estate, highways and sidewalks;
5. potholes and other dangerous conditions so long as the appropriate agency received actual written notice in advance and had a reasonable amount of time to repair the defect. No claims for property damage are allowed under this exception;
6. improper care, custody and control of animals except wild animals;
7. liquor store sales to minors, persons visibly intoxicated, insane persons or persons of known intemperate habit;
8. National Guard activities; and
9. the administration, manufacture and use of toxoids or vaccines in the Commonwealth.

The State, however, has capped its liability at an aggregate of $1,000,000.00 in damages with no one individual being able to collect more than $250,000.00. This would mean that the Commonwealth would be responsible for a state-owned bridge that collapsed due to the negligent maintenance by the Commonwealth since it falls within the exception of dangerous conditions related to state owned real estate, highways and sidewalks. However, if thirty cars happened to be on the bridge at the time of collapse, the maximum responsibility of the state would be limited to $1,000,000.00 with no one individual receiving more than $250,000.00.

Local governmental units such as cities, townships and counties in Pennsylvania allow suit in only eight areas. These areas of liability may be summarized as follows:

1. negligent operation of a motor vehicle;
2. personal property causing property damage only;
3. real property except that personal injuries sustained by intentional trespassers are not compensable;
4. dangerous conditions related to trees, traffic controls and street lighting;
5. dangerous conditions related to utilities service;
6. dangerous conditions of streets owned by local agencies or by the Commonwealth who contracted with the local agencies for maintenance;
7. dangerous conditions related to sidewalks; and
8. the care, custody and control of animals.

Damage awards against local governmental units are limited to $500,000.00 in the aggregate. An award is further offset by any insurance proceeds available to the plaintiff.

An exception to the rule of sovereign immunity does exist in Pennsylvania when the conduct of the local entity or its employees engage in tortuous actions that can be classified as willful misconduct. In that situation, immunity will not protect the individual. This was the issue in the litigation that arose out of the bombing of the MOVE compound in 1985 by the Philadelphia Police. As anyone who watched the events unfold that day will remember, the fire that was caused by the dropping of a bomb from a police helicopter, was allowed to burn until it spread to many houses in the area. A number of people died and the property damage was enormous. Suit was instituted against a number of city officials including the Police and Fire Commissioners. The issue before the court in *Africa v. City of Philadelphia* is whether the actions of the commissioners arose to willful misconduct so that they may have personal liability for the unfortunate incident.

RAMONA AFRICA V. CITY OF PHILADELPHIA
938 F. SUPP. 1278 (E.D. PA. 1996)

MAY 13, 1985 WAS A DAY OF TRAGEDY in Philadelphia. That day marked the catastrophic culmination of a stand-off between the law enforcement authorities of the City of Philadelphia and the members of a group called "MOVE."

Early in the morning, Police Commissioner Sambor, speaking through a bullhorn outside 6221 Osage Avenue, announced that the police had arrest warrants for four MOVE members and directed that those inside the house come out. That directive was not complied with. Subsequently, massive police gunfire was directed at 6221 Osage Avenue. According to the police, there was also gunfire directed at the police from the MOVE house, some of the gunfire coming from a wooden bunker on the roof. In the late afternoon, a police helicopter dropped an explosive device on the roof. The purposes of this act were to create a hole in the roof through which tear gas could be injected, and to disable the roof-top bunker. Not long after the explosive device was dropped, the roof of 6221 Osage Avenue caught fire. The fire consumed the MOVE residence and left eleven of the thirteen persons inside died. The fire spread to, and consumed scores of neighboring buildings.

Plaintiffs allege that the City, in the course of efforts to apprehend and arrest certain MOVE members, **(1)** dropped an explosive device on the MOVE house and then, **(2)** pursuant to a tactical decision taken by Police Commissioner Gregore Sambor and Fire Commissioner William Richmond, for a period of time deliberately refrained from taking effective steps to extinguish the ensuing fire

It has been the contention of the plaintiffs that the implementation of this decision to delay putting out the fire, — resulting in injuries and deaths to the MOVE members constituted a "battery."

The jury found the City of Philadelphia liable to each of the plaintiffs. The jury also found Commissioners Sambor and Richmond.

In arguing that the jury verdicts are not sufficient to establish liability, Commissioners Sambor and Richmond contend that the plaintiffs' claims must be dismissed for the reason that the batteries have not been judicially determined to constitute "willful misconduct."

In general, the liability of a local government entity for personal injury is confined to situations involving injuries arising from the operation or management of motor vehicles, streets, sidewalks, traffic control systems, utilities, reality, personality, or animals, which are possessed or controlled by the municipality. Also, as a general matter, a municipal employee sued for damages for injuries to a person resulting from acts within the scope of the employee's office or duties: **(1)** is liable for damages only to the same extent as his employing local agency; and **(2)** the person can assert certain defenses such as "official immunity."

If this were the entirety of the statutory scheme, defendants Sambor and Richmond would be wholly insulated from liability, for the reason that the batteries charged against them do not fall within any of the very limited categories of municipal liability. There is, however, a further statutory provision which, in the case of particularly egregious conduct, deprives a municipal employee of the protection contemplated by the statute. That further statutory provision provides as follows:

§ 8550. Willful misconduct

> In any action against a local agency or employee for damages on account of an injury caused by the act of the employee in which it is judicially determined that the act of the employee caused the injury and that such act constituted a crime, actual fraud, actual malice or willful misconduct, the provisions of sections 8545 (relating to official liability generally), 8546 (relating to defense of official immunity), 8548 (relating to indemnity) and 8549 (relating to limitation on damages) shall not apply.

Thus, in seeking to impose liability on Commissioners Sambor and Richmond for batteries the plaintiffs contend that the evidence establishes "willful misconduct" on their part.

The **Political Subdivision Tort Claims Act** confines the tort liability of municipalities to the very limited group of situations where the municipal employee's tortuous conduct was of a particularly egregious nature denominated, "willful misconduct."

The undisputed record seemed to establish that, after the dropping of the explosive device had caused some flames to appear on the roof of 6221 Osage, Commissioner Sambor had a conversation with Commissioner Richmond in which **(1)** the Police Commissioner asked his colleague whether, if the fire were permitted to continue until it had disabled the bunker, the fire could then be extinguished, and (2) Commissioner Richmond expressed his belief that this was feasible; the evidence seemed further to establish that in this conversation Commissioner Richmond then acquiesced in Commissioner Sambor's recommendation that the fire be permitted to spread until it disabled the bunker. The undisputed evidence also seemed to establish another conversation—one in which Managing Director Brooks, after seeing substantial flames on the roof of 6221 Osage, called Commissioner Sambor and directed him to put the fire out. At some point—vigorous firefighting efforts were undertaken; however, the fire spread out of control.

Establishing the time at which events took place is significant only to the extent that its resolution helps in establishing the sequence of events. Thus, key to plaintiffs' claim that Commissioner Sambor deliberately disregarded the directive to put out the fire is the contention that the Sambor-Richmond conversation was subsequent to the Brooks-Sambor conversation in which the Managing Director ordered that the fire be extinguished. And here arises the second difficulty in Ms. Africa's analysis of the evidence at trial. Only one person was in a position to know which conversation came first. That person was Commissioner Sambor, who was party to both conversations. Commissioner Sambor's testimony was that his conversation with Commissioner Richmond preceded his conversation with the Managing Director.

I am not persuaded that the trial testimony establishes that Commissioner Sambor was directed by Managing Director Brooks to put out the fire before Commissioner Sambor and Commissioner Richmond agreed to delay fighting the fire until the flames disabled the bunker. Accordingly, I conclude that plaintiffs have not established, that Commissioner Sambor deliberately disregarded the order of his superior, the Managing Director.

SECTION 11.6
JUDICIAL IMMUNITY

A judge has immunity from suit when he or she acts within the scope of judicial authority and in the discharge of official duties. The purpose of judicial immunity is to insure that a judge is free to render decisions on the merits without fear or influence of being sued by an aggrieved party. The concept, however, does have its limits. A judge remains liable for actions of a non-judicial nature, such as a charge of sexual harassment by a secretary or improper disciplinary actions involving an employee.

DONALD L. MEEK v. COUNTY OF RIVERSIDE
183 F. 3RD 96 (9TH CIR. 1999)

DONALD L. MEEK BROUGHT AN ACTION AGAINST the County of Riverside and two municipal court judges alleging that his right to campaign for public office had been violated when he was fired in retaliation for his seeking election to a municipal court judgeship.

Meek was appointed a Commissioner of Municipal Court. In September of 1995, Meek learned that two vacancies on the Riverside Municipal Court would occur in March and April of 1996. One of the seats was to be filled by a non-partisan election and the other by a gubernatorial appointment. Meek approached then- Commissioner Albert J. Wojcik about an arrangement whereby Meek would support Wojcik in the March, 1996, non-partisan election for the first vacant seat and Wojcik would support Meek in his efforts to obtain a gubernatorial appointment to the second seat.

Shortly after his meeting with Wojcik, Meek concluded that Wojcik would not support him in his effort to obtain the gubernatorial appointment. He also learned that Municipal Judge Curtis R. Hinman had written a letter to Governor Wilson supporting Sherill Nielsen, a close friend of Municipal Judge Rodney Walker, for appointment to the municipal court. Deciding that he had little chance of obtaining the ap-

pointment, Meek chose to run against Wojcik in the March election. During the campaign, Judge Walker allegedly stated that he would fire Meek from his position of court commissioner if Meek lost the election and that he considered Meek his political enemy.

On March 26, 1996, Wojcik was elected judge and he took office on April 23, 1996. On April 4, 1996, then-Commissioner Wojcik, Judge Walker, and Judge Hinman held a vote on whether Meek should be terminated. Wojcik and Walker voted to fire Meek and Judge Hinman abstained.

On April 8, 1996, Judge Hinman informed Meek of the vote to dismiss. Judge Hinman informed Meek that he had a right to a hearing before Wojcik and Walker, but that "it would do no good, because the outcome would be the same."

Meek filed a suit against Wojcik, Walker, and the County of Riverside claiming that he had been fired in retaliation for exercising his right to run for office. Claiming judicial immunity, Wojcik and Walker moved to dismiss the complaint.

It is well settled that judges are generally immune from civil liability. Although unfairness and injustice to a litigant may result on occasion, it is a general principle of the highest importance to the proper administration of justice that a judicial officer, in exercising the authority vested in him, shall be free to act upon his own convictions, without apprehension of personal consequences to himself.

A judge is not deprived of immunity because he takes actions, which are in error, are done maliciously, or are in excess of his authority. The rationale for granting judges immunity from liability for even intentional and malicious conduct while acting in their judicial capacity is that judges should be free to make controversial decisions and act upon their convictions without fear of personal liability. The concern for principled and fearless decision-making forms the basis for judicial immunity. Absolute judicial immunity, however, is only granted when essential to protect the integrity of the judicial process.

There are two situations in which judges are not absolutely immune from liability. First, a judge is not immune from liability for nonjudicial actions, i.e., actions not taken in the judge's judicial capacity. Second, a judge is not immune for actions, though judicial in nature, are taken in the complete absence of all jurisdiction.

The district court found that appellants were not entitled to judicial immunity because the challenged action, their decision to terminate Meek, was an administrative rather than a judicial act. The factors determining whether an act by a judge is a judicial one, relate tò the nature of the act itself, i.e., whether it is a function normally performed by a judge, and to the expectations of the parties, i.e., whether they dealt with the judge in his judicial capacity.

A state court judge is generally not entitled to absolute immunity from liability arising out of a decision to fire a subordinate judicial employee because the decision is not a judicial or adjudicative act, but rather an administrative one. In determining the scope of judicial immunity, the Court stressed that the focus must be on the function that the immunity protects. Judges are granted absolute immunity for their judicial actions in order to safeguard independent and principled judicial decision-making. Although a judge's employment decisions "may be essential to the very functioning of the courts," they are not the type of decisions that traditionally have been regarded as judicial acts meriting absolute immunity.

Appellants' decision to fire a subordinate judicial employee is an administrative decision: the district court did not err in finding that the defendants are not entitled to judicial immunity for such actions.

SECTION 11.7
CHARITABLE IMMUNITY

In the past, charitable organizations enjoyed a preferred status and were immune from tort liability. Charitable immunity was based on the idea that charities should not be concerned with liability so that they may direct their attention to public works and the public good. The courts also wanted to guarantee that the funds of charities were not depleted by judgments rendered against the charities. Most jurisdiction have abolished charitable immunity or have severally curtailed the protection since non-profit organizations may protect themselves against tort liability through insurance. *Sink v. Vinton Wesleyan Church* is a case that arises in one of the few states that still recognizes this archaic concept.

MERLIN S. SINK V. VINTON WESLEYAN CHURCH
50 VA. CIR. 361 (VA. CIR. 1999)

MERLIN S. SINK ARRANGED TO USE THE CHAPEL and social hall of Vinton Wesleyan Church for her daughter's wedding. She paid a fee of approximately $25.00 for use of the social hall facilities. Sink alleges that while at the social hall to decorate, she caught her shoe in a gap created by a detached carpet and was thrown into a brick fireplace, severely injuring herself. She has sued the church for negligence, requesting $250,000 damages.

The church has filed a plea of charitable immunity claiming that it is a charitable organization. It alleges that Sink is a beneficiary of its charitable services. In pertinent part, Sink's deposition testimony reveals that she has exclusively attended the church since she was 16 years old and considers it to be her church; she considers its pastor to be her pastor from whom she would seek spiritual guidance; and her children were raised in this Church with two or them using its social hall for their wedding receptions.

Sink contends that the doctrine of charitable immunity is not applicable because, at the time of the accident, she was a business invitee. Her argument is based upon the facts that she was not baptized a member of the church and had paid a fee for the use of the social hall. She further relies upon the fact that the social hall was used by a fee-generating child care center operated during the week by the pastor's wife and run separately from the church.

In Virginia, charitable institutions enjoy limited immunity from tort liability to their beneficiaries. While many jurisdictions have abandoned the concept of charitable immunity, the Supreme Court of Virginia has made it clear that the de-

cision to abrogate the doctrine of charitable immunity rests with the General Assembly. The justification for the doctrine of charitable immunity rests on public policy grounds.

A policy of the law which prevents him who accepts the benefit of a charity from suing it for the torts of its agents and servants, and thus taking for his private use the funds which have been given for the benefit of humanity, which shields gifts made to charity from the "hungry maw of litigation" and conserves them for purposes of the highest importance to the state, carries on its face its own justification, and, without the aid of metaphysical reasoning, commends itself to the wisdom of mankind.

The issue is whether the plaintiff is a beneficiary of the church. Charitable immunity does not extend to strangers or invitees who have no beneficial relationship to the charitable organization. To be considered a charitable beneficiary for the purpose of charitable immunity, a person must be a direct beneficiary through the receipt of money, goods, or services and not merely someone who indirectly received charitable benefits.

In the present case, Sink was utilizing the church's facilities for her daughter's wedding reception at the time that she fell. She was receiving a direct benefit of the church's charitable bounty. The fact that she was not an "official baptized member" does not remove her from the class of individuals who are beneficiaries of the church's services. She had attended the church since the age of 16, considered the pastor to be her pastor, raised her children in the church, and even used the church's facilities previously for another daughter's wedding.

Nor does the payment of a fee bar Sink from being considered a beneficiary for the purposes of charitable immunity. Sink's testimony established that she paid approximately $25.00 for the use of the fellowship hall. The payment of this nominal amount does not remove her from being a beneficiary of the church's services and facilities.

Sink also advances the argument that the church's rental of the social hall during the week to a child care center operated by the pastor's wife separate from the church should stop the church's claim of charitable immunity. There is no suggestion that the money gained by rental of the hall for the child care center is inconsistent with the church's charitable purposes. Nor was Sink's use of the social hall in any way related to the child care center. Rather, she was using the church's facilities to benefit herself and her family and friends.

Vinton Wesleyan is a charitable organization. Sink was a beneficiary of its charitable services at the time that she fell in the church's social hall. Accordingly, her claim for damages resulting from alleged negligence by the church is barred by the doctrine of charitable immunity.

SECTION 11.8
INTRA-FAMILY IMMUNITY

Traditionally, spouses could not sue one another. This spousal immunity stemmed from the idea that a husband and wife became one legal entity upon marriage. Before states began passing Married Women's Property Acts, a wife had no standing to initiate legal action against her husband. These Acts established a woman's right to property and the capacity to sue and be sued. However, spousal immunity continued to exist because courts feared that suits between spouses would be disruptive to the peace and harmony of the family unit. There was also concern that husbands and wives would fabricate fraudulent claims. Most recent decisions, however, have discarded the validity of spousal immunity and are allowing suits between husband and wives.

Most jurisdictions have also abolished immunity between parents and unemancipated children. The availability of insurance relieves parents of direct responsibility to their children in tort actions so most jurisdictions now allow the suits.

PAULA BEARDEN v. DAVID BEARDEN
499 S.E. 2D 359 (GA. APP. 1998)

PAULA BEARDEN WAS INJURED in an automobile accident while riding as a passenger in a car driven by her husband, David Bearden. She sued her husband, claiming her injuries were caused by his negligent operation of the car. The trial court granted summary judgment in favor of Mr. Bearden on the basis of the interspousal tort immunity doctrine. On appeal, Ms. Bearden claims the trial court erred in applying the doctrine because she alleges that the facts show she and her husband had not lived together for a long period of time and that no marital relationship existed between them. We agree that David Bearden was not entitled to be shielded by the doctrine of interspousal tort immunity as a matter of law, and reverse the trial court's decision.

Mr. Bearden stated that the parties married in November 1987 and separated in early 1989. He stated, however, that during the separation, he and his wife "were together frequently;...spent the night together at motels and other places,...and that, on the day of the accident, my wife and I had been together since the previous day." He stated they were returning from a swimming trip when the accident occurred.

Ms. Bearden stated that the parties have been separated since 1989 "because we could not get along with each other." She stated that during the separation, Mr. Bearden has lived with other women, and she has considered herself "unofficially divorced" from him with "no plan or hope for us getting back together." Ms. Bearden further stated "that there has not been any 'harmony' to preserve in our marriage since we separated in 1989." On the same day Ms. Bearden commenced the present action, she also filed an action seeking a divorce from Mr. Bearden.

The doctrine of interspousal immunity exists to (1) preserve the sanctity of marriage, and (2) to prevent the possibility of collusive lawsuits. This doctrine may be abrogated where there is no marital harmony or unity to preserve and where there is no possibility of collusion. Here, although Mr. and Ms. Bearden did occasionally spend the night together, such evidence without more, does not resolve the factual issue of whether there was a state of marital unity to be preserved. In light of Ms. Bearden's uncontroverted testimony that they had not lived together as husband and wife for more than six years, could not get along with each other, and had no hope or plan for reconciliation at the time of the accident, Mr. Bearden was not entitled to summary judgment as a matter of law. Our law does not presume that where there is some evidence of friendship, civility, or intimacy in a relationship, there exists as a matter of law, a de facto state of marital harmony.

Accordingly, the trial court's grant of summary judgment to Mr. Bearden on the basis of interspousal tort immunity is reversed.

SECTION 11.9
IMMUNITY BY CONTRACT

People are cavalier in their conduct and take many risks unaware of the consequences of their actions. We think nothing of leaving cars and other valuable possessions in the hands of strangers. Reflect upon the last time that you parked your car in a garage. In exchange for your automobile, the attendant provided a ticket which probably contained phrases such as, "We assume no liability for loss or damage;" "Park at your own risk;" or "We are not responsible...". These phrases are known as Immunity by Contract or more properly "exculpatory clauses."

The courts allow parties to allocate their risks by contract but will step in to invalidate exculpatory clauses which result in unfair surprise to one party. The courts examine the subject matter of the contract, the relationship between the parties, the equality of bargaining power, and whether the agreement is against public policy. For instance, exculpatory clauses relieving a party from liability for intentional misconduct or for personal injury due to negligence are not favored. On the other hand, immunity from suit for property damage claims is not so easily challenged.

The following case involves a skiing accident and focuses on the criteria that the court will use in deciding whether to enforce the exculpatory clause.

KARL KOTOVSKY V. SKI LIBERTY OPERATING CORPORATION
603 A.2D 663 (PA. SUPER. 1992)

WIEAND, Judge:

WHILE PARTICIPATING IN THE SECOND HEAT of a downhill ski race, Karl Kotovsky failed to negotiate a turn at the fourth gate and collided with a wooden fence post situated along the side of the course. As a result of this accident, he received serious injuries. Alleging negligence in failing to pad the post, Kotovsky and his wife, Sharon, commenced an action for damages against Ski Liberty Operating Corporation (Ski Liberty), the owner of the slope. In its answer to the complaint, Ski Liberty pleaded two exculpatory agreements and releases which Kotovsky had executed prior to participating in the downhill ski race. By the terms of these agreements and releases, which Kotovsky admitted, he expressly assumed the "risks, conditions and hazards which may occur whether they now be known or unknown." He also released the ski area, as well as the promoters, sponsors, organizers and others, "from any and all liability, whether known or unknown, even though the liability may arise out of negligence or carelessness on the part of persons or entities mentioned above.

The first release provided, in pertinent part, as follows:

> I agree that I am alone responsible for my safety while participating in com-

petitive events and/or training for competitive events and specifically acknowledge that the following persons or entities including the United States Ski Association, the United States Ski Team, the United States Ski Coaches Association, the ski area, the promoters, the sponsors, the organizers, the promoters, the sponsors, the organizers, the promoter clubs, the officials and any agent, representative, officer, director, employee, member or affiliate of any person or entity named above are not responsible for my safety. I specifically RELEASE and DISCHARGE, in advance, those parties from any and all liability whether, known or unknown, even though that liability may arise out of negligence or carelessness on the part of persons or entities mentioned above. I agree to accept all responsibility for the risks, conditions and hazards which may occur whether they now be know or unknown.

Being fully aware of the risks, conditions and hazards of the proposed activity as a competitor, coach or official, I HEREBY AGREE TO WAIVE, RELEASE AND DISCHARGE any and all claims for damages for death, personal injury or property damage which I may have or which may hereafter accrue to me as a result of my participation in competitive events or training for competitive events, against any person or entity mentioned above whether such injury or damage was foreseeable.

I further agree to forever HOLD HARM-LESS and INDEMNIFY all persons and entities identified above, generally or specifically, from any and all liability for death and/or personal injury or property damage result[ing] in any way from my participating in competitive events or training for competitive events.

This Acknowledgment of and Assumption of Risk and Release shall be binding upon my heirs and assigns.

The second release provided as follows.

If you do not accept fully the conditions below do not compete, officiate, coach or in any other way participate in any event.

I, the undersigned, know that alpine and nordic skiing are action sports carrying significant risk of personal injury. Racing, jumping or freestyle competition is even more dangerous. I know that there are natural and man-made obstacles or hazards, surfaces and environmental conditions, and risks which in combination with my action can cause me very severe or occasionally fatal injury. I agree that I and not the ski area or its staff or American Ski Racing Alliance, Inc. (ASRA) or its staff, am responsible for my safety while I participate in, or train for these events.

I HEREBY RELEASE and discharge, on behalf of myself, my heirs, executors, personal representatives and assigns,

ASRA, USSA, their affiliates and subsidiaries and their respective directors, officers, agents, employees, successors and assigns or any of them, from any and all actions, causes of action, claims, damages, demands, injuries and liabilities of any nature whatsoever (including reasonable attorneys fees and interest) arising out of or in any manner connected with their involvement with ski races organized, promoted or operated by ASRA.

Because of these exculpatory agreements and releases, the trial court entered judgment on the pleadings in favor of Ski Liberty. The plaintiffs appealed.

Downhill skiing is a dangerous activity. Downhill racing is even more dangerous. In recognition of the hazardous nature of such activity, the legislature has expressly provided that assumption of the risk shall be a complete defense to actions for downhill skiing injuries. 42 Pa. C.S. Section 7102(c).

This provision of the law was enacted as an amendment to the Comparative Negligence Law as follows:

(c) Downhill skiing.—

1. The General Assembly finds that the sport of downhill skiing is practiced by a large number of citizens of this Commonwealth and also attracts to this Commonwealth large numbers of nonresidents significantly contributing to the economy of this Commonwealth. It is recognized that as in some other sports, there are inherent risks in the sport of downhill skiing.

In the instant case, appellant was an experienced skier, who was well acquainted with the hazards of downhill racing. Indeed, he had previously skied on the same slope on which he received his injuries. Despite this knowledge, he expressly agreed to assume the risk of injury and released the owner and operator of the slope from all liability, even that which might result from negligence.

In *Zimmer v. Mitchell and Ness*, **385 A.2d 437 (1978),** the Superior Court laid down the following standards for a valid exculpatory agreement.

> The contract must not contravene any policy of the law. It must be a contract between individuals relating to their private affairs. Each party must be a free bargaining agent, not simply one drawn into an adhesion contract, with no recourse but to reject the entire transaction. In the instant case the validity of the agreement is apparent. However, to be enforceable, several additional standards must be met. First, we must construe the agreement strictly and against the party asserting it. Finally, the agreement must spell out the intent of the parties with the utmost particularity.

The agreement in the instant case was not one of adhesion. Appellant was not required to enter the contract, but did so voluntarily in order to participate in a downhill ski race. This activity was not essential to appellant's personal or economic well-being. See: *Valeo v. Pocono International Raceway, Inc.,* **347 Pa.Super. 230, 500 A.2d 492 (1985).**

The releases also did not contravene public policy. They were contracts between private parties and pertained only to the parties' private rights. They did not in any way affect the rights of the public. Indeed, the legislature's action in enacting 42 Pa.C.S. §7102(c) would seem to suggest that the policy in this Commonwealth is to enforce the doctrine of assumption of the risk for persons knowingly engaging in downhill skiing.

The exculpatory agreement and release in this case demonstrated clearly and unequivocally the intent of the parties. Its purpose, as stated expressly therein, was to release the "ski area" from all liability for injury to appellant caused by natural or man made obstacles on the slope, including hazards resulting form negligence by the owner. The fact that the release specifically referred to and included possible liability for acts of negligence distinguishes the release in this case from that in *Brown v. Racquetball Centers, Inc.,* **369 Pa.Super. 13, 534 A.2d 842 (1987),** where the plaintiff had slipped on a wet tile floor while exiting a shower. Because the owner of the athletic facilities had been charged with negligence, the plaintiff's action was not barred by a release which failed to absolve the owner from liability for his own negligence. In the instant case, appellee was also released from liability for its own negligence.

There was no compulsion for appellant to participate in the downhill ski race which caused his injuries. In order to participate in this hazardous event, he agreed to assume the risk of injury and released the owner of the slope, as well as others, from all liability for injuries resulting therefrom, including injuries caused by another's negligence. Appellant's exculpatory agreement and release bars the present action. Therefore, the trial court properly entered judgment on the pleadings for appellee.

Judgment affirmed.

1. Witte sold his beer distributorship in 1987. His accountant prepared Witte's tax returns. However, he did not include payments on Witte's individual income tax return for which the buyer of the business was making to an escrow account on Witte's behalf. Nevertheless, the bank reported the payments to the Internal Revenue Services which audited the seller in 1994. As the result of the accountant's negligent actions in 1987, Witte had to pay approximately $325,000 in taxes, penalties and interest. At the end of 1995, Witte sued the accountant for malpractice. The accountant argued the statute of limitations as a defense to his 1987 act of negligence. That statute of limitations in South Dakota provides that an action against an accountant for malpractice must be commenced within four years after the alleged occurrence in the absence of fraudulent concealment of the negligence advice. Is this claim for the account's malpractice barred by the statute of limitations? *Witte v. Goldey,* **590 N.W. 2d 266 (S.D. 1999).**

2. A family court judge ordered Jamerson to provide child support and health insurance for his minor children. The father defaulted on this obligation so the judge ordered Jamerson's wages attached. The father's employer sent a letter to the judge indicating that the employee had no health coverage available at work. The employer also told the judge to "get a real job" and to leave the employee "alone." The judge issued a contempt citation against the employer, which charges were subsequently dismissed. The employer then sued the judge for abuse of process. The employer claimed that the judge acted outside the scope of his jurisdiction in issuing a rule to hold the employer in contempt of court since he was not a party to the underlying litigation. Will the judge be protected by the doctrine of judicial immunity? *McEacheran v. Block,* **496 S.E. 2d 659 (S.C. 1998).**

3. Mrs. Hack was injured in automobile accident while a passenger in a car driven by her husband. She sued her husband to collect for personal injury. The negligent spouse claimed interspousal tort immunity. Will Mr. Hack be responsible to his wife for her injuries since Pennsylvania no longer recognized the doctrine of interspousal immunity? *Hack v. Hack,* **433 A.2d 859 (Pa. 1981).**

4. A father raised a window in the second story bedroom two inches in order to increase the air circulation in the room. He then left for work with the babysitter asleep on the couch. The child awoke, opened the window and fell out. The parents instituted suit against the owner of the building for negligent removal of the storm window and in failing to provide a guardrail to prevent the child's fall. In turn, the owner of the building sued the parents for contribution

or indemnification in the action brought on behalf of the child. In New York, a parent cannot be liable for contribution or indemnification unless the act of the parent violates a duty owed to the "world at large" or unless a dangerous instrumentality was entrusted to the child, the use of which caused injury or harm. Will the parents be held liable for the injuries sustained by the child in the New York lawsuit? *McNamara v. Banney,* **672 N.Y.S. 2d 569 (N.Y. App. 1998).**

SECTION 11.11
INTERNET REFERENCES

For more information on the materials contained in this chapter, see the following Internet references:

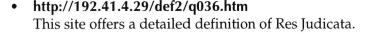

*   **http://192.41.4.29/def2/q036.htm**
    This site offers a detailed definition of Res Judicata.

*   **http://greatspirit.earth.com/taylor.html**
    This provides a discussion of an attorney's of sovereign immunity.

CHAPTER 12

REMEDIES AVAILABLE IN COURT

SECTION 12.1
AN OVERVIEW

Judicial remedies may be divided into remedies at law and remedies in equity. Remedies at law developed from common law and generally result in an award of money damages. These damages are categorized as compensatory, punitive, nominal, and liquidated.

When remedies at law are inadequate, a party may seek equitable relief. Developed in the Chancery court, equitable remedies either prohibit one from committing specified acts or require specific actions to be taken by the party. Such relief can include an injunction to force employees to return to work or specific performance to require a party to go through with the sale of a unique item such as a Picasso painting. The forms of equitable relief include restitution, reformation, injunctions, declaratory judgments and specific performance. A party who violates an equitable decree may be held in contempt of court and be subject to the payment of fines and possible imprisonment.

There is a constitutional right to trial by jury in suits at common law. No such right exists in equity cases. A party may, however, seek both legal and equitable remedies in the same suit.

JUDICIAL REMEDIES

LAW	EQUITY
Compensatory	Injunction
Punitive	Reformation
Nominal	Restitution
Liquidated	Declaratory Judgment
	Specific Performance

SECTION 12.2
COMPENSATORY DAMAGES

The purpose of compensatory damages is to award a sum of money that will return an aggrieved party to the status quo as though nothing ever happened. That is, these damages compensate a party for loss or injury.

In a **tort** action the damages should place the injured party in as substantially good a position as that occupied before the injury. Such damages, however, may be difficult to quantify.

Examine the case of Joe Hodge for having a surgical sponge left in his stomach by Dr. Feelgood. How much money should Joe receive for the doctor's mistake? The most obvious damages are the recovery of out of pocket expenses. These items would include:

1. medical expenses; **2.** lost wages; and **3.** property damage.

It is without question that Joe can recover all of the medical expenses incurred by having to undergo the second operation. Any time that he loses from work is also reimbursable.

When these items are added together, Joe will be reimbursed for all of his out of pocket expenses. Financially, he will be returned to the same position that he was in before he had to undergo the second surgery. Has Joe, however, been fully compensated for his second surgery?

Another item of recovery, known as pain and suffering is allowed in personal injury actions. Joe is entitled to be compensated for the anguish that he had to endure because of the sponge that was left in his stomach, including the trauma and pain associated with having to undergo a second operation. Pain and suffering cannot be easily calculated like other damages, which can be reduced to a mathematical certainty. Pain and suffering is subjective and determined by the fact-finder at trial. The value of each case will differ. If Joe makes a speedy recovery from the second surgery with no ill effects, his pain and suffering will be worth far less than if he suffers from the residuals of the incident for the rest of his life. As a rule, it is not uncommon to see a plaintiff recover a verdict that is 3 to 10 times the amount of the out-of-pocket expenses.

Damages in a **contract** action should place the injured party in the position he or she would have occupied had the contract not been breached. In other words, the plaintiff is entitled to receive the benefit of its bargain. Suppose Joe Hodge contracts with Dr. Feelgood to purchase the physician's boat for $20,000. On the day that Joe learns that Feelgood breached the contract, the market value of the boat is $22,000. Joe is entitled to the difference between the contract price and the market price, or $2,000. What if Joe can purchase a comparable boat for $21,500 within a reasonable time after the breach? He would be entitled to the difference between the cover price and the contract price or $1,500.

Joe Hodge is also entitled to any special damages that were caused by the breach. Special damages are limited to those losses that are foreseeable, reasonably certain, and unavoidable. For example, say that Feelgood knew that Joe needed the boat to replace a vessel for Joe's summer charter fishing business. Hodge has operated the business for five years earning approximately $8,000 each summer. If Hodge can't replace the boat before the start of the season, the doctor will be soaked for the additional $8,000 for leaving Joe high and dry.

If Joe is the breaching party, what can the aggrieved seller recover? Suppose the contract price were still $20,000 but the boat's market value had slipped to $19,000 on the scheduled date of contract performance. Feelgood's lost benefit would be the difference between the contract price and the market price or $1,000. If the seller can resell the boat, the damages will be the difference between the contract price and the resale price.

SECTION 12.3
PUNITIVE DAMAGES

The purpose of punitive damages is to punish the tort-feasor for his or her misconduct so that the types of incident in question will never occur again. Rarely are punitive damages allowed in a breach of contract claim. Such awards are more commonly found in tort actions when the defendant has engaged in outrageous or gross misconduct. Causing an accident by going through a traffic light is not sufficient to give rise to punitive damages, unless the defendant was drunk, the driver intentionally went through the light or the wrongdoer was driving at a speed far in excess of the speed limit.

Punitive damage awards can be staggering especially since some states allow a jury to consider the net worth of the defendant in calculating the verdict. According to an article from an on-line service provided by Court TV, punitive damages accounted for nearly 90% of the top 10 largest verdicts in 1999. These top ten awards amounted to a staggering $18.6 billion dollars in punitive damages. This record for punitive damages, however, was toppled in the year 2000 when a $144 billion punitive damages award was entered against the tobacco industry in Florida.

WHITNEY HOUSTON v. NEW YORK POST CO., INC.
1977 WL 10034 (S.D. N.Y. 1997)

WHITNEY HOUSTON COMMENCED THIS LIBEL ACTION after defendant New York Post falsely reported that she had been hospitalized following an overdose of diet pills. She alleges personal humiliation and "mental anguish" along with expenses for "damage control." She seeks compensatory damages of $10,000,000 and punitive damages of $50,000,000.

On Friday, June 25, 1993, David Miller, a reporter for the Post, received an anonymous phone call claiming that Houston had over-dosed on illegal drugs and had been admitted to the hospital at which the caller was employed. The caller further stated that plaintiff's husband was with her, along with Eddie Murphy. Miller called Florence Anthony at her home in an effort to confirm the story. Anthony was in Orlando, Florida that weekend. After receiving the message on Saturday morning, Anthony phoned Regina Brown to confirm the report knowing that Brown, a former publicist for Houston, maintained close contacts with members of the plaintiff's family. Defendant alleges that Brown agreed to make some calls in an effort to confirm the story, and that Brown told Anthony of plaintiff's use of diet pills and of her depression. Brown denies making these statements. Anthony claims that she made several attempts to confirm the story, calling plaintiff's public relations firm and receiving no answer, attempting to call Lois Smith, plaintiff's publicist, but not being able to obtain her phone number, and finally calling plaintiff's company, Nippy, Inc., receiving no answer.

After speaking with Brown, Florence Anthony phoned Hoffman, at the Post and relayed to him what Brown had allegedly told her. Hoffman started working on the article on Sunday, June 27, 1993. He phoned the Mount Sinai Hospital in Miami, which refused to either confirm or deny that Houston had been treated there. Hoffman claims he also attempted to contact Mr. Murphy's manager but was unsuccessful. Hoffman reviewed the Post's file of articles about plaintiff, some of which contained information about plaintiff's recent struggle controlling her weight. Hoffman then wrote the Article, which was published the next day.

The article stated that plaintiff had been hospitalized because she "overdosed on prescription diet pills" after having been severely depressed about her weight. It further stated that the overdose caused plaintiff to suffer an acute heart arrhythmia, for which she was taken to the coronary care unit of Miami's Mount Sinai Guggenheim Pavilion and released 90 minutes later. In fact, plaintiff was performing that evening in Washington, DC. She neither overdosed nor was admitted to Mount Sinai Hospital at that time. Moreover, there is no such building as the Guggenheim Pavilion at Miami's Mount Sinai Hospital. Defendant has admitted to the falsity of the article, and indeed printed a conspicuous correction on June 30, 1993.

Houston argues that the article is defamatory because "it implied to the average reader that plaintiff was so depressed and despondent that she attempted to take her life by overdosing on diet pills. Second, plaintiff argues that the article is defamatory in that it "had a tendency to injure plaintiff in her profession since it implied, a mere matter of days before she was to begin an extensive tour, that she was mentally and physically unable to perform."

In the instant case, the recklessness of the reporter is at the heart of the accusation.

Plaintiff contends that the defendant did not adequately investigate the story prior to publication. Defendant contends that they made a number of efforts to contact the plaintiff and her representatives, but those attempts were unsuccessful. Defendant says that it relied on corroborating information supplied by Regina Brown. Brown now denies the statements attributed to her.

Under New York state law, punitive damages in a libel action are appropriate where there are "circumstances of aggravation and outrage, such as spite or malice, or a fraudulent or evil motive on the part of the defendant and where plaintiff makes a showing, by clear and convincing evidence, that the wrongdoing was "intentional and deliberate." Even if every material fact is construed in a light most favorable to plaintiff, Houston, fails to meet this burden. In publishing the article, defendant omitted the most unsavory aspects of the anonymous tip, such as alleged use of illegal drugs. Moreover, within 48 hours, defendant published a conspicuous, clear, and lengthy correction. These facts, and the complete absence of any compelling evidence of evil motive presented by the plaintiff, make it clear that no reasonable person could find that the article was published with the type of personal hatred or ill will required to sustain a claim for punitive damages in a libel action. Thus, the plaintiff's punitive damages claim is dismissed.

SECTION 12.4
NOMINAL DAMAGES

Nominal damages provide a remedy where a technical wrong has been committed but no actual harm has resulted. Courts will acknowledge the legal rights of the complaining party, but will award only a trivial amount, such as one dollar, to the "injured" party. It is as if the court is saying "so what."

For example, Kathy carelessly opened her car door, putting a slight dent into Nicole's already blemished and rusted 1974 Chevy. If Nicole sues Kathy, it is likely that the court would award only nominal damages since there was no real harm to Nicole's property.

ESPN, INC. v. OFFICE OF THE COMMISSIONER OF BASEBALL
76 F. SUPP. 2D 416 (S.D. N.Y. 1999)

ON OCTOBER 15, 1999, ESPN, INC. and the Office of the Commissioner of Baseball moved to preclude the admission of certain evidence at their forthcoming trial.

Previously, I ruled that ESPN breached its 1996 telecasting agreement with Baseball when it preempted six baseball games scheduled for Sunday nights in September 1998 and September 1999 without the prior written approval of Baseball. ESPN broadcast NFL football games rather than the previously scheduled baseball games on those six nights.

Baseball claims that it has been damaged in an amount "believed to exceed millions of dollars" as a result of ESPN's breach of the 1996 Agreement.

Because Baseball received full payment from ESPN under the contract, it may only seek extra-contractual damages stemming from the six preemptions.

ESPN seeks to preclude Baseball from introducing testimony of its alleged monetary damages. ESPN contends that "there is no factual basis to support any claim for monetary damages aris-

ing from these perceived injuries, and that such claims are the product of speculation and guesswork."

Baseball argues that it has made the "requisite showing of damage" and therefore, it is "entitled to have the opportunity to prove its damages at trial."

It is well-established that a plaintiff must prove the existence of damages with certainty in order to recover for breach of contract. Although it is true that "[w]hen the existence of damage is certain, and the only uncertainty is as to its amount, the plaintiff will not be denied recovery of substantial damages," but even then the plaintiff must show "a stable foundation for a reasonable estimate" of damages.

During discovery, ESPN served Baseball with interrogatories regarding its claims for monetary damages. Among other things, ESPN asked Baseball to "state the amount of monetary damages you seek in this action and explain the basis for the computation of your claim." Baseball responded as follows: "Baseball has not quantified the amount of damages it has sustained by reason of ESPN's willful refusal to carry baseball games as required by the 1996 Agreement."

Nowhere in its response does Baseball set forth any specific dollar amount of monetary damages other than its estimate that damages are "believed to exceed millions of dollars." Nor does Baseball set forth any method of calculating its alleged damages.

Finally, this Court held oral argument on ESPN's motion to preclude damages evidence. During that argument, this Court specifically asked counsel for Baseball whether Baseball had any "concrete proof of monetary harm." Counsel for Baseball was unable to show "any loss of sponsorship, any loss of advertising, or any loss of ancillary sales or ticket sales." As counsel for Baseball conceded: "We have not shown specific losses your Honor, we agree with you 'there. What we have said is we believe it did affect us."

As the above-quoted testimony and answers to ESPN's interrogatories demonstrate, there can be no question that Baseball has failed to adequately demonstrate either the fact of damages or the amount of damages. Put simply, Baseball's subjective belief that the amount of damages is "significant" does not meet any of the required proofs set forth under New York law. To the contrary, under New York law, a claim of damages for loss of reputation and future profits must be "reasonably certain." Baseball's damages claim is based on nothing more than its own vague assertions that it was "hurt." The proffered unsupported allegations are simply inadequate to sustain a claim for damages under New York law, and therefore ESPN's motion to preclude damages evidence is granted.

Although Baseball is not entitled to an award of money damages, it may still receive nominal damages. It is a well-settled tenet of contract law that even if the breach of contract caused no loss or if the amount of the loss cannot be proven with sufficient certainty, the injured party is entitled to recover, as nominal damages, a small sum fixed without regard to the amount of the loss, if any." Accordingly, I will instruct the jury that if Baseball proves its breach of damages claim, it is entitled to an award of nominal damages.

For the reason set forth above, Baseball is precluded from presenting damages evidence at trial and is only entitled to seek an award of nominal damages.

SECTION 12.5
LIQUIDATED DAMAGES

Contracting parties can agree in advance on the amount of damages that will be paid in the event of a default or breach of contract. These amounts are known as liquidated damages and are appropriate when the damages are uncertain and difficult to prove. The stipulated sum should be a reasonable forecast of the damages, although the plaintiff may recover more or less than the actual loss. If the liquidated amount is unreasonable and grossly disproportionate to the loss incurred, a court may refuse to uphold the agreement.

A common example of a liquidated damage clause is a real estate agreement that requires the forfeiture of a deposit or down payment in the event of default.

Air travel is the subject of a number of liquidated damage clauses imposed unilaterally by the airline industry and governments of many countries. In 1929, the Warsaw Convention was ratified by a number of countries and limited compensatory damages recoverable against airlines to $75,000 per plaintiff for personal injury to passengers of international flights on a journey to or from the United States. If the trip does not have contact with this country, liability of the carrier for personal injury is limited to between $10,000 to $20,000 per passenger.

Additional protection can be obtained by purchasing insurance from a private company. Such insurance is not affected by the limitation of the carrier's liability under the Warsaw Convention, any tariff or the plane ticket.

Would an airline be allowed to limit its liability for damages for a domestic flight between two U.S. cities? That is your next assignment since the firm has received a new case on this issue. Mr. Dodge will provide you with more information.

SECTION 12.6
HODGE V.
EASTCOAST
AIRLINES

PROBLEM TWELVE

HODGE, DODGE AND LODGE
ATTORNEYS AT LAW
MEMORANDUM

To: All Law Clerks

FROM: Gregory Olan Dodge

RE: Hodge v. Eastcoast Airlines
Limitation of Liability for Lost Luggage in Domestic Travel

Joe Hodge just called and he could not stop crying over the loss of one of his most treasured possessions. Here is the story.

Joe is a big fan of "The King." It seems that when our client was a youth, he spent some time in Nashville. One night, he went to a bar to hear the band "Country Bumpkins." The lead singer looked familiar but Joe couldn't place him. He waited around until the group was finished and approached the singer. "You're great!" exclaimed Joe and asked the singer for an autograph. To his amazement, the singer said, "Son, you are a nice kid. Take this guitar and enjoy yourself." The singer then wrote "The King" on the guitar and handed Joe the instrument.

Our client recently had the guitar appraised and it was valued at $50,000. About three weeks ago, Joe was reading Rolling Stone Magazine and came across an advertisement for fans of "The King." For a nominal fee, one could travel to all the locations where "The King" had been sighted during the past year.

Joe immediately booked his trip and received a plane ticket from Eastcoast Airlines. This domestic airline is able to offer inexpensive fares because it utilizes retired pilots and offers a no-frills operation.

Joe checked his guitar with the airline along with the rest of his luggage. Unfortunately, during unexpected turbulence, the baggage door of the plane opened and the guitar was history. Our client desires to sue the airline, but Eastcoast Airlines states that its liability is limited to $1,250.00.

I reviewed the plane ticket and found the following notice on the ticket:

NOTICE OF BAGGAGE LIABILITY LIMITATIONS

Liability for loss, delay or damage to checked baggage is limited as follows unless a higher value is declared in advance and additional charges are paid: $1,250 per passenger.

Are such clauses enforceable? What policy considerations support the enforcement of such clauses? What is required for the clause to be enforced? Joe's guitar was worth $50,000 and not $1,250. This certainly seems unfair considering the airline's negligence. The Warsaw Convention is inapplicable since this was a domestic flight. A research assistant found a case on point against TWA. Read the decision and let me know what you think.

MARY MARTIN v. TRANS WORLD AIRLINES, INC.
280 A.2D 642 (PA. SUPER. 1972)

MARY MARTIN BROUGHT SUIT TO RECOVER $2,200, the stipulated value of wearing apparel contained in a piece of luggage which was lost in transit when the plaintiff was traveling on defendant's airline from New York City to Pittsburgh.

The plaintiff had checked her baggage at the East side terminal at 42nd Street, New York City, and then proceeded to the airport. The agent of the defendant gave the plaintiff a baggage claim check which recited on its front: "Baggage checked subject to the tariffs indicating limitations of liability contained therein." A similar notice was also printed on the airline ticket.

In addition to the above notices, there were notices posted in bold-face type and prominently displayed in the baggage wells at the East Side terminal and at the airline ticket counter and also at the passenger boarding gates which bore the following notation:

"Tariff regulations limit airline liability for baggage to actual value not to exceed:

Domestic - $250

International - $495

unless higher valuation declared in advance and appropriate charges paid."

Similar signs were posted at the Pittsburgh airport in the baggage wells, at the ticket counter, and at boarding gates.

The plaintiff did not declare any valuation on any of her luggage. One bag was missing. She had testified that she didn't read the small print on her ticket and the baggage check, didn't see the posted signs, and had no knowledge of the limitations. Mary Martin denied knowledge of the limitations, although in her profession as a singer, she was a seasoned traveler.

Under the Civil Aeronautics Act, an airline Carrier may by tariff limit its liability and such tariff is valid even though loss of property is the result of the company's negligence. The tariff provisions are part of the contract, and it is the duty of the passenger to declare the higher valuation and pay the higher rate if he wished protection in excess of the limited amount.

This Court held in a similar case:

> The requirement that a passenger must be offered a fair opportunity to choose between higher or lower liability before an interstate carrier can limit recovery for loss of baggage to an amount less than the actual loss sustained does not require that the passenger be actually informed that a choice of rates is available.

> The appellant had ample opportunity to discover there was a choice of rates available. The baggage check which she received made reference to the tariff regulations under which the baggage was transported. In addition, the appellee had signs posted in the bus terminal referring to the limitations of liability for checked bags and advising how travelers could increase their protection.

Unlimited liability or even common law liability for negligence would seriously affect the economic life of a transportation industry already subsidized by government to insure its healthy operation. Unlimited liability would be an open invitation to fraud.

It should be noted that the United States courts have never permitted airlines to limit their liability with regard to injury and death actions on domestic flights. The Civil Aeronautics Board has always permitted limitations on baggage liability. The Second Circuit Court has held that tickets must be delivered to the traveler "in such a manner as to afford him a reasonable opportunity to take protection against the limited liability."

Even if we were to hold that notice on the baggage check and ticket was in too small print to bring notice home to the traveler, it would not dispose of the conspicuous signs in the baggage wells, ticket office, and the boarding gates, which not only gave notice of the filing of tariffs but advised of the right to file for a higher valuation. In addition, the record shows Martin was a seasoned traveler and had many opportunities to see the posted signs, and it is highly unlikely that she had no knowledge of the value limitation on luggage and her choice to pay a fee for higher valuation. A person may not be heard to say she did not see what should have been clearly visible to her.

This record had overwhelming evidence that such notice was given to Martin. Therefore, judgment is entered in favor of the plaintiff and against the defendant in the amount of $250, the amount as limited by the filed tariff.

ANSWER SHEET
PROBLEM TWELVE

Name: _____

Please Print Clearly

1. Are such liquidated damage clauses enforceable?

_____

_____

_____

_____

_____

_____

_____

_____

_____

_____

_____

_____

_____

_____

_____

_____

_____

_____

_____

_____

_____

2. What policy considerations support the enforcement of such clauses?

_____

_____

_____

_____

_____

_____

_____

_____

_____

3. What is required for the clause to be enforced?

_____

_____

_____

_____

_____

_____

_____

_____

_____

SECTION 12.7
INJUNCTION

An injunction is an equitable order issued by a court that directs a person to do something (mandatory injunction) or to refrain from doing something (prohibitory injunction). Injunctions are further classified as: *1. permanent, 2. preliminary* and *3. temporary restraining orders* ("TRO").

A permanent injunction is a final resolution of a dispute issued after a full hearing of all relevant factors. In granting an injunction, the court will evaluate the adequacy of the remedy at law, the enforceability of the decree, and the comparative hardship to the parties.

A preliminary injunction is granted as an emergency measure before a full hearing on the merits can be held. The plaintiff must give notice to the defendant of the proceeding and the court will conduct an informal hearing to review the issue. If the plaintiff demonstrates that irreparable harm will result without such an order, the court will grant the injunction to maintain the status quo prior to a final determination of the dispute.

A TRO is an **ex parte** injunction, or an injunction granted without notice to the defendant. Because a court hears only the plaintiff's side of the case, it will grant the order only if the need for relief is so urgent that there is no time for notice and a hearing. The plaintiff must also establish that an irreparable harm will occur. Since there is no notice to the defendant, the court weighs factors more heavily against the plaintiff. These **ex parte** proceedings are always followed by a full hearing on the merits of the dispute.

Injunctive relief is a tool frequently used by employers or the government to regulate the conduct of striking employees. For instance, a prohibitory injunction can be obtained to limit the number of pickets at a facility or to prohibit violent conduct of striking employees.

Does a court of equity, however, have the power to order striking employees to return to work? In the absence of a law or provision in the collective bargaining agreement to the contrary, the court will not order striking workers to return to the job place unless the health, welfare and safety of the public is threatened. ***Jersey Shore Area School District v. Jersey Shore Education Association*, 548 A.2d 1202 (Pa. 1988)** addresses this issue in the context of a strike by school teachers.

The Pennsylvania Supreme Court balanced the following two competing interests in deciding whether to order striking school teachers back to work:

1. The Public Employees' Relation Act which gives teachers the right to strike; versus

2. The Public School Code which requires that school districts provide 180 days of pupil instruction. Failure to do so can result in non-eligibility for state funding.

The court held that loss of funding alone is insufficient to meet the immediate and irreparable harm standard. However, the court found that an injunction to force striking teachers to return to work was warranted given the potential loss of state funds coupled with the socio-economic factors impacting upon the students themselves. Falling short of the 180 days of school instruction would place seniors at a competitive disadvantage when taking the Scholastic Aptitude Test (SAT), it denied certain students free hot lunches and forced parents to experience greater difficulties and financial burdens for day-care arrangements. Therefore, a teachers' strike, which makes 180 days of pupil instruction impossible, creates a threat to the health, safety and welfare of the public, satisfying the criteria for the issuance of an injunction.

A number of record companies instituted suit against Napster in order to block the online service from making available to the public copyrighted songs. Following a decision by the 9th Circuit Court of Appeals on remand, the district court entered an order directing Napster not to allow others to copy, download, or transmit copyrighted sound recordings from its site. That order is as follows:

UNITED STATES DISTRICT COURT
NORTHERN DISTRICT OF CALIFORNIA

A&M Records, Inc., Et Al.	No. C 99-05183 MHP
v.	MDL No. C 00-1369 MHP
Napster, Inc.	**ORDER**

It is this 5th day of March, 2001, HEREBY ORDERED that, during the pendency of this action and until final judgment is entered, Napster, Inc. is enjoined as follows:

1. Napster is preliminary enjoined from engaging in, or facilitating others in, copying, downloading, uploading, transmitting, or distributing copyrighted sound recordings in accordance with this Order.

2. Plaintiffs shall provide notice to Napster of their copyrighted sound recordings providing for each work:

    (A) the title of the work;

    (B) the name of the featured recording artist performing the work;

    (C) the name(s) of one or more files available on the Napster system containing such work; and

(D) a certification that plaintiffs own or control the rights alleg-edly infringed. Plaintiffs shall make a substantial effort to identify the infringing files as well as the names of the artist and title of the copyrighted recording.

3. The Ninth Circuit held that the burden of ensuring that no copy-ing, downloading, uploading, transmitting or distributing of plaintiffs' copyrighted work occurs on the system is shared between the parties. The court "placed the burden on plaintiffs to provide notice to Napster and imposed on Napster the burden of policing the system within the limits of the system. The court anticipates that is may be easier for Napster to search the files available on its system at any particular time against lists of copyrighted record-ings provided by plaintiffs. The court deems that the result of such a search provide Napster with reasonable knowledge of specific infringing files" as required by the Ninth Circuit.

4. Once Napster "receives reasonable knowledge" of specific infring-ing files containing copyrighted sound recordings, Napster shall, within three (3) business days, prevent such files from being in-cluded in the Napster index.

5. Within three (3) business days of receipt of reasonable notice of infringing files, Napster shall affirmatively search the names of all files being made available by all users at the time those users log on, and prevent the downloading, uploading, transmitting or dis-tributing of the noticed copyrighted sound recordings.

6. Plaintiffs may provide to Napster in advance of release the artist name, title of the recording, and release date of sound recordings for which there is a substantial likelihood of infringement on the Napster system. Napster shall, beginning with the first infringe-ment file, block access to or through its system to the identified recording.

7. Within five (5) business days of the date of this Order, and within five (5) business days of service of notice by plaintiffs as provided in Paragraphs 2 or 5 of this Order, Napster shall serve upon plain-tiffs and file with the court a Report of Compliance identifying the steps it has taken to comply with this Order.

8. If in implementing this preliminary injunction the parties dispute the ability of Napster to carry out the duties established under this Order, the parties may set the matter for hearing before the court.

9. This order is effective immediately, a bond in the amount of Five Million Dollars ($5,000,000.00) already having been posted with the Court.

Judge Marilyn Hall Patel
MARILYN HALL PATEL
Chief Judge
United State District Court
Northern District of California

SECTION 12.8
RESTITUTION

The goal of restitution is to prevent one party from unfairly benefiting at the expense of another. This remedy returns to the injured party either its property that is in the defendant's possession or monetary damages. Such damages are measured by the amount the defendant benefited or was "unjustly enriched." The defendant not only has to return the plaintiff to the status quo, but must also return any "fruits" or profits that the defendant earned by use of the property.

THOMAS MITCHELL V. WILLIAM MOORE
729 A.2D 1200 (PA. SUPER 1999)

THOMAS MITCHELL AND WILLIAM MOORE first met in 1980; the two men quickly developed a romantic relationship. Moore resided in Elverson, Pennsylvania and Mitchell in South Carolina. In the spring of 1981, Mitchell accepted Moore's invitation to spend his "off season" at Moore's Chester County farm. By 1985, Mitchell had permanently moved to Elverson, where he resided at Moore's farm without paying rent, worked a full-time job with a company located in Lancaster, Pennsylvania, and assisted Moore in maintaining his house and farm. Among other things, Mitchell took care of the farm animals. In 1990, Mitchell enrolled at Penn State University for graduate studies. As a result of his academic schedule, he was unable to maintain the farm. Soon thereafter, the parties' relationship soured; Mitchell moved out of Moore's residence in June of 1994.

In 1995, Mitchell brought an action against Moore and sought restitution, for the services he rendered to Moore throughout the thirteen years the two men lived together on the farm. In his complaint, Mitchell alleged that Moore had: promised him compensation for his services rendered to maintain and operate his farm; agreed to compensate him for his help in running an antique cooperative (co-op) that Mitchell had purchased; and promised him future compensation and the devise of property in a will and codicil.

Moore filed a counterclaim seeking $139,300.00 representing reasonable rent for the 139 months Mitchell lived on his farm rent-free and as compensation for various utility and telephone bills, taxes, car payments, and other miscellaneous expenses paid by Moore on Mitchell's behalf.

Mitchell's claim for restitution lies upon the theory of unjust enrichment. "Unjust enrichment" is essentially an equitable doctrine. Where unjust enrichment is found, the law implies a contract, which requires the defendant to pay to the plaintiff the value of the benefit conferred. The elements necessary to prove unjust enrichment are:

1. benefits conferred on defendant by plaintiff;

2. appreciation of such benefits by defendant; and

3. acceptance and retention of such benefits under such circumstances that it would be inequitable for defendant to retain the benefit without payment of value. In determining if the doctrine applies, our focus is not on the intention of the parties, but rather on whether the defendant has been unjustly enriched.

The trial court determined that a benefit was conferred upon Moore as a result of the extensive labor and services Mitchell provided him on his farm and in his home. The critical question, with regard to whether Moore was unjustly enriched, was answered in the positive by the court.

Both parties concur that when Mitchell moved into Moore's home on a full- time basis, Moore paid many of Mitchell's bills, including car payments, VISA and SEARS card charges, and phone bills. Moreover, Moore claims that Mitchell became part of his own family; Mitchell, himself, admits to having celebrated all the major holidays with Moore's immediate family and received gifts from them on special occasions.

In order to prove that the defendant in the present case had been unjustly enriched by plaintiff's actions and services, there must be some convincing evidence establishing that plaintiff's services were not gratuitous.

We first note that Mitchell had complete access to a large farm house where he lived rent-free and virtually unencumbered by any utility expenses. The nature and amount of benefits that plaintiff received from living at Moore's farm rebuts any presumption that the benefit conferred upon Moore was unjust. In fact, the advantages plaintiff obtained were compensation enough for all the work he offered to do on the farm; further, Mitchell derived an obvious personal benefit by living with the defendant, his partner for thirteen years, at his farm.

Having found no evidence which would imply that Moore's services were anything but gratuitous, we cannot agree with the trial court that a theory of unjust enrichment has been proved. While defendant indisputably bequeathed plaintiff his farm (found within the provisions of two wills that were later supplanted by a codicil), the gift was exactly that, an intention to reward the plaintiff through a testamentary provision. Such bequest is not equivalent to a finding that the defendant intended to compensate the plaintiff for his services and that upon failure to remit such monies the defendant became unjustly enriched.

Furthermore, the defendant testified that the plaintiff himself suggested that he move in with the defendant because he could not afford to rent an apartment on his own at the time. He, as well as the defendant, thought such potential living arrangement would give the two men more time to foster their relationship. In fact, upon learning of plaintiff's potential job opportunity in nearby Lancaster, Pennsylvania, the defendant anticipated that the two parties would be able to grow closer in a permanent "live-in" situation—another indication that there existed no expectation of payment for plaintiff's voluntary work on the defendant's farm.

To solidify the fact that the plaintiff's actions were gratuitous services rendered during a "close, personal" relationship, the plaintiff testified that after he began to help around the farm, the defendant told him he "did a great job, that he appreciated what I [plaintiff] did, and it made the house much better looking, it kept it stable, and that we were building a future together and some day it would all be worth it for me [plaintiff]." While Mitchell would characterize the nature of the parties' relationship as a type of business venture between partners, the evidence indicates a very different aspect of their lives. As Mitchell, himself, testified, he had a "romantic or sexual aspect to his relationship with Dr. Moore." Furthermore, the parties conducted themselves around the home like parties in a loving relationship; they shared household chores, cooked dinners for each other, bestowed gifts upon one another, attended events together, and shared holidays and special occasions with Moore's family. Most potent, however, is the following language used in a letter written by Mitchell to Moore sometime in 1993, "The time I have given you breaking my back with the house and grounds were just that, a gift to our relation-

ship." To find restitution proper for services performed in such a relationship, we would curtail the freedom associated in forming new personal bonds based upon the important facet of mutual dependence.

After a review of the record in this case, we cannot find that the defendant benefited unjustly from plaintiff's services. While we do not attempt to characterize the services rendered in all unmarried couple's relationships as gratuitous, we do believe that such a presumption exists and that in order to recover restitution for services rendered, the presumption must be rebutted by clear and convincing evidence. The basis of this presumption rests on the fact that services provided by plaintiff to the defendant are not of the type for which one would normally expect to be paid, nor did they confer upon the defendant a benefit that is unconscionable for him to retain without making restitution to the plaintiff.

Accordingly, we reverse the trial court's verdict in favor of plaintiff.

SECTION 12.9
RESCISSION AND
REFORMATION

A contract can be rescinded if it is voidable for some reason such as misrepresentation, fraud, duress, undue influence, or impossibility. In that case, each party must return the property they received from the other.

Suppose though, that the contract between the parties is valid but it fails to express the real intent of the parties because of a mistake or ambiguous language. Parties can seek the equitable remedy of reformation in order to modify the written agreement to reflect their real intentions.

For example, a seller orally agrees to transfer 120 acres of land to a buyer, but the written deed conveys only 100 acres. The buyer can request that the court reform the contract to reflect the sale of 120 acres of land.

The remedy of rescission is not easily granted. A court must be satisfied that the breach of contract is material and willful, or at least so substantial and fundamental as to strongly defeat the object of the parties in making the contract. The aggrieved party must also show that the normal remedy for breach of contract, in the form of monetary damages, is inadequate. In *New Shows v. Don King Productions, Inc.,* a boxing promoter tried to rescind a contract with Don King Productions over a championship fight featuring Julio Caesar Chavez. The court did not allow rescission of the contract since monetary damages were adequate to make the aggrieved party whole.

NEW SHOWS V. DON KING PRODUCTION
1999 WL 5537 780 (S.D. N.Y. 1999)

THIS DISPUTE AROSE OUT OF THE CO-PROMOTION of a boxing event held in Monterrey, Mexico by plaintiff New Shows, S.A. de C.V. ("New Shows") and defendant Don King Productions, Inc. ("DKP"). The case was tried to a jury who returned a verdict awarding plaintiff $63,500 for breach of contract and $700,000 for fraudulent inducement to enter into a contract. Plaintiff has moved for an order requesting a judgment of rescission on the breach of contract claim.

On October 21, 1994, New Shows and DKP entered into a Co-Promotion Agreement. Pursuant to that agreement, the parties agreed to promote a boxing event in Monterrey, Mexico, featuring Julio Cesar Chavez. The agreement provided that New Shows would pay DKP a $3 million advance, and DKP would produce all of the fighters for the event and assume responsibility for the compensation of the fighters. DKP also agreed, "to a black-out in Monterrey with a radius to be determined and agreed by the parties," to cause the fighters to commence training at the site of the event in Monterrey fourteen days prior to the event; and to supply press kits and other promotion materials. New Shows would receive the proceeds of all live ticket sales for the event, as well as various sponsorship fees and other non- television revenues.

The boxing event took place in Monterrey as scheduled. New Shows contended that DKP breached the Co-Promotion Agreement in four respects: (1) DKP failed to implement a televi-sion blackout of the event within an agreed-upon seventy-five mile radius of Monterrey; (2) the fighters arrived in Monterrey eight days in advance of the event, rather than fourteen days in advance, as agreed; (3) DKP did not provide New Shows with press kits and other promotional materials sufficiently in advance of the event; and (4) DKP breached the contract's implied obligation of good faith and fair dealing.

DKP asserted that the television blackout had been implemented throughout the Monterrey area except that the event was televised on a pay-per-view basis in the City of Saltillo, approximately 55 miles from Monterrey; that it had provided promotional materials in English and Spanish in advance of the event; and that New Shows consented to the late arrival of the fighters in Monterrey.

New Shows also asserted that DKP should be held liable for inducing New Shows to enter into the Co-Promotion Agreement by false /and fraudulent representations. New Shows alleged that DKP made three separate representations not contained in the Co-Promotion

Agreement which induced it to sign the agreement: (1) DKP promised to buy $500,000 worth of tickets to the event; (2) DKP promised to give New Shows a right to receive $1 million from the Government of Nuevo Leon, in which Monterrey was located; and (3) DKP promised to arrange for the attendance at the event of Hollywood celebrities.

Plaintiff New Shows claims that it is entitled to the remedy of rescission and that the Court's failure to instruct the jury on rescission resulted in plaintiff recovering only $63,500 on the breach of contract claim, rather than $2.2 million, the amount necessary to restore plaintiff to the position it was in prior to signing the Co-Promotion Agreement. However, plaintiff was not entitled to rescission as a remedy for breach of contract, and its motion is denied.

Plaintiff failed to show that it was entitled to rescission as a remedy for defendant's breach of contract. Plaintiff's claim of widespread television viewing of the event throughout the entire Monterrey area in violation of the blackout provision was so unsupported by the evidence that a charge entitling plaintiff to rescission was not warranted. Rescission is an "extraordinary remedy," and "is to be invoked only when there is lacking complete and adequate remedy at law and where the status quo may be substantially restored." In this case, neither factor counsels in favor of rescission.

At trial, plaintiff received damages for defendant's breach of contract. The jury was properly instructed on "benefit of the bargain" damages and determined that defendant's breach of contract had caused plaintiff $63,500 in damage. As plaintiff has not demonstrated why the legal remedy was inadequate, recovery by way of rescission is inappropriate. Moreover, the status quo prior to the contract is not capable of being restored. The boxing matches involving Julio Cesar Chavez and the other fighters were performed. The event was completed and is impossible to undo. When it is not possible to substantially restore the status quo, rescission is inappropriate. Plaintiff has thus failed to demonstrate either that its legal remedy for defendant's breach was inadequate or that rescission would be the proper remedy. Furthermore, rescission may not be granted as a remedy for breach of contract unless the breach is material and willful, or, if not willful, so substantial and fundamental as to strongly defeat the object of the parties in making the contract. The evidence at trial was insufficient to demonstrate a breach of contract rising to this level. The limited violations of the television blackout provision did not go "to the root of the contract," as required to support rescission of the contract. Likewise, the delays in promoting the event attributable to the conduct of DKP, including the six-day delay in the arrival in Monterrey of the majority of the boxers, cannot reasonably be viewed as affecting the root of the contract. The fighters did appear in Monterrey eight days before the event, and twelve fights, including five world championship matches, took place as intended. There was no evidence that DKP breached the Co-Promotion Agreement in such a way as to vitiate the contract and require the exceptional remedy of rescission.

SECTION 12.10
DECLARATORY JUDGMENT

If a party's rights have been questioned, threatened, or disputed, that party may request the court to issue a declaratory judgment. The judgment does not order performance, nor is it merely advisory. Rather, it is a final determination of the rights at issue in a genuine controversy.

Suppose a twice-married man dies leaving his property to his "wife," without specifying which spouse is the recipient of the bequest. Either Wife #1 or Wife #2 may request a declaratory judgment to ascertain who is entitled to the property.

The courts are very protective and specific about entertaining an action for Declaratory Judgment. There must be an actual case and controversy that requires court intervention. This fact is demonstrated in *Gianni Sport, Ltd. v. Metallica* which involved the use of the name Metallica by a clothes manufacturer on the tag for a line of women's clothing. The court refused to hear the Declaratory Judgment action since the clothing manufacturer had stopped using the Metallica mark on the clothing.

GIANNI SPORT, LTD. V. METALLICA
2000 WL 1773511 (S.D. N.Y. 2000)

GIANNI SPORT, LTD. SEEKS A JUDGMENT declaring that it does not infringe any rights defendant Metallica may have in the "Metallica" mark.

Gianni manufactures clothing. Metallica is a band that specializes in a type of music called "heavy metal.@ The dispute between the two parties arose when Metallica learned that Gianni was using the term "Metallica" on hang tags for a line of its women's clothing. Metallica demanded that Gianni cease and desist from use of the mark and that it provide Metallica with information about sales of its allegedly infringing products. Gianni did not believe any confusion between Gianni's exclusive clothing and Metallica's products was possible.

Gianni filed this declaratory judgment action on February 8, 2000. On February 29, 2000, Metallica filed an action in the Central District of California for trademark infringement.

Metallica argues that because Gianni stopped using the term Metallica prior to filing this declaratory judgment action, Gianni fails to present an actual case and controversy. In trademark declaratory judgment actions, the actual-case-and-controversy standard has two elements. First, the defendant, Metallica must have created a real and reasonable apprehen-

sion of liability on the part of the plaintiff. Second, the plaintiff must have engaged in a course of conduct which has brought it into adversarial conflict with the defendant.

Neither party disputes that Metallica's conduct created a real and reasonable apprehension of liability on the part of Gianni. Metallica repeatedly accused Gianni of infringement and threatened legal action. However, Metallica argues that Gianni has not engaged in a course of conduct which brought Gianni into conflict with Metallica because it has not demonstrated a definite intent and apparent ability to commence use of the mark, as required in trademark cases. Gianni has ceased use of the mark, and has demonstrated no desire to resume its use. Therefore, Gianni has no "definite intent" to commence use of the mark. However, the timing of this case is different from a typical trademark case. Usually the plaintiff is seeking a declaratory judgment before marketing an allegedly infringing product. The "definite intent and apparent ability" standard was created to prevent parties with merely a vague and unspecific desire to use a mark from seeking an opinion addressing hypothetical facts. In the instant case, Gianni is not merely thinking about using the Metallica mark—it has actually used it.

A substantial controversy between Gianni and Metallica exists regarding whether Gianni has infringed Metallica's rights. The controversy is immediate and real, not hypothetical. The activity at issue has taken place. Metallica has presented an actual case and controversy before the California court in its action for damages. The case and controversy does not vanish because Gianni filed the instant action.

Although Gianni has presented an actual case and controversy, a district court possesses discretion in deciding whether to entertain a declaratory judgment action. The Supreme Court has described the Declaratory Judgment Act as creating an opportunity, rather than a duty, to grant a new form of relief.

When deciding whether to entertain a declaratory judgment action, a court considers the litigation situation as a whole. First, this action does not further the purpose of the Declaratory Judgment Act. The Declaratory Judgment Act's fundamental purpose is to allow a plaintiff not certain of his rights to avoid accrual of avoidable damages, and to afford him an early adjudication without waiting until his adversary should see fit to begin suit, after damage has accrued. Gianni, brought suit after committing the alleged infringement. Gianni has stopped using the term Metallica, and there is no suggestion that it intends to resume the use of the word "Metallica" even if it prevails here. Any damages that are due have already accrued. Therefore, Gianni will not "avoid the accrual of avoidable damages" by means of this action.

Not only does Gianni's claim fall beyond the scope of the Declaratory Judgment Act's purpose, but it was also filed in apparent anticipation of Metallica's California suit. Gianni's counsel states in his affidavit that if litigation was inevitable, we preferred that it take place where Gianni does business and keeps all its records, in New York.

Gianni argues that its filing was not anticipatory because this action was filed nine months after Metallica's initial threat to sue. However, much of the time elapsed because settlement negotiations were taking place.

Gianni filed this action on February 8, 2000, the day Metallica's first settlement offer expired. To allow Gianni's declaratory judgment action to go forward would penalize Metallica for its attempts at settlement, particularly in light of Gianni's hasty filing on the expiration date of the first settlement offer.

Furthermore, Gianni provides no justification for its haste in filing immediately following the settlement offer. Gianni suffered no prejudice by Metallica's failure to sue, as it did not intend to continue use of the mark, and was free to ignore Metallica's demands, leaving open the possibility that no lawsuit would commence.

Gianni filed this suit in anticipation of Metallica's California suit. Gianni's use of the Declaratory Judgment Act to gain a procedural advantage and preempt the forum choice of the plaintiff to the coercive action, weighs in favor of dismissal.

Gianni argues that the court is required hear its declaratory judgment action because the action would serve a useful purpose in clarifying and settling the legal relations in issue, or terminate and afford relief from the uncertainty, insecurity, and controversy giving rise to the proceedings. The action will not serve the Declaratory Judgment Act's purpose of preventing the accrual of avoidable damages. In addition, this suit is not necessary to clarify and settle the legal relations or afford relief from uncertainty, insecurity and controversy. The pending action in California will provide Gianni the opportunity to resolve the issues raised in the instant action.

For the reasons stated above, Metallica's motion to dismiss this declaratory judgment action is granted.

SECTION **12.11**
SPECIFIC PERFORMANCE

Like rescission and reformation, specific performance is an equitable remedy for breach of contract when money damages are inadequate. If a court orders specific performance, it simply tells a defendant to do that which he or she has contractually promised. Courts generally prefer to award money damages for a breach of contract. The court will, however, enforce the terms of a contract by requiring performance when the goods are unique and cannot be purchased elsewhere.

RUDDOCK v. FIRST NATIONAL BANK OF LAKE FOREST
559 N.E. 2D 483 (ILL. APP. 1990)

REINHARD, J.

MARTIN RUDDOCK BROUGHT THIS ACTION against the First National Bank of Lake Forest (Bank), as guardian of the estate of Rowland S. Stevens, and Elmer and Pauline Crum, seeking damages and specific performance of a contract for the sale of a clock belonging to Stevens' estate. Plaintiff alleges that subsequent to the formation of his contract with the Bank to purchase the clock, the Bank sold and delivered the clock to the Crums. The trial court entered judgment in favor of plaintiff in the amount of $28,000 plus costs against the Bank, denying plaintiff's claim for specific performance against the Crums. Following consideration of the Bank's post-trial motion, the trial court reduced the award of damages to $7,000. Plaintiff appeals, and the Bank and the Crums cross-appeal.

Plaintiff raises the following issues on appeal: (1) whether the trial court erred in denying plaintiff specific performance; and (2) whether the trial court erred in the computation of damages.

Evidence adduced at trial establishes the following facts. On March 30, 1982, the Bank was appointed guardian of the estate of Rowland S. Stevens. Roland Kilgus was assigned to manage Stevens' estate. During the summer of 1982 the Bank decided to sell Stevens' clock collection in order to pay for his care. Kilgus testified

that on July 13, 1982, the Bank obtained court approval to have a public sale of Stevens' clock collection conducted.

A sale was conducted on December 4, 1982. Plaintiff was in attendance at the sale and negotiated with Kilgus for the purchase of an astronomical clock which is the subject of this dispute. The price for that clock was $7,000.

On December 6, 1982, Kilgus telephoned plaintiff and informed him that he could not purchase the astronomical clock because there was a prior written agreement between Stevens and another party for the sale of the clock. Kilgus previously had a conversation with the Crums wherein they indicated that they believed they had the right to purchase the clock based upon prior negotiations with Stevens and later negotiations with the Bank.

Elmer Crum testified that he had entered into an agreement with Stevens pertaining to the clock in 1978. After learning that Stevens had been adjudicated incompetent, Crum attempted to obtain the clock from the Bank. The Bank refused to turn over the clock to Crum but informed him that if he was owed money, he could submit a bill to the estate. Crum submitted a bill for $4,200 which was paid by the estate. Crum believed that he had reached an agreement with the estate whereby he would have a right of first refusal if the clock were ever offered for sale. Kilgus testified that he verbally agreed to allow the Crums the first option to purchase the clock. Kilgus stated the estate received no consideration for the option.

Plaintiff tendered the balance due for the clocks including $7,000 for the astronomical clock. The Bank returned $7,000 to him. Thereafter, plaintiff and the Crums apparently discussed the possibility of plaintiff purchasing the clock from the Crums.

Plaintiff testified that for the past 10 years he had been conducting an in-depth study of astronomical clocks. Plaintiff testified that the subject clock represented the pinnacle of the development of the precision pendulum clock in the United States. The clock was a master clock for the Western Union Time Service. Ernest Martt, a horologist, testified that the clock was 1 of possibly 12 of its type manufactured. He testified that at the time of trial the clock was worth $40,000. Plaintiff testified that the clock was worth $30,000 to $35,000 at the time of the trial.

Section 2-716(1) of the Uniform Commercial Code (Code) provides that "[s]pecific performance may be ordered where the goods are unique or in other proper circumstances."

The requirement of uniqueness has clearly been satisfied in the present case as the evidence establishes that the clock is one of a very few of its type manufactured, may be the only one in existence, and is of historical significance. Furthermore, the Crums' attorney stipulated the clock was unique.

The Crums contend that plaintiff abandoned the contract by notifying the Crums that he did not plain to contest the title to the clock, and, therefore, pursuant to the holding in *Jones v. Dove* *(1943), 382 Ill. 445, 47 N.E. 2d 447,* plaintiff is not entitled to specific performance. The court in Jones stated as follows:

The rule in equity is that he must show that he has always been ready, willing and able to perform the contract on his part, and he is not entitled to specific performance if he has consented to a rescission of the contract or has abandoned it. Whether a contract has been rescinded or abandoned by a party to it may be deduced from circumstances or course of conduct clearly evincing such rescission or abandonment.

In the present case, plaintiff showed his willingness and ability to perform prior to the Bank's repudiation of the contract. The Crums additionally maintain that an award of damages was an adequate remedy at law and, accordingly, plaintiff was not entitled to specific performance. This position is without merit. The fact that a value can be assigned to an item of personalty does not necessarily make damages an adequate remedy. The Code's principal requirement for an order of specific performance is that the goods be unique.

The Crums also point out that they expended a fairly substantial sum of money, $2,500, restoring the clock. Nonetheless, as an equitable remedy can be fashioned to compensate the Crums for benefits conferred by restoration work, we do not view their expenditure of money as necessarily foreclosing an award of specific performance.

The Crums also contend that plaintiff is guilty of unclean hands. There is no merit to this contention.

The trial court abused its discretion in denying specific performance. In view of the fact that the Crums purchased from the Stevens estate the clock for the same amount as plaintiff contracted to pay the estate, an appropriate order of specific performance requires payment of the purchase price of $7,000 by plaintiff to the Crums. Moreover, the Crums are entitled to compensation for the benefit of the restoration work performed on the clock. Accordingly, we reverse the portion of the judgment of the circuit court denying plaintiff specific performance and awarding plaintiff damages, and the Crums are ordered to deliver the clock to plaintiff upon payment of $9,500. In other respects, the judgment of the circuit court is affirmed.

SECTION **12.12**
PROBLEM CASES

1. The New York Yankees told the City of New York that it was going to play its home opening series with the Detroit Tigers in Denver instead of at Yankee Stadium. The City of New York filed for injunctive relief to prevent the implementation of that agreement with the City of Denver. The facts show that after extensive renovations to Yankee Stadium were made by the City, it was discovered that there were certain structural flaws in the bleachers in right and left field. Additional permanent repairs were scheduled to be made between the close of the last baseball season and the opening game of the new season. Those plans were done with the approval of the Yankees. Nevertheless, the Yankees requested a guarantee that the repairs would be completed in a timely manner at the start of the new baseball season. The City stated that under the worse case scenario, only 1,000 to 2,000 seats would be unavailable for the Yankees' home opener. Nevertheless, this information lead to the Yankees scheduling their home opener in Denver. Is the City of New York entitled to an injunction to prevent the Yankees from playing in Denver even though the repairs had not been completed but only 2,000 seats would been unavailable for the Yankees home opener? *City of New York v. New York Yankees*, **458 N.Y.S. 2d 486 (N.Y. 1983)**.

2. Brett Michaels and Pamela Anderson Lee sought a Temporary Restraining Order to prevent the dissemination of a videotape in which Michaels and Lee had a registered copyright. The videotape showed the two highly profile plaintiffs engaging in sexual intercourse. Internet Entertainment Group, Inc. claimed that it obtained the videotape from a purported "agent" of Michaels, who allegedly sold the tape to the Internet Entertainment Group for $15,000. Will Michaels and Lee be successful in blocking the distribution of the tape since IEG obtained a copy of the videotape from a third person? Will the showing of the tape cause irresponsible harm? *Pamela Lee Anderson v. Internet Entertainment Group, Inc.* **5 F. Supp. 2d 823 (C.D. Cal. 1998)**.

3. The State of Washington enacted an "Erotic Sound Recordings Statute" which subjected all distributors of sound recordings to civil and criminal proceedings for distribution to minors of "erotic material." A number of recording artists filed a declaratory judgment

against the state in an attempt to have the court determine that the statute violated their substantive due process right. Is a declaratory judgment a proper action in order to invalidate a statute which is believed to be unconstitutional? *Soundgarden v. Blkenberry*, 871 P. 2d 1050 (Wash. 1994).

4. Star Magazine published an article about Rodney Dangerfield entitled, "Vegas Casino Accuses Candy Shack Funnyman; Rodney Dangerfield Swills Vodka by the Tumblerful, smokes pot all day and uses cocaine." Dangerfield sued Star Magazine for defamation and requested punitive damages. The purpose of punitive damages is to punish the wrongdoer and this is accomplished by awarding money based on the net worth of the defendant. Star Magazine's statement of operation for the fiscal year reflected a net loss. Dangerfield, however, argued that the financial condition of Star's parent owner is relevant to the tabloid's financial condition and should have been disclosed to the jury. Is the comedian correct? *Rodney Dangerfield v. Star Editorial, Inc.,* 25 Media L. Rep. 1379 (9th Cir. 1996).

SECTION 12.13
INTERNET REFERENCES

For more information on the materials contained in this chapter, see the following internet references:

A. *Punitive Damages*

- **http://www.ljextra.com/practice/arbitration/0130puni.html**
  This article from the New York Law Journal deals with punitive damages in arbitration proceedings.

- **http://www.maryalice.com/reform/punitive.html**
  An attorney provides interesting facts regarding punitive damages at this site as well as addressing the controversy dealing with reforming awards of punitive damages.

- **http://www.bleier.com/lnr/punitivedamages.htm**
  This site offers a general discussion about punitive damages.

B. *Normal Damages*

- **http://www.seyfarth.com/practice/labor/articles/ll_1221.html**
  An article about a Supreme Court decision regarding nominal damages is located at this end of this address.

CHAPTER 13

ETHICS AND THE LAW
TERRY ANN HALBERT, ESQ.

SECTION 13.1
AN OVERVIEW
OF ETHICS

Peter Christopher is walking through a park and is attracted to the sight of a pond where children are swimming. He notices that some of the children's cries sound more like desperation than enjoyment, and soon he realizes that a child is drowning. Christopher is a trained life-guard. Since he is on the way to a concert, and not in the mood to get his clothes wet, Christopher turns and walks away from the pond. Would he be violating the law by failing to help?

Surprisingly, the answer is no. Our legal system, which was greatly influenced by the notions of individual freedom, would not force a person to help a stranger in an emergency unless that person has some-how caused the problem in the first place or there was a special relationship between the parties, such as a parent and child. If, as in this example, an individual just happens to discover a stranger in grave danger, that person is legally allowed to walk on by.

This principle, the so-called "No Duty to Rescue Rule," is probably understandable in terms of the basic principles of our legal system, which generally finds a person liable for some wrong or careless **action**, not for inaction, not for something they **didn't** do. There are also practical reasons why the law backs away from demanding a rescue in these kinds of situations: Where is the line to be drawn? Who should rescue? Is everyone who hears the child screaming responsible for jump-ing in the pond to help? And how much help is enough? Suppose a person cannot swim, or suppose the pond is polluted?

But beyond the law is the concept of what is right, what is ethical. One might believe that there are ethical reasons for trying to help the drown-ing child, regardless of what the law expects. In fact, this is the major difference between law and ethics: the law is about what one **must** do to avoid liability, while ethics is about what one **should** do, about "do-ing the right thing."

Legal and ethical responsibilities do not necessarily overlap. The "No Duty To Rescue Rule" demonstrates this point. Often the ethically right decision goes beyond the expectations of the law, sometimes far be-yond. This gap between law and ethics is demonstrated in the following Pennsylvania case:

JOSEPH YANIA V. JOHN BIGAN
115 A.2D 343 (PA. 1959)

ON SEPTEMBER 25, 1957 JOHN E. BIGAN was engaged in a coal strip-mining operation in Shade Township, Somerset County. On the property being stripped were large cuts or trenches created by Bigan when he removed the earthen overburden for the purpose of removing the coal underneath. One cut contained water 8 to 10 feet in depth with side walls or embankments 16 to 18 feet in height. At this cut, Bigan had installed a pump to remove the water.

At approximately 4 p.m. on that date, Joseph F. Yania, the operator of another coal strip-mining operation, and one Boyd M. Ross went upon Bigan's property for the purpose of discussing a business matter with Bigan, and while there, were asked by Bigan to aid him in starting the pump. Ross and Bigan entered the cut and stood at the point where the pump was located. Yania stood at the top of one of the cut's side walls and then jumped from the side wall—a height of 16 to 18 feet—into the water and was drowned.

Yania's widow instituted wrongful death and survival actions against Bigan contending Bigan was responsible for Yania's death. [She] initially contends that Yania's descent from the high embankment into the water and the resulting death were caused "entirely" by the spoken words and blandishments of Bigan delivered at a distance from Yania. The complaint does not allege that Yania slipped or that he was pushed or that Bigan made any physical impact upon Yania. On the contrary, the only inference deducible from the facts alleged in the complaint is that Bigan, by the employment of cajolery and inveiglement, caused such a mental impact on Yania that the latter was deprived of his volition and freedom of choice and placed under a compulsion to jump into the water. Had

Yania been a child of tender years or a person mentally deficient then it is conceivable that taunting and enticement could constitute actionable negligence if it resulted in harm. However, to contend that such conduct directed to an adult in full possession of all his mental faculties constitutes actionable negligence is not only without precedent but completely without merit.

[The widow] next urges that Bigan, as the possessor of the land, violated a duty owed to Yania in that his land contained a dangerous condition, i.e. the water-filled cut or trench, and he failed to warn Yania of such condition. Of this condition there was neither concealment nor failure to warn, but, on the contrary, the complaint specifically avers that Bigan not only requested Yania and Boyd to assist him in starting the pump to remove the water from the cut but "led" them to the cut itself. If this cut possessed any potentiality of danger, such a condition was as obvious and apparent to Yania as to Bigan, both coal strip-mine operators. Under the circumstances herein depicted Bigan could not be held liable in this respect.

Lastly, it is urged that Bigan failed to take the necessary steps to rescue Yania from the water. The mere fact that Bigan saw Yania in a position of peril in the water imposed upon him no legal, although a moral, obligation or duty to go to his rescue unless Bigan was legally responsible, in whole or in part, for placing Yania in the perilous position. The language of this Court in *Brown v. French* is apt: "If it appeared that the deceased by his own carelessness, contributed in any degree to the accident which causes the loss of his life, the defendants ought not to have been held to answer for the consequences resulting from that accident. He voluntarily placed himself in the way of danger, and his death was the result of his own act. That his undertaking was an exceedingly reckless and dangerous one, the event proves, but there was no one to blame for it but himself. He had the right to try the experiment, obviously dangerous as it was, but then also upon him rested the consequences of that experiment, and upon no one else; he may have been, and probably was, ignorant of the risk which he was taking upon himself, or knowing it, and trusting to his own skill, he may have regarded it as easily superable. But in either case, the result of his ignorance, or of his mistake, must rest with himself—and cannot be charged to the defendants." The complaint does not aver any facts which impose upon Bigan legal responsibility for placing Yania in the dangerous position in the water and, absent such legal responsibility, the law imposes on Bigan no duty of rescue.

QUESTIONS FOR DISCUSSION:

1. What circumstances would have made this case result in liability for Bigan?

2. Yania was doing a favor for his friend Bigan. Suppose Yania was a worker being paid by Bigan to help drain the trench, and fell in by accident. Would Bigan then be legally required to help?

3. Do you think the law should be changed to require one person to help another? What would be the likely result if the rules were different?

Does a physician owe a duty to go to the aid of a sick or injured person? The Supreme Court of Indiana deals with a doctor's responsibilities to aid a patient in the following case:

GEORGE HURLEY v. GEORGE EDDINGFIELD
59 N.E. 1058 (IND. 1901)

DESMOND, Chief Judge.

THE MATERIAL FACTS ALLEGED MAY BE SUMMARIZED thus: At and for years before decedent's death appellee was a practicing physician at Mace, in Montgomery county, duly licensed under the laws of the state. He held himself out to the public as a general practitioner of medicine. He had been decedent's family physician. Decedent became dangerously ill, and sent for appellee. The messenger informed appellee of decedent's violent sickness, tendered him his fee for his services, and stated to him that no other physician was procurable in time, and that decedent relied on him for attention. Without any reason whatever, appellee refused to render aid to decedent. No other patients were requiring appellees immediate service, and he could have gone to the relief of decedent if he had been willing to do so.

Death ensued, without decedent's fault, and wholly from appellee's wrongful act. The alleged wrongful act was appellee's refusal to enter into a contract of employment. Counsel do not contend that, before the enactment of the law regulating the practice of medicine, physicians were bound to render professional service to every one who applied. The act regulating the practice of medicine provides for a board of examiners, standards of qualifications, examinations, licenses to those found qualified, and penalties for practicing without license. The act is a preventive, not a compulsive measure. In obtaining the state's license to practice medicine, the state does not require, and the licensee does not engage, that he will practice at all or on other terms than he may choose to accept.

Judgment [dismissing the complaint] is affirmed.

QUESTIONS FOR DISCUSSION:

1. What happened in this case? Why did the judge rule as he did?

2. Should people who are trained to rescue or assist others in emergency situations be held to a higher standard in these situations?

3. The Hippocratic Oath, which outlines the ethical goals of doctors, contains the following promise: "According to my power and judgment to use the medical knowledge for the benefit of those who suffer, as judged by myself to be fair, and to avoid from doing any harm or injustice." Did Dr. Hurley violate the Hippocratic Oath?

All states contain Good Samaritan statutes that protect people who are medically trained from being held liable in an emergency rescue, should they decide to help. These laws, however, do not demand that the medically-trained offer assistance in these situations. In fact, although the Hurley case is old—from 1901—it is still good law. Today a doctor may decide to "walk on by," unless she or he is already treating the patient, or is on duty in a medical facility offering treatment.

Over the years, a few exceptions to the "No Duty to Rescue Rule" have developed. There is the "Special Relationship" exception: between members of a family, between employers and employees, between providers of public transportation and passengers, or between owners of business and their customers, for instance, the law insists on a reasonable attempt at assistance in an emergency. So, if the person in the park was a father who was hearing his own drowning daughter's screams, he would have a duty to take reasonable steps to help her.

SECTION 13.2
ETHICAL THEORIES

If ethics is about choosing the right behavior, the moral way to live one's life, how does society achieve this goal? There are many different ethical beliefs individuals can hold? Abortion is just one example of an issue that separates people who have very strong but completely opposite ethical beliefs. And in a multicultural society, doesn't it become even more difficult to decide on one single ethically correct position? Who is to say which personal or cultural ethical standards is correct or is there a universal ethic?

For centuries, human beings have struggled to determine the answers to these types of questions. Within Western civilization, two major philosophical theories about ethics have evolved:

1. Utilitarian Theory: Focuses on the **consequences**—both short and long term—of any particular action for all individuals affected. Benefits and harms are balanced against one another, to determine which action produces the most happiness for the greatest number of people.

2. Rights Theory: Concerned with the **reasons** for action, not just the results. People have certain basic rights—the right to life, freedom of expression, privacy, for instance—that are of value in themselves and must be protected. This theory also includes the notion of "Universality:" Whatever we choose to do must be behavior we would be willing to have done to everyone, including to ourselves—a version of the Golden Rule.

Sometimes these two theories serve the same purpose. For example, a student who sees another student cheating on an exam employs her freedom of expression to alert the professor. Not only has she acted for ethical reasons — the Rights Theory — but she has come to the aid of the rest of the class, who benefit by having their grades accurately measured. Thus, she has also acted in accordance with the Utilitarian Theory, the greatest good (better grades) for the greatest number (the rest of the class).

Occasionally, however, the two theories are diametrically opposed to each other. The classic example is slavery, where a minority of the population is enslaved, but the rest of society benefited economically. Before the Civil War, the Southern economy prospered, providing the greatest good to the greatest number and satisfying the Utilitarian Theory. But the Rights Theory suffered, since human beings were enslaved, prevented from enjoying the same rights as the other members of society.

Can you think of other examples where the two philosophies go hand-in-hand? How about situations where they diverge? Consider these examples when you work on the following problem.

Hodge, Dodge and Lodge
Attorneys at Law
M E M O R A N D U M

To: All Law Clerks

From: Gregory Olan Dodge

Re: Kathy Hodge and Eastcoast Airlines

To facilitate Kathy's rehabilitation for drug trafficking, the judge released her from prison, with Kathy's promise that she would help society. Kathy didn't want to return to jail, so she went out and landed a job as part of the Philadelphia ground crew of Eastcoast Airlines. Her job involved a lot of customer contact and a high level of stress. But having a job seemed to stabilize Kathy. The longer she held it, the easier it was for her to remain "clean and sober."

About two years later, Kathy's training paid off: she was promoted to a middle management position with Eastcoast Airlines in its Real Estate Division. Evidently Eastcoast had tried to diversify during the 1990's, acquiring a number of properties in Florida. Kathy's mission, as part of the Real Estate Division, was to sell as many of these properties as possible. Eastcoast Airlines like so many of its competitors had been suffering substantial losses in the years since airline deregulation, and had a negative cash flow. Unless the company could control its high labor costs and increase its popularity with the flying public, bankruptcy was a possibility. Kathy's boss, Robert Stingle saw selling off the properties, as an important way of alleviating the company's financial crisis.

For months every lead Kathy had came to nothing. At last she contacted a relatively new firm, Silvertooth Inc., which was interested in turning one of Eastcoast's properties into a retirement villa. The complex Silvertooth planned would feature elaborate walking trails and outside recreation facilities.

Eastcoast had conducted a full environmental audit of the property six months earlier, and no problems were revealed. A copy of the report was given to a Silvertooth representative who also examined the property and discovered no problems.

As negotiations progressed with Silvertooth, Kathy was approached by one of her friends in the Real Estate Division at Eastcoast, Steve Flame. He told Kathy that there was now some highly toxic waste on the property that she was ready to sell. The person who told him was recently in Florida at the site, and had found several buried metal containers marked "Danger! Biohazard. Radioactive medical waste." The containers were cracked and liquid was seeping out of them onto the ground. Steve said he wanted Kathy to know about this because he was concerned that innocent people could be hurt if the sale went through.

Kathy contacted her boss, but before she could mention the containers, Stingle interrupted and told her it was vital that the sale be closed quickly, that his and Kathy's own job might well depend on it. Kathy also consulted with a lawyer who explained that Florida law does not require disclosure of hazardous substances on commercial property so long as there hasn't been a fraudulent misstatement about the condition of the property.

Kathy was very upset. She knew that Silvertooth was considering some other properties that were similar, and she thought if she mentioned the toxic spill problem that they would probably back out of the sale. Kathy figured she would be unlikely to deal with Silvertooth again regarding any future real estate sales since Eastcoast didn't own another property that was suitable for a retirement community.

The question of whether to close the sale immediately bothered Kathy so much she almost consulted her dad, but then thought the better of it.

Although there appear to be no **legal** consequences if Kathy says nothing and allows the sale to go through, from an ethical perspective the situation changes. Write an advisory memo to Kathy on the **ethics** of the choice she must make, "To Disclose or Not To Disclose?"

1. First apply the Utilitarian Theory. Who are the people affected by Kathy's decision? What choice would result in "the greatest good for the greatest number?"

2. Now do the analysis from the Rights Theory perspective. What rights do the various affected individuals and groups have in this situation? How do they weigh against one another? What would be the result if Kathy thinks about the Golden Rule?

3. Finally, summarize your own ethical opinion: If you were in Kathy's shoes, what would you do, and why?

ANSWER SHEET
PROBLEM THIRTEEN—A

Name   **Please Print Clearly**

1. First apply the Utilitarian Theory. Who are the people affected by Kathy's decision? What choice would probably result in "the greatest good for the greatest number?"

_____

_____

_____

_____

_____

_____

_____

_____

2. Now do the analysis from the Rights Theory perspective. What rights do the various affected individuals and groups have in this situation? How do they weigh against one another? What would be the result if Kathy thinks about the Golden Rule?

_____

_____

_____

_____

_____

_____

_____

_____

3. Finally, summarize your own ethical opinion: If you were in Kathy's shoes, what would you do, and why?

_____

_____

_____

_____

_____

_____

_____

_____

_____

_____

_____

_____

_____

_____

_____

_____

_____

_____

_____

_____

_____

_____

SECTION 13.4
THE WHISTLEBLOWER

Suppose Kathy decides to warn Silvertooth about the hazardous waste and the deal falls through. Kathy feels good about this outcome, but not so good when she discovers that she has been fired. Since all her other work for Eastcoast has been highly commended, Ms. Hodge believes she was fired in retaliation for letting the toxic cat out of the bag. (Under the federal "Superfund" law, Eastcoast as owner of the property will be responsible for paying for the clean up of the site.)

Kathy is a **whistleblower,** a person who feels compelled to get certain information into the hands of the people who can act to correct a problem, when it seems that the problem won't be corrected otherwise. When employees "blow the whistle," they might tell a superior, or they might go outside their company and tell government authorities, or the media.

What are Kathy's legal rights in this situation? She may have none. Unless she has an employment contract with Eastcoast for a certain stated time period, she is an "employee at will." (Most employees fall into this category.) Generally speaking, an employer can fire at-will employees at any time for any reason, or for no reason at all, unless the reason violates a statute, such as a law against discrimination on the basis of race, gender, age, handicap, etc. Kathy might also be protected if she was part of the 14 percent of American workers who belong to a union. She could then argue she was fired in violation of a collective bargaining agreement between her union and her employer. (A union contract generally provides that workers can not be fired unless for "just cause.") Finally, some state and federal laws protect whistleblowers who report violations of those laws to the government. The Superfund law, for example, would protect Kathy if she had gone straight to the Environmental Protection Agency with news about the spill. Since she told Silvertooth, she may not be protected.

Why does the law give so much freedom to employers to hire and fire as they see fit? Is "employment at will" a fair rule? How should society strike a balance between an employer's right to control and an employee's right to bring ethical concerns forward without fear of retaliation? Consider these issues as you read *Geary v. United States Steel Corporation.* In it, the Pennsylvania Supreme Court deals with the tort of "wrongful discharge," which would hold an employer responsible for firing an employee in a way that violates public policy. The case is one of first impression.

GEORGE GEARY v. UNITED STATES STEEL CORPORATION
319 A.2D 174 (PA. SUPER. 1974)

THE COMPLAINT AVERS THAT APPELLANT, George B. Geary, was continuously employed by appellee, United States Steel Corporation from 1953 until July 13, 1967, when he was dismissed from his position. Geary's duties involved the sale of tubular products to the oil and gas industry. His employment was at will. The dismissal is said to have stemmed from a disagreement concerning one of the company's new products, a tubular casing designed for use under high pressure. Geary alleges that he believed the product had not been adequately tested and constituted a serious danger to anyone who used it; that he voiced his misgivings to his superiors and was ordered to "follow directions," which he agreed to do; that he nevertheless continued to express his reservations, taking his case to a vice-president in charge of sale of the product; that as a result of his efforts the product was reevaluated and withdrawn from the market; that he at all times performed his duties to the best of his ability and always acted with the best interests of the company and the general public in mind; and that because of these events he was summarily discharged without notice. Geary asserts that the company's conduct in so acting was "wrongful, malicious and abusive."

[Geary] candidly admits that he is beckoning us into uncharted territory. No court in this Commonwealth has ever recognized a non-statutory cause of action for an employer's termination of an at-will employment relationship. Pennsylvania law is in accordance with the weight of authority elsewhere. Absent a statutory or contractual provision to the contrary, the law has taken for granted the power of either party to terminate an employment relationship for any or no reason.

We recognize that economic conditions have changed radically since [the turn of the century, when employment at will was first established.] The huge corporate enterprises which have emerged in this century wield an awesome power over their employees.

Against the background of these changes, the broad question to which [Geary] invites our attention is whether the time has come to impose judicial restrictions on an employer's power of discharge. [His] argument is an appeal to considerations of public policy. Geary asserts in his complaint that he was acting in the best interests of the general public as well as of his employer in opposing the marketing of a product which he believed to be defective. Certainly, the potential for abuse of an employer's power of dismissal is particularly serious where an employee must exercise independent, expert judgment in matters of product safety, but Geary does not hold himself out as this sort of employee. So far as the complaint shows, he was involved only in the sale of company products. There is no suggestion that he possessed any expert qualifications, or that his duties extended to making judgments in matters of product safety. In essence, Geary argues that his conduct should be protected because his intentions were good. No doubt most employees who are dismissed from their posts can make the same claim. We doubt that establishing a right to litigate every such case as it arises would operate either in the best interest of the parties or of the public.

Given the rapidity of change in corporate personnel in the areas of employment not covered by labor agreements, suits like the one at bar could well be expected to place a heavy burden on our judicial system in terms of both an increased case load. Of greater concern is the possible impact of such suits on the legitimate interest of employers in hiring and retaining the best personnel available. The ever-present threat of suit might well inhibit the making of critical judgments by employers concerning employee qualifications.

The problem extends beyond the question of individual competence, for even an unusually gifted person may be of no use to his employer if he cannot work effectively with fellow employees. Here, for example, Geary's complaint shows that he by-passed his immediate superiors and pressed his views on higher officers, utilizing his close contacts with a company vice president. The praiseworthiness of Geary's motives does not detract from the company's legitimate interest in preserving its normal operational procedures from disruption. In sum, while we agree that employees should be encouraged to express their educated views on the quality of their employer's products, we are not persuaded that creating a new non-statutory cause of action of the sort proposed by appellant is the best way to achieve this result. On balance, whatever public policy imperatives can be discerning here seem to militate against such a course.

It may be granted that there are areas of an employee's life in which his employer has no legitimate interest. An intrusion into one of these areas by virtue of the employer's power of discharge might plausibly give rise to a cause of action, particularly where some recognized facet of public policy is threatened. But this case does not require us to define in comprehensive fashion the perimeters of this privilege, and we decline to do so. We hold only that where the complaint itself discloses a plausible and legitimate reason for terminating an at-will employment relationship and no clear mandate of public policy is violated thereby, an employee at will has no right of action against his employer for wrongful discharge.

QUESTIONS FOR DISCUSSION:

1. What are the reasons for the court's decision?

2. Would the case have turned out differently if the tubular casings Geary was worried about were being manufactured in violation of federal safety regulations?

3. Do you agree with the decision?

Partly in response to this case, the Pennsylvania legislature passed the following law on whistleblowing:

> No employer may discharge, threaten or otherwise discriminate or retaliate against an employee regarding the employee's compensation, terms, conditions, location of privileges of employment because the employee...makes a good faith report or is about to report, verbally or in writing, to the employer or appropriate authority an instance of wrongdoing or waste.

> It shall be a defense to an action under this section if the defendant proves...that the action taken by the employer occurred for separate and legitimate reasons, which are not merely pretextual.

Here are some of the definitions of terms used in Pennsylvania's whistleblower law:

"Appropriate Authority:" A federal, state or local government body, agency or organization.

"Employee:" A person who performs a service for wages or other remuneration under a contract of hire, written oral, for a public body.

"Good faith report:" A report of conduct defined in this act as wrongdoing or waste which is made without malice or consideration of personal benefit and which the person making the report has reasonable cause to believe is true.

"Waste:" An employer's conduct or omissions which result in substantial abuse, misuse, destruction or loss of funds or resources belonging to or derived from Commonwealth or political subdivision sources.

"Wrongdoing:" A violation that is not of a merely technical or minimal nature of a federal or state statute or regulation or of a code of conduct or ethics designed to protect the interest of the public or the employer.

QUESTIONS FOR DISCUSSION:

1. Considering the definitions as well as the body of the law, would Kathy Hodge be protected for telling Silvertooth about the toxic spill? Why or why not? Would George Geary be protected?

2. Write your own version of a whistleblower law.

SECTION 13.5
ETHICS, LAW
AND PRIVACY

It may be granted that there are areas of an employee's life in which his employer has no legitimate interest. An intrusion into one of these areas by virtue of the employer's power of discharge might plausibly give rise to a cause of action, particularly where some recognized facet of public policy is threatened.

—**Pennsylvania Supreme Court**
Geary v. U.S. Steel

As the Court in **Geary** suggests, there are times when an employer's power to control its employees is in danger of stretching too far. For instance, should an employer have the right to insist that none of its employees smoke cigarettes? Research indicates that a smoker costs his or her employer an estimated $5,740 more annually than a nonsmoking employee. Smokers have a 50 percent greater absentee rate and produce 50 percent higher medical costs. They even do damage to the health of the nonsmoking employees who have to breathe in their smoke. But does this mean that an employer should be able to screen out and refuse to hire smokers, or fire them if they refuse to stop? And if these practices are allowed, what is to stop employers from insisting that employees change other expensive, unhealthy personal habits? What if a worker has a high cholesterol count, or is obese? Assuming that people who get regular exercise and eat sensibly are healthy and will produce fewer medical expenses, should an employer be able to insist that its workers eat salads for lunch and use a gym three times a week?

These are some of the questions raised by the conflict between employee privacy rights and an employer's interest in controlling its operations. There is also the question of testing. Workers with AIDS will end up with horrendous medical and insurance expenses: Should employers be allowed to test their workers for the AIDS virus? (This is illegal under the Americans with Disabilities Act of 1990.)

SECTION 13.6
DRUG TESTING

Illegal drug use is tremendously expensive. In 1988, the government estimated it to be a $100 billion drain on our economy, and employers can expect that drug use cost them plenty in terms of absenteeism, lower productivity, injuries and theft. Yet does this mean employers should be allowed to force their workers to undergo urinalysis testing for illegal drugs? The following materials highlight some of the issues with drug testing in the work place.

PAUL LUEDTKE v. NABORS ALASKA DRILLING, INC.
834 P.2D 1220 (ALASKA 1992)

COMPTON, Justice

THIS CASE ADDRESSES ONE ASPECT OF DRUG TESTING by employers. A private employer, Nabors Alaska Drilling, Inc. [Nabors], established a drug testing program for its employees. Paul Luedtke worked on drilling rigs on the North Slope [and] refused to submit to urinalysis screening for drug use as required by Nabors. As a result [he was] fired.

Luedtke began working for Nabors, which operates drilling rigs on Alaska's North Slope, in February 1978. [He] began as a "floorman" and was eventually promoted to "driller." A driller oversees the work of an entire drilling crew.

Luedtke started work with Nabors as a union member, initially being hired from the union hall. During his tenure, however, Nabors "broke" the union. Luedtke continued to work without a union contract. He had no written contract with Nabors at the time of his discharge.

During his employment with Nabors, Luedtke was accused twice of violating the company's drug and alcohol policies. Once he was suspended for 90 days for taking alcohol to the North Slope. The other incident involved a search of the rig on which Luedtke worked. Aided by dogs trained to sniff out marijuana, the searchers found traces of marijuana on Luedtke's suitcase. Luedtke was allowed to continue working on the rig only after assuring his supervisors he did not use marijuana.

In October 1982, Luedtke scheduled a two-week vacation. Because his normal work schedule was two weeks of work on the North Slope followed by a week off, a two-week vacation amounted to 28 consecutive days away from work. Just prior to his vacation, he was instructed to arrange for a physical examination in Anchorage. He arranged for it to take place on October 19, during his vacation. It was at this examination that Nabors first tested Paul's urine for signs of drug use. The purpose of the physical, as understood by Luedtke, was to enable him to work on offshore rigs should Nabors receive such contracts. Although Luedtke was told it would be a comprehensive physical he had no idea that a urinalysis screening test for drug use would be performed. He did voluntarily give a urine sample but assumed it would be tested only for "blood sugar, any kind of kidney failure [and] problems with bleeding." Nabors' policy of testing for drug use was not announced until November 1, 1982, almost two weeks after Luedtke's examination.

[On] November 16, Luedtke received a letter informing him that his urine had tested positive for cannabinoids. The letter informed him that he would be required to pass two subsequent urinalysis tests, one on November 30 and the other on December 30, before he would be allowed to return to work. In response Luedtke hand delivered a letter drafted by his attorney to the Manager of Employee Relations for Nabors, explaining why he felt the testing and suspension were unfair. Luedtke did not take the urinalysis test on November 30 as requested by Nabors. On December 14, Nabors sent Luedtke a letter informing him that he was discharged for refusing to take the November 30 test.

The right to privacy is a recent creation of American law. The inception of this right is generally credited to a law review article published in 1890 by Louis Brandeis and his law partner, Samuel Warren. They wrote:

> Recent inventions...call attention to the next step which must be taken for the protection of the person, and for securing to the individual ...the right "to be let alone." Instantaneous photographs and newspaper enterprise have invaded the sacred precincts of private and domestic life; and numerous mechanical devices threaten to make good the prediction that "what is whispered in the closet shall be proclaimed from the housetops."

While the legal grounds of this right were somewhat tenuous in the 1890's, American jurists found the logic of Brandeis and Warren's arguments compelling. By 1960, Professor Prosser could write that "the right of privacy, in one form or another, is declared to exist by the overwhelming majority of the American courts." He cited cases in which private parties had been held liable in tort for eavesdropping on private conversations by means of wiretapping and microphones, or for peering into the windows of homes. Eventually the right to privacy attained sufficient recognition to be incorporated in several state constitutions.

Interpreting the Constitution of the United States, the United States Supreme Court in 1965 held that a Connecticut statute banning the use of birth control devices by married couples was "repulsive to the notions of privacy surrounding the marriage relationship." *Griswold v. Connecticut*, 381 U.S. 479, 486 (1965). The Supreme Court wrote that "specific guarantees in the Bill of Rights have penumbras, formed by emanations from those guarantees that help give them life and substance. Various guarantees create zones of privacy..." Since Griswold the Supreme Court has found the federal constitutional right of privacy to apply a number of other situations. *Roe v. Wade*, 410 U.S. 113 (1973) (right of privacy broad enough to encompass a woman's decision whether or not to terminate her pregnancy); *Eisenstadt v. Baird,* **405 U.S. 438 (1972)** (regulation which made contraceptives less available to unmarried than married couples invalidated). But see *Bowers v. Hardwick,* **478 U.S. 186 (1986)** (due process clause of Fourteenth Amendment does not confer any fundamental right on homosexuals to engage in acts of consensual sodomy).

Thus, the concept of privacy has become pervasive in modern legal thought. But a clear definition of this right...has eluded both courts and legal scholars. It is the fundamental nature of the concept that leads to such great difficulty in application.

The next question we address is whether a public policy exists protecting an employee's right to withhold certain "private" information from his employer.

We believe such a policy does exist, and is evidenced in the common law, statutes and constitution of this state. Alaska law clearly evidences strong support for the public interest in employee privacy. First, state statutes support the policy that there are private sectors of employee's lives not subject to direct scrutiny by their employers. For example, employers may not require employees to take polygraph tests as a condition of employment. In addition, Alasaka Statute 18.80.200(a) provides:

> It is determined and declared as a matter of legislative finding that discrimination against an inhabitant of the state because of race, religion, color, national origin, age, sex, marital status, changes in marital status, pregnancy, or parenthood is a matter of public concern and that this discrimination not only threatens the rights and privileges of the inhabitants of the state but also menaces the institutions of the state and threatens peace, order, health, safety and

general welfare of the state and its inhabitants. [It is] unlawful for employers to inquire into such topics in connection with prospective employment. Second, as previously noted, Alaska's constitution contains a right to privacy clause. Third, there exists a common law right to privacy.

[T]here is a sphere of activity in every person's life that is closed to scrutiny by others. The boundaries of that sphere are determined by balancing a person's right to privacy against other public policies, such as "the health, safety, rights and privileges of others." Luedtke claim[s] that whether or not [he] use[s] marijuana is information within that protected sphere into which his employer, Nabors, may not intrude. We disagree. As we have previously observed, marijuana can impair a person's ability to function normally.

We also observe that work on an oil rig can be very dangerous. We have determined numerous cases involving serious injury or death resulting from accidents on oil drilling rigs. In addition, the trial court expressly considered the dangers of work on oil rigs.

Where the public policy supporting Luedtke's privacy in off-duty activities conflicts with the public policy supporting the protection of the health and safety of other workers, and even Luedtke himself, the health and safety concerns are paramount. As a result, Nabors is justified in determining whether Luedtke is possibly impaired on the job by drug usage off the job.

We observe, however, that the employer's prerogative does have limitations. First, the drug test must be conducted at a time reasonably contemporaneous with the employee's work time. The employer's interest is in monitoring drug use that may directly affect employee performance. The employer's interest is not in the broader police function of discovering and controlling the use of illicit drugs in general society. In the context of this case, Nabors could have tested Luedtke immediately prior to [his] departure for the North Slope, or immediately upon his return from the North Slope when the test could be reasonably certain of detecting drugs consumed there. Further, given Nabors' need to control the oil rig community, Nabors could have tested him at any time he was on the North Slope.

Second, an employee must receive notice of the adoption of a drug testing program. By requiring a test, an employer introduces an additional term of employment. An employee should have notice of the additional term so that he may contest it, refuse to accept it and quit, seek to negotiate its conditions, or prepare for the test so that he will not fail it and thereby suffer sanctions.

· These considerations do not apply with regard to the tests Luedtke refused to take. Luedtke was given notice of the future tests. He did not take the November 30 test. As a result, Nabors was justified in discharging him.

THE PROBLEM OF THE FALSE POSITIVE

Both employers and employees share at least one concern: whether or not urinalysis is a reliable means of uncovering drug use. Employees are concerned over the accuracy of drug testing since they may be hired or fired on the basis of results. Employers are interested because they don't want to waste time and money ferreting out innocent workers, only to spend more time and money replacing them.

There are many serious reliability problems. Certain over-the-counter drugs may register as illegal ones. Test results on people using the familiar cold remedies Contac or Sudafed have (wrongly) indicated that they were on amphetamines. The pain relievers Datril and Advil have shown up as marijuana, and cough syrups containing dextromethorphan may register as

opiate traces. False positives can be produced in the oddest ways: A person with the disease lupus (in remission) might appear to be taking amphetamines. A person who had ingested poppyseeds just before urinalysis might seem to have opium in his system. Research indicates that "passive inhalation" can also cause positive results. In other words, a person could test as a marijuana user, not because of actually smoking the drug, but because of being at a concert, a party, or on a bus where it was smoked.

How often are these mistakes made? The testing laboratories assert that the most commonly used procedures are 95-99 percent accurate. At best, then, the industry itself claims an inaccuracy rate of 1 percent. But since 4 million to 5 million people are tested annually, 40,000 to 50,000 people must be falsely accused each year.

Perhaps most telling are the results of a 1987 study performed by the National Institute on Drug Abuse, which found that 20 percent of the 50 laboratories tested reported the presence of drugs in urine specimens when no drugs were present. These mistakes were made even though each laboratory had been warned in advance that its competence was about to be evaluated by the federal government.[1]

TEST REVELATIONS

Urinalysis picks up traces of certain substances in the blood. Although drug testing cannot tell an employer whether an employee was "high" while at work (it measures the presence of a substance, not the time it was ingested), it can reveal that the employee had used marijuana sometime during the past few weeks. Some substances linger in the body longer than others: drug tests can reveal that the subject smoked one marijuana cigarette as many as 81 days earlier, while cocaine traces will be undetectable after 2-3 days, and evidence of alcohol will be flushed from the body within a half day.

Urine tests can also reveal extraneous information—whether a worker is pregnant, or is taking medication for a heart condition, asthma, epilepsy, diabetes, or manic depression, for example.

CONTROL OF PERSONAL INFORMATION

Privacy is not just a matter of minimizing the amount of information known about a person. It also involves control over that information. Employees worry that the confidentiality of test results is not guaranteed. Will they become part of a permanent, computerized file, accessible to any number of people? Will a worker be blacklisted because of a false positive, and never know why his or her career was stagnating?

SECTION 13.7
THE DRUG TESTING
OF TONY HODGE

PROBLEM THIRTEEN—B

HODGE, DODGE AND LODGE
ATTORNEYS AT LAW
MEMORANDUM

To: All Law Clerks

FROM: Gregory Olan Dodge

RE: Tony's Drug Testing Problem

In the middle of his third season with the Stallions, Tony Hodge took a short vacation during the team's off week and returned to Philadelphia to see his family. He spent Saturday night with an old girlfriend, Suzie Park. Tony and Suzy had dinner and went dancing at the Aztec Club. One thing led to another and he spent the night with Suzy at her Old City apartment. The next day it all seemed like a dream, since Tony had spent much of his night with Suzy high on something that she had given him to smoke. But it was Sunday, and he had to return to the Stallions.

Upon arriving at the practice field the next day, his coach greeted the team with a smile and a stack of small plastic specimen cups. "I hate to surprise you guys," said the coach, "But life can be surprising." Tony realized that he and his teammates were expected to line up, to go one at a time to the toilets and to produce some urine, while the assistant coach looked on. Tony felt embarrassed—but he also felt scared. Therefore, he refused the test and the team suspended him. Read *"Luedtke v. Nabors Alaska Drilling Company"* and the materials about drug testing and answer the following questions:

1. What are the chances that Tony will show "positive" results from the urinalysis test?

2. If Tony does test positive and is fired from the team, would he win a lawsuit for wrongful discharge?

3. What ethical issues are raised here and what do you think is fair in this situation?

ANSWER SHEET
PROBLEM THIRTEEN—B

Name   **Please Print Clearly**

1. What are the chances that Tony will show "positive" results from the urinalysis test?

_____

_____

_____

_____

_____

_____

_____

_____

2. If Tony does test positive and is fired from the team, would he win a lawsuit for wrongful discharge?

_____

_____

_____

_____

_____

_____

_____

_____

_____

3. What ethical issues are raised here and what do you think is fair in this situation?

_____

_____

_____

_____

_____

_____

_____

_____

_____

_____

_____

_____

_____

_____

_____

_____

_____

_____

_____

_____

_____

_____

SECTION 13.8
SEXUAL HARASSMENT

In 1964 Congress passed comprehensive Civil Rights legislation including this excerpt, known as "Title VII:"

a. It shall be an unlawful employment practice for an employer:

    1. to fail or refuse to hire or to discharge any individual, or otherwise to discriminate against any individual with respect to his compensation, terms, conditions, or privileges of employment because of such individual's race, color, religion, sex, or national origin.

The statute itself outlaws discrimination in broad, general language. The job of clarifying the statute by providing detailed examples of illegal discrimination is left to an administrative agency. In the case of Title VII, that government agency is the Equal Employment Opportunity Commission (EEOC), created by Congress to interpret and enforce the employment provisions of the Civil Rights Law.

In 1980, the EEOC adopted the following guidelines:

a. Harassment on the basis of sex consists of unwelcome sexual advances, requests for sexual favors, and other verbal or physical conduct of a sexual nature and will constitute sexual harassment when:

    1. submission to such conduct is made either explicitly or implicitly a term or condition of an individual's employment,

    2. submission to or rejection of such conduct by an individual is used as the basis for employment decisions affecting such individual, or

    3. such conduct has the purpose or effect of unreasonably interfering with an individual's work performance or creating an intimidating, hostile, or offensive working environment.

b. In determining whether alleged conduct constitutes sexual harassment, the Commission will look at the record as a whole and at the totality of the circumstances, such as the nature of the sexual advances and the context in which the alleged incidents occurred. The determination of the legality of a particular action will be made from the facts, on a case by case basis.

c. An employer is responsible for its acts and those of its agents and supervisory employees with respect to sexual harassment regardless of whether the specific acts complained of were authorized or even forbidden by the employer and regardless of whether the employer knew or should have known of their occurrence. (In its first sexual harassment case, the Supreme Court in 1986 made it clear that in cases of "hostile environment" sexual harassment an employer would only be held responsible if he knew or should have known about the harassment.)

d. With respect to conduct between fellow employees, an employer is responsible for acts of sexual harassment in the workplace where the employer (or its agents or supervisory employees) knows or should have known of the conduct, unless it can show that it took immediate and appropriate corrective action.

e. Prevention is the best tool for the elimination of sexual harassment. An employer should take all steps necessary to prevent sexual harassment from occurring, such as affirmatively raising the subject, expressing strong disapproval, developing appropriate sanctions informing employees of their right to raise and how to raise the issue of harassment under Title VII, and developing methods to sensitize all concerned.

TYPES OF SEXUAL HARASSMENT

Courts have identified two kinds of sexual harassment. The first, called quid pro quo (or "tangible benefit loss") happens when an employee is expected to give in to sexual demands or suffer the loss of some specific job benefit: a raise, a promotion, or even the job itself. Quid pro quo harassment would exist where a woman is fired for refusing to go on a date with her supervisor, for example.

The other kind of harassment, labelled hostile environment, involves less specific consequences. It occurs, for example, when a woman is constantly subjected to sexual harangues and obscenities in her workplace, or when she must repeatedly refuse unwanted sexual advances from her supervisor. Although she suffers no economic loss, she is a victim of discrimination because she must put up with a down-graded work atmosphere, pervaded with unpleasantness.

This second type of harassment has proved to be complicated: How offensive must the environment be to justify a complaint of sexual harassment? What factors should a court take into account in considering whether or not a particular workplace is so hostile to women that it discriminates against them? The next case provides contrasting views on hostile environment sexual harassment.

VIVIENNE RABIDUE V. OSCEOLA REFINING CO.
805 F.2D 611 (6TH CIR. 1986)

KRUPANSKY, Circuit Judge

THE PLAINTIFF WAS A CAPABLE, INDEPENDENT, ambitious, aggressive, intractable, and opinionated individual. The plaintiff's supervisors and co-employees with whom plaintiff interacted almost uniformly found her to be an abrasive, rude, antagonistic, extremely willful, uncooperative, and irascible personality. She consistently argued with co-workers and company customers in defiance of supervisory direction and jeopardized Osceola's business relationships with major oil companies. She disregarded supervisory instruction and company policy whenever such direction conflicted with her personal reasoning and conclusions. In sum, the plaintiff was a troublesome employee.

The plaintiff's charged sexual harassment arose primarily as a result of her unfortunate acrimonious working relationship with Douglas Henry. Henry was a supervisor of the company's key punch and computer section. Occasionally, the plaintiff's duties required coordination with Henry's department and personnel, although Henry exercised no supervisory authority over the plaintiff nor the plaintiff over him. Henry was an extremely vulgar and crude individual who customarily made obscene comments about women generally, and on occasion, directed such obscenities to the plaintiff. Management was aware of Henry's vulgarity but had been unsuccessful in curbing his offensive personality traits during the time encompassed by this controversy. The plaintiff and Henry, on the occasions when their duties exposed them to each other, were constantly in a confrontational posture. The plaintiff, as well as other female employees, were annoyed by Henry's vulgarity. In addition to Henry's obscenities, other male employees from time to time displayed pictures of nude or scantily clad women in their offices and/or work areas, to which the plaintiff and other women employees were exposed.

[T]o prove a claim of abusive work environment premised upon sexual harassment, a plaintiff must demonstrate that she would not have been the object of harassment but for her sex. It is of significance to note that instances of complained of sexual conduct that prove equally offensive to male and female workers would not support a Title VII sexual harassment charge because both men and women were accorded like treatment.

[S]exually hostile or intimidating environments are characterized by multiple and varied combinations and frequencies of offensive exposures which require the plaintiff to demonstrate that injury resulted not from a single or isolated offensive incident, comment, or conduct, but from incidents, comments or conduct which occurred with some frequency. To accord appropriate protection to both plaintiffs and defendants in a hostile and/or abusive work environment sexual harassment case, the trier of fact, when judging the totality of the circumstances impacting upon the asserted abusive and hostile environment must adopt the perspective of a reasonable person's reaction to a similar environment under essentially like or similar circumstances. Thus, in the absence of conduct which would interfere with that hypothetical reasonable individual's work performance and affect seriously the psychological well-being of that reasonable person under like circumstances, a plaintiff may not prevail. The plaintiff must also demonstrate that she was actually offended by the defendant's conduct and that she suffered some degree of injury as a result of the abusive and hostile work environment.

The trier of fact should also consider such objective and subjective factors as the nature of the alleged harassment, the background and experience of the plaintiff, her coworkers and supervisors, the totality of the physical environment of the workplace both before and after the plaintiff's introduction into its environs, coupled with the reasonable expectation of the plaintiff upon voluntarily entering that environment. As Judge Newblatt aptly stated in his opinion in the district court:

> Indeed, it cannot seriously be disputed that in some work environments, humor and language are rough hewn and vulgar. Sexual jokes, sexual conversation and girlie magazines may abound. Title VII was not meant to—or can— change this. It must never be forgotten that Title VII is the federal court mainstay in the struggle for equal employment opportunity for the female workers of America. But it is quite different to claim that Title VII was designed to bring about a magical transformation in the social mores of American workers.

In the case at bar, Henry's obscenities, although annoying, were not so startling as to have affected seriously the psyches of the plaintiff or other female employees. The evidence did not demonstrate that this single employee's vulgarity substantially affected the totality of the workplace. The sexually oriented poster displays had a de minimis effect on the plaintiff's work environment when considered in the context of a society that condones and publicly features and commercially exploits open displays of written and pictorial erotica at the newsstands, on prime-time television, at the cinema, and in other public places. In sum, Henry's vulgar language, coupled with the sexually oriented posters, did not result in a working environment that could be considered intimidating, hostile or offensive. It necessarily follows that the plaintiff failed to sustain her burden of proof that she was the victim of a Title VII sexual harassment violation.

KEITH, Circuit Judge, dissenting in part:

For seven years plaintiff worked at Osceola as the sole woman in a salaried management position. In common work areas plaintiff and other female employees were exposed daily to displays of nude or partially clad women belonging to a number of male employees at Osceola. One poster, which remained on the wall for eight years, showed a prone woman who had a golf ball on her breasts with a man standing over her, golf club in hand, yelling "Fore." And one desk plaque declared, "Even male chauvinist pigs need love..."

In addition, Computer Division Supervisor Doug Henry regularly spewed anti-female obscenity. Of plaintiff, Henry specifically remarked "All that bitch needs is a good lay" and called her "fat ass." Plaintiff arranged at least one meeting of female employees to discuss Henry and repeatedly filed written complaints on behalf of her herself and other female employees who feared losing their jobs if they complained directly. Osceola Vice President Charles Muetzel stated he knew that employees were "greatly disturbed" by Henry's language. However, because Osceola needed Henry's computer expertise, Muetzel did not reprimand or fire Henry. In response to subsequent complaints about Henry, a later supervisor, Charles Shoemaker, testified that he gave Henry "a little fatherly advice" about Henry's prospects if he learned to become "an executive type person."

In my view, Title VII's precise purpose is to prevent such behavior and attitudes from poisoning the work environment of classes protected under the Act. To condone the majority's notion of the "prevailing workplace" I would also have to agree that if an employer maintains an anti-Sematic workforce and tolerates a workplace in which "kike" jokes, displays of Nazi literature and anti-Jewish conversation "may abound," a Jewish employee assumes the risk of working there, and a court must consider such a work environment as "prevailing." I cannot. As I see it, job relatedness is the only additional factor which legitimately bears on the inquiry of plaintiff's reasonableness in finding her work environment offensive. In other words, the only additional question I would find relevant is whether the behavior complained of is required to perform the work.

QUESTIONS FOR DISCUSSION:

1. According to one survey, when people were asked how they would feel about having a co-worker express romantic interest in them when they didn't want to respond, two-thirds of the women said they would feel insulted, and two-thirds of the men said they would be flattered. This is one of many indicators that men and women view the same behavior in very different ways. What are the implications of this?

2. Remember the two ethical theories: Utilitarian, focusing on consequences for all concerned, and Rights-based, focusing on the competing rights of all concerned. How does each theory guide us in looking at sexual harassment?

3. What do you think should be done about sexual harassment?

SECTION 13.9
SHARON ROCK
v. JOSEPH HODGE

PROBLEM THIRTEEN—C

HODGE, DODGE AND LODGE
ATTORNEYS AT LAW
MEMORANDUM

To: All Law Clerks
From: Gregory Olan Dodge
Re: Sexual Harassment

Joe Hodge's construction firm is mostly male: male crew, male foremen, and Joe himself; his accountant and his lawyer are all men. Over the years the only women in the company were those who worked in the office: the receptionist, secretaries, and the bookkeeper. But last year Joe decided to hire a woman onto one of his crews. She was certified as an electrician and had had a summer's experience with another smaller construction firm. She seemed reliable, and said she was eager to get more experience with Joe's bigger, more successful company. Joe liked her. He also liked her looks and she was shapely, even in work clothes.

Things seemed to go along quite well with the new woman, Theresa Rock. After about a month though, Joe saw something that made him wonder. On one of the stalls in the bathroom he noticed, mixed in with the rest of the obscene graffiti, lewd comments about Theresa. On site about a week later he overheard some of his men laughing together about something. He thought it was a joke, and as he walked over to listen in, he noticed Theresa pushing through the knot of men, and stomping away from them. She seemed upset. Joe went up to the group and asked what was going on. "It's Mizz Sensitive," said the foreman. "What's that about?" asked Joe. "Nothing. It's about nothing, but she wants it to be something." A few of the others laughed. Joe didn't want to seem to be defending Theresa without knowing what was happening, so he changed the subject and began talking about the job at hand.

Another couple of weeks went by. Then one day he came out of his office to see Theresa herself waiting to talk with him. He was busy, but again, she seemed upset. In his office, Theresa explained that she felt she was being picked on by her co-workers. "Maybe they're jealous of me because am a really good electrician, but I think they just hate me because I'm a woman. They think it's their kingdom or something." When Joe asked who was doing what, though, she was unsure. "Someone's been taking my equipment. I'll be missing a tool, or my hardhat, things like that. And when I don't have the hat, the foreman sends me home." Joe asked her if she'd talked to the foreman. "I went to Bill right away, but he just said I was paranoid."

Joe spoke to Bill himself, after his interview with Theresa, and got nowhere. It seemed that she was imagining things, and that she couldn't take a joke. "It's rough out here with us, Joe, you know that. Maybe she can't take it."

The next time Joe saw Theresa they were both in the parking area. It was early in the morning and no one else was around. Joe thought Theresa seemed a little depressed. He said, "Theresa, what about having dinner tonight?" She looked up at him, squinted, paused and said, "Okay."

But there would be no chance to find out. Late that day Joe's secretary told him that Theresa had quit and gone home. Supposedly one of his crew operating a crane had dropped a stack of pallets from a height of about two stories down onto the ground right in front of Theresa, and she was scared to death. She had left the site in angry tears, telling Bill the foreman she would never be back.

And a few weeks later Joe received papers in a sexual harassment lawsuit that Theresa brought against him, his workers and his company. In it she alleged that the atmosphere at work had been filled with tension from the minute she arrived, that she was made to feel belittled by the sexual jokes and graffiti, by constant teasing, and by other harassing behavior, all of which, she alleged was due to the fact that she was a woman. She even accused Joe of sexual harassment for asking her out. The implication, the court papers indicated, was that Joe would use his power over her as her boss if she refused to go out with him.

Joe is shocked, horrified and nervous about Estelle's probable reaction. Based upon the materials in this section on Sexual Harassment and *Rabidue v. Osceola Refining Company*, answer the following questions:

1. What are the types of sexual harassment, and which one(s) might apply to whom in this situation?

2. What is the likely outcome if a judge follows the reasoning of Judge Krupansky in the **Rabidue** case?

3. What is the likely outcome if a judge follows the reasoning of Judge Keith in **Rabidue**?

4. Assume Joe is not liable for merely asking Theresa out on a date. Is he still liable for his behavior of his men?

ANSWER SHEET
PROBLEM THIRTEEN—C

Name   Please Print Clearly

1. What are the two types of sexual harassment, and which one(s) might apply to whom in this situation?

_____

_____

_____

_____

_____

_____

_____

_____

_____

2. What is the likely outcome if a judge follows the reasoning of Judge Krupansky in the **Rabidue** case?

_____

_____

_____

_____

_____

_____

_____

_____

_____

3. What is the likely outcome if a judge follows the reasoning of Judge Keith in **Rabidue**?

_____

_____

_____

_____

_____

_____

_____

_____

4. Assume Joe is not liable for merely asking Theresa out on a date. Is he still liable for the behavior of his men?

_____

_____

_____

_____

_____

_____

_____

_____

_____

SECTION 13.10
PROBLEM CASES

1. Butler was shopping at an Acme market when she walked towards her car in the parking lot. Suddenly, she was assaulted and her pocketbook was stolen. An investigation showed that over a period of one year, there had been seven attacks on the Acme market premises. Five of these attacks, occurred in the parking lot during the four month period immediately preceding the assault on Butler. The supermarket had hired off-duty police officers to act as security guards during the evening hours. However, there was only one security guard on duty at the time of the attack. Does the supermarket owe a duty of care to safeguard its patrons when they are in parking lot of their store? *Helen Butler v. Acme Markets, Inc.,* 426 A.2d 522 (N.J. App. 1981).

2. The car being driven by Wagner collided with a bicycle on which a ten year old boy was riding. The child's father, thinking that his son was dying, ran from the house, jumped from the porch, over the steps and onto the ground thereby fracturing his leg. The father sued the driver of the automobile on the basis that the father owed a duty to rescue his son and his injury was a natural consequence of the car driver's negligence. Wagner argued that the father rashly and unnecessarily exposed himself to danger and should be barred from recovery. Should the driver of the automobile be responsible for the father's broken leg? *Mark v. Wagner,* 307 N.E. 2d 480 (Oh. App. 1977).

3. Saltsman went to an entertainment complex in order to use the batting cage. The manager noticed a patron carrying alcoholic beverages and asked that individual to leave. In response, the patron slammed the cup of beer into the manager's face. Saltsman followed the assailant to the parking lot in order to obtain a license plate number from the assailant's vehicle. This led to a physical encounter in which Saltsman was attacked by the assailant with a golf club. Saltsman sued the entertainment complex for his injuries. An investigation showed that there had been no similar criminal activity on the premises in the past. Is the sporting complex responsible for the injuries to Saltsman? *Doug Saltsman v. Michael Corazo,* 721 A.2d 1000 (N.J. Super. 1998).

4. Estella brought a sexual harassment suit against his employer, Garage Management Corporation, for sexual harassment by a person of the same sex. The employer argued that same sex harassment does not rise to the level of a hostile work environment because the aggrieved party cannot prove that the harassment complained of was based upon his sex. Does sexual harassment of an individual by a person of the same sex, give rise to a viable cause of action? *Estella v. Garage Management Corporation,* 2000 W.L. 1228968 (S.D. N.Y. 2000).

5. A high school student was engaged in a sexual relationship with one of her teachers. She did not report that relationship to school officials. After the couple was discovered having sex, the teacher was arrested and terminated from his employment. The school district had not distributed any type of official grievance policy for lodging sexual harassment complaints as required by Federal regulations. The high school student then filed suit against the school district claiming a violation of Title IX which provides in pertinent part, "that a person cannot be subjected to discrimination under any educational program or activity which receives Federal financial assistance." An investigation into the incident revealed that no one in a supervisory power over the high school teacher knew of the affair with the student. Can the student recover damages for teacher-student sexual harassment because they failed to have a sexual harassment policy in place even though the school district officials were unaware of the teacher misconduct? *Alida Gebser v. Lago Vista, Independent School District,* **524 U.S. 274 (1998).**

SECTION 13.11
INTERNET REFERENCES

For a discussion of some of the topics contained in this chapter, see the following Internet sites:

A. *Drug Testing*

*   **http://www.mrinc.com/**
    A drug testing company maintains this site and provides news on drug testing, and provides answers to frequently asked questions about drug testing in the workplace.

B. *Sexual Harassment*

*   **http://www.uwstout.edu/affirm/sxhrs.html**
    General information about sexual harassment, including facts vs. myths may be accessed at this location.

*   **http://www.capstn.com/quiz.html**
    This site offers a quiz about sexual harassment.

*   **http://www.eeoc.gov/facts/fs-sex.html**
    The Equal Employment Opportunity Commission may be found at this address and internet users may obtain information about sexual harassment, as well as the text of Title VII of the Civil Rights Act of 1964.

*   **http://www.feminist.org/911/harass.html**
    This site lists various national hotlines for sexual harassment, including information on what to do if you or someone you know is sexually harassed.

C. Ethics

- **http://www.legalethics.com/ethics.law**
  This site provides ethics information in each state involving, lawyer ethics, confidentiality, and advertising.

- **http://www.usoge.gov/**
  The United States Office of Government Ethics Home Page is maintained at this location.

- **http://www.ljx.com/practice/professionalresponsibility/index.html**
  This site provides several interesting articles dealing with legal professional responsibility.

Footnotes   1. "Labs Err on Drug Test, Study Finds," *The Philadelphia Inquirer*, April 8, 1987, at A3, col. 1.

CHAPTER 14

BUSINESS ORGANIZATIONS[1]

SECTION 14.1
INTRODUCTION

HODGE, DODGE AND LODGE
ATTORNEYS AT LAW
MEMORANDUM

To: All Law Clerks

FROM: Gregory Olan Dodge

RE: Selecting a Business Organization

Now that your tenure at Hodge, Dodge and Lodge is about to end, it is important to consider your future business opportunities. Some of you will seek employment with established companies and others will venture out on your own. In any case, it is important to recognize the differences that exist among the different types of business organizations such as a sole proprietorship, partnership or corporation. Each business entity has its own advantages and disadvantages.

In order to demonstrate this point, I wish to share with you the success story of a client of Hodge, Dodge and Lodge who created an ice cream empire.

Jen and Barry's business started from humble beginnings, Jen behind a counter on South Street with one scoop and two flavors, chocolate and vanilla. The business was a sole proprietorship—Jen owned everything (the good news). Her federal taxes were simple; she reported the business income (and losses) on her federal income tax returns, although state and local tax returns were just as complex as if she had been incorporated. As a sole proprietor, she was responsible for everything (the bad news). Not only was she liable for all of the business' debts, including claims of anyone who suffered a personal injury due to the operation of the business (a risk for which she could insure) but she was also responsible for claims such as employment discrimination suits for which she could obtain no insurance.

After one year in the business, Jen had a dream—she should expand perhaps into strawberry, maybe even into butter almond or, thinking in the long term, perhaps mocha- beet. To actualize her ice cream dreams, Jen needed capital.

Jen persuaded her brother-in-law, Barry Able, to leave his company Able Baker and join Jen's in the partnership now known to the world as Jen & Barry's.

Jen & Barry's oral partnership agreement was never reduced to writing. Unlike the sole proprietorship, the partnership was required to file a federal tax return although this return was for information purposes only and the actual income and losses of the business were reported on Jen's & Barry's individual tax returns. The drawback to partnership was that the risks of proprietorship had not been eliminated but were now the risks of both Jen & Barry.

Unfortunately, the partners experienced a catastrophe they hadn't anticipated, a falling out. Jen wanted to expand to 28 flavors but Barry claimed that no, no, it should be 82 flavors. The differences proved irreconcilable and the partners ended up consuming all of their profits in a contentious lawsuit. It all could have been avoided if the partners had entered into a partnership agreement to provide for an orderly dissolution in the event of death or disability of one partner or an impasse between the two partners. As it was, a judge had to rule on open partnership issues such as:

Jen's buy-out price for Barry's share of the partnership; the ownership of the partnership's telephone number; and the ownership of the partnership's logo- the words "Cholesterol Free" inside a heart.

After Barry opened a competing business two doors away on South Street, Jen learned another reason for a written partnership agreement, the creation of a "non-compete" in favor of a partner, like Jen, who buys out a former partner.

The upshot of the partnership litigation was that Jen took over the business after buying Barry out. The buy-out payments reduced her liquidity and she sought a capital infusion from Joe Hodge.

Sadder but wiser, she formed a limited partnership. She was the general partner and Joe Hodge was the limited partner. Jen, as the general partner, was entitled to run the business but remained liable for all of the partnership's debts. Joe Hodge, on the other hand, as the limited partner, had no control over the operation of the business but his liability was limited to the amount of Joe's contribution to the partnership. To qualify as a limited partnership, the new business was required to file a certificate of limited partnership with the state and pay a fee.

After years of dodging the litigation bullet, a blockbuster suit was filed against the partnership by a portly man who claimed that Jen's ice cream was so addictive that it should have been labeled as a controlled substance. While Hodge, Dodge and Lodge was able to beat back the lawsuit, the litigation led to sleepless nights for Jen who feared that she, as the general partner, would have a judgment lien placed against her home, her car and all of her possessions.

Jen incorporated by having Hodge, Dodge and Lodge prepare Articles of Incorporation, paying a fee to the state, electing officers, and running annual board meetings. The paperwork involved was expensive when compared to the cost of other businesses and included annual corporate meetings, franchise tax returns and separate corporate income tax returns. Nevertheless, by following the proper corporate procedures, Jen insured that creditors could only collect the assets of the business and not her own assets.

After years of tinkering, Jen finally came up with the secret formula which put her over the top, Chocolate Chip Beet Mocha. The secret ingredient was Baco-Bits. Investors came clamoring and Jen began selling shares to those wishing to cash in on the business popularity. Jen received a salary as a corporate employee and such stock dividends as were declared by the Board of Directors. The Corporation was taxed on the remaining profits after Jen and the other employees received their salaries. The rest is history!

The following materials from *"The Legal and Regulatory Environment of Business"* by Corley, Reed, Shedd and Morehead provide a more detailed analysis of the various types of business entities.

SECTION 14.2
FACTORS TO CONSIDER

Significant factors to consider in selecting the best organizational form for a particular business activity include:

- The method of creating the organization
- The continuity or stability of the organization
- The degree of control each owner desires
- The personal liability of the owners
- The taxation of the organization's earnings and its distribution of profits to the owners

In the next five sub-sections, each of these factors is defined so that you can more easily apply their meaning in sections 14.4 thru 14.9.

1. CREATION

Through the use of this word "creation," we mean what legal steps are required to form a particular business organization. Also of importance is how much a person should expect to pay to have each form established. Exact dollar amounts are impossible to state due to the variations based on the location of professionals employed and the complexity of the organizations to be created. However, we can make some estimates of expected expenses relative to the organizational forms a person might select.

In general, unless the expense issue is of critical importance, the cost of creation is not a major factor in considering which form of business organization a person will choose to operate a business. The most significant creation-related issues are how long will it take to create a particular organization and how much paperwork is involved. These issues are addressed under the headings of each organizational form.

2. CONTINUITY

Another factor to consider when selecting the best organizational form for a business activity is the continuity of the organization. How is the organization's existence tied to its owners? By this question the meaning of the word "continuity" becomes associated with the stability or durability of the organization.

The crucial issue with this continuity factor is the method by which a business organization can be dissolved. A **dissolution** is any change in the ownership of an organization that changes the legal existence of the organization. In essence, the questions become: Is the organization easily dissolved? What impact does a dissolution of the organizational form have on the business activity of that organization? Answers to these questions are developed as each form of business organization is presented.

3. MANAGERIAL CONTROL

The factor of control concerns who is managing the business organization. Often times this issue is of vital importance to the owners. The egos of business people can cause them to insist on equal voices in management. As you study this factor under each organizational form, keep in mind the difficulties that can arise when a few strong-willed business owners disagree with one another. Usually when people are excited about getting started in a business opportunity (like a new restaurant), methods of resolving these potential deadlocks are not viewed as really important. However, consideration of potential conflict and mechanisms to resolve disputes are essential to consider when selecting a form for a business venture.

4. LIABILITY

When considering the liability factor, you should ask yourself—to what degree is the owner of a business personally liable for the debts of the business organization? Generally, business people want to limit their personal liability. While there are organizations that appear to accomplish this goal, you will see that such promises might be misleading when actually conducting business transactions. Nevertheless, this liability factor is very important and deserves significant consideration as it relates to each of the organizational forms presented below.

5. Taxation

This factor often is viewed as the most critical when selecting the form of business organization. At issue is: How is the income earned by the business taxed? How is the money distributed to the business owners taxed? Is it possible that owners may have to pay taxes on money that is attributed to them as income but which they have not actually received? The answers to these questions provide much needed guidance when deciding which form of organization is best suited for a business's operation.

People have stated that the double taxation of corporate income should be avoided by selecting a different form of organization. As you will see, there are specific advantages to creating the organizational forms that are "single taxed." However, advantages also exist when an organization is subject to the supposed "double tax."

Section 14.3
Selecting the Best
Organizational Form

Before we begin with an explanation of the various organizational forms that are available to business people, two terms that relate to the number of owners of a business organization are presented. Some organizations are owned by only a few persons. Such organizations are said to be **closely held.** Family-owned and -operated businesses are common examples of closely held organizations. Other businesses may be owned by hundreds, if not thousands, of persons. The organizations are publicly held ones. Examples of **publicly held** businesses include those whose stock is traded on a public exchange.

You should understand that the decision of selecting an appropriate organizational form usually is limited to those situations involving the few owners of a closely held business. When a business is publicly held by a large number of owners, the form of organization almost always is a corporation. The reason for this corporate form being used is that shareholders can transfer their ownership interests without interfering with the organization's management.

Possible Alternatives

Business is conducted under a variety of legal forms. The three basic forms are sole proprietors, partnerships, and corporations. Hybrid forms take on the form of both a partnership and a corporation. These forms include the limited partnership, the S corporation, and the limited liability company.

As the name implies, a **sole proprietorship** is a business owned by only one person. This is the simplest of all business organizations. The business's property belongs to the proprietor, and any income or losses are added to or deducted from that individual's personal income tax purposes. Any debts incurred by the organization actually are obligations of the proprietor. Because of its inherent limitation to one owner, a sole proprietorship cannot be a choice when two or more persons want to co-own a business.

Whenever two or more people wish to own a business together, a **partnership** is a possible organizational form. In general, a partnership is an agreement between two or more persons to share a common interest in a commercial endeavor and to share profits and losses. The word "persons" in the previous sentence should be interpreted broadly enough to allow not only individuals but also business organizations to form a partnership. For example, two or more individuals, an individual and a corporation, a partnership and a corporation, or any combination of these entities may agree to create a business organization called a partnership.

A **corporation** is an artificial, intangible entity created under the authority of a state's law. A corporation is known as a **domestic corporation** in the state in which it is incorporated. In all other states, this corporation is called a foreign corporation.

A limited partnership basically has all the attributes of a partnership except that one or more of the partners are designated as **limited partners.** This type of partner is not personally responsible for the debts of the business organization. However, these limited partners are not permitted to be involved in the control or operations of the limited partnership. The management is left in the hands of one or more **general partners** who remain personally liable for the organization's debts.

Beginning in 1958, the federal government permitted shareholders of certain corporations to unanimously elect to have their organization treated like a partnership for income tax purposes. This election is made possible through the language of subchapter S of the Internal Revenue Code. Today, organizations that are subject to this election often are referred to simply as **S corporations.**

The **limited liability company** is a relatively new organizational alternative. In 1977, Wyoming was the first state to pass a law permitting the creation of this type of business organization. Due to favorable tax rulings by the Internal Revenue Service, the use of the limited liability company has become quite popular.

These six forms of business organizations are discussed in the following Sections 14.4 thru 14.9.

SECTION 14.4
SOLE PROPRIETORSHIP

When considering the five factors introduced above, it has been said that the sole proprietorship has many virtues. However, the use of this business organization is very limited since multiple owners cannot create a proprietorship. Depending on the factual situation presented, greater continuity, less liability, and more flexible tax planning may be required than those afforded by the law of the sole proprietorship.

A sole proprietorship is the easiest and least expensive business organization to create. In essence, the proprietor obtains whatever business licenses are necessary and begins operations. Legally, no formal documentation is needed. The ease of (perhaps the lack of) the steps used to create a proprietorship makes it an attractive alternative when beginning a new business venture. However, as the other factors might dictate, a business might shift away from the proprietorship form as it becomes more successful.

A proprietorship's continuity is tied directly to the will of the proprietor. In essence, the proprietor may dissolve his or her organization at any time by simply changing the organization or terminating the business activity. The fact that the proprietorship's business activity may be more stable than the proprietor's willingness to remain actively involved in the business can indicate that the sole proprietorship is a less desirable organizational form.

The sole proprietor is in total control of his or her business's goals and operations. While the proprietor has complete responsibility for the business's success or failure, the owners of all other organizational forms usually share control to some degree. As long as this control issue is carefully thought out, there can be real value in having more than one voice in control of managing a business enterprise.

A sole proprietor is personally obligated for the debt of the proprietorship. Legally speaking, this owner has unlimited liability for the obligations of this type of business organization. The business organization's creditors can seek to hold the proprietor personally liable for 100 percent of the debts that the proprietorship cannot pay. The desire to avoid the potentially high risk of personal liability is an important reason why other organizational forms might be viewed as preferable to the proprietorship.

A sole proprietorship is not taxed as an organization. All the proprietorship's income subject to taxation is attributed to the proprietor. The initial appearance of this tax treatment may appear favorable since the business organization is not taxed. However, the individual proprietor must pay the applicable personal tax rate on the income earned by the proprietorship whether the proprietor actually receives any of the income from the organization or not.

SECTION 14.5
PARTNERSHIPS

Due to the potentially complex relationships established through a partnership, we present each factor to consider when studying the appropriateness of this organizational form under subheadings that correspond to numbers 1-5, in section 14.2.

1. CREATION

When compared to other forms of business organizations (other than the sole proprietorship), a partnership is easily formed. The cost of forming a partnership is relatively minimal. In addition, the creation of a partnership is made easier since it does not need to get permission from each state in which it does business.

The key to a partnership's existence is satisfying the elements of its definition:

1. Two or more persons,
2. A common interest in business, and
3. Sharing profits and losses.

If the parties conduct their affairs in such a way as to meet these definitional elements, a partnership exists regardless of whether the persons involved call themselves partners or not.

Since the existence of a partnership is based on the partners' agreement, it is possible that this agreement is implied from the conduct or actions of the parties. Partners should never rely on implied agreements. Rather, their agreement should be explicitly stated among the parties and drafted into a formal document. The formal agreement is called the **articles of partnership.**

Since a partnership is created by agreement, the partners select the name of the partnership. This right of selection is subject to two limitations in many states. First, a partnership may not use any word in the name, such as "company," that would imply the existence of a corporation. Second, if the name is other than that of the partners, the partners must give notice as to their actual identity under the state's **assumed name statute.** Failure to comply with this disclosure requirement may result in the partnership's being denied access to courts, or it may result in criminal actions being brought against those operating under the assumed name.

Even though an express or implied agreement of the partners may be lacking, to protect a third party, courts have held that such an organization exists. Under these circumstances the partnership is described as a **partnership by estoppel.** When a person represents himself or herself or allows others to represent him or her to third parties as being a partner, courts treat this person as a partner despite the fact that no partnership actually exists between the alleged "partners." For example, if a parent permits a child to advertise a new business venture as including the parent, a partnership by estoppel between the parent and child is necessary to protect third parties relying on the purported involvement of the parent. If this "partner" lacks knowledge of the representations made to third parties, he or she will not be estopped from denying the "partnership's" existence.

2. CONTINUITY

The partnership organizational form often is criticized for lacking stability. A general partnership is dissolved any time there is a change in the partners. For example, if a partner dies, retires, or otherwise withdraws from the organization, the partnership is dissolved. Likewise, if a person is added as a new partner, there is a technical dissolution of the organization. Therefore, it generally is said that the partnership organization is easily dissolved. Even if the partnership agreement provides that the partnership will continue for a stated number of years, any partner still retains the power to dissolve the organization. Although liability may be imposed on the former partner for wrongful dissolution in violation of the agreement, the partnership nevertheless is dissolved.

To act on the basis of a partnership's continuity being unstable is to be shortsighted. The more important question is: How will a dissolution of an organization affect the business of that organization? A dissolution does not necessarily destroy the business of a partnership. Dissolution is not the same thing as terminating an organization's business activity. Termination involves the winding up or liquidating of a business; dissolution simply means the legal form of organization no longer exists.

To prevent problems that may arise when a partner dies or withdraws from a partnership, the articles of partnership should include a **buy and sell agreement.** This agreement, which needs to be entered into when the business entity is created, provides for the amount and manner of compensation for the interest of the deceased or withdrawing owner.

Buy and sell agreements frequently use formulas to compute the value of the withdrawing partner's interest and provide for the time and method of payment. In the case of death, the liquidity needed is often provided by the cash proceeds from life insurance taken out on the life of the deceased and made payable to the business or to the surviving partner. Upon payment of the amount required by the buy and sell agreement to the estate of the deceased, the interest of the deceased ends, and all the surviving partners can continue the business.

3. MANAGERIAL CONTROL

In a general partnership, unless the agreement provides to the contrary, each partner has an equal voice in the firm's affairs, with an equal right to possess partnership property for business purposes. The partners may agree to divide control in such a way as to make controlling partners and minority partners. The decision of who has what voice in management is of crucial importance to the chances of the business's success and to the welfare of the partners' relationship with each other. The possibility of a deadlock among partners is very real, especially when there are only a few partners and they are even in number. Care should be taken to design mechanisms to avoid or at least handle the disputes that will arise when partners share managerial control.

Technical rules designate what acts of a partner are within the scope or course of the partnership. One such special rule is worthy of mention. A partner in a **trading partnership**, that is, one engaged in the business of buying and selling commodities, has the implied authority to borrow money in the usual course of business and to pledge the credit of the firm. A partner in a **nontrading partnership**, such as an accounting or other service firm, has no implied power to borrow money. In the latter case, such authority must be actual before the firm will be bound.

4. LIABILITY

Partners are liable for all transactions entered into by any partner in the scope of the partnership business and are similarly liable for any partner's torts committed while she or he is acting in the course of the firm's business. Each partner is in effect both an agent of the partnership and a principal, being capable of creating both contract and tort liability for the firm and for her or his copartners and likewise being responsible for her or his own acts.

All partners in a general partnership have unlimited liability for their organization's debts. These partners' personal assets, which are not associated with the partnership, may be claimed by the partnership's creditors. From a creditor's perspective, this personal liability of each partner extends to the organization's entire debt, not just to a pro rata share. These partners are **jointly and severally liable** for the partnership's obligations. For example, assume that a general partnership has three partners and that it owes a creditor $300,000. If it is necessary to collect the debt, this creditor can sue all three partners jointly for the $300,000. As an alternative, the creditor can sue any one partner or any combination of two for the entire $300,000. Among the partners, anyone who has to pay the creditor more than her or his pro rata share of the liability usually can seek contribution from the remaining partners.

5. TAXATION

Like proprietorship, partnerships, whether of a general or limited nature, are not a taxable entity. The fact that this type of organization pays no income tax does not mean that the profits of the partnership are free from income tax. A partnership files an information return that allocates to each partner his or her proportionate share of profits or losses from operations, dividend income, capital gains or losses, and other items that would affect the income tax owed by a partner. Partners then report their share of such items on their individual income tax returns, irrespective of whether they have actually received the items.

This aspect of a partnership is an advantage to the partners if the organization suffers a net loss. The pro rata share of this loss is allocated to each partner, and it can be used to reduce these partners' personal taxable income. However, by this same reasoning, a partnership is a disadvantage if the organization retains any profits made by the organization for the purpose of expansion. Suppose a partnership with three equal partners has $30,000 in net income. If the partnership keeps this money, there still is a constructive distribution of $10,000 to each partner for tax purposes. Assuming that these partners are in a 28 percent personal income tax bracket, they each would have to pay $2,800 in taxes even though they actually received nothing from the partnership.

SECTION 14.6
CORPORATIONS

The third basic organizational form which might be used to operate a business is the corporation. As a creature of state legislative bodies, the corporation is much more complex to create and to operate than other forms of businesses. These legal complexities associated with the corporation are presented below in a structure that parallels the preceding section so that comparisons with partnerships can be easily made.

1. CREATION

A corporation is created by a state issuing a **charter** upon the application of individuals known as **incorporators.** In comparison with partnerships, corporations are more costly to form. Among the costs of incorporation are filing fees, license fees, franchise taxes, attorneys' fees, and the cost of supplies, such as minute books, corporate seals, and stock certificates. In addition to these costs of creation, there also are annual costs in continuing a corporation's operation. These recurring expenses include annual reporting fees and taxes, the cost of annual shareholders' meetings, and ongoing legal-related expenses.

The formal application for corporate charter is called the **articles of incorporation.** These articles must contain the proposed name of the corporation. So that persons dealing with a business will know that it is a corporation, the law requires that the corporate name include one of the following words or end with an abbreviation of them: "corpora-tion," "company," "incorporated," or "limited." In addition, a corporate name must not be the same as, or deceptively similar to, the name of any domestic corporation or that of a foreign corporation authorized to do business in the state to which the application is made. Courts of equity may enjoin the use of deceptively similar names, and charters will be denied if the state believes that the names are deceptively simi-lar. The corporate name is an asset and an aspect of goodwill. As such, it is legally protected.

In addition to the proposed corporate name, the articles of incorpora-tion usually will include the proposed corporation's period of duration, the purpose for which it is formed, the number of authorized shares, and information about the initial corporate officials.. Typically, a cor-poration will apply for perpetual duration; however, a corporation can legally be created for a stated number of years. The corporate purpose stated in the articles of incorporation usually is very broad. For ex-ample, it would be better to say that a corporation is in the business of selling goods, rather than to limit this activity to either the retail or wholesale level. Stating the purpose very specifically may prohibit a growing corporation from expanding into related areas of operations.

With respect to authorized shares of stock, the articles of incorporation must indicate the class and value of stock and the number of shares of each class that will be sold. For example, incorporators may request that the state authorize 250,000 shares of $5 par value common stock of which 100,000 shares will be sold during the first year of operation. A corporation must pay taxes on the shares actually sold rather than on the shares authorized. If additional stock is sold after these initial 100,000 shares, the corporation must file a report and pay the extra taxes or fees.

Finally, the articles of incorporation must indicate the names and ad-dresses of the initial board of directors. In other words, these directors are appointed by the incorporators until such time as the shareholders can elect a board. Also appointed and specifically named in the appli-cation is the person serving as the corporation's agent to whom legal papers, such as complaints in lawsuits, may be served. Usually, the names and addresses of those persons acting as incorporators also must be included in the articles of incorporation.

Once drafted, these papers are sent to the appropriate state official (usu-ally the secretary of state), who approves them and issues a corporate charter. Notice of this incorporation usually has to be advertised in the local newspaper in order to inform the public that a new corporation has been created. The initial board of directors then meets, adopts the corporate bylaws, and approves the sale of stock. At this point, the corporation becomes operational.

If a corporation wishes to conduct business in states other than the state of incorporation, that corporation must be licensed in these foreign states. The process of qualification usually requires payment of license fees and franchise taxes above and beyond those paid during the initial incorporation process. If a corporation fails to qualify in states where it is conducting business, the corporation may be denied access to the courts as a means of enforcing its contracts.

2. CONTINUITY

In contrast to a partnership, a corporation usually is formed to have perpetual existence. The law treats a corporation's existence as distinct from its owners' status as shareholders. Thus, a shareholder's death or sale of her or his stock does not affect the organizational structure of a corporation. This ability to separate management from ownership is an often cited advantage of the corporation.

Like our analysis of continuity (or lack thereof) for partnerships, this factor may mislead people with respect to corporations. While the death of or sale of stock by a major shareholder of a corporation has no legal impact on the organization's existence, this event may have a very real adverse impact on that corporation's ability to do business. The shareholder may have been the driving force behind keeping the corporation's old customers or attracting new ones. Without this shareholder's constructive influence, the corporation's business may fail. Although the corporation may still exist, the business purpose could cease.

3. MANAGERIAL CONTROL

In the corporate form of organization, the issue of control is complicated by three groups. First, the **shareholders** elect the members of the board of directors. These **directors** set the objectives or goals of the corporation, and they appoint the officers. These **officers,** such as the president, vice president, secretary, and treasurer, are charged with managing the daily operations of the corporation in an attempt to achieve the stated organizational objectives or goals. Thus, which one of these three groups really controls the corporation?

To answer this question effectively, you must realize that the issue of who controls a corporation varies depending on the size of the ownership base of the organization. In essence, matters of managerial control require us to examine the publicly held corporation as distinct from the closely held corporation.

Publicly Held Corporations In very large corporations, control by management (a combination of the directors and officers) is maintained with a very small percentage of stock ownership through the use of corporate records and funds to solicit **proxies.** Technically, a proxy is an agent appointed by a shareholder for the purpose of voting the shares. Management can, at corporate expense, solicit the right to vote the stock of shareholders unable to attend the meetings at which the directors of the company are elected. An outsider must either own sufficient stock to elect the directors or must solicit proxies at his or her own expense. The management of a large corporation usually can maintain control with only a small minority of actual stock ownership.

In corporations having several hundred shareholders or more, a number of techniques are used by organizing investors to gain control without having a majority of the total investment. One technique is to have the corporation issue classes of stock. In some states there can be *nonvoting stock*—the investors seeking to keep control will buy *voting stock* while selling nonvoting stock to others. Preferred stock may be used to increase capital without losing control. For example, organizing investors may buy $100,000 in common stock of $1 par value each. Then the corporation will sell another $100,000 of the same common stock, requiring that for each share of common stock purchased, a $5 share of nonvoting preferred stock must be purchased. Thus, the corporation would raise $70,000, and the $100,000 original investment made by the organizing individuals would have 50 percent of the voting power. Another method of gaining and keeping control is to pool the stock of several shareholders into a voting trust so that one person gains the power, by contract, to vote all the shares in the trust.

Closely Held Corporations Unlike the situation with a large, publicly held corporation, one shareholder (or at least a small group of shareholders) may be able to control a closely held corporation. This can result because this individual (or the group) can own an actual majority of the issued shares. This majority can control the election of a board of directors. In fact, the shareholders with the largest amount of stock are often elected to this board of directors. The directors, in turn, elect officers, who again may be the shareholders with the largest interests. The directors also establish important corporate policies, such as declaring dividends and amending the bylaws. In a very real sense, those who own a majority of a closely held corporation can rule with near absolute authority.

What are the rights of those who do not possess control in a closely held corporation—the so-called minority interest? To a large degree, the owners of the minority interest are subject to the whim or caprice of the majority. The majority may pay themselves salaries that use up profits and may never declare a dividend. However, the minority interest is not without some rights, because the directors and officers stand in a fiduciary relation to the corporation and to the minority shareholders if the corporation is closely held. This relation imposes a duty on directors to act for the best interests of the corporation rather than for themselves individually.

If the majority is acting illegally or oppresses the rights of the minority shareholders, a lawsuit known as a **derivative suit** may be brought by a minority shareholder on behalf of the corporation. Such suits may seek to enjoin the unlawful activity or to collect damages for the corporation. For example, contracts made between the corporation and an interested director or officer may be challenged. If sued, the burden is on the director or officer (who may be the majority shareholder) to prove good faith and inherent fairness in such transactions.

A derivative suit cannot be used as a means of harassing management. Therefore, these actions generally cannot begin until all possible means to solve the problem within the corporate organization have been exhausted. Generally, a minority shareholder must first demand that the board of directors institute a suit to protect the corporation. However, a formal demand on the board is excused if the demand would be futile, such as when the directors are accused of the wrongdoing. In these situations, companies may appoint a disinterested committee to decide when a derivative suit filed on behalf of the company is in the organization's best interest. An independent committee balancing between the rights of the aggrieved shareholders and the needs of management may be subject to judicial review.

The basic difficulty of owning a minority interest in a closely held corporation arises from the fact that there is no ready market for the stock should the shareholder desire to dispose of it. Of course, if there is a valid buy and sell agreement, then there is a market for the stock. Thus, buy and sell agreements are absolutely essential in closely held corporations. Although shareholders have the right to attend meetings and vote for directors, they may be constantly outvoted. They have a right to any dividends that are declared but no right to have them declared. They also have a **preemptive right** to purchase their proportionate share of any new stock issue, but they may not be interested in investing more money when no dividends are being paid. Therefore, as a practical matter, the majority may be able to increase their percentage of ownership further. The minority shareholder has a right to inspect the books and records of the company, but at a proper time and place; and the books may not have much meaning without entries and account balances being analyzed by an expert.

Finally, minority shareholders have the right to their proportionate share of assets on dissolution, but they have no right to dissolution, except that they may seek it in a court of equity under circumstances that will cause a court to step in to protect creditors and the corporation.

4. LIABILITY

The legal ability to separate a corporation's shareholders from its managers means that the owners are liable for the debts of the corporation only to the extent of those shareholders' investment in the cost of the stock. Thus, corporate shareholders are said to have **limited personal liability.**

The generalization that the investors in a corporation have limited liability but those in a partnership have unlimited liability is too broad and needs qualification. To be sure, someone investing in a company listed on the New York Stock Exchange will incur no risk greater than the investment, and the concept of limited liability certainly applies. However, if the company is a small, closely held corporation with limited assets and capital, it will be difficult for it to obtain credit on the strength of its own net worth. As a practical matter, shareholders will usually be required to add their own individual liability as security for debts. For example, if the XYZ Company seeks a loan at a local bank, the bank often will require the owners, X, Y and Z to personally guarantee repayment of the loan.

This is not to say that shareholders in closely held corporations do not have some degree of limited liability. Shareholders have limited liability for contract-like obligations that are imposed as a matter of law (such as taxes). Liability also is limited when the corporate obligation results from torts committed by company employees while doing company business.

Even in these situations, the mere fact of corporate existence does not mean the shareholders will have liability limited to their investment. When courts find that the corporate organization is being misused, the corporate entity can be disregarded. This has been called **piercing the corporate veil.** When this veil of protection has been pierced, the shareholders are treated like partners who have unlimited liability for their organization's debts.

Misuse of the corporate organizational form has been defined by the courts as including several situations. First, a corporate entity is misused if it is used to defraud or avoid an otherwise valid obligation. For example, assume Alexandra sold Bennett a business, and Alexandra agreed not to compete with Bennett for two years. If, in violation of the contract, Alexandra organized a corporation and competed with Bennett, a court likely would hold that this corporation's corporate veil is pierced. Alexandra cannot do legally through a corporation what she cannot do legally personally.

Second, a corporate entity is misused if it is used to evade a statute. Assume a state law provides that a person may not hold more than one liquor license at a time. This law cannot be circumvented by forming multiple corporations. Franklin owns a restaurant, and he has a license to serve alcoholic beverages. Suppose Franklin wants to open a liquor store in a different location. To overcome the state law's limitation on liquor licenses, Franklin forms a corporation to hold the license for the store. Such a corporation cannot be used to circumvent the law. If its charter was issued by mistake or under false pretenses, the charter can be revoked by the state.

Third, a corporate entity is misused if it is organized, controlled, and conducted in a manner that makes it an instrument of another corporation. In such circumstances, one corporation is said to be the "alter ego" of another. It must be recognized that the mere relationship of a parent corporation with a subsidiary is not enough by itself to justify piercing the corporate veil. Subsidiaries are often formed in order to limit the liability of the parent corporation.

The *alter-ego theory*, by which the corporate veil can be pierced, may also be used to impose personal liability upon corporate officers, directors, and stockholders. If the corporate entity is disregarded by these officials themselves, so that there is such a unity of ownership and interest that separateness of the corporation has ceased to exist, the alter-ego theory will be followed and the corporate veil will be pierced.

Courts are not limited to these three situations when the issue is whether or not to pierce the corporate veil and hold shareholders personally liable.

5. TAXATION

Corporations must pay income taxes on their earnings. The **Corporate Tax Rate Table** on page 441 sets forth these tax rates as of the end of 1994.

The fact that there is a separate corporate income tax may work as an advantage. For example, if the corporation makes a profit that is to be retained by the corporation to support growth, no income is allocated to the shareholders. In other words, these shareholders will not have their personal taxable income increased, as would a partner in a similar situation. In addition, the corporate rate may be lower than the individual rates.

But corporations also have tax disadvantages. Suppose a corporation suffers a loss during a given tax year. The existence of the corporate tax works as a disadvantage, since this loss cannot be distributed to the shareholders in order to reduce their personal tax liability. Indeed, a net operating loss to a corporation can be used only to offset corporate income earned in other years. And the allocation of such a loss can be carried back only for three years and carried forward for fifteen years. (Note: There are many different rules concerning specialized carryover situations. The Internal Revenue Code should be examined prior to relying on the general rule just stated.)

Perhaps a greater disadvantage of the corporate tax occurs when a profit is made and the corporation wishes to pay a dividend to its shareholders. The money used to pay this dividend will have been taxed at the corporate level. It is then taxed again because the shareholder must take the amount of the dividend into his or her own personal income. The rate of this second tax depends on the personal tax rate of the shareholder receiving the dividend. This situation has been called the **double tax** on corporate income. A similar situation of double taxation occurs when a corporation is dissolved and its assets are distributed to shareholders as capital gains. Yet, as the discussion next indicates, the double tax may not be as big a disadvantage as it appears at first.

Double Taxation Corporations have employed a variety of techniques for avoiding the double taxation of corporate income. First, reasonable salaries paid to corporate officials may be deducted in computing the taxable income of the business. Thus, in a closely held corporation in which all or most shareholders are officers or employees, this technique may avoid double taxation of substantial portions of income. As might be expected, the Internal Revenue Code disallows a deduction for excessive or unreasonable compensation and treats such payments as dividends. Therefore, the determination of the reasonableness of corporate salaries is often a tax problem in that form of organization.

Second, corporations provide expense accounts for many employees, including shareholder employees. These are used to purchase travel, food, and entertainment. When so used, the employee, to some extent, has compensation that is not taxed. In an attempt to close this tax loophole, the law limits deductions for business meals and entertainment to 50 percent of the cost. Meal expenses and entertainment are deductible only if the expenses are directly related to or associated with the active conduct of a trade or business. For a deduction, business must be discussed directly before, during, or directly after the meal. Additionally, meal expenses are not deductible to the extent the meal is lavish or extravagant. Thus, the use of the expense account to avoid taxation of corporate income is subject to numerous technical rules and limitations.

Third, the capital structure of the corporation may include both common stock and interest-bearing loans from shareholders. For example, assume that a company needs $100,000 cash to go into business. If

$100,000 of stock is issued, no expense will be deducted. However, assume that $50,000 worth of stock is purchased by the owners and $50,000 is lent to the company by them at 10 percent interest. In this case, $5,000 interest each year is deductible as an expense of the company and thus subject to only one tax as interest income to the owners. Just as in the case of salaries, the Internal Revenue Code has a counteracting rule relating to corporations that are undercapitalized. If the corporation is undercapitalized, interest payments will be treated as dividends and disallowed as deductible expenses.

The fourth technique for avoiding double taxation, at least in part, is simply not to pay dividends and to accumulate the earnings. The Internal Revenue Service seeks to compel corporations to distribute those profits not needed for a business purpose, such as growth. When a corporation retains earnings in excess of $250,000, there is a presumption that these earnings are being accumulated to avoid a second tax on dividends. If the corporations cannot rebut this presumption, an additional tax of 271/2 percent is imposed on the first $100,000 unreasonably accumulated in excess of $250,000. For undistributed earnings above this amount, the penalty tax equals 381/2 percent of the unreasonable accumulation.

Corporate Tax Rates	
Income	**Tax Rate**
$0 - $50,000	15%
$50,000 - $75,000	25%
$75,000 - $10,000,000	34%
over $10,000,000	35%

SECTION 14.7
LIMITED PARTNERSHIPS

The state legislature of New York was the first body in this country to allow some partners in a partnership to be treated like shareholders of a corporation in the sense of enjoying limited liability. Since 1822, when New York passed the first Limited Partnership Act, the existence of this hybrid organization has been recognized throughout the United States.

The attributes of a general partnership and a corporation that combine to make the limited partnership an attractive alternative form of business organization are discussed under the subheadings that follow.

1. CREATION

Like a general partnership, a limited partnership is created by agreement. However, as in the case of a corporation, state law requires that the contents of a certificate must be recorded in a public office so that everyone may be fully advised as to the details of the organization. This certificate contains, among other matters, the following information: the name of the partnership, the character of the business, its location, the name and place of residence of each member, those who are to be the general partners and those who are to be the limited partners, the length of time the partnership is to exist, the amount of cash or the agreed value of property to be contributed by each partner, and the share of profit or compensation each limited partner shall receive.

The limited partnership certificate is required to be recorded in the county where the partnership has its principal place of business. An additional copy has to be filed in every community where the partnership conducts business or has an office. Whenever there is a change in the information contained in the filed certificate, a new certificate must be prepared and recorded. If an accurate certificate is not on record and the limited partnership continues its operation, the limited partners become liable as general partners. Substantial compliance with all the technical requirements of the limited partnership law is essential if the limited partners are to be assured of their limited liability.

The terms of the limited partnership agreement control the governance of the organization. These terms should be read carefully and understood by all general and limited partners before the agreement is signed. Failure of the parties to state their agreement clearly may result in a court interpreting the limited partnership agreement.

2. CONTINUITY

The principles guiding partnerships also apply to limited partnerships if there is a change in the general partners. A limited partner may assign his or her interest to another without dissolving the limited partnership.

3. MANAGERIAL CONTROL

In a limited partnership, the general partners are in control. Limited partners have no right to participate in management. The impact of this relationship on the operations of a limited partnership is discussed in detail in the next subsection.

4. LIABILITY

The true nature of the limited partnership being a hybrid is in the area of owners' liability. Traditionally, the general partners in a limited partnership have unlimited liability. However, the limited partners are not personally liable for the partnership's debts. These limited partners' liability typically will not exceed the amount of their investments.

Under the Revised Uniform Limited Partnership Act (RULPA), a limited partner's surname may not be used in the partnership's name unless there is a general partner with the same name. If a limited partner's name is used in the firm's name, that partner will become personally liable to unsuspecting creditors.

Limited partners also may not participate in the management of the limited partnership. Under the RULPA, a limited partner who participates in the organization's management becomes liable as a general partner if a third party had knowledge of the limited partner's activities. The following actions by a limited partner do not constitute participation in management in such a way that the advantage of limited liability is lost:

- Acting as an agent or employee of the partnership
- Consulting with or advising a general partner
- Acting as a guarantor of the partnership's obligations
- Inspecting and copying any of the partnership's financial records
- Demanding true and full information about the partnership whenever circumstances render it just and reasonable
- Receiving a share of the profits or other compensation by way of income
- Approving or disapproving an amendment to the partnership's certificate
- Voting on matters of fundamental importance such as dissolution, sale of assets, or change of the partnership's name
- Having contribution returned upon dissolution

5. TAXATION

During the 1980s, limited partnerships were used to finance real estate development, theatrical productions, professional sport teams, and other projects that require large amounts of capital. The limited partners trade interest in these limited partnerships in ways similar to trading stock in publicly held corporations. **Master limited partnerships** often involve thousands of limited partners. These limited partnerships become taxable organizations, like corporations, when they are publicly traded—the sale or transfer of more than 5 percent of the limited partners' interest during a taxable year.

SECTION 14.8
S CORPORATIONS

The S corporation has all the legal characteristics of the corporation previously discussed in this chapter. The one exception to this similar treatment is that shareholders in the S corporation are responsible for accounting on their individual income tax returns for their respective shares of their organization's profits or losses. In essence, these shareholders can elect to have their business organization treated, for tax purposes, as if it were a partnership. Through this election, the shareholders avoid having a tax assessed on the corporate income itself. Even though the S corporation does not pay any taxes, like a partnership, it must file an information return with the Internal Revenue Service.

S corporations cannot have more than thirty-five shareholders, each of whom must elect to have the corporate income allocated to the shareholders annually in computing their income for tax purposes, whether actually paid out or not. Only individuals are eligible to elect under subchapter S. Therefore, other forms of business organization, such as partnerships, limited partnerships, or corporations, cannot be shareholders in an S corporation.

In addition to the limitations just stated, there are many technical rules of tax law involved in S corporations. However, as a rule of thumb, this method of organization has distinct advantages for a business operating at a loss because the loss is shared and immediately deductible on the returns of the shareholders. It is also advantageous for businesses capable of paying out net profits as earned. In the latter case, the corporate tax is avoided. If net profits must be retained in the business, subchapter S tax treatment is disadvantageous because income tax is paid on earnings not received, and there is a danger of double taxation to the individual because undistributed earnings that have been taxed once are taxed again in the event of the death of a shareholder. Thus, the theoretical advantage of using an S corporation to avoid double taxation of corporate income must be carefully qualified.

SECTION 14.9
LIMITED LIABILITY
COMPANIES

In 1988, the Internal Revenue Service ruled that limited liability companies (LLCs) would be treated as nontaxable entities, much like partnerships, for federal income tax purposes. Following this ruling, states rushed to pass legislation authorizing business people to operate their businesses as LLCs. Now more than forty states recognize the LLC as a viable organizational form of business. In essence, its owners have more flexibility than with the S corporation while not having to struggle with the complexities of the limited partnership.

In the true sense of a hybrid, an LLC has characteristics of both a partnership and a corporation. For example, an LLC is created through filings much like those used when creating a corporation. **Articles of organization** are filed with a state official, usually the secretary of state. Instead of "incorporators," the term **organizers** is used. The name of any LLC must acknowledge the special nature of this organizational form by including the phrase "limited liability company," or "limited company," or some abbreviation, such as "LLC" or "LC." An LLC created in a state other than the one in which it is conducting business is called a foreign LLC. Like a foreign corporation, this LLC must apply to the state to be authorized to transact business legally. An LLC also must file annual reports with the states in which it operates.

The owners of LLCs are called **members** rather than shareholders or partners. Membership in LLCs is not limited to individuals. Unlike in the S corporation, a business organization can be an owner in any LLC. The transferability of a member's interest is restricted in the fashion of a partner as opposed to the free transferability of a corporate shareholder. Anytime a member dies or withdraws from the LLC, there is a dissolution of the business organization, in much the same way as discussed under "Partnerships" in section 8, above. However, the business of a dissolved LLC is not necessarily adversely impacted if the remaining members decide to continue business. Either as provided in the articles of organization or by agreement of the remaining members within ninety days of the withdrawing member's disassociation, the business of the LLC may be continued rather than wound up.

The managerial control of an LLC is vested in its members, unless the articles of organization provide for one or more **managers**. Regardless of whether members or managers control the LLC, a majority of these decision makers decide the direction of the organization. In a few situations enumerated in the state law authorizing LLCs, unanimous consent of the members is required for the organization to make a binding decision. Similarly to partners in a partnership, members of LLCs make contributions of capital. They have equal rights to share in the LLC's profits and losses, unless these members have agreed otherwise. When a member is in the minority with respect to decisions being made on behalf of the LLC, that dissenting member has rights very much like a dissenting shareholder in a corporation. These rights include bringing a derivative lawsuit against the controlling members of the LLC. Ultimately, a dissenting member has the right to sell the membership interest to the other members of the LLC.

For liability purposes, members do act as agents of their LLC. However, they are not personally liable to third parties. Thus, these members have attributes of both partners and shareholders with respect to liability.

Finally, state laws and the IRS recognize LLCs as nontaxable entities. While the LLC appears to have many advantages, do not forget that careful analysis is needed in every situation to determine whether this type of tax treatment is in the members' best interests. The materials in the preceding sections concerning taxation are equally applicable here.

SECTION 14.10
MAKING THE DECISION

There really is no absolutely right answer to the question—Which organizational form is best for a business's operation? The answer to this question is unique to a particular situation. Although one answer is never correct for all business opportunities, it is our hope that this chapter has presented you with some helpful material to consider when faced with the important decision about which organizational form should be used.

This analysis of selecting the best-suited organization for a business's purpose is of vital importance when a business is being started or when it encounters a substantial change, such as rapid growth. Therefore, the criteria used to select a form or organization need to be reviewed periodically. This review should be done in consultation with close advisers such as attorneys, accountants, bankers, and insurers. These people weigh the factors and costs involved and then select the most suitable organizational form for the business's needs at that time. Because this selection process balances advantages against disadvantages, the decision often is to choose the least objectionable form of organization.

SECTION 14.11
PROBLEM CASES

1. National Lumber Building Materials, Co., is a Rhode Island Corporation that has been in business for almost 50 years. A Massachusetts corporation decided to conduct business in Rhode Island and wished to file a fictitious name registration under the name of National Lumber Co., doing business as National Lumber, Co. of Massachusetts. The Rhode Island corporation filed an injunction action in order to prevent the Massachusetts firm from using the fictitious name in Rhode Island. Is the name of National Lumber Co. of Massachusetts too similar to the name of National Lumber Building Materials Co., Inc. so that it will cause confusion among customers? *National Lumber Building Materials*, Co. v. **Langevin, 2000 W.L. 1910039 (R.I. Super. 2000).**

2. Gonzalez sued both the limited and general partners of a limited partnership for breach of contract. Renovation work by Gonzalez was undertaken at the request of Chalpin and the work was performed on an apartment building owned by Excel. Excel is the limited partnership in question, which has one individual general partner, Lipkin; one corporate general partner, Tribute Music Inc.; and one limited partner, Chalpin. Chalpin, however, is also the presi-

dent of Tribute Music and is the representative who terminated Gonzalez's employment from the project. Chalpin defended the action to hold him personally liable on the basis that he was merely acting in his capacity as president of Tribute Music and not in his individual capacity as a limited partner. Will Chalpin be personally liable for the debt of the limited partnership? *Gonzalez v. Chalpin,* **565 N.E. 2nd 1253 (N.Y.S. 1990).**

3. Schmitz instituted suit for medical malpractice against The Fargo Clinic, a partnership, and some of the partners of that clinic. Schmitz, however, did not sue all of the partners in the medical practice. Is it permissible for a plaintiff to sue only a few of the partners instead of the all of the partners for a partnership debt? Will the partners that have been sued be individually liable for the entire verdict on the basis joint and several liability or will the partners that have been sued merely be responsible for a pro rata or percentage share of the judgment? *Schmitz v. St. Luke's Hospital, Inc.,* **258 F. Supp. 392 (N.D.D. 1966).**

4. Westside Sand, Inc. is a corporation and Gerald Webber is the president and stockholder of the business. An agent for Westside Sand Company purchased materials from P&L Construction Materials for use by Westside Sand Company. When the business defaulted on the payment of the bill, suit was instituted against Webber in his personal capacity. The evidence demonstrated that the agent never informed P&L that she was buying the materials for Westside Sand, Inc. Since the identity of Westside Sand, Inc. was not disclosed by the agent to P&L at the time of the purchase, does that make the president of Westside personally liable for the corporate debt? *Deroche v. P&L Construction Materials, Inc.,* **554 So.2d 717 (Ct. App. La. 1989).**

5. A&M Records sued M.V.C. Distributing Corporation and Donald Merry for the unauthorized duplication and distribution of musical recordings. Merry ran the business. These pirated or bootlegged tapes were reproductions of the original records marketed under a different record label. The record companies attempted to pierce the corporate veil of M.V.C. in order to hold Merry personally liable as a corporate officer for the music piracy. Is the officer of a business personally responsible for the improper or illegal actions of a corporation? *A&M Records, Inc. v. M.V.C. Distributing Corp.,* **574 F.2d 312 (6th Cir. 1978).**

SECTION 14.12
INTERNET REFERENCES

For more information about topics discussed in this chapter, see the following Internet sites:

A. Starting a Business

- **http://www.businesstown.com/gettingstarted/index.asp**
  This site provides a step by step process of starting a small business.

- **http://www.workingsolo.com/starting/articles/naming.thtml**
  This site offers tips for naming a business.

- **http://www.irs.ustreas.gov/bus_info/index.html**
  The IRS offers this site in order to provide tax information for businesses.

- **http://www.onlinewbc.org/Docs/finance/org_form.html**
  General information about the different forms of business and the advantages and disadvantages of each can be ascertained at this address.

- **http://www.ideacafe.com/BCdir/BCdirect.html**
  Comprehensive information about how to start a business is provided at this site, including information on starting, running and financing a business.

- **http://aol.toolkit.cch.com/**
  This is comprehensive site providing news updates, and information on planning, starting, and financing a business.

B. Starting an Internet Business

- **http://www.buildyourhomebiz.com/**
  Those interested in starting an Internet business may find this interest address helpful since it offers articles, advice, and answers to frequently asked questions about the topic.

C. Limited Liability Companies

- **http://www.llc-usa.com/**
  This site is dedicated to those interested in limited liability companies. Several links are provided to resources on the topic.

- **http://www.llcweb.com/**
  General information about limited liability companies is contained at this site.

D. Business Information

- **http://www.companiesonline.com/**
  This site allows a person to search over 900,000 public and private companies online. It also provides other links to things such as business news and business tools.

Footnotes   1. Reprinted with permission from "Business Organizations," **The Legal and Regulatory Environment of Business,** by Corley, Reed, Shedd and Morehead. Copyright 1996 by the McGraw-Hill Companies.

CHAPTER 15

INTERNATIONAL LAW[1]

SECTION 15.1
INTRODUCTION

International business transactions create additional problems for any business entity. Which country's laws shall apply and where suit must be filed in the event of a dispute are just two of the questions. In addition, a number of countries have organized their efforts to develop economic unity among their members. These organizations include the European Union and the North American Free Trade Agreement. A basic understanding of these organizations and the problems with international transactions is essential.

The following materials from *"The Legal and Regulatory Environment of Business"* by Corley, Reed, Shedd and Morehead provide a brief overview of some of the issues involving international business transactions.

SECTION 15.2
INTERNATIONAL LAW
AND ORGANIZATIONS

As you explore international business transactions, please remember that, unfortunately, international law does not consist of a cohesive body of uniform principles. Nonetheless, international law can be found in a variety of sources from U.S. domestic law to the law of other countries to international agreements and treaties and even in customary international principles found in the general practice of civilized nations.

In the famous case of *The Paquette Habana* (175 U.S. 677 [1900]), the Supreme Court held that "[i]nternational law is part of our law, and must be ascertained and administered by the courts of justice of appropriate jurisdiction as often as questions of right depending upon it are duly presented for their determination."

SECTION 15.3
SOURCES OF
INTERNATIONAL LAW

How does one go about finding the principles or rules of international law that apply to a particular contract or dispute? Generally, international law is classified as either **public international law or private international law.** Public international law examines relationships between nations and uses rules that are binding on all countries in the international community. Private international law examines relationships created by commercial transactions and utilizes treaties, agreements, and the individual laws of nations to resolve business disputes.

PUBLIC INTERNATIONAL LAW

Article 38 of the Statute of the **International Court of Justice (ICJ),** or the World Court, is the traditional place for ascertaining what is public international law. However, in contrast to what you learned regarding U.S. cases, the decisions made by the World Court do not create binding rules of law or precedent in future cases.

The ICJ is the judicial branch of the United Nations and sits at The Hague in the Netherlands. It consists of fifteen judges representing all of the world's major legal systems. The judges are elected by the U.N. General Assembly and the Security Council after having been nominated by national groups, not governments. No more than one judge may be a national of any country.

The ICJ has not been a major force in settling disputes since it began functioning in 1946. The ICJ renders, on average, only one contested decision per year and one advisory opinion every two years. There has been widespread reluctance to resort to the ICJ as a forum for resolving international disputes for several reasons. First, only countries have access to the Court. Private parties or corporations may not directly present claims before the Court. No device exists under U.S. law by which a firm or individual can compel the U.S. government to press a claim on its behalf before the ICJ. Furthermore, only countries that have submitted to the Court's jurisdiction may be parties, since there is no compulsory process for forcing a country to come before the Court. A country may choose to accept the Court's jurisdiction only when the use of the Court may suit its own interests. Moreover, the ICJ has no enforcement authority and must rely on diplomacy or economic sanctions against countries that breach international law. For these reasons, infractions of international law often are settled through diplomacy or arbitration, rather than by the presentation of formal charges to the ICJ.

Of course, deciding whether a nation has violated international law is often a very difficult question. Article 38 sets forth the following order of importance for determining what is international law in a given case:

The Court, whose function is to decide in accordance with international law such disputes as are submitted to it, shall apply:

a. *International Conventions,* whether general or particular, establishing rules expressly recognized by the contesting states;

b. *International Custom,* as evidence of a general practice accepted as law;

c. *The General Principles of Law* recognized by civilized nations;

d. *Judicial Decisions and the Teachings of the Most Highly Qualified Publicists* of various nations, as subsidiary means for the determination of rules of law.

PRIVATE INTERNATIONAL LAW

Private international law is represented by the laws of individual nations and the multilateral agreements developed between nations to provide mutual understanding and some degree of continuity to international business transactions. Even in purely domestic business deals, the law is rarely predictable or certain. When different national laws, languages, practices, and cultures are added to the transaction, the situation can become very unstable for international business. International commerce is seldom uncomplicated, and a single business transaction often involves several firms with operations in different nations. For example, in a contract dispute among a German manufacturer, an American wholesaler, and a Canadian retailer, which nation's law controls the transaction may be crucial for determining the outcome of the case.

SECTION 15.4 INTERNATIONAL ORGANIZATIONS AND AGREEMENTS AFFECTING TRADE

Several international organizations and agreements play important roles in the development of political, economic, and legal rules for the conduct of international business. They include the United Nations, the General Agreement on Tariffs and Trade, and the Convention on the International Sale of Goods.

UNITED NATIONS

The **United Nations** was established after World War II and has grown in size from fifty-one founding nations at that time to almost every nation in the world today. The Charter of the United Nations sets forth as its primary goal "to save succeeding generations from the scourge of war" and to that end authorizes "collective measures for the prevention and removal of threats to the peace, and for the suppression of acts of aggression or other breaches of the peace." Using this authority in 1991, the United States successfully led a concerted effort of nations to remove Iraq as a "threat to peace" in Kuwait.

The General Assembly is composed of every nation represented in the United Nations and permits each country to cast one vote. The real power in the United Nations rests in the Security Council, which is composed of fifteen member states. The council has the power to authorize military action and to sever diplomatic relations with other nations. The five permanent members of the Council (United States, Russia, China, France, and United Kingdom) have veto power over any action proposed in the Council.

A number of organizations affiliated with the United Nations have authority over activities that directly affect international business. The United Nations Commission on International Trade Law (UNCITRAL) was created in 1966 in an effort to develop standardized commercial practices and agreements. One of the documents drafted by the UNCITRAL is the Convention on the International Sale of Goods. The United Nations Conference on Trade and Development (UNCTAD) was created in 1964 to deal with international trade reform and the redistribution of income through trading with developing countries. The UNCTAD has drafted both the Transfer of Technology Code and the Restrictive Business Practices Code, which have gone largely ignored by most nations.

At the Bretton Woods Conference of 1944, two important agencies were also created under the auspices of the United Nations. The International Monetary Fund (IMF) encourages international trade by maintaining stable foreign exchange rates and works closely with commercial banks to promote orderly exchange policies with members. The World Bank promotes economic development in poor countries by making loans to finance necessary development projects and programs.

GENERAL AGREEMENT ON TARIFFS AND TRADE

The General Agreement on Tariffs and Trade (GATT) was originally signed by twenty-three countries after World War II and represented the determination of a war-weary world to open trade and end the protection of domestic industries.

Through the mechanism of **most-favored-nation status,** GATT prohibits discrimination in national regulations covering imports and prevents the establishment of import quotas. Under this provision, each member of GATT is obligated to treat all other GATT members at least as well as it treats the country that receives the most favorable treatment regarding imports and exports. Another provision of GATT directs that imports should be treated no worse than domestic products with regard to internal taxation or regulation.

Over the years, GATT has done remarkably well with over 100 countries subscribing to a series of agreements (rounds) that led to reduced tariffs and open markets. The completion of the Uruguay Round in 1994, named for the country where the negotiations began, marks another major turning point for GATT. The final agreement, which represents the eighth major revision of GATT since it began in 1948, consists of 22,000 pages negotiated between the United States and the other 124 member nations over seven years.

Under the Uruguay agreement, existing tariffs will be reduced by an average of 38 percent over the next ten years. The agreement also extends GATT rules to new areas like agricultural products and service industries and further restricts tariffs on textiles, apparel, and forest products. The lower tariffs are expected to make U.S. goods more competitive in many foreign markets which now impose significant duties on U.S. goods. The agreement also requires countries to upgrade their intellectual property laws to protect patents and copyrights and guard against the piracy of items like computer software and videotapes.

The new agreement, however, is not without its problems. Some critics have expressed concern over the creation of the **World Trade Organization (WTO),** which will supersede the previously weak enforcement provisions in prior GATT agreements. The WTO will adjudicate disputes between member countries and can sanction those nations that choose to ignore its decisions. The WTO troubles many environmental groups that believe that the WTO's ability to sanction a violating country may undercut U.S. environmental policies that impact free trade. For example, a 1994 GATT panel found that U.S. embargoes on imports of tuna caught by nations that use purse seine nets were inconsistent with the free-trade provisions in GATT. While the United States imposed these embargoes because these types of nets often kill and maim dolphins, the panel held that the United States may not distinguish between "environmentally friendly" products and those produced in ecologically damaging ways. Although the United States has ignored adverse GATT rulings in the past that sought to override environmental statutes, the WTO now may impose trade sanctions on countries that ignore these rulings.

CONVENTION ON THE INTERNATIONAL SALE OF GOODS

The **Convention on the International Sale of Goods (CISG)** outlines standard international practices for the sale of goods. It took several years to develop, and it represents many compromises among nations that follow a variety of practices in the area of contracts. It became effective in 1988 and has been adopted by the United States **and most of the other** countries that engage in large quantities of international trade.

The CISG applies to contracts for the commercial sale of goods (consumer sales for personal, family, or household use are excluded) between parties whose businesses are located in different nations, provided that those nations have adopted the convention. If a commercial seller or buyer in the United States, for example, contracts for the sale of goods with a company located in another country that also has adopted the CISG, the convention and not the U.S. Uniform Commercial Code (WCC) applies to the transaction.

Under the CISG, a significant degree of freedom is provided for the individual parties in an international contract. The parties may negotiate contract terms as they deem fit for their business practices and may, if desired, even opt out of the CISG entirely. One of the most interesting provisions in the CISG includes a rule that contracts for the sale of goods need not be in writing. The CISG also provides that in contract negotiations an acceptance that contains new provisions that do not materially alter the terms of the offer becomes part of the contract, unless the offeror promptly objects to the change. The CISG also sets forth the fundamental elements that will materially alter a contract such as price, payment, quality, and quantity of the goods, place and time of delivery of goods, provisions related to one party's liability to the other, and methods for settling disputes. Since international transactions typically involve sophisticated parties, the CISG also makes it easier to disclaim warranties on goods than under traditional U.S. law.

SECTION 15.5
THE EUROPEAN UNION

Probably the single most significant development affecting international business was the historic action by six European countries in 1957 to achieve economic unity by signing the Treaty of Rome, which created the European Community. Now known as the **European Union (EU), it has** grown to include fifteen member countries: Austria, Belgium, Denmark, Finland, France, Germany, Greece, Ireland, Italy, Luxembourg, the Netherlands, Portugal, Spain, Sweden, and the United Kingdom. The combined GNP of the European countries is very significant. Many Eastern European countries, such as Bulgaria, Hungary, Poland, Romania, Lithuania, Latvia, and Estonia, have expressed interest in joining the EU and have signed association agreements designed to develop economic strategies to prepare them for eventual membership. The conditions now have been set for as many as twenty-seven members in the European Union by the year 2010.

In 1987, the member states passed the Single European Act, which required each country by 1992 to complete many reforms necessary to reach the goal of a unified internal market. The 1987 act mandated the removal of many physical, technical, and tax barriers to the free movement of persons, goods, services, and capital. In 1992, the leaders of the EU member nations signed a far-reaching agreement, known as the Maastricht Treaty, designed to create a more federal system of government and further political and economic union within the KU. The Maastricht Treaty, which took effect in late 1993, will create common foreign and defense policies, establish a joint central bank, require member countries to reduce government deficits, and initiate a single currency by 1999. Moreover, under the treaty, trade barriers between member states essentially will be eliminated under a system similar to the trading policy between states in the United States. The major institutions of the EU are the Council of Ministers, the Commission, the Parliament, and the Court of Justice.

SECTION 15.6
THE NORTH
AMERICAN FREE
TRADE AGREEMENT

With passage in 1993 of the North American Free Trade Agreement (NAFTA), the United States, Mexico, and Canada set in motion increased trade and foreign investment, and unlimited opportunities for economic growth in one of the fastest-growing regions of the world. At the core of NAFTA is free trade with the reduction and eventual elimination of tariffs and other barriers to business between the three countries. NAFTA also provides for a dispute settlement mechanism that will make it easier to resolve trade disputes between the three countries. Based upon a concern that cheap labor and poor environmental controls might cause U.S. firms to relocate to Mexico, side agreements also were reached to improve labor rights and environmental protection in Mexico.

In the first year of the agreement, U.S. trade with Mexico rose by over 20 percent and U.S. trade with Canada was up nearly 15 percent. Commerce between Canada and Mexico rose by nearly 40 percent in 1994. Foreign investment from the United States in Mexico exceeded $13 billion in 1994, and over 130,000 new jobs in the United States, credited to NAFTA, were created in that same year. Nevertheless, political instability, high inflation, and an unstable currency in Mexico make the long-term future of trade uncertain.

NAFTA likely will be expanded in the near future to include other Latin American countries such as Argentina, Chile, and Colombia. Latin America already is the fastest-growing region in the world for U.S. exports, and as barriers to trade are reduced between these countries, U.S. investment and trade undoubtedly will increase substantially.

SECTION 15.7
METHODS OF TRANSACTING
INTERNATIONAL BUSINESS

A U.S. business that wants to engage in international trade is presented with an almost limitless array of possibilities. Choosing a method of doing business in foreign countries not only requires understanding the factors normally involved in selecting an organization and operating a business domestically but also demands an appreciation of the international trade perspective. Depending upon the country, type of export, and amount of export involved in a particular transaction, international trade may involve direct foreign sales, licensing agreements, franchise agreements, or direct foreign investment.

FOREIGN SALES

The simplest, least risky approach for a manufacturer to use when trying to penetrate foreign markets is to sell goods directly to buyers located in other countries. However, with foreign sales, increased uncertainty over the ability to enforce the buyer's promise to pay for goods often requires that more complex arrangements for payment be made than with the usual domestic sale. **Commonly, an irrevocable letter of credit** is used to ensure payment. Transactions using such a letter involve, in addition to a seller and buyer, an *issuing bank* in the buyer's country. The buyer obtains a commitment from the bank to advance (pay) a specified amount (i.e., the price of the goods) upon receipt, from the carrier, of a **bill of lading,** stating that the goods have been shipped. The issuing bank's commitment to pay is given, not to the seller directly, but to a *confirming bank* located in the United States from which the seller obtains payment. The confirming bank forwards the bill of lading to the issuing bank in order to obtain reimbursement of the funds that have been paid to the seller. The issuing bank releases the bill of lading to the buyer after it has been paid, and with the bill of lading the buyer is able to obtain the goods from the carrier. Use of a letter of credit in the transaction thus reduces the uncertainties involved. The buyer need not pay the seller for goods prior to shipment, and the seller can obtain payment for the goods immediately upon shipment.

There is no room in documentary transactions for substantial performance. All of the duties and responsibilities of parties must be evaluated based upon the documents tendered, and these documents must comply strictly with the letter of credit.

Licenses or Franchises

In appropriate circumstances, a domestic firm may choose to grant a foreign firm the means to produce and sell its product. The typical method for controlling these transfers of information is the **license or franchise** contract. In this manner, intangible property rights, such as patents, copyrights, trademarks, or manufacturing processes, are transferred in exchange for royalties in the foreign country. A licensing arrangement allows the international business to enter a foreign market without any direct foreign investment. Licensing often is used as a transitional technique for firms expanding international operations since the risks are greater than with foreign sales but considerably less than with direct foreign investment.

Licensing technology or the sale of a product to a foreign firm is a way to expand the company's market without the need for substantial capital. The foreign firm may agree to this arrangement because it lacks sufficient research and development capability or the management skills or marketing strategies to promote the product alone. Of course, as with all international trade agreements, there is some level of risk. The licenser must take care to restrict the use of the product or technology to agreed-upon geographic areas and must take adequate steps to protect the confidential information that is licensed to the foreign firm so that third parties cannot exploit it.

DIRECT FOREIGN INVESTMENT

As a business increases its level of international trade, it may find that creation of a **foreign subsidiary** is necessary. Most countries will permit a foreign firm to conduct business only if a national (individual or firm) of the host country is designated as its legal representative. Since this designation may create difficulties in **control and result in unnecessary** expense, the usual practice for multinational corporations is to create a foreign subsidiary in the host country. The form of subsidiary most closely resembling a U.S. corporation is known as a *societe anonyme (S.A.)* or, in German-speaking countries, an *Aktiengesellschaft (AG).* Other forms of subsidiaries may also exist that have characteristics of limited liability of the owners and fewer formalities in their creation and operation.

Creation of a foreign subsidiary may pose considerable risk to the domestic parent firm. The 1983 industrial accident in Bhopal, India, where hundreds of people were killed and thousands injured as a result of toxic gas leaks from a chemical plant, resulted in lawsuits against both the Indian subsidiary corporation and Union Carbide, the parent firm in the United States. Despite Union Carbide's paying more than $300 million to settle outstanding claims, other issues remain unresolved.

In many instances, however, the only legal or political means a firm has to invest directly in a foreign country is to engage in a **joint venture** with an entity from that host country. A host country's participant may be a private enterprise or, especially in developing countries, a government agency or government-owned corporation. Many foreign countries favor joint ventures because they allow local individuals and firms to participate in the benefits of economic growth and decrease the risk of foreign domination of local industry. Many of the developing countries require that the local partner have majority equity control of the venture and also insist on joint ventures with government participation.

SECTION 15.8
RISKS INVOLVED IN
INTERNATIONAL TRADE

Because international trade means dealing with different legal systems, cultures, and ways of doing business, there are a number of risks involved. Among them are expropriation and nationalization, export controls, pressures for bribes, and ill will resulting from U.S. antitrust laws.

EXPROPRIATION AND NATIONALIZATION

If a domestic firm is involved in a foreign country to the extent of locating assets there (whether through branches, subsidiaries, joint ventures, or otherwise), it may be subject to the ultimate legal and political risk of international business activity—expropriation. **Expropriation,** as used in the context of international law, is the seizure of foreign-owned property by a government. When the owners are not fairly compensated, the expropriation is also considered to be a *confiscation* of property. Usually, the expropriating government also assumes ownership of the property, so the process includes **nationalization** as well. In the United States, the counterpart of expropriation is called the *power of eminent domain*. This power of all governments to take private property is regarded as inherent; yet it is subject to restraints upon its exercise. The U.S. Constitution (as well as the constitutions of most states) prohibits the government from seizing private property except for "public purposes" and upon the payment of "just compensation." These constitutional safeguards are limited, however, to the taking of property by the states or the federal government. Questions arise, then, as to the legal recourse against a foreign government that has taken over ownership of property within its jurisdiction.

Of course, constitutional or statutory safeguards against expropriation may exist in other countries as well as in the United States. However, the extent of such protection varies widely. Treaties (or other agreements) between the United States and other countries may provide **additional protection** against uncompensated takings of property. It is customary for international law to recognize the right of governments to expropriate the property of foreigners only when accompanied by "prompt, adequate and effective compensation." This standard is followed by most industrialized countries; however, developing countries and socialist countries have increasingly rejected this standard in favor of a *national* standard whereby absolute supremacy is asserted with regard to nationalizations in general and compensation in particular.

Nationalization of American assets accompanied by unsatisfactory offers of compensation has led aggrieved parties to file lawsuits in the United States to seek satisfactory compensation. Two distinct but related doctrines pose serious obstacles for recovery in these situations: the act of state doctrine and the doctrine of sovereign immunity. Both doctrines demonstrate a policy of respect for the autonomy of foreign states and, if applied, lead to judicial abstention in disputes between U.S. firms and foreign countries.

Act of State Doctrine

The Supreme Court outlined the **act of state doctrine** more than ninety years ago in *Underhill v. Hernandez* and held that "[e]very sovereign State is bound to respect the independence of every other sovereign State, and the courts of one country will not sit in judgment on the acts of the government of another done within its own territory." The act of state doctrine also has constitutional underpinnings and recognizes that it is the president's responsibility to conduct foreign policy. The doctrine is the federal judiciary's response to foreign policy tensions that can be created when an American court sits in judgment of a foreign state's governmental affairs within that country's borders.

The doctrine has undergone some modification over the past century. Several exceptions to the doctrine have been recognized. The Supreme Court has held that the doctrine should not be extended to foreign governments acting in a commercial capacity and "should not be extended to include the repudiation of a purely commercial obligation owed by a foreign sovereign or by one of its commercial instrumentalities." This interpretation recognizes that governments also may act in a private or commercial capacity and, when doing so, will be subjected to the same rules of law as are applicable to private individuals. Of course, a nationalization of assets probably will be considered an act in the "public interest."

Congress outlined its narrow interpretation of the act of state doctrine in the Hickenlooper Amendment to the Foreign Assistance Act of 1964. Unless the president decides to the contrary, the amendment directs that the act of state doctrine shall *not* be applied by the courts in cases when property is confiscated, without just compensation, in violation of international law. Federal courts, however, have not received this provision enthusiastically and have applied it only to cases in which the property has returned to the United States.

The party moving for the application of the doctrine has the burden of proving that the doctrine is appropriate, however, there are limits to when the doctrine may be used.

SOVEREIGN IMMUNITY

Although inextricably related to the act of state doctrine, the doctrine of **sovereign immunity** differs fundamentally in its operation. This judicially developed doctrine provides that a foreign sovereign is immune from suit in the United States. By contrast, the act of state doctrine does not immunize anyone from suit but merely concerns the limits for determining the application and validity of a rule of law. The act of state doctrine may be relevant whether or not the sovereign nation is a direct party in the lawsuit. Under the doctrine of sovereign immunity, the foreign sovereign claims to be immune from suit entirely based on its status as a state.

Until approximately 1952, this notion was absolute. From 1952 until 1976, U.S. courts adhered to a *restrictive theory* under which immunity existed with regard to sovereign or public acts but not with regard to private or commercial acts. In 1976, Congress enacted the Foreign Sovereign Immunities Act, which codifies this restrictive theory and rejects immunity for commercial acts carried on in the United States or having direct effects in this country.

EXPORT CONTROLS

Another risk involved in doing business abroad is export controls placed on the sale of U.S. strategic products and technology abroad. Controlling the export of such items has been the cornerstone of Western policy since the conclusion of World War II. Most of the attention was focused on preventing the acquisition of technology by the former Soviet Union and its allies. However, since the end of the Cold War the policy **rationale behind** export controls has been drawn into question, with many Western countries contending they should be eliminated to increase trading opportunities with Russia, China, Eastern Europe, and the Middle East. Indeed, the Coordinating Committee for Multilateral Export Controls (COCOM), an organization created by the major Western nations (including the United States, Europe, and Japan) to control exports, came to an end in 1994. The member countries have been having difficulty reaching an agreement on a post- COCOM organization or a common understanding about the items and regions of the world where controls still are needed.

The U.S. export control system currently is regulated by the Department of State and the Department of Commerce under authority provided by the Export Administration Act (1979) and the Arms Export Control Act (1976). The Department of Defense also plays a key role in determining the technology to be controlled as does the U.S. Customs Service in the enforcement of the controls. Significant criminal and administrative sanctions may be imposed upon corporations and individuals convicted of violating the law.

The future of the U.S. system also is in some doubt with many proposals pending in Congress to reform and limit the current export control system. Over the past several years, these controls have become an extremely controversial topic in the international business community. Export controls make successful business deals more difficult because foreign buyers may be reluctant to trade with a U.S. firm due to the red tape involved in obtaining governmental approval. On the other hand, when U.S. technology is used against American troops by an enemy country, as occurred in the Persian Gulf War of 1991, many defense experts argue that export controls actually should be strengthened.

PRESSURES FOR BRIBES

Following widespread disclosure of scandalous payments by domestic firms to officials of foreign governments, Congress enacted the **Foreign Corrupt Practices Act** (FCPA) in 1977. The law is designed to stop bribery of foreign officials and to prohibit U.S. citizens and companies from making payments to foreign officials whose duties are not "essentially ministerial or clerical" for the purpose of obtaining business.

This statute has two principal requirements:

1. Financial records and accounts must be kept "which, in reasonable detail, accurately and fairly reflect the transactions and dispositions of assets" of the business.

2. The business must "devise and maintain a system of internal accounting controls sufficient to provide reasonable assurances" that transactions are being carried out in accordance with management's authorization.

These provisions are intended to correct the previously widespread practice of accounting for bribes as commission payments, payments for services, or other normal business expenses and then illegally deducting the payments on income tax returns.

Many legal observers criticized FCPA for creating a significantly chilling effect on U.S. companies seeking business in many developing countries where under-the-table payments to government officials are an accepted practice. Indeed, many civil servants in other nations are expected to supplement their salaries in this manner. The U.S. prohibition of such payments is perceived as an attempt to impose U.S. standards of morality in other parts of the world, and it has caused resentment and discrimination against U.S. businesses. Moreover, the FCPA puts U.S. firms at a competitive disadvantage with businesses in other countries that are not operating under similar constraints.

As a result of intensive lobbying by the U.S. business community, Congress amended the FCPA in 1988 in an effort to eliminate ambiguity and uncertainty over what constitutes improper conduct. While the law still prohibits bribery and corruption, the amendments establish clearer standards for firms to follow in overseas operations. The amendments limit criminal liability for violations of accounting standards to those who "knowingly" circumvent accounting controls or falsify records of corporate payments and transactions. The amendments also clarify the level of detail required in such record keeping and should improve compliance by businesses and enforcement by the government. Moreover, under the new law otherwise prohibited payments to foreign officials may be defended if they were legal under the written laws of the host country or if they cover "reasonable and bona fide" expenses associated with the promotion of the product and the completion of the contract.

Under the 1988 amendments, criminal penalties for companies violating the FCPA have been increased to a maximum of $2 million and individuals may be fined up to $100,000 and/or five years in prison.

CONFLICTS WITH U.S. ANTITRUST LAWS

The U.S. antitrust laws represent our nation's legal commitment to free markets and international competition. Perhaps no other aspect of our legal system has generated as much recent controversy and ill will abroad as the application of our antitrust laws to conduct occurring beyond the borders of the United States. To protect the welfare of the U.S. consumer, however, the government's enforcement efforts must sometimes reach foreign defendants as a means of ensuring open and free markets.

In late 1994, the Department of Justice and the Federal Trade Commission issued draft guidelines delineating the U.S. government's policy on enforcement of federal antitrust law in the international arena. The guidelines provide that anticompetitive conduct, regardless of where such conduct occurs in the world or the nationality of the parties involved, may be prosecuted if it affects U.S. domestic or foreign commerce. The guidelines also provide that imports intended for sale in the United States by definition affect the U.S. market directly and will, therefore, invariably be subject to control. For example, suppose two foreign firms organize a cartel, produce a product abroad, and agree to fix the price of the finished product sold to the United States. Under the guidelines, this type of conduct is subject to prosecution because the transaction will affect U.S. commerce. Anticompetitive conduct by a foreign firm intended to affect the exports of a U.S. business may be sanctioned as well.

SECTION 15.9
RESOLVING
INTERNATIONAL
DISPUTES

SUING FOREIGN FIRMS IN THE UNITED STATES

As foreign products and technology are imported into the United States, disputes may arise over either the terms of contract or the performance of the goods. In order to sue a foreign firm in the United States, the Supreme Court recently has held that the plaintiff must establish "minimum contacts" between the foreign defendant and the forum court. The plaintiff must demonstrate that exercise of personal jurisdiction over the defendant "does not offend traditional notions of fair play and substantial justice."

Once the plaintiff decides to sue in the United States, he or she also must comply with the terms of the Hague Service Convention when serving the foreign defendant notice of the lawsuit. The Hague Service Convention is a treaty that was formulated "to provide a simpler way to serve process abroad, to assure that defendants sued in foreign jurisdictions would receive actual and timely notice of suit, and to facilitate proof of service abroad." Thirty-two countries, including the United States, have approved the convention. The primary requirement of the agreement is to require each nation to establish a central authority to process requests for service of documents from other countries. "Once the central authority receives the request in proper form, it must serve the documents by a method prescribed by the internal law of the receiving state or by a method designated by the requester and compatible with the law."

INTERNATIONAL ARBITRATION

International businesses now are focusing on the need for new methods of resolving international commercial disputes and, as a result, are frequently resorting to the use of arbitration. The advantages of arbitration in domestic transactions are more pronounced in international transactions where differences in languages and legal systems make litigation costs still more costly.

The United Nations Convention on the Recognition and Enforcement of Foreign Arbitral Awards of 1958 (New York Convention), which has been adopted in more than fifty countries, encourages the use of arbitration in commercial agreements made by companies in the signatory countries. Under the New York Convention it is easier to compel arbitration, where previously agreed upon by the parties, and to enforce the arbitrator's award once a decision has been reached.

Once the parties to an international transaction have agreed to arbitrate disputes between them, the U.S. courts are reluctant to disturb that agreement. In the case of ***Mitsubishi Motors v. Soler Chrysler-Plymouth* (473 U.S. 614 [1985])** the Supreme Court upheld an international agreement even where it required the parties to arbitrate all disputes, including federal antitrust claims. The Court decided that the international character of the undertaking required enforcement of the arbitration clause even as to the antitrust claims normally heard in a U.S. court.

The advantages of arbitrating international disputes are many. The arbitration process likely will be more streamlined and easier for the parties to understand than litigating the dispute in a foreign court. Moreover, the parties can avoid the unwanted publicity that often results in open court proceedings. Finally, the parties can agree, before the dispute even arises, on a neutral and objective third party to act as the arbitrator. Several organizations, such as the International Chamber of Commerce in Paris and the Court of International Arbitration in London, provide arbitration services for international disputes.

SECTION 15.10
PROBLEM CASES

1. The government of Germany sought to enforce an order in the International Court of Justice which directed the United States Government to prevent Arizona from executing a prisoner who had German citizenship. The International Court of Justice had issued an Order indicating that the "United States should take all measures at its disposal to insure that Walter LaGrand is not executed pending a final decision in the International Court of Justice proceedings. Must the United States honor the request by the Government of Germany and the International Court of Justice to stay the execution? *Federal Republic of Germany v. United States,* **526 U.S. 111 (1999).**

2. Ramp filed suit against the President of the United States in order to force the government to file suit in the International Court of Justice against Russia on behalf of the persons killed when Korean airlines flight 007 was shot down by a Soviet aircraft. May an individual force the President of the United States to file a claim with the International Court of Justice? *Ramp v. President of the United States,* **758 F.2d 653 (6ᵗʰ Cir. 1985).**

3. During World War II, Jewish customers of a French Bank forfeited their accounts when those assets were turned over to the Vichy Government under a comprehensive program to "Aryanize" the property owned by Jewish individuals. Suit was instituted in New York Federal Court by the decedents of the Jewish customers whose assets were forfeited by certain French financial institutions. The New York suit was based upon the fact that most of the customers, who assets were expropriated during the war, had moved to New York and the French financial institutions maintained offices in that state. Does the court in New York have jurisdiction over these claims? *Fernande Bodner v. Banque Paribas,* **114 F. Supp 2d 117 (E.D. N. Y. 2000).**

4. The North American Free Trade Agreement provides preferential tariff treatment to member countries if the imported goods originate in the territory of a NAFTA party. When a good is not "wholly obtained or produced entirely" in the territory of a NAFTA country, the product will not enjoy the full protection of the treaty. Brazil manufactured molded crank shafts for cars from alloy steel. These products were then shipped to Mexico for processing into finalized crank shafts that were ultimately shipped into the United States. Does this product enjoy tariff protection under the North American Free Trade Agreement? *Cummins v. United States of America,* **83 F. Supp. 2d 1366 (U.S. Ct. Int. T. 1999).**

5. Subsequent to Mexico joining the North American Free Trade Agreement, that country joined in a lawsuit by migrant workers in Maine seeking to hold companies in that state responsible for alleged unlawful employment practices. The plaintiffs were either Mexican citizens or American citizens of Mexican ancestry. Does the North American Free Trade Agreement have within its contemplation the ability of a foreign country to maintain a lawsuit in the United States for unfair employment practices in this country? *Estados Unidos Mexicanos v. De Coster*, 59 F. Supp. 2d 120 (D. ME. 1999)

SECTION 15.11
INTERNET REFERENCES

For more information about the materials contained in this chapter, see the following Internet sites:

A. *International Court of Justice*

- **http://www.icj-cij.org/**
  The International Court of Justice provides decisions, recent cases, and general information at this site.

B. *United Nations*

- **http://www.un.org**
  This is the United Nations' official site and offers general information, international law, humanitarian affairs, peace and security, human rights, economic and social development, as well as conferences and events, about the UN's work around the world.

C. *Other International Organizations*

- **http://www.usitc.gov**
  The International Trade Commission's web site is located at this address and provides news releases, tariffs, and trade resources.

- **http://www.wto.org**
  This is the World Trade Organization's official site which discusses intellectual property and environmental issues, trade policy, and dispute settlement.

- **http://www.ita.doc.gov**
  The International Trade Administration maintain this address and provides information about trade rights, tariffs, exports, and answers to frequently asked questions.

- **http://www.nato.int/**
  The North Atlantic Treaty Organization's (NATO) official site is maintained at this location.

- **http://www.europa.eu.int/index-en.htm**
  This is the European Union's site, giving news, basic information about the European Union, its policies, and its institutions.

- **http://www.dfait-maeci.gc.ca/nafta-alena/menu-e.asp**
  To learn background information about NAFTA, the text of that agreement, as well as information on dispute settlement, trade agreements, and answers to frequently asked questions, visit this address.

D. *Foreign Corrupt Practices Act*

- **http://www.tannedfeet.com/Business/Importing_and_ Exporting/Foreign_Corrupt_Practices_Act/foreign_ corrupt_practices_act.html**
  This site offers an explanation of the Foreign Corrupt Practices Act.

- **http://www.abanet.org/cle/articles/turza.html**
  An article about the Foreign Corrupt Practices Act, is maintained at this address including information about the elements of a violation and an introduction to due diligence.

E. *International Arbitration*

- **http://www.iccwbo.org/home/menu_ international_ arbitration.asp**
  The International Chamber of Commerce provides information on the International Court of Arbitration, the rules of arbitration, and other news about the organization at this address.

- **http://www.internationaladr.com/**
  The International Alternative Dispute Resolution page offers information and links about treaties, arbitrators and arbitration laws, and recent awards and decisions.

- **http://arbiter.wipo.int/neutrals/index.html**
  This site is another comprehensive site, which focuses on arbitration and mediation.

F. *International Business*

- **http://www.iccwbo.org/**
  This is a comprehensive site, dealing with all aspects of international business.

Footnotes   1. Reprinted with permission from *"International Law,"* **The Legal and Regulatory Environment of Business,** by Corley, Reed, Shedd and Morehead. Copyright 1996 by the McGraw-Hill Companies.

APPENDIX

During your tenure with the firm, your input and advice will be sought on a number of issues. Several matters will require a written response in the nature of a legal memorandum. As law clerks, your answers must conform to the format as established by this office.

I am providing you with a sample memo and answer that was written by James Jones, a former associate. The matter deals with a lawsuit filed against Joseph Hodge for palimony that was brought to a successful conclusion. You will never have to have to do independent research to answer a problem. Our research is computer generated and will be given to you with each assignment. In the palimony case, the associate was provided with a case involving a suit for palimony against the rock star, Peter Frampton. He merely had to read the case and provide a written answer to the problem presented. By the way, this was the only assignment ever completed by Mr. Jones. He never returned from lunch after his first day on the job. I expect more from you.

HODGE, DODGE AND LODGE
ATTORNEYS AT LAW
SAMPLE MEMORANDUM

To: James Jones

From: Gregory Olan Dodge

Re: Mary Smith v. Joe Hodge
Palimony Suit

In the past, Joe Hodge had some momentary lapses in judgment. There was a time when he drank too much. As a result, his work suffered and so did his marriage. During this difficult period, he and the bartender at Cheers became quite friendly. Now that Joe is a millionaire, this old pal, Mary has resurfaced, demanding half of Joe's new-found wealth. She claims that Joe promised to support her if she would leave her husband and four children to live with him in a "love nest" above the bar. Mary further claims to have complied with Joe's request, thereby accepting his offer. Joe, of course, denies all of the bartender's allegations. He does admit that they were friends.

I do not think that Mary has a good case for breach of contract even if her allegations are true. Please read *McCall v. Frampton* and assess this situation. Your memorandum should address the following questions:

1. Is this contract enforceable?
2. Why might this contract be against public policy?
3. Does it matter whether Joe actually made these promises to Mary?

McCall v. Frampton
415 New York Supplement, 2d 754 (1979)

GAGLIARDI, Joseph F., Justice

This is an action brought by plaintiff to recover damages for breach of an oral contract allegedly made between plaintiff and defendant in 1973. The complaint alleges that in and prior to 1972 plaintiff had expertise and was engaged in the business of promotion and management of musicians involved in "Rock and Roll" or "Rock" and, during that period, besides doing so for compensation engaged in those activities without compensation for others; that plaintiff met defendant in 1972 when defendant was a member of the musical group known as "Humble Pie" and when plaintiff was married to the group's manager (a Mr. Brigden); that in 1973 defendant "requested that McCall leave her then husband and her then employment… and that she become associated with and work with Frampton in the promotion of Frampton as a musician representing to McCall that if she did so they would be equal partners in all proceeds from his employment in that field" (Emphasis supplied); that in reliance upon these representations plaintiff left her husband and her employment and went to live with defendant, "thereafter devoting all her resources, time and effort to the promotion and success of Frampton in his endeavors;" that beginning in 1973 plaintiff, at defendant's request, used all of her financial resources to support herself and

defendant, and engaged in performing various services for defendant "including, but not limited to, public relations and promotion work; aiding in costuming of Frampton and his associates; managing Frampton's personal finances and traveling with Frampton during tours conducted by him;" that at various times from 1973 to 1978, defendant acknowledged plaintiff's efforts both in public and in private and shared his receipts from his business with plaintiff, as well as bank accounts and other credit sources, and that both charged expenses incurred for the benefit of each to accounts maintained for that purpose "in accordance with their prior agreement;" in sum, that the parties were equal partners from 1973 through July, 1978.

The complaint requests an accounting of defendant's earnings from 1973 to date and a judgment equally dividing those earnings between the parties.

In support of her argument that the complaint should not be dismissed, plaintiff relies principally upon the following cases: *Marvin v. Marvin,* 18 Cal.3d 660, 134 Cal. Rptr. 815, 557 P.2d 106; *Dosek v. Dosek* (Conn.Sup.Ct., decided October 4, 1978, reported in 4 Family Law Reporter, October 31, 1978, p. 2828); *McCullon v. McCullon,* 96 Misc.2d 962, 410 N.Y.S.2d 226 [Sup.Ct., Erie County 1978]; *Hewitt v. Hewitt,*

62 Ill. App.3d 861, 20 Ill.Dec. 476 380 N.E.2d 454; *Carlson v. Olson,* 256 N.W.2d 249 [Minn. 1977]. These cases are all distinguishable for there is no allegation herein that plaintiff and defendant ever intended to marry each other, that they held themselves out to the public as husband and wife, or that the plaintiff and defendant were ever free to marry each other. There is no allegation that plaintiff ever changed her surname to that of defendant. (Apparently no children were born as a result of the sexual relationship between the parties.)

This court holds that the contract between the plaintiff and defendant is void and unenforceable as a matter of public policy. Plaintiff pleads as the consideration for this agreement the commission of adultery on her part; that she leave her husband and live with defendant and become associated with him. This contract was, therefore, in derogation of her existing marriage and prohibited by section 255-17 of the Penal Law: "A person is guilty of adultery when he engages in sexual intercourse with another person at a time when he has a living spouse, or the other person has a living spouse." (The papers submitted leave no doubt that there was an illicit sexual relationship between the parties. There is no indication that plaintiff has ever been divorced from her husband. Apparently, defendant was divorced from his wife during the time when the parties lived together.)

It is settled that agreements against public policy are unlawful and void. This rule is not based on a desire to benefit the party who breaches an illegal contract, but on a desire to protect the common wealth, the general welfare of society being damaged by the very making of such a contract. By refusing to enforce such a contract and leaving the parties without a legal remedy for breach, society is protected by discouraging the making of contracts contrary to the common good.

To define public policy is often difficult, for it is a concept which is flexible. The Court has recently addressed this point:

"Controversies involving questions of public policy can rarely, if ever, be resolved by the blind application of sedentary legal principles. The very nature of the concept of public policy itself militates against an attempt to define its ingredients in a manner which would allow one to become complacent in the thought that these precepts which society so steadfastly embraces today will continue to serve as the foundation upon which society will function tomorrow. Public policy, like society, is continually evolving and those entrusted with its implementation must respond to its ever-changing demands."

It is the opinion of this court that the contract, as alleged by plaintiff, is clearly subject to the defense of illegality. It is contrary to the public policy of this state, which recognizes the state of marriage and the protection thereof as essential to the welfare of our society. It requires, in its performance, the commission of adultery which remains a crime in this state. The plaintiff's Complaint is therefore dismissed.

SAMPLE ANSWER

James Jones

Name: James Jones   **Please Print Clearly**

According to *McCall v. Frampton,* the alleged contract between Joe and Mary to engage in an adulteress relationship is unenforceable because it is against public policy. As the court noted, "It is settled that agreements against public policy are unlawful and void." **Frampton**, at 755. The court goes on to explain that these types of contracts are harmful to the welfare of society. "By refusing to enforce such a contract and leaving the parties without a legal remedy for breach, society is protected by discouraging the making of contracts contrary to the public good." **Frampton**, at 755. Thus, it is clear that once this contract is classified as being against public policy, Mary has no legal remedy regardless of the truthfulness of her allegations.

Although the **Frampton** court does explain the difficulties involved in determining which agreements are unenforceable, Joe and Mary's alleged contract is strikingly similar to the one made in **Frampton**. That court explained that "...the public policy of this state...recognizes the state of marriage and the protection thereof as essential to the welfare of society." **Frampton**, at 756. A contract in which Mary agrees to leave her husband and children in return for Joe's support would clearly undermine marriage and the family unit. While the **Frampton** court didn't discuss family life, we may assume that the state is as interested in promoting a stable family relationship as it is in marriage. After all, part of the reason our society protects marriage is because of it's effect on American family life.

Whether or not Joe actually made these promises to Mary is irrelevant. Even if he did, the contract is unenforceable because it violates public policy. Furthermore, an agreement to create an adulteress relationship is illegal and illegal contracts are not enforced by the courts. Like the complaint in **Frampton**, this action should be dismissed.

SECTION A.2
ALTERNATE PROBLEM
LEGISLATION TO REGULATE
EXPLICIT ROCK LYRICS

State legislatures are reacting to the public's concern with explicit rock music lyrics. For instance, Washington enacted a law designed to keep children from buying recordings that contain "erotic lyrics." The law allows a county prosecutor to ask a judge to declare that a recording offends community standards. If a judge agrees, the recording must be labeled for "adults only." The penalty is a $500 fine and six months in jail. The Supreme Court found the statute unconstitutional because it infringes on the free-speech of adults and violates music sellers' rights to due process. The Court ruled on a lawsuit filed on behalf of dozens of musicians, including Nirvana and Pearl Jam.

Public concern against explicit rock music lyrics, however, might not be unfounded. In Austin, Texas, an admitted murderer blamed rap music for his shooting of a Texas state trooper. His attorneys asked that the state not seek the death penalty because he was improperly influenced by the music. The 19-year-old shot the trooper in the neck after he was stopped for a missing headlight. Before the killing, the defendant contends that he had driven 120 miles listening to Tupac Shakur's *2pacalypse Now*, a "gansta rap" recording. Gansta rap focuses on drugs, sex, violence, and a hatred for police.

Estelle Hodge has become involved with the problem and has requested our help. Her concerns are presented in the following problem.

HODGE, DODGE AND LODGE
ATTORNEYS AT LAW
MEMORANDUM

To: All Law Clerks

FROM: Gregory Olan Dodge

RE: Drafting of Legislation to Regulate Explicit Rock Lyrics

The State Legislature is again considering the adoption of a bill requiring warning labels to be placed on music containing "explicit lyrics" not suitable for children. Support for the legislation had waned given the surge of voluntary compliance by record companies. The controversy, however, has resurfaced because of the intense lobbying efforts by Estelle Hodge.

What prompted Estelle's outrage? It seems that her youngest child, Greg, purchased a tape for her for Mother's Day. What Greg thought was Marie Osmond's "Paper Roses" was in actuality a copy of Guns and Roses latest album. Unaware of the error, Estelle settled back in her armchair to listen to her favorite recording artist. Instead of hearing the soothing voice of Marie Osmond, she was startled by loud guitar music and shrieking vocals. What troubled Estelle the most were the lyrics of the songs on the cassette. Estelle called the record store visited by Greg and bombarded them with questions on how they could sell such music to a small child. The manager could not understand why Mrs. Hodge was so angry but they offered to exchange the cassette for another of her choice. Estelle was not satisfied with this offer and contacted her good friend, Senator Earl. She convinced the Senator to resume efforts to pass a law requiring labels to be prominently displayed on record covers whose songs contain explicit lyrics.

The Senator was troubled by the constitutionality of any such law and informed Estelle of his concerns. How was one to define "explicit lyrics" and how could the law be enforced? Estelle wasn't interested in technicalities and took matters in her own hands. She asked Senator Earl to send her any information she could use to revive the campaign. Mrs. Hodge was a woman with a mission. She put together a flyer which contained information regarding the need for the legislation.

She listed in the flyer titles of songs whose lyrics she found offensive. These included George Michael's "I Want Your Sex;" Ozzy Osbourne's "Suicide Solution;" Guns and Roses' "Rocket Queen;" Mötley Crüe's "Shout At The Devil;" Madonna's "Like a Virgin;" 2 Live Crew's "Me So Horny;" Eric Clapton's "Cocaine;" Naughty By Nature's "O.P.P.;" Prince's "Sexy M.F.s;" and Ice-T's "Cop Killer."

Estelle visited the malls and shopping centers to round up support for her mission. She promptly dubbed the group of homemakers who agreed with her position, "M.A.L.L." or "Mothers Against Lousy Lyrics." The group banded together with the objective to picket any record store which sold this "trash" and to have the legislature pass a law addressing the concerns of "M.A.L.L." As you can imagine, the record stores were upset by the picketing and responded with their own flyer. It stated that the record industry had voluntarily taken remedial measures by placing labels on records that contained explicit lyrics. The retailers claim that they can't be the judge of what constitutes inappropriate lyrics on songs and to punish them for selling the tapes and discs to children is wrong. Besides, retailers assert the labels are sufficient to put parents on notice of the explicit nature of the lyrics, and the parents should police what records their children buy.

The retailers and the record industry claim that such a law is ludicrous because the literal interpretation of many of the old standards would require warning notices. These would include such songs as "Mac the Knife" (violence); "She'll Be Coming Around the Mountain" (incest); "Clementine" (suicide); "Hundred Bottles of Beer on the Wall" (alcoholism); "Old Man River" (alcohol abuse); "Teen Angel" (morbid violence); and "Can't Buy Me Love" (prostitution). The record industry warns that compulsory legislation in this area is an exercise in futility since minors become more intrigued when such things are labeled taboo.

Estelle contacted Hodge, Dodge and Lodge to help M.A.L.L. draft a bill for Senator Earl to introduce in the next session. She maintains that not all record companies label their music and that the final responsibility for preventing children from buying this trash must rest with the retailers. After all, stores are not allowed to sell liquor, cigarettes or obscene magazines so why not require them to regulate the sale of records containing explicit rock lyrics as well. Estelle mentions some things we should include in the draft of the proposed legislation. She wants the law to be directed to those who sell the music and not to the children who purchase the tapes. The bill will be tacked on to Title 18 of the Penal Code.

The task of drafting the statute has been assigned to you. Please write the statute and focus on four aspects:

1. **Definitions.** Who would be responsible under the legislation (i.e. clerks, managers, retail owners) to place labels on the records and what constitutes explicit lyrics (i.e. sexual activity, violence, drugs, suicide, bestiality, murder, etc.). This section will need careful attention to detail to prevent a constitutional challenge due to vagueness.

2. Define what acts or conduct are prohibited. As I mentioned before, Estelle believes the retailer should be prevented from selling the music unless the record contains the appropriate parental warning notice.

3. Draft a sample warning label that should be placed on the records and state where the label should be displayed.

4. What penalties should be imposed for violating the statute? Please remember that the penalty should not be overly harsh because of the nature of the proposed offense. You should review the Graffiti Statute for reference.

I have prepared the following outline for you to use in drafting the legislation which will become **Section 5905 of Title 18 of the Code:**

1. Definitions
2. Prohibited conduct
3. Required label
4. Penalty

Name   **Please Print Clearly**

Section 5905 Regulation of Explicit Rock Lyrics

1. Definitions
2. Prohibited Conduct
3. Required Label.
4. Penalty

1. Definitions:

_____

_____

_____

_____

_____

_____

_____

_____

_____

_____

2. Prohibited Conduct

_____

_____

_____

_____

_____

_____

_____

_____

_____

3. **Required Label:** _____

_____

_____

_____

_____

_____

_____

_____

_____

_____

_____

4. **Penalty** _____

_____

_____

_____

_____

_____

_____

_____

_____

_____

_____

SECTION A.3
CONSTITUTION

THE CONSTITUTION OF THE UNITED STATES

We the people of the United States, in order to form a more perfect union, establish justice, insure domestic tranquility, provide for the common defense, promote the general welfare, and secure the blessings of liberty to ourselves and our posterity, do ordain and establish this Constitution for the United States of America.

ARTICLE I

SECTION 1

All legislative powers herein granted shall be vested in a Congress of the United States, which shall consist of a Senate and House of Representatives.

SECTION 2

1. The House of Representatives shall be composed of members chosen every second year by the people of the several States, and the electors in each State shall have the qualifications requisite for electors of the most numerous branch of the State legislature.

2. No person shall be a representative who shall not have attained to the age of twenty-five years, and been seven years a citizen of the United States, and who shall not, when elected, be an inhabitant of that State in which he shall be chosen.

3. Representatives and direct taxes[1] shall be apportioned among the several States which may be included within this Union, according to their respective numbers, which shall be determined by adding to the whole number of free persons, including those bound to service for a term of years, and excluding Indians not taxed, three fifths of all other persons.[2] The actual enumeration shall be made within three years after the first meeting of the Congress of the United States, and within every subsequent term of ten years, in such manner as they shall by law direct. The number of representatives shall not exceed one for every thirty thousand, but each State shall have at least one representative; and until such enumeration shall be made, the State of New Hampshire shall be entitled to choose three, Massachusetts eight, Rhode Island and Providence Plantations one, Connecticut five, New York six, New Jersey four, Pennsylvania eight, Delaware one, Maryland six, Virginia ten, North Carolina five, South Carolina five, and Georgia three.

4. When vacancies happen in the representation from any State, the executive authority thereof shall issue writs of election to fill such vacancies.

5. The House of Representatives shall choose their speaker and other officers; and shall have the sole power of impeachment.

Section 3

1. The Senate of the United States shall be composed of two senators from each State, chosen by the legislature thereof,[3] for six years; and each senator shall have one vote.

2. Immediately after they shall be assembled in consequence of the first election, they shall be divided as equally as may be into three classes. The seats of the senators of the first class shall be vacated at the expiration of the second year, of the second class at the expiration of the fourth year and of the third class at the expiration of the sixth year, so that one third may be chosen every second year; and if vacancies happen by resignation, or otherwise, during the recess of the legislature of any State, the executive thereof may make temporary appointments until the next meeting of the legislature, which shall then fill such vacancies.[4]

3. No person shall be a senator who shall not have attained to the age of thirty years, and been nine years a citizen of the United States, and who shall not, when elected, be an inhabitant of that State for which he shall be chosen.

4. The Vice President of the United States shall be President of the Senate, but shall have no vote, unless they be equally divided.

5. The Senate shall choose their other officers, and also a president pro tempore, in the absence of the Vice President, or when he shall exercise the office of the President of the United States.

6. The Senate shall have the sole power to try all impeachments. When sitting for that purpose, they shall be on oath or affirmation. When the President of the United States is tried, the chief justice shall preside: and no person shall be convicted without the concurrence of two thirds of the members present.

7. Judgment in cases of impeachment shall not extend further than to removal from office, and disqualifications to hold and enjoy any office of honor, trust or profit under the United States: but the party convicted shall nevertheless be liable and subject to indictment, trial, judgment and punishment, according to law.

Section 4

1. The times, places, and manner of holding elections for senators and representatives, shall be prescribed in each State by the legislature thereof: but the Congress may at any time by law make or alter such regulations, except as to the places of choosing senators.

2. The Congress shall assemble at least once in every year, and such meeting shall be on the first Monday in December, unless they shall by law appoint a different day.

SECTION 5

1. Each House shall be the judge of the elections, returns and qualifications of its own members, and a majority of each shall constitute a quorum to do business; but a smaller number may adjourn from day to day, and may be authorized to compel the attendance of absent members, in such manner, and under such penalties as each House may provide.

2. Each House may determine the rules of its proceedings, punish its members for disorderly behavior, and, with the concurrence of two thirds, expel a member.

3. Each House shall keep a journal of its proceedings, and from time to time punish the same, excepting such parts as may in their judgment require secrecy; and the yeas and nays of the members of either House on any question shall, at the desire of one fifth of those present, be entered on the journal.

4. Neither House, during the session of Congress, shall, without the consent of the other, adjourn for more than three days, nor to any other place than that in which the two Houses shall be sitting.

SECTION 6

1. The senators and representatives shall receive a compensation for their services, to be ascertained by law, and paid out of the Treasury of the United States. They shall in all cases, except treason, felony, and breach of the peace, be privileged from arrest during their attendance at the session of their respective Houses, and in going to and returning from the same; and for any speech or debate in either House, they shall not be questioned in any other place.

2. No senator or representative shall, during the time for which he was elected, be appointed to any civil office under the authority of the United States, which shall have been created, or the emoluments whereof shall have been increased, during such time; and no person holding any office under the United States shall be a member of either House during his continuance in office.

SECTION 7

1. All bills for raising revenue shall originate in the House of Representatives; but the Senate may propose or concur with amendments as on other bills.

2. Every bill which shall have passed the House of Representatives and the Senate, shall, before it become a law, be presented to the President of the United States; If he approves he shall sign it, but if not he shall return it, with his objections, to that House in which it

shall have originated, who shall enter the objections at large on their journal, and proceed to reconsider it. If after such reconsideration two thirds of that House shall agree to pass the bill, it shall be sent, together with the objections, to the other House, by which it shall likewise be reconsidered, and if approved by two thirds of that House, it shall become a law. But in all such cases the votes of both Houses shall be determined by yeas and nays, and the names of the persons voting for and against the bill shall be entered on the journal of each House respectively. If any bill shall not be returned by the President within ten days (Sundays excepted) after it shall have been presented to him, the same shall be a law, in like manner as if he had signed it, unless the Congress by their adjournment prevent its return, in which case it shall not be a law.

Every order, resolution, or vote to which the concurrence of the Senate and the House of Representatives may be necessary (except on a question of adjournment) shall be presented to the President of the United States; and before the same shall take effect, shall be approved by him, or being disapproved by him, shall be repassed by two thirds of the Senate and House of Representatives, according to the rules and limitations prescribed in the case of a bill.

SECTION 8

THE CONGRESS SHALL HAVE THE POWER

1. To lay and collect taxes, duties, imposts, and excises, to pay the debts and provide for the common defense and general welfare of the United States; but all duties, imposts, and excises shall be uniform throughout the United States;

2. To borrow money on the credit of the United States;

3. To regulate commerce with foreign nations, and among the several States, and with the Indian tribes;

4. To establish an uniform rule of naturalization, and uniform laws on the subject of bankruptcies throughout the Untied States;

5. To coin money, regulate the value thereof, and of foreign coin, and fix the standard of weights and measures;

6. To provide for the punishment of counterfeiting the securities and current coin of the United States;

7. To establish post offices and post roads;

8. To promote the progress of science and useful arts, by securing for limited times to authors and inventors the exclusive right to their respective writings and discoveries;

9. To constitute tribunals inferior to the Supreme Court;

10. To define and punish piracies and felonies committed on the high seas, and offenses against the law of nations;

11. To declare war, grant letters of marque and reprisal, and make rules concerning captures on land and water;

12. To raise and support armies, but no appropriations of money to that use shall be for a longer term than two years;

13. To provide and maintain a navy;

14. To make rules for the government and regulation of the land and naval forces;

15. To provide for calling forth the militia to execute the laws of the Union, suppress insurrections and repel invasions;

16. To provide for organizing, arming, and disciplining the militia, and for governing such part of them as may be employed in the service of the United States, reserving to the States respectively, the appointment of the officers, and the authority of training the militia according to the discipline prescribed by Congress;

17. To exercise exclusive legislation in all cases whatsoever, over such district (not exceeding ten miles square) as may, by cession of particular States and the acceptance of Congress, become the seat of the government of the United States, and to exercise like authority over all places purchased by the consent of the legislature of the State in which the same shall be, for the erection of forts, magazines, arsenals, dockyards, and other needful buildings; and

18. To make all laws which shall be necessary and proper for carrying into execution the foregoing powers, and all other powers vested by this Constitution in the government of the United States, or any department or officer thereof.

Section 9

1. The migration or importation of such persons as any of the States now existing shall think proper to admit, shall not be prohibited by the Congress prior to the year one thousand eight hundred and eight, but a tax or duty may be imposed on such importation, not exceeding ten dollars for each person.

2. The privilege of the writ of hàbeas corpus shall not be suspended, unless when in cases of rebellion or invasion the public safety may require it.

3. No bill of attainder or ex post facto law shall be passed.

4. No capitation, or other direct, tax shall be laid, unless in proportion to the census or enumeration hereinbefore directed to be taken.[5]

5. No tax or duty shall be laid on articles exported from any State.

6. No preference shall be given by any regulation of commerce or revenue to the ports of one State over those of another: nor shall vessels bound to, or from, one State be obliged to enter, clear, or pay duties in another.

7. No money shall be drawn from the treasury, but in consequence of appropriations made by law; and a regular statement and account of the receipts and expenditures of all public money shall be published from time to time.

8. No title of nobility shall be granted by the United States: and no person holding any office of profit or trust under them, shall, without the consent of the Congress, accept of any present, emolument, office, or title, of any kind whatever, from any king, prince, or foreign State.

SECTION 10

1. No State shall enter into any treaty, alliance, or confederation; grant letters of marque and reprisal; coin money; emit bills of credit; make any thing but gold and silver coin a tender in payment of debts; pass any bill of attainder, ex post facto law, or law impairing the obligation of contracts, or grant any title of nobility.

2. No State shall, without the consent of the Congress, lay any imposts or duties on imports or exports, except what may be absolutely necessary for executing its inspection laws: and the net produce of all duties and imposts laid by any State on imports or exports, shall be for the use of the treasury of the United States; and all such laws shall be subject to the revision and control of the Congress.

3. No State shall, without the consent of the Congress, lay any duty of tonnage, keep troops, or ships of war in time of peace, enter into any agreement or compact with another State, or with a foreign power, or engage in war, unless actually invaded, or in such imminent danger as will not admit of delay.

ARTICLE II SECTION 1

1. The executive power shall be vested in a President of the United States of America. He shall hold his office during the term of four years, and, together with the Vice President, chosen for the same term, be elected, as follows:

2. Each State shall appoint, in such manner as the legislature thereof may direct, a number of electors, equal to the whole number of senators and representatives to which the State may be entitled in the Congress: but no senator or representative, or person holding an office of trust or profit under the United States, shall be appointed an elector.

The electors shall meet in their respective States, and vote by ballot for two persons, of whom one at least shall not be an inhabitant of the same State with themselves. And they shall make a list of all the persons voted for, and of the number of votes for each; which list they shall sign and certify, and transmit sealed to the seat of the government of the United States, directed to the president of the Senate. The president of the Senate shall, in the presence of the Senate and House of Representatives, open all the certificates, and the votes shall then be counted. The person having the greatest number of votes shall be the President, if such number be a majority of the whole number of electors appointed; and if there be more than one who have such majority, and have an equal number of votes, then the House of Representatives shall immediately choose by ballot one of them for President; and if no person have a majority, then from the five highest on the list the said House shall in like manner choose the President. But in choosing the President, the votes shall be taken by States, the representation from each State having one vote; a quorum for this purpose shall consist of a member or members from two thirds of the States, and a majority of all the States shall be necessary to a choice. In every case, after the choice of the President, the person having the greatest number of votes of the electors shall be the Vice President. But if there should remain two or more who have equal votes, the Senate shall choose from them by ballot the Vice President.[6]

3. The Congress may determine the time of choosing the electors, and the day on which they shall give their votes; which day shall be the same throughout the United States.

4. No person except a natural born citizen, or a citizen of the United States, at the time of the adoption of this Constitution, shall be eligible to the office of President; neither shall any person be eligible to that office who shall not have attained to the age of thirty-five years, and been fourteen years a resident within the United States.

5. In case of the removal of the President from office, or his death, resignation, or inability to discharge the powers and duties of the said office, the same shall devolve on the Vice President, and the Congress may be law provide for the case of removal, death, resignation or inability, both of the President and Vice President, declaring what officer shall then act as President, and such officer shall act accordingly, until the disability be removed, or a President shall be elected.

6. The President shall, at stated times, receive for his services a compensation, which shall neither be increased nor diminished during the period for which he shall have been elected, and he shall not receive within that period any other emolument from the United States, or any of them.

7. Before he enter on the execution of his office, he shall take the following oath or affirmation: "I do solemnly swear (or affirm) that I will faithfully execute the office of President of the Untied States, and will to the best of my ability, preserve, protect, and defend the Constitution of the United States."

SECTION 2

1. The President shall be commander in chief of the army and navy of the United States, and of the militia of the several States, when called into the actual service of the United States; he may require the opinion, in writing, of the principal officer in each of the executive departments, upon any subject relating to the duties of their respective offices, and he shall have power to grant reprieves and pardons for offenses against the United States, except in cases of impeachment.

2. He shall have power, by and with the advice and consent of the Senate, to make treaties, provided two thirds of the senators present concur; and he shall nominate, and by and with the advice and consent of the Senate, shall appoint ambassadors, other public ministers and consuls, judges of the Supreme Court, and all other officers of the United States, whose appointment are not herein otherwise provided for, and which shall be established by law: but the Congress may by law vest the appointment of such inferior officers, as they think proper, in the President alone, in the courts of law, or in the heads of departments.

3. The President shall have power to fill up all vacancies that may happen during the recess of the Senate, by granting commissions which shall expire at the end of their next session.

SECTION 3

He shall from time to time give to the Congress information of the state of the Union, and recommend to their considerations such measures as he shall judge necessary and expedient; he may, on extraordinary occasions, convene both Houses, or either of them, and in case of disagreement between them with respect to the time of adjournment, he may adjourn them to such time as he shall think proper; he shall receive ambassadors and other public ministers; he shall take care that the laws be faithfully executed, and shall commission all the officers of the United States.

SECTION 4

The President, Vice President, and all civil officers of the United States, shall be removed from office on impeachment for, and conviction of, treason, bribery, or other high crimes and misdemeanors.

ARTICLE III   **SECTION 1**

The judicial power of the United States shall be vested in one Supreme Court, and in such inferior courts as the Congress may from time to time ordain and establish. The judges, both of the Supreme and inferior courts, shall hold their offices during good behavior, and shall, at stated times, receive for their services, a compensation, which shall not be diminished during their continuance in office.

SECTION 2

1. The judicial power shall extend to all cases, in law and equity, arising under this Constitution, the laws of the United States, and treaties made, or which shall be made, under their authority;—to all cases affecting ambassadors, other public ministers and consuls;—to all cases of admiralty and maritime jurisdiction;—to controversies to which the United States shall be a party;[7]—to controversies between two or more States;—between a State and citizens of another State;—between citizens of different States;—between citizens of the same State claiming lands under grants of different States, and between a State, or the citizens thereof, and foreign States, citizens or subjects.

2. In all cases affecting ambassadors, other public ministers and consuls, and those in which a State shall be party, the Supreme Court shall have original jurisdiction. In all the other cases before mentioned, the Supreme Court shall have appellate jurisdiction, both as to law and fact, with such exceptions, and under such regulations as the Congress shall make.

3. The trial of all crimes, except in cases of impeachment, shall be by jury; and such trial shall be held in the State where the said crimes shall have been committed; but when not committed within any State, the trial shall be at such place or places as the Congress may by law have directed.

SECTION 3

1. Treason against the United States shall consist only in levying war against them, or in adhering to their enemies, giving them aid and comfort. No person shall be convicted of treason unless on the testimony of two witnesses to save overt act, or on confession in open court.

2. The Congress shall have power to declare the punishment of treason, but no attainder of treason shall work corruption of blood, or forfeiture except during the life of the person attained.

ARTICLE IV   SECTION 1

Full faith and credit shall be given in each State to the public acts, records, and judicial proceedings of every other State. And the Congress may by general laws prescribe the manner in which such acts, records and proceedings shall be proved, and the effect thereof.

SECTION 2

1. The citizens of each State shall be entitled to all privileges and immunities of citizens in the several States.[8]

2. A person charged in any State with treason, felony, or other crime, who shall flee from justice, and be found in another State, shall on demand of the executive authority of the State from which he fled, be delivered up to be removed to the State having jurisdiction of the crime.

3. No person held to service or labor in one State under the laws thereof, escaping into another, shall in consequence of any law or regulation therein, be discharged from such service or labor, but shall be delivered up on claim of the party to whom such service or labor may be due.[9]

SECTION 3

1. New States may be admitted by the Congress into this Union; but no new State shall be formed or erected within the jurisdiction of any other State; nor any State be formed by the junction of two or more States, or parts of States, without the consent of the legislatures of the States concerned as well as the Congress.

2. The Congress shall have power to dispose of and make all needful rules and regulations respecting the territory or other property belonging to the United States; and nothing in this Constitution shall be so construed as to prejudice any claims of the United States, or of any particular State.

SECTION 4

The United States shall guarantee to every State in this Union a republican form of government, and shall protect each of them against invasion; and on application of the legislature, or of the executive (when the legislature cannot be convened) against domestic violence.

ARTICLE V   The Congress, whenever two thirds of both Houses shall deem it necessary, shall propose amendments to this Constitution, or, on the application of the legislatures of two thirds of the several States, shall call a convention for proposing amendments, which in either case shall be valid to all intents and purposes, as part of this Constitution, when ratified by the legislatures of three fourths of the several States, or by conventions in three fourths thereof, as the one or the other mode of ratification may be proposed by the Congress; Provided that no amendment which may be made prior to the year one thousand eight hundred and eight shall in any manner affect the first and fourth clauses in the ninth section of the first article; and that no State, without its consent, shall be deprived of its equal suffrage in the Senate.

Article VI 1. All debts contracted and engagements entered into, before the adoption of this Constitution, shall be as valid against the United States under this Constitution, as under the Confederation.

2. This Constitution, and the laws of the United States which shall be made in pursuance thereof; and all treaties made, or which shall be made, under the authority of the United States, shall be supreme law of the land; and the Judges in every State shall be bound thereby, any thing in the Constitution or laws of any State to the contrary notwithstanding.

3. The senators and representatives before mentioned, and the members of the several State legislatures, and all executive and judicial officers, both of the United States and of the several States, shall be bound by oath or affirmation to support this Constitution; but no religious test shall ever be required as a qualification to any office or public trust under the United States.

Article VII The ratification of the conventions of nine States shall be sufficient for the establishment of this Constitution between the States so ratifying the same.

Done in Convention by the unanimous consent of the States present the seventeenth day of September in the year of our Lord one thousand seven hundred and eighty-seven, and of the independence of the United States of America the twelfth. In witness whereof we have hereunto subscribed our names.

Amendment I [First Ten Amendments ratified in 1791]

Congress shall make no law respecting an establishment of religion, or prohibiting the free exercise thereof; or abridging the freedom of speech, or the press; or the right of the people peaceably to assemble, and to petition the government for a redress of grievances.

Amendment II

A well regulated militia, being necessary to the security of a free State, the right of the people to keep and bear arms, shall not be infringed.

AMENDMENT III

No soldier shall, in the time of peace be quartered in any house, without the consent of the owner, nor in time of war, but in a manner to be prescribed by law.

AMENDMENT IV

The right of the people to be secure in their persons, houses, papers, and effects, against unreasonable searches and seizures, shall not be violated, and no warrants shall issue, but upon probable cause, supported by oath or affirmation, and particularly describing the place to be searched, and the persons or things to be seized.

AMENDMENT V

No person shall be held to answer for a capital, or otherwise infamous crime, unless on a presentment or indictment of a grand jury, except in cases arising in the land or naval forces, or in the militia, when in actual service in time of war or public danger; nor shall any person be subject for the same offense to be twice put in jeopardy of life or limb; nor shall be compelled in any criminal case to be a witness against himself; nor be deprived of life, liberty, or property, without due process of law; nor shall private property be taken for public use, without just compensation.

AMENDMENT VI

In all criminal prosecutions, the accused shall enjoy the right to a speedy and public trial, by an impartial jury of the State and district wherein the crime shall have been committed, which district shall have been previously ascertained by law, and to be informed of the nature and cause of the accusation; to be confronted with the witnesses against him; to have compulsory process for obtaining witnesses in his favor, and to have the assistance of the counsel for his defense.

AMENDMENT VII

In suits at common law, where the value in controversy shall exceed twenty dollars, the right of trial by jury shall be preserved, and no fact tried by a jury shall be otherwise reëxamined in any court of the United States, than according to the rules of the common law.

AMENDMENT VIII

Excessive bail shall not be required, nor excessive fines imposed, nor cruel and unusual punishments inflicted.

AMENDMENT IX

The enumeration in the Constitution of certain rights shall not be construed to deny or disparage others retained by the people.

AMENDMENT X

The powers not delegated to the United States by the Constitution, nor prohibited by it to the States, are reserved to the States respectively, or to the people.

AMENDMENT XI [RATIFIED IN 1798]

The judicial power of the United States shall not be construed to extend to any suit in law or equity, commenced or prosecuted against one of the United States by citizens of another State, or by citizens or subjects of any foreign State.

AMENDMENT XII [RATIFIED IN 1804]

The electors shall meet in their respective States, and vote by ballot for President and Vice President, one of whom, at least, shall not be an inhabitant of the same State with themselves; they shall name in their ballots the person voted for as President, and in distinct ballots, the person voted for as Vice President, and they shall make distinct lists of all persons voted for as President and of all persons voted for as Vice President, and of the number of votes for each, which lists they shall sign and certify, and transmit sealed to the seat of the government of the Untied States, directed to the President of the Senate;—The President of the Senate shall, in the presence of the Senate and House of Representatives, open all the certificates and the votes shall then be counted;—The person having the greatest number of votes for President, shall be the President, if such number be a majority of the whole number of electors appointed; and if no person have such majority, then form the persons having the highest numbers not exceeding three on the list of those voted for as President, the House of Representatives shall choose immediately, by ballot, the President. But in choosing the President, the votes shall be taken by States, the representation from each State having one vote; a quorum for this purpose shall consist of a member or members from two thirds of the States, and a majority of all the States shall be necessary to a choice. And if the House of Representatives shall not choose a President whenever the right of choice shall devolve upon them, before the fourth day of March next following, then the Vice President shall act as President, as in the case of the death or other constitutional disability of the President. The person having the greatest number of votes as Vice President shall be the Vice President, if such number be a majority of the whole number of electors appointed, and if no person have a majority, then from the two highest numbers on the list, the Senate shall choose the Vice President; a quorum for the purpose shall consist of two thirds of the whole number of Senators, and a majority of the whole number shall be necessary to a choice. But no person constitutionally ineligible to the office of President shall be eligible to that of Vice President of the United States.

AMENDMENT XIII [RATIFIED IN 1865]

SECTION 1

Neither slavery nor involuntary servitude, except as a punishment for crime whereof the party shall have been duly convicted, shall exist within the United States, or any place subject to their jurisdiction.

SECTION 2

Congress shall have power to enforce this article by appropriate legislation.

AMENDMENT XIV [RATIFIED IN 1868]

SECTION 1

All persons born or naturalized in the United States, and subject to the jurisdiction thereof, are citizens of the United States and of the State wherein they reside. No State shall make or enforce any law which shall abridge the privileges or immunities of citizens of the United States; nor shall any State deprive any person of life, liberty, or property, without due process of law; nor deny to any person within its jurisdiction the equal protection of the laws.

SECTION 2

Representatives shall be apportioned among the several States according to their respective numbers, counting the whole number of persons in each State, excluding Indians not taxed. But when the right to vote at any election for the choice of electors for President and Vice President of the United States, representatives in Congress, the executive and judicial officers of a State, or the members of the legislature thereof, is denied to any of the male inhabitants of such State, being twenty-one years of age, and citizens of the United States, or in any way abridge, except for participating in rebellion, or other crime, the basis or representation therein shall be reduced in the proportion which the number of such male citizens shall bear to the whole number of male citizens twenty-one years of age in such State.

SECTION 3

No person shall be a senator or representative in Congress, or elector of President and Vice President, or hold any office, civil or military under the United States, or under any State, who having previously taken an oath, as a member of Congress, or as an officer of the United States, or as a member of any State legislature, or as an executive or judicial officer of any State, to support the Constitution of the United States, shall have engaged in insurrection or rebellion against the same, or given aid or comfort to the enemies thereof. But Congress may by a vote of two thirds of each House, remove such disability.

SECTION 4

The validity of the public debt of the United States, authorized by law, including the debts incurred for payment of pensions and bounties for services in suppressing insurrection or rebellion, shall not be questioned. But neither the United States nor any State shall assume or pay any debt or obligation incurred in aid of insurrection or rebellion against the United States, or any claim for the loss or emancipation of any slave; but all such debts, obligations, and claims shall be held illegal and void.

SECTION 5

The Congress shall have power to enforce, by appropriate legislation, the provisions of this article.

AMENDMENT XV [RATIFIED IN 1870]

SECTION 1

The right of citizens of the United States to vote shall not be denied or abridged by the United States or by any State on account of race, color, or previous condition of servitude.

SECTION 2

The Congress shall have power to enforce this article by appropriate legislation.

AMENDMENT XVI [RATIFIED IN 1913]

The Congress shall have power to lay and collect taxes on incomes, from whatever source derived, without apportionment among the several States, and without regard to any census or enumeration.

AMENDMENT XVII [RATIFIED IN 1913]

The Senate of the United States shall be composed of two senators from each State, elected by the people thereof, for six years; and each senator shall have one vote. The electors in each State shall have the qualifications requisite for electors of the most numerous branch of the State legislature.

When vacancies happen in the representation of any State in the Senate, the executive authority of such State shall issue writs of election to fill such vacancies: *Provided*, That the legislature of any State may empower the executive thereof to make temporary appointments until the people fill the vacancies by election as the legislature may direct.

This amendment shall not be so construed as to affect the election or term of any senator chosen before it becomes valid as part of the Constitution.

AMENDMENT XVIII[10] [RATIFIED IN 1919]

After one year from the ratification of this article, the manufacture, sale, or transportation of intoxicating liquors within, the importation thereof into, or the exportation thereof from the United States and all territory subject to the jurisdiction thereof for beverage purposes is thereby prohibited.

The Congress and the several States shall have concurrent power to enforce this article by appropriate legislation.

This article shall be inoperative unless it shall have been ratified as an amendment to the Constitution by the legislature of the several States, as provided in the Constitution, within seven years from the date of the submission hereof to the States by Congress.

AMENDMENT XIX [RATIFIED IN 1920]

The right of citizens of the United States to vote shall not be denied or abridged by the United States or by any State on account of sex.

Congress shall have the power to enforce this article by appropriate legislation.

AMENDMENT XX [RATIFIED IN 1933]

SECTION 1

The terms of the President and Vice President shall end at noon on the 20th day of January, and the terms of Senators and Representatives at noon on the 3rd day of January, of the years in which such terms would have ended if this article had not been ratified; and the terms of their successors shall then begin.

SECTION 2

The Congress shall assemble at least once in every year, and such meeting shall begin at noon on the 3d day of January, unless they shall by law appoint a different day.

SECTION 3

If, at the time fixed for the beginning of the term of President, the President-elect shall have died, the Vice President-elect shall become President. If a President shall not have been chosen before the time fixed for the beginning of his term, or if the President-elect shall have failed to qualify, then the Vice President-elect shall act as President until a President shall have qualified; and the Congress may by law provide for the case wherein neither a President-elect nor a Vice President-elect shall have qualified, declaring who shall then act as President, or the manner in which one who is to act shall be selected, and such person shall act accordingly until a President or Vice President shall have qualified.

SECTION 4

The Congress may by law provide for the case of the death of any of the persons from whom the House of Representatives may choose a President whenever the right of choice shall have devolved upon them, and for the case of the death of any of the persons from whom the Senate may choose a Vice President whenever the right of choice shall have devolved upon them.

SECTION 5

Sections 1 and 2 shall take effect on the 15th day of October following the ratification of this article.

SECTION 6

This article shall be inoperative unless it shall have been ratified as an amendment to the Constitution by the legislatures of three-fourths of the several States within seven years from the date of its submission.

AMENDMENT XXI [RATIFIED IN 1933]

SECTION 1

The Eighteenth Article of amendment to the Constitution of the United States is hereby repealed.

SECTION 2

The transportation or importation into any State, Territory, or possession of the United States for delivery or use therein of intoxicating liquors in violation of the laws thereof, is hereby prohibited.

SECTION 3

This article shall be inoperative unless it shall have been ratified as an amendment to the Constitution by conventions in the several States as provided in the Constitution, within seven years from the date of the submission thereof to the States by the Congress.

AMENDMENT XXII [RATIFIED IN 1951]

No person shall be elected to the office of the President more than twice, and no person who has held the office of President, or acted as President, for more than two years of a term to which some other person was elected President shall be elected to the office of President more than once.

But this article shall not apply to any person holding the office of President when this article was proposed by the Congress, and shall not prevent any person who may be holding the office of President, or acting as President, during the term within which this article becomes operative from holding the office of President or acting as President during the remainder of such term.

This article shall be inoperative unless it shall have been ratified as an amendment to the Constitution by the legislatures of three-fourths of the several States within seven years from the date of its submission to the States by the Congress.

AMENDMENT XXIII [RATIFIED IN 1961]

SECTION 1

The District constituting the seat of Government of the United States shall appoint in such manner as the Congress may direct:

A number of electors of President and Vice President equal to the whole number of Senators and Representatives in Congress to which the District would be entitled if it were a State, but in no event more than the least populous State; they shall be in addition to those appointed by the States, but they shall be considered, for the purposes of the election of President and Vice President, to be electors appointed by a State; and they shall meet in the District and perform such duties as provided by the twelfth article of amendment.

SECTION 2

The Congress shall have power to enforce this article by appropriate legislation.

Amendment XXIV [Ratified in 1964]

Section 1

The right of citizens of the United States to vote in any primary or other election for President or Vice President, for electors for President or Vice President, or for Senator or Representative in Congress, shall not be denied or abridged by the United States or any State by reason of failure to pay any poll tax or other tax.

Section 2

The Congress shall power to enforce this article by appropriate legislation.

Amendment XXV [Ratified in 1967]

Section 1

In case of the removal of the President from office or his death or resignation, the Vice President shall become President.

Section 2

Whenever there is a vacancy in the office of the Vice President, the President shall nominate a Vice President who shall take office upon confirmation by a majority vote of both Houses of Congress.

Section 3

Whenever the President transmits to the President pro tempore of the Senate and the Speaker of the House of Representatives his written declaration that he is unable to discharge the powers and duties of his office, and until he transmits to them a written declaration to the contrary, such powers and duties shall be discharged by the Vice President as Acting President.

Section 4

Whenever the Vice President and a majority of either the principal officers of the executive departments or of such other body as Congress may by law provide, transmit to the President pro tempore of the Senate and the Speaker of the House of Representatives their written declaration that the President is unable to discharge the powers and duties of his office, the Vice President shall immediately assume the powers and duties of the office as Acting President.

Thereafter, when the President transmits to the President pro tempore of the Senate and the Speaker of the House of Representatives his written declaration that no inability exists, he shall resume the powers and duties of his office unless the Vice President and a majority of either the principal officers of the executive departments or of such other body as Congress may by law provide, transmit within four days to the President pro tempore of the Senate and the Speaker of the House of Representatives their written declaration that the President is unable to discharge the powers and duties of his office. Thereupon Congress shall decide the issue, assembling within forty-eight hours for that purpose if not in session. If the Congress, within twenty-one days after receipt of the latter written declaration, or, if Congress is not in session, within twenty-one days after Congress is required to assemble, determines by two-thirds vote of both Houses that the President is unable to discharge the powers and duties of his office, the Vice President shall continue to discharge the same as Acting President; otherwise, the President shall resume the powers and duties of his office.

AMENDMENT XXVI [RATIFIED IN 1971]

SECTION 1

The right of citizens of the United States, who are eighteen years of age or older, to vote shall not be denied nor abridged by the United States or by any State on account of age.

SECTION 2

The Congress shall have power to enforce this article by appropriate legislation.

AMENDMENT XXVII [RATIFIED IN 1992]

No law, varying the compensation for the services of the Senators and Representatives, shall take effect, until an election of Representatives shall have intervened.

Footnotes

1. Altered by the 16th Amendment.
2. Altered by the 14th Amendment
3. Superseded by the 17th Amendment.
4. Altered by the 17th Amendment.
5. Superseded by the 16th Amendment.
6. Superseded by the 12th Amendment.
7. Cf. the 11th Amendment.
8. Superseded by the 14th Amendment, Sec. 1
9. Voided by the 13th Amendment.
10. Repealed by the 21st Amendment.

SECTION A.4
KEY TERMS

CHAPTER ONE

Plaintiff
Defendant
Burden of Proof
Wager of Law
Compurgation
Trial by Ordeal
Caption
Common Law
Statutory Law
Appellee

Appellant
Citation
Majority Opinion
Concurring Opinion
Dissenting Opinion
Affirmed
Reversed
Remanded
Status and Process
Stare Decisis

CHAPTER TWO

Public Law
Private Law
Criminal Law
Treason
Felony
Misdemeanor
Summary offense
Mens Rea
Beyond a Reasonable Doubt
Constitutional Law
Constitutional Relativity
Administrative Law
Administrative Agencies
Federal Register

Contract Law
Offer
Acceptance
Consideration
Capacity
Legality
Tort
Intentional Tort
Negligence
Real Property
Personal Property
Tangible Property
Intangible Property

CHAPTER THREE

Jury
Voir Dire
Challenge for Cause
Peremptory Challenge
Jurisdiction
Venue
Forum Non Conveniens
Standing
Full, Faith and Credit
Comity
District Court
Circuit Court of Appeals
Court of Federal Claims

United States Supreme Court
Certiorari
Activist
Judicial Restraint Oriented
Allocator
Municipal Court
Common Pleas Court
Superior Court
Commonwealth Court
State Supreme Court
Arbitration
Mediation

CHAPTER FOUR

Due Process
Substantive Law
Procedural Law

Substantive Due Process
Procedural Due Process
Bill

CHAPTER FIVE

Tort
Negligence
Duty of Care
Breach of Duty
Proximate Cause
Good Samaritan Statute
Trespasser
Licensee
Business Visitor
Contributory Negligence
Comparative Negligence
Assumption of Risk

Comparative Negligence
Independent Contractor
Intentional Tort
Assault
Battery
Invasion of Privacy
Defamation
Libel
Slander
False Imprisonment
Product Liability

CHAPTER SIX

Civil Procedure
Pleading
Fee Arrangement
Contingent Fee
Retainer
Subpoena
Set Price
Quantum Meruit
Service of Process
Complaint
Answer
New Matter
Affirmative Defense
Counterclaim
Preliminary Objection
Confidential Communication

Deposition
Production of Documents
Submission to a Medical
    Examination
Request for Admission
Rules of Evidence
Direct Examination
Cross Examination
Redirect Examination
Hearsay
Opinion Testimony
Relevant Evidence
Authentication
Discovery
Irrelevant Evidence
Interrogatory

CHAPTER SEVEN

Criminal Procedure
Crime
Homicide
Justifiable Homicide
Excusable Homicide
Criminal Homicide
First Degree Murder
Malice
Aforethought
Second Degree Murder
Third Degree Murder
Voluntary Manslaughter
Involuntary Manslaughter
Rape
Carnal Knowledge
Statutory Rape
Burglary
Cruel and Usual Punishment

Arson
Robbery
Receiving Stolen Property
Polygraph
Fifth Amendment
Custodial Interrogation
Miranda Warnings
Voluntary Statement
Search and Seizure
Fourth Amendment
Preliminary Arraignment
Preliminary Hearing
Trial
Sentencing
Grand Jury
Bail
Eighth Amendment

CHAPTER EIGHT

Contract
Offer
Acceptance
Consideration
Capacity
Legality
Liquidated Damages
Bilateral Contract

Unilateral Contract
Valid Contract
Void Contract
Voidable Contract
Unenforceable Contract
Express Contract
Implied Contract

CHAPTER NINE

Real Property
Personal Property
Title
Intestacy
Joint Tenancy
Tenancy by the Entirety
Encumbrance
Personal Property
Chattel
Good
Inter Vivos
Bailment
Bailor
Bailee
Bailee Lien
Real Property
Estate

Fee Simple Absolute
Eminent Domain
Fee Simple
Life Estate
Reversionary Interest
Remainder
Lease
Waste
Lessor
Lessee
Implied Warranty of
    Habitability
Lease
Gift
Adverse Possession
Purchase
Escheat

CHAPTER TEN

Copyright Law
Federal Registration
Fair Use
Trademark Infringement
Lanham Act
Fanciful Marks
Suggestive Marks
Descriptive Marks
Generic Marks
Domain Name
Anti-Cybersquatting
    Consumer Protection Act
Internet Corporation For
    Assigned Names and
    Numbers
World Intellectual Property
    Organization
Federal Trademark Dilution Act
e-Defamation
Communication Decency Act
e-Privacy
Electronic Communications
    Privacy Act
e-Contracts
Clickwrap Agreement
Digital Signature
Statute of Frauds
Electronic Signatures in Global
    and National Commerce Act
Shrinkwrap Agreement

CHAPTER ELEVEN

Res Judicata
Double Jeopardy
Statute of Limitations
Sovereign Immunity
Judicial Immunity
Charitable Immunity
Intra-Family Immunity
Immunity by Contract

CHAPTER TWELVE

Judicial Remedies
Remedies at Law
Remedies in Equity
Compensatory Damages
Punitive Damages
Nominal Damages
Liquidated Damages
Injunction
Reformation
Restitution
Declaratory Judgement
Specific Performance
Preliminary Injunction
Permanent Injunction
Temporary Restraining Order
Mandatory Injunction
Prohibitory Injunction

CHAPTER THIRTEEN

Ethics
Special Relationship
Utilitarian Theory
Rights Theory
Whistle Blower
Good Faith Report
Waste

Drug Testing
Sexual Harassment
Title VII
EEOC
Quid Pro Quo
Hostile Work Environment

CHAPTER FOURTEEN

Closely Held Companies
Publicly Held Companies
Sole Proprietorship
Partnership
Subchapter S Corporation
Articles of Incorporation
Incorporators
Limited Partnership
Dissolution
Buy and Sell Agreements
Trading Partnership
Non-Trading Partnership
Shareholders

Directors
Officers
Proxies
Non-Voting Stock
Preferred Stock
Derivative Suit
Preemptive Right
Revised Uniform Limited
Partnership Act
Piercing the Corporate Veil
Alter-Ego Theory
Master Limited Partnerships
Double Taxation

CHAPTER FIFTEEN

International Law
Public International Law
Private International Law
International Court of Justice
United Nations
Convention on International
    Sale of Goods

General Agreement on
    Tariffs and Trade
Most Favored Nations Status
European Community
U.S. - Canada Free
    Trade Agreement
North American Free-Trade
    Agreement

Section A.5

Administrative Agency–a governmental body charged with administering and implementing particular legislation; administrative agencies have legislative, executive, and judicial powers.

Adverse Possession–a means of acquiring title by possessing and using property for a required statutory period of time in a way that is adverse, actual, open, and exclusive.

Affirm–when a decision is affirmed, the appellate court determines that the lower court reached the correct decision.

Alter-Ego Theory–piercing of the corporate veil in order to impose personal liability upon corporate officers, directors and stockholders.

Anticybersquatting Consumer Protection Act–Federal Legislation which protects businesses and consumers against the improper registration of a domain name.

Appellee–party against whom the appeal is filed.

Appellant–person who appeals the lower court's decision.

Arbitration- a form of alternate disputed resolution often used in a commercial setting where both parties agree to have a third party or arbitrator resolve a controversy.

Articles of Incorporation–the formal application for a corporate charter which articles must contain the proposed name of the business, the term, purpose, number of shares, and information about the initial corporate officials.

Assault–the intentional tort consisting of an act intended to put another in fear of an immediate battery.

Assumption of the Risk–a defense to a negligence action asserting that when the plaintiff knows of the danger but voluntarily exposes himself to the harm, the plaintiff will be barred from recovery.

Bailee–the person in possession of personal property in a bailment.

Bailee's Lien–a bailee may retain possession of an item until a bailor pays the bailee's compensation.

Bailment–the delivery of personal property by the owner to another person usually for a particular purpose.

Bailor–the owner of personal property in a bailment.

Battery–the intentional tort consisting of an intentional touching of the body of another or an object closely associated with the body in an offensive or harmful manner.

Bench Trial–a trial with no jury where the judge decides both factual and legal questions.

Bill–the form used for the introduction of proposed legislation.

Burglary–the entering of a building or occupied structure not open to the public at the time with the intent to commit a crime.

Business Visitor–one who enters the premises for a business purpose.

Buy and Sell Agreement–provides for manner of compensation for the interests of the deceased or withdrawing owner.

Caption–part of a case that identifies the parties to the lawsuit.

Charging the Jury–the situation where the judge explains what law the jury must consider in reaching a verdict.

Chattel–all forms of personal property: animate (living), inanimate, tangible (physical) or intangible.

Clickwrap License–an agreement that is provided by the distributor or manufacturer of software which is contained in the packaging of the product and contains non-negotiable terms and conditions imposed by the seller.

Closely Held Organization–a business owned by only a few people.

Closing Speech–a speech given by each side after the evidence has been heard arguing to the jury how and why the evidence supports their view or theory of the case.

Comity–the principle that allows the recognition of the rules and laws of a foreign jurisdiction in this country.

Communication Decency Act–legislation to protect interactive computer services from the growing number of lawsuits being filed against internet providers as a result of the improper conduct of its customers.

Comparative Negligence–a defense to a negligence action that as long as the plaintiff's negligence is not greater than the defendant's, the plaintiff may recover damages, but the verdict will be reduced by the percentage of the plaintiff's negligence.

Compensatory Damages–a sum of money that will return an aggrieved party to the status quo as though nothing ever happened.

Compurgation–one of the three English pre-jury methods of trial that was necessary when a person's oath was questioned; compurgation required the accused person to bring forward 11 supporters, called compurgators, making 12 people in all who would be willing to take an oath on behalf of the accused.

Compurgators–the 11 persons who would swear on behalf of the accused in a compurgation; they did not swear that what the accused said was true but served more as character witnesses.

Concurrent Ownership–a term used when ownership to property is shared and title is held by two or more people (see also "joint ownership").

Concurring Opinion–an opinion written by a judge who agrees with the outcome of the case but wants to note a difference in logic for reaching the decision.

Conditional Fee–a form of ownership which conveys all the rights of ownership so long as the owner complies with a certain condition (see also "fee simple defeasible" or "qualified fee").

Constitutional Relativity–the concept that the constitution was intentionally written in broad vague terms to ensure that the constitution could adapt to changing times.

Continuance–a situation in which a case is postponed until a later date.

Contract–the exchange of promises voluntarily made by those whose agreement is enforceable in court; the five essential elements of a contract are offer, acceptance, consideration, capacity, and legality.

Contributory Negligence–a defense to a negligence action asserting the failure of the plaintiff to act as a reasonable person under the circumstances.

Convention on the International Sale of Goods–outlines standard international practices for the sale of goods.

Copyright–the granting of property rights, including the exclusive ability to reproduce and distribute copyrighted materials, to display the work publicly or to create a derivative product, such as the development of a screen play from a novel.

Copyright Infringement–the authorized distribution of a copyrighted work.

Corporation–an artificial entity created under the authority of a state's law whose ownership is not necessarily tied with the management of the corporate organization.

Crime–a violation of those duties which an individual owes to the community and for breach of which the law requires that the offender make satisfaction to the public; an offense against society or the state that violates a penal law and carries a possible punishment of imprisonment.

Criminal Complaint–a statement of facts about a crime which later becomes the basis for formal charges against the accused.

Criminal Homicide–a unlawful killing of another; includes murder and manslaughter.

Defamation–a statement that is false and tends to harm the reputation of another or to lower him in the estimation of the community.

Defendant–party who is being sued.

Derivative Suit–litigation brought by a minority shareholder on behalf of the corporation to contest the illegal or improper acts of the majority.

Descriptive Mark–cannot identify the source of goods. Rather, it describes some feature or characteristic of the product.

Directors–individuals whose set the objectives or goals of the corporation, and appoint the officers.

Dissenting Opinion–a judge writes a dissent when he or she disagrees with the result reached by the majority; the dissent has no value as precedent.

Dissolution–a change in the ownership of an organization that changes the legal existence of the organization.

Documents of Title–used to prove ownership, e.g. title to a car, a deed to a house, or a bill of sale for merchandise.

Double Jeopardy–the right guaranteed by the Fifth Amendment of the United States Constitution that no person shall be tried twice for the same offense.

Duty of Care–establishes the type of behavior a person must exhibit in a given situation; the basic rule is that a person must conform to the standard of care of a "reasonable person under the circumstances."

e-Contract–voluntary exchange of promises between two or more people that constitutes a legal obligation which contract is created through an internet transmission.

e-Defamation–defamatory message transmitted through the internet.

Electronic Communications Privacy Act–provides the primary statutory protection against the interception of electronic communications, including e-mail transmissions.

Electronic Signatures in Global and National Commerce Act–legislation that will make online transactions the equivalent of a signed paper contract.

Encumbrance–any right or interest that someone has in another's property.

Escheat–the doctrine under which property will be transferred to the state if there are no legal heirs.

Estate–the extent of a person's interests or rights in real property.

European Community–an organization comprised of European countries whose purpose is to achieve economic unity and whose objectives include the free movement of goods, services, labor, transportation and capital among member states.

Excusable Homicide–a killing by accident or mistake where the wrongdoer does not have criminal culpability.

Fair Use–an exception to the Copyright Act which permits the utilization of copyrighted work for the restricted purpose of criticism, comment, news reporting, teaching, scholarship or research.

False Imprisonment–the unlawful detention of a person against his or her will.

Fanciful Mark–consists of made up words which serve as a product's brand name.

Fee Simple Absolute Estate–the most complete form of ownership of real property which includes the right to possess, use, exclude others, encumber and alienate the property.

Fee Simple Defeasible Estate–a form of ownership which conveys all the rights of ownership so long as the owner complies with a certain condition (see also "conditional fee" or "qualified fee").

Federal Trademark Dilution Act–legislation to protect the owner of a famous mark from dilution regardless of the likelihood of confusion between the products.

Felony Murder–an unintentional killing of another committed during the commission of a felony; also called "second degree murder."

First Degree Murder–an unlawful killing of another with malice aforethought and the specific intent to kill.

Forum non conveniens–means that the place of the trial is inconvenient for the parties and the witnesses involved in the trial.

General Agreement on Tariffs and Trade–an international treaty that requires member countries to abide by certain rules of trade, prohibits discrimination in national regulations covering imports and prevents the establishment of import quotas.

Generic Mark–merely describes a type of product regardless of its source.

Gift–a transfer of title to property without payment or compensation.

Good–personal property that is both tangible and movable.

Homicide–the killing of another human.

Hostile Environment–a type of sexual harassment that does not involve specific consequences like economic loss, but under which a victim suffers a down-graded work atmosphere, pervaded with unpleasantness.

Implied Warranty of Habitability–the right of a residential tenant to insist that the premises are fit for human habitation.

Imputed Negligence–the concept that because of a special relationship that exists between the parties, one person can be held liable for the negligence of the other; also called vicarious liability.

Incorporators–individuals who apply for the charter to start a corporation.

Independent Contractor–one who undertakes to perform the act requested on his own and is not subject to the control of an employer.

Injunction–an equitable order issued by a court that directs a person to do something (mandatory injunction) or not to do something (prohibitory injunction).

Insanity–a defense to a crime based on the criminal's failure to appreciate what he or she did is wrong or the person did not know the difference between right and wrong because of some mental disease or defect.

Intangible Property–property that is not a physical object, e.g. a patent or trademark.

Intentional Tort–when a wrongdoer purposely sets out to harm another.

International Court of Justice–the judicial branch of the United Nations and consists of fifteen judges representing all of the world's major legal systems.

International Monetary Fund–encourages international trade by maintaining stable foreign exchange rates and works closely with commercial banks to promote orderly exchange policies with members.

Internet Corporation for Assigned Names and Numbers–a non-profit corporation recognized by the United States Government as the business which coordinates the management of the internet domain name system and IP address numbers.

Inter Vivos–a gift made while the donor is alive.

Intoxication–not a defense to a criminal act unless it negates a specific mental state.

Invasion of Privacy–the intentional tort consisting of an unwarranted intrusion upon a person's right to be left alone.

Involuntary Manslaughter–an unintentional killing of another which is the result of outrageous conduct or gross negligence.

Joint Ownership–a term used when ownership to property is shared and title is held by two or more people (see also "concurrent ownership").

Joint Tenancy with the Right of Survivorship–a form of concurrent or joint ownership in which the co-owners have essentially equal rights to the property; if one co-owner dies, her share will pass to the surviving co-owner.

Judge–the person who presides over the trial and decides questions of law.

Judgment on the verdict–the final pronouncement by the court of a defendant's guilt or innocence after the verdict has been announced.

Judicial Immunity–a judge has immunity from suit when he or she acts within the scope of judicial authority and in the discharge of official duties.

Jurisdiction–refers to the power of a court to determine the merits of a dispute and to grant an aggrieved party relief.

Jury–the individuals who decide questions of fact.

Justifiable Homicide–a killing in self-defense or an execution carried out by court order.

Lanham Act–federal registration that regulates trademark law.

Larceny–the taking and carrying away of property of another without consent and with the intention of depriving the other of the goods permanently.

Lease–an encumbrance upon property where a landlord holds property as a fee simple absolute but has given a tenant the rights to possess and use the property exclusively.

Legal Capacity–the capacity of the organization to sue and be sued in its own name.

Lessee–a tenant who is given the rights to possess and use the property exclusively by a landlord who holds property as a fee simple absolute.

Lessor–a landlord who holds property as a fee simple absolute but has given a tenant the rights to possess and use the property exclusively.

Libel–the publication of defamatory matter by written or printed words.

Licensee–a person who comes on the property of another with the owner's consent or with a legal right to be on the land.

Life estate–an ownership interest which is limited to the life of the person holding it.

Limited Partnership–a hybrid between a general partnership and a corporation which has the attributes of a partnership except that the limited partners are not permitted to be involved in the control or operation of the business.

Liquidated Damages–a sum of money agreed upon by contracting parties that will be paid in the event of a default or breach of contract.

Majority Opinion–a decision reached by more than half of the judges of an appellate court panel; a decision rendered by the majority of the court which is the law.

Malice Aforethought–describes the conduct that exhibits a wanton disregard for the safety of others.

Mediation–a form of alternate dispute resolution used primarily in disputes between labor and management; mediation is advisory in nature.

Mens Rea–the necessary state of mind that a perpetrator must have to be found guilty of committing a particular crime; criminal intent.

Mini-trial–a form or alternate dispute resolution where the parties submit their case to a panel of experts or neutral advisor who suggest the likely outcome if the case were to go to court.

Negligence–the failure to do what a reasonable person would do under the circumstances; the three elements of negligence are 1) a duty, 2) breach of duty, and 3) the negligence must be the proximate cause of the harm.

Neighborhood Justice Centers–programs where local cases, usually neighborhood or family disputes, are decided by a panel of local residents.

No Duty to Rescue Rule–the rule under which the law does not force a person to help a stranger in an emergency unless that person has somehow caused the problem or has a special relationship to the party.

Nominal Damages–provide a remedy where a technical wrong has been committed but no actual harm has resulted.

Non-binding Trial–see "mini-trial."

Officers–individuals who manage the daily operations of the corporation.

Opening Statement–a speech given by each side at the beginning of the case describing what the evidence will prove.

Partnership–an agreement between two or more people to share a common interest in a commercial enterprise and to share profits and losses.

Permanent Injunction–a final resolution of a dispute issued after a full hearing of all relevant factors.

Personal Property–consists of all property that is not land or attached to land; the two kinds of personal property are tangible and intangible; includes such things as a car, book, clothes, and furniture as well as bank accounts, stocks, bonds, patents and copyrights.

Piercing the Corporate Veil–when the corporation is being misused so that the shareholders are treated like partners and have unlimited liability for the organization's debts.

Plaintiff–party who initiates the case.

Precedent–the process whereby judges apply the decision and rules or prior cases to the present case over which they are presiding; see also *"stare decisis."*

Preliminary Injunction–an order granted as an emergency measure before a full hearing on the merits can be held.

Private International Law–exams relationships created by commercial transactions and utilizes treaties, agreements, and the individual laws of nations to resolve business disputes.

Private Judging–a form of alternate dispute resolution used when parties are constrained by time and can afford to hire a private judge; private judging proceeds as a normal trial would be conducted.

Private Law–involves matters between individuals; most common forms are contract, tort, and property law.

Procedural Law–the way that substantive law is made, enforced, and administered.

Products Liability–the concept of holding sellers of defective products liable for harm caused to the user, consumer, or his property even though the seller has exercised all possible care in the preparation and sale of the product; also called strict liability.

Property–everything that may be owned, either as real property or personal property.

Property Law–deals with the rights and duties that arise out of the ownership or possession of real or personal property; defines and enforces the rights and responsibilities that accompany ownership.

Proximate Cause–requires that there be a reasonable connection between the negligence of the defendant and the harm suffered by the plaintiff.

Proxy–an agent appointed by a shareholder for the purposes of voting the shares.

Public International Law–exams relationships between nations and uses rules that are binding on all countries in the international community.

Public Law–involves the rights of society as a whole, and those interests are usually handle by a government agency; most common forms are criminal, constitutional, and administrative law.

Publicly Held Organization–a business owned by many people and includes those whose stock is traded on a public exchange.

Punitive Damages–a sum of money awarded to punish the tort-feasor for his or her misconduct so that the type of incident in question will never occur again.

Purchase–the transfer of title from one owner to another for payment or compensation.

Qualified Fee–a form of ownership which conveys all the rights of ownership so long as the owner complies with a certain condition (see also "fee simple defeasible" or "conditional fee").

Quid Pro Quo–a type of sexual harassment where an employee is expected to give in to sexual demands or suffer the loss of some specific job or benefit.

Quiet Title Action–with respect to real property, a suit in which the court is asked to determine who among several contenders has ownership rights to a given piece of property.

Rape–the unlawful carnal knowledge of a person another through force or the threat of force and without consent.

Real Property–land and everything attached to the land.

Receiving Stolen Property–intentionally obtaining property of another that has been stolen, or believed to be stolen.

Reformation–a remedy that allows modification of a contract that does not reflect the true intention of the parties.

Remainder–the future rights of ownership held by a party who will acquire title to a life estate when the current holder dies.

Remand–the appellate court remands—or sends back—a case to the trial court when the appellate court finds that the trial judge committed an error in deciding the case or additional evidence must be obtained.

Res Judicata–"the thing has been decided."

Rescission–the voiding of a contract for some reason such as misrepresentation, fraud, duress, undue influence or impossibility, under which each party must return the property they received from the other.

Restitution–a remedy to prevent one party from unfairly benefiting at the expense of another.

Reverse–the appellate court reverses a decision when it finds that the lower court's decision was incorrect.

Reversionary Interest–the future rights of ownership held by a party who will acquire title to a defeasible estate if the current users do not comply with the stated conditions.

Rights Theory–the ethical theory that focuses on the reasons for actions.

Robbery–larceny with the additional requirement that the taking be accomplished by force or threat of force.

Second Degree Murder–an unintentional killing of another committed during the commission of a felony; also called felony murder.

Security Council–consists of fifteen countries, has the power to authorize military action and to sever diplomatic relations with other nations.

Self-defense–the right of a person unlawfully attacked to use reasonable force to protect himself.

Slander–a defamatory statement that is verbal or oral in nature.

Sole Proprietorship–a business owned by only one person.

Sovereign Immunity–the concept that prohibits suits against any level of the government unless the sovereign gives its expressed consent to the litigation.

Standing–the concept that a plaintiff in a lawsuit must have a direct and substantial interest in the outcome of the case that he or she intends to bring.

Stare Decisis–the process whereby judges apply the decision and rules or prior cases to the present case over which they are presiding; (see also "precedent").

Statute of Frauds–requirement that certain agreements be in writing in order to enforceable by the court.

Statute of Limitations–the time period within which an aggrieved party must institute suit or the claim will be forever barred.

Statutory Rape–generally occurs when a man over the age of 16 has sexual relations with the consent of a girl under sixteen; her consent is presumed meaningless because of her young age.

Strict Liability–see "products liability."

Subchapter S Corporation–has all the characteristics of a corporation except that its shareholders must report profit and losses on their individual tax returns.

Substantive Due Process–the requirement that the law be fundamentally fair; legislation must be capable of serving a legitimate public interest, and the law cannot be vague.

Substantive Law–the "actual law" which defines the duties and rights of members of society.

Suggestive Mark–requires imagination in order to figure out the nature of the product which the mark represents.

Tangible Property–a physical object.

Tenancy by the Entirety–a special form of co-ownership for married couples which carries the right of survivorship; however, neither spouse can convey his or her interest in the property since each spouse owns a 100 percent interest in the property.

Tenancy in Common–a form of concurrent or joint ownership in which the co-owners have essentially equal rights to the property; if one co-owner dies, his share will pass to his heirs.

Third Degree Murder–a killing of another with malice aforethought but with no specific intent to kill and not occurring during the commission of a felony.

Title–the right of ownership.

Trespasser–one who comes upon the premises of another without consent and with no legal right to be on the property.

TRO–(temporary restraining order) an injunction granted without notice to the defendant.

Tort–a private or civil wrong against an individual for which the court will award money damages; torts are classified into the categories of negligence or intentional torts.

Tort Damages–a sum of money that should place the injured party in as substantially a good position as she occupied before the injury.

Trademark–is a word, name, symbol or slogan which identifies the origins or a product or services from those of a competitor.

Trademark Infringement–occurs when there is a likelihood of confusion as to the source, origin, or sponsorship of a product in a commercial environment.

Trial by Cold Water–a form of trial by ordeal where the accused was bound and placed in a body of water that had been purified by prayer. If he sank, he was considered innocent because the water would "accept" one who was pure; floating indicated that the accused's body was polluted by sin by rejecting it.

Trial by Fire–a form of trial by ordeal where the accused was tested with some type of fire, for example holding a hot iron or walking across hot coals. The accused was guilty if burned or innocent if not burned; sometimes the test was not whether the person was burned but how well the burn healed.

Trial by Hot Water–a form of trial by ordeal where the accused would remove a ring from a cauldron of boiling water after being cleansed by prayer; if he was burned he was considered guilty, and if he was unharmed he was considered innocent.

Trial by Ordeal–an old fashioned method of determining justice where the accused was subject to some sort of physical test, the results of which were supposed to indicate guilt or innocence; e.g. trial by hot water, trial by cold water, trial by fire.

U.S. - Canada Free Trade Agreement–a pact to phase out all tariffs and quotas between the two countries and guarantees equal treatment for those that invest across the border.

United Nations–its primary goal is to "save succeeding generations from the scourge of war" and authorizes "collective measures for the prevention and removal of threats to peace, and for the suppression of acts of aggression or other breaches of the peace."

United Nations Commission on International Trade Law–develops standardized commercial practices and agreements.

United States Constitution–the legal document which establishes the fundamental rights of United States citizens and protects them from unlawful governmental interference.

Utilitarian Theory–the theory of ethics that focuses on the consequences of actions.

Venue–the place where a case should be heard.

Verdict–the decision regarding a defendant's guilt or innocence made by either a judge or jury.

Vicarious Liability–see "imputed negligence."

Voir Dire–process for selecting a jury by which members of the jury are questioned by the judge or attorneys to ascertain whether they are suitable to serve at trial; issue of prejudice, conflicts of interest, and philosophies of life are explored.

Wager of Law–one of the three English pre-jury methods of trial that simply required the accused person to take an oath, swearing to a fact.

Whistleblower–a person who feels compelled to get certain information into the hands of people who can act to correct a problem when it seems that the problem cannot be corrected otherwise.

World Bank–promotes economic development in poor countries by making loans to finance necessary development projects and programs.

World Intellectual Property Organization–the leading dispute resolution service for disagreements arising out of the registration or use of internet domain names.

STUDENT NOTES